The Impact of HIV/AIDS on Criminology and Criminal Justice

International Library of Criminology, Criminal Justice and Penology - Second Series

Series Editors: Gerald Mars and David Nelken

Titles in the Series:

Gender and Prisons
Dana M. Britton

Quantitative Methods in Criminology
Shawn Bushway and David Weisburd

Detecting Deception
David Canter and Donna Youngs

Offender Profiling
David Canter and Michael Davis

Insurgent Terrorism
Gerald Cromer

Criminal Courts
Jo Dixon, Aaron Kupchick and Joachim Savelsberg

Crime and Security
Benjamin Goold and Lucia Zedner

Crime and Regulation
Fiona Haines

Recent Developments in Criminological Theory
Stuart Henry

Gun Crime
Richard Hobbs and Robert Hornsby

The Criminology of War
Ruth Jamieson

The Impact of HIV/AIDS on Criminology and Criminal Justice
Mark M. Lanier

Burglary
Robert Mawby

Domestic Violence
Mangai Natarajan

Women Police
Mangai Natarajan

Crime and Immigration
Graeme Newman and Joshua Freilich

Surveillance, Crime and Social Control
Clive Norris and Dean Wilson

Crime and Social Institutions
Richard Rosenfeld

The Death Penalty, Volumes I and II
Austin Sarat

Gangs
Jacqueline Schneider and Nick Tilley

Corporate Crime
Sally Simpson and Carole Gibbs

Green Criminology
Nigel South and Piers Beirne

Crime and Deviance in Cyberspace
David Wall

The Impact of HIV/AIDS on Criminology and Criminal Justice

Edited by

Mark M. Lanier

University of Central Florida, USA

Routledge
Taylor & Francis Group
LONDON AND NEW YORK

First published 2006 by Ashgate Publishing

Reissued 2018 by Routledge
2 Park Square, Milton Park, Abingdon, Oxon, OX14 4RN
711 Third Avenue, New York, NY 10017, USA

Routledge is an imprint of the Taylor & Francis Group, an informa business

A Library of Congress record exists under LC control number: 2005053092

ISBN 13: 978-0-815-39783-0 (hbk)
ISBN 13: 978-1-351-14648-7 (ebk)

Contents

PART V FUTURE TRENDS, GLOBAL IMPACT AND ETHICAL ISSUES

Acknowledgements

The editor and publishers wish to thank the following for permission to use copyright material.

American Medical Association for the essay: Lawrence O. Gostin and David W. Webber (1998), 'HIV Infection and AIDS in the Public Health and Health Care Systems: The Role of Law and Litigation', *Journal of the American Medical Association*, **279**, pp. 1108–13.

American Public Health Association for the essay: Richard Parker (2002), 'The Global HIV/AIDS Pandemic, Structural Inequalities, and the Politics of International Health', *American Journal of Public Health*, **92**, pp. 343–46. Copyright © 2002 APHA.

Blackwell Publishing for the essays: Delphine Valette (2002), 'AIDS Behind Bars: Prisoners' Rights Guillotined', *Howard Journal*, **41**, pp. 107–22. Copyright © 2002 Blackwell Publishers Ltd.

Elsevier for the essays: Mark M. Lanier and Scott Gates (1996), 'An Empirical Assessment of the AIDS Risk Reduction Model (ARRM) Employing Ordered Probit Analyses', *Journal of Criminal Justice*, **24**, pp. 537–47. Copyright © 1996 Elsevier Science Ltd; Johanna Crane, Kathleen Quirk and Ariane van der Straten (2002), '"Come Back when You're Dying:" The Commodification of AIDS Among California's Urban Poor', *Social Science and Medicine*, **55**, pp. 1115–27. Copyright © 2002 Elsevier Science Ltd; Janine Pierret (2000), 'Everyday Life with AIDS/HIV: Surveys in the Social Sciences', *Social Science and Medicine*, **50**, pp. 1589–98. Copyright © 2000 Elsevier Science Ltd; José Esparza, Marie-Louise Chang, Roy Widdus, Yvette Madrid, Neff Walker and Peter D. Ghys (2003), 'Estimation of "Needs" and "Probable Uptake" for HIV/AIDS Preventive Vaccines Based on Possible Policies and Likely Acceptance (a WHO/UNAIDS/IAVI study)', *Vaccine*, **21**, pp. 2032–41.

Emerald Group Publishing Limited for the essays: R. Alan Thompson and James W. Marquart (1998), 'Law Enforcement Responses to the HIV/AIDS Epidemic: Selected Findings and Suggestions for Future Research', *Policing: An International Journal of Police Strategies and Management*, **21**, pp. 648–65. Copyright © 1998 Emerald Group Publishing Limited; Terry D. Edwards and Richard Tewksbury (1996), 'HIV/AIDS: State Police Training Practices and Personnel Policies', *American Journal of Police*, **15**, pp. 45–62. Copyright © 1996 Emerald Group Publishing Limited.

Lippincott Williams and Wilkins for the essays: Esther Sumartojo (2000), 'Structural Factors in HIV Prevention: Concepts, Examples, and Implications for Research', *AIDS*, **14**, pp. S3–S10. Copyright © 2000 Lippincott Williams and Wilkins, Inc.; Raffaele D'Amelio, Emmanuelle Tuerlings, Olga Perito, Roberto Biselli, Sergio Natalicchio and Stuart Kingma (2001), 'A

Global Review of Legislation on HIV/AIDS: The Issue of HIV Testing', *Journal of Acquired Immune Deficiency Syndromes*, **28**, pp. 173–79. Copyright © 2001 Lippincott Williams and Wilkins, Inc.

Matthew Bender and Company, Inc. for the essay: Richard Tewksbury, Gennaro F. Vito and Scott Cummings (1998), 'Injection Drug Users and HIV Risk Behaviors: Criminal Justice Professionals' Role in Identifying and Responding to Risk Behaviors', *Journal of Crime and Justice*, **22**, pp. 1–22.

Sage Publications for the essays: Barbara H. Zaitzow (2001), 'Whose Problem is it Anyway? Women Prisoners and HIV/AIDS', *International Journal of Offender Therapy and Comparative Criminology*, **45**, pp. 673–90. Copyright © 2001 Sage Publications; Michael Welch (2000), 'The Correctional Response to Prisoners With HIV/AIDS: Morality, Metaphors, and Myths', *Social Pathology: A Journal of Reviews*, **6**, pp. 121–42. Copyright © 2000 Sage Publications, Inc.; Kato B. Keeton and Cheryl Swanson (1998), 'HIV/AIDS Education Needs Assessment: A Comparative Study of Jail and Prison Inmates in Northwest Florida', *Prison Journal*, **78**, pp. 119–32. Copyright © 1998 Sage Publications, Inc.; Anthony J. Lemelle, Jr (2003), 'Linking the Structure of African American Criminalization to the Spread of HIV/AIDS', *Journal of Contemporary Criminal Justice*, **19**, pp. 270–92. Copyright © 2003 Sage Publications.

Springer for the essays: Oscar Grusky, Hongjie Liu and Michael Johnston (2002), 'HIV/AIDS in China: 1990–2001', *AIDS and Behavior*, **6**, pp. 381–93. Copyright © 2002 Plenum Publishing Corporation; Maria L.A. Tiamson (2002), 'Challenges in the Management of the HIV Patient in the Third Decade of AIDS', *Psychiatric Quarterly*, **73**, pp. 51–58. Copyright © 2002 Human Sciences Press, Inc.; Edison J. Trickett (2002), 'Context, Culture, and Collaboration in AIDS Interventions: Ecological Ideas of Enhancing Community Impact', *Journal of Primary Prevention*, **23**, pp. 157–74. Copyright © Human Sciences Press, Inc.

Taylor & Francis Group for the essays: Nilanjana R. Bardhan (2002), 'Accounts from the Field: A Public Relations Perspective on Global AIDS/HIV', *Journal of Health Communication*, **7**, pp. 221–44. Copyright © 2002 Taylor & Francis; A. Liau and G.D. Zimet (2001), 'The Acceptability of HIV Immunization: Examining Vaccine Characteristics as Determining Factors', *AIDS Care*, **13**, pp. 643–50. Copyright © 2001 Taylor & Francis.

University Publishing Group for the essay: David W. Webber (2004), 'Self-Incrimination, Partner Notification, and the Criminal Law: Negatives for the CDC's "Prevention for Positives" Initiative', *AIDS & Public Policy Journal*, **19**, pp. 54–66. Copyright © 2004 University Publishing Group.

Every effort has been made to trace all the copyright holders, but if any have been inadvertently overlooked the publishers will be pleased to make the necessary arrangement at the first opportunity.

Preface to the Second Series

The first series of the International Library of Criminology, Criminal Justice and Penology has established itself as a major research resource by bringing together the most significant journal essays in contemporary criminology, criminal justice and penology. The series made available to researchers, teachers and students an extensive range of essays which are indispensable for obtaining an overview of the latest theories and findings in this fast changing subject. Indeed the rapid growth of interesting scholarly work in the field has created a demand for a second series which like the first consists of volumes dealing with criminological schools and theories as well as with approaches to particular areas of crime criminal justice and penology. Each volume is edited by a recognised authority who has selected twenty or so of the best journal articles in the field of their special competence and provided an informative introduction giving a summary of the field and the relevance of the articles chosen. The original pagination is retained for ease of reference.

The difficulties of keeping on top of the steadily growing literature in criminology are complicated by the many disciplines from which its theories and findings are drawn (sociology, law, sociology of law, psychology, psychiatry, philosophy and economics are the most obvious). The development of new specialisms with their own journals (policing, victimology, mediation) as well as the debates between rival schools of thought (feminist criminology, left realism, critical criminology, abolitionism etc.) make necessary overviews that offer syntheses of the state of the art.

GERALD MARS
Visiting Professor, Brunel University, Middlesex, UK

DAVID NELKEN
Distinguished Professor of Sociology, University of Macerata, Italy;
Distinguished Research Professor of Law, University of Cardiff, Wales;
Honourary Visiting Professor of Law, LSE, London, UK

Introduction

In a relatively short time period the 'new' disease of human immunodeficiency virus (HIV) and its more serious developmental manifestation, acquired immunodeficiency syndrome (AIDS), have dramatically altered every aspect of justice systems worldwide. For example, due to this physiological ailment, law enforcement personnel now search, book and handle suspects differently from past procedures. Trauma cases, including the use of CPR, are treated much more gingerly that they were just 15 years ago. Some police officers have distanced themselves from the public they serve due to a fear of infection. Correctional systems have had to completely revise their structure and practice. Issues such as testing for HIV status, segregation of infected inmates and staff protection have taken on new significance. Courts have had to deal with a tangle of legal issues, such as segregation, healthcare and criminal culpability for infecting others with an illness. Never before has a health problem so widely impacted criminal justice.

This collection of essays seeks to provide a broad overview of the myriad issues surrounding HIV/AIDS and the criminal justice 'system'. I should be explicit in stating that by 'system' I do not mean a unified, coherent system of justice with uniform objectives; rather, I refer to the loose, coexisting constellation of entities, dealing with crime, criminals and justice issues, that some have called a 'loose coupling' (Paoline, personal correspondence, 21 September 2004).

The Incidence of HIV/AIDS

The World Health Organization cites 1981 as the year when the first cases of HIV/AIDS appeared (although a case involving a teenage boy reportedly occurred as early as 1958 in Philadelphia – a re-examination of frozen skin tissue revealing the presence of the AIDS virus in this previously undiagnosed death). Since that time more than 20 million people have died from AIDS and between 34.6 and 42.3 million are living with HIV (UNAIDS, 2004). In 2003 almost 5 million people became newly infected with HIV (UNAIDS, 2004).

By the late 1990s, due to a combination of antiretroviral therapy and public health efforts, the numbers of new HIV cases and AIDS-related deaths declined. However, many people are infected with HIV and do not know it. Some estimates are that only one person in ten knows of their infection. There is also often a lengthy incubation period. Once infection with HIV becomes known, 39 per cent of cases progress to the more serious AIDS within 12 months (CDC, 2003, p. 6). Death often quickly follows.

The distribution of cases is far from uniform. The continent of Africa has suffered the most devastation. An estimated 25 million people have HIV in sub-Saharan Africa – nearly two-thirds of all cases worldwide – yet only around 10 per cent of the world's population lives in this part of Africa (UNAIDS, 2004). In 2003, 3 million people became newly infected and 2.2 million died (UNAIDS, 2004). Recently India has been identified as another region with large amounts of infection; some even argue that India surpasses Africa in the number of cases.

In Latin America around 1.6 million people are living with HIV, and, within this region, the distribution of cases is also far from uniform. In Brazil the national incidence is less than 1 per cent but some major cities report that over 60 per cent of drug injectors are infected. The fact that the disease can only spread amongst the general population from this infected group is not, however, a reason for complacency. Close by, in the three Caribbean island countries of the Bahamas, Haiti and Trinidad/Tobago, HIV prevalence rates are 3 per cent, or 430 000 people.

One of the fastest growing regions to be infected with the HIV virus is Eastern Europe and Central Asia. In 1995 there were 160 000 cases of HIV; by 2003 this had increased to around 1.3 million. Even more alarming is the fact that over 80 per cent of those infected are under the age of 30. The countries most affected are Estonia, Latvia, Ukraine and Russia (UNAIDS, 2004).

In the United States an estimated 1.3 to 1.4 million people were infected with HIV between 1981 and 2001; 816 149 have AIDS and 467 910 have died. At the end of 2002, 384 906 persons were living with AIDS in the United States. Of these, 43 per cent were between 35 and 44 years of age; 42 per cent were African-American, 37 per cent were white and 77 per cent were male (CDC, 2003). Urban areas are often much harder hit than rural areas, and three states (California, Florida and New York) reported 44 per cent of all cumulative AIDS cases and 38 per cent of the cases in 2002 (CDC, 2003:8). The relevance of these demographics is that they virtually mirror individuals in contact with justice systems worldwide.

Clearly the distribution of cases is not uniform in terms of demographic or geographic factors. As shown already, certain countries are impacted more than others; regions are differentially impacted; and, furthermore, males and minorities are disproportionately affected.

What Does the Research Show?

Just as disease trends are disparate, there are also wide disparities in the available research dealing with HIV/AIDS and criminal justice agencies. As this volume shows, there is a plethora of studies examining correctional issues and relatively few dealing with law enforcement issues. Close consideration of the targeted populations suggests one reason: namely, that the police are often viewed as being moral, peacekeepers, the 'thin blue line', and so on, whereas institutionalized individuals are one of society's most ostracized groups. I have previously made the analogy that:

> . . . much like leper colonies of the 18th century today's 'correctional' facilities segregate the disempowered, the poor, drug users and the violent from the rest of society. Also like leper colonies, inhabitants of these institutions face serious medical threats including acquired immunodeficiency syndrome (AIDS) and human immunodeficiency virus (HIV). Unlike leper colonies, however, most of the inhabitants of modern penal colonies will one day reenter society – some infected with these serious, contagious diseases, and many unarmed with knowledge about the disease and prevention. Like lepers, in addition to physical separation, the stigma associated with institutionalization further isolates the incarcerated from 'mainstream' society. Victims of HIV and AIDS also face considerable stigma and social isolation even when not incarcerated. In addition, in our society women and people of color have a history of being marginalized, and disempowered by sexism and racism. When any individual is simultaneously a member of each of these groups, the psychological and physical pressures are immense.

> Persons who belong to these high-risk groups (drug users, economically disadvantaged and people of color) are concentrated in correctional institutions. (Lanier, 1999, pp. 413–14)

The public and many researchers focus on the downtrodden; thus offenders are scrutinized more closely than law enforcement personnel. Many inmates have HIV/AIDS, many more are at risk, while in the United States not one law enforcement officer has ever tested positive for HIV due to work-related exposure (Thompson and Marquart, 1998). From the late 1980s until 1995, AIDS was the second leading cause of deaths in American state prisons (Maruschak, 2002), and was identified as the leading cause of death in some correctional systems (New York State Commission, 1986; 'Florida: AIDS Primary Cause', 1989). Furthermore, all those who are incarcerated had initial contact with law enforcement and then progressed through the courts. Consequently, more discussion is directed at correctional issues than to law enforcement.

At this point, it might be useful to draw a connection between the disproportionate burden of HIV/AIDS on communities of colour and the disproportionate rates of incarceration among members of these same communities. These disparities hold true for almost every category of infectious and chronic disease found in correctional facilities. By and large, the people incarcerated in jails and prisons come from communities of colour and/or economic disadvantage. The high-risk behaviours associated with substance use and dependency, other criminal behaviours, sex work or trading, and 'life on the streets' place these groups at high risk of acquiring HIV/AIDS, Hepatitis B and C, and other sexually transmitted diseases (STDs).

The United States provides an illustrative example. By the end of 2002 over 2 million individuals were incarcerated in the United States. The Bureau of Justice Statistics (BJS) census of prison and jail inmates reveals that minority-status individuals comprised over 63 per cent of all male inmates. African-American males comprised the largest single group (45 per cent) of incarcerated individuals (in jails, African-Americans accounted for 40.6 per cent of the population). How are these individuals treated by justice systems? Unfortunately, the treatment they receive is neither uniform, nor is it always just.

HIV/AIDS Medical Treatment

Healthcare worldwide is not evenly distributed. Wealthier nations fare much better than economically stressed areas. For example, in sub-Saharan Africa 4.3 million people are in need of home-based care and only 12 per cent receive it; in South Asia only 2 per cent receive the needed home-based care (UNAIDS, 2004).

In recent years, medical advances have greatly increased the longevity (life span) of AIDS patients. Ironically, increased longevity compounds, rather then decreases, the burdens faced by criminal justice officials. This trend should continue as medications improve and knowledge increases. A complete cure or preventive vaccine remains elusive, however.

People who work in justice systems worldwide will come into contact with large numbers of at-risk and infected individuals. How does the system respond? What are the legal issues? What are the medical issues? What are the ethical obligations? This volume hopes to address these and other issues.

Physiological, Medical and Disease Trends

Part I documents the physiological effects, medical treatments and disease trends. The opening essay by Richard Parker provides an overview of the problems created by structural inequalities that cause the poor and undeveloped nations to bear a disproportionate burden of HIV and AIDS. Parker concludes the discussion by reviewing recent United Nations iniatives. In Chapter 2, Esther Sumartojo relates economic, social policy and organizational factors to individuals' preventive behaviours. This is followed by an essay by Nilanjana Bardhan, which examines the public relations perspective from a global perspective. Agenda-setting and news 'framing' is discussed relative to the HIV problem. Like the first two essays in this section, this author takes a large-scale approach. The focus then turns to issues related to immunizations and vaccines. José Esparza *et al.* (Chapter 4) provide a quantitative estimation of the amount of vaccine required and, in Chapter 5, Liau and Zimet consider the acceptability of HIV immunization. The final essay in Part I by Oscar Grusky *et al.* (Chapter 6) links these issues and provides an illustrative case study focusing on emerging problems in China. This is not because China is any more or less impacted by HIV; rather, the essay was selected because the problems discussed mirror those found elsewhere and discussed in the preceding essays.

Legal, Policy and Administrative Care Issues

Part II discusses the legal, policy and custody issues surrounding HIV/AIDS. Issues examined include; whether inmates who are HIV-positive should be segregated; whether staff should be made aware of an inmate's health status; and what are treatment obligations. Like Part I, Part II starts with a global view and then becomes more specific. In Chapter 7 Raffaele D'Amelio *et al.* provide a global review of the issue of HIV testing with a focus on military applicants. Delphine Valette (Chapter 8) then provides an illustrative summary of the European Convention on Human Rights (ECHR) and examines how this should impact the rights of HIV-positive European prisoners. In Chapter 9 Lawrence Gostin and David Webber present a summary of the 600-plus legal cases involving HIV and AIDS brought before American courts. In a closely related essay Webber (Chapter 10) updates the law relative to the recent CDC 'Prevention for Positives' initiative. This essay presents some of the ethical and legal problems that well-intended policy may inadvertently create. The final essay in Part II, by Barbara Zaitzow, ties it all together with a perceptive and comprehensive look at HIV-positive female inmates and the unique problems they face while incarcerated in the United States. She provides a case study and concludes by discussing the more controversial issues such as screening and testing, segregation, financial issues and HIV status disclosure. Her concluding policy recommendations address the issues raised by the preceding essays.

Custody, Supervision and Treatment Issues

Part III is closely related to Part II in that custodial and treatment issues are raised, but theoretically driven pieces and empirical research are used to expand on the issues raised in Part II. In Chapter 12 Maria Tiamson discusses issues related to the increasing longevity of

HIV patients, in part due to highly active anti-retroviral therapy (HAART). The next essay, by Sarah Chippindale and Lesley French (Chapter 13), describes the basics of HIV counselling and the psychosocial management of HIV patients. In Chapter 14 Michael Welch describes the political economy and the impact of 'conservative' notions about morality and drug use and discusses how these factors serve to disadvantage HIV-positive inmates. This theoretically driven critical analysis is perceptive and important for all readers, not just those interested in HIV/AIDS. In the fourth and final essay of Part III, Mark Lanier and Scott Gates statistically test the dominant theoretical strategy for reducing the spread of HIV/AIDS and point out the flawed assumptions, namely that people are rational and health-seeking.

Behavioural Interventions, Knowledge and Attitudes

The focus of Part IV shifts to specific policies, both law enforcement and correctional. The role of knowledge and attitudes are featured here. In Chapter 16 Alan Thompson and James Marquart provide an overview of the literature of law enforcement policies dealing with AIDS/HIV. They supplement this with a study of police officers from Texas and show how perceptions impact their handling of suspects. In Chapter 17 Jeanne Flavin examines perceptively how the threat of HIV infection is perhaps exaggerated compared to the reality of the risks faced by law enforcement personnel. The third essay in this section by Richard Tewksbury, Gennaro Vito and Scott Cummings identifies the role of 'criminal justice professionals' with reducing the occurrence of HIV risk behaviours. The next essay, by Terry Edwards and Richard Tewksbury (Chapter 19), offers an empirical view of training practices among almost 50 American police agencies. Finally, Kato Keeton and Cheryl Swanson (Chapter 20) examine the impact and role of education in north-west Florida jails and prisons.

Future Trends, Global Impact and Ethical Issues

The collection of essays concludes with a look towards future trends, global impact and related ethical issues. Part V also critically considers the role of community and race/ethnicity in the context of society's response. Anthony Lemelle begins, in Chapter 21, with a disturbing and, to some, controversial argument that African-Americans in the United States are differentially treated by the criminal justice and social systems. This type of treatment greatly increases their risk not only of incarceration, but also HIV infection. Johanna Crane, Kathleen Quirk and Ariane van der Straten continue this critical analysis in Chapter 22, but focus on how the economically disadvantaged are disproportionately impacted by HIV and the 'war on drugs'. They provide forceful qualitative research support for their arguments. The next essay, by Edison Trickett (Chapter 23), describes some refreshing and positive efforts at community AIDS intervention that account for culture and context. The fourth and final essay, which also concludes the volume, discusses some methodological difficulties associated with HIV research. Janine Pierret offers suggestions on how knowledge of HIV-positive individuals' needs may be enhanced.

Conclusion

Some caveats should be made explicit. First, societies, cultures and people vary greatly around the world. Whenever possible, essays with an international focus were included. Unfortunately, an overabundance of peer-reviewed essays located focused on the United States. Some may find this troubling, and to those I apologize. However, the etiology of HIV/AIDS is uniform for all peoples. Many of the issues examined by American researchers apply, or will apply, to justice systems in other countries as well. Second, my goal was to include the most recently published essays dealing with a particular subject. This goal was met in most cases, but a few exceptions were made for older essays that were exceptionally well-written and which remained germane. Finally, readers will note that journals external to criminal justice and criminology were included. This is due to the fact that HIV/AIDS is not restricted to criminal justice settings. A related observation is that there is an overlap between the essays that appear in the five Parts: for example, some papers dealing with legal issues may also address custodial concerns. Essays which were exceptionally well executed were selected for inclusion, although, in some readers' opinions, they may be miscatagorized. Despite these flaws, I hope that you find the collection useful and that the content stimulates renewed debate and ultimate progress.

References

Centers for Disease Control (2003), 'Advancing HIV Prevention: New Strategies for a Changing Epidemic – United States, 2003', *Morbidity and Mortality Weekly Report*, **18**, **52**(15), pp. 329–32.

'Florida: AIDS Primary Cause of Death in Prison' (1989), *CDC Weekly*, 6 November.

Lanier, Mark (1999), 'HIV-Related Issues for Incarcerated Women in the Twenty-First Century: Statistical, Medicinal and Theoretical' in Roslyn Muraskin and Albert Roberts (eds), *Visions for Change: Crime and Justice in the Twenty-First Century*, 2nd edn, New York: Prentice-Hall

Maruschak, Laura M. (2002), *HIV in Prisons, 2000*, Washington, DC: Bureau of Justice Statistics (NCJ 196023).

New York State Commission of Corrections (1986), *Acquired Immunodeficiency Syndrome: A Demographic Profile of New York State Mortalities 1982–1985*, Albany, NY: New York State Commission of Corrections.

Thompson, R. Alan and Marquart, James W. (1998), 'Law Enforcement Responses to the HIV/AIDS Epidemic: Selected Findings and Suggestions for Future Research', *Policing*, **21** (4), pp. 648–60.

UNAIDS (2004), 'Report on the Global AIDS Epidemic – Executive Summary', World Health Organization at: www.unaids.org/bangkok2004.

Part I
Physiological, Medical and Disease Trends

[1]

The Global HIV/AIDS Pandemic, Structural Inequalities, and the Politics of International Health

In spite of recent advances in treatment and care available in most developed countries, the HIV/AIDS pandemic continues to spread throughout the developing world.

Structural inequalities continue to fuel the epidemic in all societies, and HIV infection has increasingly been concentrated in the poorest, most marginalized sectors of society in all countries. The relationship between HIV/AIDS and social and economic development has therefore become a central point in policy discussions about the most effective responses to the epidemic.

Important progress has been made in recent United Nations initiatives. Maintaining long-term commitment to initiatives such as the Global Fund to Fight AIDS, Tuberculosis and Malaria is especially important in the wake of September 11 and ensuing events, which threaten to redirect necessary resources to seemingly more urgent security concerns.

| Richard Parker, PhD

AS THE HIV/AIDS EPIDEMIC enters its third decade, much of the sense of urgency that accompanied discussions of AIDS only 10 or 15 years ago seems to be disappearing.[1] Thanks to the development of new antiretroviral treatments capable of transforming HIV infection into a chronic but manageable health condition, mortality rates due to AIDS have fallen throughout the industrialized or "developed" world, and even in some of the more privileged "developing" countries.[2]

The worst types of discrimination and human rights violations against people living with HIV and AIDS (or suspected to be at risk for HIV infection), which occurred regularly during the early years of the epidemic, seem to have declined as well. Legal systems and official structures have been pushed to respond to the epidemic by reaffirming the basic rights of all human beings, independent of serostatus. And both governmental and civil society organizations in countries around the world have gradually mobilized resources and developed programs to overcome what once was described as "AIDS exceptionalism,"[3] increasingly mainstreaming programmatic responses to the epidemic at international, national, and local levels. Indeed, as we have turned the page on the past century and entered the new millennium, and as we head into the third decade of the HIV/AIDS epidemic, the progress made in responding to AIDS over the past decade seems to give reason for guarded optimism.

STRUCTURAL INEQUALITIES

When we turn our gaze beyond our own borders to focus on the HIV/AIDS pandemic in the most resource-poor countries of the developing world, however, the picture is considerably worse. The Joint United Nations Program on AIDS (UNAIDS) estimates that by the end of 2000 approximately 36.1 million people had been infected with HIV globally.[2] Of these, approximately 34.7 million are adults—16.4 million are estimated to be women—and 1.4 million are children. Since the beginning of the epidemic, 21.8 million people are estimated to have died—17.5 million adults (roughly 9 million women) and 4.3 million children. In 2000 alone, 3 million deaths were attributed to AIDS, and 5.3 million new infections are believed to have occurred—2.2 million among women and nearly 570000 among children.[2]

These current estimates are enough to give us pause, but it is also important to remember that there is little likelihood that the situation will improve any time soon. On the contrary, UNAIDS and the World Bank predict that HIV, which was responsible for 8.6% of deaths from infectious disease in the developing world in 1990, will be responsible for 37.1% of such deaths among adults between the ages of 15 and 59 by 2020.[4] If treatment advances and other recent scientific advances give us reason for optimism, there is equally good reason for concern, as HIV/AIDS continues to stand as one of the most significant global health problems that must be confronted in the new millennium.

Beyond the sheer weight of the numbers, what is perhaps most important about the shape of the HIV pandemic is the fact that the global distribution of infection has been anything but equal. It is estimated that approximately 920000 people have been infected in North America, for example, with 540000 infections in Western Europe and another 15000 in Australia and New Zealand.[2] In sub-Saharan Africa, by contrast, it is estimated that as many as 25.3 million persons have been infected by HIV. Another 5.8 million have been infected in South and Southeast Asia, and 1.4 million have been infected in Latin America.[2] In short, the vast majority of HIV infections can be found in the poorest regions of the world, in developing countries already facing a wide range of other serious public health problems.

This concentration of HIV infection in the countries of the developing world becomes even more worrisome if we look again at societies such as the United States, where disproportionate levels of HIV infection have been documented among racial and ethnic minority populations. Rates are especially high among gay and bisexual men in communities of color and among heterosexual women living in poverty in the inner cities.[5]

Indeed, if we bring together the available data on HIV/AIDS in the developing world with the most recent trends on HIV infection in countries such as the United States, it is impossible not to be impressed by the extent to which a range of structural inequalities intersect and combine to shape the character of the HIV/AIDS epidemic everywhere, both North and South, in developed as well as developing countries. In all societies, regardless of their degree of development or prosperity, the HIV/AIDS epidemic continues to rage—but it now affects almost exclusively the most marginalized sectors of society, people living in situations characterized by diverse forms of structural violence.[6]

[A] range of structural inequalities intersect and combine to shape the character of the HIV/AIDS epidemic everywhere.

It is in the spaces of poverty, racism, gender inequality, and sexual oppression that the HIV epidemic continues today—in large part unencumbered by formal public health and education programs, let alone by the advances in treatment that might otherwise convince us that the emergency has passed. The context in which the HIV/AIDS epidemic continues to expand in countries around the world is one of growing polarization between the very rich and the very poor, increasing the isolation of some segments of the population at a time when others are perversely integrated into the criminal economics of international drug smuggling and the like, and increasing social inequalities that seem to be an integral part of globalization based on neoliberal economic policies.[7]

These structural factors, which shape the HIV/AIDS epidemic within the contours of specific societies, even in the resource-rich industrialized countries, are the same factors that shape the global epidemic, particularly in the resource-poor and often economically dependent countries of the developing world. Indeed, perhaps no other major international public health problem so clearly reflects the social, political, and economic architecture of what has been described as the new world order: a post–Cold War international system in which, at least until very recently, the gravest threats to human security seemed to stem less from state-controlled and state-inflicted violence (such as the threat of nuclear war) than from the dismantling of previously existing health, education, and welfare systems in many of the most advanced industrial societies and from diverse forms of structural adjustment that have been imposed on many developing countries.[8]

THE POLITICS OF INTERNATIONAL HEALTH

Given these trends, it is worthwhile to note a number of recent developments and to question the ways in which they may continue to evolve, particularly in light of the still largely unpredictable consequences of the post–September 11 world. First, there is the growing role of the World Bank as one of the lead "development" agencies responsible not only for the global response to HIV/AIDS but for international health more broadly. Established as part of the Bretton Woods accords following World War II, the World Bank has emerged as the most wide-reaching and powerful international development agency in the world. It is responsible for efforts to combat poverty and promote economic development throughout Africa, Asia, and Latin America, as well as in the post-socialist countries of Eastern Europe and the former Soviet Union.

Since the early 1990s, in part as a response to critics who called attention to the frequently negative consequences of structural adjustment programs promoted by the World Bank together with the International Monetary Fund, the World Bank has increasingly focused on health-related issues, opening up new lending programs and expanding the resources available for projects focusing on population, nutrition, and similar issues throughout the developing world.[9]

And nowhere has the institution's growing involvement in health-related work been more visible than in response to the HIV/AIDS pandemic.[4] By early 2001, a total of US $1.7 billion had been made available for HIV/AIDS-related work through World Bank loans to developing countries, with significant increases in the commitment of resources in recent years.[10] Indeed, in fiscal year 2001, the World Bank expected to commit an additional US $744 million for new HIV/AIDS prevention and control efforts, making its loans the single most important source of financial resources for the global fight against the epidemic.

As potentially important as these resources have been, however, the World Bank's growing role in international health has not gone unquestioned. Precisely because structural adjustment policies have often resulted in greatly reduced spending for health, education, and welfare programs, the role of structural adjustment in contributing to the HIV/AIDS epidemic, especially in sub-Saharan Africa, has been a major focus of debate in recent years.[11] The fact that the World Bank seems increasingly to rival the World Health Organization as the most influential international agency involved in health-related work has been cited as a cause for concern.[1]

Despite the fact that World Bank loans for HIV/AIDS prevention and control are generally made at the most favorable interest rates possible, there is concern that they are still loans, rather than donations, and thus they contribute to increasing the national debt of many developing countries—countries that are already forced to commit significant portions of their annual gross national products to service existing debt obligations.[12] And although the negative impact of HIV/AIDS on economic development has been clearly articulated by the World Bank and others as a reason for greater mobilization on a global level in response to the epidemic, concern has nonetheless grown about the possibility that relatively crude cost–benefit calculations or overly economic notions of "development" may replace a broader public health framework as the basis for decisions about the design of programs and the allocation of resources.

Equally important, in the effort to develop a fuller understanding of social and economic development in relation to public health within this context, the broader implications and consequences of already existing levels of debt in the developing world must be addressed. Increasingly, treatment activists and others, in both the North and the South, have begun to call for debt relief as the only way to enable many low-income countries to increase their public health budgets to a level that will allow the implementation of adequate care and treatment programs. Without significant reforms in the current global financial system, even the most basic international public health goals may be unattainable, and nowhere are these dilemmas more clearly exposed than in the case of HIV/AIDS.

In light of these concerns, however, it is also important to note some significant progress in recent efforts to build a renewed response to the global HIV/AIDS epidemic. In mid-2001, for example, UNAIDS helped to orchestrate a groundbreaking Special Session of the United Nations General Assembly to reinforce HIV/AIDS as a priority in the international policy agenda. While there is still much to be done to transform policy into practice, the Declaration of Commitment on HIV/AIDS that emerged from that special session marked an important step.

Equally important, as part of this process, United Nations Secretary-General Kofi Annan has exercised leadership in international policy debates about HIV/AIDS and global health more broadly. Annan's role has been crucial in launching a broader debate about the social and economic roots and consequences of AIDS, as well as in supporting an innovative new funding mechanism that may have a long-term impact on restructuring financial support for the response not only to HIV/AIDS but to other serious international health problems: the Global Fund to Fight AIDS, Tuberculosis and Malaria. With Annan's active backing, the creation of this special fund received widespread international support in June 2001, when representatives from more than 50 countries, multilateral agencies, and nongovernmental organizations met at the Special Session of the United Nations General Assembly.[13]

The specific details of the governance, administration, and underlying principles of the Global Fund to Fight AIDS, Tuberculosis and Malaria are still being finalized. However, early signs suggest that the fund may offer important advances in terms of better coordination of efforts to confront disease, greater transparency in relation to the distribution of resources, and greater decentralization of decision making in relation to program design and implementation than has been the case in previous multilateral agency responses to HIV/AIDS and related issues.

Unfortunately, the initial response in terms of commitment of resources to the fund has been disappointing. Although Annan originally estimated that US $7 to $10 billion would be needed by 2005 to meet expected demand, as of November 2001 only slightly more than US $1.5 billion had been committed by governments, nongovernmental organizations, and private donors. This amount includes only US $300 million committed thus far by the government of the United States.[14]

The relatively disappointing response of the United States should be cause for alarm for anyone concerned about HIV/AIDS or issues of international health more broadly. As the richest nation in the world—and as one of the chief beneficiaries of the current global economic order, which has done so much to shape the HIV/AIDS pandemic as a product of structural inequalities both within and between nations—the United States is unquestionably the key point of reference for other nations, as well as for private-sector organizations and individuals, in evaluating their own contributions to the global effort to respond to HIV/AIDS and other major international health problems.

Without renewed and expanded commitment from the Bush administration and the US Congress, the likelihood is that the Global Fund to Fight AIDS, Tuberculosis and Malaria will fall far short of its goal, and one of the most innovative opportunities in the response to HIV/AIDS globally will be lost. At a time when health care around the world is increasingly privatized, and when banks have increasingly become the arbiters of international health policy, losing this chance to reaffirm a vision of health as a fundamentally public good would be a terrible loss—not only for those who are living with or vulnerable to HIV infection, but for all who understand that questions of health can never be separated from broader struggles for responsibility, fairness, and social justice.

MAINTAINING COMMITMENT

The risk of a lack of ongoing commitment to HIV/AIDS internationally, and to the Global Fund to Fight AIDS, Tuberculosis and Malaria in particular, has of course become all the more serious in the wake of the terrible terrorist attacks on September 11 and the ensuing military response of the United States. As the international system struggles to come to grips with the many changes that have been brought about by these events, public attention has understandably turned to questions of our immediate security in a world that now seems physically unsafe in a new and very different way, and our ability to maintain interest in the seemingly more long-term and distant security concerns of issues such as HIV/AIDS is threatened.

Although the United Nations leadership has stood firm in emphasizing the continued importance of the Global Fund and the high priority that must be given to struggles against infectious diseases, issues such as terrorism and bioterrorism have understandably taken precedence in many of the most recent debates about human well-being and safety within the broader context of international relations. Within this rapidly changing context, we can only hope that new concern will emerge, as well, with the fundamental inequities that have been such an integral part of recent processes of globalization—in particular, with the ways in which such inequities have contributed to the terrible new forms of risk and insecurity that confront us today in a world that often seems to be spinning out of control.[7]

Now, more than ever, it is crucial that we work to analyze and understand the social and economic processes that have not only produced extreme forms of physical violence, but that have exacerbated the health threats that face so much of the world's population on a daily basis. Clearly, public health research and analysis has a key role to play in building the intellectual bridges that will be necessary to understand the health consequences of the development models that have been pursued in recent decades—and the ways in which these models may have contributed to new forms of insecurity that are omnipresent in today's world.

In a policy context that is increasingly conditioned by fear—and, because of this fear, by urgent demands for immediate solutions—one of our greatest challenges is to build an understanding of the broader structural forces that have shaped not only the first epidemics of a truly globalized world, but also its most recent political and ideological challenges.[15] And in a historical moment in which our most pressing dangers have come so close to home, one of our most urgent priorities must be to keep alive, as well, the broad range of public health issues that must be confronted as we march into the new millennium. The future of the global HIV/AIDS epidemic, and of the millions of lives affected by it, will depend on the ways in which we confront these dilemmas. ■

About the Author

Richard Parker is with the Department of Sociomedical Sciences, Mailman School of Public Health, Columbia University, New York, NY.

Requests for reprints should be sent to Richard Parker, PhD, Department of Sociomedical Sciences, Mailman School of Public Health, Columbia University, 600 W 168th St, New York, NY 10032 (e-mail: rgp11@columbia.edu).

This commentary was accepted November 30, 2001.

References

1. Parker R. Administering the epidemic: HIV/AIDS policy, models of development, and international health. In: Global Health Policy, Local Realities: The Fallacy of the Level Playing Field. Boulder, Colo: Lynn Reinner Publishers; 2000:39–55.

2. UNAIDS. AIDS epidemic update—December 2000. Available at: http://www.unaids.org. Accessed November 15, 2001.

3. Kirp D, Bayer R, eds. AIDS in the Industrialized Democracies. New Brunswick, NJ: Rutgers University Press; 1992.

4. World Bank. Confronting AIDS: Public Priorities in a Global Epidemic. New York, NY: Oxford University Press; 1997.

5. Karon JM, Fleming PL, Steketee RW, DeCock KM. HIV in the United States at the turn of the century: an epidemic in transition. *Am J Public Health.* 2001;91:1060–1068.

6. Farmer P, Connors, M, Simmons J, eds. Women, Poverty and AIDS: Sex, Drugs and Structural Violence, Monroe, Me: Common Courage Press; 1996.

7. Castells M. End of Millennium. Oxford, England: Blackwell; 1998.

8. Beck U. What Is Globalization? Cambridge, Mass: Polity Press; 2000.

9. World Bank. World Development Report 1993: Investing in Health. New York, NY: Oxford University Press; 1993.

10. World Bank. HIV/AIDS. Available at: http://www.worldbank.org/HDN. Accessed August 1, 2001.

11. Lurie P, Hintzon P, Lowe RA. Socioeconomic obstacles to HIV prevention and treatment in developing countries: the roles of the International Monetary Fund and the World Bank. *AIDS.* 1995;9:539–546.

12. Galvão J. A AIDS no Brasil. Rio de Janeiro, Brazil: Editora 34/ABIA; 2000.

13. Fact sheet: a global AIDS and health fund. Available at: http://www.un.org/ga/aids/ungassfactsheets/html/fsfund_en.htm. Accessed November 15, 2001.

14. Office of the Spokesman for the Secretary General. Contributions pledged to the Global Fund to Fight AIDS, Tuberculosis and Malaria. Available at: http://www.un.org/News/ossg/aids.htm. Accessed November 15, 2001.

15. Castells M. The Power of Identity. Oxford, England: Blackwell; 1997.

[2]

Structural factors in HIV prevention: concepts, examples, and implications for research

Esther Sumartojo

Introduction: HIV-prevention behavior is affected by the environment as well as by characteristics of individuals at risk. HIV-related structural factors are defined as barriers to, or facilitators of, an individual's HIV prevention behaviors; they may relate to economic, social, policy, organizational or other aspects of the environment.

Impact of structural interventions: A relatively small number of intervention studies demonstrates the potential of structural interventions to increase HIV prevention in the United States and internationally. The promise of structural interventions has also been shown in studies of interventions to prevent disease or promote public health in areas other than HIV.

Framework of structural factors: Frameworks help define and exemplify structural barriers and facilitators for HIV prevention. One framework developed at Centers for Disease Control and Prevention gives examples of structural facilitators in terms of the economic resources, policy supports, societal attitudes, and organizational structures and functions associated with governments, service organizations, businesses, workforce organizations, faith communities, justice systems, media organizations, educational systems, and healthcare systems. Frameworks should assist researchers and health officials to identify important areas for structural research and programming.

Conclusions: A structural approach is timely and innovative. Despite limitations, including the challenge of a new perspective on prevention and the difficulty of evaluating their effects, researchers and public health officials are urged to pursue structural interventions to prevent HIV.

Keywords: HIV prevention, structural factors, risk factors

Introduction

HIV-related structural factors are defined as barriers to, or facilitators of, an individual's HIV-prevention behaviors. They directly or indirectly affect an individual's ability to avoid exposure to HIV. These factors have different names in the literature — environmental, structural, societal, super-structural, policy, contextual and others — often reflecting the disciplines and experiences of the writers. The broad term 'structural' is used in this paper, with the assumption that its meaning will become clearer and more differentiated as work in this area progresses.

International research demonstrates the potential of structural interventions for reducing HIV risk [1]. Specific examples include: the 80% increase in condom use among commercial sex workers following a policy requiring the use of condoms in brothels in Thailand [2]; a 45% difference in HIV prevalence among intravenous drug users in two cities in Scotland, attributed to differing enforcement of paraphernalia laws [3]; a 10% increase in requests for HIV tests by pregnant women following provision of testing in south-eastern France [4]; and increases in reports of condom use between steady partners by up to 24% and between casual partners by up to 48% following implementation of a comprehensive national prevention policy in Switzerland [5]. Additional studies have linked structural factors and HIV prevention in the United States [6–13], and review articles have assessed collections of studies and confirmed the importance of structures to HIV risk [1,14–19]. Studies addressing disease prevention and health promotion in other areas of public health, including infectious diseases, food-borne illnesses, environmental health, chronic disease, infant mortality, and injury and violence prevention corroborate the importance of structures to prevention [20].

Increasingly, writers envision changes that would remove barriers to or erect facilitators for effective prevention [17,19,21–38], and that would address HIV by increasing human rights [38–40]. The purpose of this paper is to help support and direct research that will characterize existing structural facilitators and barriers to prevention, and evaluate the impact of structural changes on HIV risk behaviors and infection.

Research on structural factors and interventions

Research on HIV prevention needs to target multiple levels, including individuals and the environments that influence their behavior. Biomedical and behavioral research have addressed HIV primarily at the level of individuals, providing treatment and prevention for HIV and AIDS, and behavioral interventions such as education, counseling and testing, small group counseling and skills development, and information and prevention motivation provided by peers in a community context. These behavioral approaches have been summarized by various reviewers [22,41–48]. Although there are relatively few rigorous experimental studies of behavioral interventions to prevent HIV [22,46], there is sufficient evidence to support the replication and dissemination of individually focused strategies [49]. In addition to these individual-level studies, researchers are called to examine family-focused strategies [10,50–52], community-level interventions [16,53–55], inequality among social and demographic groups [34–36,40,56], and interventions to build prevention capacity and sustainability in affected communities [10,57].

Research that demonstrates the relationship between structural factors and HIV is rare, particularly in the United States. However, several published studies exemplify how structural factors may facilitate or inhibit HIV prevention. Albert *et al.* [6] studied a structurally mandated intervention targeting female brothel workers and their clients. In 1988, the state of Nevada passed a law requiring condom use in legal brothels. This law allowed women working in the brothels to insist on condom use with clients, and to devise strategies to serve clients who were reluctant to use condoms. It also led brothel owners to install safeguards such as buzzers in rooms or security personnel to help women deal with uncooperative clients. Because income for the women was dependent on keeping the brothels open, there was economic pressure for them to comply with the law. Very few clients (2.7%) refused to use condoms, and there was no incidence of HIV and negligible incidence of sexually transmitted diseases among the brothel workers after the condom law was passed.

Two studies provide examples of interventions that facilitated prevention behaviors by instituting policies related to HIV testing. In 1985, the Department of Public Health in San Francisco began contacting the partners of index cases and offering them HIV information, counseling and testing [11]. Only 12% of the partners who were contacted refused to be interviewed. Of those interviewed, all elected some form of follow-up, and 58% elected to be tested for HIV. The health department policy increased the likelihood that exposed persons would know of their risk, and seek follow-up services and testing. At about the same time, in 1986, 25 Oregon counties initiated anonymous HIV counseling and testing [9]. During pretest counseling, clients could choose confidential or anonymous testing. Over three times as many clients were tested during the 3 months following the new policy compared with the preceding 3 months. Of those tested after the new policy, 29% of clients overall, and 49% of men who have sex with men, reported that they would not have accepted testing if their identities were confidential but not anonymous. The new policy removed a significant barrier to an important preventive behavior.

Cost may be a structural barrier to the acquisition and use of condoms. Researchers interviewed patrons of local stores in a community in Louisiana, and asked how they obtained condoms and whether they used them during their last sexual encounter [8]. Surveys were conducted while condoms were freely available in these businesses, and after a small (25 cent) charge was imposed. The researchers found that individuals who reported picking up free condoms were significantly more likely to report using condoms during their last sexual encounter than those who reported not picking up free condoms. Persons with two or more sex partners were significantly more likely to

Table 1. Comparison of frameworks of factors affecting HIV prevention

Framework author(s)	Individual micro-level factors	Structural intermediate-level factors	Structural macro-level factors
Diez-Roux [26]		Area-based treatment center and neighborhood characteristics; poverty and deprivation	Socio-economic status of populations
Sweat and Denison [17]	Individual level knowledge of HIV risk and prevention	Structural level laws, policies, standard operating procedures; environmental conditions and resources of individuals	Superstructural economic underdevelopment, gender inequality
Tawil *et al.* [19]	Individual characteristics targeted in prevention programs	Economic conditions or policies	
Mann and Tarantola [39]	Personal vulnerabilities such as knowledge and skills	Programmatic vulnerabilities such as education and social services	Societal vulnerabilities such as discrimination of HIV-positive
Zierler and Krieger [38]			Class, race, gender, sexuality inequalities

report using condoms when they were free than when they had to pay the low price. The authors concluded that cost is a barrier to condom use, and that free condoms should be available to persons at risk for HIV.

Another study described the impact on HIV-related behaviors of a structurally imposed barrier to prevention. Researchers assessed the impact of the closure of a needle-exchange program for intravenous drug users in a town in Connecticut. Before closure, 14% of interviewed intravenous drug users reported unsafe sources for syringes and 16% reported sharing a syringe in the past 30 days. After closure of the exchange, those reporting unsafe sources increased to 51% and those reporting sharing a syringe increased to 34%. After closure, the rate of reusing syringes doubled among those surveyed [7,13].

Educational interventions, such as teaching people about HIV or how to be safe from infection, are not structural *per se*. However, policies supporting the provision of education or information may be structural. Examples might be hospital policies to teach universal precautions to staff or to provide information to mothers on prevention of perinatal transmission, or a policy adopted by a nonprofit organization to inform local legislators about the impact of discrimination and stigmatization on HIV risk among minorities or men who have sex with men. Researchers in Seattle instituted an organizational system to train and remind physicians and other providers to conduct HIV-risk assessments and counseling with outpatient patients in a health maintenance organization setting. In follow-up surveys, patients in the intervention arm reported significantly more discussions of HIV risk and prevention with their physicians [58]. This structural intervention involved a policy change that gave administrative support for the provision of prevention services, including patient education.

Frameworks of factors associated with HIV

Various writers have developed frameworks to differentiate and define levels or types of environmental influences on HIV and other health behaviors (Table 1). Diez-Roux [26] discussed the impact on public health of the socio-economic status of a population, area-based characteristics such as poverty and deprivation, neighborhood-level characteristics, and treatment-center characteristics. Sweat and Denison [17] used examples from developing countries to differentiate environmental factors in terms of the range of their influence over HIV-prevention or risk behaviors. According to this framework, superstructural factors such as economic underdevelopment or gender inequality might affect an entire nation. Structural factors such as laws, policies and standard operational procedures might affect the behavior of a segment of the society, such as commercial sex workers or recipients of publicly funded services. Environmental factors might have an impact on the conditions and resources of individuals, such as whether work camps could accommodate the families of male workers. Individual-level factors might influence whether people know about HIV and risk behaviors, and methods to avoid exposure. Tawil *et al.* [19] differentiated between individual-level prevention approaches that attempt to persuade individuals to change their HIV-risk behaviors, and economic conditions or policies that may either remove barriers or erect barriers to safe behaviors. Frameworks have also differentiated among social, economic and political types of influence that impact on HIV rates in a society or social subgroups. For example, Mann and Tarantola [39] introduced the concept of vulnerabilities: HIV risk is affected by personal vulnerabilities, such as individual knowledge and skills; programmatic vulnerabilities, such as education and social services; and societal vulnerabilities, such as discrimination directed at persons with AIDS. Zierler and Krieger [38] attributed the distribution of HIV among women to inequalities associated with class, race, gender and sexuality.

As shown in Table 1, these frameworks distinguish individual- from structural-level factors that affect HIV prevention. They also describe structural factors as having a more immediate or proximal impact on individuals (at the intermediate level) or a more distal impact (at the macro level). This is an important distinction because it characterizes differing views of HIV experts about how structural factors relate to HIV risk and where interventions need to be targeted. At the macro level, the vulnerability of persons to HIV is influenced by broad social structural characteristics. These 'core' or distal causes may be far removed from individuals' control, but impact their lives through economic inequalities, racism, sexism, discrimination and stigmatization directed towards groups at high risk for HIV. At the intermediate or more proximal level, barriers are more closely linked to specific behaviors, such as when they influence the availability of legal and accessible prevention services or products to reduce the likelihood of infection. This distinction has important implications because the focus of structural research and prevention programming will depend on which level is accepted as causal of HIV outcomes or as the most promising target for interventions. In addition, if the causal link between distal influences and HIV risk is unclear to fund providers and policy-makers, they may be unwilling to support structural research and interventions. The intermediate-level barriers may be easier to study and change, and causal links to HIV risk may be more direct, but they may also fail to address the important core issues. Most of the frameworks shown in Table 1 include both levels.

During 1998, a workgroup of Centers for Disease Control and Prevention staff developed a framework to help define and provide parameters for structural barriers and facilitators of HIV prevention, and a list of barriers or facilitators that might inhibit or support HIV prevention. (Contributing members of the workgroup were Kim Boyd, Scott Damon, Lynda Doll, Patricia Martins, Scott McCoy, Ann O'Leary, Esther Sumartojo, and Linda Wright-Deaguero.) The criteria for barriers and facilitators were that they are part of the context or environment surrounding individuals, but outside their direct control. The workgroup developed a two-dimensional framework of structural factors (see Table 2). One dimension comprised four levels of barriers or facilitators: economic, such as funding to support risk-reduction strategies; policy, including laws and regulations; societal, including community norms, cultural beliefs, and expressions of broad social attitudes such as discrimination or stigmatization targeting specific groups; and organizational, including the structures and functions of service organizations or their capacity to sustain prevention programs. The second dimension comprised the systems that implement and support each type of structural barrier or facilitator: government (of all types); service organizations such as community-based organizations, professional or nonprofit organizations; business or for-profit organizations; workforce organizations such as labor unions; faith communities or organizations such as individual religious institutions or denominations; justice systems such as courts or law-enforcement systems; media organizations; educational systems such as school districts or universities; and healthcare systems such as provider organizations or hospitals.

The Centers for Disease Control and Prevention framework is not meant to be exhaustive, but to provide a model of the scope and character of structural factors related to HIV prevention. For example, an economic barrier to HIV prevention erected by a state or federal government might be limitations on funding for HIV prevention and treatment in prisons. A business-related policy that could facilitate HIV prevention might be self-imposed controls by chemical producers on the sale of products used in 'street' or illicit drugs. A societal barrier to HIV prevention might be promulgated by a community where institutions such as schools, churches, and the police fail to address discrimination or stigmatization directed at men who have sex with men. At an organizational level, a facilitator of HIV prevention through a healthcare system might be the integration of HIV and sexually transmitted disease treatment services, or a requirement that providers discuss HIV testing and prevention with their patients. These facilitators and barriers would be indirectly related to HIV prevention behaviors on the part of individuals but would help to create an environment that supports or inhibits prevention.

Despite the differences among the frameworks described in this article, there appears to be consensus that effective prevention will require a continu-

Table 2. Examples of structural facilitators affecting HIV prevention

System	Economic resources	Policy supports	Societal conditions	Organizational structures and functions
Government	Housing assistance for high-risk homeless	Policies on partner notification (see also [11])	Constituent attitudes about local government role in prevention	Overlap in research mission among agencies
Service organization	Financial assistance for families at risk	Policies on advocacy activities	Community sensitivity toward persons at risk	Mission and capacity for prevention programs (see also [55])
Private business	Funds for new product development (see also [8])	Health-promotion policies targeting workers (see also [2])	Attitudes of pharmacists on sale of syringes to IDUs (see also [18])	Mission and capacity for programs targeting employees (see also [6])
Workforce organization	Funds to support advocacy for worker safety	Policies on HIV-positive workers	Attitudes on discrimination against high-risk groups	Mission and capacity for programs targeting workers
Faith community	Funds for soup kitchens, shelters	Policies on contraception, ordination of gay clergy	Attitudes on stigmatization of MSM, gender equality	Mission and capacity for community prevention programs
Justice system	Funds for prison job training	Policies on HIV testing and condoms in prisons (see also [12,13])	Police attitudes about sex workers, IDU, MSM	Mission and capacity for prison prevention programs; integration of prison and community resources (see also [3])
Media	Free broadcasts promoting HIV-prevention behaviors	Policies on advertising of condoms (see also [5])	Representation of gender stereotypes and violence	Mission to address discrimination, stigma using popular media
Educational system	Funds for school and college prevention	Policies on education on sexual health, violence	Attitudes on gender roles, HIV-positive persons	School-board mission to promote prevention
Healthcare system	Funds for accessible and high-quality healthcare	Policies on confidentiality of patient information (see also [4,9,11])	Approaches to sexuality, patient communication	Mission and capacity to provide prevention targeting high-risk patients (see also [58])

IDU, injecting drug users; MSM, men who have sex with men.

um of approaches targeting the structures and environments that influence individual behavior. Consistent terminology, clear explanations of how structural factors influence individual behavior, and realistic ideas for structural and environmental intervention strategies are needed. In particular, research must hypothesize and demonstrate causal relationships between changes in structural conditions and HIV outcomes.

Issues related to structural approaches to HIV prevention

Even if they are meant to facilitate prevention, structural interventions may be seen by some as limiting individual choice or coercing individuals in unacceptable ways. For example, a law to quarantine infected persons, although structural, would be considered an unacceptable loss of individual rights. Laws to remove private rooms in bathhouses have met with strong opposition, partly for this reason [59]. When it was first introduced, named reporting of partners of HIV-infected persons raised concerns about loss of confidentiality [60,61]; this policy has now met greater acceptance as it helps public-health officials identify and offer treatment to newly infected persons [62]. Structural interventions may also inadvertently lead to stigmatization if, for example, they call attention to groups at high risk; for example, when restrictions on HIV-infected immigrants lead to stigmatization of national groups or when regulations preventing blood donations increase stigmatization of high-risk groups.

A second issue is that structural approaches require a shift in our thinking about how to change behavior. Many view behavior as personally motivated or resulting exclusively from a person's conscious decisions. The role of the structural environment is therefore often overlooked. In this way, interventions may aim to change an individual's knowledge or motivations without also addressing the root causes or the context that encourages HIV risk [63].

An additional issue is the difficulty of assessing the impact of structural interventions and describing how they affect behavior. Structural interventions are difficult to evaluate because they do not conform easily to conventional experimental designs, and effects are difficult to measure. Researchers may be hampered by a lack of methodologies for studying the complex relationship between the context of health and health outcomes. The effectiveness of structural approaches will therefore be hard to defend scientifically without new and rigorous research methods.

Structural interventions may also be perceived as going beyond the traditional role of public health. Indeed, this work will require greater participation by experts in organizational structure and function, lawyers, policy analysts, sociologists and others.

A structural perspective needs to be workable, not just idealistic. Otherwise, the area may be so broadly defined that interventions become impossible. Dowsett [64] stated: "We could easily produce wondrous arguments on the effects of poverty, the impact of structural adjustment policies on public health infrastructure, the effects of global gender inequalities, the universal vulnerability of young people, the oppression of minorities, or the immoral effects of the international drug marketeers. All true, but they would provide little insight into where to start in developing local public health HIV/AIDS/STD policy or useful, on-the-ground, health promotion interventions to prevent infection and to improve the lives of the infected. The challenge is to come up with a macrosocial view that adds to a workable response to the pandemic instead of one that overwhelms our capacity to act."

Conclusion

It is time for HIV research and interventions to address the structures that influence risk or that limit the impact of other prevention strategies. Ideas and justifications for research and programming will emerge from epidemiological observations, the innovative ideas of HIV experts, research reports, and opportunities for natural experiments provided by new laws, regulations, policies and societal changes. Researchers and health officials, with guidance from affected groups and communities, must determine what research is needed and how it should be prioritized, the types of disciplines and expertise needed, the most promising theories or models, and the most appropriate research methods. There is an urgency to these activities because of the power of structural interventions to affect the HIV epidemic.

At the same time, research will be difficult and controversial. It will be challenging to study multiple interacting levels of behavioral causation while also attending to issues of equality and human rights that are usually involved at the level of structural factors and interventions. Taking a structural approach to preventing HIV implies a much broader role for public-health scientists and providers. It will require a shift in perceptions about how to influence HIV risk behaviors, and new and interdisciplinary research methodologies.

In the Soho region of London, there is a pub that serves as a kind of Mecca for epidemiologists. Its namesake, John Snow, ended a cholera outbreak in that region by removing the handle from the pump that had been delivering contaminated water [65]. Snow did not conduct focus groups, distribute pamphlets or hold skill-building seminars in order to motivate residents to avoid using water from that pump. He simply removed the handle, a kind of structural intervention that would probably be impossible today. There is no pump handle to stop HIV, but there are ways to change the environment through the structures affecting HIV risk. Finding, studying and implementing these approaches are some of the most important challenges facing HIV researchers, health providers and affected communities.

Acknowledgments

The author acknowledges those colleagues who provided recommendations for the development and revision of this paper: Lynda Doll, Steve Jones, Robert Kohmescher, Richard Parker, Dan Wohlfeiler and Richard Wolitski.

References

1. Parker R, Easton D, Klein C. **Structural barriers and facilitators in HIV prevention: a review of international research.** *AIDS* 2000, **14(suppl 1)**:S22–S32.
2. Hanenberg RS, Rojanapithayakorn W, Kunasol P, *et al.* **Impact of Thailand's HIV-control programme as indicated by the decline of sexually transmitted diseases.** *Lancet* 1994, **344**:243–245.
3. Convisier R, Rutledge JH. **Can public policies limit the spread of HIV among IV drug users.** *J Drug Issues* 1989, **19**:113–128.
4. Rey D, Carrieri MP, Obadia Y, *et al.* **Mandatory prenatal screening for the human immunodeficiency virus: the experience in south-eastern France of a national policy, 1992–1994.** *Br J Obstet Gynaecol* 1998, **105**:269–274.

5. Dubois-Arber F, Jeannin A, Konings E, *et al.* **Increased condom use without other major changes in sexual behavior among the general population in Switzerland.** *Am J Public Health* 1997, 87:558–566.
6. Albert AE, Warner DL, Hatcher RA, *et al.* **Condom use among female commercial sex workers in Nevada's legal brothels.** *Am J Public Health* 1995, **85**:1514–1520.
7. Broadhead RS, Van Hulst Y, Heckathorn DD. **Termination of an established needle-exchange: a study of claims and their impact.** *Social Problems* 1999, **46**:48–66.
8. Cohen, D, Scribner R, Bedimo R, Farely TA. **Cost as a barrier to condom use: the evidence for condom subsidies in the United States.** *Am J Public Health* 1999, **89**:567–568.
9. Fehrs LJ, Foster LR, Fox V, *et al.* **Trial of anonymous versus confidential human immunodeficiency virus testing.** *Lancet* 1988, **2**:379–382.
10. Fullilove RE, Green L, Fullilove MT. **The family to family program: a structural intervention with implications for the prevention of HIV/AIDS and other community epidemics.** *AIDS* 2000, **14(suppl 1)**:S63–S67.
11. Rutherford GW, Woo JM, Neal DP, *et al.* **Partner notification and the control of human immunodeficiency virus infection.** *Sex Transm Dis* 1991, **18**:107–110.
12. Koester SK. **Copping, running, and paraphernalia laws: contextual variables and needle risk behavior among injection drug users in Denver.** *Hum Org* 1994, **53**:287–295.
13. Groseclose SL, Weinstein B, Jones ST, Valleroy LA, Fehrs LJ, Kassler WJ. **Impact of increased legal access to needles and syringes on practices of injecting-drug users and police officers — Connecticut, 1992–1993.** *J Acquir Immune Defic Syndr Hum Retrovirol* 1995, **10**:82–89.
14. Des Jarlais DC. **Structural interventions to reduce HIV transmission among injecting drug users.** *AIDS* 2000, **14(suppl 1)**. S41–S46.
15. Marks G, Burris S, Peterman TA. **Reducing sexual transmission of HIV from those who know they are infected: the need for personal and collective responsibility.** *AIDS* 1999, **13**:297–306.
16. Rotheram-Borus MJ. **Expanding the range of interventions to reduce HIV among adolescents.** *AIDS* 2000, **14(suppl 1)**.S33–S40.
17. Sweat MD, Denison JA. **Reducing HIV incidence in developing countries with structural and environmental interventions.** *AIDS* 1995, **9**:S251–S257.
18. Taussig J, Weinstein B, Burris S, Jones ST. **Syringe laws and pharmacy regulations are structural constraints on HIV prevention in the US.** *AIDS* 2000, **14(suppl 1)**:S47–S51.
19. Tawil O, Verster A, O'Reilly KR. **Enabling approaches for HIV/AIDS prevention: can we modify the environment and minimize the risk?** *AIDS* 1995, 9:1299–1306.
20. Blankenship KM, Bray SJ, Merson MH. **Structural initiatives in public health.** *AIDS* 2000, **14(suppl 1)**:S11–S21.
21. Coates TJ. **Strategies for modifying sexual behavior for primary and secondary prevention of HIV disease.** *J Consult Clin Psychol* 1990, **58**:57–69.
22. Choi K-H, Coates TJ. **Prevention of HIV infection.** *AIDS* 1994, 8:1371–1389.
23. Stryker J, Coates TJ, DeCarlo P, Haynes-Sanstad K, Shriver M, Makadon HJ. **Prevention of HIV infection: looking back, looking ahead.** *JAMA* 1995, **272**:1143–1148.
24. Brownson RC, Newschaffer CJ, Ali-Abarghoui F. **Policy research for disease prevention: challenges and practical recommendations.** *Am J Public Health* 1997, **87**:735–739.
25. Schmid TL, Pratt M, Howze E. **Policy as intervention: environmental and policy approaches to the prevention of cardiovascular disease.** *Am J Public Health* 1995, **85**:1207–1211.
26. Diez-Roux AV. **Bringing context back into epidemiolgy: variables and fallacies in multilevel analysis.** *Am J Public Health* 1998, **88**:216–222.
27. Wallace R, Wallace D. **The coming crisis of public health in the suburbs.** *Milbank Q* 1993, **71**:543–564.
28. Susser M. **The tribulations of trials – intervention in communities [editorial].** *Am J Public Health* 1995, **85**:156–158.
29. Sampson RJ, Raudenbush SW, Earls F. **Neighborhoods and violent crime: a multilevel study of collective efficacy.** *Science* 1997, **277**:919–924.
30. Pappas G. **Elucidating the relationships between race, socioeconomic status, and health.** *Am J Public Health* 1994, **84**:892–893.
31. Diehr P, Koepsell T, Cheadle A, *et al.* **Do communities differ in health behaviors?** *J Clin Epidemiol* 1993, **46**:1141–1149.
32. Blank D. **Social determinants of health — socioeconomic status, social class, and ethnicity [editorial].** *Am J Public Health* 1995, **85**:903–906.
33. Link BG, Phelan JC. **Understanding sociodemographic differences in health — the role of fundamental social causes [editorial].** *Am J Health Promotion* 1996, **86**:471–473.
34. Aggleton P. **Global priorities for HIV/AIDS intervention research.** *Int J STD AIDS* 1996, **7**:13–16.
35. Amaro H. **Love, sex, and power.** *Am Psychol* 1995, **50**:437–447.
36. Gupta GR, Weiss E. **Women's lives and sex: implications for AIDS prevention.** *Culture Med Psychiatr* 1993, **17**:399–412.
37. Merson MH. **International perspective on AIDS prevention research.** In *NIH Consensus Development Conference. Interventions to Prevent HIV Risk Behaviors: Program and Abstracts.* Washington, DC: National Institutes of Health; 1997:101–106.
38. Zierler S, Krieger N. **Reframing women's risk: social inequalities and HIV infection.** *Annu Rev Public Health* 1997, **18**:401–436.
39. Mann JM, Tarantola DJM. *AIDS in the World II.* New York: Oxford University Press; 1996.
40. Farmer P, Connors M, Simmons J. *Women, Poverty, and AIDS: Sex, Drugs, and Structural Violence.* Monroe, ME: Common Courage Press; 1996.
41. Booth RE, Watters JK. **How effective are risk-reduction interventions targeting injecting drug users?** *AIDS* 1994, **8**:1515–1524.
42. Exner TM, Seal DW, Ehrhardt AA. **A review of HIV interventions for at-risk women.** *AIDS Behavior* 1997, **1**:93–124.
43. Ickovics JR, Yoshikawa H. **Preventive interventions to reduce hererosexual HIV risk for women: current perspectives, future directions.** *AIDS* 1998, **12**:S197–S208.
44. Wolitski RJ, MacGowan RJ, Higgins DL, *et al.* **The effects of HIV counseling and testing on risk-related practices and help-seeking behavior.** *AIDS Educ Prev* 1997, **9**:52–67.
45. Coates TJ, Collins C. **HIV prevention: a 10-point program to protect the next generation.** *Sci Am* 1998, **279**:96–97.
46. Oakley A, Fullerton D, Holland J. **Behavioral interventions for HIV/AIDS prevention.** *AIDS* 1995, **9**:479–486.
47. Office of Technology Assessment. *The Effectiveness of AIDS Prevention Efforts.* Washington, DC: American Psychological Association Office on AIDS; 1996.
48. National Institutes of Health. *NIH Consensus Development Conference. Interventions to Prevent HIV Risk Behaviors: Program and Abstracts.* Washington, DC: National Institutes of Health; 1997:1–106.
49. Sogolow E, Semaan S, Johnson W, *et al.* **Effects of US-based HIV interventions on safer sex: meta-analyses, overall and for populations, age, groups, and settings.** In *12th World AIDS Conference.* Geneva, Switzerland; June–July 1998:239 [abstract 14283].
50. Miller KS, Kotchick BA, Forehand R. **Adolescent sexual behavior in two ethnic minority samples: the role of family variables.** In *12th World AIDS Conference.* Geneva, Switzerland; June–July 1998:979 [abstract 44217].
51. de Loye GJ, Henggeler SW, Daniels CM. **Developmental and family correlates of children's knowledge and attitudes regarding AIDS.** *J Pediatr Psychol* 1993, **18**:209–219.
52. Sigelman CK, Derenowski EB, Mullaney HA, Siders AT. **Parents' contributions to knowledge and attitudes regarding AIDS.** *J Pediatr Psychol* 1993, **18**:221–235.
53. The CDC AIDS Community Demonstration Projects Research Group. **Community-level HIV intervention in 5 cities: final outcome data from the CDC AIDS community demonstration projects.** *Am J Public Health* 1999, **89**:336–345.
54. Kelly JA. **Community-level interventions are needed to prevent new HIV infections.** *Am J Public Health* 1999, **89**:299–300.
55. Valdiserri RO, Aultman TV, Curran JW. **Community planning a national strategy to improve HIV prevention programs.** *J Community Health* 1995, **20**:87–100.
56. Singer M. **AIDS and the health crisis of the US urban poor; the perspective of critical medical anthropology.** *Social Sci Med* 1994, **39**:931–948.
57. Guenther-Grey C, Sumartojo E. **Developing a comprehensive community-level intervention for young men who have sex with men: the CITY project.** In *National HIV Prevention Conference.* Atlanta, GA, 1999 [abstract 196].

58. Dodge WT, BlueSpruce J, Grothaus Louis, Rebolledo V, McAfee TA, Thompson RS. **Enhancing primary care based HIV prevention behaviors: impact of a comprehensive clinical intervention in managed care.** In *APHA Annual Meeting: Abstracts*. Chicago, IL, November 1999 [abstract 2149]
59. Wohlfeiler D. **Structural and environmental HIV prevention for gay and bisexual men.** *AIDS* 2000, 14(suppl 1):S52–S56.
60. Gostin LO, Hodge JG Jr. **Piercing the veil of secrecy in HIV/AIDS and other sexually transmitted diseases: theories of privacy and disclosure in partner notification.** *Duke J Gender Law Policy* 1998, 5:9–88.
61. Richardson L. **Wave of laws aimed at people with HIV.** *New York Times* September 25, 1998.
62. Centers for Disease Control and Prevention. **Evaluation of HIV case surveillance through the use of non-name unique identifiers — Maryland and Texas, 1994–1996.** *MMWR Weekly* 1998, 46:1254–1271.
63. O'Leary A, Martins P. **Structural factors affecting women's HIV risk: a life-course example.** *AIDS* 2000, 14(suppl 1):S68–S72.
64. Dowsett G **The indeterminate macro-social: new traps for old players in HIV/AIDS social research.** *Culture, Health Sexuality* 1999, 1:95–102.
65. Snow J. *On the Mode of Communication of Cholera*. London: Churchill; 1855.

[3]

Accounts from the Field: A Public Relations Perspective on Global AIDS/HIV

NILANJANA R. BARDHAN

Department of Speech Communication
Southern Illinois University at Carbondale
Carbondale, Illinois, USA

This study is a theoretical as well as empirical exploration of the power and cultural differentials that mark and construct various intersecting discourses, specifically media discourse, on global AIDS/HIV. It applies the language and concepts of public relations to understand how the press coverage of the pandemic is associated with the variables that impact the newsmaking process as well as the public and policy implications of macro news frames generated over time. Theoretical work in the areas of agenda setting and news framing also instruct the conceptual framework of this analysis. Narrative analysis is used as a methodology to qualitatively analyze three pools of accounts—from people either living with AIDS/HIV, involved in AIDS/HIV work, or discursively engaged in the media construction of the pandemic; from transnational wire service journalists who cover the issue at global and regional levels; and policy shapers and communicators who are active at the global level. These three communities of respondents represent important stakeholders in the AIDS/HIV issue. The findings are analyzed from a public relations standpoint. Perhaps the most important finding of this study is that the public relations approaches used to address AIDS/HIV related issues need to be grounded in context-specific research and communicative practices that bring out the lived realities of AIDS/HIV at grassroots levels. The findings also posit that those situated at critical junctions between various stakeholders need to cultivate a finely balanced understanding of the etic and emic intersections and subjectivities of global/local AIDS/HIV.

Introduction

The AIDS/HIV pandemic is a phenomenon that is as socially, symbolically, and communicatively constructed as it is a biomedical "reality." The meanings attributed to it are culturally diverse and multiperspectival (O'Neill, 1991), and they emanate from the lived as well as mediated experiences of those directly and indirectly involved in its discursive and retroviral folds. However, it is the views, values, and perspectives that are privileged and endorsed at larger societal levels that rhetorically and politically shape the future courses of action, policy, and signification (Treichler, 1988). This study is, in part, a theoretical as well as empirical exploration of the power and cultural differentials that mark and construct the various intersecting discourses, specifically media discourse, on global AIDS/HIV.

My sincerest thanks to the coparticipants who provided "accounts" from the field, and to Dr. Hugh Culbertson, Dr. Joseph Bern, and Dr. Lenore Langsdorf for their guidance and helpful insight.

Address correspondence to Nilanjana R. Bardhan, Ph.D., Assistant Professor, Department of Speech Communication, Mailcode 6605, Southern Illinois University at Carbondale, Carbondale, IL 62901-6605, USA. E-mail: bardhan@siu.edu

There is much that is understood and a lot more not understood about how to socially and medically cope with AIDS/HIV. On a global note from UNAIDS (Piot, Bartos, Ghys. Walker, & Schwartländer, 2001), an international organization specifically dedicated to addressing the pandemic:

> Responding to HIV/AIDS on a scale commensurate with the epidemic is a global imperative. The task has barely begun, but at least we are at the end of the beginning, with the needs recognized together with the proven elements of an effective response. (p. 973)

If it has taken twenty years to reach the "end of the beginning," then it remains necessary to keep exploring why it has taken this long. This is a large and interdisciplinary area for investigation. This article adopts a critical cultural approach to examining the social and global construction of AIDS/HIV, and it does so mainly using the language of public relations. There is a growing acknowledgment that the AIDS/HIV issue needs to be understood as a cultural phenomenon, that the media's role is a significant part of this culture (Airhihenbuwa & Obregon, 2000), that exploration of the various contexts of the pandemic at global as well as local levels is necessary (Airhihenbuwa, Makinwa, & Obregon, 2000), and that overall, communication is central to all prevention efforts (Rogers, 2000). Thus, this article is an attempt to dilute the boundaries that prevent holistic understanding of the pandemic since an ecological approach is necessary to move closer to more humane, expeditious, and responsible communicative action (and policy).

The first part of this article is a compact analysis of some of the prominent sociological, cultural, economic, geopolitical, mass media, and human communications trends related to the pandemic. It makes a case that global AIDS/HIV lends itself well to analysis from a public relations standpoint, specifically international/intercultural public relations. It also uses the theoretical concepts of agenda setting and news framing to understand the media construction of the pandemic and claims that in addition to the more visible mainstream media narratives, there is a need to unpack the meanings of the more embedded narratives that are either shaped by or explain the construction of the AIDS/HIV mainstream media narratives. This is an attempt to situate media content as a point along a continuum of a much larger and complex process of social construction that includes various other levels of communicative action. With the intention of drawing out the lived experiences of those who are vectors of these more embedded AIDS/HIV narratives, analysis of narrative is used as a qualitative methodology to examine three pools of responses—from people either living with AIDS/HIV, involved in AIDS/HIV work, or discursively engaged in the media construction of the pandemic; from transnational wire service journalists who cover the issue at global and regional levels; and policy shapers and communicators who are active at the global level. The findings are finally analyzed from a public relations standpoint.

Global AIDS/HIV

The worldwide picture of the pandemic is sobering. Currently 36.1 million people are infected and 21.8 million have succumbed to AIDS/HIV (UNAIDS, 2000). Because infection spreads primarily through human contact, the patterns of the latter half of the twentieth century, such as increased global trade, travel, and migration have all contributed to increases in the spread of infection (Gallo, 1991). However, this spread is not homogenous in character, and the epidemic exhibits different behavioral and cultural patterns of transmission in various regions of the world (Brown & Xenos, 1994). But an overwhelming fact remains that the virus is taking its heaviest toll in specific developing regions of the world, that is, sub-Saharan Africa, South and Southeast Asia, and now Eastern Europe (Piot et al., 2001). In the West, the virus is now spreading faster among less privileged groups in society (Shelton, 1999). There are still myriad complexities surrounding vaccine development (Nabel, 2001; Stephenson, 2001), and prevention is the only known method for checking the spread of HIV. The expensive antiretroviral drugs that are distant dreams for 90 percent of those affected (Purvis, 1996/1997) are not cures but ways of prolonging lives, accessible to the more economically privileged.

Since the 1980s, the global effort to stem the tide of AIDS/HIV has moved through various phases of multilateral, bilateral, nongovernmental, voluntary and private programs and initiatives. The World Health Organization started the Global Programme on AIDS in 1987—this was the first international institutional effort to contain AIDS/HIV. Once the complex nature of the pandemic was realized, UNAIDS, a joint body of six UN organizations, was formed in 1994. The three main goals of the UNAIDS mission are policy development and research, technical support, and advocacy (UNAIDS: Mission and Roles, 1995).

For much of the last 20 years of the pandemic, there was a general lack of cohesiveness and clarity in the direction of global planning. Some reasons for this ambiguity were the difficulties of worldwide data collection; the scarcity of funds for sustaining long-term programs; inordinate allocation of available funding to expensive drug treatment research; complacency and lack of effective leadership in many countries; diverse cultural interpretations of AIDS/HIV; interorganizational confusion about the scope of each unit's work; and an overall fuzzy picture of worldwide AIDS (Christakis, 1989; Mann, Tarantola, & Netter, 1992).

Policies over the past two decades have reflected the course of international discourse and agendas. The early panic frame led to the identification of "risk groups" (instead of risk behaviors), and some countries implemented repressive policies such as segregation in "sidatorios" in Cuba (O'Connor, 1991) and tight immigration controls in Russia (Kraft, 1994). Next came the heterosexual scare phase that exploded the derogatory gay disease label. Policies began to reflect wider social, cultural, economic, ethical, prevention, and education related issues and concerns. In addition, there was much cultural resistance out of many countries, specifically in Asia, that took the form of governmental denial and lack of commitment toward policy development (Bonacci, 1992). The biomedical frame has been consistent throughout the two decades, especially in the economically developed West, and has heavily influenced policy, research, and funding allocation (McAllister, 1992). Differing combinations of these phases have existed at any given point in time in various countries (Gordenker, Coate, Jönsson, & Söderholm, 1996).

The General Assembly of the United Nations held its first ever gathering to discuss the future of a disease in June 2001, and issues of culture and allocation of funds for treatment and prevention research were the focus of attention. The meeting concluded on the note that any global action needs to be respectful of the cultural traditions in many parts of the world, which includes the use of culturally appropriate language and culturally sensitive treatment of issues such as homosexuality, commercial sex work, intravenous drug use, and condom use. This meeting also made headway in terms of garnering a commitment from national governments to work with a global blueprint that sets specific policy and preventive action goals for the years 2003 and 2005. Secretary General Kofi Annan clearly endorsed a grassroots culture-specific approach by emphasizing that women and nongovernmental organizations (NGOs) need to be at the helm of the global prevention initiative (Harris, 2001). Other current issues on the global plate involve pharmaceutical companies and patent legalities that make it difficult for economically underprivileged and hard hit nations to access therapy drugs (Boseley & Astill, 2001), and the global call for a commitment from the G-8 nations to explore how corporations can increase their contributions to the worldwide effort (Beattie & Fidler, 2001).

A Public Relations Perspective

There are several parallels between the global AIDS/HIV situation and the current directions of international/intercultural public relations theory and practice. An analysis of these parallels holds practical value for a better understanding of the pandemic from the perspective of communicative relationship-building efforts to achieve the larger goals of prevention and context-friendly policy and research.

Public relations, a communications profession and practice that mainly developed in the United States in response to market needs, is predominantly understood as a corporate management function (Grunig & Hunt, 1984). However, literature in the area has evolved to include many diverse definitions for public relations. Any planned communicative action that aims to develop "mutually beneficial relationships" between clients and their significant publics (Cutlip, Center, & Broom, 1994) can be defined as public relations. For the purpose of this article, clients and publics are referred to as "stakeholders" (Wartick & Wood, 1998) because there is no primary client, in an organizational or corporate sense, in the global AIDS matrix.

From a macro perspective, some of the key stakeholders in the global AIDS issue are national governments; international organizations such as the UN and its arm UNAIDS; NGOs; the media (global as well as local); people living with AIDS/HIV (who may be divided into subgroups); activist groups, pharmaceutical companies; insurance companies and other corporate stakeholders; service-providing organizations; and researchers and policymakers at various levels. Some of these stakeholders work together and some work in opposition to others and they all contribute to shaping the responses to the pandemic at micro and macro levels that involve human as well as mediated communication efforts.

An Analysis of the Power Relations Between Stakeholders

The matrix of relationships between global AIDS/HIV stakeholders may be examined from the perspective of the four models of public relations that evolved in the West (Grunig & Hunt, 1984). According to the first model, the *press agentry/publicity model*, public relations activities aim to get the attention of relevant publics often through sensationalism and distortion of information. The power to initiate communicative action is perceived to be with the client. According to the second model, the *public information model*, the client aims to inform its publics about itself through dissemination of accurate information. The power to initiate communication is still perceived to be with the client. The third model, the *two-way asymmetrical model*, emphasizes feedback from the publics so that the client may strategize its communication activities to systematically and scientifically persuade its publics. Although feedback from the publics is crucial, the purpose of this feedback is to empower the client and not the provider of the feedback. The last model, the *two-way symmetrical model*, reconfigures the tradition of focus on the client and emphasizes a transactional approach to public relations where relationship building is the primary goal. Both client and publics, within this model, are open to the ideas of change and mutual adaptation. This model values the diminishing of power differentials. A mix of all four models is usually in operation at any given point in time; however, which model dominates depends on the cultural and ideological, as well as national, contexts of practice.

When applied to global AIDS/HIV, shades of the first three models are evident in how different stakeholders have been more (or less) visible or active during various social phases and in different contexts. The power relationships between stakeholders signified through these models have also played out somewhat concurrently.

The communicative phenomena of silence, denial, hype, and distortion of information are characteristic of the first model. For example, in many parts of the world, distinct silence from national governments, heads of state, and policymakers marked the early to mid-1980s. In the United States, the first speech about AIDS from the president and the first report from the surgeon-general did not come until after the mid-1980s (Rogers, Dearing, & Chang, 1991). At an international level at that time, bodies such as the World Health Organization were struggling to set up a response in the face of a fuzzy picture of worldwide infection (Christakis, 1989). In many parts of Asia and Africa (Sabatier, 1988; Bonacci, 1992), national governments were in denial about AIDS and labeled it as a "foreign" disease. The mainstream media were unsure about how to report in the face of overall confusion and uncertainty (Shilts, 1987; Kinsella, 1989; Klaidman, 1990). Discriminatory responses in the United States included labeling AIDS as a "gay disease" or blaming Haiti (or Haitian immigrants) as being the source of the virus (Grmek, 1990). Misinformation about how the virus can be contracted came from official (Fauci, 1983) as well as other sources. Much fear and uncertainty surrounded the issue, and overt stigmatization of people living with AIDS/HIV was prevalent (Sontag, 1989). Thus the relationships between the stakeholders were mostly marked by conflict, uncertainty, blame attribution, and a general lack of cultural sensitivity. Apart from a few prominent activist groups such as the AIDS Coalition for Unleashing Power (ACT-UP), the stakeholders whose lives were most affected by the virus were most invisible and powerless in this early rhetorical and social construction of the pandemic. An effort to elicit their "feedback" was not very evident.

Shades of the public information model became apparent once the heterosexual scare phase (Albert, 1989) mutated into the "normalization" and "medicalization" phase (Nelkin, 1991; McAllister, 1992) in the latter half of the 1980s. Dissemination of accurate information through the media became a priority. Governments around the world were paying better attention to the issue, and the international response began to take clearer shape (Sepulveda, Fineberg, & Mann, 1992). Biomedical researchers in the West, drawing societal endorsement from cultural dependence on science as a quick-fix for most problems (Nelkin, 1987; Wilkins, 1995), searched for a miracle cure while policymakers began speaking the language of education and prevention. According to a study of the coverage of AIDS by the *Washington Post*, the *New York Times*, the *Los Angeles Times*, and the *Chicago Tribune* between 1983 and 1989 (Walters & Walters, 1996), 90 percent of the stories were drawn from mainstream medical journals and publications. Alternative stories were restricted to the alternative media (McAllister, 1990). Although activist and nongovernmental groups were gaining more presence and voice, the more traditional or "official" voices of authority (Gans, 1979) continued to shape the grand discourse of the pandemic (Bardhan, 2001). Efforts to include feedback from the least powerful stakeholders—those most situated in the life world of AIDS/HIV—were still not very evident.

The second model gradually evolved into the third or the two-way asymmetrical model in the late 1980s and the 1990s. With some lessening of social stigma and more open discussions in global and local forums, behavior-based research and persuasive programs aimed at prevention and changing harmful health beliefs and practices became more visible. Nonetheless, feedback was obtained for the main purpose of designing theory-driven top-down programs (Airhihenbuwa & Obregon, 2000) and policies. These initiatives were two-way but mostly asymmetrical in the sense that feedback was elicited to fit a priori planning. At the global level, UNAIDS was formed and work in this area picked up momentum. Ironically, it was about this time that the mainstream media started struggling to find novel frames for an ongoing issue. Overall, coverage declined and became routine (Hernandez, 1994; Princeton Survey Research Associates, 1996; Bardhan, 2001). Human interest stories involving celebrities and the occasional medical hope story would inspire sporadic surges in coverage (Princeton Survey Research Associates, 1996). In many parts of the developing world, stigmatization of groups was still very evident (Bonacci, 1992; Netter, 1992; Lim, 1995; Rogers, 2000). The theme of prevention received scant coverage, as did the globally interconnected dimensions of the pandemic. Policymakers gained ground as spokespersons, and biomedical authority remained undisturbed (Bardhan, 2001); however, the voices of the majority stakeholders still remained muted despite increasing involvement of NGOs and other grassroots organizations. Overall, the agency and the resources to communicate, determine the direction of research and funding, initiate and devise policy/programs, and shape the content of information disseminated remained with the traditional authorities, and the position of the less powerful "unknown" (Gans, 1979) stakeholders did not change much.

The application of these public relations models to the various phases of the pandemic must be understood as broad strokes; and the intention is not to simplify a complex situation. However, these broad strokes do enable us to see that the dominant representation of the pandemic has primarily been shaped by the more powerful stakeholders (minority) although the lived experiences of those whose lives are most touched by AIDS/HIV (majority) remain embedded at the micro level in this stakeholder matrix.

This brings us to the fourth model, the two-way symmetrical model. Conscious adoption of this model would be a progressive step toward grassroots empowerment and involvement, that is, a transfer of power to the less privileged majority stakeholders through increased co-participation in shaping the programs and discourses that affect their lives. This model would not change the stakeholders, but it would require that the traditionally powerful stakeholders be more inclusive of the lived experiences of those most affected by the pandemic. The global discourse at present is leaning toward this model; however, it is still exogenous to the extent that it ultimately requires the local to conform to the global blueprint for action (Harris, 2001). This is where the problematic nature of the notion of "symmetry" becomes apparent.

Symmetry between clients and their publics is an ideal and never possible. Holtzhausen (2000) and Duffy (2000) propose that instead of striving for a mythical equal playing field, stakeholders (publics and clients) should work on openly identifying points of conflict, differences, or tensors and work toward communicative relationship building and maintenance strategies from this less airbrushed perspective. This critique, when applied to global AIDS/HIV, makes good sense because there are more tensors than points of convergence in the ongoing attempts at dialogue between different stakeholders. This leads us to the internationally and interculturally oriented models of public relations.

An International/Intercultural Approach

Since the escalation of globalization and free market philosophies in the latter part of the twentieth century, there has been a tendency to contextually export Western style public relations concepts to various nations around the world. This tendency has been criticized as ethnocentric (Al-Enad, 1990; Van Leuven & Pratt, 1996), and more context-sensitive and polycultural approaches have been offered.

Botan (1992) developed the public relations matrix approach that posits that the meaning of public relations in any given country or cultural context can be best understood by examining the four indicators of level of national development, primary client for public relations, the legal/political context, and the history of the development of public relations in that environment. Such an analysis, according to Botan, provides an endogenous explication of how public relations is conceptualized and practiced in a particular country and its unique environment. Wartick and Wood (1998) propose the institutional–ideological model with reference to multinational corporations and global business. They suggest that technology and ecology (natural environment) form the core of any environment (or culture) of operation and that the business, government, and public institutions and the social, political, and economic ideologies that drive these institutions are shaped, constrained, and fueled by these two core dimensions. Thus, imposing top-down communication strategies before understanding the institutional and ideological textures of any environment amounts to unwise or myopic strategy.

Banks (1995) applies intercultural theorizing to international public relations and suggests that the local/global/local approach should replace the global/local mindset. With this approach, the conceptualization of communicative public relations action starts at the local or emic level instead of at the global or etic level, thus giving preference to context over a priori strategizing. Berkowitz and Muturi (1999) make a case for participatory public relations, and they do so specifically in the context of the population control program in Kenya. They identify women as primary stakeholders in this issue and state that "Participatory communication strategies pertain to creating conditions for and facilitating dialogue between programs and the stakeholders" (p. 2).

These ground up approaches to public relations can be useful in the current struggle to negotiate the global and local dimensions of AIDS/HIV. As Banks (1995) suggests, the locus of power and decision making needs to shift more to the local level. There is an urgent need to tap into the symbolic realities of those who are traditionally *targeted* by AIDS/HIV initiatives—how do they perceive, understand, and subjectively interpret their experiences? What kinds of programs do they think would work best for them? This sentiment is also evident in the current rhetoric emerging from the UN and UNAIDS. Between 1997 and 1999, in a concerted effort to review past and current theoretical approaches to communicative action for prevention, practitioners and researchers representing different world regions came to the conclusion that five vital contextual domains—government and policy, socioeconomic status, gender relations, culture, and religion—need to be addressed in the attempt to build global and regional frameworks for action that will provide structure and direction and yet be flexible enough to incorporate change depending on contextual needs. This process included experiential input from some of the hardest hit regions in the world (Airhihenbuwa, Makinwa, & Obregon, 2000).

If these domains are to be respected, then more research needs to be conducted to include voices of experience from the field—the voices of the traditionally less powerful stakeholders in the pandemic. Some scholarly efforts in this direction include a recent volume edited by Elwood (1999) that investigates talk and conversation at several communicative, political, and cultural levels. to bring out various lived AIDS/HIV realities for a better understanding of risk behavior. It privileges the viewpoint that the interpretations of AIDS/HIV that are most important from the perspective of formative research reside in those who are most immersed in the pandemic. Another study analyzes the conversations of women who use drugs with their social supporters in the attempt to endogenously locate their social support and illness management needs

(Falkin & Strauss, 2000). In order to more completely comprehend how people living with AIDS/HIV subjectively interpret available treatment options, their own sexual behavior, and manage illness, Bartos and McDonald (2000) conducted in-depth conversational style interviews with respondents in Australia. Along a similar vein, Frey, Adelman, Flint, and Query, Jr. (2000) explored the communicative practices that residents at a facility for people living with AIDS/HIV participate in for the purpose of symbolically constructing a sense of community in order to cope with disease and illness. Similarly, Reeves (2000) conducted a qualitative study to explore how, in the absence of institutional support, people living with AIDS/HIV use the Internet to search for resources and build (and participate in) a sense of (cyber) community.

Programs communicatively infused with culturally sensitive and ground-up research on risk behaviors tend to empower and provide a sense of ownership for health to those most affected or at risk, and they tend to have high success rates. Some examples include peer promotion programs in Ghana (Wolf, Tawfik, & Bond, 2000), needle exchange programs for intravenous drug users in Australia and Britain (Roane, 1997), condom use promotion and awareness campaigns in Thailand that are embedded in the cultural mores and practices of that country, and Veshya AIDS Muquabla Parishad (VAMP) in India, a grassroots collective initiative that empowers commercial sex workers through peer education and action (Caron, 1999).

From a public relations standpoint, it can be argued that because AIDS/HIV is a polycultural phenomenon, it makes sense to follow polycultural and emic approaches to negotiate the relationships between various stakeholders and the tensions between the global, regional, and local interpretations of the pandemic. This approach is more of an attitude than a method. The willingness to cooperate (in working toward a common goal) on what is really a valence issue (Dearing & Rogers, 1996) is a mindset that is necessary for all stakeholders involved. At the same time, the global momentum cannot be sustained without commitment from national levels and in many nations, community level agency is difficult without government (national level) support. This suggests that there is a need for a fine balance between the agendas of all these multilevel units, between the etic and the emic levels of action and understanding, and that "interdependence" is the key word in this stakeholder matrix.

The Role of the Mass/News Media

So far, the main argument of this article has been that for successful communicative relationship building to occur between the various stakeholders involved in the AIDS/HIV pandemic, there needs to occur a significant transfer of agency from macro to grassroots levels. The role of the mass media, a stakeholder in the issue by virtue of its sociological involvement in the public opinion and policy process (Dearing & Rogers, 1996), is crucial in how these power relationships between stakeholders are continuously constructed, endorsed, maintained, negated, or amplified. This framing, in turn, has an impact on how these relationships are negotiated/shaped at human interactional levels.

Many of the stakeholders in the global AIDS/HIV pandemic are also active "claim-makers" (Best, 1989):

> Claim-making is an act of communication. Claim-makers address different audiences: Some hope to identify and organize the people directly affected by the conditions described in their claims; others try to educate the general public; and still others approach the policymakers who can do something about the conditions. While some meet their audiences face-to-face, many

> contemporary claim-makers use the mass media to reach their audiences. If the press can be convinced that their claims are newsworthy, the media will spread their message. (p.1)

Thus the media construction and response to AIDS/HIV becomes inextricably intertwined with matters such as which claims/stakeholders are accorded privilege or credence and the symbolic and ideological content of these claims. This brings us to the concepts of news framing and agenda setting.

News Framing

Tuchman (1978) borrowed the term "frame" from Goffman (1974) who used frame analysis to phenomenologically analyze the social organization of human experience, and applied it to the newsmaking process. She posited that news, especially news about phenomena that is beyond an individual's direct experience,

> . . . is a window to the world. But, like any frame that delineates a world, the news frame may be considered problematic. The view through a window depends upon whether the window is large or small, has many panes or few, whether the glass is opaque or clear, whether the window faces a street or a backyard. (p. 1)

In a similar move to make apparent the process-oriented nature of newsmaking, and to point out that news content is simultaneously a dependent as well as independent variable, Shoemaker and Reese (1996) offer the hierarchical model for influences on media content. According to this model, the interplay of five levels of influence—the individual, media routine, organizational, extramedia, and ideological levels—give shape to media content. At the individual level, the personal beliefs and values of the reporter, despite professional conditioning, influence decision making. At the media routine level, the set routines of information gathering and processing, for instance, the ritual of mostly relying on expert, authoritative, or official sources (Gans, 1979; Soloski, 1989), shape the final news product. At the organizational level, the structures, policies, rules, and goals of news organizations form yet another layer of influence. The extramedia influences include the public relations efforts of various groups, advertisers, and various forms of government control. The last level, the ideological level, infuses the entire process with the dominant ideologies of the times. Thus, this model lends further support to the thesis that the manner in which an issue is constructed by the media is a fluid process that can be strategically influenced by various stakeholders because "Unlike physical scientists, journalists observe phenomena that can fight back, dispute the way they are described, and set rules for their observation" (Reese, 1990, p. 393).

Most of the several studies that have examined the news framing of AIDS/HIV have tracked the patterns of coverage, but have stopped short of analyzing the practical/theoretical implications of the frames or of offering suggestions for public (specifically media) relations strategies to prosocially influence coverage.

A donation request packet received by the author from the American Foundation for AIDS Research in 2000 contained a decal that proclaimed, "AIDS. This may be the most dangerous time yet." It also included a timeline graph for the United States that locates 1980 to be the year of confusion, the mid-1980s to be the era of hysteria, the early 1990s to be the time of ignorance, and it marks the year 2000 as the point of complacency. The macro media frames of coverage display a similar timeline, thereby indicating an interplay between media and social construction.

This macro pattern, which has become evident in most parts of the world (Netter, 1992), is documented empirically. Studies conducted of the press coverage in various countries in Africa (Sabatier, 1988; Lester, 1992), North America (Rogers, Dearing, & Chang, 1991; Clarke, 1992; Princeton Survey Research Associates, 1996), Asia (Lim, 1995: Bonacci, 1992; Netter, 1992), Australia (Lupton, 1993), and Britain and Europe (Grube & Boehme-Deurr, 1989; Semetko & Goldberg, 1993; Traquina, 1996) unpack the following frames. The early phase of coverage is usually scant and marked by fear and ignorance. The focus is on identifying "risk groups" rather than "risk behaviors." Blame attribution and lack of political support from heads of state also mark this phase. The second phase is one of exploration and understanding and an attempt to move beyond labels and blame attribution (Rogers, Dearing, & Chang, 1991; Princeton Survey Research Associates, 1996). There is more of an acceptance that HIV can affect anybody and everybody. This phase shifts to one that amplifies biomedical and policy matters (McAllister, 1992; Watts, 1993). To this may be added a last phase (the 1990s onward) of routine wherein events such as World AIDS Day and international conferences are accorded perfunctory coverage (Princeton Survey Research Associates, 1996; Traquina, 1996). The routine is rippled by the occasional celebrity story, scandal angle, or biomedical discovery (Princeton Survey Research Associates, 1996). This phase, it has been opined (Sepulveda et al., 1992), generates a false sense of security by recasting what remains an urgent issue into a mold of routine. Focus on prevention programs and the globally interrelated nature of AIDS/HIV is minimal (Bardhan, 2001).

"Official" sources (Gans, 1979) and stakeholders such as biomedical researchers and policymakers continue to control and shape the grand contours of the news narrative. Although activists and people living with AIDS/HIV have gained more ground as sources through the 1990s, this has not been a significant shift in voice (Princeton Survey Research Associates, 1996; Bardhan, 2001). June 2001 marked the twentieth anniversary of HIV/AIDS, and once again there was a routine upward surge in the media graph indicating attention to the issue. However, the graph line subsided quickly, and the meta news narrative of the pandemic did not step off the "beaten path."

Agenda Setting

What are the theoretical, public opinion, and policy implications of these macro level AIDS/HIV news frames? According to Gitlin (1980), "*Media* frames, largely unspoken and unacknowledged, organize the world for both the journalists who report it, and, in some important degree, for us who rely on their reports" (emphasis in original, p. 7). According to Brown (1992), "... [reporting about] AIDS carries with it another obligation—thrusting onto the media the often unwanted and ambiguous role of an audience that, by and large, relies on the press for nearly all it knows about AIDS" (p. 721). These statements imply an agenda-setting effect.

With initial seeds in Lippmann's (1922) assertion that the media shape "pictures in our heads," research in agenda setting has come a long way. It no longer proposes a linear causal relation between media, public, and policy agendas but problematizes this relationship using the language of social construction. Initial theorizing proposed that the media agenda is causally linked to the public agenda because the news tells us "what to think about" (Cohen, 1963, p. 13). Studies over the last 30 years show that the relationship is not that straightforward, that various contingent factors and alternate agendas make the media agenda a dependent variable (McCombs, 1992) as well as an independent variable because "media framing suggests that the media not only tell us what to think about, but also how to think about it, and consequently what to think" (McCombs, 1993, p. 65).

According to Dearing and Rogers (1996), "The agenda-setting process is an ongoing competition among issue proponents [stakeholders] to gain the attention of media professionals, the public and policy elites" (p. 1–2). Through a comprehensive review of landmark studies in this area, they point out that "real-world indicators" have no causal relationship with media salience accorded to issues or with issue attention cycles, that trigger events spark coverage, that high salience is accorded to an issue when all three agendas are at a peak, and that repetition in the media does keep an issue on the public agenda. They also emphasize the need for more longitudinal studies that track the agenda-setting effects for single issues. In an agenda-setting study of AIDS/HIV between 1981 and 1988, Rogers, Dearing and Chang (1991) found that there were no linear effects between media (coverage by the *New York Times, Los Angeles Times, Washington Post*, and the national television networks NBC, CBS and ABC), science (prestige science journals), public (measured through national poll responses) and policy (federal funding for research) agendas as well as real-world indicators (mortality rates). All these agendas were linked in non-causal combinations during different phases. However, as already described earlier in this article, it is evident that when analyzed from a macro perspective (as opposed to micro unit analysis), there are several links between the sociological (includes public and policy agendas) and the media frames of global AIDS/HIV, thus lending support to the social and symbolic-issue construction argument.

Although there is not much evidence for causal links between media/public and policy agendas (Dearing & Rogers, 1996), some studies do exist that are pertinent to the AIDS/HIV issue. O'Heffernan (1994), through in-depth interviews with senior policy-makers, found that most policymakers tend to accord high importance to media coverage of issues, especially in the early stages of an issue or if it is a crisis/conflict situation. Also, the level of accountability in coverage may significantly impact policy agendas. According to Pritchard (1992), when accountability is not clear-cut and news stories are passive, even a high volume of coverage may not lead to any policy outcomes. The nature of an issue is also a factor. Research indicates that global issues such as AIDS/HIV, human rights, international refugee migration, and global warming have more of an impact on policy agendas and that "The key element in the salience of these issues is the intensity, duration, and type of media coverage they can garner. Those that generate stories in prestige media . . . are defined as politically important and are given attention" (O'Heffernan, 1993, p. 194). Brown and Xenos (1994) emphasize that policymakers need to see and learn about developments in local and global AIDS initiatives in order to be concerned about effective policy change. Thus,

> the media identification and definition of public problems work not only on mass audiences. Policymakers are very attentive to news coverage. They are more likely to respond to highly salient issues, even those that provoke considerable conflict, and they do so largely in the context of the frame that the media have provided. The media's construction of AIDS thus has influenced not merely how we as individuals will react but also how we as a society and as a polity will respond. (Colby & Cook, 1991, p. 219)

With recent moves toward social constructionist thinking in agenda-setting research, it makes good methodological sense to explore the process through qualitative approaches that enable in-depth investigation of lived experiences. Thus, an analysis of the personal narratives of stakeholders situated at various points in the global AIDS/HIV agenda-setting or social construction process should provide some useful qualitative insights that could be useful for future media coverage, media relations, policy outcomes, and program planning.

Narratology (Methodology)

> . . . my thinking and writing about AIDS has been done, to invoke one of the only metaphors by which AIDS can be understood, at the level of everyday involvements. (Grover, 1992, p. 230)

Human beings are storytelling creatures (Fisher, 2001). Through their narratives they organize their everyday lived experiences and provide situated accounts of these experiences. Storytelling then is a form of subjectively assigning meaning to experiences. Although some narratives are offered voluntarily, others are elicited (Hinchman & Hinchman, 2000). The tradition of narrative-knowing hails primarily from the work of historians, literary critics, and psychologists. There are various approaches to gleaning meanings from narratives; however, there is general agreement among scholars of narratology that narratives are not mirror reflections of peoples' internal realities—people narratively organize their experiences, share these with others (or co-construct with others), and these narrative accounts are yet again coded (or interpreted) by others (such as researchers) (Polkinghorne, 1988). This implies that there are various cognitive levels of narrative construction and meaning attribution at play in the process of narrative knowing, and that the process is not static.

Narratives can be organized at various levels such as the personal (identity) level as well as at the community level. At the community level, "The stories that individuals create often strike variations upon a repertoire of socially available narratives that, in turn, legitimize the community and guarantee its continued existence" (Hinchman & Hinchman, 2000, p. xvii). Narratives are political (teleological), and the context in which they are offered, and the relationship between the participants in the narrative construction process all contribute to the shaping of the accounts. Working out of this theoretical approach, this study elicited narratives from three communities of stakeholders in the AIDS/HIV pandemic:

- Internet discussion groups devoted to AIDS/HIV and journalism issues (this community of respondents includes individuals who live with AIDS/HIV or are involved in AIDS/HIV work);
- Journalists who cover AIDS/HIV for transnational wire services;
- AIDS/HIV policy shapers and communicators who work at the global level.

By tapping into these three communities of stakeholders, it was the intention of the author to communicatively co-construct narratives in the global playing field of AIDS/HIV. The first community represents the majority ("unknowns") stakeholders whereas the other two communities are the voices of the traditionally more powerful stakeholders.

An open-ended questionnaire was designed for each community of respondents. Questions for the transnational wire service correspondents focused on exploring the forces that shape the coverage (Shoemaker & Reese, 1996) of AIDS/HIV at a global level. The Internet discussion groups and the policy shapers and communicators were mostly asked to provide their views on the implications of current trends in coverage for social perception and global action. Contact between each respondent and the author was limited to one or two sessions. Because these open-ended respondent interviews followed a certain order and were at the same time designed to encourage the participants to freely share their narratives, they were, in this sense, semi-directive (Lindlof, 1995).

A purposive approach was followed to build the entire sample of respondents. Eighteen correspondents who cover AIDS/HIV for the transnational wire services Reuters, the Associated Press (AP), Agence France-Presse (AFP), Telegrafenoye Agentsvo Sovetskovo Soyuza (ITAR-TASS), and Inter Press Service (IPS) were identified and contacted. The first four wire services were selected because they are the world's leading mainstream wire services responsible for the bulk of the news and information that flows through the arteries of the global news web (Alleyne & Wagner, 1993). IPS was included as an alternative wire service that focuses primarily on third world issues and concerns (Boyd-Barrett & Thussu, 1992). A total of five correspondents agreed to be interviewed—two from Reuters, and one each from AFP, ITAR-TASS, and IPS. Electronic mail and/or telephone interviews were conducted with each of these correspondents.

The three Internet discussion groups selected were sci.med.aids, misc.health.aids, and alt.journalism. These discussion groups were located by using the services of Deja News, Inc., an Internet newsgroup facilitator that coordinates these cyber public spheres that are open to participants from all over the world. A total of 15 detailed responses were received, 9 from the 2 AIDS discussion groups, and 6 from alt.journalism. Participation was voluntary, and the interview questions were posted on the "bulletin boards" of each of these discussion groups.

Seventeen specific individuals at the World Health Organization and other member units of UNAIDS and at the PANOS Institute, another organization involved in global prevention and policy efforts, were contacted for the third pool of narratives. Two individuals responded and interviews were conducted by telephone and electronic mail.

Confidentiality was offered and assured to all individuals wishing to remain unidentified. Names of most respondents have been left out to accommodate such requests. All interviews were started and completed during the months of April and May, 1998.

Analysis of narrative (Polkinghorne, 1995) was used as a method to qualitatively analyze the narratives (responses) elicited from each of these three communities of stakeholders. This approach applies the notion of "paradigmatic cognition" to analyze narratives. According to Polkinghorne, paradigmatic cognition involves "... classifying a particular instance as belonging to a category or concept ... Paradigmatic reasoning is a primary method by which humans constitute their experience as ordered and consistent" (pp. 9,10). Polkinhorne's theory was cast into method form and used to qualitatively thematize the narratives, and crystallize categories of structured opinions, arguments, and experiences in order to understand how these stakeholders narrate the media and social construction of global AIDS/HIV. The attempt was to arrive at "best fit" explanations that incorporated the commonalties that emerged from each of the three sets of stakeholder narratives.

Overall, the following were the main research questions:

1. How does each community of stakeholders narrate the media and social construction of global AIDS/HIV?
2. Are there any significant overlaps in the narrative constructions of these three communities of stakeholders?
3. What do these narratives tell us about the media and social construction of global AIDS/HIV that is useful feedback from a public relations standpoint, specifically for the purpose of improving the quality of relationships between various stakeholders?

Accounts from the Field (Results)

Cyber Community

The respondents from this stakeholder community provided the majority of the narratives. There was an overall agreement that the manner in which the news media construct global AIDS/HIV has definite consequences for public opinion, policy, and prevention strategies at local and global levels.

Most of the respondents felt that the dominant impression conveyed by the current coverage of worldwide AIDS is that the epidemic is over, under control, or declining in intensity. Other words used to describe the coverage were "inadequate," "uninformed," "simplistic," and "misleading." There was also consensus that the coverage focuses heavily on the United States and Western Europe, the biomedical research hubs of the world. According to one respondent from the United States, "I cannot recall the last mainstream story I saw on the epidemic outside the United States even though by absolute numbers the United States is far from the majority of cases reported worldwide." According to a respondent from England, "I don't see any coverage of the world here, to speak of."

Several narrative explanations were offered for this lack of global focus. These included "xenophobic" tendencies of the mainstream Western press; the economic and political "insignificance" of some of the countries being hit the hardest; reporters' general lack of understanding of the global proportions of the pandemic; and their propensity to "slavishly" rewrite press releases from mainstream authoritative sources. "There is probably more to be learned from Thailand and Uganda and China (or the South Bronx) than anywhere else," wrote one respondent who described himself as a "long-termer" who did not start antiviral drug therapy until 1996. "In addition, by far the biggest 'news draw' today is the drugs, and most of that work is taking place in the U.S., Canada and Western Europe," he added.

Some respondents who work for non-profit organizations in the United States that are involved in prevention efforts expressed that the quality of global coverage is a "disservice" to the global AIDS reality. They criticized the press for practicing "parachute journalism" while covering the third world. "There is little or no coverage of programs that have worked in other countries but that would be controversial here [U.S.]—such as Thailand's all out government-led education and condom distribution effort," explained one of these respondents.

According to an editor of textbooks on AIDS/HIV, the Western press tends to pit the issues into a "healthy us" versus the "diseased other" frame and AIDS is presented as a scourge of the third world. "There may be mention of the epidemic in an article that is describing life in India or Bosnia, but it seems to be only in an effort to show how hopeless someplace is," reiterated another respondent. Regarding the overall framing of the pandemic, the narratives converged on the opinion that there is a definite lack of critical reporting. According to one respondent, "I think that the news media either repeats the dogma provided by major agencies or by leading researchers, without even questioning how much sense it makes." Many agreed that the main reason for the prominence of the biomedical theme is the "general Western public" that wants a "magic bullet" cure for everything including AIDS/HIV. According to an attorney who practices AIDS advocacy, the dominant focus on drug news skews the perceptions of those not directly in contact with the pandemic. "This is why we are having such a tough time in the courts," she explained. "Like everyone else, judges only hear about new drugs, new treatments, new therapeutic discoveries. The CDC stats never get the same amount of attention, so the fact that 33 people were infected with HIV today escapes everyone's notice, but the fact that Pfizer has some new 4th generation protease inhibitors (PI) going into human trials will be in the news."

Most respondents felt that although biomedical views are important, they should not overshadow the equal, if not greater importance of prevention and education. According to a psychology professor from a Midwestern university in the United States, prevention gets reported but usually in the context of conflict over methods of prevention such as sex education and needle exchange programs. According to another respondent living with HIV, "Real news would have to cover the things that even prevention agencies aren't totally comfortable with, and these are typically even more taboo for media coverage—drug use, moralism, harm-reduction, philosophies, relapse, reinfection, and sex itself." The editor of the textbooks wrote, "There is such taboo around accurate and clear discussion of gender issues as well as sexual issues, that no news item can be understood as it is sent. So none of the experts for whom I edit textbooks can comfortably discuss gender inequity, female genital mutilation, economic stratification and access to sexuality, reproductive rights, racist assumptions, anal sex, sexual assault and slavery of children and young women, homosexual sex, etc.—with disastrous consequences for intercultural understanding and AIDS intervention."

Other respondents living with AIDS felt that the biomedical view is more top-down than ground up and misleading to the general public. "Now the new superdrugs, while they are keeping us alive, have made many aspects of our lives—and other peoples' lives—much more complicated, and this is newsworthy in many ways," was one account. According to another account, aspects of political corruption in funds allocation and services provided are hardly ever explored or questioned. "I am a person living with HIV now that the new cocktail drugs have improved my health from AIDS status. I have some perspective about news media coverage and what is really happening in the world we patients live in. I have found service providers to be self serving. They openly discriminate against people with AIDS who will not babble their undying devotion to providers. I see use and abuse of funds for over staffed service provider salaries. Guidelines are recommended and not enforced. I think many people with AIDS/HIV are afraid to speak their mind. They have found it does directly relate to the services which are received."

In terms of the main sources used, the collective view was that biomedical sources, scientists, researchers, and policymakers dominate and shape the global AIDS story. According to a respondent living with HIV, there is a need to include more voices from within the pandemic in order to reinvigorate the current news frames. Too many sources, according to this respondent, represent "simple minds making simple statements concerning complex issues whose solutions belong with those more qualified to devise them." Regarding volume of coverage, the unanimous view was that AIDS has lost its "shock value" for the media. A more caustic note from one respondent was that the interest (hence volume of coverage) has declined because HIV infections are now spreading fastest among the economically underprivileged sectors of the world. "The amount of coverage has decidedly decreased as the demographics of the epidemic change to poor people of color in the cities. The epidemic is out of control in countries such as Thailand and Romania, but there doesn't seem to be much interest. These populations can't afford the medications, and the drug companies aren't exactly falling all over themselves to help," commented an AIDS counselor. According to another AIDS counselor, "I talked to one, very good reporter, who said that unless the story shows a real 'breakthrough,' or better yet, a cure, the editors don't want to print it." On an analytical note, one respondent offered the following explanation:

"The news media look for 'news.' There isn't always a lot of news that is immediately discernible as news—science tends to progress in small steps—so instead, information gets hyped."

From the Wires

The responses from the four wire service correspondents constituted narrative explications from journalists who are involved in the process of covering global AIDS/HIV news. Overall, their collective input supported the thesis that coverage of the issue is subject to various extramedia and intramedia forces.

According to Shoemaker and Reese (1996), the personal worldview and opinions of reporters and editors influence the coverage (or lack of coverage) of issues and events. The correspondents provided mixed responses on this point. "Individual views are important because in terms of feature and soft news, reporters have a lot of flexibility in what they cover. If they are interested in AIDS/HIV, then they are likely to do more research on the subject," wrote the AFP correspondent based in China. "Individual opinions and worldviews affect press coverage of everything," reiterated the IPS correspondent based at the wire's Washington, D.C. bureau. Reuters and ITAR-TASS correspondents took the opposite stance that the individual opinions and worldviews of reporters and editors are neither wanted nor included in news stories.

At the media routine level, space, time, and structural constraints emerged as important factors that determine how much coverage AIDS/HIV gets, what world regions get covered the most, and who speaks for the pandemic. According to the Reuters correspondents based in Washington, D.C., "We have a limit of 60 lines on most stories, 100 for a feature. That means a lot of explanation and background cannot go in. We rely heavily on major journals such as *Nature* or *Science*, and one reporter is assigned to each of these (among other things). If that reporter is out of town for a week, the stories are often missed." According to the AFP correspondent, AIDS is a "long-term problem," and unless there is a major medical breakthrough, the topic takes a back seat to more immediate issues. "AIDS remains high on our agenda, but given competing stories, we cover it as much as we can," contributed the ITAR-TASS correspondent based in Washington, D.C.

All correspondents except those from Reuters and IPS could not pinpoint any organizational level policies that specifically influence their wire's coverage of global AIDS/HIV. The Reuters correspondent based in Germany quoted organizational policy from the Reuters stylebook. "Handle all stories with new threats to health or reputed cures for AIDS, cancer and other scourges with great care. They play on the hopes and fears of millions of people." According to the IPS correspondent, IPS clearly covers news from a "third world" perspective, and this perspective includes the coverage of AIDS, a predominantly third world phenomenon. However, he qualified this point by adding, "We are clearly skeptical of the 'out of Africa' narrative, which most of us regard as off the point at best, and gratuitously inflammatory, at worst."

All the correspondents agreed that non-newsroom forces such as organized demonstrations, news releases, conferences, and the miscellaneous public relations efforts of various interest and activist groups affect the coverage of the pandemic. According to the AFP correspondent, they provide "easy-access story materials" to reporters. Giving the example of "several original actions" of ACT-UP at the 1993 Berlin international AIDS conference, which he covered, the Reuters correspondent out of Germany explained that activists can get the attention of reporters, and help journalists "report on aspects other than the agenda set up by organizers."

Regarding sources used most often, both Reuters correspondents stated that biomedical researchers and scientists carry authority. "If David Ho says something, it doesn't matter where it is—it gets covered," was one view. The other was that authoritative sources carry weight and "journalists with tight deadlines and limited space" mostly turn to them for information. The AFP correspondent's comment was that source selection depends on who is most cooperative and that this, in turn, is dependent on the government structure of a region. The ITAR-TASS correspondent explained that source selection depends on the nature of the story, and the IPS correspondent emphasized that his wire tends to approach "alternative" sources such as activists and social organizations.

Regarding the coverage of AIDS in various world regions, the two Reuters correspondents provided the infrastructure argument—that the regions with more reporters and bureaus get covered the most. One Reuters correspondent noted that for this reason, although most HIV cases are in Africa and South Asia, most coverage emanates out of Europe and the United States. The AFP correspondent's view was similar, but the IPS correspondent's view was more optimistic—that coverage around the world has improved with increase in awareness.

None of the correspondents had a clear perspective on the dominant frames that prevail in current global AIDS/HIV coverage. "Hard to say," and "I don't know—I have not analyzed this," were some of the comments. However, all correspondents agreed that issues such as prevention, education, and society's response to people living with AIDS/HIV are important topics for coverage. There was also consensus on the matter that there has been a significant decline in volume of coverage since the 1990s, and this consensus was captured well by the IPS correspondent. "As with any other subject of news coverage, there's a 'spike' when the issue is considered new. Subsequently, coverage levels off," he explained. "I would say interest has perhaps declined as the search for a cure proves more and more elusive, and the tangible success goals seem more difficult to attain," added the Reuters correspondent based in Germany.

Policy Notes

"The manner in which the news media of the world cover AIDS/HIV has a significant impact at various levels on the effort to coordinate worldwide prevention strategy," offered Dr. Michael Merson, director of the World Health Organization's Global Programme on AIDS between 1990 and 1995 and currently dean of the School of Public Health at Yale University. First, he explained, the press helps to get the right scientific information to the public at large. Second, he emphasized, the manner in which the stories are framed can motivate or demotivate policymakers. "The way the stories are written can influence their reaction to the pandemic. If the projection is worrisome, policy makers can be spurred into action."

Merson noted that the news coverage of the last decade has focused mostly on cure and treatment, unfortunately at the expense of prevention themes. He also stated that biomedical voices shape the news to a great extent, and emphasized the need for more critical coverage such as analyses of sexual behavior among high-risk behavior groups. It was his opinion that the press needs to be a true watchdog of policy. "There was hardly any critical coverage, for instance, of the Clinton administration's refusal to fund needle exchange programs in the United States. The press needs to treat AIDS/HIV as a public health crisis and not as a morality issue. The need of the hour is to save lives." He stressed the importance of highlighting successful prevention strategies from around the world, and by way of suggestion, he stated that more interaction is needed between reporters, editors, and those working on prevention.

According to Chris Powell, audiovisual and public relations coordinator at the Geneva headquarters of the World Health Organization, "The news media, especially the western wire services, are generally reluctant to cover AIDS as an issue in developing countries." AIDS, he reiterated like many of the other stakeholders, has become just another story. "Of course there will be on-off issues like a new drug or reduction in mother-to-child transmission. But basically, dealing with HIV/AIDS from here on is a long slog. Long hauls rarely make news except at the beginning and the end." Powell also added narrative support to the view that biomedical research personalities and issues make the headlines most of the time. His suggestion was to investigate other communication approaches such as social marketing to spread awareness and prevention information about AIDS/HIV.

A Public Relations Challenge? (Discussion and Conclusion)

Revisiting the research questions helped further crystallize these narratives, mark paradigmatic overlaps in the stakeholder meanings attributed to the media and social construction of AIDS/HIV, and generate discussion about the public relations (public, policy, and cultural) implications of the same.

1. *How does each community of stakeholders narrate the media and social construction of global AIDS/HIV?*

The cyber community of respondents, which included miscellaneous stakeholders who mostly live with AIDS/HIV or are directly immersed in the pandemic's life world clearly endorsed the view that the manner in which the issue is framed by the media affects understanding and action at many levels, and that the macro coverage lacks critical perspective. They qualified "lack of critical perspectives" by accounting how many emic realities and newsworthy angles embedded in peoples' lived experiences are invisible to the press, and that there is a general lack of openness and moral squeamishness displayed by the media when it comes to matters related to sex and controversy. There was agreement that this airbrushed coverage makes lives difficult for people living the pandemic because it affects public opinion and policy. They further elaborated that the main news frames are imbued with Western cultural assumptions, which include privileging biomedical authority. AIDS/HIV, this community opined, seems to have become a stale topic for the media, and the important aspect of prevention is not explored adequately. Overall, the narrative diktat of these stakeholders was that there never has been or will be any real-world indicator connects between AIDS/HIV and its media and social construction.

The community of wire service journalists mostly agreed that extra and intramedia forces do affect coverage of AIDS/HIV. They particularly felt that the public relations efforts of various stakeholders do play a significant role in how the issue gets shaped, and agreed that there is an inherent ritualistic tendency to approach (rely on) mainstream credible authorities as sources. They also agreed that there are no real-world indicator connects between AIDS and how it gets covered and how much gets covered, that there has been a definite decline in coverage because AIDS is not a new issue any more, and that its on-going and process-oriented nature is not suitable for everyday "spot" reporting. Due to the everyday imperative of their work, they explained that it is hard to keep track of the main frames that get created through overall reporting; however, they also agreed that aspects that get missed out or receive less attention (such as prevention, education, and the sociocultural aspects of AIDS/HIV) need more coverage.

The two policy shapers and communicators felt that there is a lack of critical reporting, that the biomedical frame dominates understanding, and that AIDS has become an old story that is difficult to revive. These stakeholders also felt that more coverage should be accorded to prevention issues, that the press should not treat AIDS/HIV as a morality narrative, and that the stories need to be such that they hold policymakers more accountable in order to induce action.

2. *Are there any significant overlaps in the narrative constructs of these three communities of stakeholders?*

Most of the overlaps between the narrative constructs were between the cyber community stakeholders and the policy shapers and communicators. These overlaps were the views that coverage has declined, that important aspects such as prevention receive inadequate attention, that the press is squeamish about covering ground realities that they find socially "uncomfortable," that there is a dominant focus on the biomedical frame, that AIDS/HIV is a hard issue to revive, and that overall, there is a general lack of critical reporting. All agreed that AIDS should not be a morality story.

The wire service journalists overlapped with the other two groups in agreeing that coverage has declined, that AIDS is a difficult story to revive, that there is a propensity to focus on biomedical and other authority sources, and that there is a need to cover many important aspects of the pandemic that do not get covered due to various everyday and professional constraints. They agreed with the cyber community that there are no real-world indicator connects between AIDS and how or how much of it gets covered. The voice from IPS, the alternative wire service, however, was more self-reflexive and congruent with those of the other two communities in its critical tone.

3. *What do these narratives tell us about the media and social construction of global AIDS/HIV that is useful feedback from a public relations standpoint, specifically for the purpose of improving the quality of relationships between various stakeholders?*

A public relations analysis of these findings generated these final suggestions:

- AIDS/HIV is an on-going pandemic, its urgency has not declined, and much still needs to be accomplished in the area of preventive action in order to slow and reverse its forward progression. From a communicative action perspective, it needs to be kept on the public, policy, and media agendas. The challenge, however, is that the on-going nature of the issue does not lend itself well to the everyday pace (and constraints) of the newsmaking process in most cultures. Also, current frames need to be revitalized, the claims need to be diversified, and more voices need to emerge from the field. Therefore the main problem query becomes: Since public and policy agenda are impacted by media construction, how do we keep AIDS/HIV on the media agenda and how can the current, mostly topdown frames be regenerated?
- Because the media is an important conduit for shaping views and agendas, media relations needs to be a significant area of focus. The current challenge is that the media routinely approach traditional authoritative claim-makers/stakeholders. Creative media relations skills need to be cultivated by grassroots stakeholders that will help them interface more effectively with media personnel. Suggestions include being more accessible to and proactive with the media; making strategic claims that can shape certain issues (channeling funding, holding policymakers more accountable, increasing the credibility of nontraditional sources); developing a savvy understanding of the art of news release writing and distribution, and synchronizing

that understanding with what is considered newsworthy in a given context; understanding how the media work in different environments; using new technologies (interactive web sites that provide "easy-access" materials to journalists); getting the maximum public relations mileage out of "trigger" events; positioning and training spokespersons; and overall, remembering that real-world AIDS/HIV indicators are not enough to draw journalists' attention.

- Other public relations suggestions would be increasing the level of human interaction between the various stakeholders (especially conflicting ones); strategic planning of events including fundraisers; and creating mutually beneficial ties with traditional (authority) and corporate stakeholders, and having them represent grassroots people and issues. This latter strategy could contribute toward diluting the dichotomies that currently exist between these stakeholders and improving the quality of these relationships.
- Policymakers need to be more in touch with the ground realities of AIDS/HIV—this means that they need to be less reliant on mass mediated projections and work more directly with various other stakeholders.
- The press needs to be less squeamish about addressing the controversial aspects of the pandemic, and news organizations need to institute specific policies about AIDS/HIV coverage. It needs to be more accepting of the social responsibility it willy-nilly has in covering the pandemic, be more proactive, and appoint reporters who are more connected to and knowledgeable about the pandemic to cover its many diverse facets.
- Programs and campaigns need to involve flexible blueprints and set measurable goals at micro as well as macro levels. Context-specific formative research is imperative for quantitatively and qualitatively understanding a given situation, or tensor, or relationship, or problem and so on.
- Much research still needs to be conducted that can modify or add to this list.

In conclusion, AIDS/HIV is a polycultural phenomenon that involves the agendas, interactions, and interpretations of various cultural groups/stakeholders. In this sense, it is also an intercultural phenomenon. Thus, those people who operate at boundary spanning (Burk, 1994), transition nodes along the global/local continuum, and the etic and emic (intra as well as inter) dimensions that connect different cultural groups/stakeholders play a crucial communicative relationship-building role that requires cultural sensitivity and open-minded creativity, initiative, superior leadership qualities, and a finely balanced understanding of the top-down and ground up intersections and subjectivities of AIDS/HIV. A topic for future research could be more in depth analysis of this role of the intercultural AIDS/HIV communicative boundary spanner.

The "sample size" of this study may be considered its limitation. However, as many qualitative researchers would claim—"I take qualitative research to be that which examines the qualities (attributes, characteristics, properties) of communication phenomena. Data tend to be continuous rather than discrete, and the emphasis is on description and explanation more than on measurement and prediction" (Fitch, 1994, p. 32). The obvious weakness of this study is that only two policy shapers and communicators responded and also, the cyber community comprised only voices of people living the reality of AIDS/HIV in the Western cultural context—no accounts emerged from the life world of the hardest hit (lesser developed) nations of the world. The obvious reason for this was that the Internet, accessible mostly to those living in technologically privileged countries, was used as a tool to access narratives. These weaknesses could also be springboards for future research.

Acknowledgment

My sincerest thanks to the coparticipants who provided "accounts" from the field, and to Dr. Hugh Culbertson, Dr. Joseph Bern, and Dr. Lenore Langsdorf for their guidance and helpful insights.

References

Airhihenbuwa, C., & Obregon, R. (2000). A critical assessment of theories/models used in health communication for HIV/AIDS. *Journal of Health Communication, 5* (Supplement), 5–15.

Airhihenbuwa, C., Makinwa, B., & Obregon, R. (2000). Toward a new communication framework for HIV/AIDS. *Journal of Health Communication, 5* (Supplement), 101–111.

Albert, E. (1989). AIDS and the press: The creation and transformation of a social problem. In J. Best (Ed.), *Images of issues: Typifying contemporary social problems* (pp. 39–54). Hawthorne, NY: Aldine de Gruyter.

Al-Enad, A. (1990). Public relations roles in developing countries. *Public Relations Quarterly, 35*(1), 24–26.

Alleyne, M., & Wagner, J. (1993). Stability and change at the "Big Five" news agencies. *Journalism Quarterly, 70*, 40–50.

Banks, S. (1995). *Multicultural public relations: A social-interpretive approach.* Thousand Oaks, CA: Sage Publications.

Bardhan, N. (2001). Transnational AIDS/HIV news narratives: A critical exploration of overarching frames. *Mass Communication & Society, 4*, 283–310.

Bartos, M., & McDonald, K. (2000). HIV as identity, experience or career. *AIDS Care, 12*(3), 299–306.

Beattie, A., & Fidler, S. (2001, July 21). G-8 health fund pledges "inadequate." *Financial Times*, p 7.

Berkowitz, D., & Muturi, N. (1999, August). *Refining the participatory approach to development communication through the public relations excellence model.* Paper presented at the annual meeting of the Association for Education in Journalism and Mass Communication, New Orleans, LA.

Best, J. (1989). Claims. In J. Best (Ed.), *Images of issues: Typifying contemporary social problems* (pp. 1–3). Hawthorne, NY: Aldine de Gruyter.

Bonacci, M. (1992). *Senseless casualties: The AIDS crisis in Asia.* Washington, DC: Asia Resource Center.

Boseley, S., & Astill, J. (2001, June 16). Dying for drugs: Battle over cheap drugs goes to WTO. *The Guardian*, p. 1.

Botan, C. (1992). International public relations: Critique and reformulation. *Public Relations Review, 18*, 149–159.

Boyd-Barrett, O., & Thussu, D. (1992). *Contra-flow in global news.* London: John Libbey & Company Ltd.

Brown, J., & Xenos, P. (1994). AIDS in Asia: The gathering storm. *Asia Pacific Issues*, No. 16. Honolulu, HI: East-West Center.

Brown, P. (1992). AIDS in the media. In J. M. Mann, D. M. J. Tarantola, & T. W. Netter (Eds.), *AIDS in the world* (pp. 720–732). Cambridge, MA: Harvard University Press.

Caron, M. (1999). The politics of life and death: Global responses to HIV/AIDS. *World Watch, 12*(3), 30–38.

Christakis, N. (1989). Responding to a pandemic: International interests in AIDS control. *Daedalus, 118*(2), 113–134.

Clarke, J. (1992). Cancer, heart disease, and AIDS: What do the media tell us about these diseases? *Health Communication, 4*(2), 105–120.

Cohen, B. (1963). *The press and foreign policy.* Princeton, NJ: Princeton University Press.

Colby, D., & Cook, T. (1991). Epidemics and agendas: The politics of nightly news coverage of AIDS. *Journal of Health Politics, Policy and Law, 61*, 215–249.

Cutlip, S., Center, A., & Broom, G. (1994). *Effective public relations*, 7th ed. Englewood Cliffs, NJ: Prentice Hall.

Dearing, J., & Rogers, E. (1996). *Agenda-setting*. Thousand Oaks, CA: Sage Publications.

Duffy, M. (2000). There's no two-way symmetric about it: A postmodern examination of public relations textbooks. *Critical Studies in Mass Communication, 17*, 294–315.

Elwood, W. (Ed.). (1999). *Power in the blood: A handbook on AIDS, politics, and communication*. Mahwah, NJ: Lawrence Erlbaum Associates.

Falkin, G. P., & Strauss, S. M. (2000). Drug-using women's communication with social supporters about HIV/AIDS issues. *Journal of Drug Issues, 4*, 801–822.

Fauci, A. (1983, May 6). Acquired immune deficiency syndrome: The ever broadening clinical spectrum. *Journal of the American Medical Association, 250*, 2375–2376.

Fisher, W. (2001). Narration, reason, and community. In L. Hinchman & S. Hinchman (Eds.), *Memory, identity, community: The idea of narrative in the human sciences* (pp. 307–327). Albany: State University of New York Press.

Fitch, K. (1994). Criteria for evidence in qualitative research. *Western Journal of Communication, 58*, 32–38.

Frey, L., Adelman, M., Flint, L., & Query, J., Jr. (2000). Weaving meanings together in an AIDS residence: Communicative practices, perceived health outcomes, and the symbolic construction of community. *Journal of Health Communication, 5*, 53–72.

Gallo, R. (1991). *Virus hunting—AIDS, cancer, and the human retrovirus: A story of scientific discovery*. New York: Basic Books.

Gans, H. (1979). *Deciding what's news*. New York: Pantheon.

Gitlin, T. (1980). *The whole world is watching*. Berkeley: University of California Press.

Goffman, E. (1974). *Frame analysis: An essay on the organization of experience*. New York: Harper & Row, Publishers.

Gordenker, L., Coate, R., Jönsson, C., & Söderholm, P. (1996). *International cooperation in response to AIDS*. New York: Printer Publishers.

Grmek, M. D. (1990). *History of AIDS: Emergence and origin of a modern pandemic*. (R. C. Maulitz & J. Duffin, Trans.). Princeton: Princeton University Press. (Original work published 1989)

Grover, J. (1992). AIDS: Keywords, and cultural work. In L. Grossberg, C. Nelson, & P. Treichler (Eds.), *Cultural studies* (pp. 227–239). New York: Routledge.

Grube, A., & Boehme-Deurr, K. (1989). AIDS in international magazines. *Journalism Quarterly, 66*, 686–689.

Grunig, J., & Hunt, T. (1984). *Managing public relations*. New York: Holt, Rinehart & Winston.

Harris, R. (2001, June 28). *Morning edition*. Washington, DC: National Public Radio.

Hernandez, D. (1994, August 20). AIDS fades. *Editor & Publisher, 127*, 16–17.

Hinchman, L., & Hinchman, S. (2000). Introduction. In L. Hinchman & S. Hinchman (Eds.), *Memory, identity, community: The idea of narrative in the human sciences* (pp. xiii–xxxii). Albany: State University of New York Press.

Holtzhausen, D. (2000). Postmodern values in public relations. *Journal of Public Relations Research, 12*, 93–114.

Kinsella, J. (1989). *Covering the plague: AIDS and the American media*. New Brunswick, NJ: Rutgers University Press.

Klaidman, S. (1990). How well the media report health risk. *Daedalus, 119*(4), 119–132.

Kraft, S. (1994, December 2). 42 nations vow to protect AIDS patients. *San Francisco Chronicle*, p. D3.

Lester, E. (1992). The AIDS story and moral panic: How the Euro-African press constructs AIDS. *Howard Journal of Communication, 7*(1), 1–10.

Lim, K. (1995). Reporting AIDS: News representations in the Malaysian newspapers. *Journal of Development Communication, 6*(1), 79–86.

Lindlof, T. (1995). *Qualitative communication research methods*. Thousand Oaks, CA: Sage Publications.

Lippmann, W. (1922). *Public opinion*. New York: The Macmillan Company.

Lupton, D. (1993). AIDS risk and heterosexuality in the Australian press. *Discourse and Society, 4*, 307–328.

Mann, J., Tarantola, D., & Netter, T. (Eds.). (1992). *AIDS in the world*. Cambridge, MA: Harvard University Press.

McAllister, M. P. (1990). *Medicalization in the news media: A comparison of AIDS coverage in three newspapers*. [CD-ROM]. Abstract from: ProQuest File: Dissertation Abstract Item: 9114339.

McAllister, M. (1992). AIDS, medicalization, and the news media. In T. Edgar, M. A. Fitzpatrick, & V. S. Freimuth (Eds.), *AIDS: A communication perspective* (pp. 195–221). Hillsdale, NJ: Lawrence Erlbaum Associates.

McCombs, M. (1992). Explorers and surveyors: Expanding strategies for agenda-setting research. *Journalism Quarterly, 69*, 813–824.

McCombs, M. (1993). The evolution of agenda-setting research: Twenty-five years in the marketplace in ideas. *Journal of Communication, 43*, 58–67.

Nabel, G. (2001, April 19). Challenges and opportunities for development of an AIDS vaccine. *Nature, 410*, 1002–1007.

Nelkin, D. (1987). *Selling science: How the press covers science and technology*. New York: W. H. Freeman and Company.

Nelkin, D. (1991). AIDS and the news media. *The Milbank Quarterly, 69*, 293–307.

Netter, T. W. (1992). The media and AIDS: A global perspective. In J. Sepulveda, H. Fineberg, & J. Mann (Eds.), *AIDS: Prevention through education—a world view* (pp. 241–253). New York: Oxford University Press.

O'Connor, A. (1991, August 18). Lifting quarantine/Cuba relaxes policy of strict segregation of AIDS carriers. *Houston Chronicle*, p. 16.

O'Heffernan, P. (1993). Mass media and U.S. foreign policy: A mutual exploitation model of media influence in U.S. foreign policy. In R. J. Spitzer (Ed.), *Media and public policy* (pp. 187–211). Westport, CT: Praeger Publishers.

O'Heffernan, P. (1994). Mass media roles in foreign policy. In D. A. Graber (Ed.), *Media power in politics*, 3rd ed. (pp. 325–336). Washington, DC: Congressional Quarterly Press.

O'Neill, J. (1991). *Plato's cave*. Norwood, NJ: Ablex Publishing Company.

Piot, P., Bartos, M., Ghys, P., Walker, N., & Schwartländer, B. (2001, April 19). The global impact of HIV/AIDS. *Nature, 410*, 968–973.

Polkinghorne, D. (1988). *Narrative knowing and the human sciences*. Albany: State University of New York Press.

Polkinghorne, D. (1995). Narrative configuration in qualitative analysis. *International Journal of Qualitative Studies in Education, 8*(1), 5–23.

Princeton Survey Research Associates (1996, July/August). Covering the epidemic: AIDS in the news media, 1985–1996. *Columbia Journalism Review, 35* (Special supplement), 1–12.

Pritchard, D. (1992). The news media and public policy agendas. In J. D. Kennamer (Ed.), *Public opinion, the press, and public policy* (pp. 103–112). Westport, CT: Praeger.

Purvis, A. (1996/1997, December 30/January 6). The global epidemic. *Time, 148/149*, 76–78.

Reese, S. D. (1990). The news paradigm and the ideology of objectivity: A socialist at the *Wall Street Journal. Critical Studies in Mass Communication, 7*, 390–409.

Reeves, P. (2000). Coping in cyberspace: The impact of Internet use on the ability of HIV-positive individuals to deal with their illness. *Journal of Health Communication, 5* (Supplement), 47–59.

Roane, K. (1997, April 27). Making the case for clean needles. *The New York Times*, p. 6.

Rogers, E. (2000). Introduction. *Journal of Health Communication, 5* (Supplement), 1–3.

Rogers, E., Dearing, J., & Chang, S. (1991). AIDS in the 1980s: The agenda-setting process for a public issue. *Journalism Monographs, 126*.

Sabatier, R. (1988). *Blaming others: Prejudice, race and worldwide AIDS*. Philadelphia, PA & Washington, DC: New Society Publishers and The Panos Institute.

Semetko, H., & Goldberg, E. (1993). Reporting AIDS in the U.S. and Britain. In R. Spitzer (Ed.), *Media and public policy* (pp. 171–186). Westport, CT: Praeger.

Sepulveda, J., Fineberg, H., & Mann, J. (1992). *AIDS: Prevention through education—A world view*. New York: Oxford University Press.

Shelton, D. (1999, September 20). Progress against AIDS stalls, in prevention and treatment. *American Medical News, 42*, 24–26.

Shilts, R. (1987). *And the band played on: Politics, people, and the AIDS epidemic*. New York: St. Martin's Press.

Shoemaker, P., & Reese, S. (1996). *Mediating the message: Theories of influences of mass media content*, 2nd ed. White Plains, NY: Longman Publishing.

Soloski, J. (1989). News and professionalism: Some constraints on the reporting of news. *Media, Culture and Society, 11*, 207–228.

Sontag, S. (1989). *AIDS and its metaphors*. New York: Farrar, Straus and Giroux.

Stephenson, J. (2001). 20 years after AIDS emerges, HIV's complexities still loom large. *Journal of the American Medical Association, 285*, 1279–1282.

Traquina, N. (1996, August). *Portuguese journalism and HIV/AIDS: A case study in news*. Paper presented at the annual convention of the Association for Education in Journalism and Mass Communication, Anaheim, CA.

Treichler, P. (1988). AIDS, homophobia, and biomedical discourse: An epidemic of signification. In D. Crimp (Ed.), *AIDS: Cultural analysis/Cultural activism* (pp. 31–70). Cambridge, MA: MIT Press.

Tuchman, G. (1978). The news net. *Social Research, 45*, 253–276.

UNAIDS. (2000). *AIDS epidemic update: December 2000*. Retrieved on 7/13/2001 from the World Wide Web: http://www.unaids.org/wac/2000/wad00/files/WAD_epidemic_ report.htm

UNAIDS: Mission and Roles. (1995). *Global AIDSNEWS, 3/4*, 1–2.

Van Leuven, J., & Pratt, C. (1996). Public relations' roles: Realities in Asia and in Africa south of the Sahara. In H. Culbertson and N. Chen (Eds.), *International public relations: A comparative analysis* (pp. 93–105). Mahwah, NJ: Lawrence Erlbaum Associates.

Walters, L., & Walters, T. (1996, August). *Life on the edge of the precipice: Information subsidy and the rise of AIDS as a public issue, 1983–1989*. Paper presented at the annual convention of the Association for Education in Journalism and Mass Communication, Anaheim, CA.

Wartick, S., & Wood, D. (1998). *International business and society*. Malden, MA: Blackwell Publishers.

Watts, L. (1993). Coverage of polio and AIDS. *Ohio Journalism Monographs, 4*.

Wilkins, D. (1995, August). *Science, journalism, and the public sphere: An oppositional model of knowledge construction*. Paper presented at the annual convention of the Association for Education in Journalism and Mass Communication. Washington, DC.

Wolf, R., Tawfik, L., & Bond, K. (2000). Peer promotion programs and social networks in Ghana: Methods for monitoring and evaluating AIDS prevention and reproductive health programs among adolescents and young adults. *Journal of Health Communication, 5* (Supplement), 61–80.

[4]

Estimation of "needs" and "probable uptake" for HIV/AIDS preventive vaccines based on possible policies and likely acceptance (a WHO/UNAIDS/IAVI study)

José Esparza [a,*], Marie-Louise Chang [a], Roy Widdus [b], Yvette Madrid [c], Neff Walker [d], Peter D. Ghys [d]

[a] *WHO-UNAIDS HIV Vaccine Initiative, Health Technology and Pharmaceuticals, World Health Organization, 20 Avenue Appia, 1211 Geneva 27, Switzerland*
[b] *Access Project, International AIDS Vaccine Initiative, ICC, Block G, 3rd Floor, 20 Route de Pre-Bois, 1215 Geneva 15, Switzerland*
[c] *Access Project, International AIDS Vaccine Initiative, 30 Rue de la Gabelle, 1227 Carouge, Geneva, Switzerland*
[d] *United Nations Programme on HIV/AIDS (UNAIDS), 20 Avenue Appia, 1211 Geneva 27, Switzerland*

Received 1 May 2002; received in revised form 4 October 2002; accepted 26 November 2002

Abstract

Once an effective HIV vaccine is discovered, a major challenge will be to ensure its world wide access. A preventive vaccine with low or moderate efficacy (30–50%) could be a valuable prevention tool, especially if targeted to populations at higher risk of HIV infection. High efficacy vaccines (80–90%) could be used in larger segments of the population.

Estimated "needs" for future HIV vaccines were based on anticipated policies regarding target populations. Estimated "needs" were adjusted for "accessibility" and "acceptability" in the target populations, to arrive at an estimate of "probable uptake", i.e. courses of vaccine likely to be delivered. With a high efficacy vaccine, global needs are in the order of 690 million full immunization courses, targeting 22 and 69%, respectively, of the 15–49 years old, world wide and in sub-Saharan Africa, respectively. With a low/moderate efficacy vaccine targeted to populations at higher risk of HIV infection, the global needs were estimated to be 260 million full immunization courses, targeting 8 and 41%, respectively, of the world and sub-Saharan African population aged 15–49 years.

The current estimate of probable uptake for hypothetical HIV vaccines, using existing health services and delivery systems, was 38% of the estimated need for a high efficacy vaccine, and 19% for a low/moderate efficacy vaccine. Bridging the gap between the estimated needs and the probable uptake for HIV vaccines will represent a major public health challenge for the future. The potential advantages and disadvantages of targeted versus universal vaccination will have to be considered.

Keywords: Vaccines; HIV; AIDS

1. Introduction

A safe, highly effective and accessible preventive HIV vaccine represents the best long-term hope for controlling the HIV/AIDS pandemic, although its development has encountered a number of unprecedented scientific challenges [1,2]. Despite these uncertainties, a number of experimental vaccines are being developed in the laboratory, and many have already progressed to clinical trials. Two candidate vaccines based on the outer envelope protein of HIV-1 (gp120) of two different genetic subtypes of HIV-1 (B and E) are currently undergoing phase III efficacy evaluation in North America and Thailand, and the final results from these trials are expected within the next 1–2 years. At least one additional phase III trial, using a prime-boost regime (a canarypox-HIV vector followed by gp120), is being planned to start in 2003 in Thailand, with results expected by 2007.

Once an effective vaccine is developed, a major challenge for the international community will be to ensure its access to all populations in need, without unnecessary delays. For this, a number of actions need to be taken now, including the identification of policies and strategies for vaccine introduction and use in different communities, countries and regions. These policies should be based, among others, on the characteristics of the vaccine (including level of efficacy and cost), as well as on the epidemiological situation and availability of other preventive interventions in the different

* Corresponding author. Tel.: +41-22-7914392; fax: +41-22-7914865. *E-mail address:* esparzaj@who.int (J. Esparza).

communities or countries. Determination of policies and strategies is also essential to estimate needs and potential demand for future vaccines. Such estimates are critical to assure adequate supply and financing for future HIV vaccination programmes.

The World Health Organization (WHO), the Joint United Nations Programme on HIV/AIDS (UNAIDS) and the International AIDS Vaccine Initiative (IAVI) have begun to address the issue of access to future vaccines. In June 2000, IAVI issued a blueprint outlining a comprehensive access strategy [3]. In October 2000, WHO and UNAIDS organized a consultation to identify specific steps to be taken to ensure future access to HIV vaccines [4]. One of the recommendations from the WHO-UNAIDS consultation was to explore with countries critical policy issues related to future use of HIV vaccines, and to initiate a process to obtain initial credible estimates of needs and probable uptake for future HIV vaccines. This paper reports on the results from a collaborative project jointly implemented in 2001 by WHO, UNAIDS and IAVI.

2. Methods

2.1. Regional workshops

Information on policy issues and initial estimates of needs and currently delivery capacity for HIV vaccines were obtained from four regional workshops convened by WHO-UNAIDS in collaboration with IAVI and several local organizations. The workshops took place between April and June 2001 in Florianópolis, Brazil (for Latin America and the Caribbean); Entebbe, Uganda (for Africa); Seoul, Republic of Korea (for Asia and the Pacific); and Geneva, Switzerland (for North America and Europe). Each workshop was attended by an average of 25 participants from the relevant region, representing several disciplines, including epidemiologists, immunization experts, national decision makers, and community representatives (participants listed in Appendix A). The outcome of these four consultations was reviewed by the WHO/UNAIDS/IAVI Secretariat and external experts and subsequently presented to the vaccine industry in a WHO-UNAIDS consultation held in November 2001.

2.2. Vaccine efficacy scenarios

After a general discussion on HIV vaccines and trials, workshop participants reviewed concepts related to potential vaccine-induced protection (e.g. protection against infection or protection against disease) and levels of efficacy (e.g. percentage of infections and/or disease prevented by vaccination). Two hypothetical scenarios of vaccine efficacy were considered: low/moderate (30–50%) and high (80–90%) efficacy. Levels of efficacy represented a combination of prevention of infection (sterilizing immunity) and prevention of disease (decrease in virus load in vaccines who subsequently become infected).

In both scenarios the following vaccine characteristics were assumed: that a full vaccination course will require three intramuscular injections during the first year; that the vaccine was safe, even for HIV-infected people, although it would not have any "therapeutic effect" if given to an HIV-infected person; and that the vaccine is effective against the HIV strain(s) circulating in the country or community where it is used.

It would have been ideal to examine vaccine demand through a range of cost, but this proved impractical given time constraints. It was decided to choose one scenario that removes vaccine affordability as a constraint to access, assuming that vaccines were provided to countries free of charge (due to external support), but that costs of vaccine distribution were borne by countries.

The subsequent brainstorming discussion served to identify potential strategies for the use of HIV vaccines of low/moderate and high efficacy in the context of the epidemiological situation in different countries and communities, and its possible co-ordination and complementation with other HIV preventive interventions. The approach used was to initiate the discussion focusing on a "pilot" country from which a large amount of information was available (i.e. Brazil, Uganda and Thailand), in order to later extend and adapt the conclusions to other countries in the region.

2.3. Estimating needs and probable uptake for HIV vaccines

Once the key policy issues were identified, participants engaged in calculations on needs and probable uptake for future HIV vaccines of either low/moderate or high efficacy. "Needs" was defined as the size of the target population that ideally could benefit from a future HIV vaccine, based on epidemiological considerations. "Probable uptake" was defined by a more realistic estimate of vaccine usage, influenced by its accessibility and acceptability by the target population.

Estimates for both scenarios were obtained through a sequential process. First, participants identified the target populations (specific groups at risk) in need of vaccination. For each of these groups estimates were made of the size of the populations. For age groups, 2001 estimates of population size were used [5]. Estimates of the size of groups at higher risk for each country were compiled prior to the regional workshops. These groups included men who have sex with men (MSM), men and women with sexually transmitted infections (STI) [6], female commercial sex workers (CSW), and injecting drug users (IDU). For countries where there were no estimates for these groups, regional averages were used to make an estimate for the country. In addition to these four groups, other groups where also considered (e.g. health care professionals, military recruits) and calculations were made by using national estimates or estimates drawn for other sources.

Once the "needs" were established for each country, the probable uptake was calculated based on "accessibility" and "acceptability" by the target population. Accessibility was defined as the percentage of people in each group that could be reached by an existing service or organization through which the vaccine would be provided. Acceptability referred to the percentage of people accessed who would agree to be vaccinated and who would receive the recommended course of at least three doses of the vaccine (i.e. the potential drop-out rate is included here). The estimated global need for each of the two vaccine scenarios (low/moderate and high) was the sum of the groups that were identified as needing a vaccine. The estimated probable uptake was the total number of people in each group that had a need for a vaccine, corrected by accessibility and acceptability rates. Country-specific estimates were aggregated by region, for both efficacy scenarios.

2.4. Estimating needs for subtype-specific vaccines

At the present time it is not known what could be the relevance of HIV genetic subtypes in terms of vaccine-induced protection [7]. In this process, we assumed that the vaccine was effective against the strain(s) prevalent in the target populations. However, a scenario that must be considered for the estimation of needs is that vaccines could exhibit subtype specificity, protecting only against the HIV genetic subtype used to manufacture the candidate vaccine. For that reason needs estimates were also obtained for vaccines protecting only against the major envelope genetic subtypes of HIV-1 (A–E). The prevalence and incidence of different envelope subtypes of HIV-1 during 2000 has been estimated by WHO-UNAIDS [8] and that information was used to calculate the needs for subtype-specific vaccines. In regions where a single subtype predominates (representing more than 90% of all infections) the needs for the subtype specific vaccine is equivalent to the overall HIV vaccine needs. In regions with more than one prevalent subtype (with individual subtype prevalence of more than 10%) it was assumed that the target population would need to be vaccinated with vaccines based on each of the prevalent subtypes, doubling or tripling the initial needs estimates if two or three subtypes were present in the population.

3. Results

3.1. Potential use of vaccines with low/moderate or high efficacy

Most participants in the regional workshops agreed that even a preventive HIV vaccine with low or moderate efficacy could be a valuable prevention intervention, especially if used in specific populations at higher risk of HIV infection. These populations, however, differed from region to region. In most regions, MSM, IDU and CSW were identified as potential beneficiaries of vaccines with low/moderate efficacy. STI patients were also identified as a potential target population for low/moderate efficacy vaccines in Latin America and Africa. Participants from Africa identified additional potential target populations for a low/moderate efficacy vaccine, including truck drivers, post-natal women and, in some areas with high HIV incidence, all adolescents and young adults (aged 15–24 years old), especially if other preventive interventions were not widely available in the community.

High efficacy vaccines could be used in larger segments of the population, including adolescents and young adults, health care workers, discordant couples (with respect to their HIV infection status), military recruits, and prisoners. Regional differences were evident, correlating with the severity of the epidemic and the relative success of other preventive interventions. This was particularly evident for Asia, the Pacific and Eastern Europe, where due to the generally low HIV prevalence, there was a reluctance to recommend mass vaccination programmes, especially with low efficacy vaccines.

3.2. Global and regional estimates of needs

If an HIV vaccine with low/moderate efficacy is initially targeted to populations considered at higher risk of HIV infection, the global need for such a vaccine was estimated to be 260 million full immunization courses (or individuals to be vaccinated) (Table 1). That estimate targets 8% of the total world population of those aged 15–49 years, although in some regions, such as sub-Saharan Africa, the estimated needs targets 41% of the population in the same age group. An immunization programme with a high efficacy vaccine would target a larger proportion of the population, with a total global estimate of 690 million immunization courses, targeting 22% of the world population aged 15–49 years, and 69% of that population in sub-Saharan Africa. The above-mentioned estimates represent the catch-up needs, where all target populations and age groups would be vaccinated within the first 5 years of a vaccination campaign. A maintenance programme to vaccinate new cohorts would follow this. Furthermore, the estimates reflect the current situation with regard to the capacity to deliver a vaccine to the target population and the likely acceptance within them. It is believed that over time the infrastructure to deliver a vaccine and the acceptance level will increase.

The difference between the estimates of needs for low/moderate and high efficacy vaccine (430 million full immunization courses) is because with a low/moderate efficacy vaccine most regions may consider vaccinating only individuals at higher risk of HIV infection, while with a higher efficacy vaccine both higher-risk and lower-risk populations would be vaccinated. Indeed, most regions suggested using a high efficacy vaccine for all young people, through school-based vaccination programmes. It is

Table 1
Regional estimates of need and probable uptake for HIV vaccines

Region	Adult population 15–49 (M)	Low/moderate efficacy			High Efficacy		
		Need (M)	Probable uptake (M)	%, Probable uptake (M)/ need (M)	Need (M)	Probable uptake (M)	%, Probable uptake (M)/ need (M)
Sub-Saharan Africa[a]	290	120	37	30.83	200	86	43.00
South and South-East Asia[b]	1000	89	4.3	4.83	140	32	22.86
Latin America[c]	260	34	2.6	7.65	120	28	23.33
North Africa and Middle East[d]	180	1.1	0.013	1.18	54	36	66.67
Eastern Europe and Central Asia[e]	210	0	0	0.00	50	37	74.00
Western Europe[f]	200	11	3.2	29.09	45	21	46.67
North America[g]	160	11	1.6	14.55	38	12	31.58
East Asia and Pacific[h]	830	0.22	0.04	18.18	27	1.5	5.56
Carribean[i]	18	2.4	0.41	17.08	8.5	2.3	27.06
Australia and New Zealand	12	2.5	0.098	3.92	5.9	2.6	44.07
Global total	3200	260	49	18.85	690	260	37.68

[a] Sub-Saharan Africa: Angola, Benin, Botswana, Burkina Faso, Burundi, Cameroon, Cape Verde, Central African Republic, Chad, Comoros, Congo, Cote d'Ivoire, Democratic Republic of Congo, Djibouti, Equatorial Guinea, Eritrea, Ethiopia, Gabon, Gambia, Ghana, Guinea, Guinea-Bissau, Kenya, Lesotho, Liberia, Madagascar, Malawi, Mali, Mauritania, Mauritius, Mozambique, Namibia, Niger, Nigeria, Reunion, Rwanda, Senegal, Sierra Leone, Somalia, South Africa, Swaziland, Togo, Uganda, United Republic of Tanzania, Zambia, Zimbabwe.

[b] South and South-East Asia: Afghanistan, Bangladesh, Bhutan, Brunei Darussalam, Cambodia, East Timor, India, Indonesia, Iran (Islamic Republic of), Lao People's Democratic Republic, Malaysia, Maldives, Myanmar, Nepal, Pakistan, Philippines, Singapore, Sri Lanka, Thailand, Viet Nam.

[c] Latin America: (Central America) Costa Rica, El Salvador, Guatemala, Honduras, Mexico, Nicaragua, Panama. (South America) Argentina, Bolivia, Brazil, Chile, Colombia, Ecuador, Paraguay, Peru, Uruguay, Venezuela.

[d] North Africa and Middle East: Algeria, Bahrain, Cyprus, Egypt, Iraq, Israel, Jordan, Kuwait, Lebanon, Libyan Arab Jamahiriya, Morocco, Occupied Palestinian Territory, Oman, Qatar, Saudi Arabia, Sudan, Syrian Arab Republic, Tunisia, Turkey, United Arab Emirates, Yemen.

[e] Eastern Europe and Central Asia: Armenia, Azerbaijan, Belarus, Bosnia and Herzegovina, Bulgaria, Croatia, Czech Republic, Estonia, Georgia, Hungary, Kazakhstan, Kyrgyzstan, Latvia, Lithuania, Poland, Republic of Moldova, Romania, Russian Federation, Slovakia, Tajikistan, Turkmenistan, Ukraine, Uzbekistan.

[f] Western Europe: Albania, Austria, Belgium, Denmark, Finland, France, Germany, Greece, Iceland, Ireland, Italy, Luxembourg, Malta, Netherlands, Norway, Portugal, Slovenia, Spain, Sweden, Switzerland, TFYR Macedonia, United Kingdom, Yugoslavia.

[g] North America: Canada, United States of America.

[h] East Asia and Pacific: China, Democratic People's Republic of Korea, Fiji, Hong Kong, Japan, Macao, Mongolia, Papua New Guinea, Republic of Korea.

[i] Caribbean: Bahamas, Barbados, Belize, Bermuda and Cayman Islands, Cuba, Dominican Republic, Guyana, Haiti, Jamaica, Netherland Antilles and Aruba, OECS, Suriname, Trinidad and Tobago.

noteworthy that participants analysing Eastern European and Asian countries indicated that a low-efficacy vaccine might not be used at all, not even in the groups at higher risk. Arguments in support of this policy included the fact that vaccines of low efficacy would not be acceptable to the health authorities, and the fact that low-efficacy vaccines would have only marginal effects in countries with very low HIV prevalence.

3.3. Estimates of probable uptake

For a low/moderate efficacy vaccine, for which we estimated a need of 260 million full immunization courses, the probable uptake was estimated to be of only 49 million immunization courses, or 19% of the needs (Table 1). Likewise, for a high efficacy vaccine for which we estimated a need of 690 million immunization courses, global estimated probable uptake was of 260 million immunization courses, or 38% of the needs.

It is noteworthy that for a low/moderate efficacy vaccine the highest estimated probable uptake to need ratio was for sub-Saharan Africa (31%), while most other regions have relatively low ratios (Fig. 1). This higher ratio for Africa may reflect a perceived higher public health importance of an HIV vaccine and that the target population would be the general population rather than specific groups at higher risk.

The estimated probable uptake to need ratio for a high efficacy vaccine was significantly higher for most regions (from 23 to 74%), with the exception of East Asia and the Pacific (6%).

3.4. Estimates of needs for subtype-specific vaccines

While the global needs for a broadly protective vaccine of low/moderate and high efficacy were estimated to be 260 and 690 million immunization courses, respectively, the needs for individual subtype specific vaccines would be lower, depending on the geographical distribution and prevalence of the different HIV-1 subtypes (Table 2). On the other hand, because of the co-circulation of several HIV subtypes in different regions, the total number of immunization courses with subtype specific vaccines, perhaps used in combination, would be higher than with a broadly protective vaccine.

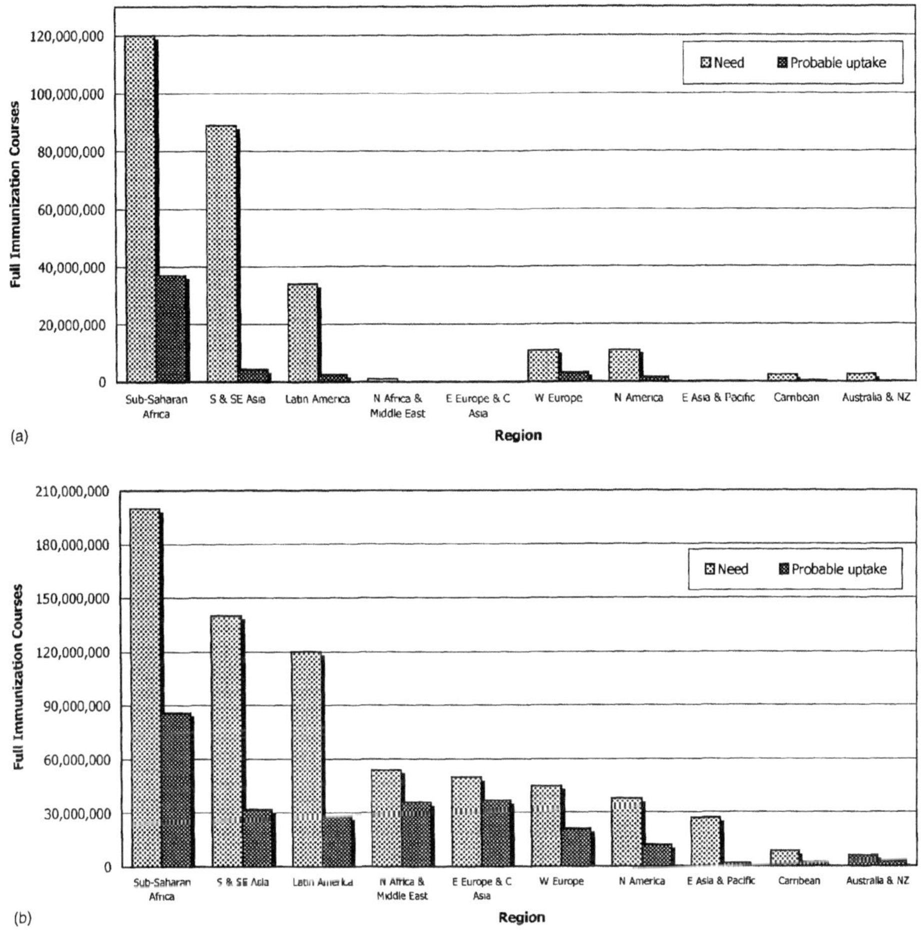

Fig. 1. Regional gap between estimated need and probable uptake of HIV vaccines: (a) low/moderate efficacy; (b) high efficacy vaccine.

Table 2
Estimated global need for subtype specific vaccines

Envelope (Env) subtype	Low/moderate efficacy (million)	High efficacy (million)
Env_A	94	270
Env_B	91	380
Env_C	82	140
Env_D	36	67
Env_E	30	61
Env_G	35	65
Total	370	990

For instance, the needs for a high efficacy subtype E-specific vaccine was estimated to be of 61 million full immunization courses because its use, at least with the present epidemiological situation, would be limited mostly to South East Asian countries. Likewise, a high efficacy subtype C-specific vaccine would be used in Southern Africa, the horn of Africa and India, with a total estimate of 140 million full immunization courses. The highest need estimate was for a high efficacy subtype B-specific vaccine (380 million full immunization courses), because of the presence of this particular subtype in several regions of the world, including some countries with the resources required to implement mass vaccination programmes.

4. Discussion

The results presented in this paper were obtained after extensive consultation with key informants from different regions of the world (Appendix A). It is appreciated, however, that workshop participants were not officially representing any country, nor were they making formal recommendations for future vaccine use. They were also aware that the estimates of needs and probable uptake were only preliminary figures, which will need to be validated or corrected with additional exercises conducted at the regional and country level.

Likely policies for use are difficult to predict because of uncertainties on vaccine characteristics, and policy makers are likely to err on the side of caution. Better information on the potential benefits may make use policies less conservative. A number of important issues emerged, the most important one being that future HIV vaccination programmes be fully integrated within the overall HIV/AIDS prevention. Vaccines were not considered as "magic bullets" against HIV/AIDS, but as an additional components of future comprehensive HIV/AIDS preventive packages. Two important additional findings were the moderate enthusiasm for the use of low/moderate efficacy vaccines (with the possible exception of sub-Saharan Africa), and a general preference for targeted vaccination of populations at high-risk of HIV infection.

Although the ultimate goal is to develop a highly effective HIV-1 vaccine that confers sterilizing immunity against all HIV strains, the most realistic scenario is the introduction of a first generation of HIV preventive vaccine that will only be partially protective. Our findings suggest that a low/moderate efficacy vaccine would be accepted by public health authorities, although it would most likely be recommended for populations at higher risk of HIV infection [9]. A high efficacy vaccine, however, would be more readily accepted and could gather more political support. This must be an incentive to continue research towards the ultimate goal of developing better products [10].

Although a targeted vaccination approach was often favored, the difficulties in accessing high-risk population were fully recognized. Additionally, a targeted vaccination strategy could result in stigmatization and discrimination of the populations selected for vaccination. An alternative strategy to be considered, is that of universal vaccination. An interesting point of comparison is with Hepatitis B immunization, where initial targeted strategies have largely been replaced by universal vaccination, which is now considered a more effective strategy, both from the economic and the public health point of view [11,12].

Another identified concern, especially regarding low efficacy vaccines, was the possibility of "behavioral reversals", resulting in higher HIV incidences in the target population [13]. This situation, however, has not been documented during the ongoing phase III HIV vaccine trials in North America and Thailand [14,15]. In any case, it would be essential to continue and strengthen general HIV prevention efforts during a vaccination programme.

The estimates of probable uptake of HIV vaccines, given current delivery systems and acceptance levels, represent only 19 and 38% of the targeted needs for vaccines of low/moderate and high efficacy, respectively. This is unsatisfactory and provides ample opportunities to expand the use of HIV vaccines even within the currently identified needs. Bridging the gap between what it is deliverable today and the estimated needs will be a critical public health challenge in the future. In some areas of the world, such as in Africa, the major reason for the difference between needs and probable uptake of vaccine could be the lack of appropriate delivery systems and infrastructures to bring the vaccine to the target populations. It is evident that there is an urgent need for donor agencies to allocate budgets to build up and strengthen infrastructures and systems, essential for future HIV vaccine introduction. Information is needed to define the minimum criteria required to have an operational health care infrastructure appropriate for HIV vaccination.

Acceptance can also be increased by education. Vaccination of adolescents requires the development of innovative strategies that are ethical, legal and logistically feasible. In other regions, the reason for the gap between needs and probable uptake of vaccines might be the perception that existing interventions are adequate, and that vaccination against HIV would not be cost effective. Country-specific studies are needed to validate or reject the above perceptions, and to better identify and develop country policies and vaccination strategies. Such a study has already been initiated in Thailand [16]. In this regard it is important to indicate that our analysis considered the present epidemiological situation in different regions of the world. It is possible, however, that HIV spread in Asia and the Pacific, or in other regions of the world, could increase the perceived need for a vaccine in those and other regions.

Although the relevance of the genetic variability of HIV-1 in terms of potential vaccine-induced protection is not known, this variability is perceived as an obstacle for the development of broadly protective vaccines [7]. It is believed that envelope based vaccines (such as gp120), aimed at inducing neutralizing antibodies, would be more subtype-specific than vaccines designed to induce cell-mediated immunity to more conserved epitopes of HIV. Our estimates for subtype-specific vaccines were made for individual vaccines, although it is recognized that antigens for different subtypes (or immunotypes) could be combined together on broadly protective cocktail vaccines. In any case, a subtype-specific vaccine would only be an intermediate step on HIV vaccine development because the ideal vaccine would need to protect against all HIV subtypes and strains. This would be an important goal both for individuals, who travel from region to region, and for communities, since the subtype distribution is very dynamic and it is continuously changing over time.

Our estimates were based on vaccine procurement and distribution by the public sector, and we did not explore the potential private market, although a range of public/private financing and distribution mechanisms may be used by countries. It would be important to ensure that the private market in industrialized countries does not limit the availability and access to vaccines in developing countries, where more than 95% of all HIV infections are occurring [17].

It was also assumed that the vaccine would be provided at zero cost to certain countries, and that they would face distribution costs, although it is likely that some countries will receive substantial subsidies to strengthen their delivery systems. It is likely that a global immunization campaign would require substantial funding, which should be discussed in the context of the estimated US$ 9 billion per year estimated to be needed to mount an effective global response to the HIV/AIDS pandemic [18]. The present estimates were made without an a priori consideration of the capacity to produce the required number of doses, and a dialogue with industry is urgently required to ensure swift, world wide availability of the vaccines.

Future decisions about introduction and use of HIV vaccines will be based not only on vaccine efficacy, but also on the cost-benefit of vaccination, including costs associated with vaccine procurement and distribution and efficiency of existing preventive interventions. Since the introduction of an HIV vaccine, especially one with low efficacy, would have to be accompanied with intense social marketing and behavioral counselling, overall AIDS prevention and control costs will increase significantly, to account for the extra expenses related to vaccine procurement and distribution, and for the additional behavioral interventions which would have to be strengthened. We believe, however, that this extra investment in HIV/AIDS prevention and control would pay back after a few years, by implementing an effective campaign that will finally result in the interruption of the chain of transmission of the virus. That campaign will only succeed if communities are supportive and engaged.

Finally, when an effective HIV vaccine is discovered, the international community and the affected countries will have to make many critical decisions on how to use the vaccine. These decisions will have to be taken with a considerable degree of uncertainty, although mathematical modelling could provide useful insights [19–22]. For instance, several years will pass before definitive information regarding duration of protective immunity, or efficacy against different HIV-1 subtypes and strains, become available. Moreover, vaccine availability may be limited at the beginning, forcing national authorities to decide what populations should be prioritized for vaccination. Strategies for vaccine introduction should also consider the possibility of conducting selected phase IV effectiveness trials, to address the uncertainties about the practical generalizability of vaccine performance [23], although these trials should not be a bottleneck to early access to future HIV vaccines.

The numbers provided in this study should encourage donor agencies as well companies involved in HIV vaccine development, to plan for the budgets needed to be able to produce and distribute the necessary number of doses once an HIV vaccine is licensed.

Acknowledgements

We thank Drs. Saladin Osmanov, Julie Milstien, Mark Miller and Timothy Mastro for their valuable comments and advice in the preparation of the manuscript, and Mr. Efren Fadriquela for his help with the analysis of the databases. The study was funded by the Joint United Nations Programme on HIV/AIDS and the World Health Organization.

Appendix A. List of participants in the different consultations

A.1. Florianópolis, Brazil; 16–17 April 2001. Co-sponsored by the Brazilian AIDS Programme

Barros T	UNAIDS, Brazil
Brigido de Macedo LF	National AIDS Programme, Ministry of Health, Brazil
Camara B	Special Programme on STIs, Caribbean Epidemiology Centre, Trinidad and Tobago
Carvalheiro JR (Chair)	Institutes of Research, Sao Paulo, Brazil
Chateaubriand Domingues R	National Vaccine Committee, Brasilia, Brazil
de Moura Filho EA	National Programme on Immunization, Brazil
Girade H	UNAIDS Theme Group/UNICEF, Brazil
Greco DB	HIV Vaccine Center, Minas Gerais, Brazil
Irons B	Caribbean Epidemiology Centre, Trinidad and Tobago
Luna E	Faculty of Science, São Paolo, Brazil
do Valle Menezes A	Grupo Pela Vidda/RJ, Brazil (IAVI consultant)
de Oliva O (Co-chair)	Pan American Health Organization, Division of Vaccines and Immunization, USA
Nascimento MVL	National Programme on Immunizations, Brazil
Spink MJP	Catholic University of São Paulo, Brazil
Szwarcwald CL	Oswaldo Cruz Foundation Brazil
Weissenbacher M	National Reference Center on AIDS, Argentina
Yih K	Pan American Health Organization, Brazil

A.2. Entebbe, Uganda; 18–19 June 2001. Co-sponsored by the Uganda AIDS Commission

Asther A	World Health Organization, Uganda
Gershy-Damet G-M	Regional Office for Africa, World Health Organization, Zimbabwe
Jacobi J	UNAIDS, Uganda
Kihumuro Apuuli D (Chair)	Uganda AIDS Commission, Uganda
Kizza Mayanja H	Mulago Hospital and Makerere University, Uganda
Korukiiko Ndyomugyenyi L	Uganda AIDS Commission, Uganda
Makumbi I (Co-chair)	Expanded Program on Immunization, Ministry of Health, Uganda
Mbidde E	Uganda Cancer Institute, Uganda
Mugarura C	Ministry of Health, Uganda
Mugerwa R	Mulago Hospital and Makerere University, Uganda
Musinguzi J	AIDS Control Programme, Ministry of Health, Uganda
Mwesigwa Kindyomunda R	Uganda AIDS Commission, Uganda
Nielsen LE	International AIDS Vaccine Initiative, Uganda
Obodozie O (Co-chair)	National Institute for Pharmaceutical Research and Development, Nigeria
Omaswa F	Health Services, Uganda
Pallangyo K	Muhumbili Medical Centre, Tanzania
Rwomushana J (Co-chair)	Uganda AIDS Commission, Uganda
Sassan-Morokro M	Projet RETRO-CI, Côte d'Ivoire
Sekatawa E	Makere University, Uganda
Swaya W	Ministry of Finance, Uganda
Tafesse Y	Ethiopian Health and Nutrition Research Institute, Ethiopia
Walker O	World Health Organization, Uganda

A.3. Seoul, Republic of Korea, 4–5 June 2001. Co-sponsored by the International Vaccine Institute (IVI)

Acosta C	International Vaccine Institute, Republic of Korea
Clemens J (Chair)	International Vaccine Institute, Republic of Korea
Chitwarakorn A	Ministry of Public Health, Thailand
Gorna R	Australian Federation of AIDS Organizations, Australia
Hossain MM	International Vaccine Institute, Republic of Korea
Kilgore P	International Vaccine Institute, Republic of Korea
Lee J	National Institute of Health, Ministry of Health and Welfare, Republic of Korea
Kunanusont C	UNFPA Office for East and South East Asia, Thailand
Limpakarnjanarat K	Thai Ministry of Health-US Centers for Disease Control and Prevention (CDC) Collaboration, Ministry of Public Health, Thailand
Monzon O	AIDS Society of the Philippines, Philippines
Oh M-D	Seoul National University College of Medicine, Republic of Korea
Phoolcharoen W	Health Systems Research Institute, Ministry of Public Health, Thailand
Rugpoa S	Department of Communicable Disease Control, Ministry of Public Health, Thailand
van Seidlein, L	International Vaccine Institute, Republic of Korea
Sung YC	Department of Life Sciences, Pohang University of Science and Technology, Republic of Korea
Suraratdecha C	School of Economics, Sukhothai Thammathirat Open University, Thailand
Xu Z-Y	International Vaccine Institute, Republic of Korea
Yi Z	Institute of Virology, People's Republic of China

A.4. Geneva, Switzerland; 28–29 June 2001

Brunet J-B	Cellule d'appui Scientifique (C.A.S.), Direction Générale de la Santé, France
Casabona Barbarà J	Hospital Universitari Germans Trias i Pujol, Barcelona, Spain
Dehne KL	UNAIDS, Austria
van den Hoek JAR	Municipal Health Service, Amsterdam, The Netherlands
King K (Chair)	Communicable Disease Branch, Department of Health, UK
Kobyshcha Y	UNAIDS, Division for Europe and America, Austria
Kruglov Y	Ministry of Health, Ukraine
Mastro TD (Chair)	HIV Vaccine Section, Division of HIV/AIDS Prevention, Centers for Disease Control and Prevention, Atlanta, USA
Miller M	Fogarty International Center, National Institutes of Health, USA
Pokrovsky V	Russia AIDS Centre, Russia
Rezza G	Istituto Superiore di Sanità, Italy
Smolskaia T	North-Western District AIDS Centre of Russian Ministry of Health, Russia
Van den Boom F	European Policy, IAVI, The Netherlands

A.5. Geneva, Switzerland; 19–20 November 2001

Bartholow B	HIV Vaccine Section, Division of HIV/AIDS Prevention, Centers for Disease Control and Prevention, Atlanta, USA
Berger J	Aventis Pasteur, France
Van den Boom F	IAVI, The Netherlands
Casabona Barbarà J	Hospital Universitari Germans Trias i Pujol, Barcelona, Spain
Cunningham G	Merck Vaccine Division, Merck & Co. Inc., USA
Donnelly J	Chiron Research and Development, Chiron Corporation, USA
Ehreth J	Aventis Pasteur, France
Francis DP	VaxGen, USA
Gershy-Damet G-M	Regional Office for Africa, WHO, Zimbabwe
Gold D	IAVI, USA
Gordon L	VaxGen, USA
Hayashi C	WHO, Switzerland
van den Hoek JAR	Municipal Health Service, Department of Infectious Diseases, The Netherlands
Hombach J	GlaxoSmithKline, Belgium
Jaatar H	Morocco
King K	Communicable Disease Branch, Department of Health, Public Health Group, UK
LaSalvia T	Scientific Information and Program Planing, NIAIDS/Division of AIDS, NIH, Bethesda, USA
Limpakarnjanarat K	The Thai Ministry of Health-US Centers for Disease Control and Prevention Collaboration, Ministry of Public Health, Thailand
Longini I	Department of Biostatistics, the Rollins School of Public Health, Emory University, Atlanta, USA
do Valle Menezes A	Grupo Pela Vidda, Brazil
Miller M	Fogarty International Center, National Institutes of Health, USA
Milstien J (Co-chair)	World Health Organization (WHO), Switzerland
Mukasa-Monico S	International Council of AIDS Service Organizations, Canada
de Oliva O (Co-chair)	Pan American Health Organization/Pan American Sanitary Bureau, Division of Vaccines and Immunization, USA
Pallangyo K	Muhumbili Medical Centre, Tanzania
Phoolcharoen W	Health Systems Research Institute, Ministry of Public Health, Thailand
Shin S-I	VaxGen, USA
Vandermissen W	GlaxoSmithKline, Belgium
Xu Z-Y	International Vaccine Institute, Republic of Korea
Young P	AlphaVax Inc., USA

A.6. Secretariat

Chang M-L	WHO-UNAIDS HIV Vaccine Initiative/WHO, Switzerland
Esparza J	WHO-UNAIDS HIV Vaccine Initiative/WHO, Switzerland
Ghys PD	UNAIDS, Switzerland
Madrid Y	Access Project, IAVI, Switzerland
Nixon S	WHO-UNAIDS HIV Vaccine Initiative/WHO, Switzerland
Osmanov S	WHO-UNAIDS HIV Vaccine Initiative/WHO, Switzerland
Pattou-Markovic C	WHO-UNAIDS HIV Vaccine Initiative/WHO, Switzerland
Touré C	WHO-UNAIDS HIV Vaccine Initiative/WHO, Switzerland
Walker N	UNAIDS, Switzerland
Widdus R	Initiative on Public–Private-Partnerships for Health, Switzerland

References

[1] Esparza J, Bhamarapravati N. Accelerating the development and future availability of HIV-1 vaccines: why, when, where, and how. Lancet 2000;355:2061–6.
[2] Esparza J. An HIV vaccine: how and when? Bull World Health Organ 2001;79:1133–6.
[3] International AIDS Vaccine Initiative. AIDS vaccines for the world: preparing now to assure access. New York: IAVI; 2000.
[4] WHO-UNAIDS. Future access to HIV vaccines. Report from a WHO-UNAIDS Consultation. Geneva, 2–3 October 2000. AIDS 2000;15:27-W44.
[5] UNAIDS. Estimates of populations at higher risk of HIV infection, unpublished data.
[6] Gerbase AC, Rowley JT, Heymann DH, Berkley SF, Piot P. Global prevalence and incidence estimates of selected curable STDs. Sex Transmitted Infect 1998;74(1):S12–6.
[7] WHO-UNAIDS. Approaches to the development of broadly protective HIV vaccines: challenges posed by the genetic, biological and antigenic variability of HIV-1. Report from a meting of the WHO-UNAIDS Vaccine Advisory Committee. Geneva, 21–23 February 2000. AIDS 2000;15:W1–25.
[8] Osmanov S, Pattou C, Walker N, Schwartlander, Esparza J. and the WHO-UNAIDS Network for HIV Isolation and Characterization. Estimated global distribution and regional spread of HIV-1 genetic subtypes in the year 2000. J. Acquired Immune Def. Syndrome 2002;29:184–90.
[9] Makgoba MW, Solomon N, Tucker TJ. The search for an HIV Vaccine. Br Med J 2002;324:211–3.
[10] Batson A, Ainsworth M. Private investment in AIDS vaccine development: obstacles and solution. Bull World Health Organ 2001;79:721–7.
[11] Da Villa G, Picciottoc L, Elia S, Peluso F, Montanaro F, Maisto T. Hepatitis B vaccination: universal vaccination of newborn babies and children at 12 years of age versus high risk groups. A comparison in the field. Vaccine 1995;13:1240–3.
[12] Beutels P. Economic evaluations of hepatitis B immunization: a global review of recent studies (1994–2000). Health Econ 2001;10:751–74.
[13] Blower SM, McLean AR. Prophylactic vaccines, risk behaviour change, and the probability of eradicating HIV in San Francisco. Science 1994;265:1451–4.
[14] Bartholow B, Buchbinder S, McKirnan D, Goli V, Celum C, The VaxGen Study Team. HIV risk behaviour change in a phase-III HIV vaccine efficacy trial. AIDS Vaccine 2001, Philadelphia, 5–8 September 2001. p. 132 [abstract 324].
[15] Migasena S, Vanichseni S, van Griensven F, Phonrat B, Keawkangwal J, Hiranrus K, et al. Risk behaviour monitoring among injecting drugs users (IDUs) participating in the AIDSVAX B/E vaccine trial in Bangkok. In: Proceedings of the Sixth Internationl Congress on AIDS in Asia and the Pacific. Melbourne, 5–10 October 2001. p. 220 [abstract 0386].
[16] Tangcharoensathien V, Phoolcharoen W, Pitayangsarit S, Kongsin S, Kasemsup V, Tantivess S, et al. The potential demand for an AIDS vaccine in Thailand. Health Policy 2001;57:111–39.
[17] Piot P, Bartos M, Ghys PD, Walker N, Schwartlander B. The global impact of HIV/AIDS. Nature 2001;410:968–73.
[18] Schwartlander B, Stover J, Walker N, Bollinger L, Gutierrez JP, McGreevey W, et al. AIDS. Resource need for HIV/AIDS. Science 2001;292:2434–6.
[19] Anderson RM, Swinton J, Garnett GP. Potential impact of low efficacy HIV-1 vaccines in populations with high rates of infection. Proc R Soc London B Biol Sci 1995;22:147–51.
[20] Anderson RM, Garnett GP. Low-efficacy HIV vaccines: potential for community-based intervention programmes. Lancet 1996;348: 1010–3.
[21] Barth-Jones DC, Longini IM. Epidemic and vaccine factors influencing optimal HIV vaccination distribution policies. In: Proceedings of the 2001 Congress of Epidemiology, Toronto, Canada, 13–16 June 2001. Am. J. Epidemiol. 2001;153(11):S190.
[22] Bogard E, Kuntz KM. The impact of a partially effective HIV vaccine on a population of intravenous drug users in Bangkok, Thailand: a dynamic model. J Acquired Immune Def Syndrome 2002;29:132–41.
[23] Brenner R, Rao M, Tafari N, Lowe C. Evaluating new vaccines for developing countries. Efficacy or effectiveness? J Am Med Assoc 1996;275:390–7.

[5]

The acceptability of HIV immunization: examining vaccine characteristics as determining factors

A. LIAU & G. D. ZIMET

Indiana University School of Medicine, Indianapolis, USA

Abstract *The acceptance of a future HIV vaccine may be influenced, in part, by the characteristics of the vaccine itself. This study evaluated the relationship of vaccine characteristics to acceptability of hypothetical HIV immunization. Subjects were 549 undergraduates (18–56 years of age); 70.3% were female, and 80.4% were non-Hispanic white. Subjects completed a self-administered questionnaire assessing a series of 12 hypothetical vaccines that varied along the dimensions of efficacy (80 or 50%), cost (free or $300) and social saturation or percentage of the population already vaccinated (10, 50 or 90%). The vaccines were each rated on an 11-point scale ranging from zero ('I will never get this vaccine') to 100 ('I will definitely get this vaccine'), in increments of ten. All three dimensions were significantly associated with probability of vaccine acceptance, particularly vaccine efficacy and cost. The highest rated vaccine (free, 80% efficacious, 90% saturation level) received a mean acceptability score of 83.4, whereas the lowest rated vaccine ($300, 50% efficacious, 10% saturation level) received a mean score of 32.8. The mean acceptability rating across all 12 vaccines was 55.14. These findings indicate the potential importance of considering the influence of vaccine characteristics in future HIV immunization programmes.*

Introduction

This past decade has seen a dramatic increase in our understanding of the biology and action of the human immunodeficiency virus (HIV). It is imaginable, therefore, that an effective HIV vaccine will be developed and made available in the future (Grady, 1999). However, the availability of such a vaccine may not necessarily lead to successful prevention of acquired immunodeficiency syndrome (AIDS). For instance, various studies on existing vaccines have demonstrated relatively low rates of acceptance for the prevention of influenza and hepatitis B infection (Barie *et al.*, 1994; Centers for Disease Control, 1991; Fedson, 1994). As such, it is reasonable to anticipate that many people may also not accept an HIV vaccine.

Prior research on acceptability of HIV vaccination has demonstrated that health beliefs, such as perceived susceptibility to infection and perceived barriers to immunization, were significant predictors of vaccine acceptability (Liau *et al.*, 1998; Liau & Zimet, 2000; Zimet *et al.*, 1997; 1999). However, characteristics specific to the vaccine itself may also affect acceptability of HIV immunization. Even if the vaccine is quite safe, its degree of

Address for correspondence: Gregory D. Zimet, PhD, Section of Adolescent Medicine, Indiana University School of Medicine, 575 N. West Drive, Room 070, Indianapolis, IN 46202-5225, USA. Tel. + 1 (317) 274-8812; Fax: + 1 (317) 274-0133; E-mail: gzimet@iupui.edu

efficacy may strongly influence attitudes about immunization. This issue is of particular importance since even the most promising HIV vaccines may not provide as much protection against strains of HIV as once thought (Cohen, 1994). Studies on hepatitis B virus (HBV) vaccination found that individuals who had doubts about the efficacy of HBV vaccine were less likely to accept immunization (Bodenheimer *et al.*,1986; Crossley *et al.*, 1985; Israsena *et al.*, 1992). Furthermore, preliminary studies on HIV vaccination found that vaccine efficacy strongly influenced probability of acceptance for HIV immunization (Liau *et al.*, 1998; Zimet *et al.*, 2000). Liau *et al.* (1998) found that vaccines described as 90% efficacious had a mean probability of acceptance of nearly 70%, but for those described as 50% efficacious, the mean probability of acceptance was only 39%. These findings suggest that there may be a threshold level of efficacy below which most people will not accept the vaccine. Many individuals may ask whether the limited or questionable benefits of a vaccine with less than a desirable level of efficacy can outweigh the real and/or imagined risks associated with getting vaccinated.

Another characteristic of an HIV vaccine that may affect its acceptability is its cost. Harward *et al.* (1988) found that one reason for voluntary HBV vaccination among medical and surgical residents was that the vaccine was free. Cost of the vaccine was also cited as a reason for medical residents who were not vaccinated. Similarly, Pennie *et al.* (1991) reported that as the cost of HBV immunization increased from $15 to $100, acceptability among health discipline students dropped from 94% to 35%. Herold *et al.* (1992) also found cost to be a deterrent to complying with a rubella vaccination among medical students. Results from a preliminary study on acceptability of hypothetical HIV vaccination indicated that increases in cost (free to $25 to $100) led to statistically significant, though not substantial, decreases in acceptability (Liau *et al.*, 1998). The range of costs described may not have been sufficient to substantially influence acceptability.

A vaccine characteristic that may also affect HIV vaccine acceptance but has not been studied is the percentage of a population that has already been vaccinated (i.e. social saturation). Diffusion theory proposes that acceptance of an innovation increases with the increased social saturation of the innovation (Rogers, 1983). One would therefore predict that individuals would rate an HIV vaccine as more acceptable as the proportion of the population immunized for HIV increases.

The purpose of this research was to expand on the earlier study (Liau *et al.*, 1998) by examining the effects of social saturation and whether specifying a larger range of cost may more strongly influence acceptability. Specifically, it was predicted that HIV vaccine acceptability would be influenced by the dimensions of cost (free or $300), social saturation (10, 50 or 90%) and efficacy (50 or 80%).

Method

Subjects and setting

Subjects for this study were 551 undergraduate volunteers, at least 18 years of age, attending an urban, Midwestern university and taking psychology courses at the lower undergraduate level. Usable data from 549 subjects indicated that females comprised 70.3% of the sample. Subjects ranged in age from 18 to 56 years (mean = 23.4, SD = 7.35). Non-Hispanic whites comprised the largest ethnic group (80.4%). Other demographic data showed that singles (i.e. never married) comprised the largest group (79.2%), followed by married persons (15.8%). With respect to sexual orientation, heterosexuals comprised 94.8% of the entire

Table 1. *Hypothetical HIV vaccines: acceptability score means and standard deviations presented in order of increasing acceptability*

Vaccine #*	Cost	Efficacy (%)	Social saturation (%)	Mean†	Standard deviation
Vaccine #8:	$300	50	10	32.8	29.9
Vaccine #10:	$300	50	50	35.2	30.3
Vaccine #12:	$300	50	90	38.9	31.0
Vaccine #2:	$300	80	10	47.8	31.1
Vaccine #7:	Free	50	10	51.5	33.4
Vaccine #4:	$300	80	50	52.3	30.8
Vaccine #9:	Free	50	50	53.2	32.4
Vaccine #6:	$300	80	90	58.1	31.8
Vaccine #11:	Free	50	90	58.2	33.0
Vaccine #1:	Free	80	10	72.4	27.7
Vaccine #3:	Free	80	50	77.3	26.9
Vaccine #5:	Free	80	90	83.4	25.1

* Number refers to order of presentation.
† Vaccines rated on a scale of 0 to 100, in increments of 10, reflecting probability of acceptance.

sample. Due to the skewed nature of these distributions, no further analyses were computed with race, marital status or sexual orientation.

Procedure/instrumentation

Students took part in the experiment in a classroom setting. Written informed consent was obtained from all participants and the study was approved by the university's Institutional Review Board. After completing the anonymous, self-administered questionnaires, an envelope was provided for each subject to return the questionnaires.

Measures and data analysis

Subjects were asked to rate the acceptability of a series of hypothetical HIV vaccines. Each vaccine was uniquely defined along three dimensions: cost, social saturation and efficacy. Cost consisted of two attributes (free or $300), efficacy consisted of two attributes (50 or 80%) and social saturation consisted of three attributes (10, 50 or 90%). Vaccines, therefore, were described as consisting of different combinations of these attributes.

Given that cost and efficacy have two attributes each, and that social saturation has three attributes, the various combinations of attributes resulted in 12 hypothetical vaccines presented (see Table 1). Order of presentation was not varied across subjects. However, a randomization procedure was used to develop the initial ordering of the vaccines, thereby ensuring that vaccine ratings and order of presentation would not be substantially confounded. For each vaccine presented, students rated the probability that they would get that vaccine. An 11-point scale was used, ranging from zero ('I will never get this vaccine') to 100 ('I will definitely get this vaccine'), in increments of ten units. A five-way ANOVA ($3 \times 2 \times 2 \times 2 \times 2$) was used to calculate the within-subjects effects of social saturation, cost and efficacy, and the between-subjects effects of age group (18–20 years of age; 21 years of age and older) and gender.

Results

Mean acceptability rating and demographic variables

Across all 12 hypothetical vaccines presented, the mean acceptability rating for all subjects was 55.14 out of a possible 100. Age was the only significant demographic predictor of acceptability $r = -0.123$, $p < 0.05$), indicating that younger participants were more likely to give higher ratings to the hypothesized vaccines presented than older participants. The most desirable vaccine (free, 80% efficacious, 90% social saturation) received a mean rating of 83.4 (SD = 25.1), whereas the least desirable vaccine ($300, 50% efficacious, 10% social saturation) received a mean rating of 32.8 (SD = 29.9). See Table 1 for a listing of the mean and standard deviation of acceptability scores for each of the 12 vaccines.

Main effects

The ANOVA revealed significant main effects for all three dimensions. Free vaccines (M = 66.0) were preferred over $300 vaccines (M = 44.3): $F(1,530) = 475.7$, $p < 0.001$. The 80% efficacious vaccines (M = 65.2) were preferred over the 50% efficacious vaccines (M = 45.0): $F(1,530) = 486.3$, $p < 0.001$. Subjects also preferred vaccines with 90% social saturation (M = 59.7) over those with 50% saturation (M = 54.6) or 10% saturation (M = 51.1): $F(2,1060) = 147.8$, $p < 0.001$.

Interaction effects

Although three significant two-way interactions were identified, none of them substantially modified the main effects. One interaction was between gender and vaccine efficacy: $F(1,530) = 11.7$, $p < 0.001$. Both males and females rated 50% efficacious vaccines lower than 80% efficacious vaccines; however females rated the 50% efficacious vaccine significantly lower than males. See Figure 1 for a graphic representation of this interaction effect.

A second interaction was between efficacy and social saturation: $F(2,1060) = 13.3$, $p < 0.001$. Mean acceptability ratings were higher for vaccines that were 80% efficacious than for vaccines that were 50% efficacious at every level of social saturation. However, the rise in vaccine acceptability across social saturation levels was greater for 80% efficacious vaccines. See Figure 2 for a graphic representation of this interaction effect.

There was also an interaction between efficacy and cost: $F(1,530) = 41.0$, $p < 0.001$. Mean acceptability ratings were higher for 80% efficacious vaccines than for 50% efficacious vaccines regardless of whether the vaccines were free or cost $300. However, the drop in vaccine acceptability with increased cost was greater for 80% efficacious vaccines. See Figure 3 for a graphic representation of this interaction effect.

Discussion

The results of this study suggest that many individuals may have reservations about HIV immunization. Although the most attractive vaccine (80% efficacious, 90% social saturation, free) was rated as very acceptable by the majority of subjects, acceptability began to drop steeply as vaccine characteristics began to deviate from this ideal configuration. The finding regarding a negative reaction to low efficacy vaccines is particularly noteworthy, given that future HIV vaccines are likely to have limited efficacy (Cohen, 1994). Moreover, this finding is consistent with the results from the earlier study (Liau *et al.*, 1998).

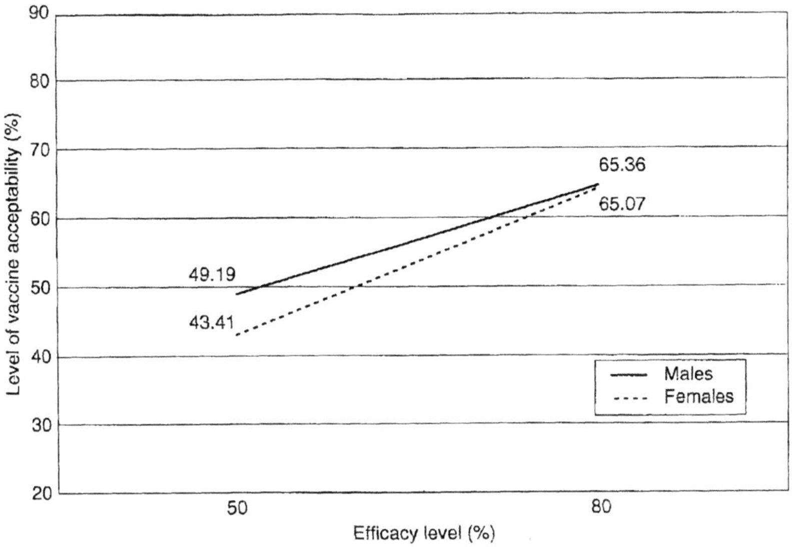

FIG. 1. *Interaction effect between vaccine efficacy and gender.*

The acceptability of HIV immunization also was strongly influenced by vaccine cost. This finding serves to extend the results of the earlier study (Liau *et al.*, 1998), in which a lower range of cost (free to $100) had a statistically significant, but modest effect on acceptability. Taken in conjunction with the previous study, the results of the current study suggest that the cost of a vaccine may become a particularly influential issue as it rises above $100. Given that cost is a vaccine characteristic that can be adjusted when the vaccine is marketed, policy makers may wish to consider cost as a highly relevant factor in influencing people's willingness to get immunized.

Although there was a statistically significant main effect for social saturation, this particular vaccine characteristic did not influence acceptability of the vaccine as strongly as efficacy or cost. Social saturation ultimately may be a salient issue for HIV immunization, however, it may be difficult now for people to imagine what it will be like for a certain percentage of the population to be immunized for a vaccine that does not yet exist.

The interaction effects of efficacy with cost and efficacy with social saturation suggest a synergistic effect across these dimensions. This set of findings suggests that it may be important to optimize, as much as possible, the positive attributes of a future HIV vaccine in order to increase its likelihood of acceptability.

Finally, the results derived from the two-way interaction effect of efficacy and gender indicated that males and females were equally likely to choose an 80% effective vaccine. At the same time, males were more likely than females to accept a vaccine that was 50% effective. These findings suggest that women may be more sensitive than men to issues of vaccine efficacy. Future HIV immunization programmes, therefore, may wish to consider possible gender-based differential acceptance of limited efficacy HIV vaccines.

This study continues to lay the groundwork for understanding factors that ultimately may be related to HIV vaccine acceptance and suggests some key areas that may be important

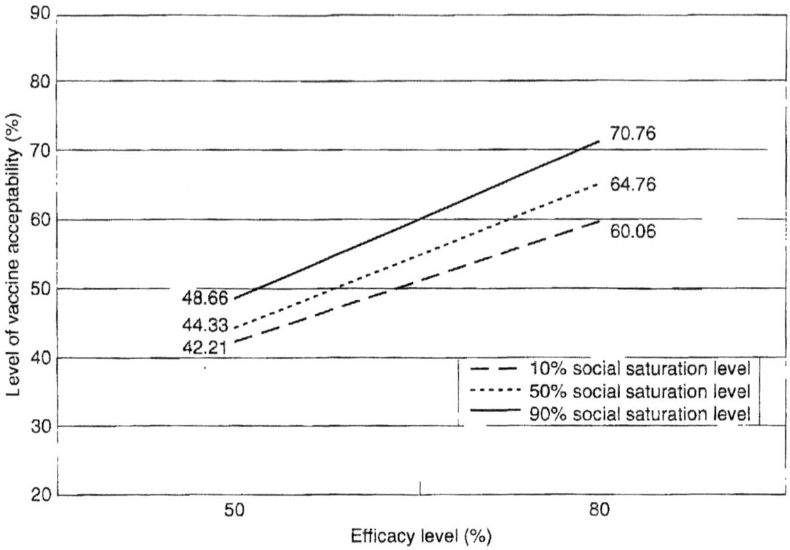

FIG. 2. *Interaction effect between vaccine efficacy and level of social saturation.*

to consider in the development of HIV immunization programmes. However, there are some limitations, including the fact that no HIV vaccine currently exists. It may be difficult for subjects to imagine what sort of an HIV vaccine will be available and to conceptualize the social/psychological context of future HIV immunization. As a result, the attitudes we

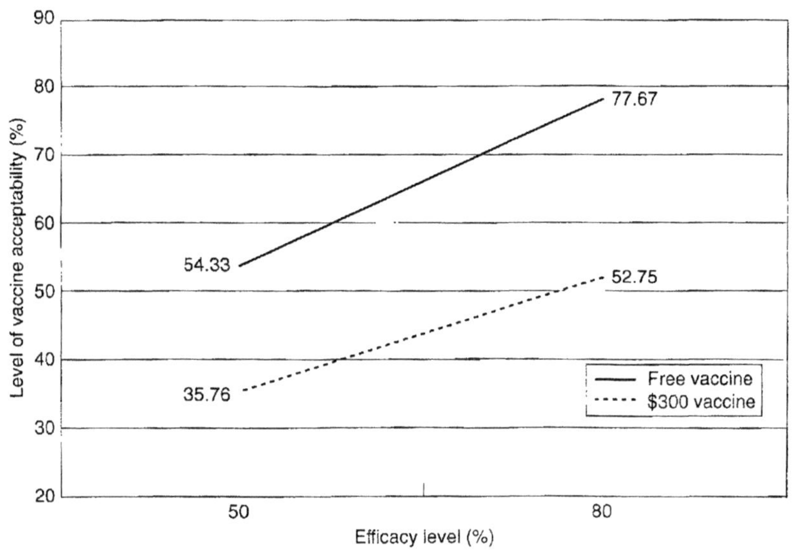

FIG. 3. *Interaction effect between vaccine efficacy and cost of vaccine.*

measured regarding vaccine acceptability may not be highly correlated with actual behaviour once the vaccine is made available. However, the hypothetical nature of the vaccine in some regards is a strength, in that it allows us to begin to understand people's attitudes and beliefs, as well as identify potential barriers to HIV vaccination, prior to the introduction of such an immunization programme.

Another limitation is the use of college students as a sample group, in that it is not clear how the results from this study may generalize across other, high-risk, subject groups. It is noteworthy that the findings from the current study are consistent with the results of a similar study with urban adolescents, in which vaccine efficacy and cost substantially influenced HIV vaccine acceptability (Zimet *et al.*, 2000). In addition, college students are relevant to the study of HIV immunization. The documented high prevalence of risky sexual behaviours among university undergraduates (Prince & Bernard, 1998), combined with the low prevalence of HIV in this group, make them, in many ways, an ideal target for HIV immunization programmes. Furthermore, it is unlikely that HIV immunization programmes will be targeted only at so-called high-risk groups. Widespread vaccination coverage will have to be achieved, particularly with a low-efficacy vaccine, to reduce the incidence of infection.

The current study is one of the few research efforts that has examined vaccine characteristics as potential determinants of HIV vaccine acceptability. As with the earlier studies, the results suggest that people may have reservations about accepting an HIV vaccine and that these reservations may be associated, in part, with particular characteristics of the vaccine (efficacy, cost, social saturation). Although the current study does not apply to all individuals, it is hoped that the results obtained from this study will lay the groundwork for additional, more comprehensive studies. In addition, vaccine characteristics beyond those examined in the present study may prove to be important factors in HIV vaccine acceptability (e.g. type of vaccine; number of injections required; potential side-effects). In two of our previous research studies, for example, subjects expressed antipathy toward the idea of a live-attenuated HIV vaccine (Liau *et al.*, 1998; Zimet *et al.*, 2000). Failure to continue to study issues of HIV vaccine acceptance may lead to inadequate vaccine coverage, delays in immunization programme implementation and unnecessary expenditure of substantial sums of money and resources on ineffective immunization efforts (Levin, 1993).

References

Barie, P S., Dellinger, E.P., Dougherty, S.H. & Fink, M.P. (1994). Assessment of hepatitis B virus immunization status among North American surgeons. *Archives of Surgery, 129*, 27–32.

Bodenheimer, H.C., Fulton, J.P. & Kramer, P.D. (1986). Acceptance of hepatitis B vaccine among hospital workers. *American Journal of Public Health, 76*, 252–255.

Centers for Disease Control and Prevention (1991). Successful strategies in adult immunization. *Morbidity and Mortality Weekly Report, 40*, 700–709.

Cohen, J. (1994). The HIV vaccine paradox. *Science, 264*, 1072–1074.

Crossley, K.B., Gerding, D.N. & Petzel, R.A. (1985). Acceptance of hepatitis B vaccine by hospital personnel. *Infection Control, 6*, 147 149.

Fedson, D S. (1994). Adult immunization: summary of the National Vaccine Advisory Committee report. *Journal of the American Medical Association, 272*, 1133–1137.

Grady, C. (1999). Grappling with global concerns in the search for an HIV vaccine. *Journal of the Association of Nurses in AIDS Care, 10*, 17–20.

Harward, M.P., Kaiser, D.L. & Fedson, D.S. (1988). Acceptance of hepatitis B vaccine by medical and surgical residents. *Journal of General Internal Medicine, 3*(2), 150–155.

Herold, A.H., Roetzheim, R.G., Pamies, R.J., Woodard, L.J., Van Durme, D.J. & Manning, R. (1992). Matriculants' compliance with a required preventive health program. *Academic Medicine, 67*, 403–405.

Israsena, S., Kamolratanakul, P. & Sekulramrung, R. (1992). Factors influencing acceptance of hepatitis B vaccination by hospital personnel in an area hyperendemic for hepatitis B. *American Journal of Gastroenterology, 87,* 1807–1809.

LEVIN, M.A. (1993). The day after an AIDS vaccine is discovered: management matters. *Journal of Policy Analysis and Management, 12,* 438–455.

LIAU, A. & ZIMET, G.D. (2000). Undergraduates' perception of HIV immunization: attitudes and behaviours as determining factors. *International Journal of STD and AIDS.*

LIAU, A., ZIMET, G.D. & FORTENBERRY, J.D. (1998). Attitudes about human immunodeficiency virus immunization. *Sexually Transmitted Diseases, 25,* 76–81.

PENNIE, R.A., O'CONNOR, A.M., GARVOCK, M.J. & DRAKE, E.R. (1991). Factors influencing the acceptance of hepatitis B vaccine by students in health disciplines in Ottawa. *Canadian Journal of Public Health, 82,* 12–15.

PRINCE, A. & BERNARD, A.L. (1998). Sexual behaviors and safer sex practices of college students on a commuter campus. *Journal of American College Health, 47,* 11–21.

ROGERS, E.M. (1983). *Diffusion of innovation,* 3rd edition. New York: Free Press.

ZIMET, G.D., BLYTHE, M.J. & FORTENBERRY, J.D. (2000). Vaccine characteristics and acceptability of HIV immunization among adolescents. *International Journal of STD and AIDS, 11,* 143–149.

ZIMET, G.D., FORTENBERRY, J.D. & BLYTHE, M.J. (1999). Adolescents' attitudes about HIV immunization. *Journal of Pediatric Psychology, 24,* 67–75.

ZIMET, G.D., LIAU, A. & FORTENBERRY, J.D. (1997). Health beliefs and intention to get immunized for HIV. *Journal of Adolescent Health, 20,* 354–359.

HIV/AIDS in China: 1990–2001

Oscar Grusky,[1,3] Hongjie Liu,[2] and Michael Johnston[1]

Received Nov 7, 2001; revised July 11, 2002; accepted July 17, 2002

China is facing a major crisis because of the increasing epidemics of HIV/AIDS and other sexually transmitted diseases (STDs). The purpose of this paper is to enhance understanding of the crisis by analyzing the capacity of China's health care system, its governmental HIV/AIDS policies, and the published literature on the epidemiology of HIV/AIDS during the period 1990–2001. HIV/AIDS and other STDs are rapidly increasing. The situation is urgent and requires comprehensive preventive actions. China's health care system is decentralized and underfunded, and access to treatment by the poor is seriously limited. There is a lag in public knowledge and in knowledge among health care workers about HIV/AIDS. The HIV/AIDS epidemic emerged initially in rural areas by means of intravenous drug use. Paid blood donors and blood recipients account for a significant portion of the persons infected by the HIV virus, especially in rural areas. Sexual risk behaviors in rural and urban areas are of increasing importance as a method of transmission of the virus.

KEY WORDS: China; HIV/AIDS; STDs; transmission routes.

INTRODUCTION

It has been estimated by the World Health Organization and UNAIDS that HIV/AIDS worldwide to date has resulted in 19 million deaths, 13 million orphans, and over 55 million HIV-infected persons. Every day 16,000 new infections are reported. Developing nations are the location of over 95% of new infections. Southeast Asia, and China and India in particular because of their vast populations, constitute, after Africa, the next major and most vulnerable area of the world. Attention is naturally focused on China because it is the most populous nation on earth. The nature of the epidemic in China, in large part because of its demographic features and its social, economic, and political institutions, is strikingly different from that of two smaller Southeast Asian nations, Thailand and Australia, which have mounted comparatively effective strategies for coping with the disease.

Over the past century infectious diseases have accounted for the largest portion of human mortality. They remain the leading causes of mortality among children and young adults in poor nations. Poverty, lack of access to clean drinking water, crowding, inadequate access to sanitary waste disposal, and poor education combine to contribute to high infectious disease morbidity and mortality (Merson *et al.*, 2001).

Several factors are essential to understanding the basic contours of HIV/AIDS in China: the epidemiologic features of the epidemic and its demographic and geographic characteristics, and the structure and functioning of the nation's social institutions, in particular its health care system, economic structure, family system, and political system, including the approach of its political leaders to the epidemic.

Yu *et al.* (1996) presented data on the distribution of HIV/AIDS in China from 1985 to 1994. Detels (1997) provided an insightful social epidemiologic essay on HIV in China. The goal of the present paper is to update and expand their work by analyzing what is known from the published literature on China's health care system, governmental HIV/AIDS policies, and

[1]Department of Sociology, University of California at Los Angeles, Los Angeles, California.
[2]School of Public Health, The Chinese University of Hong Kong, Hong Kong, China.
[3]Correspondence should be directed to Oscar Grusky, Ph.D., Department of Sociology, University of California at Los Angeles, Box 951551, Los Angeles, California 90095-1551; e-mail: grusky@ucla.edu.

the epidemiology of HIV/AIDS during the period 1990–2001.

METHODS

A literature search was undertaken that involved the following steps. First, six electronic databases relevant to HIV/AIDS (AIDSLINE), medicine (Medline), sociology (Sociological Abstracts), psychology (PsychINFO), nursing (Cumulative Index of Nursing and Allied Health Literature, CINAHL), and education (Education Resources Information Center, ERIC-Cambridge version were searched to find published and unpublished studies on HIV/AIDS in China. Second, we examined reference sections of selected retrieved studies to identify additional studies. Third, we examined Yu *et al.*'s (1996) review of the literature and other articles for additional English and Chinese references. The key words used initially included HIV/AIDS, sexual risk-taking, health care delivery, health care services, and China. We later did an additional search for articles on blood safety and injection drug use. Initially 67 research reports were identified in English and in Chinese in Medline, 74 in AIDSLINE, 72 in PsychINFO, 39 in CINAHL, and 74 in ERIC. However, most were unpublished conference papers and were not deemed pertinent. Selected magazine and newspaper reports published in the United States and in Hong Kong and the Peoples Republic of China were added.

All tables and figures rely on official Chinese Ministry of Health reports even though a number of UNAIDS/WHO experts have suggested that they seriously underestimate the true rates (Editorial, 2001). Unfortunately, UNAIDS and WHO do not provide specific information regarding the bases for their higher estimates. A report issued by the Monitoring the AIDS Pandemic (MAP) Network (2001) also claims rapidly increasing rates of STDs in China, but fails to provide national data on HIV/AIDS. The data shown in Figure 3 on the rapid increase in other STDs, combined with the estimates of a large number of injection drug users and sex workers, undermines confidence in the official numbers of HIV/AIDS cases. A recent article (Gill *et al.*, 2002) estimates that China has 1.2 million persons in Henan province alone infected with HIV. The authors also assert that China will have between 6.4 and 10 million people with HIV/AIDS in 2010. However, no specifics are provided concerning how those numbers were determined.

FINDINGS AND DISCUSSION

China's Health Care System

The capacity of a nation to cope with HIV/AIDS and other infectious diseases such as STDs depends in large part on the state of its health care system. Roemer (1991) defined a health care system as the "combination of resources, organization, financing and management that culminate in the delivery of health services to the population." Although each nation's health care system has unique features, these four aspects capture its core elements. China's health care system is seriously limited in resources. This has resulted in significant problems of access to health care for most of the rural population in need and for many, if not most, poor urbanites. Confidential and anonymous HIV testing and antiretroviral treatment are virtually unavailable (H. Liu *et al.*, 2001a).

Each province in China has considerable fiscal independence. The nation is subdivided into counties (2,182), townships (47,000), and villages (740,000). As these numbers suggest, China is predominantly rural, with about 70–75% of its population of about 1.3 billion persons living in the countryside. The same percentage of the population resides in those urban and rural sectors where the epidemiologic transition from infectious to chronic and degenerative diseases has taken place.

Hsiao (1995) summarized the leading causes of death in China from 1957 to 1987. Over that period, infectious diseases declined in rank in urban areas from the second leading cause of death to the ninth. Infectious diseases in rural areas also ranked ninth in 1987. Infectious diseases accounted for about 2% of total deaths in 1987 in urban and rural areas combined. Basic immunization remains free in China, although fees are frequently charged for "administrative costs" and for needles and syringes.

In 1989, China allocated 3.6% of its gross domestic product (about U.S. $10 billion) for health care (Ministry of Public Health, 1991). Health care financing in 1989 (Ministry of Public Health, 1991) was primarily by means of work and government insurance (39%) and direct patient payments (36%). Provinces and local counties provided 19%. Cooperative medical insurance paid 5% and the central government only about 1%. China's health care costs increased rapidly from 1990 to 1997 and this made medical care too expensive for most poor rural residents. As a result, tuberculosis cases and infant mortality increased.

Due to budgetary problems, in part due to state enterprise failures, China has been compelled to cut back on national health care expenditures. The replacement of collective farming also led to the demise of many village health stations. Rural health care in China consists of three tiers: village, township, and county health units. Government health reforms led to the replacement of the communes with a system of household responsibility. Consequently, the village, which formerly subsidized medical services, no longer does so, and was replaced by fee-for-service medical care for peasants (Zheng and Hillier, 1995). Because there was less money available, the number of health care personnel in villages also declined. The control of township hospitals was switched from county health units to townships. In addition, each county also has a Chinese traditional medicine hospital.

At the same time, hospitals have been forced to become more and more financially independent. The private ownership of clinics and health facilities has increased. In 1991 (Ministry of Public Health, 1991), 68% of the 1.9 million beds in regional or county hospitals were under government control. State enterprises ran the remainder. Even government-controlled hospitals must generate most of their revenue from user fees.

The Ministry of Public Health provides some top-level policy guidelines, but because it lacks financial responsibility for health care, its influence is reduced. Many ministries and at least 11 commissions participate in one form or another in health policy formulation. For example, there is the Ministry of Finance, the Ministry of Labor and Personnel, the Family Planning Commission, and the Central Price Commission, which sets the prices for health service payments. In fact, the management of health care has been largely decentralized to the provincial and the county levels. This may have created problems in attempts to control the HIV/AIDS and other STD epidemics, particularly with regard to the supply and distribution of donated plasma and blood.

Ho (1995) described China's health care system as having three formal systems: (1) a publicly funded system for civil servants, those who work in universities and public agencies, and certain ranked handicapped military officers; these categories included 29 million persons in 1993; (2) employees of state and collective enterprises and their family members (who receive partial coverage), which included 144 million persons in 1993; and (3) those under the cooperative medical care scheme in rural areas, which covers "about 20% of workers in the agricultural sector" (Ho, 1995). Ho estimated that, in 1993, 845 million persons were without medical insurance.

An eight-province household survey of about 16,000 individuals undertaken in 1989 found that the poor and those residing in rural areas were significantly less likely to have medical insurance (Henderson *et al*., 1995). Hsiao (1995) estimated that by 1985 only 5.4% of rural communities were maintaining cooperative-financed medical care. He estimated that, as of 1995, only 10% of the rural population was covered by prepayment methods or insurance of any kind. Ho and Hsiao concur that the large bulk of rural inhabitants lack health insurance.

This huge number, 845 million uninsured people, may be placed in some perspective by contrasting the situation in China with that of the United States. WHO recently ranked the U.S. 37th in the world in overall quality of health care, in part because of the large number of persons who are uninsured, a number estimated to be about 40 million (World Health Organisation, 2000). China has more than 21 times as many persons who are uninsured than does the United States. The purpose of the contrast is simply to point out how critical this problem is for China. Dahlman and Aubert (2001) also compared China and the United States in their systematic study of methods for transforming the Chinese economy to one based on knowledge.

China has for some time had different organizations delivering health care in rural and urban areas. In rural areas, as noted above, village stations, township health centers, and county hospitals are the principal components. Urban hospitals quickly dominated care delivery in cities, as most large enterprises had their own well-equipped hospitals with a trained staff. These hospitals were apparently quick to adopt technological advances in medicine and more expensive medications in order to attract patients and increase revenue (X. Liu and Hsiao, 1995).

In about 12% of the villages, mainly in the poorest geographic areas, there are no village stations. Because the staff in village stations are usually part-time, have relatively little training, and are not well-equipped, those farmers who have the funds go directly to county and area hospitals, where better facilities and better trained staff are available. China has experimented with urban health care reform and there is evidence that in Zhengjiang city some changes were cost-effective (G. G. Liu *et al*., 1999). Reforms have also been carried out in hospitals at the county level with mixed results. For example, the length of a hospital stay is influenced by a peasants insurance status, with the uninsured being charged more and having a shorter stay (Zheng and Hillier, 1995).

Choi *et al.* (1999), in a study of 939 STD patients in Guangzhou and Shenzen, found that seeking treatment from private physicians was associated with treatment delay. They also found diagnostic deficiencies and inappropriate treatment. They cite other studies (e.g. Yuen, 1992) suggesting that "a majority of Chinese physicians in China are not well-qualified to treat STD patients" (p. 314) because of inadequate medical training.

H. Liu *et al.* (2002) assessed the accuracy of laboratory testing and diagnoses by physicians in four STD clinics in Hefei, the capital of Anhui province. They reported that STDs, including syphilis and herpes simplex virus, were sometimes incorrectly diagnosed as non-STDs and other times overdiagnosed. In addition, they found that more than half of the patients previously infected were not given information to prevent reinfection. The study concluded that "the quality of clinic laboratory testing was not high and physicians often misdiagnosed STDs."

In summary, China's health care system faces resource, policy, and organizational and management problems. Other important problems stem from lack of knowledge of HIV/AIDS and other STDs among health care providers (Li *et al.*, 1993; Wu *et al.*, 1999), people at risk (Wang *et al.*, 2001a), and the general population (Liao *et al.*, 1997; Treise *et al.*, 1996), stigmatization of persons living with HIV/AIDS, and health care system decentralization. We were unable to find studies of HIV/AIDS stigmatization in China, but H. Liu *et al.* (2001b) studied stigma among STD patients. In some areas these factors, fueled by concern over the impact of the epidemic on economic development, may have led to HIV/AIDS underreporting or in some areas to no reporting at all. A fundamental challenge to China's ability to deal effectively with HIV/AIDS lies in its poorly developed public health system and major disparities in health care distribution and access between rich and poor, among minorities, between urban and rural populations, and between different geographic regions. HIV/AIDS prevention is also challenged by the lack of confidential and anonymous testing, effective substance use programs, and antiretroviral treatment programs.

Government Policies on HIV/AIDS

The ability and willingness of the government to confront the HIV/AIDS epidemic is a key factor influencing its impact. This issue was first addressed by Detels (1997), who characterized the Chinese government as beginning "a major effort to control HIV." He described the Chinese government's response to the HIV/AIDS epidemic as having six components: establishment of a national sentinel surveillance system, condom promotion, blood supply screening starting in 1996, making HIV/AIDS a notifiable disease in 1987, including HIV/AIDS in the ninth Five-Year Plan, and strengthening AIDS prevention and control in 1995. Nevertheless, it was not until August 2001 that a high-ranking government official, Deputy Health Minister Yin Dakui, publicly acknowledged the seriousness of the HIV/AIDS epidemic (Rosenthal, 2001a).

The Chinese national surveillance of HIV/AIDS was established in 1995 under WHO guidance and support. As of 1998 the national sentinel surveillance system had expanded to 98 sentinel sites (Zheng, 1999). By the year 2000, 101 sentinel population sites were established in 31 provinces, autonomous regions, and directly administered municipalities. The target populations are attendees of sexually transmitted infection clinics, underground female sex workers, injection-drug users, long-distance truck drivers, antenatal women, and blood and plasma donors. Cross-sectional surveys of these populations have been conducted twice yearly to monitor HIV-infection trends, except for long-distance truck drivers, who are surveyed yearly. The sample size for each target group is between 250 and 400. Sentinel surveillance data include social demographics, HIV prevalence, number of injection-drug users, proportion of drug users who share needles, and sexual behaviors (Qu *et al.*, 2000).

HIV testing is provided by government STD clinics and anti-epidemic stations in cities. HIV testing in rural areas is rare. Because antiretroviral drugs are very expensive, virtually no access to this treatment exists for the HIV-infected population. We were able to find only one study of vertical transmission. Among 619 children up to 7 years old who were tested, 11 were HIV positive, with a prevalence of 1.8%. The authors state that because none of the infected children had a history of blood transfusion, the probable transmission route was from mother to child (Wang *et al.*, 2001).

Condom promotion is undertaken by the government, but, as Detels (1997) noted, this is being accomplished in a cautious fashion. Since the early 1970s, when China initiated a major family planning program, use of male condoms has been encouraged.

Hence, Chinese women can suggest condom usage to avoid pregnancy more easily than women in many other cultures (Choi *et al.*, 2000). According to J. Wang *et al* (2001b, p. 651) "In China, condoms are readily available in pharmacies, at places of employment, and through government family planning programs." Nevertheless, two thirds of the 498 male STD patients studied in 1998 by J. Wang *et al.* (2001b) reported never using condoms even when having sex with a person other than their spouse or friend.

In 1998, the State Council issued a national medium-and long-term strategic plan for HIV/AIDS prevention and control. The plan stresses prevention and health education. It develops indicators for activities and goals for public education. According to the plan, by 2002 HIV transmission through blood collection and supply will be eliminated, the rapid spread of HIV among drug users will be contained, and the annual increase of STD incidence is targeted to be less than 15%. In addition, the plan proposes that by 2010 the annual incidence of STDs will have halted or declined and the number of HIV infections will be kept to within 1.5 million. In 2001, China issued an action plan for reducing and preventing the spread of HIV/AIDS (Ministry of Health, Communicable Disease Control Division, 2001). This document acknowledged that HIV/AIDS and other STD epidemics are spreading, that intravenous drug use is not yet controlled, and that HIV transmission through blood transfusion remains a problem because of illegal blood and blood plasma collection. It also acknowledged that leaders in some regions failed to comprehend the threat of the epidemic. The document specified implementation principles and an action plan to reduce HIV/AIDS and other STD infection rates by closing illegal blood plasma collection stations, increasing the HIV and STD training of medical workers, expanding treatment of HIV-infected persons, and developing an HIV/AIDS and STD information network, national comprehensive surveillance and laboratory testing systems, and policies designed to reduce risky behaviors of those in high-risk groups. Other positive signs are China's establishment of a Center for Disease Control and Prevention and its recent willingness to cooperate in its HIV/AIDS prevention efforts with the U.S. Centers for Disease Control and Prevention (Rosenthal, 2001b). The Chinese government has actively, although selectively, supported the development of nongovernmental organizations in sensitive health education matters, such as HIV/AIDS.

The Phases and Geography of the HIV/AIDS Epidemic

The first AIDS case in China was reported in 1985. By the end of 2000, 21,870 HIV cases and 800 AIDS cases were reported from all 31 provinces, autonomous regions, and directly-administered municipalities.

Conceptually, the HIV/AIDS epidemic in China can be divided into three phases (Zheng, 1999). The first phase, which began in 1985 and ended in 1988, was that of a sporadic epidemic. The first phase was marked by a small number of imported cases. The majority of infected persons during this time were foreigners or overseas Chinese. Cases appeared intermittently in coastal cities.

The epidemic's second phase (1989–1993) was focused in a few rural counties in Yunnan province that border Myanmar. It began in October 1989 with the identification of HIV infection in 146 drug users in southwest Yunnan. In this phase, the majority of reported HIV infections in China were among drug users in Yunnan. Prevalence among drug injectors was high. The estimated prevalence of HIV was 70–80% among known drug injectors in Ruili county, 40% in Longchuan county, and 0–5% in Luxi county. At the same time, a small number of HIV infections were reported among laborers returning from abroad, STD patients, and commercial sex workers.

The third phase of the epidemic (1994 onward) is the rapid spread phase and began in late 1994 when HIV transmission spread beyond Yunnan province. A considerable number of HIV infections were reported among drug users and commercial plasma donors from various regions, and national figures for HIV infection quickly grew. Increasing numbers of drug-related HIV infections were reported in Sichuan province in 1995, in Xinjiang province in 1996, and in Guangxi province in 1997 (J. Zhang, 1999). At the same time, HIV infection by sexual contact increased, but remained relatively infrequent, and had not yet reached epidemic proportions (Sun, 1999).

In this phase, HIV/AIDS cases were reported from all provinces, autonomous regions, and directly administered municipalities. Table 1 displays the estimated HIV adult prevalence rate for all of China from 1990 to 2001. Figure 1 shows the distribution of HIV and AIDS and its rapid increase from 1985 to 2000. Figure 2 shows the HIV distribution by province. Figure 3 shows the rapid increase of STDs over this same period of time. The increase in STD cases is significant because STDs increase the efficiency of HIV

Table I. Estimated HIV Adult Prevalence Rate[a]

Variable	1990 1995	1996 1997	1998 1999	2000 2001
Estimated total adult HIV	10,000	100,000	500,000	> 1,000,000
Adult HIV prevalence	< 0.002%	< 0.02%	< 0.1%	< 0.2%
Male/female ratio	9:1	7:1	5:1	4:1
Male HIV prevalence	< 0.01%	< 0.05%	< 0.2%	< 0.5%
Female HIV prevalence	< 0.001%	< 0.01%	< 0.02%	< 0.01%

[a] All estimates are based on official estimates by the Ministry of Health and the Chinese Academy of Preventive Medicine.

transmission by 10- to 20-fold (Fleming and Wasserheit, 1999).

Five high-prevalence HIV-infected provinces are Yunnan, Xinjian, Guangxi, Sichuan, and Henan. The majority of cases from Yunnan and Xinjiang provinces are among injection-drug users. Qinghai was the last province to report the epidemic (Zheng, 1999). The overall reported HIV infection rate in China is relatively low, with infections clustered in particular areas. The majority of HIV cases are from rural areas (Figure 2). As Table II indicates, over three fourths of the HIV/AIDS cases are concentrated among the 20- to 39- year-old age group. Among 22,326 reported HIV/AIDS cases, 82.71% were male and 17.29% were female. The ratio of male to female cases was 4.78.

Illegal Blood Donor Centers and the Blood Supply System

The case of Shen Jieyong and his poor, rural family consisting of himself, his wife, and their 3-year-old daughter is tragically illustrative of what can go wrong in the blood supply system (Rosenthal, 2001c). The wife contracted HIV/AIDS from a blood transfusion given in a hospital when she was pregnant. The child contracted the disease from her mother and the husband presumably contracted it by means of sexual relations with his wife. The mother died of AIDS and the father and daughter are seriously ill with the disease. The family lost its livelihood, was ostracized by their village, and was compelled to move. The father reported suffering "intense discrimination." Although some limited funds were obtained by the father as a result of a legal judgment, their funds have run out and no medical treatment is available to him or his child.

In some provinces of central China, such as Henan, a significant number of HIV infections are among commercial plasma donors. Plasma donors are often at greater risk of infection than those donating

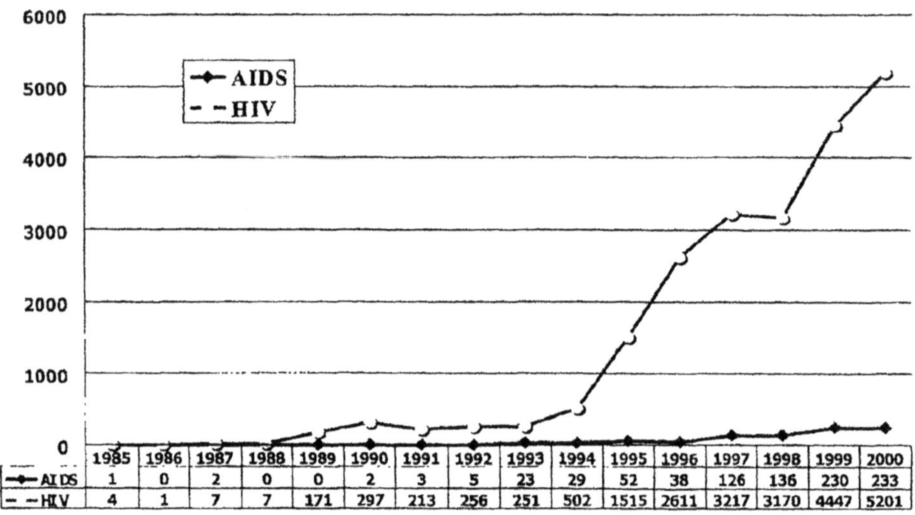

	1985	1986	1987	1988	1989	1990	1991	1992	1993	1994	1995	1996	1997	1998	1999	2000
AIDS	1	0	2	0	0	2	3	5	23	29	52	38	126	136	230	233
HIV	4	1	7	7	171	297	213	256	251	502	1515	2611	3217	3170	4447	5201

Fig. 1. Reported HIV/AIDS cases by year in China

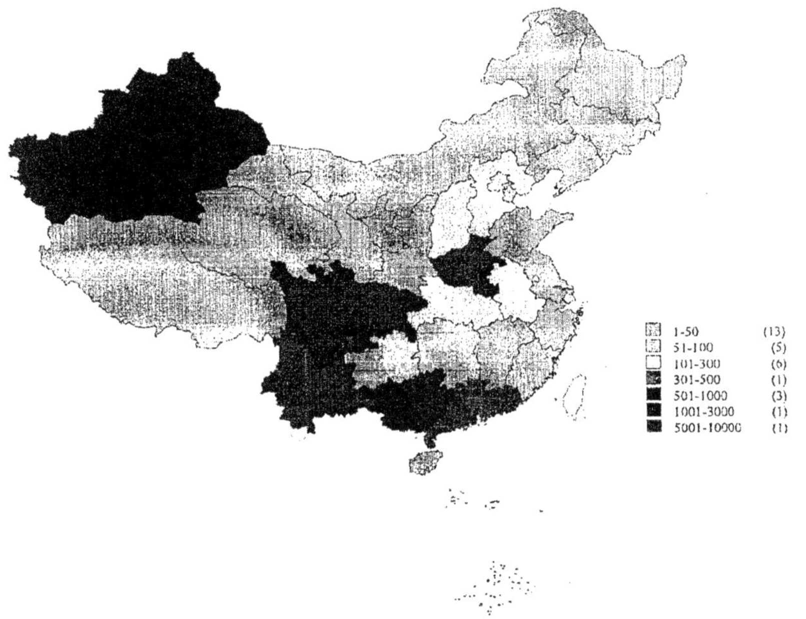

Fig. 2. HIV infection distribution by province in China.

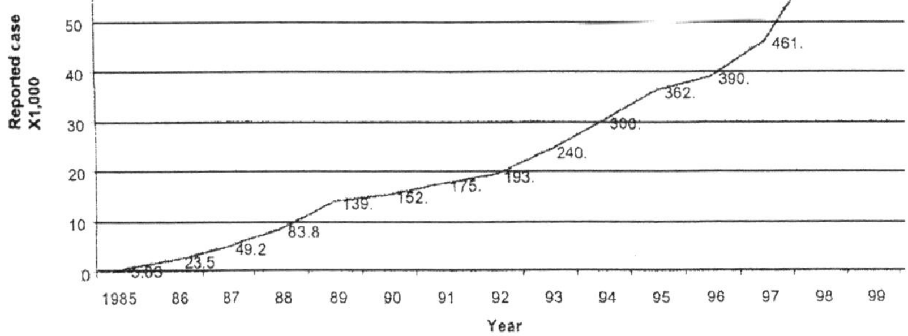

Fig. 3. Reported STD cases in China 1985 2000.

Table II. Age Distribution of HIV/AIDS[a]

Age group (years)	Number of HIV/AIDS cases	%
<15	148	0.65
16–19	1,701	7.5
20–29	12,695	56.0
30–39	5,563	24.54
40–49	1,251	5.52
>50	359	1.58
Unknown	953	4.2

[a]See footnote to Table I.

Table III. HIV/AIDS Transmission[a]

Route	Number of HIV/AIDS cases	%
Injection drug use	15,991	70.54
Heterosexual	1,542	6.8
Homosexual	39	0.17
Blood/blood products	184	0.81
Mother to child	23	0.1
Unknown	4,891	21.57

[a]See footnote to Table I.

whole blood because the blood of plasma donors is transfused, that is, returned to the donor after the plasma has been filtered from the blood (Zheng, 2000). A recent study conducted in a county in central China reported that the HIV prevalence rate was 9.1% among paid blood donors and 25.9% among paid plasma donors (Yan *et al.*, 2000). These commercial plasma donors are often recruited by illegal plasma-collecting companies from among mobile migrant populations, who sometimes also engage in prostitution and drug abuse. In a number of instances, HIV infection was traced to contaminated needles and equipment used in illegal commercial plasma collection settings.

The U.S. Embassy in Beijing provided a detailed account of the spread of HIV/AIDS in rural areas from blood donors (U.S Embassy Beijing, 2000). Illegal blood donation centers in Beijing, Hebei, and Henan provinces were discussed. A Henan province blood donor village where 80 of 140 persons tested HIV-positive was described (J. Zhang and Zi, 2000; Rosenthal, 2001a). The U.S. Embassy report cited serious shortages of blood needed for transfusions in Guangzhou, Shanghai, and other areas. China also exports products made from blood plasma, with the demand for blood plasma increasing 7–10% each year. About one fourth of Guangzhou's blood comes from voluntary donors. The embassy report cited a 1998 *Peoples Daily* article reporting that the prevalence of hepatitis B virus infections in paid blood donation was 8–13% overall and in migrant workers' blood donations was as high as 40–50%. According to the report, after a number of cases where hospital patients were infected with HIV/AIDS came to the attention of the government, China made an effort to improve its blood supply practices. Henan province, which has 90 million people, reportedly had 287 legal blood collection stations and many illegal ones. Numerous peasant farmers with marginal incomes reportedly supported themselves by selling their blood (Aifang, 2000; J. Zhang and Zi, 2000).

This may be an example of how the decentralization of the health care system contributed to its inability to stem HIV/AIDS and other STD epidemics. The provincial health agencies' personnel and their budget come from the provinces. Likewise, the regional or county health departments' personnel and budget come from local sources. This local control may weaken the upward flow of information and hence the control of the Ministry of Health. Local agencies can suppress the upward flow of information to authorities, as was allegedly the case with the Henan Provincial Department of Health (Aifang, 2000; J. Zhang and Zi, 2000).

As shown in Table III, official figures show that for over one-fifth of the cases (21.57%), the route of HIV transmission is unknown. The vice minister of health reported that a significant percentage of these cases were from blood collection irregularities (Aifang, 2000; Editorial, 2001; Rosenthal, 2001a).

A Close Look at HIV/AIDS Transmission by Injecting-Drug Users and by Sexual Behavior

The three main methods of the spread of HIV/AIDS in China are intravenous drug use, blood collection methods, and sexual risk behaviors (predominantly heterosexual). As noted, the first route, intravenous drug use, particularly in Yunnan province, played a leading role in the earliest stage of the epidemic, and continues to play a significant role (Detels, 1997). Although documentation is limited, blood collection has also played a part (Zheng, 2000). Heterosexual intercourse appears to be of increasing significance as a transmission method (Qu *et al.*, 2000). Gill *et al* (2002) estimate that 5–7% of the male population is gay. They assert that homosexual intercourse is another source of HIV transmission in China, but no evidence is cited.

Yu *et al*'s review of the HIV/AIDS literature from 1985 to 1994 concluded: "HIV infection and

AIDS in China began as a highly regionalized and largely rural problem in Yunnan Province. However, HIV infection and AIDS have become an emerging urban problem" (Yu *et al.*, 1996, p. 1116). This statement merits careful examination.

As noted above, HIV infection was first identified as a serious problem in rural Yunnan counties bordering Myanmar (Zheng *et al.*, 1994). In the mid-1980s, HIV/AIDS received little attention in China. After discovering a handful of HIV/AIDS cases in 1985, the Chinese government initiated surveillance in eight cities: Beijing, Shanghai, Guangzhou, Fuzhou, Hangzhou, Xi'an, Shenyang, and Nanning (Xia *et al.*, 1994). In 1986, the Ministry of Public Health listed AIDS as a notifiable communicable disease (Xia *et al.*, 1994). Still, as noted above, only a small number of HIV/AIDS cases had been identified in China by the end of 1988. There was a dramatic turning point in October 1989, when nearly 100 HIV infections were identified among participants in a county drug detoxification center in Ruili county, Yunnan province (Xia *et al.*, 1994).

Researchers speculated that the Golden Triangle area, which includes Myanmar and Laos and is within 1 day's travel of Yunnan province, was the ultimate source of the epidemic. In the early 1990s, Xia *et al* (1994) suggested that Chinese villagers near the border had contracted HIV by means of intravenous drug use and were now spreading it the same way.

The importance of intravenous drug use as the main mechanism of spreading HIV/AIDS among drug users in rural villages in counties adjacent to Myanmar is now widely accepted (Yu *et al.*, 1996). Wu *et al.* (1996, 1997) substantially strengthened understanding of the HIV epidemic in rural Yunnan by undertaking a cross-sectional survey of 1,548 respondents in 1994. Based upon a multivariate logistic regression of their retrospective data, they found that having been encouraged by friends or others to try drugs had the strongest effect on initiation of drug use. Attributing the proportion of drug use caused by a particular factor, they found that, among the overlapping causal factors, 70.8% was related to encouragement by others, 50% to cigarette smoking, 24% to membership in the Jingpo ethnic group, 13.5% to pre/extramarital sex, 8.3% to a family member who used drugs, and 2% to being divorced, widowed, or separated.

HIV/AIDS is no longer an almost entirely rural phenomenon, and the mechanism of transmission is no longer exclusively through intravenous drug use. At the same time HIV/AIDS continues to have a significant rural character. Moreover, intravenous drug use continues to play an important role in spreading the disease There apparently are two main drug routes, one that originates in the Golden Triangle (Myanmar and neighboring nations) and the other in the Golden Crescent (Central Asia). The Golden Triangle route enters China in Yunnan province, from which it snakes through several western provinces until it reaches Xinjiang province and intersects with the Golden Crescent route. Both drug routes pass through rural areas, thus spreading the epidemic through them. The Golden Crescent drug route will likely become more traversed as the government implements infrastructure improvements designed to strengthen the linkage between Xinjiang province and Central Asia and Eastern Europe. The Golden Triangle drug route from Yunnan through Guangxi (or from Vietnam to Guangzi) to Guangdong and then to Hong Kong also largely passes through rural areas and seems to be responsible for transmitting the virus to rural areas in Guangxi, Guizhou, and perhaps even Guangdong.

There were reportedly 681,000 registered drug users in China in 1999, although most experts believe that this figure greatly underestimates the true number (State Council, 2000). There are also reportedly 914 compulsory methadone detoxification centers in China. Two studies conducted in China found that over 90% of detoxified drug users relapse (Jin, 1996; Tie *et al.*, 1999).

As noted, tragically, health professionals have probably played a role in spreading HIV in rural China. Officials responsible for collecting plasma (filtering the blood to remove plasma and transfusing it to the contributor) in central China have not been sterilizing the equipment between contributors (Aifang, 2000; Editorial, 2001; U.S. Embassy Beijing, 2000).

In 1994, HIV infection in China again dramatically increased. Aside from the aforementioned mechanisms (intravenous drug use and contaminated blood products), researchers identified sexual risk behavior as an important mechanism for spreading HIV (Gil, 1994). This mechanism has implications for both urban and rural China.

In 1988, the first Chinese case of sexually transmitted HIV was discovered in a person who acknowledged homosexual intercourse with a tourist (Gil, 1994). By the end of 1990, there were still no reported cases of HIV among commercial sex workers or their clients, nor was there any case record evidence of a connection between STD patients and HIV (Gil,

1994). However, according to 69 of 82 medical and epidemiology personnel, "the most significant growth in *new* HIV cases during 1992–1993 occurred in sexual transmission categories" (Gil, 1994, p. 213, italics in original).

Sexual behavior in China is becoming much freer than in the past few decades (K.-L. Zhang *et al.*, 1999). Many young people view sexual experimentation and cohabitation as an acceptable lifestyle (Gil, 1994). D. Liu's (1992) large-scale ($n = 20,000$) survey on sexual behavior in China confirmed that premarital sex is popular. Homosexuality remains strongly stigmatized and little is known about sexual risk behavior among men who have sex with men.

A consecutive sample of 1,371 STD clinic patients (drawn from 12 of the 22 national surveillance system STD clinics in 1997 that agreed to participate) reported by Choi *et al.* (2000) shed additional light on nationwide sexual behaviors. During the year previous to being surveyed, men had a median of two sexual partners (range 0–43). Although the median is not reported for women, the range is 0–50. The authors also note a gender difference in the kinds of sexual partners, with 97% of the women versus 93% of the men reporting relationships with spouse, fiance, or boy/girlfriend. This contrasts with 50% of the men who reported sexual relationships with classmates, coworkers or acquaintances versus 42% of the women. Many more men than women (65% versus 16%) reported sexual relationships with attendants at hotels, karaoke bars, coffee shops, or massage parlors, street prostitutes, or hairdressers. Few reported using condoms during their first sexual intercourse (men 12%, women 15%). Men 35 years or older who had initiated sex at an earlier age were most likely to have had multiple sexual partnerships. Young persons with nonsteady partners who had used condoms in their first sexual encounter were more likely than others to have used condoms in the last year.

Though commercial sex work was abolished in 1955, it has reemerged and resurged since the initiation of economic reforms in 1979. According to national and provincial police records, the police dealt with over 580,500 cases of people involved in prostitution from 1981 to 1991 (Gil *et al.*, 1996). The growth of commercial sex work seems to have accelerated with the deepening of economic reforms from 1992 onward. China's very large (over 100 million) migrant worker population also expanded during this period (W. M. Zhang *et al.*, 1998), an unknown number of whom engage in high risk sexual behavior. Most commercial sex workers have at least one kind of sexually transmitted disease (van den Hoek *et al.*, 2001). Gill *et al.* (2002) claim that the cultural preference for male children in China is producing a demographic imbalance that limits opportunities for men and increasingly fuels the demand for commercial sex workers.

The number of STD cases has risen dramatically since the initiation of economic reforms. In 1979, there were few STD cases. By 1990, there were 204,077 reported cases (Gil *et al.*, 1996). According to the Ministry of Public Health, from one half to two thirds of the infections occurred among nonmarried individuals (Gil *et al.*, 1996).

A random sample of patients from STD clinics in Jinan, Shandong province, in 1998 (J. Wang *et al.* 2001b), provided information regarding sexual behavior in urban China. The majority of the sample did not use condoms consistently and engaged in high-risk sexual behaviors. The mean age at which first sexual intercourse took place was in the early 20s. Most patients had multiple sexual partners and many men reported paying for sex.

Risky sex may be more frequent in urban than rural areas because of greater opportunities for anonymity in urban areas when engaging in sexual behaviors. There are many more private clinics in urban areas, so that STD cases are more likely to be underestimated for urban than rural areas (Gil *et al.*, 1996). On the other hand, the quality of reporting in urban areas is relatively better than in rural areas. STD cases are underreported throughout China. Chen *et al.* (2000) described the epidemiology of STDs in China from 1989 to 1998. During this period, STD incidence increased significantly in men and women. Incidence increased more in women (4.20 times) than men (3.79 times). Syphilis incidence increased approximately 20 times at an average annual rate of 52.7%. Gonorrhea increased 2.6 times at an average annual rate of 11.4% and reached a plateau from 1994 to 1997. Extramarital transmission as source of STD infection significantly increased from 1995 to 1998. The incidence of STDs continued to increase in China from 1989 to 1998. The epidemic patterns are different from rates in developed counties in which behavioral interventions have been successfully implemented, suggesting the need for active behavioral intervention programs in China. At the same time, the government surveillance system is based in cities, as are the STD clinics. Yet, research by H. Liu *et al.* (1998) on a rural county in Anhui province in central China reported that a significant proportion of rural residents engage in activities that carry an elevated risk of HIV infection. They observed that 27.1% of the sampled men and 18.9% of the sampled women reported premarital sex and that sexual activities began in the early 20s. However, they also find that an overwhelming majority of people (94.9%) reported that their first sexual partner was their spouse and only 7.8% of the people reported multiple sexual partners in their entire life (primarily younger men and older women).

Evidence concerning the intermingling of sexual risk behaviors and intravenous drug use is mixed. On the one hand, Gil *et al.* (1996) reported that there is no evidence of commercial sex workers engaging in drug use of any kind. On the other hand, Wu *et al.* (1997; citing Zheng *et al.*, 1991) reported that intravenous drug users in Longchuan county, a rural county in Yunnan, are sexually promiscuous. Additional study of this problem is needed. Nevertheless, it is reasonable to be very concerned about the potential spread of HIV from the intravenous drug population to other sectors of society.

Yu *et al.* (1996) characterized HIV as an emerging urban problem in China. If so, the slowness with which HIV is being identified in urban areas may be due to inadequate access to health care, inadequate knowledge of HIV/AIDS, stigmatization of persons with HIV/AIDS, low motivation to test because of lack of treatment, and inexperience among health care workers in testing and diagnosis (Detels, 1997).

CONCLUSIONS

This paper reviewed the literature, English and Chinese, on HIV/AIDS and other STDs in China. The health care system was described, as were the responses of the Chinese government to these epidemics. A detailed analysis of the social epidemiology of HIV/AIDS and other STDs was presented based on official reports. The methods of HIV/AIDS transmission were closely examined.

Several trends typify the HIV/AIDS epidemic:

1. HIV/AIDS and other STDs are rapidly increasing. The situation is urgent and requires rapid, comprehensive, and systematic preventive actions at the national and the local levels. Recent indications of government awareness of the epidemics' seriousness are a positive sign.
2. China's health care system is decentralized and underfunded, and access to treatment by the poor is seriously limited. This greatly complicates the situation. Relatively few individuals have health insurance. Overall, the local system response to HIV/AIDS is not as informed as that at the national level.
3. There has been a serious lag in public knowledge and in knowledge among health care system officials about HIV/AIDS and other STDs. Stigmatization of HIV-infected persons is a serious problem.
4. The epidemic emerged initially in rural areas in Yunnan by means of intravenous drug use and this remains the major route of HIV infection.
5. Blood collection problems account for a significant portion of the persons infected by the HIV virus.
6. Sexual risk behaviors in rural and urban areas appear to be of increasing importance as a method of transmission of the virus.

ACKNOWLEDGMENTS

This study was supported in part by NIMH Grant T32 MH19127 awarded to Oscar Grusky. The authors acknowledge the helpful comments and contributions of Mary Jane Rotheram-Boris, Ph.D., Zunyou Wu, M.D., Ph.D., and Chy Tran. Of course, these persons are not responsible for the views expressed in this study. We are very grateful to the journal's anonymous reviewers for their insightful comments and suggestions on the manuscript.

REFERENCES

Aifang H. (2000). Revealing the "blood wound" of the spread of HIV/AIDS in Henan Province Written on the eve of the first AIDS Day of the new millennium. Available in Chinese at http://hbscity.com/news/rdxw/forum.html (November 28). English translation at http://www.usembassy-china.org.cn/english/sandt/henan-htm.

Chen, X., Gong, X. D., Liang, G. J., and Zhang, G. C. (2000) Epidemiologic trends of sexually transmitted diseases in China. *Sexually Transmitted Diseases*, 27. 138 142.

Choi K. H., Zheng, X., Zhou, H., Chen, W., and Mandel, J. (1999). Treatment delay and reliance on private physicians among patients with sexually transmitted diseases in China *International Journal of STD and AIDS*, *10*, 309 315.

Choi K. H., Zheng, X., Qu, S., Yiee, K., and Mandel, J. (2000). HIV risk among patients attending sexually transmitted disease clinics in China. *AIDS and Behavior*, *4*, 111-119.

Dahlman, C. J., and Aubert, J.-E. (2001). *China and the knowledge economy: Seizing the 21st century*. Washington, DC: World Bank.

Detels, R. (1997). HIV in China: The epidemic is now. *ISOP Intercom*, *20*, 1 11.

Editorial. (2001). China faces AIDS. *Lancet*, *358*, 773.

Fleming, D. T., and Wasserheit, J. N. (1999). From epidemiological synergy to public health policy and practice: The contribution of other sexually transmitted diseases to sexual transmission of HIV infection. *Sexually Transmitted Infections*, *75*, 3-17.

Gil, V. E. (1994). Sino conundrum: A history of HIV/AIDS in the People's Republic of China. *Journal of Sex Research, 31*, 211-217.

Gil, V. E., Wang, M. S., Anderson, A. F., Lin, G. M., and Wu, Z. O. (1996). Prostitutes, prostitution and STD/HIV transmission in mainland China. *Social Science and Medicine, 42*, 141-152.

Gill, B., Chang, J., and Palmer, S. (2002). China's HIV crisis. *Foreign Affairs, 2002(March/April)*, 96-110.

Henderson, G., Jin, S., Akin, J., Li, Z., Wang, J., Ma, H., He, Y., Zhang, X., Chang, Y., and Ge, K. (1995). Distribution of medical insurance in China 1995. *Social Science and Medicine, 41*, 1119-1130.

Ho, S. L. (1995). Market reforms and China's health care system. *Social Science and Medicine, 41*, 1065-1072.

Hsiao, W. C. L. (1995). The Chinese health care system: Lessons for other nations. *Social Science and Medicine, 41*, 1047-1055.

Jin, B. (1996). The development of opiate-drug relapse prevention in China. *Chinese Journal of Drug Dependence, 3*, 2-5.

Li, V. C., Cole, B. L., Zhang, S. Z., and Chen, C. Z. (1993). HIV-related knowledge and attitudes among medical students in China. *AIDS Care, 5*, 305-312.

Liao, S.-S., Choi, K.-H., Zhang, K.-N., Hall, T. L., Qi, B.-X., Deng, Y.-J., Yang, Y., Kay, J., Qin, Z., Liu, W., and Mandel, J. S. (1997). Extremely low awareness of AIDS, sexually transmitted diseases and condoms among Dai ethnic villagers in Yunnan province, China. *AIDS, 11*(Suppl. 1), S27-S34.

Liu, D. (1992). *Sexual behavior in modern China. A report of the nationwide sex civilization survey on 20,000 subjects in China* ([cofacilitated by M. L. Ng, W. L. Liu, and P. K. Yao] Shanghai: SJPC Publishing in Mandarin).

Liu, G. G., Cai, R., Zhao, Z., Yuen, P., Xiong, X., Chao, S., and Wang, B. (1999). Urban health care reform initiative in China: Findings from its pilot experiment in Zhengjiang city (1). *International Journal of Economic Development, 1*, 504-525.

Liu, H., Detels, R., Li, X., and Ma, E. (2001b). *Stigma, delayed treatment, and spousal notification among male STD patients in China*. Manuscript submitted.

Liu, H., Detels, R., Yin, Y., Li, X., and Visscher, B. (2002). *Do STD clinics correctly diagnose STDs? An assessment of STD management in Hefei, China*. Manuscript submitted.

Liu, H., Ma, Z., Yu, W., Xie, J., and Detels, R. (2001a). Acceptability of voluntary HIV testing and result disclosure among rural residents of China. *Journal of Chinese Preventive Medicine, 35*, 30-32.

Liu, H., Xie, J., Yu, W., Song, W., Gao, Z., Ma, Z., and Detels, R. (1998). A study of sexual behavior among rural residents of China. *Journal of Acquired Immune Deficiency Syndrome and Human Retrovirology, 19*, 80-88.

Liu, X., and Hsiao, W. C. L. (1995). The cost escalation of social health insurance plans in China: Its implication for public policy. *Social Science and Medicine, 41*, 1095-1101.

Merson, M., Black, R. E., and Mills, A. J. (Eds.) (2001). *International Public Health*. Gaithersburg, MD: Aspen.

Ministry of Health, Communicable Disease Control Division. (2001). China's action plan for reducing and preventing the spread of HIV/AIDS, 2001-2005. Available at http://www.usembassy-china.org.cn/english/sandt/AIDS-actionplantranslation.htm.

Ministry of Public Health. (1991). Annual Statistical Report Beijing.

Monitoring the AIDS Pandemic (MAP) Network. (2001). The status and trends of HIV/AIDS/STI epidemics in Asia and the Pacific Available at http://www.unaids.org/hivaidsinfo/statistics/MAP/.

Qu, S., Sun, X., Zheng, X., and Shenjie, H. (2000). National sentinel surveillance of HIV infection in China from 1995 to 1998. *Chinese Journal of Epidemiology, 21*, 7-9.

Roemer, M. I. (1991). *National health systems of the world*. Vol. 1. *The countries*. New York: Oxford University Press.

Rosenthal, E. (2001a, August 24). China now facing an AIDS epidemic, a top aide admits. *New York Times*.

Rosenthal, E. (2001b, August 30). U.S. agency will help China fight AIDS. *New York Times*.

Rosenthal, E. (2001c, September 16). A Chinese family's ordeal in a nation in denial of AIDS. *New York Times*.

State Council of People's Republic of China. (2000). News Office. Anti-drugs in China. Beijing p. 8.

Sun, X. (1999). The HIV/AIDS epidemic and key initiatives for HIV/AIDS prevention and control in China in 1998. *Chinese Journal of Prevention and Control of STD and AIDS, 5*, 97-99.

Tie, F., Zeng, H., Jin, J., Xu, B., Sun, Z., Wang, Y., Chen, J., and Zhang, Y. (1999). An epidemic investigation on relapse and relapse reasons after detoxification. *Chinese Journal of Drug Dependence, 8*, 305-309.

Treise, D., Walsh-Childers, K., Dai, S., and Swain, K. (1996). AIDS knowledge, attitudes and beliefs among Chinese college students: Implications for PSA development. *Health Marketing Quarterly, 13*, 87-107.

U.S. Embassy Beijing (2000). PRC blood donors and the spread of rural AIDS. Available at http://www.usembassy-china.org.cn/english/sandt/AIDSblood.htm

Van den Hoek, A., Yuliang, F., Dukers, N. H., Zhiheng, C., Jiangting, L., Lina, Z., and Xiuxing, Z. (2001). High prevalence of syphilis and other sexually transmitted diseases among sex workers in China: Potential for fast spread of HIV. *AIDS, 15*, 753-759.

Wang, J., Jiang, B., Siegal, H., Falck, R., and Carlson, R. (2001a). Level of AIDS and HIV knowledge and sexual practices among sexually transmitted disease patients in China. *Sexually Transmitted Diseases, 28*, 171-175.

Wang, J., Jiang, B., Siegal, H., Falck, R., and Carlson, R. (2001b). Sexual behavior and condom use among patients with sexually transmitted diseases in Jinan, China. *American Journal of Public Health, 91*, 650-651.

Wang, L., Zheng, X., and Li, D. (2001). The survey of HIV prevalence among children between 0-7 years old in one county in China. *Chinese Journal of Epidemiology*, 22, 38-39.

World Health Organization (2000). *The World Health Report 2000. Health Systems: Improving Performance*. Available at http://www.who.org.

Wu, Z., Detels, R., Zhang, J., Duan, S., Cheng, H., Li, Z., Dong, L., Huang, S., Jia, M., and Bi, X. (1996). Risk factors for intravenous drug use and sharing equipment among young male drug users in Longchuan County south-west China. *AIDS, 10*, 1017-1024.

Wu, Z., Qi, G., Zeng, Y., and Detels, R. (1999). Knowledge of HIV/AIDS among health care workers in China. *Aids Education and Prevention, 11*, 353-363.

Wu, Z., Zhang, J., Detels, R., Li, V. C., Cheng, H., Duan, S., Li, Z., Dong, L., Huang, S., Jia, M., and Bi, X. (1997). Characteristics of risk-taking behaviors, HIV and AIDS knowledge, and risk perception among young males in southwest China. *AIDS Education and Prevention, 9*, 147-160.

Xia, M., Kreiss, J. K., and Holmes, K. K. (1994). Risk factors for HIV infection among drug users in Yunnan province, China: Association with intravenous drug use and protective effect of boiling reusable needles and syringes. *AIDS, 8*, 1701-1706.

Yan, J., Zheng, X., Zhang, X., Liu, S., Zhangyi, Wang, C., and Liu, S. (2000). A survey of prevalence of HIV infection among paid blood donors in one county in China. *Chinese Journal of Epidemiology, 21*, 10-12.

Yu, E. S. H., Xie, Q., Zhang, K., Lu, P., and Chan, L. L. (1996). HIV infection and AIDS in China, 1985 through 1994. *American Journal of Public Health, 86*, 1116-1122.

Yuen, P. P. (1992). Private medicine in socialist China: A survey of the private medical market in Guangzhou. *International Journal of Health Planning Management, 7*, 211-221.

Zhang, J. (1999). HIV/AIDS epidemic, and the strategies for prevention and control. *Chinese Journal of Epidemiology, 20*, 234–236.

Zhang, L. and Zi, S. (2000). *The mystery of how nearly 100 people caught a "strange illness."* Available at http://www.usembassy-china.org.cn/english/sandt/AIDSblood.htm.

Zhang, K.-L., Li, D., Li, H., and Beck, E. J. (1999). Changing sexual attitudes and behaviour in China: Implications for the spread of HIV and other sexually transmitted diseases. *AIDS Care, 11*, 581–589.

Zhang, W. M., Li, X. R., Ye, L. Q., Xie, G., and Hu, Y. (1998). Migration in China. *Economic Research Conference, 1117*, 2–18.

Zheng, X. (1999). HIV/AIDS epidemic, and its prevention and control in China. *Chinese Journal of Epidemiology, 20*, 131–134.

Zheng, X. (2000). Control of HIV infections transmitted though blood transfusion. *Chinese Journal of Epidemiology, 21*, 1.

Zheng, X., and Hillier, S. (1995). The reforms of the Chinese health care system: County level changes: The Jiangxi study. *Social Science and Medicine, 41*, 1057–1064.

Zheng, X., Tian, C., Choi, K.-H., Zhang, J., Cheng, H., Yang, X., Li, D., Lin, J., Qu, S., Sun, X., Hall, T., Mandel, J., and Hearst, N. (1994). Injecting drug use and HIV infection in southwest China. *AIDS, 8*, 1141–1147.

Zheng, X., Tian, C. J., Yang, G., Xia, M., Zhu, L., Zhang, G., Zhang, J., Cheng, H., Lin, J., Kou, J., Li, Z., Zhao, S., Yag, W., Duan, Y., Zeng, Y., Wang, Z., and Lin, X. (1991). A preliminary study on the behavior of 225 drug abusers and risk factors of HIV infection in Ruili County Yunnan Province. *Chinese Journal of Epidemiology, 12*, 12–14.

Part II
Legal, Policy and Administrative Care Issues

[7]

A Global Review of Legislation on HIV/AIDS: The Issue of HIV Testing

*†Raffaele D'Amelio, *Emmanuelle Tuerlings, †Olga Perito, †Roberto Biselli, †Sergio Natalicchio, and ‡Stuart Kingma

*World Health Organization, Department of Communicable Disease Surveillance and Response, Geneva, Switzerland; †Ministero della Difesa, Direzione Generale Sanità Militare, Rome, Italy; and ‡Civil-Military Alliance to Combat HIV and AIDS, Rolle, Switzerland

Objective: Critical review of worldwide legislation on HIV/AIDS, with a focus on the issue of HIV testing, mainly in a military context.

Design: Analysis of health legislation on HIV/AIDS among 121 of the 191 member states of the World Health Organization (WHO), representing 85% of the world's population.

Methods: The WHO Directory of Legal Instruments Dealing with HIV Infection and AIDS has been the main source consulted. Relevant findings of two global surveys were used to examine HIV testing in the military.

Results: AIDS cases are reportable in 60% of the 121 countries, whereas HIV infections in no more than 26%.

Notifications are kept confidential by law in 20% of countries. Only 17% have developed HIV-specific legislation against social discrimination, whereas 10% have passed legislation establishing financial reimbursement to those who have acquired HIV infection after injection of HIV-contaminated biologic material, support for occupational risk, and/or social protection for patients.

Only 42% of the 121 countries report having legal instruments that require screening of donated blood. Legislative measures that address, generally in a prescriptive but sometimes also in a protective way, vulnerable groups, such as commercial sex workers, men who have sex with men, injecting drug users, and recipients of multiple transfusions of blood or blood-derivatives, are reported in 27% of countries. Other categories considered potentially vulnerable, for which specific legislation has been passed, include immigrants (17% of countries), prisoners (5%), and health personnel (14%). Further legislative measures for HIV prevention address testing pregnant women in the prenatal period (7% of countries), supporting condom promotion (11%), measures requiring quarantine, isolation, or coercive hospitalization of HIV-infected people or AIDS patients (9%), or imposing penal sanctions for HIV-infected people who deliberately expose others to the risk of transmission (10%). A National AIDS Committee responsible for addressing issues related to HIV/AIDS has been established by law in 39% of the 121 countries.

Global surveys show that 27 countries carry out compulsory HIV screening on recruitment of military personnel.

Conclusions: These data represent a useful tool to make governments aware of the problem of underreporting of legal instruments to the WHO and of the need to promote legislation in line with the idea that public health and human rights are complementary, not conflicting, goals.

Key Words: Legislation–HIV/AIDS–HIV testing–Military.

Address correspondence and reprint requests to R. D'Amelio, University of Rome "La Sapienza," II Faculty of Medicine and Surgery, Piazza Sassari 3, 00161 Rome, Italy; e-mail: raffaele.damelio@flashnet.it

R. D'Amelio is currently affiliated with the University of Rome "La Sapienza" II Faculty of Medicine and Surgery, Rome, Italy.

Manuscript received February 6, 2001; accepted July 10, 2001

The production of legal instruments on HIV/AIDS began in 1982 (very early, considering the mean time interval between the establishment of baseline epidemiologic data and the production of specific health legislation) (1) in industrialized countries, a few months after the first description of the syndrome (2–3). It shows two peaks (1985 and 1987), the first reflecting the introduction of laws on the notification of cases and the second on the compulsory screening of donated blood. In developing countries, legislation started 2 years later and reached a peak in 1987 (4). Therefore, the production of legal instruments was generally increased by progression of the epidemic, that is the reaching of a certain level of prevalence (which may widely differ among countries) or the fear of spreading the infection, as a consequence of rapid increase of cases over a short time, even if exceptions to this general rule do exist (5).

CURRENT SITUATION

In 1997, the World Health Organization (WHO), with the support of the Joint United Nations Program on HIV/AIDS (UNAIDS), updated the Directory of Legal Instruments Dealing with HIV Infection and AIDS (6). Of the 191 member states of the WHO, information on specific legislation is available for only 121, but this subtotal represents 85% of the world population (7). It should be noted however that the listing in this directory is not necessarily exhaustive. Some countries that are not listed as reporting may well have laws and regulations in force that do cover HIV/AIDS-related matters (4).

LEGISLATION ADDRESSING REPORTING REQUIREMENTS FOR HIV/AIDS

Among the 121 countries for which information is available, 60% (56% of the world's population) have enacted a specific law or regulation, making AIDS a disease that requires official notification (Table 1). Given the stigma attached to the disease, in this controversial area it could be argued that compulsory notification might deter people from testing, education, and counseling. Other methods for monitoring the epidemic, such as sentinel surveillance, may thus be considered by some countries more effective than compulsory reporting. However, unlinked anonymous testing within HIV sentinel surveillance has also been recently criticized, because of the absence of the individual's explicit consent (8).

The problem is even more sensitive in terms of notification of HIV infection, because of the maintenance of privacy concerning HIV status in apparently healthy people. Knowing the epidemiologic pattern of HIV transmission is essential to understand the dynamics of viral spreading properly, particularly after the introduction of the highly active antiretroviral therapy (HAART). HAART, in fact, dramatically modified the timing of the progression from HIV infection to AIDS and from AIDS to death, from which points the estimates of HIV incidence in industrialized countries were derived through the method of back-calculation (9). Only 31 countries (but representing 43% of the world's population) report the notification of HIV infection, all but one together with the notification of AIDS cases. Even within the United States, this measure varies from state to state (10,11).

TABLE 1. *Legislation addressing reporting requirements for HIV/AIDS*

				Year	
Type of legislation	No./total[a]	%	%[b]	Range	Mean
Compulsory notification system	72/121	60	56	(82–93)	87
Only AIDS	41/121	34	13		
AIDS + HIV-infected[c]	31/121	26	43		
Not confidential	48/121	40	28		
Confidential	24/121	20	28		

[a] Number of countries with specific laws out of total countries (121) for which information is available.
[b] Percentage of world's population is expressed is this column.
[c] One country notifies only cases of HIV infection, not of AIDS.

LEGISLATIVE MEASURES FOR THE PROTECTION OF HUMAN RIGHTS

Of the 72 countries requiring notification of HIV infection and/or AIDS cases, only 24 (28% of the world's population, but only 3.6% of the global estimated HIV-infected subjects) have explicitly required confidentiality (Table 2). Confidentiality is generally ensured by different types of code or by making the reports anonymous.

Moreover, only 17% of the 121 reporting countries, which represent 16% of the world's population but only 5.5% of the global estimate of HIV-infected people, have developed specific legislation against social discrimination of those with HIV infection or AIDS. Most countries, thus, do not state that they have specific legislation to protect HIV-infected people from discrimination in

TABLE 2. *Legislative measures for the protection of human rights*

				Year	
Type of legislation	No./total[a]	%	%[b]	Range	Mean
Against discrimination	21/121	17	16	88–96	91
Financial aid to HIV-infected people	12/121	10	13	88–95	91

[a] Number of countries with specific laws out of total countries (121) for which information is available.
[b] Percentage of world's population as expressed in this column.

access to jobs or in maintaining their employment, or in access to schools, sports, housing, public services, and other social activities. This is the case despite specific recommendations included in the International Guidelines on HIV/AIDS and Human Rights (12). Only 10% of the 121 countries, with 13% of the world's population but only 3.6% of the global estimated HIV-infected subjects, have passed legislation establishing either financial reimbursement to those who have acquired HIV infection following injection of HIV-contaminated biologic material, or support for occupational risk and/or social protection for patients.

These figures show that legislation aimed at protecting the human rights of persons with HIV infection remains a low priority for most countries, although it has by now been clearly demonstrated that such protection of human rights will reduce transmission of the virus by encouraging people with HIV/AIDS to access HIV education programs (12). Moreover, the observation that a low percentage of the global estimated HIV-infected population is protected by specific laws and regulations is even more worrying, considering the nearly total absence of such guarantees in developing countries with high HIV prevalence. Such a situation emphasizes the difficulty encountered by international organizations in stimulating member states to promote legislation for the protection of human rights, even though we are 20 years into the HIV/AIDS epidemic.

LEGISLATION ABOUT PREVENTION OF HIV/AIDS TRANSMISSION

After 1985, when diagnostic tests to recognize HIV specific antibodies were cleared for marketing by the U.S. Food and Drug Administration, there was a flowering of legislation that predominantly addressed the issue of mandatory screening of donated blood as a means to stop HIV transmission through legal transfusion of blood or blood derivatives (Table 3). Currently, however, only an unexpectedly low 42% of the 121 countries but representing 66% of the world's population, have as yet reported legislation that provides for the compulsory screening of donated blood. It must be stressed, however, that not all countries in the world have functional systems of blood donation, so the proper common denominator is missing from these figures. The observation that most large and populous countries of the world do report specific legislation in this field, and that many countries are probably screening of donated blood, despite not reporting legislation on this matter, may help explain the low estimated proportion (<5%) of HIV transmission in this means (13,14).

TABLE 3. *Legislation addressing the prevention of HIV/AIDS transmission*

Type of legislation	No./total	%	%[a]	Year: Range	Year: Mean
Compulsory testing of blood donors	51/121	42	66	85–95	88
Vulnerable groups	33/121	27	14	85–96	89
Immigrants	20/121	17	40	86–92	88
Prisoners	6/121	5	7	88–93	90
Health personnel	17/121	14	15	84–95	88
Pregnancy	9/121	7	6	85–94	90
Condom promotion	13/121	11	10	86–96	89
Quarantine/coercive hospitalization	11/121	9	25	85–93	88
Penal code	12/121	10	11	87–94	90
National AIDS committee	47/121	39	30	85–95	89
Testing of military personnel on recruitment	27/52	52	44	85–96	94

[a] Percentage of world's population is expressed in this column.

Some countries (27% of the 121, representing 14% of the world's population), have focused legislative attention on vulnerable groups, such as commercial sex workers, men who have sex with men, injecting drug users, and recipients of multiple transfusions of blood or blood-derivatives. The legislation that was passed, in most cases, involves mandatory screening of these groups, prohibits specific risk activities (e.g., donating blood, prostitution) or obliges participation in preventive programs, such as needle-exchange schemes for injecting drug-users. Other at-risk categories considered potentially vulnerable, for which specific legislation has been passed, include immigrants (17% of the 121, but 40% of the world's population), prisoners (5% of the 121, 7% of the world's population) and health care personnel (14% of the 121, 15% of the world's population).

Further legislative measures to support HIV prevention, identified in this review, address requirements for, or offers of, prenatal testing of pregnant women, (9 of 121 [7%], 6% of the world's population); condom promotion (liberalization of condom advertising as means for reducing sexually transmitted diseases [STDs] transmission, availability of condoms in hotels and motels, standardization of technical requirements for condoms, condom provision to prisoners) as protection against sexual transmission (13 of 121 [11%], 10% of the world's population); requirement for quarantine, isolation, or coercive hospitalization of HIV-infected people or AIDS patients or patients with STDs in general (11 of 121 [9%], covering 25% of the world's population); imposition of penal sanctions for HIV-infected people who deliberately expose others to the risk of transmission (12 of 121 [10%], 11% of the world's population). Three countries have legislated obligatory premarital HIV testing, and two others impose HIV screening on all hospitalized patients. These data emphasize the need that legislation be adopted after a balanced discussion between social and public health considerations and in close adherence to the International Guidelines on HIV/AIDS and Human Rights (12). The observation that 25% of the world's population still lives with laws requiring quarantine, isolation, or coercive hospitalization, measures that heavily infringe on human rights without any documented public health justification, compared with a very much lower percentage that require screening for pregnant women and encouraging the use of condoms, measures the preventive capability of which has been well documented, is a further dismal confirmation of the scarce impact of the international institutions on the legislative activity of member states.

Forty-seven of the 121 countries (39%, 30% of the world's population) have formally established a national body responsible for addressing issues related to HIV/AIDS, such as a National AIDS Committee of experts, generally convened by the country's ministry of health. A survey performed by Mann and Tarantola in 1994 (15) found that some 85% of 118 countries (75% of world's population), had established some form of a national AIDS committee. The disparity in these two estimates stems, at least in part, from the fact that not all such committees are as yet established as statutory, legislated bodies. However, even though a considerable number of countries feel the need to discuss the best measures to be adopted against this health and social threat, the situation that is emerging from the current analysis emphasizes the lack of capability of several governments to go beyond general statements of good intentions.

ISSUE OF HIV TESTING

This panoply of legal instruments, often mandating the HIV screening of vulnerable groups as a preventive measure, poses sensitive ethical and legal questions, some of which involve serious human rights issues. They revolve around the crucial issue of the right of refusal in the context of informed consent. They are further compounded by the fact that identification of someone as having been infected with HIV is so often followed by one or another form of stigma or discriminatory consequence.

Public health is recognized as a societal good that may at times call for measures that restrict human rights to some extent (16). Nonetheless, any such restrictions are considered acceptable only if they are:

1. "Provided for and carried out in accordance with the law;
2. Based on a legitimate interest, as defined in the provisions guaranteeing the rights;
3. Proportional to that interest and constituting the least intrusive and least restrictive measure available and actually achieving that interest in a democratic society (12,17).

Public health is most often cited by states as a basis for restricting human rights in the context of HIV/AIDS. Many such restrictions, however, infringe on the principle of non-discrimination" (17). Moreover, "coercive [public health] interventions can be justified in only 3 cases: to avert a risk of serious harm to other persons, to protect the welfare of incompetent persons, and, most controversially, to prevent a risk to the person himself/herself" (18).

In 1997, UNAIDS reaffirmed the position, adopted earlier by the Global Program on AIDS of WHO, that it was not possible to justify the imposition of mandatory HIV testing on public health grounds (19). This position, respective of the human rights, should not prevent, however, consideration of new scientific achievements, which may encourage closer examination of how HIV testing and counseling can be made more widely available and used (20,21). These achievements include greater reliability of current diagnostic tests, decreasing costs of testing (22), new perspectives in therapy with triple or more drug regimens (23–25), success in reducing the rate of HIV transmission between mother and fetus by using antiretroviral drugs (26) and elective caesarean section (27), and by avoiding breast-feeding (28). Two recent reports, the first from the Institute of Medicine (29) and the other from the European Commission (30), suggest that HIV testing should be consistently available for all U.S. or European pregnant women. A report from the U.K. Department of Health "estimates that about 55 babies in the UK were born with HIV infection in 1999. If testing had been offered to, and accepted by, all mothers, the numbers could have been as low as 10, it says. If no one had been offered or accepted testing, the figure could have been as high as 100" (31). The very problem is that, in less-developed countries, even for very effective interventions, such as short-course antiretroviral therapy to reduce mother-to-fetus transmission, "provision of HIV-1 counseling and testing remains a major barrier to implementation" (32). In particular, counseling should not be a barrier to HIV testing (33). In such critical situations, in fact, the possibility of only providing testing without any counseling should probably be considered, if instrumental to a easier reaching of the target.

MILITARY CONTEXT

The military represents a population at special risk of contracting STDs, both at home and in the course of foreign deployment. Prevalence of STDs has in fact been two to three times higher in among U.S. military troops than among their civilian counterparts and up to one hundred times higher in wartime (34). The special vulnerability of the military to STDs has again been recently demonstrated in a large epidemiologic analysis in the U.S. Army (35–36). This consideration makes the military a natural target for HIV containment policies, through different approaches, such as HIV testing, training, condom promotion, and research. Moreover, the military has unique characteristics in terms of well organized and disciplined population, so that reliable epidemiologic studies may easily be performed and the relevance of public health strategies to reduce HIV prevalence (37) may more easily be evaluated than in other at-risk populations.

During the 1980s, mandatory testing was only performed during recruitment by the U.S. Army, on the premise that protection of individual and public health required the diagnosis of HIV infection as early as possible. The rationale was also based on certain military-specific concerns: administration of live vaccines (38); potential exposure to exotic infections; maintenance of a safe walking blood bank; military readiness; and worldwide deployability. Introduction of mandatory testing was stimulated by the death of a seropositive recruit due to generalized vaccinia after smallpox vaccination (39). A survey carried out among North Atlantic Treaty Organization (NATO) countries in 1991 (40) showed that some other countries were then performing mandatory screening, but only for specific categories of military personnel, such as pilots.

Two more recent independent surveys gave information on the HIV screening on recruitment in the military context. The first was carried out on 119 countries by UNAIDS and the Civil-Military Alliance to Combat HIV and AIDS in 1995 and 1996, and 63 replies were received (41). The second was administered by WHO on 107 countries in 1996 and 1997, and 52 countries replied, representing 58% of the world's population (42). These studies showed that mandatory HIV testing on recruitment was performed by the armed forces of at least 27 countries, representing 44% of the world's population. The dramatic increase in the number of countries performing HIV testing from only one in the second half of 1980s to at least 27 in the second half of 1990s probably depends on the following factors.

First, the burden of high HIV seroprevalence in the military of some African countries, eroding the ranks of officers and conscripts alike, reducing readiness in key battalions, and making heavy demands on the military health care budget, has compelled a number of African ministries of defense to consider excluding those who test positive during recruitment procedures.

Second, the practice of some armed forces is to test and exclude those who are HIV-positive from certain occupations and activities that have high performance requirements (43). Among these, the most frequently reported are piloting aircraft, combat duties, and peacekeeping operations.

There is accumulating evidence of subtle cognitive impairment in early HIV infection, as measured by neuropsychologic tests, even before the onset of AIDS. Some studies (44,45) report the appearance of subsyndromic neurocognitive impairment in a median of 35% of HIV-infected individuals, compared with a median of 12% among appropriately matched, HIV-uninfected controls. In high performance duties, such as piloting an airplane, it is recommended that HIV-positive individuals undergo neurocognitive evaluation on a periodic basis, such as every 6 months (46).

The actual or potential presence of HIV-positive individuals in the ranks becomes more important in conflict situations. It calls into question the safety of the walking blood bank supplies in field circumstances.

The management of United Nations peacekeeping operations has renewed debate on the testing question, as recently reported (47). These operations bring with them the particular demands of a community of soldiers coming from different countries, which may differ widely in the level of HIV seroprevalence. Peacekeeping missions also must face delicate relationships with the local population. The potential risk of HIV infection being transmitted from peacekeepers to the local population, or from the local population to the peacekeepers (48), has fueled debate on the testing question once again. However, the realization that HIV testing is not an effective prevention measure, even in this setting, means that intensive prevention education with the peacekeepers and with the local population deserves renewed and greater attention.

In the late 1990s, debate on these issues within UNAIDS suggested that, to justify mandatory testing (invasion of an individual's right to privacy) and its consequences (discriminatory treatment), in the military or in other particular circumstances, one should have to:

1. Demonstrate compelling aspects of the workplace concerned (military or otherwise) that make it differ-

ent from other workplaces (where mandatory testing is unacceptable);

2. Show that mandatory testing (together with its consequences of rejection, limitation on employment options, dismissal) is the least restrictive means available, and that it will actually achieve the goals being sought, that is, achieve those goals more effectively than voluntary testing, counseling and prevention programs; and/or
3. Show that HIV/AIDS is not being singled out for such treatment as compared with similar diseases that raise comparable issues.

CONCLUSIONS

Infection by HIV is peculiar in that, for a long time after onset of the infection, the person infected feels well and can conduct a normal life. This commonly results in infected people transmitting the virus to others while still unaware that they are infected. And when the principal modes of transmission of this virus, through heterosexual and homosexual contact, are taken into consideration, legal and normative instruments touch on even greater sensitivities.

The rapid evolution of scientific research and development in this field imposes even greater difficulties as social norms and legislation try to keep up with that pace (1). As an example, a major argument against widespread screening has been the lack of effective therapeutic means to offer those being tested. However, as effective therapies become more and more available, the relevant legal instruments would have to be modified accordingly, at least for those situations involving persons who may immediately benefit by the knowledge of serostatus, such as pregnant women (49), and people living in those countries that are able to afford the high cost of therapies. Early HIV testing, in fact, allows entering medical care early in the course of HIV infection (21). Moreover, in the military, a sample population at high risk for STDs, the increasing use of HIV testing in over just the last few years is a consequence of a series of factors, probably including a growing and more diffuse sensitivity to the needs of the community at large, not only of the individual.

Data here reported represent a useful tool for increasing awareness of the already emphasized (50) problem of underreporting of legal instruments to the WHO. It can also increase awareness of the need to promote legislation in line with the idea that public health and human rights are complementary, not conflicting, goals.

Acknowledgments: The authors wish to thank Stefano Lazzari of WHO for helpful criticism, and Livia Primerano, Direzione Generale Sanità Militare, Rome, for excellent secretarial assistance.

REFERENCES

1. Sadetzki S, Modan B. Epidemiology as a basis for legislation: how far should epidemiology go? *Lancet* 1999;353:2238–9.
2. Gottlieb MS, Schorff R, Schanker HM, et al. *Pneumocystis carinii* pneumonia and mucosal candidiasis in previously healthy homosexual men. *N Engl J Med* 1981:305:1425–31.
3. Masur H, Michelis RA, Green JB, et al. An outbreak of community-acquired *Pneumocystis carinii* pneumonia. Initial manifestations of cellular immune disfunction. *N Engl J Med* 1981;305:1431–8.
4. Jayasuriya DC. *Health law. International and regional perspectives. HAR-ANAND.* Publications PVT LTD.1997:90–4.
5. Mann JM, Tarantola DJM, Netter TW. In *AIDS in the world. A global report.* Mann JM, Tarantola DJM, Netter TW, eds. Cambridge, MA: Harvard University Press. 1992:547.
6. WHO/UNAIDS/ *Directory of legal instruments dealing with HIV infection and AIDS* (HLE97.1). Geneva: World Health Organization, 1997.
7. WHO/Division of Health Situation and Trend Assessment. *Demographic data for health situation assessment and projections 1998* (HST/HSP/98.4) Geneva: World Health Organization, 1998.
8. Kessel A, Watts C, Weiss HA. Bad blood? Survey of public's views on unlinked anonymous testing of blood for HIV and other diseases. *BMJ* 2000;320:90–1.
9. UNAIDS/WHO-1999. *AIDS epidemic update: December 1999* (UNAIDS/99.53E-WHO/CDS/CSR/EDC/99.9-WHO/FCH/HIS/99.6). Geneva: World Health Organization, 1999.
10. Gostin LO, Ward JW, Baker AC. National HIV Case Reporting for the United States. A Defining Moment in the History of the Epidemic. *N Engl J Med* 1997:337:1162–7.
11. Guidelines for national human immunodeficiency virus case surveillance, including monitoring for human immunodeficiency virus infection and acquired immunodeficiency syndrome. *MMWR Morb Mortal Wkly Rep* 1999;48(RR-13):1–27.
12. HIV/AIDS and Human Rights Commission (organized jointly by the Office of the United Nations High Commissioner for Human Rights and the Joint United Nations Program on HIV/AIDS). *International Guidelines. Second International Consultation on HIV/AIDS and Human Rights. Geneva, 23–25 September 1996.* New York and Geneva: United Nations, 1998.
13. Kallings LO. HIV infection in the nineties. *Vaccine* 1993;11:525–8.
14. Adler MW. Clinical review. ABC of AIDS. Development of the epidemic. *BMJ* 2001;322:1226–9.
15. Governmental National AIDS Programs. In Mann JM, Tarantola DJM, eds. *AIDS in the world II Global dimensions, social roots, and responses. The Global AIDS Policy Coalition.* New York and Oxford: Oxford University Press, 1996:315–325.
16. The Siracusa principles on the limitation and derogation provisions in the International Covenant on Civil and Political Rights. Annex to U.N. Doc. E/CN.4/1985/4, September 28, 1984. New York and Geneva: United Nations, 1984.
17. Sieghart P. *AIDS & human rights—a UK perspective.* London British Medical Association Foundation for AIDS, 1989:12.
18. Gostin LO. Public health law in a new century. Part III: Public health regulation: a systematic evaluation *JAMA* 2000;283:3118–22.
19. UNAIDS Policy on HIV Testing and Counseling. *UNAIDS Policy Statement* (UNAIDS 97.2). Geneva and New York: United Nations, 1997.
20. The World Health Organization. News from the Vancouver conference. Geneva: World Health Organization, 1996:2.
21. Freedberg KA Samet JH. Why physicians should lower their threshold for HIV testing. *Arch Intern Med* 1999;159:1994–2000.

22. Brown AE, Burke DS. Cost of HIV testing in the US Army. *N Engl J Med* 1995;332:963.
23. Hammer SM, Katzenstein DA, Hughes MD, et al. A trial comparing nucleoside monotherapy with combination therapy in HIV-infected adults with CD4 cell counts between 200 and 500 per cubic millimeter. *N Engl J Med* 1996;335:1081–90.
24. Fauci AS. The AIDS Epidemic. Considerations for the 21st Century. *N Engl J Med* 1999:341:1046–50.
25. Carpenter CCJ, Cooper DA, Fischl MA, et al. Antiretroviral therapy in adults. Updated recommendations of the International AIDS Society—USA Panel. *JAMA* 2000;283:381–90.
26. Connor EM, Sperling RS, Gelber R, et al. Reduction of maternal-infant transmission of human immunodeficiency virus type 1 with zidovudine treatment *N Engl J Med* 1994;331:1173–80.
27. Kind C, Rudin C, Siegrist CA, et al. Prevention of vertical HIV transmission: additive protective effect of elective caesarean section and zidovudine prophylaxis. *AIDS* 1998;12:205–10.
28. Nduati R, John G, Mbori-Ngacha D, et al. Effect of breastfeeding and formula feeding on transmission of HIV-1 a randomized clinical trial. *JAMA* 2000;283:1167–74.
29. Institute of Medicine. *Reducing the odds: preventing perinatal transmission of HIV in the United States*. Washington DC: National Academy Press, 1998.
30. European Commission. Recommendations for the management of HIV infected women and their infants. A European consensus. By Experts in the field of pediatric AIDS research. Presented at the meeting of European Communities, Turin, Italy, October, 1999.
31. Ferriman A. Antenatal testing reduces vertical transmission of HIV. *BMJ* 2000:321:1430.
32. Mofenson LM, McIntyre JA. Advances and research directions in the prevention of mother-to-child HIV-1 transmission. *Lancet* 2000;355:2237–44.
33. U.S. Centers for Disease Control and Prevention. Draft. Revised Guidelines for HIV Counseling, Testing, and Referral. Atlanta: U.S. Centers for Disease Control and Prevention, 2000:32.
34. Tramont EC, Burke DS. AIDS/HIV in the Military. Vaccine 1993; 11:529–33.
35. Temoshock LR, Kingma SJ. HIV exposure risk in military populations, an uncharted prevention frontier [Track C.36]. Presented at the XI International Conference on AIDS, Vancouver, British Columbia, Canada, July 7–12, 1996.
36. Temoshock LR, Patterson TL. Risk of HIV transmission in infected US military personnel. *Lancet* 1996;347:697.
37. Nelson KE, Celentano DD, Eiumtrakol S, et al. Changes in sexual behavior and a decline in HIV infection among young men in Thailand. *N Engl J Med* 1996;335:297–303.
38. Talbot EA, Perkins MD, Fagundes S, et al. Disseminated bacille Calmette-Guérin disease after vaccination: case report and review. *Clin Infect Dis* 1997;24:1139–46.
39. Redfield R, Wright DC, James WD, et al. Disseminated vaccinia in a military recruit with human immunodeficiency virus (HIV) disease. *N Engl J Med* 1987;316:673–6
40. D'Amelio R. Allergic, Immunological and infectious disease problems in aerospace medicine. 72nd AMP/AGARD Symposium, Rome, Italy, October 21–25, 1991. *Vaccine* 1993;11:492–5.
41. Yeager R, Hendrix C, Kingma S. International military human immunodeficiency virus/acquired immunodeficiency syndrome policies and programs: strengths and limitations in current practice. *Mil Med* 2000;165:87–92.
42. D'Amelio R, Heymann DL. Can the military contribute to the fight against infectious diseases? *Emerg Infect Dis* 1998;4:708–9.
43. Sharma DC. Court ruling favors Indian Navy's HIV policy. *Lancet* 2000:356.2166.
44. White DA, Heaton RK, Monsch AU, and the HNRC Group. Neuropsychologic studies of asymptomatic human immunodeficiency virus-type 1 infected individuals. *J Int Neuropsychol Soc* 1995;1: 304–15.
45. Martin A, Heyes MP, Salazar MA, et al. Progressive slowing of reaction time and increasing cerebrospinal fluid concentrations of quinolinic acid in HIV-infected individuals. *J Neuropsychiatr Clin Neurosci* 1992;4:270–9.
46. UNAIDS Expert Consultation on Cognitive and Neuropsychologic Impairment in Early HIV Infection. Presented at UNAIDS conference, Washington D.C., June 3–4, 1997.
47. Final Report. First United Nations International Conference on Medical Support for Peace-Keeping Operations. Geneva, Switzerland. March 24–26, 1997.
48. Brodine SK, Mascola JR, Weiss PJ, et al. Detection of diverse HIV-1 genetic subtypes in the USA. *Lancet* 1995;346:1198–9.
49. Guay LA, Musoke P, Fleming T, et al. Intrapartum and neonatal single-dose nevirapine compared with zidovudine for prevention of mother-to-child transmission of HIV-1 in Kampala, Uganda HIV-NET 012 randomised trial. *Lancet* 1999;180:290–8.
50. Fluss SS The role of WHO in health legislation: some historical perspectives. *Int Dig Health Leg* 1998;49:113–30.

[8]

AIDS Behind Bars: Prisoners' Rights Guillotined

DELPHINE VALETTE
PhD, Faculty of Law, University of Bristol

Abstract: A man is condemned to jail for a crime. End of the Story. Who cares about what is going on behind bars? That is the reality of the society in which we live. In the mind of the public, an individual sent to prison seems to lose identity and life. Too often one forgets that there is a life behind bars, a new life in another community with different rules, with spatial limits, and that according to individual human rights standards, a prisoner does not cease to be an individual entitled to be treated humanely and with dignity as each human being is. In the UK, the coming into force of the Human Rights Act 1998 is expected to make some considerable difference to the treatment of prisoners. It is questioned whether it will go sufficiently far, especially by reference to some of the limitations of the European Convention on Human Rights (ECHR). The object of this article is to examine, in the light of international experiences, how the ECHR may be used to secure prisoners' rights in the context of AIDS.

If you are interested to assess the degree of civilisation of a country then don't visit its parliament or theatres but its prisons. (Editor's choice, *British Medical Journal*, 5 July 1997, p. 315)

When one considers prisoners as human beings and not as persons convicted for crimes, then one realises that we have to ensure that a person behind bars is not deprived of fundamental human rights alongside their liberty. Due to the stigma and discrimination associated with HIV/AIDS (De Bruyn 1998; Schulman 1998), being known to be HIV positive (a person can be HIV+ and asymptomatic or symptomatic) or having AIDS (last stage of HIV infection) in prison means 'being a specific pariah class within the general pariah class of prisoners' (Young and McHale 1992, p. 91), being 'the least worthwhile of the undeserving' (p. 91). For those who are not infected with HIV (commonly called 'seronegative'), prison seems to be an ideal breeding ground for HIV transmission due to overcrowding, sexual activities and injection drug use. As a result, seronegative prisoners are at an exceptional risk for infection with HIV. This article will examine the situation of prisoners who have to bear the burden of being infected with HIV or of having AIDS behind bars, as well as the situation of prisoners exposed to high risks of HIV transmission. I will consider these issues by adopting a comparative approach of three main countries (UK, Australia, USA and Canada) and by relying on international human rights material which deals with prisoners' human rights and the issue of AIDS in prison.

Prisoners' Rights as Human Rights

Whilst imprisonment involves the loss of the right to liberty, individuals are sentenced to prison as punishment and not for punishment, and thus should retain as many civil rights as possible.[1]

It has only been over the past 30 years that an interest in prisoners' rights has developed and that the traditional conception of a prisoner as a 'slave of the state' with no right but that of life behind bars has been condemned. Today, prisoners' human rights are clearly protected under the main international human rights standards, mainly the International Covenant on Civil and Political Rights (ICCPR) and the European Convention on Human Rights (ECHR) which both contain provisions of particular relevance in relation to prisoners' rights, especially the prohibition of torture and cruel, inhuman, or degrading treatment or punishment. However, the most comprehensive guidelines remain the 1955 United Nations Standard Minimum Rules for the Treatment of Prisoners (SMR).[2] Other documents dealing with conditions of detention include the Body of Principles for the Protection of All Persons under Any Form of Detention or Imprisonment (adopted by the UN General Assembly on 9 December 1988, UN Doc. A/43/49 (1988)) whose Principle 1 reads:

> All persons under any form of detention or imprisonment shall be treated in a humane manner and with respect for the inherent dignity of the human person.

Furthermore, recommendations as regards HIV/AIDS in prisons have been issued by the United Nations Programme on HIV/AIDS (UNAIDS 1996, 1997a, 1997b). The World Health Organisation (WHO 1993) has published guidelines on HIV infection and AIDS in prisons that should be considered as supplementing and clarifying human rights standards as regards prisoners' rights. I shall refer to their provisions as regards the issues dealt with in this article.

Testing for HIV in Prison

Mandatory/Compulsory Testing

It is a well-established principle that prisoners retain all their rights – except for those inherently limited or withdrawn by their imprisonment – and it is arguable that under international human rights law, HIV-testing of prisoners on a mandatory basis may amount to a violation of prisoners' right to bodily/physical integrity (art. 8 ECHR) and freedom from torture or cruel, inhuman or degrading treatment or punishment (art. 3 ECHR). It is also noteworthy that both the WHO (1993, at para. B) and the UNAIDS (1996) have condemned compulsory testing of prisoners, arguing in favour of the development of voluntary HIV-testing programmes carried out with the informed consent of the person and with adequate pre- and post-test counselling. Furthermore, numerous community-based groups in several countries, especially the Canada's Expert Committee on AIDS and Prisons, have also condemned compulsory or mandatory HIV-testing.

However, despite its condemnation by numerous international organisations and its prohibition in some countries, mandatory or compulsory HIV-testing of inmates is not rare and is carried out, *inter alia*, in the United States and Australia. Mandatory HIV-testing of prisoners was initially authorised in all Australian jurisdictions, either specifically or through general provisions. However, some changes have recently taken place in New South Wales after the introduction of a voluntary HIV/hepatitis testing programme as part of an induction programme for new prisoners.[3] In Western Australia, only prisoners considered to be 'high risk' are tested and Victoria and ACT have an official policy of voluntary blood testing, with a compliance rate in Victoria of more than 99%! Yet, in the Northern Territory, Tasmania and South Australia, compulsory HIV-testing is carried out upon admission and after three months (Magnusson 1995; Malkin 1995). In the United States, the US Federal Bureau of Prisons tests certain classes of prisoners, such as inmates involved in community activities, a random selection of 5% of new prisoners, and all inmates at least 60 days before their release. Furthermore, 18 state prisons carry out mandatory testing (*Kaiser Daily Report*, 29 July 1998) and usually adopt, to various degrees, a policy of segregation of those who test positive. HIV-testing of persons convicted of sexual assault is also sometimes carried out (see Jürgens 1998).[4]

Challenging HIV-Testing under Article 8 ECHR

The prohibition of mandatory medical examinations has been made clear by the Convention case law under art. 8 (right to privacy) which has been interpreted as covering interference with bodily integrity (*X and Y* v. *Netherlands* (1986) 8 EHRR 235, at para. 22), for example by subjecting an individual to compulsory medical or psychological examinations (*X* v. *Austria* 18D and R 154 1979).

Under the ECHR, the right of privacy is not absolute and can be subjected, under art. 8(2), to restrictions on grounds of public security, public health and the protection of rights of others. In the context of mandatory HIV-testing, governments could argue that such a policy is justified on grounds of public health. Indeed, it has been submitted that prisons should screen for HIV in order to identify HIV+ prisoners and take the necessary steps to provide adequate care and protect staff, fellow inmates and third parties with whom HIV+ prisoners are likely to have contact after being released. Thus, in reference to the ECHR, a government would have to show that the interference with prisoners' right of privacy was: (i) in accordance with the law; (ii) necessary in a democratic society; and (iii) for the protection of a 'legitimate aim' (in this case public health). Furthermore, it would have to show that there was a 'pressing social need', and that the restriction was proportionate to that need, weighed both against its adverse effects on the prisoners and against the protection of others.

The UN International Guidelines on HIV/AIDS state that '[t]here is no public health or security justification for mandatory HIV-testing of prisoners . . .' (UNAIDS 1996, para. 131) and several arguments can be put forward to support this view.

First, testing all prisoners for HIV cannot detect all prisoners that are HIV+ due to delayed seroconversion. A prisoner may be infected but tests negative because seroconversion has not yet occurred. Therefore, in order to identify all prisoners infected with HIV in the perspective of protection of public health, testing would need to be continually repeated on those who test negative. Second, there is the problem of false positive results and should a prison segregate HIV+ prisoners, a prisoner who wrongly tested positive may be exposed to segregation. Third, it is now known that HIV transmission occurs in prison, especially because of needle sharing among injecting drug users and consensual or coerced sex without protection (Gore and Bird 1995; Dolan 1998). As a result, without an effective campaign of education and prevention, HIV-testing in unlikely to have any benefits for the protection of public health. The question is not 'who is HIV+?' but 'how to prevent HIV transmission?' Fourth, the argument in favour of the protection of staff, fellow inmates and third parties supposes the communication of test results to all the persons concerned, which is only likely to result in discrimination, stigmatisation and segregation of HIV+ prisoners. And finally, since the informed consent and counselling of patients is recommended in the general community, there is no reason why the same standard should not apply to prisoners.

In the absence of case law dealing with this specific issue, it is difficult to predict whether the European Court of Human Rights (ECtHR) would apply the same standards as it would in the case of mandatory HIV-testing in the general community or if it would allow a wider margin of appreciation to the states by considering the issue of mandatory HIV-testing in prison as distinct from mandatory testing outside, due to the specific factors linked to the situation of imprisonment.

Yet, from the case law of the ECHR on drug testing in prison, one can argue that the Court might decide to consider HIV-testing in the general community and in prison as two distinct issues. Drug testing was at stake in *Peters* v. *The Netherlands* (App. No 21132/93, Decision of 6 April 1994, Inadmissible) where a prisoner was required to undergo a urine test because he was suspected of using drugs. In *Galloway* v. *UK* (App. No 34199/96, Decision of 9 September 1998, Inadmissible) another prisoner was chosen to take part in a random mandatory drug testing (provision of urine sample). All applicants argued that the compulsory imposition of a mandatory examination violated art. 8 of the Convention.

In all cases, the Commission stated or recalled that a compulsory medical intervention, even if it is of minor importance, must be considered as an interference with an individual's right of privacy. No contestation was made by the Commission about the legal basis of the interference. As regards the other elements of the justification test for interference with art. 8(1), the Commission stated that a distinction had to be drawn between violations of art. 8(1) which took place in the community and those which occurred in prison. In the latter case, the Commission mainly explained the justification of the interference with the prisoners' right of privacy by recalling the special context of imprisonment, stating that imprisonment may justify wider measures of interference in the case of a prisoner than in that of a person at liberty.

Challenging HIV-Testing Under Article 3 ECHR

Under human rights law, an individual's physical/bodily and mental integrity is also protected by the prohibition of inhuman and/or degrading treatment under art. 3 ECHR. Though the ECtHR has not dealt with mandatory HIV-testing in prison under art. 3, it seems that such a policy could amount to a violation of a prisoner's right to be free from inhuman and degrading treatment as prohibited under this article. The ECtHR stated that the assessment to determine whether an act falls under art. 3 ECHR is relative and depends on all the circumstances of the case such as the physical and mental effects of the treatment (cf. *Ireland* v. *UK* (1978) Series A No. 25, para. 162). Furthermore, in a case decided the same year, the Court went on to state that the nature and context of the punishment (and arguably treatment) itself and the manner or method of its execution were also to be taken into consideration when determining whether an act was degrading (see *Tyrer* v. *UK* (1978) Series A, No. 26, para. 30). Whilst the European Commission asserted that the absence of consent does not constitute a decisive element of the prohibition of art. 3 (see *X* v. *Denmark*, Appl. 9974/82. D.R. 32 (1983), pp. 283–4), it has also noted that it is a relevant factor.

Whilst according to the reasoning of the Court, the absence of consent does not necessarily amount to a breach of art. 3 ECHR, three main arguments may be put forward in order to argue that testing prisoners for HIV without their informed consent is to be deemed a *prima facie* violation of their rights under art. 3 ECHR.

First, the initial vulnerability of a prisoner linked to his detention and the presumed absence of pre- and post-counselling are likely to increase the far-reaching psychological and emotional consequences of a positive test. Furthermore, the fear of discrimination and stigmatisation and the lack of moral support may cause detrimental mental and emotional troubles and lead for example to suicidal attempts. And finally, as one shall see below, a positive HIV-test may result in discrimination and segregation and impact on a prisoner's mental and physical health. Thus, arguably, the consequences of a positive HIV-test might result in the infliction of severe mental suffering under art. 3 ECHR defined by the Commission in the *Greek* case as 'creating a state of anguish and stress by means other than bodily assault' (*Greek* Case 1969 Yearbook XII, p. 461).

Yet, it is noteworthy that the European Court of Human Rights has generally interpreted art. 3 ECHR in a very narrow way, and as noted by Starmer (1999), most of applications brought by prisoners under art. 3 have failed, mainly because the Court found the conditions complained of were justified by reference to the aim pursued by their imposition.

Whether the Court would interpret art. 3 ECHR as prohibiting mandatory HIV-testing of prisoners is doubtful. The fact that it has been stated by the Commission that a failure to comply with the Minimum Rules for the Treatment of Prisoners does not automatically lead to a finding that art. 3 ECHR has been violated (see *Eggs* v. *Switzerland*, 6 DR 170) makes it clear that the interpretation of this article in relation to the conditions of prisoners is to be extremely narrow.

Violation of Confidentiality

The issue of confidentiality in relation to a prisoner's HIV status is akin to the problem of HIV-testing and deals with an individual's right of privacy. It has been made clear in international guidelines that information regarding the HIV status of a prisoner should only be disclosed in specific circumstances if, with due regard to medical ethics, such a disclosure is warranted to ensure the safety and wellbeing of staff and fellow prisoners (WHO 1993, para. E). The violation of secrecy of a prisoner's HIV status is likely to result in harassment and discrimination from both staff and fellow inmates and may lead to a risk of segregation such as solitary confinement or to the exclusion of the seropositive prisoners from activities in prison (Jürgens 1999). However, the violation of prisoners' right of confidentiality by prison officers and even prison medical personnel is common and has been well documented by various reports or case law. In its report on HIV and AIDS related discrimination, the New South Wales Anti-Discrimination Board (1992) noted that the right of confidentiality of seropositive prisoners is violated by prison officers quite routinely:

> ... for example, lists of *AIDS prisoners* are sometimes posted in semi-public places, individual prisoners are referred to as having AIDS in conversations with visitors or in the presence of visitors or other prisoners. (p. 56)[5]

The issue of confidentiality in relation of HIV/AIDS in prison has only been considered by the European Commission in *T. V.* v. *Finland* (1979) 18 EHRR CD 179, where it stated that access by prison and medical staff to information regarding a prisoner's HIV status constitutes an interference with his right to respect for his private life. Furthermore, the respect for confidentiality in relation to an individual's HIV status was further considered in *Z* v. *Finland* (1998) 25 EHRR 371, where the European Court of Human Rights recognised that the respect for medical confidentiality was a 'vital principle' crucial to privacy, in particular as regards a person's HIV status:

> ... [t]he protection of personal data, not least medical data, is of fundamental importance to a person's enjoyment of his or her right to respect for privacy ... as guaranteed by Article 8 of the Convention (...). Without such protection, those in need of medical assistance may be deterred from revealing such information of a personal and intimate nature as may be necessary in order to receive appropriate treatment and, even, from seeking such assistance, thereby endangering their own health and, in the case of transmissible diseases, that of the community (...) The above consideration are especially valid as regards protection of the confidentiality of information about a person's HIV infection (...). (para. 95)

It is interesting to have a look at the US case law in relation to the disclosure of prisoners' HIV status since the courts have not only reasserted a prisoner's right of privacy but have also strongly argued for the protection of confidentiality as regards inmates' HIV status by emphasising the link between AIDS and stigma and the negative effects of an unnecessary disclosure.

For example, in *Woods* v. *White* 689F. Supp. 874 (W.D. Wis. 1988), the Court found that the right of privacy extended to a prisoner's HIV status because a prisoner 'retains his right to privacy, although he is incarcerated. The right to privacy is not terminated by conviction for a crime' (para 876).[6] The necessity to protect prisoners against non-consensual disclosure of their HIV status was reiterated in *Doe* v. *Coughlin* 697F. Supp. 1234 (N.D.N.Y. 1988), where the Court, stressing the link between AIDS and stigma, concluded that an individual should have control over the disclosure of their HIV status (para. 1237).

Since the respect for confidentiality falls within the scope of the right of privacy, it also may be subjected to limitations. The argument in favour of the disclosure of prisoners' HIV status is similar to that for justification of mandatory HIV-testing; that is public health and protection of others. In *Z* v. *Finland* (1998) 25 EHRR 371, the European Court of Human Rights emphasised the importance of respecting the confidentiality of a person's HIV status and stated that, in the case of disclosure:

> The interests in protecting the confidentiality of such information [someone's HIV status] will therefore weigh heavily in the balance in determining whether the interference was proportionate to the legitimate aim pursued. (para. 96)

As noted above, *Z* v. *Finland* did not deal with the specific issue of confidentiality within the prison setting. However, it is arguable that the statement of the Court could be equally applied in relation to the disclosure of a prisoner's HIV status. Indeed, as it may sometimes be necessary to disclose a patient's HIV status in the general community, the disclosure of the seropositivity of a prisoner may be justifiable if that prisoner puts others at significant risk of infection.

Furthermore, as regards the specific issue of disclosure to third parties (arguably prisoners' partners included), it has been stated that:

> [p]artner notification carried out mandatorily is a relatively ineffective means of 'breaking the chain of transmission' when there is considerable delay before contacts can be traced, when sex with partners other than the regular partner is common, and when health services are inaccessible or unacceptable to clients (. . .). The evidence that partner notification approaches are more effective when carried out on a voluntary rather than mandatory basis stems from combined experience in the history of sexually transmitted diseases and, more recently, HIV. (WHO and UNAIDS 1999, section II)

Finally, as noted above, whilst prison systems do not necessarily apply a policy of disclosure, the promise of confidentiality is often broken. Yet, the promise of confidentiality between prisoners and prison medical officers is essential to the promotion of public health. Without it, a prisoner who has not been tested for HIV but believes he may be infected may be deterred to come forward and seek care by fear of the repercussions that he may have to face if his HIV status is disclosed. And this is clearly where the public health argument is relevant.

Denial of Adequate HIV Medical Treatment

Reports and cases have documented the denial of prisoners' rights of care and dignity in sickness and the violation of their freedom from being subject to inhuman and degrading treatment and in extreme cases of their right to life. One example of the appalling treatment of prisoners with HIV/AIDS has been revealed by the inquest into the death of Billy Bell, a prisoner who died of AIDS-related cryptococcal meningitis at the Regional Hospital Unit (Ontario Region, Canada) of Kingston Penitentiary (Lines 1997/98). The testimony of a specialist HIV clinic at the Kingston General Hospital revealed how the prison failed to provide Billy Bell with the quality care that patients outside prison benefit from (lack of AZT which prevented the prisoner from taking his dose days at a time, difficulty in accessing proper pain management medication, lack of compassion from staff, and dangerous delays in the diagnosis of AIDS-related illnesses).

Under the Convention, the issue of the right of prisoners to adequate care has been dealt with under art. 3 ECHR which has been read as encompassing an obligation to provide adequate medical treatment of detainees. In *Hurtado* v. *Switzerland* (1994) A/280-A, the Commission confirmed that art. 3 imposes upon the state a specific positive obligation to protect the physical wellbeing of persons deprived of their liberty. Furthermore, in *Tanko* v. *Finland* (1994, Appl. 23634/94, Inadmissible), the Commission did not exclude 'that a lack of proper care in a case where someone is suffering from a serious illness could in certain circumstances amount to treatment contrary to Article 3' (para. 1). More recently, in *D* v. *UK* (1997) 24 EHRR 423, the Court made it clear that the withdrawal or termination of existing medical treatment in serious cases might amount to a violation of art. 2 ECHR (right to life) or art. 3. In this case, the applicant who suffered from AIDS was to be deported to St. Kitts, where no adequate medical facilities necessary to his condition were available. The Court considered that the critical stage of the applicant's illness and the dramatic consequences that would result from his deportation meant that 'the decision to remove him to St. Kitts would amount to inhuman treatment by the respondent State in violation of article 3' (para. 54). Whilst the case dealt with deportation, it is arguable that the Court's interpretation of art. 3 could be similarly applied to the context of HIV medical care in detention. As a result, in contrast with the uncertainty as regards the interpretation of art. 3 of the Convention in the context of mandatory HIV-testing of prisoners, there is no doubt that a state has a positive obligation to provide adequate care to a prisoner with HIV/AIDS and that a failure to do so is likely to amount to a violation of art. 3 ECHR.

Furthermore, it is arguable that the right of care and the right to be treated with dignity extend to the final stage of a disease such as full-blown AIDS. However, despite being recommended by the WHO (1993, para. L) compassionate release for prisoners with AIDS has so far only been unevenly implemented, and most often, on a case-by-case basis (Jürgens 1996; Kantor 1998).

Denial of Protection against HIV Transmission

With evidence of HIV seroconversion within the prison setting,[7] statistics showing higher HIV seroprevalence in prison than in the general population and the recognition of the high risk of HIV transmission in prison (Dolan 1998; Taylor *et al.* 1995), there is a strong argument that the denial or lack of preventive measures against HIV transmission in prison may amount to a violation of prisoners' rights to life and security as supplemented by the right to protection against inhuman and degrading treatment or punishment under international human rights law.

Sexual HIV Transmission

Coerced or consensual, sexual contacts between inmates are common. Male homosexual activity occurs inside as it would outside as a consequence of homosexual orientation but also as a consequence of the denial of female company. Heterosexual sex is also occurring, either between male and female inmates or between female inmates and prison staff. Rapes are not rare and are sometimes even considered as a sort of institutionalised initiation where it can take the form of gang rapes (Wooden and Parker 1982; Donaldson 1995; Human Rights Watch 2001). The risks of sexual assaults are also enhanced by the violent and unstable nature of some inmates especially in overcrowded institutions. Finally, prostitution is also going on, proving that sex in prison is a micro-representation of the illegal sexual activities happening outside. As a result, sex in prison raises two main issues: the provision of condoms and lubricants and the introduction of measures to combat aggressive sexual behaviour, including rape.[8]

Despite the extent of sexual activity in prison, sex behind bars is by definition illegal and the provision of condoms to avoid HIV transmission might be seen as condoning it. It is sometimes argued that consensual homosexual sex between inmates is illegal because prisons are public places not private. As a result, whilst prisoners' access to condoms has been introduced in numerous prisons, the provision of condoms is still denied or limited in a number of countries, and not necessarily the poor under-developed ones (see the recent decision of the UK High Court in *R* v. *Secretary of State for the Home Department ex p. Fielding*, England and Wales Queen's Bench Divisional Court, [1999] TNLR No 543).

The right of prisoners to receive health care, including prevention measures, has been strongly asserted by the international community. For example, the WHO (1993) guidelines on HIV/AIDS in prisons state that:

> [p]reventive measures for HIV/AIDS in prison should be complementary to and compatible with those in the community (. . .). Prison administrations have a responsibility to define and put in place policies and practices that will create a safer environment and diminish the risk of transmission of HIV to prisoners and staff alike (. . .). Since penetrative sexual intercourse occurs, even in prison, even when prohibited, condoms should be made available to prisoners throughout their period of detention. (paras. 4, 8, 20)

The issue of condoms in prison was brought before an Australian Court in what has been referred to as the 'Condom Case' (*Prisoners A to XX inclusive* v. *State of NSW*, Supreme Court of NSW, Dunford J, 5 October 1994). The case was a civil action undertaken on behalf of 52 inmates from two prisons against the state of NSW over its refusal to permit prisoners to have access to condoms. The action sought a mandatory injunction to force the government to reform its policies, the prisoners' lawyer arguing that it was no proper part of the punishment of prisoners that their access to preventive means to protect their health is impeded. Arguably, partly because of this legal action, the NSW government has since decided to make condoms available in three prisons on a trial basis. Whilst the legal action is still ongoing, the prisoners involved have decided not to push the case. If there is general introduction of condoms in NSW prisons at the end of the trials, the case will likely be dropped. Since this case, further actions have been considered or taken in other Australian states.

In the US, only a small minority of prison systems makes condoms available. In 1995, condoms to male prisoners were only distributed in five jurisdictions (Mahon 1995). No new development seems to have taken place within the past six years. The situation is not better in the UK where condoms and lubricants are only prescribed by medical officers 'when in their clinical judgment there is a known risk of HIV infection as a result of HIV risk sexual behaviour'.[9] In Canada's federal prisons, condoms were made available in 1992 but their access remained limited in some prisons. However, following the recommendations of the Expert Committee on AIDS and Prisons, the federal prison system announced that condoms, dental dams and water-based lubricant would become more easily and discreetly available. The situation is quite different in Canadian provincial prisons where condoms are not available in some prisons or not easily accessible (Canadian HIV/AIDS Legal Network 2001).

There is a strong argument for interpreting the failure to provide prisoners with condoms as a violation of the right to be protected against inhuman and degrading treatment under art. 3 ECHR. As examined above, it has been held that art. 3 of the Convention imposes a duty on state authorities to take appropriate measures where an individual may be exposed to torture, inhuman or degrading treatment/punishment, for example in relation to the lack of health care (*D* v. *UK*). By failing to provide prisoners with condoms, a state not only violates the right of prisoners to health care, including protection against the transmission of diseases, but it also puts their lives and dignity at stake by exposing them to the risk of contracting a fatal disease. As a result, it is argued that positive obligations under art. 3 ECHR should include preventive measures in prisons, such as the provision of condoms, and failure to provide prisoners with condoms should be held to be a violation of this article.

Furthermore, as noted by Watt (2000), the argument for the provision of condoms in prisons may be put forward on the basis of the right of privacy under art. 8 ECHR. Indeed, the European Court of Human Rights has stated that art. 8 may require positive measures to be taken by the states 'to secure respect for private life even in the sphere of the relations of individuals between themselves' (see *X & Y* v. *The Netherlands* (1985) Series A, vol. 91, para. 23). Thus, in this case, it is arguable that respect for private life requires authorities to take the necessary steps to protect prisoners from contracting sexually transmitted diseases, arguably via the provision of condoms.

The right of prisoners to be free from cruel, inhuman and degrading treatment in the context of sexual HIV transmission is also jeopardised in the context of coerced sex, and both the protection of prisoners from HIV transmission and the necessity to protect them from sexual abuse clearly impose positive obligations on the states. Indeed, the perpetrators of rapes or sexual assaults are not likely to use condoms (Siegal 1992). That means that the victim will not only be subject to a sexual crime, but he might also become infected with HIV as a result of the attack. As a result, states' actions should rest upon the introduction of adequate measures to combat aggressive and violent sexual behaviours (WHO 1993, para. 21). Such measures may include adequate staffing, supervision, disciplinary sanctions and housing. In contrast, it is frequently reported that prison authorities ignore the problem of prisoner-on-prisoner rape or even react hostilely to inmates' complaints of rape (Human Rights Watch 2001). Failure to take appropriate measures exposes prisoners to inhuman and degrading treatment inflicted by physical and emotional pain linked to the act and the emotional and psychological consequences resulting from HIV infection.

HIV Transmission by Injection

The problem of HIV transmission in prison is mainly raised as regards injecting drug use (Dolan *et al.* 1995; Taylor *et al.* 1995). Similar to sexual activities in prison, drug use is illegal and yet does go on. Drug use is already a habit for some prisoners when they come in and it becomes a means of coping with the incarceration for some others. Yet, the result is the same: the sharing of non-sterile injecting equipment makes of the phenomenon of injecting in prison an ideal breeding ground for HIV transmission. The available data as regards the extent of drug injection in prison provide a strong argument for the introduction of measures aimed at preventing this form of HIV transmission (Dolan *et al.* 1995). For example, in Australia, in a survey on HIV risk-taking behaviour of male drug injectors while in custody, 75% of respondents reported having injected drugs at least once. The extent of use and availability of injectable drugs has also been highlighted in a study carried out in the United Kingdom (Correctional Service Canada 1994; Gore *et al.* 1995).

The arguments for the introduction of measures to prevent HIV transmission via drug injunction are similar to those discussed above in relation to sexual transmission of HIV, that is the right to be free from cruel, inhuman and degrading treatment and punishment which includes the duty of care for prisoners and the respect for prisoners' dignity and life at stake in the absence of appropriate measures to prevent HIV transmission. International experiences have shown that the introduction of specific measures such as the provision of bleach, needle exchange programmes, or the implementation of prison methadone maintenance programmes have had a beneficial impact. For example, in Switzerland, the 1994 one-year Hindelbank Pilot Project became a long-term programme after its success. The experiment was based on the provision of clean needles in a women's prison with most of the prisoners serving sentences for drug offences. The programme provided for dispensing machines of sterile needles set up in various accessible locations. Prisoners were allowed to keep one piece of injecting equipment in a specifically designated cabinet. At the end of the first year, no new cases of HIV or hepatitis had been shown and the prisoners' health had improved. Furthermore, a significant decrease in needle sharing was observed, there had been no evident increase in drug consumption and needles had not been used as weapons (Stöver 2000).

Segregation

At the beginning of the AIDS epidemic, governments have adopted a punitive approach as a response to HIV/AIDS, and whilst the segregation of people with HIV/AIDS is now rare in the general community, it continues to take place in prisons as a standard practice, and is also sometimes endorsed by the courts. Recently, the US Supreme Court (Cert denied 10 January 2000, SC, No 98–9663 (sub nom *Davis* v. *Hopper*); 2000 WL 29361), left intact a ruling of the 11th Circuit Court of Appeals allowing Alabama prison officials to segregate inmates with HIV and denying them a range of programmes and services (such as sports competitions, educational programmes, religious services) on the grounds that uninfected inmates would be placed at a 'significant risk' of contracting HIV (*Onishea* v. *Hopper* 171 F3d 1289 (1999)).

However, the segregation of HIV+ prisoners has been judged unlawful in an Australian case. Two prisoners infected with HIV alleged discrimination under the Equal Opportunity Act 1984 (WA) and the Federal Disability Discrimination Act 1992 on the grounds that the segregation policy operating in Western Australian prisons amounted to discrimination on grounds of HIV status. The 'Prisons Infectious Disease Management Procedure' (Director General's Rule 3Q) required HIV+ prisoners to be treated as a special segregated group, to be accommodated in the Infectious Diseases Unit of a maximum-security prison's infirmary (where all HIV+ prisoners had to be placed), subject to close supervision when outside this unit, and more restricted in their movements, and activities within the prison than other prisoners. The Equal Opportunity Tribunal of WA found that the complainants had been discriminated against on the ground of their HIV status under the Equal Opportunity Act 1984 (see *The Complainant & The Complainant* v. *The State of Western Australia* (1994) EOC 92–610). A similar ruling was made by the Human Rights and Equal Opportunity Commission (HREOC) which considered the complaint under the DDA 1992 (cf. *X & Y* v. *State of Western Australia* [1996] HREOCA 32).[10] The HREOC held that only in extreme cases such as severely mentally disturbed prisoners or persons engaging in clearly dangerous behaviours, may segregation be justified (see para. 3.4 of the judgment).

Though there has been no case in relation to the segregation of seropositive inmates brought under the ECHR, as noted above, the European Commission of Human Rights has adopted a restrictive approach with regard to the conditions of prisoners. It has repeatedly stated that the segregation of a prisoner from the prison community does not in itself constitute inhuman treatment under art. 3 ECHR and has often tolerated extreme forms of social isolation imposed on grounds of security, order, discipline or the prevention of crime (see for example, *Kröcher and Möller* v. *Switzerland*, Comm. Report, 16 December 1982 D.R. 34). Furthermore, the Commission's approach in relation to the segregation of prisoners has indicated that the conditions must have been deliberately designed to debase or humiliate so as to destroy the victims' personality or break down their resistance in order for art. 3 to be successfully challenged (cf. *Ensslin, Baader and Raspe* v. *FRG* (1979) 14 DR 64). In the cases considered by the Commission, segregation resulted from the crimes of the complainants, and was necessary, according to the governments, in the interest of security, to preserve order or discipline or prevent crime. Arguably, the segregation of HIV+ prisoners is different from the conditions of detention dealt with by the Commission, in the sense that the policy applies to prisoners infected with HIV regardless of their crimes, and as a result, amounts to discrimination *vis-à-vis* HIV negative inmates. Furthermore, the severity of the physical and psychological consequences of the segregation of seropositive prisoners, as highlighted in the Australian case discussed above, provides a strong argument for the interpretation of art. 3 ECHR as prohibiting the segregation of HIV+ prisoners, mainly due to the physical and psychological consequences it has on prisoners:

> You can get irrational behaviour when you have people with such a serious problem [HIV/AIDS] segregated . . . Segregation causes severe psychological problems and this alters the natural history of the disease . . . [Isolation] adds enormously to mental suffering, no matter how good the physical situation (. . .) (*X & Y* v. *State of Western Australia*, Evidence of Dr Dwyer, at para. 3.11) [A]ny stress has an effect on a person's natural immunity, particularly continuing stress which isn't relieved. The problem with stress in a unit like that [Infectious Diseases Unit] is that it is going to directly cause some deterioration in their immune system (. . .) (Evidence of Dr Bockman, at para. 3.13) The segregation and close supervision policy is wrong because it leads to the affected prisoners being stigmatised . . . The segregation and close supervision policy is wrong because it has the potential to damage the health, by damaging the immune system and mental health, of those subjected to it. (Evidence of Dr Hames, at para. 3.2)

Conclusion

This article has demonstrated how the ECHR may be used to prevent AIDS-related violations of human rights in prison. Under international human rights law, states have duties to promote and protect prisoners' rights on a double rationale; that is human rights and public health. To do so, prisoners' right of privacy should be guaranteed, in particular via the introduction of voluntary HIV-testing and the non-disclosure of the HIV status of prisoners. As examined above, mandatory HIV-testing is not likely to prevent HIV transmission by the identification of all HIV+ prisoners (problem of delayed seroconversion, HIV transmission whilst in jail) and is likely to have detrimental psychological consequences on the prisoners tested positive, especially in the absence of pre- and post-counselling, and the risk of stigmatisation and discrimination. Similarly, the breach of confidentiality of

HIV-test results is very likely to deter prisoners from coming forward to seek advice and care if they believe that they may be infected with HIV by fear of being stigmatised and discriminated against by both the prison staff and the other inmates. Furthermore, the public health argument also requires prison authorities to provide adequate HIV medical treatment to prisoners with HIV/AIDS and a better protection against HIV transmission within the prison settings, in particular by providing prisoners with condoms and lubricants, measures to prevent rapes and the introduction of needle exchange programmes. Finally, segregation of prisoners with HIV/AIDS should be forbidden. It is not justified on grounds of prevention of HIV transmission and may have significant physical and psychological consequences on the segregated prisoners.

International human rights standards provide for an extensive scope of protection of prisoners' rights in the context of HIV/AIDS and urge for governmental actions to promote and guarantee the rights of those, who, despite being deprived of their liberty, remain human beings with fundamental rights.[11]

Notes

1 See for example ECHR case law, *Golder* (1975) Series A, No 18, (1979) 1 EHRR 524.

2 Adopted by the First United Nations Congrèss on the Prevention of Crime and the Treatment of Offenders held in Geneva in 1955.

3 Until early 1995, mandatory HIV-testing of prisoners was carried out.

4 In Tasmania, HIV-testing is mandatory where a person has been charged with a crime of sexual nature, including rape and indecent assault (s. 10(1) of the HIV/AIDS Preventive Measures Act 1993). Many US statutes have introduced mandatory HIV-testing of people convicted of sex-related offences or injection drug use as a condition of probation or parole.

5 See also the Report of the Canadian Expert Committee on AIDS and Prisons, *HIV/AIDS in Prisons: Final Report*, Ottawa: Minister of Supply and Services Canada, March 1994. As the Report observes, '[l]ittle goes on in prisons that is not almost immediately known by almost all inmates and staff, and it has been said that when a HIV-positive person is in prison, her or his health status is usually circulated among both correctional officers and inmates'.

6 The Court further stated that interference with privacy had to be balanced, on a case-by-case basis, against the government's interest in disclosure. In this case, interference with the inmate's right of privacy was not justified.

7 Evidences of HIV transmission in prisons in France, Scotland, the United States, Australia and other countries have been released. In 1994, a study undertaken in Glenochil prison for adult male offenders in Scotland provided evidence that an outbreak of HIV infection had occurred. Twelve of 27 inmates who admitted having injected drugs in Glenochil tested positive. Certain characteristics of the positive test results showed that in most, if not all cases, the infection had occurred in prison. A first case of custodial seroconversion was confirmed in Australia (Jürgens 1996).

8 The issue of sex, either consensual or coerced, between inmates and prison staff, will not be considered here, but the author wishes to emphasise that too often abuses of prisoners by prison staff are disregarded. Actions should be taken in order to punish those who abuse their power.

9 Policy on condoms, DDL (95) 10.

10 At the time of the decision, the respondent had undertaken the revision of the policy that had been held discriminatory by the Equal Opportunity Tribunal. The HREOC found that the complainants had been discriminated against on the ground of their seropositivity.

11 *Acknowledgements*: I would like to thank Bob Watt, senior lecturer in law at Essex University, and from the University of Bristol, Dr Steven Greer, reader in law and Dr Tonia Novitz, lecturer in law, for their valuable help and comments.

References

Canadian HIV/AIDS Legal Network (2001) Info sheet 4, *HIV/AIDS in Prisons*, Prevention: Condoms, (available at www.aidslaw.ca).

Correctional Service Canada (1994) *HIV/AIDS in Prisons: Final Report of the Expert Committee AIDS and Prisons*, Ottawa: Minister of Supply and Services Canada.

De Bruyn, T. (1998) *HIV/AIDS and Discrimination: A Discussion Paper*, Montréal: Canadian HIV/AIDS Legal Network and Canadian AIDS Society.

Dolan, K. (1998) 'Evidence about HIV transmission in prisons', *Canadian HIV/AIDS Policy and Law Newsletter*, *3*(4)/*4*(1), 32–5.

Dolan, K. *et al.* (1995) 'AIDS behind bars: preventing HIV spread among incarcerated drugs injectors', *AIDS*, *9*(8), 825–32.

Donaldson, S. (1995) *Rape of Incarcerated Americans: A Preliminary Statistical Look* (available at www.spr.org/doc/stats.htm).

Gore, S. M. and Bird, A. G. (1993) 'Transmission of HIV in prisons', *British Medical Journal*, *307*, 147–8.

Gore, S. M. *et al.* (1995) 'Drug injection and HIV prevalence in inmates of Glenochil Prison', *British Medical Journal*, 310, 295–6.

Human Rights Watch (2001) *No Escape: Male Rape in US Prisons*, New York: HRW Report.

Jürgens, R. (1996) *HIV/AIDS in Prisons: Final Report*, Montreal: Canadian HIV/AIDS Legal Network and Canadian AIDS Society.

Jürgens, R. (1998) *HIV Testing and Confidentiality: Final Report*, Montreal: Canadian HIV/AIDS Legal Network and Canadian AIDS Society.

Jürgens, R. (1999) 'HIV/AIDS in prisons: new developments', *Canadian HIV/AIDS Policy and Law Newsletter*, 4(4), 61–6.

Kantor, E. (1998) 'AIDS and HIV infection in prisoners', in: *The AIDS Knowledge Base* (available at www.hivinsite.ucsf.edu/akb/1997/01pris/).

Lines, R. (1997/98) 'Death exposes treatment of prisoners living with HIV/AIDS', *Canadian HIV/AIDS Policy and Law Newsletter*, *3* and *4*, 29–30.

Magnusson, R. (1995) 'A decade of HIV testing in Australia: Part 1: a review of current legal requirements', *University of New South Wales Law Journal*, *18*, 341–63.

Mahon, N. (1995) 'Transmission and advocacy for harm reduction in US prisoners and jails', *Canadian HIV/AIDS Policy and Law Newsletter*, *2*(1), 24–5.

Malkin, I. (1995) 'Tort law's role in preventing prisoners' exposure to HIV infection while in Her Majesty's Custody', *Melbourne University Law Review*, *20*, 423–80.

New South Wales Anti-Discrimination Board (1992) *Report of the Inquiry into HIV and AIDS Related Discrimination*, Sydney: The Board.

Schulman, D. (1998) 'AIDS discrimination: its nature meaning and function', *Nova Law Review*, *12*(3), 1113.

Siegal, D. M. (1992) 'Rape in prison and AIDS: a challenge for the eighth amendment framework of *Wilson* v. *Seiter*', *Stanford Law Review*, *44*, 6.

Starmer, K. (1999) *European Human Rights Law*, London: Legal Action Group.

Stöver, H. (2000) 'Evaluation of needle exchange pilot projects shows positive results', *Canadian HIV/AIDS Policy and Law Newsletter, 5*(2/3).

Taylor, A. *et al.* (1995) 'Outbreak of HIV infection in a Scottish prison', *British Medical Journal, 310*, 289–92.

UNAIDS (1996) *International Guidelines on HIV/AIDS and Human Rights*, Geneva: UNAIDS.

UNAIDS (1997a) *UNAIDS Technical Update: Prisons and AIDS*, Geneva: UNAIDS.

UNAIDS (1997b) *Prisons and AIDS, UNAIDS Point de Vue*, Geneva: UNAIDS.

Watt, B. (2000) 'HIV/AIDS and European Human Rights Law, *European Human Rights Law Review, 1*, 54–65.

WHO (1993) *Guidelines on HIV Infection and AIDS in Prisons*, Geneva: WHO.

WHO and UNAIDS (1999) *Questions and Answers, Reporting, Partner Notification and Disclosure of HIV Serostatus and/or AIDS, Public Health and Human Rights Implications*, Geneva: WHO.

Wooden, W. S. and Parker, J. (1982) *Men Behind Bars: Sexual Exploitation in Prison*, New York: Plenum.

Young, A. and McHale, J. V. (1992) 'The dilemmas of the HIV positive prisoner', *Howard Journal, 31*, 89–104.

Date submitted: April 2001
Date accepted: August 2001

[9]

HIV Infection and AIDS in the Public Health and Health Care Systems

The Role of Law and Litigation

Lawrence O. Gostin, JD; David W. Webber, JD

The AIDS Litigation Project has reviewed nearly 600 reported cases involving individuals with human immunodeficiency virus (HIV) infection and acquired immunodeficiency syndrome (AIDS) in the federal and state courts in the United States between 1991 and 1997. Cases were identified through a federal and 50-state computer and library search. An important subset of litigation relates to HIV/AIDS in the public health and health care systems, since the law affects health care institutions and professionals, patients, and public health policy in America. This subset of HIV/AIDS litigation includes testing and reporting; privacy, the duty to warn, and the right to know; physician standards of care in prevention and treatment; and discrimination and access to health care. In broad terms, the review demonstrates a reliance on voluntary testing and protection of patient privacy through HIV-specific statutes and the common law. Negligence with potential civil and criminal liability has been alleged in cases of erroneous or missed diagnosis of HIV infection. In the first AIDS case to be considered by the Supreme Court, the Court will decide whether patients with asymptomatic HIV infection are protected under the Americans With Disabilities Act. Considerable progress has been made, both socially and legally, during the first 2 decades of the epidemic, but much still needs to be accomplished to protect privacy, prevent discrimination, and promote tolerance.

THE EPIDEMIC of human immunodeficiency virus (HIV) infection and the acquired immunodeficiency syndrome (AIDS) has had powerful personal, social, and economic effects throughout America—in employment, housing, insurance, education, prisons, and many other aspects of life.[1] Yet, perhaps the most profound effects of the epidemic have been in the public health and health care systems.[2] Public health and medicine have responsibilities to monitor, prevent, and treat HIV infection. At the same time, the nation has struggled with the task of reconciling patients' rights to privacy and nondiscrimination with collective rights to public health protection.

Given the high degree of ongoing social conflict caused by the epidemic, it is not surprising that, unlike past infectious disease outbreaks, attempts to resolve contentious issues consistently involve the courts and legislatures at all levels. Furthermore, because of the high level of patient activism and advocacy, as well as immediate public access to new developments in scientific and medical information, including that available via the Internet, law and policymaking have not been the exclusive preserve of medical experts or other professional specialists. The resulting democratization of policymaking processes has heightened the impact that legislatures and courts have had on the public health and health care systems.

Deeply divisive questions have emerged relating to informed consent for HIV testing, named HIV reporting, confidentiality vs the duty to warn, and an HIV-infected physician's right to practice. These and many other questions have come to be decided by legislatures and courts. The results are by no means uniform or consistent. Court decisions in similar cases sometimes conflict, and legislatures in different jurisdictions at times take markedly different approaches. Nevertheless, legislation and litigation provide a window through which the HIV epidemic's troubling questions, arising in relation to the delivery of health care services and the formulation of complex public health policy, can be examined.

This article is part of the AIDS Litigation Project,[3,4] which has reviewed nearly 600 cases reported in the federal and state courts in the United States between 1991 and 1997. The methods involved a federal and 50-state computer and library search of all reported cases involving HIV infection or AIDS. This article discusses an important subset of litigation relating to HIV/AIDS in the public health and health care systems. (The complete AIDS Litigation Project report can be found in the Library section of the HIV/AIDS Information Center at http://www.ama-assn.org.)

IDENTIFYING CASES OF HIV INFECTION: TESTING AND REPORTING

Issues of law and public policy take on new urgency as the HIV/AIDS epidemic experiences a paradigm shift. Combination antiviral therapies and clinical prophylaxes provide for the first time an opportunity for a longer, higher quality of life for persons living with HIV.[5] Combination therapies have markedly reduced the incidence of AIDS,[6] have lowered rates of perinatal transmission,[7,8] and potentially may diminish infectiousness by decreasing viral load. With these new treat-

From the Georgetown/Johns Hopkins Program on Law and Public Health, Washington, DC, and Baltimore, Md (Mr Gostin). Mr Webber is in private practice in Philadelphia, Pa

Reprints: Lawrence O Gostin, JD, Georgetown University Law Center, 600 New Jersey Ave NW, Washington, DC 20001 (e-mail: gostin@law georgetown edu).

Health Law and Ethics section editors: Lawrence O. Gostin, JD, the Georgetown/Johns Hopkins University Program on Law and Public Health, Washington, DC, and Baltimore, Md; Helene M Cole, MD, Contributing Editor, *JAMA*.

ment opportunities, it becomes critically important to identify persons at the earliest stages of HIV infection and to ensure full and fair access to the health care system.

Testing, since the approval of an HIV antibody test in early 1985,[9] has been considered essential for HIV prevention. With more recent advances in antiviral and prophylactic treatments, testing has also become important as an entrée into the health care system. Public health and medical authorities recommend that all persons at risk should know their serologic status, and many want to see the "routinization" of HIV testing. A broad range of testing services are desirable, such as testing by primary care clinicians and hospitals, public clinics, "alternative" (anonymous) test sites, and home testing. The technological development of "rapid" tests and analyses of saliva and urine will make testing easier for the public.

Despite the manifest clinical and public health benefits, testing may result in loss of privacy, increased social stigma, and discrimination. As a result, many state legislatures have enacted special requirements for HIV testing. State legislation requires informed consent, often in writing, as well as pretest and posttest counseling. While counseling and consent are thought to be important to enhance patient autonomy, ironically, they do make it more burdensome for health care professionals to "routinize" HIV testing and bring it into the mainstream of medicine.

Voluntary testing is almost universally recommended, and most states have abided by an ethic of voluntarism. Compulsory, nonconsensual testing has been undertaken only in limited circumstances and principally for nonmedical purposes. Thus, mandatory tests are imposed, for example, on US military[10] and foreign service personnel,[11] immigrants,[12] and certain sex offenders.[13,14] In the health care setting, however, compulsory testing violates statutory and common law requirements for informed consent and may violate nondiscrimination statutes[15] or constitutional prohibitions against unreasonable searches and seizures.[16] Although a Pennsylvania court held that HIV testing without patient consent or knowledge did not violate state common law doctrines of informed consent or invasion of privacy,[17] that ruling was subsequently overturned by statute.[18]

Some states permit nonconsensual HIV testing of patients in limited circumstances. An Alabama statute, for example, allows testing without consent if (1) the patient is at "high risk" of infection; (2) knowledge of the patient's serologic status is necessary for medical care; or (3) knowledge of HIV status is needed for the protection of health care personnel. A federal district court found the high-risk classification to be unconstitutional because a patient could be arbitrarily classified, but upheld the other 2 classifications.[19] Many states allow compulsory testing to determine the HIV status of a patient in the event of an injury to a health care worker, emergency response employee, or corrections officer that poses a risk of HIV transmission.

Scientific evidence that anti-HIV therapy could significantly reduce perinatal transmission, together with new treatment opportunities for newborns, has led legislatures to consider mandatory testing of pregnant women and newborn infants. Under federal law, states must at a minimum follow Centers for Disease Control and Prevention (CDC) guidelines recommending counseling and voluntary testing for all pregnant women. If federally set targets for reduction of perinatal HIV transmission are not met, mandatory measures ensue.[20] At the state level, several legislatures have enacted laws that mandate counseling and make voluntary testing available. These federal and state statutes may set a standard of care in tort, so that failure to counsel and offer testing to pregnant women may result in physician liability for wrongful life or wrongful birth in the event that the infant is born with HIV infection.[21] New York has enacted a law requiring mandatory testing of newborns, even though a positive antibody test reveals the serologic status of the mother. New York's law also requires disclosure to the mother and protects confidentiality.[22] That law is currently under court challenge on constitutional grounds.[23]

Since the earliest moments of the epidemic, all states have required named reporting of CDC-defined AIDS. By contrast, 28 states require HIV reporting,[24] and 3 additional states conduct HIV surveillance for pediatric cases only.[25] All HIV reporting states except Maryland and Texas are name based.[26] The CDC recently recommended that all states move to a system of HIV surveillance.[6] The CDC also recommends that states (unless otherwise required by state law) provide alternative test sites where names of persons with HIV infection are not reportable. Ten states proscribe nonreportable, anonymous testing.[27] North Carolina's closure of publicly funded anonymous HIV test sites was upheld as a valid exercise of the state's public health powers.[28]

The predominantly voluntary approach to HIV testing and the absence of a national HIV surveillance system has resulted in concerns that HIV/AIDS has acquired a special or "exceptional" status.[29] In New York State, prominent medical organizations sued to compel the health commissioner to include HIV in the official list of sexually transmitted diseases (STDs). By failing to classify HIV as an STD, the commissioner declined to trigger his powers for compulsory testing, reporting, and contact tracing. New York's highest court held that the classification of diseases was within the commissioner's discretion and affirmed the reasonableness of his belief that the exercise of mandatory powers would not serve an important public health purpose.[30]

PRIVACY, DUTY TO WARN, AND THE RIGHT TO KNOW

Privacy of HIV data has been thought to be necessary for both patient autonomy and public health.[31] Privacy safeguards against social stigma and discrimination and allows each person to make decisions for herself concerning disclosure. Privacy also supports trusting clinical relationships and participation in public health services such as testing, counseling, and partner notification. Most states have HIV-specific statutes requiring confidentiality of HIV data.[32] Litigation claiming wrongful disclosure of HIV-related information has been commenced against numerous individual and institutional providers during the course of the epidemic, including hospitals,[33] physicians,[34] and health departments.[35]

Guided by the mandates of the provider-patient privilege and state HIV confidentiality laws, health care professionals are generally prohibited from revealing a patient's HIV-related information.[36] In fact, some state privacy statutes specifically protect HIV information within the health care or social service setting.[37] Intentional disclosure is only 1 way to breach confidentiality. A health care facility's negligent failure to protect a medical record from disclosure may also violate privacy.[38] However, not all disclosures result in liability. If the health care provider can present a compelling reason for disclosure, a court may allow it. The courts balance the need for the disclosure against the harm done to both the individual's privacy and the public interest and often have little difficulty finding against the individual's privacy right. Using such a test, a Pennsylvania court authorized a hospital to disclose a physician's HIV status to 280 patients who had received invasive procedures.[39] In another case, a court held that a public health agency's disclosure of confidential HIV information to aid in a criminal prosecution was permissible; the criminal activity was deemed a waiver of confidentiality.[40] In contrast, another court prohibited law enforcement access to public health records.[41]

A major tension exists between confidentiality and the "right to know." Health care workers and others who perceive themselves to be at risk for HIV infection in the workplace claim the right to know the HIV status of patients or others. Generally, because infection control precautions in the health care setting are both the standard of practice and highly effective, right-to-know claims are difficult to maintain. For example, a surgeon's lawsuit alleging emotional distress caused by learning, after the fact, that his surgical patient was HIV positive was rejected.[42] Similarly, if morticians and emergency response employees use universal infection control precautions, the risk of HIV transmission is negligible. Nevertheless, federal law authorizes, under certain circumstances, disclosure of HIV information to morticians and emergency response workers upon their request.[43] But whether right-to-know claims will be successful in generating damage awards seems questionable. In a West Virginia case, a mortician filed a tort action against a hospital for failing to inform him that a corpse he had handled was contaminated with HIV. The court found no liability in the absence of actual exposure.[44]

Fear of HIV Exposure in the Health Care Setting

Many cases have been filed by patients claiming that individual or institutional health care providers are liable for exposing them to the risk of HIV transmission without their knowledge. Patients argue that health care professionals negligently caused them emotional distress by failing to warn or failing to prevent some contact that is perceived to pose a risk of transmission. These plaintiffs seek compensation for their mental distress and anguish. Recognizing the litigious nature of American society, many courts limit fear of HIV claims by requiring proof that the plaintiff's mental distress is a result of circumstances posing an actual risk of HIV transmission. Plaintiffs who fear an objectively nonexistent or unprovable risk generally will not be compensated.[45,46] Furthermore, many courts limit compensation to distress occurring during the "window of anxiety," the period between learning of possible exposure and obtaining a reliable HIV-negative test result.[47] In 1 case, a surgical patient provided her own blood for transfusion, but the surgeon transfused another donor's blood. This negligence caused emotional distress that, in light of plaintiff's precautions, was in the court's view both reasonable and foreseeable.[48]

HIV-Infected Health Care Professional's Duty to Disclose

Several courts have held that health care professionals have a duty to disclose their HIV status to patients or health authorities, assuming that their professional activities pose a risk of transmission to patients. The Maryland Court of Appeals ruled that a surgeon has a duty to inform his patients of his infection; even if the patient has not actually been exposed and tests HIV negative, the contact with the surgeon may subsequently give rise to a claim for the infliction of mental distress due to fear of transmission.[49] Courts justify orders to disclose based on a duty to protect patients and on the doctrine of informed consent.[39] Requiring disclosure to patients, of course, can severely jeopardize a health care professional's career. To avoid this result, some states allow the professional to continue practicing, with appropriate restrictions and supervision, but without disclosing his or her HIV status.

The Duty to Warn Third Parties at Risk

Many state laws permit, but do not require, disclosure by physicians to third parties known to be at significant future risk of HIV transmission from patients known to be infected.[50] Thus, if a physician reasonably believes that a patient will share drug injection equipment or have unprotected sex without informing a partner of the risk, the physician has discretion to inform the partner. Under some disclosure laws, the physician is required to first counsel the patient to refrain from the risk behavior, and, in providing the third-party warning, the physician is prohibited from disclosing the patient's identity. In the absence of state laws permitting such disclosure, physicians may be held liable for breach of confidentiality for disclosing patient information to sex partners.[51]

The "duty to warn" may extend to nonpatient third parties in other contexts, based on the provider's primary duty to the patient. Thus, health care professionals have a duty to inform patients that they have been transfused with HIV-contaminated blood, and this duty may extend to third parties. A physician in 1 case failed to inform a teenager or her parents that she had been transfused with HIV-contaminated blood. When the young woman's sexual partner tested positive for HIV, the court upheld his claim against the physician based on the physician's failure to inform the patient.[52] Similarly, courts have held that a health care professional's duty to inform a patient of his or her HIV infection may extend to those the patient foreseeably puts at risk such as a spouse[53] or family member caregiver.[54] On the other hand, courts have ruled that disclosure is wrongful in cases in which the third party, such as a family member, is not at actual risk of infection, or the physician has no knowledge that the patient has failed to disclose to the partner.[55]

PREVENTION AND TREATMENT: PHYSICIAN STANDARDS OF CARE

Negligent Diagnosis of HIV/AIDS

Patients who have been erroneously informed that they are HIV-infected, when in fact they are not, have filed suit against their health care providers for negligent infliction of emotional distress. Some of these plaintiffs have argued that an HIV-positive diagnosis is a "death sentence" that inflicts extreme psychological harm. To limit recovery to only those cases involving a significant claim for compensation, some courts have refused to award damages unless the mental distress arose from or led to physical injury. For example, courts have held that increased blood pressure is not an adequate injury, but that adverse effects of AIDS treatments or a patient's attempt at suicide would suffice to justify liability.[56] Other courts have not imposed a physical injury requirement.[57]

Providers may also be liable for negligently failing to diagnose HIV infection. In 1 case, a jury awarded more than $1 million in a case in which an earlier diagnosis would have delayed by 1 year the onset of symptoms, disability, and death.[58] A physician may also be liable for unnecessary delay in notifying a patient of exposure to HIV[59] and may be liable to the patient's sexual partner who is subsequently infected.[52] However, providers have not been held liable for failure to diagnose and effectively treat HIV unless the plaintiff has shown a causal connection between their failure and the injury suffered.[60] In the early years of the epidemic, failure to diagnose HIV infection did not expose the provider to significant liability, since treatment options and likelihood of success in treatment were limited. But as treatments for HIV illness develop to higher levels of efficacy, failure to render a prompt diagnosis or failure to initiate prompt and appropriate treatment may expose providers to increasing liability.

Distribution of Drug Injection Equipment

Public health[61] and medical[62] authorities recommend that physicians counsel drug users to use a new syringe and needle for every injection. Syringe exchanges have been established at the state and local levels to prevent transmission of HIV and other blood-borne pathogens.[63] Nevertheless, a web of state statutes create criminal offenses for the sale, distribution, or possession of syringes and needles.[64,65] These laws pose the threat of prosecution to public health officials and community activists who distribute sterile needles and syringes, and, in some cases, prosecutions have resulted. The Washington Supreme Court, however, upheld syringe exchange as a valid public health measure. The court reasoned that the health department had acted in pursuance of an AIDS statute that granted the department the general power to implement prevention strategies.[66] Federal law prohibits use of federal funds for syringe exchange until the secretary of health and human services certifies that exchanges are effective in preventing HIV infection and do not encourage drug use.[67]

DISCRIMINATION AND ACCESS TO CARE

The HIV epidemic has been characterized by a high level of social opprobrium against those infected or suspected of being infected. As a result, individuals with HIV infection routinely encounter discrimination in many aspects of their lives. Discrimination in the health care setting, however, is especially pernicious, depriving patients of necessary services and undermining their trust in the system's commitment to provide them with the care they need. If individuals fear discrimination in health care, they may forgo testing or fail to discuss their health and risk behaviors. Furthermore, because health care professionals are viewed by the general public as being well informed, their actions set a poor example for others attempting to respond to the epidemic in a nondiscriminatory fashion.

Institutional health care providers and other employers have a duty to provide a reasonably safe workplace. The use of barrier techniques on a universal basis has been the officially sanctioned approach to workplace safety. As a result, discrimination against patients is rarely, if ever, justified by a provider's fear of transmission. The Occupational Safety and Health Administration's (OSHA's) blood-borne pathogen safety standard[68] has been challenged as overly broad,[69] but remains the primary safety standard. Although employer noncompliance with infection control standards may give rise to a justifiable refusal to work, the underlying fear must have an objective basis.[70] Employee claims of occupational transmission (or fear of occupational transmission) are generally covered by worker compensation statutes,[71] which provide exclusive remedies for work-related claims against employers.[72]

Definition of "Disability" Under the ADA: The Supreme Court's First AIDS Case

An array of laws at the federal, state, and local levels prohibit discrimination on the basis of a person's disability or health status.[1] The primary federal nondiscrimination statute is the Americans With Disabilities Act (ADA) of 1990,[73,74] although the laws of many states and localities also specifically prohibit discrimination against individuals living with HIV/AIDS.

The ADA provides that no individual "shall be discriminated against on the basis of disability in the full and equal enjoyment of the goods, services, facilities, privileges, advantages, or accommodations of any place of public accommodation."[75] The ADA's definition of "public accommodation" specifically includes hospitals and professional offices of health care providers.[76] Similarly, New York's highest court ruled that the offices of private dentists are considered places of public accommodation under New York law.[77]

A critically important issue under the ADA is whether persons with asymptomatic HIV infection have a "disability" and thus are protected under the ADA.[78] Disability is defined as a physical or mental impairment that substantially limits 1 or more of the major life activities of the individual, a record of such impairment, or being regarded as having such an impairment.[79] In the past, many courts have ruled or assumed as undisputed that HIV infection, as the underlying cause of a life-threatening illness, is a disability. However, several recent court decisions have held that HIV does not automatically qualify as a disability, and in each case there must be an individualized determination as to whether the infection actually limits, in a substantial way, a major life activity. Given the advent of new combination therapies that significantly delay the onset of disabling symptoms, this judicial view could markedly undermine legal protection against discrimination for persons with asymptomatic or mildly symptomatic HIV infection. The ADA's legislative history, however, indicates that Congress intended to include HIV infection within the definition of disability, and the Equal Employment Opportunity Commission's regulations embody that view.[80] In its first AIDS case ever, the Supreme Court will decide whether and to what extent persons with HIV infection are protected under the ADA.

In *Abbott v Bragdon*,[81] a dentist refused to fill a dental cavity of an HIV-infected patient. The patient then brought suit alleging that the refusal violated the ADA. The dentist conceded that his professional office was covered by the ADA, but argued that providing services to the infected patient, because of the risk of HIV transmission, would pose a direct threat to his health. Additionally, he argued that the plaintiff, who did not have symptoms of HIV illness, was not an individual with a disability under the ADA. The lower courts rejected the dentist's defenses, concluding that the dentist was unable to show that in 1994, when the case arose, there was evidence that treating an infected patient posed a significant risk. The plaintiff's infection, which she testified resulted in her decision against becoming pregnant, was viewed as substantially limiting the major life activity of reproduction. The Supreme Court has agreed to consider 3 questions presented by the case: (1) whether reproduction is a major life activity; (2) whether asymptomatic HIV infection is a per se disability under the ADA; and (3) whether the courts should defer to a health care provider's reasonable professional judgment.

The ADA's coverage also extends to individuals merely regarded as having a disability. Thus, it is unlawful to discriminate against an individual based on the misperception that the person is infected with HIV under the ADA as well as under the laws of many states.[82] Persons discriminated against because of their association with a person with HIV infection are also protected,[83] as are persons retaliated against because of their opposition to discrimination.[84]

The Health Care Professional's Duty to Treat

Courts have consistently held that health care professionals have a legal duty to treat patients living with HIV/AIDS.[85] Health care professionals must, of course, exercise appropriate clinical judgment. If a professional lacks the skill appropriate to render competent care, she may legally refuse to treat the person and may lawfully refer him elsewhere.[86] A clinician cannot, however, simply reject or refer an HIV-infected patient solely because of his or her HIV status.

The courts have had to decide the difficult question whether and to what degree a health care professional can treat HIV-infected persons differently from other patients. Although CDC and OSHA standards require use of "universal" precautions applicable to all patients without regard to infection status, imposition of special precautions for HIV-infected patients has been upheld.[87] One court, finding that special precautions may be necessary for certain procedures, ruled that a dentist may lawfully refuse to treat a patient who refuses to reveal HIV-related information.[88] But another court ruled that the use of special precautions, which resulted in delay of services, beyond those recommended by the CDC constituted unlawful discrimination.[89]

Nondiscrimination in Health Insurance

Access to health care is often contingent on the ability to pay or the availability of insurance coverage. Federal and state law provides little or no protection from adverse coverage decisions provided the insurance company uses sound actuarial data. However, an employer's decision to place severe limits on coverage for HIV/AIDS, but not on comparable diseases, may be unlawful under the ADA.[90,91] A central question in determining the extent of health insurance coverage is whether certain services are "medically necessary." In an important case, the Eleventh Circuit Court of Appeals held that skilled nursing care was "medically necessary" and should be reimbursed under an employer's self-funded health benefits plan.[92]

HIV-Infected Health Care Professionals

Federal law[93] requires states to comply with CDC guidance[94] that recommends an individualized determination of whether HIV-infected physicians engaging in "exposure-prone" procedures can safely practice. At present the CDC and the American Medical Association are reevaluating their policies in light of epidemiologic evidence showing that the risk to patients, even from invasive procedures, is negligible. The judiciary has had to decide whether HIV-infected health care professionals pose a significant risk to their patients, and thus are not qualified to continue to practice. Several courts have upheld decisions to prohibit HIV-infected health care professionals who perform invasive procedures.[95,96] These courts have reasoned that the severity of harm if HIV infection were transmitted justifies practice restrictions. However, the Ninth Circuit Court of Appeals held that a physician's practice could not be restricted if he did not primarily perform invasive procedures. The physician, a general internist, was employed by the Federal Bureau of Investigation (FBI). The agency refused to refer patients to the physician after suspecting that he was HIV positive. The court ruled that the FBI had failed to make adequate inquiries about the physician's infection control procedures: "The record shows that Dr. Doe and the hospital were entirely forthcoming about these procedures, but that their explanations fell on deaf ears."[97]

Prisoner Health Care

Access to adequate health care for prison inmates living with HIV/AIDS has been a long-term problem.[98] Gross inadequacies in state prison health care systems may rise to a constitutional violation.[99] In New York, inmates living with HIV/AIDS challenged the state's delivery of medical, mental health, educational, and prevention services. The court ordered the state to release records enumerating the inmates, both living and deceased, who had been diagnosed as having AIDS or AIDS-related illnesses, in order to aid in the court's determination as to whether the prison authorities deliberately neglected the inmates' health care needs.[100] Inadequate medical care and lack of HIV education services resulted in a court-imposed remedial plan in another case.[101] But when a showing of deliberate indifference is lacking, federal constitutional claims against prison officials will fail.[102]

CONCLUSION

Considerable progress has been made—socially and legally—during the first 2 decades of the HIV/AIDS epidemic. Reductions in social stigma and new statutes to protect privacy and proscribe discrimination have emerged. The serious consequences of the epidemic, however, are not over. While instances of gross abuse are less frequent, intolerance and animus stubbornly persist. Even legal advances have been eroded with some courts denying antidiscrimination protection for persons with asymptomatic HIV infection, and upholding discrimination against HIV-infected health care professionals despite the extremely low risks.

Systematic efforts to confront the HIV/AIDS epidemic are needed: (1) expanded and nondiscriminatory access to health care; (2) expansion of counseling, testing, and other prevention services; (3) educational campaigns to promote tolerance and reduce social stigma; and (4) better laws to protect privacy and prohibit discrimination. The health care and public health systems need these and other kinds of new strategies to reduce the deep personal and social burdens of HIV disease in the United States.

References

1. Webber DW, ed. *AIDS and the Law*. 3rd ed. New York, NY: John Wiley & Sons Inc; 1997.
2. Gostin LO, ed. *AIDS and the Health Care System*. New Haven, Conn: Yale University Press; 1990.
3. Gostin LO. The AIDS Litigation Project: a national review of court and Human Rights Commission decisions, I: the social impact of AIDS. *JAMA*. 1990;263:1961-1970.
4. Gostin LO. The AIDS Litigation Project: a national review of court and Human Rights Commission decisions, II: discrimination in education, employment, housing, insurance, and health care. *JAMA*. 1990;263:2086-2093.
5. Carpenter CCJ, Fischl MA, Hammer SM, et al. Antiretroviral therapy for HIV infection in 1997. *JAMA*. 1997;277:1962-1969.
6. Centers for Disease Control and Prevention. Update: trends in AIDS incidence—United States, 1996. *MMWR Morb Mortal Wkly Rep*. 1997;46:861-867.
7. Peckham C, Gibb D. Mother-to-child transmission of the human immunodeficiency virus. *N Engl J Med*. 1995;333:298-302.
8. Fiscus SA, Adimora AA, Schoenbach VJ, et al. Perinatal HIV infection and the effect of zidovudine therapy on transmission in rural and urban counties. *JAMA*. 1996;275:1483-1494.
9. Centers for Disease Control. Provisional Public Health Service interagency recommendations for screening donated blood and plasma for antibody to the virus causing acquired immunodeficiency syndrome. *MMWR Morb Mortal Wkly Rep*. 1985;34:1-5.
10. 32 CFR §§58.1-58.6 (1997).

11. *American Fed'n of Gov't Employees, Local 1812 v US Dep't of State*, 662 F Supp 50 (DDC 1987).
12. Gostin LO, Cleary PD, Mayer K, Brandt A, Chittenden E. Screening and exclusion of international travelers and immigrants for public health purposes: an evaluation of United States policy. *N Engl J Med.* 1990;322:1743-1746.
13. *US v Ward*, 131 F3d 335 (3d Cir 1997).
14. Gostin LO, Lazzarini Z, Alexander DD, et al. HIV testing, counseling, and prophylaxis after sexual assault. *JAMA.* 1994;271:1436-1444.
15. *T.E.P. v Leavitt*, 840 F Supp 110 (D Utah 1993).
16. *Glover v Eastern Neb Community Office of Retardation*, 686 F Supp 243 (D Neb 1988), *aff'd*, 867 F2d 461 (8th Cir), *cert denied*, 493 US 932 (1989).
17. *Doe v Dyer-Goode*, 566 A2d 889 (Pa Super Ct 1989).
18. Pa Stat Ann tit 35, §7607.
19. *Hill v Evans*, No. 91-A-626-N, 1993 WL 595676 (MD Ala Oct 7, 1993).
20. 42 USC §300ff-34.
21. *Anastosopoulos v Perakis*, 644 A2d 480 (Me 1994).
22. New York Department of Health, Maternal-Pediatric HIV Prevention and Care Program. *HIV Counseling and Testing of Newborns as Part of the Comprehensive Newborn Testing Program.* Albany: New York Dept of Health Maternal-Pediatric HIV Prevention and Care Program; 1997. Memorandum 97-2.
23. *R.Z. v Pataki*, Index No. 97-112960 (Sup Ct NY County, complaint filed July 18, 1997).
24. Alabama, Arizona, Arkansas, Colorado, Florida, Idaho, Indiana, Louisiana, Michigan, Minnesota, Mississippi, Missouri, Nebraska, Nevada, New Jersey, New Mexico, North Carolina, North Dakota, Ohio, Oklahoma, South Carolina, South Dakota, Tennessee, Utah, Virginia, West Virginia, Wisconsin, Wyoming.
25. Connecticut, Texas, and Oregon.
26. Gostin LO, Ward JW, Baker, AC. National HIV case reporting for the United States. *N Engl J Med.* 1997;337:1162-1167.
27. Alabama, Idaho, Michigan, Nevada, North Carolina, Ohio, South Carolina, South Dakota, Tennessee, and Wyoming.
28. *ACT-UP Triangle v Comm'n for Health Servs*, 483 SE2d 388 (NC 1997), *rev'g* 472 SE2d 605 (NC Ct App 1996).
29. Bayer R. Public health policy and the AIDS epidemic: an end to HIV exceptionalism. *N Engl J Med.* 1991;324:1500-1503.
30. *New York State Soc'y of Surgeons v Axelrod*, 572 NE2d 605 (NY 1991).
31. *Report of the Presidential Commission on the Human Immunodeficiency Virus Epidemic.* Washington, DC: US Government Printing Office; 1988.
32. Gostin LO, Lazzarini Z, Neslund VS, et al. The public health information infrastructure: a national review of the law on health information privacy. *JAMA.* 1996;275:1921-1927.
33. *Doe v Methodist Hosp*, 639 NE2d 683 (Ind Ct App 1994).
34. *Doe v Marselle*, 675 A2d 835 (Conn 1996), *rev'g* 660 A2d 871(Conn App Ct 1995).
35. *Estate of Benson v Minnesota Bd of Medical Practice*, 526 NW2d 634 (Minn Ct App 1995).
36. *Doe v Roe*, 588 NYS2d 236 (Sup Ct Onondaga County 1992), *rev'd in part*, 599 NYS2d 350 (App Div 1993), *subsequent opinion*, 620 NYS2d 666 (App Div 1994).
37. NY Pub Health Law §2782.
38. *Estate of Behringer v Medical Ctr*, 592 A2d 1251 (NJ Super Ct Law Div 1991).
39. *In re* Milton S. Hershey Medical Ctr, 634 A2d 159 (Pa 1993), *aff'g* 595 A2d 1290 (Pa Super Ct 1991).
40. *State v Stark*, 832 P2d 109 (Wash Ct App 1992).
41. *State v J. E.*, 606 A2d 1160 (NJ Super Ct Law Div 1992).
42. *Ordway v County of Suffolk*, 583 NYS2d 1014 (Sup Ct Suffolk County 1992).
43. 42 USC §300ff-76(4).
44. *Funeral Servs by Gregory, Inc v Bluefield Community Hosp*, 413 SE2d 79 (WVa 1991), *overruled in part by Courtney v Courtney*, 437 SE2d 436 (WVa 1993).
45. *Kaufman v Physical Measurements, Inc*, 615 NYS2d 508 (App Div 1994).
46. *Barrett v Danbury Hosp*, 654 A2d 748 (Conn 1995).
47. *Madrid v Lincoln County Medical Ctr*, 923 P2d 1154 (NM 1996), *aff'g* 909 P2d 14 (NM Ct App 1995).
48. *Hoffman v Brandywine Hosp*, 661 A2d 397 (Pa Super Ct 1995).
49. *Faya v Almaraz*, 620 A2d 327 (Md 1993).
50. Gostin LO, Hodge J. Piercing the veil of secrecy in HIV/AIDS and other sexually transmitted diseases: theories of privacy and disclosure in partner notification: contact tracing, the "right to know," and the "duty to warn." *Duke J Gender Law & Policy.* In press.
51. *N. O. L. v District of Columbia*, 674 A2d 498 (DC 1996).
52. *Reisner v Regents of Univ of Cal*, 37 Cal Rptr 2d 518 (Ct App 1995).
53. *Garcia v Santa Rosa Health Care Corp*, No. 13-94-482-CV, 1996 Tex App LEXIS 824 (Tex App 13 Dist 1996), *substituted opinion upon reh'g*, 1996 Tex App LEXIS 2513 (Tex App 13 Dist June 20, 1996).
54. *J. B. v Sacred Heart Hosp*, 635 So2d 945 (Fla 1994), *certified question at* 996 F2d 276 (11th Cir 1993).
55. *Diaz Reyes v US*, 770 F Supp 58 (DPR 1991), *aff'd without opinion*, 971 F2d 744 (1st Cir), *cert denied*, 504 US 957 (1992).
56. *R. J. v Humana of Fla, Inc*, 652 So2d 360 (Fla 1995).
57. *Bramer v Dotson*, 437 SE2d 773 (WVa 1993).
58. *Doe v McNulty*, 630 So2d 825 (La Ct App 1993), *cert denied*, 631 So2d 1167 (La 1994).
59. *Mixon v Cason*, 622 So2d 825 (Ala 1993).
60. *Baker v English*, 894 P2d 505 (Ore Ct App 1995), *aff'd in part & rev'd in part*, 932 P2d 57 (Ore 1997).
61. Centers for Disease Control and Prevention. *HIV Prevention Bulletin: Medical Advice for Persons Who Inject Illicit Drugs.* Atlanta, Ga: Centers for Disease Control and Prevention; May 9, 1997.
62. Normand J, Vlahov D, Moses LE, eds. *Preventing HIV Transmission: The Role of Sterile Needles and Bleach.* Washington, DC: National Academy Press; 1995.
63. Burris S, Finucane D, Gallagher H, Grace J. The legal strategies used in operating syringe exchange programs in the United States. *Am J Public Health.* 1996;86:1161-1166.
64. Gostin LO, Lazzarini Z, Jones TS, et al. Prevention of HIV/AIDS and other blood-borne diseases among injection drug users: a national survey on the regulation of syringes and needles. *JAMA.* 1997; 277:53-62.
65. Gostin LO, Lazzarini Z. Prevention of HIV/AIDS among injection drug users: the theory and science of public health and criminal justice approaches to disease prevention. *Emory Law J.* 1997;46:587-696.
66. *Spokane County Health Dist v Brockett*, 839 P2d 324 (Wash 1992).
67. Pub L No. 105-78, Title V, §§505-506, 1997 USCCAN (111 Stat) 1467, 1515.
68. Occupational Safety and Health Administration. Blood borne pathogens. 29 CFR §1910.1030 (1997).
69. *American Dental Ass'n v Martin*, 984 F2d 823 (7th Cir 1993).
70. *Armstrong v Flowers Hosp*, 33 F3d 1308 (11th Cir 1994), *aff'g* 812 F Supp 1183 (MD Ala 1993).
71. Miller P, Tereskerz D, Jagger J. Occupationally acquired HIV. *Am J Public Health.* 1997;87:1558-1562.
72. *Elliott v Dugger*, 579 So2d 827 (Fla Dist Ct App 1991), *prior opinion*, 542 So2d 392 (Fla Dist Ct App 1989).
73. 42 USC §§12101 *et seq.*
74. Gostin L, Beyer H, eds. *The Americans With Disabilities Act: What It Means for All Americans.* Baltimore, Md: Brookes Publishing Co; 1993.
75. 42 USC §12182(a).
76. 42 USC §12181(7).
77. *Cahill v Rosa*, 674 NE2d 274 (NY 1996), *rev'g* 632 NYS2d 614 (App Div 1995).
78. Parmet WE, Jackson DH. No longer disabled: the legal impact of the new social construction of HIV. *Am J Law Med.* 1997;23:7-44.
79. 42 USC §12102(2).
80. 29 CFR §1630, appendix at 339 (1996).
81. *Abbott v Bragdon*, 107 F3d 934 (1st Cir 1997), *aff'g* 912 F Supp 580 (D Me 1995), *cert granted*, 118 SCt 554 (1997).
82. *Sanchez v Lagoudakis*, 486 NW2d 657 (Mich 1992), *subsequent opinion*, 552 NW2d 472 (Mich Ct App 1996).
83. *Finley v Giacobbe*, 827 F Supp 215 (SD NY 1993).
84. *Sherer v Foodmaker, Inc*, 921 F Supp 651 (ED Mo 1996).
85. *Howe v Hull*, 873 F Supp 72 (ND Ohio 1994).
86. *Schulman v State Div of Human Rights*, 641 NYS2d 134 (App Div 1996), *rev'd*, 677 NE2d 284 (NY 1997), *on remand*, 658 NYS2d 70 (App Div 1997).
87. *North Shore Univ Hosp v Rosa*, 657 NE2d 483 (NY 1995), *aff'g* 600 NYS2d 90 (App Div 1993).
88. *Doe v Kahala Dental Group*, 808 P2d 1276 (Haw), *reconsideration denied*, 841 P2d 1074 (Haw 1991).
89. *Sharrow v Bailey*, 910 F Supp 187 (MD Pa 1995).
90. *EEOC Interim Guidance on Application of the ADA to Health Insurance.* Washington, DC: Equal Employment Opportunities Commission; June 8, 1993.
91. *Carparts Distrib Ctr, Inc v Automotive Wholesalers Ass'n*, 37 F3d 12 (1st Cir 1994), *rev'g* 826 F Supp 583 (D NH 1993).
92. *Florence Nightingale Nursing Serv v Blue Cross & Blue Shield*, 832 F Supp 1456 (ND Ala 1993), *aff'd*, 41 F3d 1476 (11th Cir), *cert denied*, 115 S Ct 2002 (1995).
93. Pub L No. 102-141, Title VI, §633, 1991 USCCAN (105 Stat) 834, 876-77, *reprinted in note to* 42 USC §300ee-2.
94. Centers for Disease Control and Prevention. Recommendations for preventing transmission of human immunodeficiency virus and hepatitis B virus to patients during exposure-prone invasive procedures. *MMWR Morb Mortal Wkly Rep.* 1991;40(RR-8):1-9.
95. *Bradley v Univ of Tex M. D. Anderson Cancer Ctr*, 3 F3d 922 (5th Cir 1993) (per curiam), *cert denied*, 114 SCt 1071 (1994).
96. *Mauro v Borgess Medical Ctr*, 886 F Supp 1349 (WD Mich 1995).
97. *Doe by Lavery v Attorney Gen'l*, 44 F3d 715 (9th Cir 1995), *superseded without opinion*, 62 F3d 1424 (9th Cir), *vacated and remanded sub nom Reno v Doe by Lavery*, 116 SCt 2543 (1996).
98. Burris S. Prisons, law and public health: the case for a coordinated response to epidemic diseases behind bars. *Univ Miami Law Rev.* 1992;47:291-329.
99. *Hetzel v Swartz*, 917 F Supp 344 (MD Pa 1996).
100. *Inmates of NY State With HIV v Cuomo*, No. 90-CV-252, 1991 US Dist LEXIS 1488 (ND NY Feb 7, 1991).
101. *Madrid v Gomez*, 889 F Supp 1146 (ND Cal 1995).
102. State *ex rel Peeples v Anderson*, 653 NE2d 371 (Ohio 1995).

[10]

Self-Incrimination, Partner Notification, and the Criminal Law: Negatives for the CDC's "Prevention for Positives" Initiative

David W. Webber

ABSTRACT

On 18 April 2003, the Centers for Disease Control and Prevention (CDC) announced a new HIV prevention initiative, "Prevention for Positives," which emphasizes partner-notification activities for individuals who have already been diagnosed with HIV. The CDC failed, however, to address significant criminal law issues that are presented by this initiative. The proposed partner notification activities involve patients' voluntary identification of contacts at risk for HIV transmission. But because all states have laws that make it a crime to knowingly expose another person to HIV, information provided by patients for partner-notification purposes is in most cases evidence of a crime. Little if any confidentiality protections prevent law enforcement officials from obtaining test results, records of counseling sessions, or similar information from the records of health or social service providers. Prevention for Positives thus exposes patients to an unacknowledged risk of criminal prosecution, which may severely inhibit future cooperation among those infected. This problem should be addressed by law and policy reforms, including enhanced confidentiality of partner-notification records and the availability of "use and derivative use" immunity that bars prosecution of patients based on the information they provide in partner-notification programs.

David W. Webber, JD, is Editor in Chief of *APPJ* and currently is of counsel to the AIDS Law Project of Pennsylvania, a nonprofit, public interest law firm he founded in 1988, *dwwebber@critpath.org*.

In a major policy shift announced on 18 April 2003, the CDC initiated a "new strategy" in HIV prevention efforts: Prevention for Positives, that focuses on changing the sexual and syringe-sharing behavior of persons already identified as being infected with HIV.[1] The CDC's new strategy is intended to reduce the infection rate that has remained at 40,000 annually for more than the past decade in the United States. Partner notification is an integral part of this initiative. Although partner notification programs are already in place in some states such as New York,[2] the CDC's initiative, which includes increased funding for such programs on the state and local levels, promises to extend this approach to a national level. This article assesses the CDC's failure to address significant criminal law issues in implementing its initiative.

As the CDC acknowledges, not all of the new HIV infections are the result of transmission from those who are not aware of their infection. For example, studies of treatment-resistant infection among the newly infected indicate that a small percentage of individuals diagnosed and being treated for HIV infection with retroviral medications are infecting others.[3] A recent survey of HIV-infected individuals shows a similar result.[4] But the extent to which new HIV infections are actually the result of nondisclosure of HIV status by those aware of their infection is apparently not known.

The Prevention for Positives strategy involves first identifying patients to be "at greatest risk for transmitting HIV."[5] These patients are then provided with "behavioral risk-reduction interventions"—referrals for counseling, education, and provision of condoms. Perhaps the most important element, however, is partner notification, which is to be facilitated through partner counseling and referral services (PCRS). As described by the CDC, patients' identification of their partners is voluntary and is to include both current and former partners. Partner notification can be done by the patient, but more often notification is done by health department personnel. When clinic staff or health department personnel make the disclosure, the patient's identity is not disclosed to the partner. Re-notification is recommended, particularly in cases when the partner has concluded that someone else was the infected partner. The program also seeks to identify infections among persons at risk for HIV, primarily by increasing HIV testing and then through partner notification activities.

Whether Prevention for Positives is an effective policy choice is a discussion well beyond the scope of this article, although the CDC itself concedes that "No studies have directly shown that PCRS prevents disease in a community."[6] One recent partner notification study reports a high rate of relationship dissolution and acquisition of new partners among those participating in partner notification, which could result in new infections.[7] But that study also questions causality, suggesting that dissolution rates in general are high, and that, therefore, partner notification "may not have much influence on the breakup of partnerships."[8] Partner notification programs have been criticized in the past for both their confidentiality risks and lack of practical value,[9] but those criticisms have not extended to the criminal law implications of partner notification.

There has been a curious congruence between the CDC's policy change and the news media and popular culture. The day before the CDC described its Prevention for Positives initiative in its *Morbidity and Mortality Weekly Report*, the *Indianapolis Star* published an examination of the role of HIV confidentiality laws in the context of persons with HIV who knowingly expose others, contrasting the public health approach (civil proceedings, secrecy) with that of law enforcement (criminal proceedings, public notification).[10] Two weeks later, an article in the *New York Times Magazine* described the activities of African-American men "on the down low"—seemingly heterosexual men who lead secret bisexual lives in which they eschew safe sex, or even embrace high-risk sex.[11] During this same time period, best-selling novelist E. Lynn Harris, whose books feature situations in which bisexual African-American men are involved with women who are not aware of the risk of being infected with HIV, was on a highly publicized national book tour to promote his new memoir.[12] In reporting on the prosecution of five people who were charged

Acronyms Used in this Article

CARE Act	Comprehensive AIDS Resources Emergency Act
CDC	Centers for Disease Control and Prevention
PCRS	partner counselling and referral services

with selling their HIV-infected blood plasma, the *Indianapolis Star* emphasized in July 2003 that the state HIV confidentiality law delayed the identification of the individuals who were subsequently charged in the case.[13] Then, in September 2003, news coverage of the prosecution of a former San Francisco Health Commissioner, Ron Hill, for intentionally infecting a sex partner with HIV, suggested that the fox was guarding the henhouse.[14] In reporting on this case, the *San Francisco Chronicle* made a direct connection between the CDC's Prevention for Positives initiative and "holding those who are already infected responsible for the health of people with whom they have consensual sex."[15] The subsequent dismissal of the intentional transmission charge in the Hill case provided further opportunity for law enforcement officials to bemoan the inadequate HIV exposure criminal laws in California.[16] Finally, the *New York Times* ran what was ostensibly a news story with the ominous headline "HIV Secrecy Is Proving Deadly,"[17] about the publication of Klitzman and Bayer's *Mortal Secrets: Truth and Lies in the Age of AIDS*.[18] In fact, that book discusses the criminal law response to the epidemic as a potential option, but stops short of explicitly endorsing it. Although this is not an exhaustive survey of news media coverage of HIV prevention and criminal law issues, it gives a fair indication of the way that the media frequently frame discussion of these issues.

In this broader context, the CDC's new policy might easily be viewed as abandoning the long-accepted precept that the prevention of HIV transmission is the responsibility of both the infected and uninfected. The focus on the already diagnosed suggests that the epidemic is fueled by individuals who know their infected status and fail to disclose it or take measures to prevent infection to others, a suggestion that opens the door to holding such individuals legally accountable. We do that by defining their conduct as criminal, then prosecuting, convicting, and punishing them for those crimes.

The history of the epidemic thus far indicates that the use of the criminal law to address HIV transmission has had limited use, even if the occasional case results in banner headlines. As Lazzarini and her colleagues show in a survey of print news media coverage and case reports of HIV exposure criminal prosecutions nationwide from 1986 to 2001, the number of reports of prosecutions has remained extremely low in comparison to the estimated number of individuals with HIV and the number of new infections each year.[19] The years 1986-1988 and 2000-2001 had the lowest numbers of reported prosecutions, with 10 or fewer in each of those years, while there were no more than 20 prosecutions in most other years. The highest level of reported prosecutions occurred in 1998 (more than 50) and 1993 (30). The authors suggest that their total is probably an underestimate of the true number of cases; indeed, whether judicial case and media reports are a reliable measure of the actual number of cases prosecuted is very likely a question that cannot be answered. In terms of the trends in numbers of cases prosecuted, whether there are fewer prosecutions or merely less media coverage of the prosecutions, perhaps as a result of declining sensational impact of such stories, also is not known. But what this study indicates is that, in a significant portion of the criminal prosecutions (at least 24 percent), defendants receive significant jail time (in 135 cases with minimum sentences of less than life, the median sentence was six years) for having engaged in conduct that did not involve any risk of HIV transmission.

The Lazzarini study and its valuable web site counterpart, the HIV Criminal Law Project,[20] document that every state has criminal laws adequate to prosecute any HIV-infected person who, aware of his or her infection, engages in sexual activity, shares hypodermic needles, or otherwise puts others at risk for infection. This should come as no surprise, because Congress required states to certify as much in order to receive funding under the Ryan White Comprehensive AIDS Resources Emergency (CARE) Act as enacted in 1990.[21] Significantly, however, the Lazzarini study found "no systematic enforcement of HIV exposure laws" and concluded that a criminal prosecution is the result of "the accident of being caught and brought to the attention of a willing prosecutor." The study, however, does not take account of race or class as factors that influence the "accidental" nature of law enforcement in this area. The study also concludes that, at this point, criminal prosecutions have not been shown to reduce HIV transmission. Of course, advocates of a criminal law response to the epidemic might respond by pointing out that deterrence would increase with more effective and systematic enforcement, and that the rate of HIV transmission would be even higher if there were no prosecutions.

One way that what Lazzarini called "the accident of being caught" can take place is when the possessor of confidential HIV information is authorized by law to disclose that information to a third party who is at risk for infection. Unlike the Prevention for Positives initiative, which relies on patients' cooperation, partner notification in a number of states can take place without a patient's consent. In fact, it can take place over the explicit objection of the patient. The law of confidentiality, which usually applies to health information, has been modified to allow such disclosure in many circumstances. On the federal level, the Health Insurance Portability and Access Act (HIPAA) regulations include a broad general exception to confidentiality in the partner notification context by authorizing the disclosure of so-called protected health information to a "person who may have been exposed to a communicable disease or may otherwise be at risk of contracting or spreading a disease or condition, if the covered entity or public health authority is authorized by law to notify such person."[22] In particular, spouses of the HIV infected, presumed to be unaware of the risk of HIV infection and thus particularly vulnerable, have been the subjects of protective legislation on both the federal and state levels. The 1996 amendments to the CARE Act, for example, included a spousal notification requirement.[23] To be eligible for CARE Act funding, states must take "administrative or legislative action to require that a good faith effort" is made to notify the spouse of a known HIV-infected patient of the spouse's potential exposure to HIV. Illinois, New York, and Texas, for example, authorize non-consensual disclosure of HIV status to the patient's spouse.[24] For veterans who receive healthcare services from the Veterans Administration, spousal notification of HIV infection is permitted, although it is not mandatory.[25] Some legislatures are more careful than others to make the concept of "spouse" equivalent with "at actual (past or future) risk." In contrast, Congress took an expansive view of the "spouse at risk" by defining that term to include any "marriage partner" of the HIV-infected patient at any time within the 10-year period prior to diagnosis. Many states, however, authorize the disclosure of HIV information that would otherwise be confidential not just to spouses, but to non-spousal sex or needle-sharing partners.[26]

Case law on third-party notification does not exist in all jurisdictions, but the outcome in the few reported cases is dependent on the statutory and common law standards that vary from state to state. In *N.O.L. v. District of Columbia*, for example, a husband's emotional distress claim against the hospital that failed to disclose his wife's HIV status was held to be barred by a confidentiality statute prohibiting disclosure of reportable diseases.[27] But in *Chizmar v. Mackie*, disclosure of an HIV test result that turned out to be a false positive to the patient's husband was held to be proper and not a basis for suit.[28] Often, in the absence of a statutory standard, general tort law principles favor disclosure of information in circumstances in which the disclosure is intended to prevent the commission of a future crime. Because knowing exposure to HIV is criminal in all jurisdictions, this principle would serve as a defense against a claim of invasion of privacy.[29] But despite the laws that authorize disclosure to third parties at risk, without authorization from the patient, the extent to which partner notification actually takes place may vary significantly from jurisdiction to jurisdiction.

Although it is reasonable to suppose that clinicians will encounter situations in which a patient withholds consent for partner notification yet admits behavior that has placed or will place a known partner at risk for HIV infection, the CDC offers no specific guidance on how that situation might be handled. While acknowledging that some health departments require the reporting of any partner at risk, the CDC simply advises that clinicians should "know and comply with" any state law or health department partner notification laws.[30] But this is not much guidance for clinicians in jurisdictions where the disclosure is discretionary, not mandatory. Furthermore, disclosure of a patient's HIV status to a partner without the patient's consent, even without disclosure of the patient's identity, risks undermining the therapeutic relationship. It may also damage the individual or institutional careprovider's reputation for commitment to patients' confidentiality more widely in the community, thus making patients' cooperation with partner notification efforts in the future less likely.

In contrast to laws and regulations that authorize partner notification without the patient's consent, the CDC's approach to partner notification relies explicitly on patients' cooperation. The HIV-infected patient identifies the contact who was or is at risk for infection. When the patient identifies the contact, at a time when the patient was aware of his or her HIV infection, however, the patient is admitting a criminal offense. In many jurisdictions that offense is a felony, for which consequences may be severe. The Lazzarini study reports that the average minimum sentence the patient would receive upon conviction, assuming it is less than a life sentence, is 14.3 years. Unless covered by an applicable evidentiary privilege or statutory protection, any record of the information provided by the patient about the contact might later be used in a criminal prosecution as evidence. Thus, patients' cooperation in the CDC's PCRS context poses an entirely different criminal prosecution risk than does partner notification activities undertaken at the point when a patient first tests positive. In the latter circumstance, the patient's identification of past contacts would not pose the risk of criminal prosecution, because, at the time of the contact, the patient was not aware or his or her HIV infection.

Although the CDC's reliance on patients' cooperation makes the disclosure of partners to clinic staff consensual, provision of information regarding the criminal law implications of identifying the partner at past or future risk is not required in obtaining the patient's cooperation. On that account, the consent of the patient may be invalid. If an *informed* consent were required prior to the patient's disclosure of a partner in a clinical setting, there would be little question that the patient should be informed about and understand the potential criminal law implications of the disclosure.

Perhaps the authors of the CDC's Prevention for Positives guidelines were unaware of this issue. Perhaps it is an issue that the CDC would rather not introduce into the discussion. After all, who would cooperate with the partner notification process with awareness of the criminal law implications? In its blueprint for Prevention for Positives, the CDC simply fails to mention, yet alone discuss, this significant difficulty with its latest initiative for HIV-infected patients.

While it can be said that partner notification is a way that an individual with HIV "gets caught" for having committed the offense of knowing (or intentional) transmission, perhaps primarily by their own doing, what remains in Lazzarini's formulation is for that person to be "brought to the attention" of law enforcement authorities. In regard to the Prevention for Positives initiative, the patient's HIV information is disclosed to a third party (the past or current partner) over whom neither the clinical staff, public health officials, nor the patient himself or herself has any control. Even without being told who the source patient was, the notified partner may be able to infer with ease that individual's identity. Although the notified contact might appreciate the patient's act of solicitude, the contact may as likely respond angrily and have powerful motives to invoke the criminal law against the patient. The partner may, for example, seek retribution, particularly in the case where the partner learns of his or her own HIV infection as a result of the notification and believes that the patient was the reckless or even intentional source of his or her infection. Or the partner may feel an altruistic desire to deter or prevent the patient, or others, from engaging in risk behaviors involving another partner in the future. Pursuing the criminal option may entail nothing more than telephoning local police or prosecutors. In jurisdictions that allow the filing of private criminal complaints, the process can be initiated directly by the notified contact (even then, many jurisdictions allow the prosecutor's office to veto private complaints). Ironically, in situations in which the patient's identity is known to the notified contact, as is the case under many laws that authorize disclosure of the HIV status of sexual assault defendants to complainants, the law often requires that the complainant not further disclose that information. Of course, the complainant may have his or her own self-interest in not disclosing, but in reality such confidentiality provisions may be largely unenforceable. In terms of partner notification, in contrast, the identity of the contact is not directly disclosed, and thus the laws do not impose any confidentiality duty on the notified contact. Even if they did, it is not clear how such confidentiality standards could be enforced. Moreover, once one criminal complaint is made and publicized, including the fact of the defendant's HIV infection, other contacts of the defendant may come forward, resulting in additional charges against the defendant. In early 2003, for example, Adam Musser was charged in the first of four separate cases involving knowingly transmitting HIV in the Iowa City, Iowa, area. He was subsequently convicted in all four cases and sentenced to 25 years in each.[31] Three of the cases involved former sexual partners who apparently came forward after learning of Musser's HIV status from publicity resulting from his initial arrest. One of the complainants, who tested HIV positive after having sexual contact with Musser, appeared on local television to encourage additional complainants to contact prosecutors.[32]

While there would appear to be no limits on subsequent disclosure by the notified contact, there may nevertheless be limitations on law enforcement access to confidential information about the patient's HIV status and behavior involving a risk of HIV transmission. One factor contributing to a prosecutor's willingness to bring a case against a patient with HIV is the degree of likelihood of conviction, and that question turns on the nature of readily available evidence of the crime. The precise elements of HIV transmission offenses may vary somewhat from jurisdiction to jurisdiction, but in general, a complainant's statement that the potential defendant had, for example, unprotected sexual contact on a specific date establishes at least one element of the offense. In addition to evidence of that element, all a prosecutor would need, under most such laws, is evidence that on that date, the defendant knew he or she was infected with HIV and knew that his or her behavior posed a risk of transmission. What better way to obtain that evidence than from records of HIV testing and counseling, perhaps from a private clinic's files or those of other careproviders, or from a local or state health department?

Although criminal prosecutions of individuals with HIV are relatively rare, concerns about the use of confidential healthcare or public health information in such prosecutions are by no means hypothetical. Several such cases have been reported, contrary to the finding of the Lazzarini study.[33] In some cases, confidential HIV information has been disclosed directly from public health officials to law enforcement. In 1992, in the first reported case of this sort, *State v. Stark*,[34] the Court of Appeals of Washington affirmed Calvin Stark's 10-year sentence upon conviction of intentionally exposing his sexual partners. In that case, Stark was alleged not to have complied with a civil cease-and-desist order issued by the county public health authority, and as a result the county health officer contacted the county prosecutor to seek enforcement of that order by way of a confidential civil proceeding resulting in civil commitment, as then authorized by Washington State law. The prosecutor, however, used the information provided by the public health officer concerning Stark's HIV status and history of counseling to commence a public criminal prosecution and obtain Stark's conviction and sentence. Treating the public health official's disclosure as though it was made for criminal enforcement purposes, the Court of Appeals ruled that although the applicable Washington statute did not explicitly authorize disclosure of confidential HIV public health information to prosecutors for criminal enforcement purposes, that disclosure was impliedly authorized by the legislature's enactment of the criminal HIV intentional exposure statute. The ruling sets no limits on when or under what circumstances confidential public health information can be disclosed from public health to law enforcement authorities. Apparently, under *State v. Stark*, any disclosure intended to result in enforcement of the criminal statute is permissible. Such information sharing takes other forms as well. In another case involving public health authorities' collaboration with law enforcement, the Supreme Court of South Carolina affirmed a conviction based on evidence of the defendant's HIV status that the prosecutor obtained by court order from the state health department.[35] In that case, "John Doe" was charged with knowingly exposing a sexual partner to HIV in violation of a state statute. The state health department agreed that there was a "compelling need" for its disclosure of HIV test results and records indicating that the defendant had acknowledged receiving HIV counseling, and thus that issue was not in dispute. The court's holding, however, that the records of test results could be admitted into evidence as "business records" (a category of evidence also applicable to government records, in which the matters set forth in those records can be taken as true even without live witness testimony), and that the state need not establish any chain of custody for them, significantly eased the evidentiary burden on the prosecution.

In the context of criminal law enforcement, federal or state confidentiality statutes offer little if any protection in most circumstances. Federal healthcare confidentiality standards, as set forth in the Health Insurance Portability and Access Act (HIPAA) regulations, provide a broad exception for law enforcement access to so-called protected health information (PHI).[36] Covered entities may disclose PHI to federal, state, or local law enforcement officials in compliance not only with a court order or court-ordered warrant, but also to comply with "an administrative request, including an administrative subpoena or summons, a civil or an authorized investigative demand, or similar process authorized under law," provided that the information sought is "relevant and material to a legitimate law enforcement inquiry." Disclosure of PHI under this provision requires neither the patient's authorization nor notice to the patient providing an opportunity to agree or object. Whether or not the covered entity receiving the "request" or "demand" for PHI could challenge its relevance or materiality, or the "legitimacy" of the inquiry, the entity may have little incentive to do so.

Some states have a similar lack of confidentiality for HIV information sought for law enforcement purposes. In one such case, *Weaver v. State*,[37] the Court of Appeals of Arkansas affirmed three concurrent 30-year sentences for violation of an Arkansas statute that prohibited exposing another person to HIV. The conviction was based on the defendant's medical records, which the prosecutor obtained from the county health department by issuing an investigative subpoena, which, under state law, did not even require court approval. The subpoena was issued by the prosecutor to investigate "reports that [Weaver] had exposed others to the HIV virus" in violation of state law. The court of appeals held that the prosecutor's use of the investigative subpoena to obtain medical records from the health department was proper as authorized by statute, and that a judicially issued search warrant based on probable cause was not required.

State general health information or HIV-specific confidentiality laws frequently include exceptions allowing law enforcement access.[38] Or, even when such authorization is not explicit, the courts have found such authorization implicit in the statutes. The Supreme Court of Missouri affirmed the convictions of two defendants, Charles Mahan and Sean Sykes, who were prosecuted for exposing their sex partners to HIV.[39] Mahan received a sentence of five years; Sykes was given two consecutive five-year terms. The state supreme court rejected their challenges to their convictions, which were based on municipal health department records of their HIV test results, explaining that a "prosecutor who is contemplating bringing charges against someone under [the Missouri statute] needs to know the HIV status of that individual."

State statutes frequently allow access to confidential HIV information by court order. In some jurisdictions, the law does not define the circumstances under which a request for a court order should be granted.[40] In many states, however, the release of HIV information can be ordered by a court only upon a showing of a "compelling need,"[41] a standard that a criminal investigation or prosecution is likely to meet.[42] The few reported cases rely on interpretations of these state laws. In *People v. Hawkrigg*, for example, a local court in New York State held that absent a statutory exception or the patient's waiver of the statutory right, it is improper to admit medical records before a grand jury.[43] Nevertheless, the court concluded that the defendant's disclosure of HIV status to sexual partners constituted a waiver of the confidentiality right. Even when a prosecutor fails to comply with statutory confidentiality standards, however, that violation of the law may be irrelevant to a successful prosecution. In *State v. Gonzalez*,[44] the Ohio Court of Appeal affirmed the conviction under a failure to disclose statute, resulting in a sentence of 16 years. The court concluded that the prosecutor's failure to obtain court authorization on a "compelling need" basis to disclose the HIV information violated the state's HIV confidentiality statute. That statutory violation, however, was deemed "harmless error," given the other evidence of the defendant's HIV status. In one of the few cases to preserve patients' confidentiality, *State v. J.E.*, a New Jersey court concluded that, without statutory authorization for disclosure of the defendant's HIV information to the complainant in a sexual assault case, the defendant's interest in confidentiality of the physician-patient relationship outweighed the need for disclosure.[45] That case, however, turned on the fact that eight months had passed since the alleged assault, and thus the complainant's own HIV antibody tests would determine whether he or she was infected with HIV.

The Fourth Amendment requires that prosecutors must obtain a search warrant based on a neutral and impartial judge's finding of probable cause that a crime has been committed (in this case, knowing exposure to HIV) and that evidence of the crime (proof of the suspect's knowledge of his or her HIV infection) is to be found in the location specified in the warrant (the suspect's HIV testing and counseling records) at the time of the search. Thus, in very few cases does the Fourth Amendment's probable cause requirement pose an impediment to law enforcement demands for confidential information.

The Supreme Court's recent Fourth Amendment ruling in the context of hospital records, *Ferguson v. City of Charleston*, has little relevance to the confidentiality of HIV information sought for law enforcement purposes.[46] The Court held that the Fourth Amendment prohibits a state hospital's program of taking urine samples from pregnant women suspected of illegal drug use for the undisclosed purpose of giving the test results to criminal prosecutors. What made the underlying urine testing a "search" for Fourth Amendment purposes was the predetermined plan of disclosure for law enforcement purposes. The Court did not address the issue of a law enforcement demand, authorized under state law, for records made by health agencies in the ordinary course of their activities.[47] Furthermore, the precedent applies only to government agencies' disclosures, not those of private, nongovernmental hospitals or clinics. Thus, even if a nongovernmental clinic, for example, were to seek out HIV information for the primary but undisclosed purpose of turning it over to prosecutors, the Fourth Amendment would not be implicated. Based on a notified contact's complaint of sexual contact without disclosure of HIV status, on the other hand, prosecutors may have little difficulty in obtaining a valid search warrant.[48] Only if constrained by a state constitutional or statutory prohibition on the use of such information will a prosecutor's search for and use of the resulting evidence be limited.[49] Such constraints appear to be rare.[50]

The Fifth Amendment protects individuals from being compelled by the government to answer questions that may tend to incriminate them. But when patients participate in partner notification activities, the participation is voluntary, not compulsory, and thus the right against self-incrimination would not apply. The Fifth Amendment privilege against self-incrimination also offers only limited protection against the forced disclosure of confidential health information for law enforcement purposes.[51] But, in most cases, law enforcement officials seek the information not from records in the patient's possession, but from those in the possession of a corporate or governmental entity, such as a clinic or other careprovider or a public health agency. The patient would have no Fifth Amendment privilege against production of records that are not in his or her personal possession, nor could the custodian of the records assert the privilege on the patient's behalf.[52] The custodian of the records could, however, assert that they are protected by a physician-patient or similar privilege, but the existence and scope of such a privilege would be defined by state law and thus may vary from state to state.[53] Agencies involved in partner notification and similar activities should consider, as a matter of their own professional ethics, how they will respond in the event that law enforcement officials attempt to obtain records pertaining to their patients.

Some advocates for a law enforcement response to the epidemic would argue that exceptions to confidentiality for criminal law enforcement purposes are appropriate. Those who knowingly violate the law by placing others in deadly danger, they would argue, should lose its protection. That view, however, collides directly with the premise of the CDC's Prevention for Positives initiative. After all, many of the patients participating in the Prevention for Positives initiative are admitting the commission of criminal offenses, thus risking prosecution, yet the CDC pins its hopes for success of its program on their cooperation. Not only do the criminal laws and lack of confidentiality for incriminating evidence provide a potent disincentive for cooperation, in the event that a patient involved in Prevention for Positives is prosecuted, the nature of the risks involved in participating will be widely and rapidly publicized.

There are several ways to respond to these potential problems both through policy and law reform. First, if the CDC wants people with HIV to incriminate themselves in the process of preventing new infections, the information they provide should not be available to law enforcement for criminal prosecution. This can be accomplished simply by closing the significant confidentiality loopholes that currently exist in many states. For example, Texas has addressed this problem in part by with a statute mandating that "partner names" can be used exclusively for public health investigation and notification, not for law enforcement.[54] This is an important first step, but it does not help when a prosecution is based not on information directly obtained from partner notification activities, but from information that reaches law enforcement indirectly, as is the case when the notified contact seeks a criminal prosecution and law enforcement authorities look to a source other than the partner notification records for confirming evidence of the potential defendant's test result and counseling records. New York's partner notification program, on the other hand, includes broad confidentiality standards and a public pledge on the department of health's web site that the "Department will NOT disclose this information [about an HIV-infected patient] to other government or private agencies like the . . . police."[55] At least one commentator has recommended limitations on evidence to be used in HIV criminal prosecutions in general, so that confidential medical records are not used.[56] This outcome might depend entirely on a prosecutor's exercise of discretion in declining to prosecute cases based on such medical records. Other commentators have recommended that public health agencies avoid direct collaboration with law enforcement.[57] These are all potential means of remedying the problem; none are mentioned, yet alone recommended, by the CDC.

Putting aside the general and entirely legitimate question of whether someone with HIV should ever be prosecuted for an HIV transmission offense,[58] we should confront directly the more specific question of whether anyone with HIV who cooperates with authorities in identifying their partners should ever be prosecuted. If the government wants information in the nature of an admission of a crime, and cannot ensure the confidentiality of that information, then why should the patient not receive immunity from prosecution for providing it? Indeed, an offer of immunity would serve as a powerful incentive for individuals to identify contacts, if the patient knows that once the contact is identified, then no resulting complaint from the named contact will result in prosecution. The granting of what is called "use and derivative use" immunity—that is, no prosecution could use information provided by the patient, or evidence derived directly or indirectly from the information provided by the patient—would accomplish this purpose.[59] Such a practice also is fair. If an individual discloses her or his HIV status to a contact or former contact, she or he should at least have the assurance that the disclosure will not result in a criminal prosecution. On a practical level, public health officials do not have the authority to grant immunity from prosecution. Nevertheless, public health officials are in the position to negotiate with local prosecutors regarding their exercise of prosecutorial discretion and adopt immunity policies in favor of encouraging cooperation from persons with HIV.

In the past, the CDC has not been shy about recommending policies and legal reforms at the state or local levels that will, in the CDC's view, serve the public health.[60] In the case of Prevention for Positives, however, the CDC has failed to address critical issues that may affect the success of the initiative. Moreover, the initiative unfairly puts participating patients at risk for criminal prosecution, particularly at a time when public frustration with the seemingly intractable nature of the epidemic may make prosecution an attractive official response. The CDC's silence on this issue also results in a lack of guidance for clinicians and public health officials involved in implementing the initiative at the local level on the potentially thorny ethical and legal questions regarding their relationship with criminal law enforcement authorities. To date, there apparently have not been prosecutions directly resulting from increased partner notification activities under Prevention for Positives. But if such prosecutions take place, the adverse impact on the success of the initiative could be enormous.

ACKNOWLEDGMENT

The author thanks Peter Goldberger and Catherine Hanssens for their valuable comments on earlier drafts of this article.

NOTES

1. CDC, "Advancing HIV Prevention: New Strategies for a Changing Epidemic—United States, 2003," *Morbidity and Mortality Weekly Report* 52, no. 15 (2003): 329-32.

2. N.Y. Comp. Codes R. & Regs. tit. 10, § 63.4(b) (West 2001) *www.health.state.ny.us/nysdoh/rfa/hiv/full63.htm* (requiring physicians to notify known contacts, including spouses, of patients diagnosed with HIV and to report to health commissioner the identity of known contacts for partner notification purposes).

3. A.M.J. Wensing et al., "Analysis from More than 1600 Newly Diagnosed Patients with HIV from 17 European Countries Shows that 10% of the Patients Carry Primary Drug Resistance: The CATCH-Study," (abstract of the International AIDS Society *www.iasociety.org/abstract/show.asp?abstract_id=11112*).

4. D.H. Ciccarone et al., "Sex Without Disclosure of Positive HIV Serostatus in a US Probability Sample of Persons Receiving Medical Care for HIV Infection," *American Journal of Public Health* 93, no. 6 (2003): 949-54 (finding 13 percent of serodiscordant partnerships involved unprotected anal or vaginal sex without disclosure).

5. CDC, "Incorporating HIV Prevention into the Medical Care of Persons Living with HIV," *Morbidity and Mortality Weekly Report* 52, no. RR-12 (2003): 1-24.

6. See note 5 above, p. 15.

7. P.J. Kissinger et al., "Partner Notification for HIV and Syphilis: Effects on Sexual Behaviors and Relationship Stability," *Sexually Transmitted Diseases* (January 2003): 75-82.

8. See note 7 above, p. 81.

9. R. Doughty, "The Confidentiality of HIV-Related Information: Responding to the Resurgence of Aggressive Public Health Interventions in the AIDS Epidemic," *California Law Review* 82 (1994); 111-84, pp. 167-75.

10. C. Kightlinger, "Privacy vs. Protection: Lack of HIV Disclosure Places Some at Risk," *Indianapolis Star,* 17 July 2003.

11. B. Denizet-Lewis, "Double Lives on the Down Low," *New York Times Magazine,* 3 August 2003.

12. E. Wellington, "A Coming Out," *Philadelphia Inquirer,* 15 July 2003.

13. J. Tuohy and D. Penner, "Privacy Law Hurt Plasma Case," *Indianapolis Star,* 19 July 2003 (quoting prosecutor's comment that the delay allegedly caused by the HIV confidentiality law was "ridiculous" and that "privacy concerns may have put the public at risk").

14. J. Van Derbeken, "Ex-S.F. Official Jailed on HIV Charge," *San Francisco Chronicle,* 18 September 2003.

15. S. Russell, "Shift in AIDS Prevention Strategy: Emphasis Now on Accountability of Those Infected," *San Francisco Chronicle,* 21 September 2003.

16. J. Van Derbeken, "HIV Transmission Case Tossed Out," *San Francisco Chronicle,* 10 December 2003 (referring to prosecutors' lament that "the state Legislature set the bar high on the law so that someone could not be prosecuted simply for withholding his or her HIV status from a partner").

17. H. Markel, "HIV Secrecy Is Proving Deadly," *New York Times,* 25 November 2003.

18. R. Klitzman and R. Bayer, *Mortal Secrets: Truth and Lies in the Age of AIDS* (Baltimore, Md.: Johns Hopkins University Press, 2003).

19. Z. Lazzarini et al., "Evaluating the Impact of Criminal Laws on HIV Risk Behavior," *Journal of Law, Medicine & Ethics* 30 (2002): 239-53; see also S.J. Bray, "Criminal Prosecutions for HIV Exposure: Overview and Analysis," *Yale University Center for Interdisciplinary Research on AIDS* 3, no. 1 (2003) (available from HIV Criminal Law Project, *www.HIV criminallaw.org*).

20. HIV Criminal Law Project, *www.HIV*

criminallaw.org.

21. 42 U.S.C. § 300ff-47, *repealed by* Ryan White CARE Act Amendments of 2000, Pub. L. No. 106-345, § 301(a), 2000 U.S.C.C.A.N. (114 Stat.) 1319, 1345.

22. 45 C.F.R. § 164.512(b)(1)(iv) (2003).

23. 42 U.S.C. § 300ff-27a.

24. 410 Ill. Comp. Stat. Ann. 305/9(a) (West 1997 & Supp. 2004) (authorizing physician disclosure to spouse if spouse is not otherwise informed); N.Y. Pub. Health Law §§ 2780, 2782 (West 2002) (authorizing physician disclosure to spouse); Tex. Health & Safety Code Ann. § 81.103(7) (West 2001) (same).

25. 38 U.S.C. § 7332(f).

26. E.g., Cal. Health & Safety Code Ann. § 121015 (West 1996) (exception to confidentiality for physicians' disclosure of HIV test result to person reasonably believed to be the sex partner of the patient); N.Y. Pub. Health Law §§ 2780, 2782 (West 2002) (authorizing physician's disclosure to spouse, or sex or needle-sharing partner); S.C. Code Ann. § 44-29-146 (physicians and state agencies exempt from liability for disclosure to spouse or other known contact).

27. 674 A.2d 498 (D.C. 1996).

28. 896 P.2d 196 (Alaska 1995).

29. Restatement (Second) of Torts § 595, Comment g (1977) (general privilege to report that "another intends to . . . commit some . . . serious crime against a third person"); ibid. § 652G (privilege applies to invasion of privacy tort). See also Bartnicki v. Vopper, 532 U.S. 514, 539 (2001) (Souter, J., concurring) ("Where publication of private information constitutes a wrongful act, the law recognizes a privilege allowing the reporting of threats to public safety").

30. See note 5 above, p. 16.

31. "Man Found Guilty on 4th HIV Count," *Iowa City Press-Citizen,* 13 April 2004.

32. "Woman Who Contracted HIV Speaks," 13 WHO-TV (Des Moines, Iowa), 17 May 2004, *www.whotv.com/global/story.asp?s=1874442.*

33. Z. Lazzarini et al., "Evaluating the Impact of Criminal Laws on HIV Risk Behavior," *Journal of Law, Medicine & Ethics* 30 (2002): 239-253 (finding no reported cases involving disclosure of public health data to law enforcement officials).

34. 832 P.2d 109 (Wash. Ct. App. 1992).

35. Department of Health and Environmental Control v. Doe, 565 S.E.2d 293 (S.C. 2002).

36. 45 C.F.R. § 164.512(f) (2003).

37. 990 S.W.2d 572 (Ark. Ct. App. 1999).

38. E.g., N.J. Rev. Stat. § 26:5C-9(a), (b) (West 1996) ("criminal investigation" exception to HIV confidentiality).

39. State v. Mahan, 971 S.W.2d 307 (Mo. 1998).

40. E.g., Va. Code Ann. § 32.1-36.1 (Matthew Bender 2004) (allowing access by "court order").

41. E.g., Cal. Health & Safety Code Ann. § 120292(a)(2) (West Supp. 2004) (judicial order required for disclosure of confidential HIV information in criminal proceeding); Fla. Stat. Ann. § 381.004(3)(e) (West Supp. 2004) ("compelling need" required for judicial authorization of disclosure of or access to confidential HIV information); N.Y. Pub. Health Law § 2785 (West 2002) (same); Pa. Stat. Ann. tit. 35, § 7608 (West 2003) (same).

42. Department of Health and Environmental Control v. Doe, 565 S.E.2d 293 (S.C. 2002) (public health agency conceded "compelling need" for its disclosure of HIV information for law enforcement purpose); In re Gribetz, 605 N.Y.S.2d 834 (Rockland County Ct. 1994) (disclosure of defendant's HIV information to provide evidence of crime); People v. Anonymous, 582 N.Y.S.2d 350 (Monroe County Ct. 1992) (same); see also Community Healthcare Centerone, Inc. v. Florida, 852 So. 2d 322 (Fla. Dist. Ct. App. 2003) (allowing prosecutor's subpoena for HIV patient records in Medicaid fraud investigation on basis that criminal investigation is a "compelling need" justifying invasion of patients' privacy rights), appeal denied, 868 So. 2d 522 (Fla. 2004).

43. 525 N.Y.S.2d 752 (Suffolk County 1988).

44. 796 N.E.2d 12 (Ohio Ct. App. 2003).

45. 606 A.2d 1160 (N.J. Super. Ct. 1992).

46. 532 U.S. 67, 78 (2001) ("The reasonable expectation of privacy enjoyed by the typical patient undergoing diagnostic tests in a hospital is that the results of those tests will not be shared with nonmedical personnel without her consent.").

47. The reliance on *Ferguson v. City of Charleston by Lazzarini et al.,* see note 33 above, for the principle that "information gathered for health purposes should not be used by law enforcement" is therefore misplaced.

48. In re Gribetz, 605 N.Y.S.2d 834 (Rockland County Ct. 1994) (disclosure of defendant's HIV information to provide evidence of crime); People v. Anonymous, 582 N.Y.S.2d 350 (Monroe County Ct. 1992) (same).

49. See, e.g., 28 C.F.R. §§ 59.1-59.6 (2004) (self-imposed restrictions on issuance of federal search warrants for professional records that implicate the privacy rights of third parties).

50. See, e.g., Limbaugh v. Florida, No. 4D03-4973, 2004 WL 2238978, 2004 Fla. App. LEXIS 14653 (Fla. Dist. Ct. App. Oct. 6, 2004) (state's seizure of medical records pursuant to validly issued search warrant is not limited by state constitutional right to privacy).

51. United States v. Hubbell, 530 U.S. 27 (2000).

52. Braswell v. United States, 487 U.S. 99 (1988); Rogers v. United States, 340 U.S. 367 (1951).

53. See Northwestern Memorial Hosp. v. Ashcroft, 362 F.3d 923 (7th Cir. 2004) (discussing Illinois medical record privilege law, asserted by hospital on behalf of its patients, in context of a federal government subpoena for hospital records in civil litigation).

54. Tex. Health & Safety Code Ann. § 81.051(c) (West 2001).

55. New York State Department of Health, "HIV Reporting and Partner Notification: What You Need to Know About the Law," *www.health.state.ny.us/nysdoh.hivaids/hivpartner/qanda.htm.*

56. D.L McColgin, *Criminal Law,* in *AIDS and the Law* § 7.1, ed. D.W. Webber (New York: Wiley, 1997), 264-65.

57. J.G. Hodge and L.O. Gostin, "Handling Cases of Willful Exposure Through HIV Partner Counseling and Referral Services," *Women's Rights Law Reporter* 23, no. 1 (2001): 45-62.

58. Although it is not relevant to the thesis of this article, it should be noted that taking the position that persons with HIV infection have a moral and ethical duty to avoid transmitting HIV to others does not compel the conclusion that they should be criminally prosecuted for doing so. For an detailed review of this issue, see L.E. Wolf and R. Vezina, "Crime and Punishment: Is There a Role for Criminal Law in HIV Prevention Policy?" *Whittier Law Review* 25 (2004): 821-86.

59. This grant of immunity is more limited than "transactional" immunity, which provides complete immunity for the offense to which the patient's information relates. See Kastigar v. United States, 406 U.S. 441 (1972).

60. For an example of the CDC's role in recommending law reforms at the state level, see Model State Public Health Privacy Law, *http://www.critpath.org/msphpa/privacy.htm.*

[11]

Whose Problem Is It Anyway? Women Prisoners and HIV/AIDS

Barbara H. Zaitzow

Abstract: *One of the pressing public health concerns facing correctional systems today is HIV/AIDS. Although no segment of the incarcerated population is immune to this infection, an alarming number of female inmates have been shown to test positive for HIV at higher rates than male inmates. As women in prison have different treatment needs and problems than their male counterparts, the impact of such inmates on correctional health care services represents a potentially critical issue confronting correctional managers and correctional health service administrators. This article highlights the need for the corrections community to address the special needs of female inmates infected with the HIV/AIDS virus and to acknowledge the impact of HIV/AIDS on all imprisoned women in the United States.*

A rising tide of infectious diseases in the nation has affected jails and prisons as infected inmates enter correctional systems. Administrators are concerned about the potential spread of infectious diseases in their facilities due to close living arrangements in often overcrowded conditions, the cost of medical care, and the potential spread of such diseases to a community upon an inmate's release. In addition to tuberculosis (TB), one of the pressing public health concerns facing correctional systems today is HIV/AIDS.

Although no segment of the incarcerated population is immune to this infection, certain populations show a higher frequency of HIV infection. Lachance-McCullough, Tesoriero, Sorin, and Stern (1994) noted, "Minorities are disproportionately impacted by the AIDS epidemic. In fact, the sociodemographics of HIV/AIDS look strikingly similar to the sociodemographics of American prisons" (p. 200). Olivero (1992) stated, "Most of those infected in prison are disproportionately members of minority groups; they tend to be Black and Hispanic" (p. 50). In addition, HIV cases in prison also show a difference by gender. According to a 1997 study by the Department of Justice, male HIV cases far outnumbered those of females (20,200 compared to 2,200), but the numbers are misleading because there are so many more male prisoners. When computed as a percentage of the total population in custody, 2.2% of the male inmates and 3.5% of the female inmates were HIV positive. The percentage of HIV-positive women has been higher than the male percentage in every year since 1991 (Maruschak, 1999). Numerous other studies support this trend. The purpose of this article is to explore the policy ramifications of various options designed to minimize the impact of HIV/AIDS on imprisoned women in the United States.

CHARACTERISTICS OF FEMALE OFFENDERS

Although women comprise only a small proportion of the total incarcerated population in the United States today, the growing numbers of women being sent to prison have increased, but the increase is disproportionate to their involvement in serious crime. Women imprisoned in state and federal correctional institutions throughout the United States totaled 84,427 (with 3,600 holdbacks for lack of beds) at year-end 1998, increasing at a faster rate during 1997 and 1998 than did male inmates. Overall, the rate of growth for female prison inmates exceeded that for males for each of the past 14 years. From 1990 to 1996, the male population increased by 51%, and the female population gained by 73%. Despite the fact that female prisoner population growth outpaced that of males, females comprise less than 7% of the imprisoned offenders (Gilliard, 1999, p. 4).

Like their male counterparts, female inmates are young (about two thirds are younger than 34 years old), minority-group members (more than 60%), unmarried (more than 80%), undereducated (about 40% were not high school graduates), and underemployed (Beck & Mumola, 1999). Unlike men, large majorities are unmarried, mothers of children younger than 18, and daughters who had grown up in homes without both parents present. Moreover, a distinguishing characteristic of incarcerated females is their significantly increased likelihood of having survived sexual and/or physical violence, particularly by a male relative or intimate partner (Fletcher, Rolison, & Moon, 1993; Sargent, Marcus-Mendoza, & Yu, 1993). Research also shows that women in prison have experienced unusually high rates of extremely abusive "discipline" from parents, involvement in drugs, and prostitution, whether they were imprisoned for these crimes or not (Harlow, 1999).

As noted in Harlow's (1999) Survey of Inmates of State Correctional Facilities (SISCF), most of the women in prison were convicted for a nonviolent offense and had only nonviolent offenses as prior convictions. The women who were serving a sentence for a violent crime were most likely to have victimized a relative, an intimate (husband, ex-husband, boyfriend), or some other acquaintance. In fact, the women in prison were more likely to have committed their violent offense against someone close to them than were their male counterparts (36% to 16%). The tendency for violent crimes by women, including homicides, to have been committed against intimates and relatives (nearly 50% of the cases) may be the result of women responding to a history of physical and psychological abuse by that relative or intimate. Several studies have suggested that many women in prison for violent crimes are serving sentences for killing abusive husbands, ex-husbands, or boyfriends (see Moyer, 1993; Owen & Bloom, 1995, for reviews of the studies). The SISCF did not address this point specifically, but it did find that more women inmates (43%) than men (12%) reported having been physically or sexually abused before their current incarceration.

Whether as direct consequence of abuse or other contributing factors, female inmates may suffer from a loss of self-respect, hiding their pain in substance abuse (McKinney, 1994). A significant number of female inmates report having substance abuse problems. Before their incarceration, women prisoners used more drugs and used those drugs more frequently than did men in prison. Women prisoners are also more likely to report that they were under the influence of drugs at the time of their current offense and to claim that they committed the offense to obtain money to buy drugs (Greenfeld & Snell, 1999).

The picture that emerges of the female inmate is troubling. Female criminal behavior appears to be the product of continuing social problems—the impact of physical and emotional abuse and extreme disadvantage, exacerbated by economic problems as well as drug and alcohol abuse.

MEDICAL SERVICES FOR WOMEN IN PRISON

Health services delivery within prisons has been increasingly strained over the past decade, resulting primarily from (a) more inmates coming into the prisons and (b) new inmates being less healthy than their counterparts of just a decade ago. Although research shows that during the past two decades medical services for incarcerated women improved (Lillis, 1994), the implementation of innovative in-house medical treatment for women has not kept pace with the diverse needs of the ever-increasing population.

Women often require more medical attention than men, and women's prisons must deal with a greater demand for adequate health care. In particular, women experience health problems related to their reproductive systems, especially true of those who are pregnant and require prenatal care when they enter prison. A host of other problems related to health care exists in women's prisons, including the availability of specific medications. Because women's prisons are relatively small institutions, policy makers believe that installing extensive medical services in the prison cannot be justified. Consequently, women inmates who require greater medical attention than the prison provides must be transported to hospitals that can enhance their access to care. Furthermore, when the prisons are located in rural areas, transporting inmates to urban medical centers can be problematic, thereby posing greater risks for the inmate-patient. Such issues have been the subject of litigation. Even when the courts uphold the inmates' petition for better medical attention, prison administrators react slowly to those court orders (Muraskin, 1993).

The quality and quantity of health care received by all inmates have been questioned and generally have been found in need of reconsideration. Because women commonly need and avail themselves of more medical services than men, the problem of poor medical services for the female inmate is even greater than it is for the male. The street lifestyle of many female inmates (e.g., drug and alcohol abuse, poor diet, possibly indiscriminate sexual behavior, restricted access to medical services, and the tendency to neglect medical problems) means that women entering prison are likely to require significant medical attention and education to help them take better care of themselves on release to the community (Acoca, 1998).

HEALTH CARE FOR IMPRISONED WOMEN WITH HIV/AIDS

HIV/AIDS is only transmitted in one of three ways: (a) via sexual activity with an infected person, (b) through contact with infected blood by sharing an intravenous needle with an infected person, and (c) from an infected mother to a newborn infant. The virus is not transmitted through casual everyday contact such as holding hands or having a face-to-face conversation. In the majority of states and in every region of the United States except the West, female inmates had a higher HIV-positive infection rate than male inmates (Maruschak, 1999). The high rates of HIV infection and AIDS among women offenders are essentially the result of intravenous drug use, trading sex for drugs and money, sexual abuse, living under conditions of poverty, and other gender-specific conditions of their lives that make them more prone to HIV infection (DeGroot, Leibel, & Zierler, 1998). However, it is important to note that the information known about HIV-infected inmates is limited by jurisdictional differences with respect to testing protocol and reporting practices. Therefore, the actual number of HIV and AIDS cases may be much higher than corrections officials are reporting. Additional cases may be concealed by the lengthy incubation period of the disease (sometimes as long as several years). Thus, it is likely that there are many more AIDS cases than have actually been detected at this time. Still, the increasing numbers of women in prison with HIV/AIDS is a serious concern. Although levels of activity vary among facilities, many inmates engage in the types of high-risk behavior (e.g., illicit sex and drug injection) during incarceration that pose a significant danger of viral transmission (Mahon, 1996).

Corrections professionals must be prepared for offenders who are suffering from the long-term debilitating effects of previous drug use. Besides addiction, drug use may lead to a variety of chronic physical problems. Alcoholic offenders may have serious liver damage or health problems precipitated by years of poor nutrition. Opiate usage, which is known to impair immune response, may increase narcotic-dependent persons' susceptibility to the various infections that accompany use of unsterile, often shared injection equipment (Snell & Morton, 1994). Injecting drugs has been associated with viral hepatitis, infection and inflammation of the heart or valves, pneumonia, blood poisoning, meningitis, and, in recent years, with HIV infection. The problem of HIV infection and AIDS is especially serious for incarcerated women, who often receive the smallest piece of the resource pie. Women at high risk of infection (drug abusers and the economically disadvantaged) are concentrated in prison populations. Studies have shown that AIDS has been identified as the eighth leading cause of death among women (in the United States) aged 15 to 44 (Lanier, 1999).

Women who are HIV-positive are especially vulnerable to opportunistic infections such as TB (Lanier, 1999). TB, an airborne disease transmitted via droplet nuclei (e.g., droplets from sneezes or coughs), poses a much greater health risk among prison populations than does HIV because it spreads relatively easily through the air: "TB can be transmitted through repeated exposure in crowded, poorly ventilated environments; it does not require intimate contact" (Wilcock, Hammett, Widom, & Epstein, 1996, p. 5). The health concern presented by TB to corrections officials is related to the fact that many prisoners—both men and women—come from segments of the community with high rates and risk of TB attributable to poverty, poor living conditions, substance abuse, and HIV/AIDS. Overcrowding in a correctional facility increases the potential for close and repeated contact with an active case of TB.

Complicating the matter is the high incidence of false-negative TB skin tests among those also infected with HIV. When an individual is co-infected with both HIV and TB, the purified protein derivative skin test for TB often comes out negative, and the infected individual (logically) is not treated. Furthermore, TB can become resistant to the leading medications, and the resistant strain may be spread among the other inmates and staff. Just as corrections has a responsibility to protect society from those who have wronged it, so too does it have a responsibility to protect society against the spread of infection by inmates who have acquired TB while incarcerated and might spread the disease among the community. In addition, diseases carried by drug-using offenders can place the rest of the inmate population at risk.

Beyond the physical effects of drug use, addicted offenders may suffer from numerous psychological and emotional effects. Mental health problems, including suicidal thoughts, attempts, or completion; depression; poor conduct; and personality disorders are but a few of the drug-related mental health challenges facing correctional mental health workers today.

SPECIAL NEEDS OF WOMEN PRISONERS WITH HIV/AIDS

Some persons infected with HIV may be asymptomatic, not even knowing they have the virus. Others may know they are HIV-positive but may appear just as healthy as noninfected inmates. Still others, however, may have developed AIDS or other health problems as a result of the virus and may need substantial medical treatment. Inmates in the terminal stage of AIDS will need intensive medical care. Because HIV compromises the body's ability to fight infection and resist disease, those who are infected, whatever their stage of the disease, must be removed from inmates with contagious illnesses and other conditions that might overwhelm their suppressed immune systems. However, when segregation is used to isolate HIV-infected inmates, these inmates need to be properly cared for; they should not be denied services or programming available to the general prison population.

Counseling issues must be handled with much care and sensitivity, depending on whether the inmate is uninfected but at risk for HIV infection, HIV-positive but asymptomatic, or has full-blown HIV infection or AIDS. The concerns expressed most frequently by HIV-positive women inmates are fear of becoming ill, fear of transmitting HIV to their sexual partners and children, difficulty in communicating with potential sexual partners while remaining sexually active, and being unable to bear children for fear the offspring will become infected. Unlike women in the other groups, those who have symptomatic HIV infection and AIDS must deal with grief over the loss of their previous body image, sexual freedom, and potential for childbearing. They must also address the imminent loss of their own lives. Grief and other emotions triggered by the HIV/AIDS diagnosis can be profound. Moreover, there may be as many as 80,000 mothers in local, state, and federal jails and prisons, and their dependents may total 150,000 people (Johnston, 1995). The legal and practical restrictions imposed on women prisoners infected with HIV/AIDS, as they try to maintain relationships with their children, significantly affect their physical and emotional well-being. The dramatic growth in the number of women in correctional settings during the past decade who have either tested positive for HIV/AIDS or are presumed to have HIV/AIDS and their need for gender-specific services has prompted researchers and advocates to call for increased attention to correctional programming for women and increased use of community-based interventions and alternatives.

Although life is rarely easy for any inmate, it is often more difficult for those who are HIV-positive. Lachance-McCullough et al. (1994) noted, "That dangers exist in being a known HIV-positive prison inmate, ranging from social isolation to physical abuse, has been well documented in the literature" (p. 213). Likewise, Olivero (1992) stated, "It appears that inmates and some prison administrators share society's repulsion of AIDS victims. Prisoners found to be infected with AIDS are an 'outgroup' and are stigmatized within the prison community" (p. 50).

A REAL-LIFE EXAMPLE: LINDA

Although prisoner advocates assert that women prisoners have a harder time getting treatment than men do, it is difficult to generalize about HIV/AIDS care in prison because it is not standardized across the nation. Each state system has its own set of policies and procedures for treating inmates, and the federal prison system operates under its own guidelines as well. Even within each state, the quality of treatment programs varies widely from facility to facility. To understand the seriousness of the problems confronting women prisoners with HIV/AIDS, meet Linda.

Linda, incarcerated at the Central California Women's Facility (CCWF) in Chowchilla in 1995, was diagnosed with AIDS. Arrested in January 1994 in Riverside County for possession of an unregistered firearm and violation of her parole, Linda spent almost 3 years in CCWF before compassionate release sent her home in December 1996. While at CCWF, she developed AIDS-related herpes zoster on her leg, which looked like a series of dark red, blistering cigarette burns. The doctor, however, did not admit her to the infirmary. The herpes spread to her eyes, and she went blind. But Linda's bad luck did not end there. After she was returned to her old cell, she says that no one acknowledged that she could not see or taught her how to get around or even made sure that she got breakfast. When she was brought a breakfast tray, no one told her it was there. When she finally left prison in December 1996, Linda weighed 92 pounds, was unable to walk, and was convinced that she was about to die. "My care at Chowchilla?" said Linda recently, "I'll put it like this: If you were dying of thirst and I stuck you in the desert with no water, how would you feel? You would die from dehydration." She paused and then continued, "To put it even more bluntly, they didn't give a fuck."

After leaving prison, Linda was treated at the University of Southern California Medical Center in Los Angeles, where she was given AIDS medications, taught how to use her legs again, and placed on an appropriate diet. Since then, she has learned how to manage the HIV by herself, regained weight, and begun working with the Braille Center to become self-sufficient (Siegal, 1998).

Stories of negligence and abuse are repeated again and again across the nation. In some cases, inmates with HIV may be sent to the nearest outside hospital, whether or not it has an infectious-disease specialist. Nevertheless, many inmates in state and federal prisons simply go untreated and find themselves in prison infirmaries or hospitals, where they are left to die.

CONTROVERSIAL ISSUES FOR CORRECTIONAL ADMINISTRATORS

The increasing number of inmates who test positive for HIV or who have AIDS has presented correctional authorities at all levels with a range of problems and challenges. These problems affect systemwide or institutional policies, medical care, housing, inmate and staff rights, inmate and staff safety, employee training, and release considerations. Several issues must be taken into account in the development of correctional policies for HIV/AIDS.

Screening and testing inmates for HIV is controversial. Perhaps the most highly charged and controversial issue is the debate over forced or mandatory HIV testing for inmates. Proponents argue that identifying infected inmates will facilitate administration of antiviral medications such as zidovudine (AZT) and didanosine (ddI), which are used for preemptive or early intervention treatment and may help sustain better health over a period of time (Hammett, Harrold,

Gross, & Epstein, 1994). It is also argued that testing is the best way to identify HIV-infected inmates, offering an opportunity to educate them about protecting against further spread of the disease. Furthermore, it has been posited that mass screening will offer corrections officials a better understanding of the scope of the problem so they can plan for more effective institutional responses (Blumberg, 1990).

Opponents argue that because any testing method may produce inaccurate results—positive cases testing negative and negative cases testing positive—it is not possible to identify all potentially infectious inmates. This could produce a false sense of security over who may or may not have AIDS. It can also unnecessarily stigmatize inmates and place them in the pariah-like status that comes with being identified as HIV-positive.

The issue of mass testing raises many questions with few or no clear answers for correctional administrators. Although policies vary widely, all 50 states, the District of Columbia, and the Federal Bureau of Prisons have at least one policy for prison HIV testing. The most prevalent policy (used in 44 of the jurisdictions in 1997) is to test inmates if they exhibit HIV-related symptoms or if they ask to be tested (Maruschak, 1999). Other common policies require testing of inmates who are involved in an incident that might have increased their exposure risk (29 jurisdictions). Fifteen states test inmates who belong to designated high-risk groups. Eighteen states test all inmates upon admission, and 4 states (as well as the Bureau of Prisons) test inmates at release.

Most states house HIV-infected inmates with the general inmate population. Until 1988, virtually every correctional institution segregated HIV-positive inmates. By 1993, however, there was an almost universal move away from such blanket policies (Hammett, Harmon, & Maruschak, 1999). The prevailing policy today is to segregate inmates with AIDS from the general prison population only when their medical needs require separate housing.

All HIV-infected inmates were segregated from the general population in eight prison systems in 1985, but by the year 2000, only three systems kept inmates known to have HIV infection from the general inmate population. Those three systems—Alabama, Mississippi, and South Carolina—have mandatory HIV-antibody testing of all incoming inmates; thus, they identify and segregate a large percentage of HIV-infected inmates (Greenhouse, 2000; Hammett et al., 1999). Alabama's procedure was upheld in 1999 by the United States Court of Appeals for the 11th Circuit *(Onishea v. Hopper)* and left intact by the United States Supreme Court in 2000 *(Davis v. Hopper).*

Housing and segregation policies for HIV-positive or AIDS-symptomatic inmates, in which inmates are forcibly housed apart from the general population, raise a number of issues. Proponents of segregation assert that it is necessary to prevent transmission of HIV within the prison setting. Here, advocates note that various types of high-risk activities occur in correctional institutions. Segregation has also been supported on grounds that HIV-infected inmates who have weakened immune systems are at greater risk of becoming ill. Therefore, they need to be protected against exposure to illnesses from the general inmate population. Finally, this policy can protect other inmates and staff members from HIV-positive inmates who may become violently, sexually, or otherwise assaultive; engage in consensual sex; or expose others to their infected blood during an encounter. These concerns have been the basis for lawsuits brought by both staff and inmates.

Civil libertarians, on the other hand, are opposed to the practice of segregation except for valid medical reasons or in cases involving protective custody. They argue that segregation undermines the basic public health message that HIV is not transmitted through casual contact but through high-risk behaviors. Moreover, many HIV-positive inmates who are not ill will complete their sentences in a relatively short period of time. This has significant implications for how they should be treated while in prison. It makes little sense to segregate low-risk inmates and make the prison experience more difficult than it ordinarily would be.

Precautionary measures can protect staff and inmates from infection. Correctional systems must continue to address the fears and concerns of staff and inmates regarding the possibility of exposure to the HIV virus from an infected inmate. Reasonable precautions must be taken to protect inmates and staff. As more is learned about how AIDS is spread, concerns voiced by both prison staff and inmates have declined. The Centers for Disease Control and Prevention (CDC) has issued a series of guidelines for health care and public safety workers, including correctional officers, concerning steps that should be taken as precautions when working with individuals who may potentially be HIV-positive or who may have other communicable diseases such as hepatitis B. Known as universal precautions, these are basic medical standards of safety and care designed to reduce the spread of infectious diseases. The CDC recommends that all personnel treat all prisoners as though they were HIV infected to protect staff and inmates from the possibility of exposure to the HIV virus. Institutions must adopt policies for their employees regarding how to respond to occurrences, such as dealing with exposure to needles and other sharp instruments, hand washing, cleaning up blood spills or other body fluids, and using protective equipment such as gloves for body and cell searches (Hammett, 1988).

Correctional systems are experiencing financial pressures concerning the care of AIDS-ill inmates. Security and medical costs are dominant issues in prison medicine. The increasing number of AIDS-symptomatic inmates has resulted in a major escalation in medical costs as a budget item for institutions. This increased financial burden results from the fact that inmates are not eligible for Medicaid, which is the prime public health method of financing AIDS-related treatment; hence, the costs of health care for HIV/AIDS inmates must be borne entirely by the systems in which they are incarcerated.

In recent years, a new class of drugs called protease inhibitors has been developed. This treatment has reduced the number of deaths from this disease and may change HIV/AIDS from a fatal to a chronic condition. However, it is important to recognize that these drugs are not a cure. Many questions remain unanswered, including whether the virus will eventually become resistant to this medication.

Protease inhibitors are rapidly becoming the standard of care for seropositive individuals in the community. However, prisons and jails face enormous difficulty in trying to provide this treatment. The annual retail cost of providing this medication to one individual is between $12,000 and $16,000 (Waldholz, 1996, p. 1). Correctional institutions with large numbers of HIV-infected inmates could easily see their entire health care budget consumed by this expense. In addition, persons receiving this treatment must take between 14 and 20 pills each day in accordance with a rigid dosing schedule and often must adhere to strict dietary restrictions. These requirements can pose serious logistical problems for correctional institutions.

Policies vary widely with respect to protease inhibitors. New York City expected to spend $5.4 million in 1998 to provide these drugs. On the other hand, Louisiana reserves this treatment for inmates who were already receiving this medication prior to incarceration (Purdy, 1997). Given the efficacy of these drugs, there is clearly an ethical obligation on the part of medical personnel to provide inmates with this treatment. Whether there is also a legal obligation is uncertain. Although the United States Supreme Court has ruled that inmates have a constitutional right to adequate medical care (*Estelle v. Gamble*, 1976), this decision did not grant inmates "unqualified access to health care." Furthermore, lower courts have subsequently interpreted this standard to mean that inmates rarely have a right to the best medical care (Vaughn & Carroll, 1996).

There are other factors that complicate the treatment of seropositive inmates. To date, many of the important advances in the treatment of HIV/AIDS have come from experimental medications. However, many states forbid inmates from participating in experimental trials of new drugs. In those jurisdictions that do allow such trials, few inmates actually participate (Collins, Baumgartner, & Henry, 1995). Although the rules that prevent prisoners from participating in experimental research were initially designed to protect incarcerated individuals, it is clear that these policies now prevent some inmates from receiving potentially beneficial treatments.

Finally, it should be noted that the treatment of HIV/AIDS has become quite complex. Outside the correctional setting, the management of this disease has increasingly become the responsibility of specialists (Purdy, 1997). Unfortunately, many prisons and jails are forced to rely on primary care doctors who sometimes lack the necessary expertise to provide the most up-to-date care. For these reasons, it is not surprising that the level of care varies dramatically between jurisdictions and sometimes even varies between different facilities within the same correctional system. In fact, the best care is provided by those institutions that are operating under court order to improve medical care (Purdy, 1997).

Federal inmates, like those in state prisons, suffer from a variety of ailments that are not addressed until they are confined in a correctional institution. Yet, the customary health care model in federal corrections is similar to health maintenance organizations, where general practitioners (GPs) evaluate and treat most patients and refer serious and chronic cases to medical specialists. The Bureau of Prisons hires GPs, who are then trained as correctional workers. These physicians, among other federal prison health care providers, are the mainstay of inmate medical care in mainline prisons. Medical staff always includes a GP and licensed physician assistants. Where medical care need is extensive, institutions also employ either licensed registered nurses or licensed practical nurses, or both. There are other institutions whose medical staff includes public health service physicians and/or dentists; these federal government medical workers can choose career tracks in different settings, including federal prisons.

The federal GP model of health care is able to reduce medical costs by consulting medical specialists, such as oncologists or orthopedic surgeons, only when they are needed. These specialists are then compensated under the terms of a negotiated contract. These contract physicians treat inmate-patients in prison or, under particular circumstances, at their offices or a local hospital to which inmate-patients are transported. Moreover, security concerns, which are a primary concern in corrections even during the delivery of medical care to inmates, are enhanced with the GP model. A federal GP becomes familiar with his or her caseload in the same manner as a family physician in a community medical practice. This familiarity with inmate-patients reduces the likelihood that inmates will successfully manipulate an unsuspecting physician into prescribing particular types of addictive drugs or into authorizing a trip into the community to implement the first step in an escape plot.

Until recently, very few women were confined in federal prisons. As a result, the Bureau had little experience in coping with women inmates, and few policies offered explicit instructions for managing issues associated with their confinement. That inexperience extended to female inmates' medical care. Even the opportunity for medical transfers to a medical center close to the place of residence raised issues of parity. Today, the Bureau is achieving parity in medical care for female inmates, which means that female inmates have access to medical treatment that is equal to that of males in both quality and quantity of services. Hopefully, the current trend of intergovernmental exchanges of information and services will extend to the health care delivery systems for women inmates.

Disclosure of an inmate's HIV status generally is limited to those with a need to know. Issues as to who should receive information regarding inmates' HIV test results are difficult and legally complex. Although inmates and staff members have asserted their right to know the status of those who are HIV-positive, AIDS-infected individuals have asserted their right to privacy (Hammett et al., 1994). Decisions concerning whether to release such test results are governed by legal and policy standards and mandates within a given jurisdiction.

Lawsuits brought by infected and uninfected inmates based on constitutional challenges to prison policies and procedures have met with little success. Correctional officials have effectively defended these cases based on *Turner v. Safley*, decided by the U.S. Supreme Court in 1987. In *Turner*, the Court articulated the standard to be applied in cases alleging constitutional claims brought by prisoners. The Court determined that institutional policies and procedures are valid if they are "reasonably related to legitimate penological interests" (p. 89). This requirement of reasonableness, as opposed to more stringent standards of substantial or compelling interest, has made it considerably easier for correctional officials to implement policies that restrict prisoners' rights. In applying the *Turner* standard to HIV-related cases, lower courts have consistently upheld prison policies that restrict the rights of both infected and uninfected inmates.

Most of the suits brought by infected inmates allege differential treatment or the denial of privileges. In *Dunn v. White* (1989), mandatory screening of inmates for HIV infection was challenged on grounds that testing constituted an unreasonable search and seizure and was therefore prohibited by the Fourth Amendment. The court upheld the prison's screening policy and, applying the *Turner* standard, concluded that there was a logical connection between mandatory testing and the prison's goal of preventing the spread of AIDS. Mass screening for the purpose of segregating infected prisoners in HIV dormitories has also been upheld under the same rationale (*Harris v. Thigpen*, 1991). Courts have reached similar results in cases in which individual inmates had been singled out for testing after an incident that posed a risk of transmission, as in cases of prison rape. A policy of not testing inmates after potential transmission occurrences has likewise been upheld (*Lile v. Tippecanoe County Jail*, 1992).

Prison policies regarding the segregation of HIV-positive inmates have provided fertile ground for litigation as well. Despite a consistent trend in mainstreaming seropositive prisoners into the general population, the courts have taken a hands-off position on the issue and left housing policy decisions to prison officials. Whether the institution chooses segregation or mainstreaming, the policy has been upheld. Thus, infected inmates who bring suit to challenge mandatory segregation policies have not been successful. Courts have also upheld segregation policies against constitutional challenges based on the following claims: cruel and unusual punishment under the Eighth Amendment (*Cordero v. Coughlin*, 1984); equal protection under the Fourteenth Amendment (*Moore v. Mabus*, 1992); and due process under the Fifth and Fourteenth Amendments (*Harris v. Thigpen*, 1991). The case of *Nolley v. County of Erie* (1991) represents a rare departure from those decisions upholding mandatory segregation of infected prisoners. Nolley, solely on the basis of her status as an HIV-positive inmate, was forced into a segregation unit for prisoners who were suicidal or mentally disturbed. Evidence in the case made it clear that she was not placed in the unit to receive medical care or for her safety. The court found merit in Nolley's assertions that her due process and right of privacy protections were violated. *Nolley* is distinguishable from other cases, however, because the institution failed to follow its own policies regarding the placement of seropositive inmates.

Inmates have also brought suit alleging the unauthorized disclosure of their HIV status. This claim is based on the fact that individuals in the free world have a constitutional right to protect their medical records from unauthorized disclosure (Vaughn & Carroll, 1996). However, the courts have ruled that this principle does not apply to incarcerated individuals and that disclosing an inmate's HIV-positive condition to correctional personnel and other inmates does not violate the constitutional right of privacy (*Anderson v. Romero*, 1995).

In other areas as well, courts have applied the *Turner* standard and afforded prison administrators wide discretion in making decisions that have an effect on infected inmates. Courts have upheld prison policies against challenges by inmates asserting differential treatment or a denial of privilege in cases involving exclusion from a community work program (*Williams v. Sumner*, 1986) and prohibiting work in prison cafeterias and hospitals (*Farmer v. Moritsugu*, 1990).

Attempts to invoke the protections of federal statutes have also met with limited success. For example, in *Gates v. Rowland* (1995), infected inmates claimed that their exclusion from certain work assignments violated Section 504 of the Rehabilitation Act of 1973. Courts have ruled that seropositive individuals fall under the protection of this Act. Section 504 provides that handicapped persons are entitled to a reasonable accommodation of their employment needs and other activities if they are otherwise qualified to perform the work or participate in the activities. The question in *Gates* was how the Rehabilitation Act should be applied to correctional institutions. The court's opinion applied the same test to this statutory claim that it applied to constitutional claims, namely the *Turner* standard. The court found that the exclusion of infected inmates from prison programs, arguably in violation of the Rehabilitation Act, was permissible because the policy was reasonably related to the prison's goal of promoting the safety of inmates.

Although decisions to disclose the HIV status of inmates will be decided by state legislatures and the courts, current correctional practices permit disclosure of AIDS-related medical information to those with a need to know. These include correctional administrators, physicians, other medical staff, probation officers, and the infected inmate. A variety of related issues can be raised as well. How will HIV information be used? Who has access to it? Should public health authorities or relatives be notified? Correctional administrators will continue to confront these and other complex confidentiality issues.

Issues of segregation, access to programs, and health care as they relate to inmates with HIV or AIDS have been working their way through the nation's courts for over a decade. The most recent decisions concern whether prisoners with HIV or AIDS are covered under the Americans With Disabilities Act. If they are—and the decision of the Supreme Court in *Pennsylvania Department of Corrections v. Yeskey* (1998) suggests that they are—rulings under the Act will affect the way prisoners with HIV or AIDS are managed (Hammet et al., 1999).

POLICY RECOMMENDATIONS

For the past 10 years, much concern has been voiced about communicable diseases and health and safety in the workplace. With the emergence of HIV/AIDS and the resurgence of TB, these concerns are certainly justified. Since the beginning of the HIV/AIDS epidemic, the disease has struck incarcerated populations extraordinarily hard. Notwithstanding the fact that incarcerated women have been identified as being at higher risk for contracting the HIV virus and that their symptoms and treatment needs are substantially different from those of men, HIV/AIDS-related treatment resources for women in prisons are limited or nonexistent. Based on the variety of policies and practices currently in use throughout U.S. correctional systems, several areas of continued attention are needed to develop a comprehensive and sustained strategy to actively promote the health of incarcerated women.

1. Continue to educate and communicate with inmates and staff in all correctional institutions. The following are the most effective tools in dealing with anxiety and curtailing risky behavior associated with transmission of communicable diseases:
   - Implement a comprehensive HIV/AIDS education and training program.
   - Provide individual and/or group counseling for HIV-infected inmates.
2. Institution staff must implement the required health and safety programs concerning air- and blood-borne pathogens and must implement universal precautions as well.
   - There is a need to develop policies and procedures that teach officers how to conduct searches in a manner that minimizes their likelihood of injury.
   - Improve the prison's physical plant in terms of ventilation and equipping staff with appropriate barrier masks and respirators whenever TB outbreaks are noted.
   - Correctional staff members need to follow all prescribed infection control guidelines issued by the CDC.
3. Inmates should be screened for communicable diseases at booking/admission to, during, and on release from a facility, and there should be annual examinations of correctional employees for communicable diseases.
   - Early identification of HIV-infected inmates is important. Recent scientific advances have contributed to a significant reduction in the fatality rate among HIV/AIDS-infected individuals who receive these medications in a timely fashion.
   - As the frequency of transmission of HIV/AIDS and other communicable diseases to other inmates and staff members within the institution has yet to be determined, continued monitoring is recommended for the health and safety of all who live and/or work in penal settings.
4. Correctional management teams, comprising custody and medical management, must make informed decisions about the numerous treatment approaches that are now available for HIV/AIDS (such as protease inhibitors).

- These treatment regimens are very costly, but they have become a part of the minimal standard of practice in treating HIV/AIDS. Therefore, we are obligated by the correctional health care standards (continuity of care and special medical needs) to make these regimens available.
- Guidelines are needed to determine which protease inhibitors to stock and use in treatment initiated in the institution and to develop effective communications with treating physicians on the outside to facilitate continuity.
- Establishing contacts, and perhaps contracts, with community organizations (e.g., in-prison hospice and hospice services) that may be able to assist inmates and their family members with "death with dignity" issues and correctional staff members with their continued exposure to inmate deaths.

5. Alleviating prison overcrowding because it is a significant contributor to the spread of TB.
   - Referring TB- and HIV-infected inmates to community-based service agencies upon release. It has been suggested that many of the women currently serving prison terms could safely and more economically serve their sentences in community-based programs. Female offenders may be an ideal population for community-based correctional programs in light of the fact that they (a) commit crimes that, although unacceptable, pose little threat to public safety; (b) are less likely to reoffend; and (c) respond favorably to community-based programs. Health-related programs for women inmates must be integrated into the release plans in which prison-based assistance can be linked to the free community.

CONCLUSION

Although the crisis atmosphere surrounding AIDS in prison and jails seems to have dissipated, the disease remains a serious issue for correctional administrators and their health care systems. Concern has shifted significantly from short-term matters, such as fear of casual transmission, to long-term issues, such as housing, programming, and medical care for inmates with HIV infection.

As the population ages, and as determinate sentencing and strict sentencing guidelines continue, inmates—in particular, women—will age within our facilities. We will see more women of childbearing age who are infected. The historic differences between federal offenders and offenders within state, city, or county systems have become blurred by the issue of drug trafficking. These offenders tend to be less educated and from predominantly urban and depressed socioeconomic backgrounds. The frequent victimization of these female offenders also increases the risk for heterosexual disease transmission.

HIV infection and resulting AIDS cases pose particular problems for corrections in terms of staff and inmates. Staff have been alarmed by the introduction of AIDS into prison, and initially little was done through education or training to reduce levels of irrational fear. Institutional policies will need to be developed and reconsidered in the areas of diagnosing, managing, and treating HIV infection. Additional policy development and implementation will be necessary in the areas of staff training and education, inmate counseling, pretest and posttest counseling, voluntary (versus mandatory) testing, medical parole, and discharge and aftercare services (for parole and community supervision). Infection control policies will be necessary for dentists, nurses, physicians, and security and treatment staff.

Contracts for medical care with private health care providers are considered an option for cost-effective and quality medical care. This requires a competitive bidding process under which health care providers submit proposals detailing the services they will provide. Under this system, the company selected provides medical care at a fixed cost per year. Private providers claim there are economic advantages to contracting for these services, but, at this point, there is no independent research that confirms this assertion, especially as this relates to the budget allocations for local and state correctional institutions. Nevertheless, contractors have a vested interest in hiring quality doctors and nurses who can provide good care because this will minimize liability and ultimately reduce inmate health care costs. Also, large health care organizations may be better able to provide specialty care by temporarily transferring staff to a correctional facility.

There are also some potential problems associated with private health care providers. For-profit organizations may have strong motives to cut costs so that they can increase profits. This may result in measures that discourage inmate complaints and appearances at sick call, cause delay in or failure to take inmates from one health care unit to another, and transfer inmates who are expensive or difficult to treat to state facilities. Thus, care must be taken to ensure that profit motives do not jeopardize the adequacy of medical care. Strict supervision by the contracting agency and prior contractual arrangements are the keys to dealing with these potential problems (Anno, 1991).

Given the projected rise in HIV-seropositive inmates in the next decade and the continuing threat of inmate litigation, it appears that the correctional health care crisis will continue for some time. The medical and custodial needs of HIV/AIDS inmates will be one of the most, if not the single most, important considerations for correctional administrators well into the 21st century.

There is no doubt that the provision of health-related services to inmates will provide increasing burdens for the nation's correctional systems. Their response to this challenge will be influenced by fiscal realities, court mandates, humanitarian concerns, and the public beliefs as to the treatment deserved by inmates. But there is also a dire need for evaluations of HIV/AIDS service delivery in correctional settings. Particularly, methodologically sound research into the efficacy of prison-based HIV education programs at stimulating risk reduction of inmates upon release is needed. Correctional administrators should also work together with community leaders to develop more extensive linkage to community-based HIV services for inmates being released. Such linkages are severely lacking in most states today.

Why should we care about these prisoners? It must be remembered that most prisoners are released from prison and reenter the free society. Without programs to address the unique physical, emotional, sexual, and drug-related problems of female inmates and prisoners in general, our prisons will be returning high-risk (not in a criminal sense) individuals to the free community.

REFERENCES

Acoca, L. (1998). Defusing the time bomb: Understanding and meeting the growing health care needs of incarcerated women in America. *Crime & Delinquency, 44*, 49-70.

Anderson v. Romero, 72 F.3d 518 (7th Cir. 1995).

Anno, B. J. (1991). *Prison health care: Guidelines for the management of an adequate delivery system.* Washington, DC: National Institute of Corrections.

Beck, A. J., & Mumola, C. (1999). *Prisoners in 1998.* Washington, DC: Government Printing Office.

Blumberg, M. (1990). Issues and controversies with respect to the management of AIDS in corrections. In M. Blumberg (Ed.), *AIDS: The impact of the criminal justice system* (pp. 195-210). Columbus, OH: Merrill.

Centers for Disease Control. (1993). *HIV/AIDS surveillance quarterly report: Year-end edition.* Atlanta, GA: Author.

Collins, A., Baumgartner, D., & Henry, K. (1995). U.S. prisoners' access to experimental HIV therapies. *Minnesota Medicine. 78*, 45-48.

Cordero v. Coughlin, 607 F. Supp. 9 (S.D. N.Y. 1984).

Davis v. Hopper, No. 98-9663 (2000).

DeGroot, A. S., Leibel, S. R., & Zierler, S. (1998). A standard of HIV care for incarcerated women: A northeastern United States experience. *Journal of Correctional Health Care, 5*(2), 139-176.

Dunn v. White, 880 F.2d 1188 (10th Cir. 1989), cert denied, 110 S. Ct. 871 (1990).

Estelle v. Gamble, 429 U.S. 97 (1976).

Farmer v. Moritsugu, 742 F. Supp. 525 (W.D. Wis. 1990).

Fletcher, B. R., Rolison, G. L., & Moon, D. G. (1993). The woman prisoner. In B. R. Fletcher, L. D. Shaver, & D. G. Moon (Eds.), *Women prisoners: A forgotten population* (pp. 15-26). Westport, CT: Praeger.

Gates v. Roland, 39 F.3d 1439 (9th Cir. 1995).

Gilliard, D. (1999). *Prison and jail inmates at midyear 1998.* Washington, DC: U.S. Department of Justice.

Greenfeld, L. A., & Snell, T. L. (1999). *Women offenders* (NCJ 175688, special report). Washington, DC: Bureau of Justice Statistics.

Greenhouse, L. (2000, January 19). Justices allow segregation of inmates with HIV [Online]. *The New York Times.* Available: www.nytimes.com

Hammett, T. M. (1988). *Precautionary measures and protective equipment: Developing a reasonable response.* Washington, DC: National Institute of Justice.

Hammett, T. M., Harmon, P., & Maruschak, L. M. (1999). *1996-1997 update: HIV/STDs, and TB in correctional facilities.* Washington, DC: National Institute of Justice.

Hammett, T. M., Harrold, L., Gross, M., & Epstein, J. (1994). *1992 update: AIDS in correctional facilities: Issues and opinions.* Cambridge, MA: U.S. Department of Justice.

Harlow, C. (1999). *Prior abuse reported by inmates and probationers.* Washington, DC: U.S. Department of Justice.

Harris v. Thigpen, 941 F.2d. 1495 (11th Cir. 1991).

Johnston, D. (1995). Child custody issues of women prisoners: A preliminary report from the CHICAS project. *The Prison Journal 75.* 222.

Lachance-McCullough, M. L., Tesoriero, J. M., Sorin, M. D., & Stern, A. (1994). HIV infection among New York State female inmates: Preliminary results of a voluntary counseling and testing program. *The Prison Journal, 73*. 198-219.

Lanier, M. (1999). HIV-related issues for incarcerated women in the twenty-first century. In R. Muraskin & A. R. Roberts (Eds.), *Visions for change: Crime and justice in the twenty-first century* (2nd ed.). Upper Saddle River, NJ: Prentice Hall.

Lile v. Tippecanoe County Jail, 844 F. Supp. 1301 (N.D. Ind. 1992).

Lillis. J. (1994). Programs and services for female inmates. *Corrections Compendium 29* (2), 6-13.

Mahon, N. (1996). New York inmates' HIV risk behaviors: The implications for prevention policy and programs. *American Journal of Public Health, 86*, 1211-1215.

Maruschak, L. (1999). HIV in prisons, 1997. *Bureau of Justice Statistics Bulletin*. Washington, DC: U.S. Department of Justice.

McKinney, J. D. (1994). *A descriptive case study of the impact of social learning experiences on adult female inmates*. Paper presented at the annual meeting of the American Society of Criminology, Miami, FL.

Moore v. Mabus, 976 F.2d 268 (5th Cir. 1992).

Moyer, I. L. (1993). Women's prisons: Issues and controversies. In R. Muraskin & T. Alleman (Eds.), *It's a crime: Women and justice* (pp. 193-210). Englewood Cliffs, NJ: Regents/Prentice-Hall.

Muraskin, R. (1993). Disparate treatment in correctional facilities. In R. Muraskin & T. Alleman (Eds.), *It's a crime: Women and justice*. Englewood Cliffs, NJ: Regents/Prentice-Hall.

Nolley v. County of Erie. 776 F. Supp. 715 (W.D. N.Y 1991).

Olivero, J. M. (1992). AIDS in prisons: Judicial and administrative dilemmas and strategies. In P. J. Benekos & A. V. Merlo (Eds.), *Corrections: Dilemmas and directions* (pp. 37-55). Cincinnati, OH: Anderson.

Onishea v. Hopper, No. 96-6213 (11th Cir. 1999).

Owen, B., & Bloom, B. (1995). Profiling women prisoners: Findings from national surveys and a California sample. *The Prison Journal, 75*, 165-185.

Pennsylvania Department of Corrections v. Yeskey. 524 U.S. 206 (1998).

Purdy. M. (1997, May 26). As AIDS increases behind bars, costs dim promise of new drugs. *The New York Times*, p. 1.

Sargent, E., Marcus-Mendoza, S., & Yu, C.H. (1993). Abuse and the woman prisoner. In B. R. Fletcher, L. D. Shaver, & D. G. Moon (Eds.), *Women prisoners: A forgotten population* (pp. 55-64). Westport, CT: Praeger.

Siegal, N. (1998. November). Lethal Lottery [Online]. *POZ*. Available: www.thebody.com/poz/survival

Snell, T. L., & Morton, D.C. (1994, March). Women in prison: Survey of state prison inmates, 1991 (NCJ-145321, Bureau of Justice Statistics special rep.). Washington, DC: U.S. Department of Justice.

Turner v. Safley, 482 U.S. 78 (1987).

Vaughn, M., & Carroll, L. (1996). *Separate and unequal: Prison versus free-world medical care*. Paper presented at the annual meeting of the American Society of Criminology, Chicago.

Waldholz. M. (1996, July 3). New AIDS treatment raises tough question of who will get it. *Wall Street Journal*, p. 1.

Wilcock, K., Hammett, T. M., Widom, R., & Epstein, J. (1996). Tuberculosis in correctional facilities 1994-1995. *National Institute of Justice, Research in Brief* (July, NCJ-157809). Washington, DC: U.S. Department of Justice.

Williams v. Sumner, 648 F. Supp. 510 (D. Nev. 1986).

Barbara H. Zaitzow, Ph.D.
Associate Professor
Department of Political Science and Criminal Justice
Appalachian State University
Boone, North Carolina 28608
USA

Part III
Custody, Supervision and Treatment Issues

[12]

CHALLENGES IN THE MANAGEMENT OF THE HIV PATIENT IN THE THIRD DECADE OF AIDS

Maria L.A. Tiamson, M.D.

The epidemic of AIDS has been increasingly recognized as a major health and socioeconomic problem, not only in the United States or Africa, but also the rest of the world. The face of the epidemic has changed. The role that mental health providers play has also significantly grown as the epidemic continues on. Prior to the introduction of Highly Active Anti-Retroviral Therapy (HAART) and other advances in HIV care, the patients faced issues that related to death and dying. These advances brought with them renewed hope and resurrected lives. The patients fought with issues related to living new lives with HIV no longer an imminent death threat. In the third decade of AIDS, the struggles of the post-HAART era continue but bring with it more challenges. Mental health providers need to familiarize themselves with these issues so that they can better help HIV patients cope with this devastating disease.

KEY WORDS: HIV/AIDS; pre-HAART issues; post-HAART issues; role of mental health providers.

Maria L.A. Tiamson is Assistant Professor, Psychiatry, New York Medical College, and Director, Psychiatric Services, AIDS Care Center, Westchester Medical Center.

Address correspondence to Maria L.A. Tiamson, New York Medical College, Valhalla, NY 10595.

INTRODUCTION

AIDS first reared its ugly head in the United States in June 1981 when a rare pulmonary disease called pneumocystis carinii pneumonia was found in homosexual men in Los Angeles. The HIV virus was finally discovered in 1984 and HIV testing was made possible. We have come a long way since. The availability of highly active antiretroviral therapy (HAART) which was introduced in 1996, the development of new diagnostic technologies (viral load, genotypic and phenotypic resistance testing, etc.) and other advances in HIV prevention and management have altered the lives of patients with HIV and brought significant changes to their care. We have erstwhile considered AIDS synonymous with a progressively terminal disease. In the third decade of AIDS, we now consider it to be a chronic disease. Like the HIV virus that mutates so rapidly, the management of the HIV patient has also evolved with each new advance or change in circumstances that surround the epidemic.

THE NEW FACES OF THE EPIDEMIC

Through June 2000, there have been 753,907 cases of AIDS in the United States (1). While men still consist the majority of people infected with AIDS, the rate in women has increased. It is also notable that more than half of US AIDS cases were among blacks and Hispanics. Among adult and adolescent women with HIV, 81% were blacks or Hispanics. Between 1985 and 1999, the number of cases due to Men-having-Sex-with-Men (MSM) has gradually decreased but this remains as the most common route of transmission in the United States. Injection drug use (IDU) and heterosexual contact have steadily increased during the same period. We are also seeing an increasing number of AIDS patients "over fifty." What is alarming is the increasing prevalence of the virus in young gay men who engage in unsafe sexual behavior because they no longer see HIV as a death threat.

The AIDS epidemic is not just a problem for the United States. We should, in fact, be cognizant of the fact that there is a world pandemic of AIDS. In Africa, more than 20% of the population aged 15–49 years old is infected with HIV. Ten years hence, there will be approximately 40 million AIDS orphans in Africa. What this will do to the economies and social structures of the countries that AIDS has devastated because of the death of men and women in their prime is incomprehensible.

PRE-HAART ISSUES

Prior to the introduction of Highly Active Antiretroviral Therapy (HAART), patients with HIV/AIDS were dealing with issues related to death and dying. Like patients with cancer, they go through a series of stages preparing for death. This has been previously described in the literature (2,3). These stages do not necessarily occur in order or in clear-cut and definite stages. They do help in providing a framework that psychiatrists can use when working with HIV patients. The stages include the following: *Initial crisis*: After being diagnosed, the patients are in a stage of shock, and intense emotions are present, particularly denial, anger, guilt and depression. The predominant emotion is denial and this may interfere with treatment. It is not unusual for some to request for a second test to confirm their serostatus. It is important to realize that patients may be unable to process and retain information that has been given them when they are in such an emotional state. *Transitional state*: This is a period of distress during which patients feel very anxious and oftentimes distressed and confused. There may be such anger that some patients engage in unsafe sexual behavior and/or increased drug use in reaction to the diagnosis. Some patients may be preoccupied with guilt for their behavior and become depressed and suicidal. *Acceptance*: At this stage, patients are able to accept the fact that they have the disease and form new identities. It is at this point that we see the development of their fighting spirit, as well as the reassessment of their lives, their priorities, their values. One of the remarkable outcomes of this is the birth of AIDS activism. AIDS activism set a new standard in advocacy around the disease and it has become a model for other diseases. AIDS activism was also responsible for changing standards in drug development and the unprecedented availability of various benefits to people affected by the disease. For example, no other disease entity has a federally funded drug assistance program exclusive to those that have the disease who fall between the Medicaid eligible and those with good insurance coverage. What has also emerged from this is the fact that as a group, AIDS patients were the most informed on their disease, including experimental trials going on and advances in the field compared to other patient groups. *Preparatory Stage*: At this time patients prepare for their impending death. They take care of unfinished business and make their wills, healthcare proxies and funeral services. They reunite with estranged family and friends and make amends. Although most patients continue to fight for their life, at this point, for some, suicide becomes an alternative to a lingering and long suffering death that they have witnessed their friends go through.

Faced with imminent death, patients often turn their lives around. They decide to make drastic lifestyle changes. They struggle to maintain sobriety. They try to live healthy, quite often using alternative and complementary medicine to help them keep longer lives. They become quite vigilant with whatever happens to their bodies. As far as they are concerned, the key to survival is taking care of themselves and preventing opportunistic infections from taking over what is left of their life. They have come to accept that they have shortened lifespans and make the most of what they have.

POST-HAART ISSUES

Soon after HAART became available in 1996, the astounding impact they had on patients became obvious. This was a significant turning point in the lives of patients with HIV/AIDS. AIDS death rates in the United States started declining in 1997. No longer facing certain mortality, patients are now dealing with living. Like the biblical figure, Lazarus, who was dead and brought back to life, patients discovered that their lives have been renewed (4). No longer facing death's door, they now recognize they have to face living again (5–7). The struggle has shifted and is now centered on maintaining health insurance and prescription benefits. The patients who have become healthier and ready to return to work are quite fearful of losing their benefits that provide them with the drugs that made them live longer lives. They have to redefine themselves and their relationships. Their hope has been rekindled and they can look forward to the future again.

But with the good news comes the bad. Medication issues are prominent in the minds of patients with HIV/AIDS. One important dilemma for them is whether to start or not start the treatment. This can be brought about by other issues such as mistrust based on past history, fear of being identified as AIDS patients, fear of disclosure among other things. Living longer with AIDS means having to take a lot of medications, each with its restrictions such as taking pills with or without food or water, or taking them two hours before or after meals. Adherence becomes a priority issue with these complicated instructions particularly since the virus mutates so rapidly and resistance can develop even after only day or two of not taking the medications. For those who are relatively healthy, the fact that they are reminded each time they take a pill that they are not healthy, that they have the virus, a fact that they would rather forget. They have to readjust their daily routine around the pills. They also need to be careful about drug interactions. Patients with HIV often have several medications, such as prophylactic drugs for opportunistic infections, psychotropic drugs, drugs used to treat other medical conditions such as diabetes, heart disease, and herbal and over the counter medications. On top of these, some patients also use street drugs.

Combination treatment with HAART is not a cure. Patients with HIV, while appearing healthy, live their lives with much uncertainty that can lead to clinical anxiety and depressive syndromes. These drugs were approved within a relatively short period and long term complications of these treatments are yet to be determined. At this point, we do know that metabolic parameters are increased so that there is an increased risk of diabetes, stroke and cardiovascular disorders secondary to increased cholesterol, triglycerides and blood sugar. There are also severe GI side effects that make them intolerable. There is maldistribution of fat or lipodystrophy that cause disfiguring body changes such as the protease paunch and the buffalo hump. This can wreck havoc on the patient's self esteem and body image. In addition, the drugs also cause neuropsychiatric side effects that complicate the psychiatric morbidity.

Along with the advent of HAART came advances in technology in relation to the virus. Viral load testing, along with CD4 counts, also impact on the psychological well being of patients. At times, mood swings can be traced to what these numbers are. There was a false belief that having undetected viral loads means they no longer have HIV. On the other side, there is also a false belief that if they have high viral loads, they will die soon. Both these beliefs have been addressed by education efforts.

ISSUES IN THE THIRD DECADE OF AIDS

New issues have come up after HAART has been available for several years (6). The long term effects of antiretroviral drug combinations are now surfacing. The opportunistic infections have decreased in incidence in those who are treated with HAART. Hospitalization rates for AIDS patients have gone down. However, patients on HAART now have to deal with the complications of medications such as lipodystrophy, hypercholesterolemia, diabetes and neuropsychiatric disorders.

We have also known for some time that HAART regimens do not always succeed. Maintaining hope while treatment is failing is a difficult task for any physician. Salvage regimens have been created and even these are not guaranteed to work. The recommendations for treatment are always evolving, probably due to the increasing numbers of new drug developments and treatment advances as well as evidence of treatment failures with various combination regimens (10). The current recommendation is not to start HAART unless the t-cell count is 300 and below. What this means to those asymptomatic patients who have been on HAART for many years and are now being told to stop has yet to be determined. Some patients are going to be very glad to stop while others are quite fearful of stopping treatment for fear of progression of the disease.

One important issue in the third decade of AIDS is the resurgence of high risk behavior despite education efforts regarding prevention of HIV. Both HIV negative and HIV positive persons engage in this high risk behavior because of their belief that HIV is no longer an immediate death sentence. For some HIV negative individuals, engaging in unprotected sex ("bug-chasing") carries with it some element of excitement and danger. For others, particularly the younger population, the message of risk reduction and HIV prevention does not carry with it the same dire prognosis that it had in the 80's and early 90's. The pressure of peer groups and social fads affect the decision of others to go "barebacking" (sex without condoms).

For the HIV positive individual with undetectable viral loads, engaging in high risk behavior "normalizes" them and sustain their belief that they are not sick. We have also noted an increase in substance use in patients who have managed to maintain sobriety for a long period of time. As they live longer and deal with the issues of rebuilding their lives, they cope with their difficulties in the only way they know how: using drugs.

One of the important issues that have emerged since the advent of new therapies is the desire for family. The patients who have benefited from these treatments are reestablishing their lives and their priorities. Among these include having children, especially among discordant couples. This is complicated by several factors. It has been known that the majority of babies of HIV infected mothers do not develop HIV if they were treated with treatment protocols. Sexual dysfunction has been a complication of HIV and its treatments and this impacts on the desire to gain a sexual life. The HIV negative partner of a discordant couple also places his or her life at risk if they decide to conceive.

For patients who are living longer and are relatively healthy, returning to work or going back to school are complicated by the fear of disclosure. The stigma of HIV still exists despite the wide range education efforts by various AIDS organizations and by the government. This has become a stumbling block for some patients in their efforts to renew their lives.

THE ROLE OF THE MENTAL HEALTH PROVIDERS

Mental health providers should be able to understand the context in which HIV infected individuals find themselves. The prevalence of psychiatric disorders is high in HIV/AIDS. However, even in those who do not have clinically significant psychiatric disorders, the importance of mental health treatment cannot be dismissed. There are multiple psychosocial issues such as those discussed above. As the epidemic progresses, the role of mental health providers become even more essential as the patients grapple with these issues. Of particular relevance is the role of the mental health provider in promoting adherence to treatment as well as HIV prevention and risk reduction. The mental health provider is a significant part of the multidisciplinary team treating HIV infected individuals. Discussing the patients' sexual lives, drug use, family planning and need for HIV testing should be part of routine mental health care, no matter how old the patient is. It is important that mental health providers identify their own countertransference issues when treating the HIV infected individuals who knowingly infect others as well as the uninfected who put themselves at risk for HIV. Finally, the mental health provider should collaborate and have open communication with the other health providers involved in the patients they care for.

REFERENCES

1. Centers for Disease Control and Prevention. HIV/AIDS Surveillance Report. US HIV and AIDS cases reported through June 2000. Midyear edition Vol. 12, No. 1.
2. Forstein M: The psychosocial impact of acquired immune deficiency syndrome. Semin Oncol 11:77–82, 1984.
3. Nichols S: Psychosocial reactions of persons with the acquired immune deficiency syndrome. Ann Intern Med 103:765–767, 1985.
4. Scott S, Constantine LM: The lazarus syndrome: a second chance for life with HIV infection. J Am Pharm Assoc 39(4):462–6, Jul–Aug 1999.
5. Trainor A, Ezer H: Rebuilding life: the experience of living with AIDS after facing imminent death. Qual Health Res 10(5):646–60, Sep 2000.
6. Brechtl JR, et al: The use of highly active antiretroviral therapy (HAART) in patients with advanced HIV infection: impact on medical, palliative care and quality of life outcomes. J Pain Symptom Manage 21(1):41–51, Jan 2001.
7. Brashers DS, et al: 'In an important way, I did die': uncertainty and revival in persons living with HIV and AIDS. AIDS Care 11(2):201–19, Apr 1999.

8. Forstein M: Psychosocial issues in antiretroviral treatment. New Dir Ment Health Serv (87):17–24, Fall 2000.
9. Kelly JA, et al: Implications of HIV treatment advances for behavioral research on AIDS: Protease inhibitors and new challenges in HIV secondary prevention. Health Psychol 17(4):310–9, Jul 1998.
10. Boyle B: Can a broken HAART be mended? AIDS Reader 8(3):114–120, 1998.

[13]

ABC of AIDS

HIV counselling and the psychosocial management of patients with HIV or AIDS

Sarah Chippindale, Lesley French

This article has been adapted from the forthcoming 5th edition of ABC of AIDS. *The book will be available from the BMJ bookshop and at www.bmjbooks.com*

What is HIV counselling?

Counselling in HIV and AIDS has become a core element in a holistic model of health care, in which psychological issues are recognised as integral to patient management. HIV and AIDS counselling has two general aims: (1) the prevention of HIV transmission and (2) the support of those affected directly and indirectly by HIV. It is vital that HIV counselling should have these dual aims because the spread of HIV can be prevented by changes in behaviour. One to one prevention counselling has a particular contribution in that it enables frank discussion of sensitive aspects of a patient's life—such discussion may be hampered in other settings by the patient's concern for confidentiality or anxiety about a judgmental response. Also, when patients know that they have HIV infection or disease, they may suffer great psychosocial and psychological stresses through a fear of rejection, social stigma, disease progression, and the uncertainties associated with future management of HIV. Good clinical management requires that such issues be managed with consistency and professionalism, and counselling can both minimise morbidity and reduce its occurrence. All counsellors in this field should have formal counselling training and receive regular clinical supervision as part of adherence to good standards of clinical practice.

When is HIV counselling necessary?

Pre-test discussion

A discussion of the implications of HIV antibody testing should accompany any offer of the test itself. This is to ensure the principle of informed consent is understood and to assist patients to develop a realistic assessment of the risk of testing HIV antibody positive. This process should include accurate and up to date information about transmission and prevention of HIV and other sexually transmitted infections. Patients should be made aware of the "window period" for the HIV test —that a period of 12 weeks since the last possible exposure to HIV should have elapsed by the time of the test.

Patients may present for testing for any number of reasons, ranging from a generalised anxiety about health to the presence of HIV related physical symptoms. For patients at minimal risk of HIV infection, pre-test discussion provides a valuable opportunity for health education and for safer sex messages to be made relevant to the individual. For patients who are at risk of HIV infection, pre-test discussion is an essential part of post-test management. These patients may be particularly appropriate to refer for specialist counselling expertise. In genitourinary medicine clinics where HIV antibody testing is routinely offered as a part of sexual health screening, health advisers provide counselling to patients who have been identified as high risk for testing HIV positive.

The importance of undertaking a sensitive and accurate sexual/and or injecting drug risk history of both the patient and their sexual partners cannot be overstated. If patients feel they cannot share this information with the physician or counsellor then the risk assessment becomes meaningless; patients may be inappropriately reassured, for example, and be

Aims of counselling in HIV infection

Prevention
- Determining whether the lifestyle of an individual places him or her at risk
- Working with an individual so that he or she understands the risks
- Helping to identify the meanings of high risk behaviour
- Helping to define the true potential for behaviour change
- Working with the individual to achieve and sustain behaviour change

Support
- Individual, relationship, and family counselling to prevent and reduce psychological morbidity associated with HIV infection and disease

Different HIV counselling programmes and services

- Counselling before the test is done
- Counselling after the test for those who are HIV positive and HIV negative
- Risk reduction assessment to help and prevent transmission
- Counselling after a diagnosis of HIV disease has been made
- Family and relationship counselling
- Bereavement counselling
- Telephone "hotline" counselling
- Outreach counselling
- Crisis intervention
- Structured psychological support for those affected by HIV
- Support groups

Pretest discussion checklist

Indications for further counselling and referral to counsellor
- People who have been sexually active in areas of high HIV prevalence
- Men who have sex with men
- Current or previous sexual partners HIV positive
- Client presenting with clinical symptoms of HIV infection
- High risk sexual behaviour
- High risk injecting drug practices
- Learning or language difficulties

Points for counsellor and/or physician to cover
- What is the HIV antibody test (including seroconversion)
- The difference between HIV and AIDS
- The window period for HIV testing
- Medical advantages of knowing HIV status and treatment options
- Transmission of HIV
- Safer sex and risk reduction
- Safer injecting drug use
- If the client were positive how would the client cope: personal resources, support network of friends/partner/family
- Who to tell about the test and the result
- Partner notification issues
- HIV status of regular partner, is partner aware of patient testing?
- Confidentiality
- Does client need more time to consider?
- Is further counselling indicated?
- How the results of the test are obtained (in person from the physician or counsellor)

unable to disclose the real reason for testing. Counselling skills are clearly an essential part of establishing an early picture of the patient and his/her history and of how much intervention is needed to prepare him or her for a positive result, and to further reinforce prevention messages. It is at this stage that potential partners at risk are identified which will become an important part of the patient's management if HIV positive.

Post-test counselling

HIV results should be given simply, and in person. For HIV negative patients this may be a time where the information about risk reduction can be "heard" and further reinforced. With some patients it may be appropriate to consider referral for further work on personal strategies to reduce risks—for example one to one or group interventions. The window period of 12 weeks should be checked again and the decision taken about whether further tests for other sexually transmitted infections are appropriate.

HIV positive patients should be allowed time to adjust to their diagnosis. Coping procedures rehearsed at the pre-test discussion stage will need to be reviewed in the context of the here and now; what plans does the patient have for today, who can they be with this evening? Direct questions should be answered but the focus is on plans for the immediate few days, when further review by the counsellor should then take place. Practical arrangements including medical follow up should be written down. Overloading the patient with information about HIV should be avoided at this stage. Sometimes this may happen because of the health professional's own anxiety rather than the patient's needs. Counselling support should be available to the patient in the weeks and months following the positive test results.

Counselling during combination antiretroviral therapy

Significant developments in combination antiretroviral therapy have led to a surge of optimism about long term medical management of HIV infection, and people are now living much longer with HIV. Patient adherence is an important factor in the efficacy of drug regimens. However, taking a complicated drug regimen—often taking large numbers of tablets several times a day—is a constant reminder of HIV infection. The presence of side effects can often make patients feel more unwell than did the HIV and some may be unable to cope with the side effects. Counselling may be an important tool in determining a realistic assessment of individual adherence and in supporting the complex adjustment to a daily routine of medication.

Psychological responses to an HIV positive result

Many reactions to an HIV positive diagnosis are part of the normal and expected range of responses to news of a chronic, potentially life threatening medical condition. Many patients adjust extremely well with minimal intervention. Some will exhibit prolonged periods of distress, hostility, or other behaviours which are difficult to manage in a clinical setting. It should be noted that serious psychological maladjustment may indicate pre-existing morbidity and will require psychological/psychiatric assessment and treatment. Depressed patients should always be assessed for suicidal ideation.

Effective management requires allowing time for the shock of the news to sink in; there may be a period of emotional "ventilation", including overt distress. The counsellor should provide an assurance of strict confidentiality and rehearse, over time, the solutions to practical problems such as who to tell, what needs to be said, discussion around safer sex practices and adherence to drug therapies. Clear information about medical

Counselling is a core element in the care of HIV infected patients

Causes of uncertainty

- The cause of illness:
  Progression of disease
  Management of dying
  Prognosis
  Reactions of others (loved ones, employers, social networks)
- Effects of treatment
- Long term impact of antiretroviral therapy
- Impact of disclosure and how this will be managed

Coping strategies

- Using counselling
- Problem solving
- Participation in discussions about treatment
- Using social and family networks
- Use of alternative therapies, for example relaxation techniques, massage
- Exploring individual potential for control over manageable issues
- Disclosure of HIV status and using support options

and counselling follow up should be given. Counselling may be of help for the patient's partner and other family members.

Counselling can also be offered to patients and their partner together.

Counselling patients and partners together

This should only take place with the patient's explicit consent, but it may be important for the following reasons:

- Adjustments to sexual behaviour and other lifestyle issues can be discussed and explained clearly to both.
- If the patient's partner is HIV negative (ie a serodiscordant couple) particular care and attention must be paid to emotional and sexual consequences in the relationship.
- Misconceptions about HIV transmission can be addressed and information on safer sex given.
- The partner's and the patient's psychological responses to the diagnoses or result, such as anxiety or depression, can be explained and placed in a manageable perspective
- There may be particular issues for couples who have children or who are hoping to have children or where the woman is pregnant.

Partners and family members sometimes have greater difficulty in coming to terms with the knowledge of HIV infection than the patients do themselves. Individual counselling support is often required to manage this, particularly role changes within the relationship, and other adjustment issues that may lead to difficulties. This is part of a holistic approach to the patient's overall health care.

In many cases the need for follow up counselling may be episodic and this seems appropriate given the long term nature of HIV infection and the different challenges a patient may be faced with. The number of counselling sessions required during any of these periods largely depends on the individual presentation of the patient and the clinical judgment of the counsellor.

The worried well

Patients known as the "worried well" present with multiple physical complaints which they interpret as sure evidence of their HIV infection. Typically, fears of infection reach obsessive proportions and frank obsessive and hypochondriacal states are often seen. This group shows a variety of characteristic features, and they are rarely reassured for more than a brief period after clinical or laboratory confirmation of the absence of HIV infection. A further referral for behavioural psychotherapy or psychiatric intervention may be indicated, rather than frequent repetition of HIV testing.

Coping strategies

The importance of encouraging and working towards coping strategies involving active participation (to the extent the patient can manage) in planning of care and in seeking appropriate social support has been demonstrated clinically and empirically. Such an approach includes encouraging problem solving, participation in decisions about their treatment and care, and emphasising self worth and the potential for personal control over manageable issues in life.

Many patients diagnosed with HIV some years ago are now feeling well enough to return to work and to study and are, paradoxically, learning to readjust to living, as they had formally adjusted to the possibility of dying. Patients also have to deal with the uncertainty which remains about the long term efficacy of current medical treatment, and there are some who will fail on combination therapy. Even with the significant medical advances in patient management, counselling remains an integral part of the management of patients with HIV, and their partners and family.

Psychological issues in HIV/AIDS counselling

Shock
- of diagnosis
- recognition of mortality
- of loss of hope for the future

Fear and anxiety
- uncertain prognosis
- effects of medication and treatment/treatment failure
- of isolation and abandonment and social/sexual rejection
- of infecting others and being infected by them
- of partner's reaction

Depression
- in adjustment to living with a chronic viral condition
- over absence of a cure
- over limits imposed by possible ill health
- possible social, occupational, and sexual rejection
- if treatment fails

Anger and frustration
- over becoming infected
- over new and involuntary health/lifestyle restrictions
- over incorporating demanding drug regimens, and possible side effects, into daily life

Guilt
- interpreting HIV as a punishment; for example, for being gay or using drugs
- over anxiety caused to partner/family

Characteristics of the worried well

- Repeated negative HIV tests
- Low risk sexual history, including covert and guilt inducing sexual activity
- Poor post adolescence sexual adjustment
- Social isolation
- Dependence in close relationships (if any)
- Multiple misinterpreted somatic features usually associated with undiagnosed viral or postviral states (not HIV) or anxiety or depression
- Psychiatric history and repeated consultation with general practitioners or physicians
- High levels of anxiety, depression, and obsessional disturbance
- Increased potential for suicidal gestures

BMJ 2001;322:1533-5

[14]

The Correctional Response to Prisoners With HIV/AIDS: Morality, Metaphors, and Myths

MICHAEL WELCH
Rutgers University

Rather than adhering to a medical approach, the criminalization of drug use in the United States tragically compounds the problem of incarcerating persons infected with HIV/AIDS. Correspondingly, the correctional response to prisoners with HIV/AIDS continues to be shaped by a criminalization model along with conservative notions of morality and theological metaphors of punishment. In this article, a critical examination reveals patterns of discrimination against prisoners with HIV/AIDS, most significantly the emergence of added forms of retribution, a phenomenon we call "fringe punishments." As a correctional response to HIV/AIDS, fringe punishments often are justified by popular myths aimed at demonizing drug use, promiscuity, and homosexuality. Implications to the political economy and its role in reproducing problem populations also are addressed.

The war on drugs has delivered a dual impact on the nation's correctional system. Quantitatively, more drug violators are being sentenced to prison now than at any other point in U.S. history. Qualitatively, the incarceration of intravenous (IV) drug users infected with acquired immunodeficiency syndrome (AIDS) and human immunodeficiency virus (HIV), the asymptomatic infection that leads to AIDS, is significantly transforming the role of corrections in social control. Prisons and jails continue to serve as human warehouses predominately reserved for society's impoverished, given that the vast majority of drug violators behind bars are economically marginalized. Moreover, due to the debilitating and lethal nature of HIV/AIDS, correctional facilities are increasingly—albeit reluctantly—assuming the traditional function of infirmaries, in effect, becoming repositories for infectious diseases (Welch, 1999).

By exploring HIV/AIDS at different levels of analysis, this article unveils related key concepts in the spheres of macrosociology, mesosociology, and microsociology. Fittingly, connections are drawn between the following: the production of deviance in capitalist society, the process of stigmatizing problem populations, and the establishment of social control mechanisms designed to manage those who are marginalized. This examination further contextualizes HIV/AIDS ideologically by attending to adverse societal reactions dependent on metaphors in creating distinct cultural meanings. For example, a prominent ideological theme in popular depictions of HIV/AIDS is a moralizing of the illness, insinuating that those infected are being judged and punished by a higher power for indulging in illicit drugs, promiscuity, or homosexuality.

These ideological connotations also are prevalent in corrections where prisoners with HIV/AIDS are stigmatized and often ostracized. As a result, their incarceration experience is marked by a greater degree of suffering, commonly traced to discrimination and various other fringe punishments. Whereas fringe benefits denote extra rewards, fringe punishments refer to added forms of retribution. Throughout key periods in correctional history, prison reformers have struggled to improve the conditions of confinement: By making penal institutions more humane, they are better equipped to reform and rehabilitate their prisoners. Over the past few decades, however, the penal harm movement has emerged as the antithesis of prison reform. Currently, these campaigns lobby legislators to make prison conditions harsher by eliminating or scaling down what they call amenities and luxuries, including personal clothing, televisions, recreation, educational programs, and even medical care (Clear, 1994; Cullen, 1995; Flanagan, 1996; Johnson, Bennett, & Flanagan, 1997; Vaughn & Carroll, 1998; Welch, 1997, 1999). Proposals to abolish amenities are rooted in the perception that incarceration is not sufficiently harsh; therefore, by imposing fringe punishments, supplemental doses of retribution are intended to maximize suffering. In this article, it is argued that prisoners with HIV/AIDS are subjected to numerous fringe punishments, most notably victimization, discrimination, and the denial of adequate medical attention. Altogether, these fringe punishments produce a level of suffering for prisoners with HIV/AIDS rarely experienced by other inmates.

From an institutional perspective, correctional policies and practices have the potential to exacerbate or alleviate inmate suffering. Hence, one objective of this article is to enumerate the ways that correctional management—intentionally or unintentionally—contributes to hardship for prisoners with HIV/AIDS. In doing so, we remain mindful of the mesosociological and organizational forces affecting the incarceration experience. Relatedly, this discussion also encompasses the microsociological elements of imprisonment, exploring phenomenology and the role that temporality plays in shaping the contours of suffering. Setting the stage for a multilayered and critical analysis of HIV/AIDS, we begin with a macrosociological examination of deviance production in capitalist society.

The Production of Problem Populations in Capitalist Society

A critical discussion of problem populations, including prisoners with HIV/AIDS, should acknowledge the production of deviant classes at a broader level of society, especially considering the dialectical nature of capitalism. Among the contradictions of capitalism is the production of deviance that marginalizes—rather than absorbs—some people from economic activity (Spitzer, 1975). Unemployed workers are the most recognizable manifestations of the internal contradictions of capitalism—a system that ironically requires a certain level of unemployment to function properly.

Still, unemployed workers (the surplus population) do not become a problem until they threaten the social relations of production; when that occurs, they are labeled a problem population by the state. More specifically, problem populations become eligible for social control when they disrupt or challenge the following components of a capitalist society:

- the capitalist modes of appropriating the product of human labor (e.g., when the poor steal from the rich),
- the social conditions under which capitalist production takes place (e.g., those who refuse or are unable to perform wage labor),
- patterns of distribution and consumption in capitalist society (e.g., those who use drugs for escape and transcendence rather than sociability and adjustment),
- the process of socialization for productive and nonproductive roles (e.g., youths who refuse to be schooled or those who deny the validity of family life), and
- the ideology that supports the functioning of capitalist society (e.g., proponents of alternative forms of social organization) (Spitzer, 1975, p. 642).

As the problem population swells, it is in the interests of the state and its political economy to devise mechanisms of class (social) control in an effort to preserve the social order and status quo. In particular, two major groupings within the problem population are identified: *social junk* and *social dynamite*. From the perspective of the state, *social junk* are viewed as costly but relatively harmless to the social order. "The discreditability of social junk resides in the failure, inability or refusal of this group to participate in the roles supportive of the capitalist society" (Spitzer, 1975, p. 645). The category of social junk is composed of the elderly and the physically and mentally handicapped. Because social junk are deemed harmless, social control mechanisms in the form of therapeutic and welfare agencies serve to regulate rather than eliminate or suppress them. Conversely, the portion of the problem population labeled *social dynamite* is believed to pose a serious threat to the existing social and economic order. Due to their presumed volatility, those in the social dynamite group are processed through the coercive components of the social control apparatus, namely, the criminal justice system.

Despite these seemingly discrete categories within the problem population, the social control apparatus operates equivocally in that members of the problem population, including the impoverished, drug users, and problem children, are processed as alternatively either social junk or social dynamite. Gays and lesbians also are subjected to deviance processing because they represent a threat to the validity of the bourgeois family, essential to capitalism as a unit for consumption, socialization, and reproduction of the labor force (Frankford & Snitow, 1972; Secombe, 1973; Zaretsky, 1973a, 1973b). Indeed, gay and lesbian activists have been routinely funneled through the criminal justice machinery after being arrested at gay rights demonstrations.

It has been commonly observed that jails (even more so than prisons) fail to consistently distinguish between harmless social junk (or rabble, see Irwin, 1985) and menacing social dynamite; consequently, jails serve as unspecialized catch basins for both types of the problem population (Irwin, 1985; Shover & Einstadter, 1988; Welch, 1991b, 1994). Accounting for this lack of uniformity in processing deviance, Spitzer (1975) notes that social control is patterned by the political, economic, and ideological priorities that are continuously subject to change; likewise, Marx (1967) characterized capitalism as dynamic rather than static, a political economy in constant transformation. A key economic transformation in the United States during the past four decades has been the shift from industrial to corporate capitalism, resulting in the erosion of jobs formerly occupied by blue-collar workers in the inner city (many of whom are people of color). In brief, this economic transformation has contributed to the growth of the surplus population, prompting the state to invest greater resources in coercive mechanisms of social control—the criminal justice and correctional systems. Indeed, containment has emerged as an increasingly expansive measure of social control, as currently evidenced by the largest incarceration rate in U.S. history and the world (Welch, 1996, 1999; Welch, Fenwick, & Roberts, 1997, 1998).

AIDS, Metaphors, and Morality

In her book *AIDS and Its Metaphors*, Susan Sontag (1989) offers an interpretive narrative of AIDS, blending historical and literary references that parallel the sociologies of knowledge, medicine, and deviance. Much of her discussion underscores the processes and consequences of stigma and social control by illuminating the potency of metaphors, that is, the tendency to give a thing a name that belongs to something else. Sociologically, the construction of metaphors is an initial process of labeling; this reification allows those who are perceived as different from so-called normal people to be stigmatized and marginalized (Becker, 1963; Goffman, 1963; Schur, 1971). Sontag (1980), drawing on her previous work, *Illness as Metaphor*, reminds us of society's propensity to interpret diseases through the prism of morality and punishment. Still, AIDS is not confined solely to moral and punitive connotations, but rather, it is subject to an array of metaphors.

> AIDS has a dual metaphoric genealogy. As a micro-process, it is described as cancer is: an invasion. When the focus is transmission of the disease, an older metaphor, reminiscent of syphilis, is invoked: pollution. (One gets it from the blood or sexual fluids of infected people or from contaminated blood products.) (Sontag, 1989, p. 17)

In a sense, this metaphor moves in opposite directions: Inwardly, AIDS attacks the body of the infected, whereas outwardly, it poses a threat to others. Whereas stigma is imposed on those infected, it is the outward threat (contagiousness) posed by AIDS that spawns a different type of societal reaction, that is, moral panic—a turbulent and exaggerated response to a social problem (Cohen, 1973). Returning to the notion of morality, AIDS is subject to demonization, evangelical condemnation, and judgments. In a nationally televised sermon, Jerry Falwell of the Moral Majority proclaimed that AIDS with regard to homosexuals represented a "lethal judgment of God on America for endorsing this vulgar, perverted and reprobate life-style" (Bayer & Kirp, 1992, p. 34). Moreover, integrating moral metaphors with medical constructs produces another common reference to AIDS: The disease is brought on by the lack of moral hygiene. This notion insinuates that homosexual sex is both immoral and unhealthy.

An understandable reaction to AIDS is fear; thus, we turn to the scientific community to help us understand the nature of the illness, not only in the hope of eventually developing a cure but also to learn how to protect ourselves from infection. Regrettably, not all members of the scientific community have acted responsibly, and some researchers have inaccurately characterized AIDS only to inflame fears and incite hysteria among the public. For example, the famous sex researchers Masters and Johnson (with Kolodny) published a popular book about AIDS in 1988. In *Crisis: Heterosexual Behavior in the Age of AIDS*, the authors made false statements about the nature of the transmission of AIDS, claims which ran counter to what was known about the disease at the time. Masters et al. asserted that AIDS had "clearly broken out" among heterosexuals and that AIDS could be contracted from saliva and hard substances such as toilet seats. When confronted by the Presidential Commission on AIDS about such claims, Masters et al. conceded that they had no independent data to support their conclusions (Sirica, 1988). Critics charged that Masters et al. knowingly disseminated false information about AIDS in an effort to capitalize commercially from book profits. As a result, Masters et al. fueled fear among the public and reinforced the myths and misconceptions about AIDS (see Thomas, 1985; Welch, 1989).

Originating from the traditional enforcement of conventional morality, stigma is a mark of social disgrace. In ancient Greece, unusual bodily markings were construed as signs of moral inferiority; similarly, lawbreakers were deliberately branded for the purpose of exposing their moral defects. During early Christian times, bodily signs in the form of eruptive blossoms on the skin were interpreted as being emblematic of holy grace, suggesting supernatural qualities. However, less aesthetic imperfections were believed to be indicative of physical and moral defects. Nathaniel Hawthorne's novel, *The Scarlet Letter*, remains a compelling lesson on how colonial communities publicly punished and humiliated women for moral—especially sexual—transgressions. Our contemporary understanding of stigma is largely indebted to the work of sociologist Erving Goffman (1963). In *Stigma: Notes on the Management of Spoiled Identity*, Goffman delineates the processes and products of stigma that devalues and disqualifies some people from full social acceptance. Stigma has numerous sources: physical (e.g., illnesses, injuries, disfigurements), documentary or character (e.g., mental illness, chronic unemployment, a prison record), and contextual (e.g., keeping bad company). Stigma also may be ascribed or assigned to a person at birth—known as tribal (or class) stigma in which all members of a particular race, ethnic group, or religion are tainted. Tribal stigma also connotes moral transgressions because it is inherited from the sins of one's parents.

Stigma attached to prisoners with HIV/AIDS is actually a configuration of several attributes. The complex makeup of their stigma is physical, documentary or character, contextual, and tribal, all of which are interpreted through the lens of morality. Physically, inmates with HIV/AIDS are devalued because they are inflicted with a fatal and contagious illness. Prisoners with HIV/AIDS typically became infected by injecting illicit drugs into their bodies with unclean needles or by having sexual contact with infected partners, either heterosexually or, even more stigmatizing, homosexually. As a result of the ways in which they contracted HIV/AIDS, these inmates are further discredited for their lack of moral character and for keeping bad company. The stigma of HIV/AIDS is potent, which explains why many of those infected refuse testing and treatment. Sheila Morris, an HIV-positive prisoner in Washington, D.C., reports,

> You have a lot of people who know they're [HIV] positive who are in denial. I am surprised by people who are sick and won't admit it. They're more willing to admit they're drug addicts or murderers or pedophiles than admit they're sick and get care for it. (Purdy, 1997, p. 28)

Compounding their stigma, prisoners with HIV/AIDS are convicted felons and, in many cases, are ascribed tribal (class) stigma: The vast majority are impoverished people of color from the inner city.[1] Given the proportion of inmates with HIV/AIDS who are non-White and urban, additional commentary about racism and HIV/AIDS is apropos. Throughout history, the interpretation of plagues and epidemics are typically twofold. First, plagues are depicted in moral terms, sent by a higher power as a punishment for society's sins; second, plagues come from somewhere else. Sontag (1989) reminds us that the syphilis epidemic in Europe during the 15th century, the bubonic plague during the 18th century, and the outbreaks of cholera during the 19th century were all characterized as dreaded foreigner diseases. Literally and figuratively, plagues are reified as pollution from alien and exotic lands.

> AIDS is thought to have started in the 'dark continent,' then spread to Haiti, then to the United States and to Europe, then. . . . It is understood as a tropical disease: another manifestation from the so-called Third World. (Sontag, 1989, pp. 51-52)

Popular beliefs on the origin of HIV/AIDS—commonly but inaccurately described as a plague—has fueled anti-African (Black) prejudice in the Americas, Europe, and Asia.

> The subliminal connection made to notions about a primitive past and the many hypotheses that have been fielded about possible transmission from ani-

mals (a disease of green monkeys? African swine fever?) cannot help but activate a familiar set of stereotypes about animality, sexual license, and blacks. (Sontag, 1989, p. 52; also see Huber & Schneider, 1992; Schneider, 1992)

Throughout history, urbanization also has been blamed for plagues, epidemics, and the spread of numerous diseases. Whereas rural communities have been long cherished as pure, simple, and wholesome, cities represented the embodiment of crime, vice, and disease—aggravated by an influx of minorities and immigrants. Not surprisingly, HIV/AIDS is currently viewed by conservative extremists as another symptom of the immorality of urban life, in particular, homosexuality and illicit drug use (see Shilts, 1987).

Prisoners With HIV/AIDS as a Problem Population for Corrections

Perhaps not so coincidentally, the term *problem population* also abounds in the field of corrections, referring to prisoners who require special (in many cases medical) attention, including the infirm, the elderly, the pregnant, and inmates with various psychiatric needs. Among the most pressing issues in correctional management today is dealing with problem populations, especially prisoners with HIV/AIDS. The equivocal tendencies of social control are clearly evident in the harsh treatment of prisoners with HIV/AIDS, who are not only regarded as harmless social junk but, given the contagious and fatal nature of their illness, also characterized as costly social dynamite (Welch, 1989) (incidentally, many prisoners with HIV/AIDS fit also into Irwin's, 1985, rabble category). For instance, in 1995, the Special Officer for the Court of the District of Columbia released a document describing the abominable conditions concerning the delivery of medical care for inmates with HIV/AIDS. In particular, the report featured an account of the death of a male prisoner with AIDS who had remained neglected in his cell for 10 days: "The inmate died while being transported to the hospital strapped in a wheelchair and wrapped in a urine and feces stained sheet" (Perez, 1996, p. 8). Processed as social junk and social dynamite, prisoners with HIV/AIDS occupy the lowest stratum in the correctional caste system. As we shall discuss further, these inmates are likely to experience greater suffering than are other prisoners, including discrimination and various fringe punishments.

The most recent data available indicate that in 1997, 2.1% of all state and federal inmates were known to be infected with HIV. The infection rate was down slightly from 2.2% in 1996. In 1997, a total of 23,548 prisoners were HIV positive, and 6,184 were confirmed AIDS cases. Also in 1997, there were 538 AIDS-related deaths in state prisons, a figure that is three times the rate in the general population. Other statistics show that confirmed AIDS cases in prison more than doubled from 1991 to 1997 and that the rate of AIDS in prison is at least five times the rate in the general population (Bureau of Justice Statistics, 1999; Hammett, Harmon, & Maruschak, 1999). It is commonly believed that the actual number of HIV (and AIDS) cases is much higher in prisons than officially recorded due to the high concentration of IV drug users; moreover, many cases remain concealed by the lengthy incubation period of the disease, sometimes lasting several years (Hammett, Harrold, Gross, & Epstein, 1994) (also compounding this health crisis behind bars are prisoners coinfected with HIV and tuberculosis, see Hammett & Harrold, 1994).

Discrimination and Fringe Punishments

HIV and AIDS generate special medical and psychological needs, and the degree of suffering from these illnesses is generally determined by how adequately such needs are met. In prison, medical and psychological needs are complicated by the very nature of incarceration, including the adverse conditions of confinement (Welch, 1991a). Although being infected with HIV/AIDS is physically and emotionally debilitating in and of itself, imprisonment merely adds to the suffering by exacerbating depression, helplessness, worthlessness, and grief. Even worse, at the later stages of AIDS, neurological deficits develop along with encephalopathy, dementia, psychomotor retardation, disorientation, and seizures (McArthur, 1987). Understandably, prisoners with HIV/AIDS not only direct their anger at the disease but also direct it at the institution for rejection, discrimination, and the denial of adequate medical care (Gostin & Lazzarini, 1997; Lawrence & Zwisohn, 1991; Potler, 1988).

As previously noted, many prisoners with HIV/AIDS are stigmatized by society according to a larger constellation of disreputable attributes: Typically, they are lawbreakers who are impoverished, urban, a minority, IV drug users (and in some cases gay), and infected with a terminal and contagious illness. Within the prison world, inmates with HIV/AIDS are devalued by both staff and other inmates to the extent that they become institutional outcasts, subjected to a level of suffering rarely found among their free world counterparts. Even though persons with HIV/AIDS in the free world also are subjected to prejudice and discrimination, the degree of fear and hostility often is magnified in prison and jail due to the nature of captivity. "Additional factors, unique to the incarcerated, aggravate that stress. Segregation and isolation, witnessing the deteriorating health and eventual death of fellow inmates, and the fear—heightened in the total institution of the prison—that health care is inadequate cause additional anxiety" (Juvelis, 1995, p. 6). Under such adverse conditions, myths and misconceptions about HIV/AIDS take on a life of their own, manifesting in prison fiction that is used to justify mistreating unpopular inmates. Ostracizing—and worse, victimizing—prisoners with HIV/AIDS serve the function of informally controlling the pariahs of the prison society, thus reinforcing the hierarchy and status boundaries between different classes of inmates (see Akerstrom, 1986). Victimization occurs in the form of harassment and physical attacks against inmates with HIV/AIDS, and in some incidents, their prison cells are flooded with water or set afire (Potler, 1988; Welch, 1989, 1991a, 1991b).

Institutional policies and practices have the potential to either alleviate or exacerbate the suffering of prisoners with HIV/AIDS. With this in mind, policies and practices that contribute directly or indirectly, intentionally or unintentionally, to the pain and suffering of prisoners with HIV/AIDS shall be referred to as fringe punishments, including victimization, lack of adequate medical care, and various other forms of discrimination. In the next section, we shall examine significant aspects of prison and jail management while attending to policies and practices that result in fringe punishments for prisoners with HIV/AIDS.

Myths, Misconceptions, and the Correctional Response to HIV/AIDS

After more that 15 years of medical and scientific research demonstrating that HIV/AIDS cannot be transmitted through casual contact, many criminal justice and security personnel still behave on the basis of myths and misconceptions. For example, in 1995, 50 gay and lesbian officials were invited to the White House where four security guards wore plastic gloves while conducting routine security checks on briefcases and other personal belongings (Kappeler, Blumberg, & Potter, 1996). In corrections, many staff also stray from medical and scientific knowledge and rely more on exaggerated fears in shaping their views of HIV/AIDS; contributing to these misconceptions are deep-seated anxieties and prejudices against the impoverished, urban minorities, IV drug users, and homosexuals. A common fear among correctional officers is contracting HIV while carrying out their duties despite the fact that the Centers for Disease Control and Prevention (CDC) has not documented a single case of occupational transmission among correctional officers (or police officers) (Hammett et al., 1994; also see Flavin, 1998). Nevertheless, some offenders with HIV have been sentenced harshly by the courts for engaging in assaultive behaviors that pose relatively little danger to others; appellate courts in Georgia, Indiana, New Jersey, and Texas have upheld attempted homicide charges against seropositive offenders who bit or spat on correctional staff. In addition to spitting and biting, two other types of assaults by HIV-positive offenders have recently become subjects of controversy in corrections: injuries sustained in altercations and being stabbed with an infected hypodermic needle (Kappeler et al., 1996).

In scenarios involving spitting, laboratory tests reveal that HIV is present in saliva but only in very few infected persons (Ho, Byington, Schooley, Flynn, Rota, & Hirsch, 1985). Still, the quantity of HIV in saliva is minute, making transmission extremely unlikely (CDC, 1988). In Texas, an HIV-positive prisoner was convicted of attempted murder for spitting in the face of a correctional officer and was sentenced to life imprisonment (*Weeks v. Texas*, 1992). Curtis Weeks testified at trial that he was provoked to spit at the guard after being denied bathroom facilities while being transported between two prisons. An expert witness for the prisoner testified that it is impossible to transmit HIV by spitting and reported that there has never been a documented case of such transmission, but it was to no avail.

Contracting HIV through biting is also remote. Researchers Richman and Richman (1993) have concluded that "the transmission of HIV through human bites is biologically possible but remains unlikely, epidemiologically insignificant, and as yet, not well documented" (p. 402). In New Jersey, an HIV-positive prisoner was convicted of attempted murder for biting a correctional officer and was sentenced to 25 years (*New Jersey v. Smith*, 1993). The Appellate Division was not concerned with whether HIV can be transmitted by biting as long as the inmate believed that it could. During the scuffle in which the officer was bitten, the inmate was reported to have shouted, "Now die, you pig! Die from what I have" (Sullivan, 1993, p. B7). The trial judge instructed the jury as follows: "Impossibility is not a defense to the charge of attempted murder. That is because our law, our criminal statutes, punish conduct based on state of mind" (Sullivan, 1993, p. B7). The prosecution maintained that whether the biting could transmit HIV was legally irrelevant, but the appellants argued that Smith "was as likely to have caused the death of [corrections officers] by biting them as he was to have caused their deaths by sticking pins in dolls bearing their likenesses" ("NJ Inmate Argues for Reversal," 1992, p. 1). Attorneys for the inmate insisted that the guilty verdict and 25-year sentence were not driven by current medical evidence or sound legal reasoning but rather by public hysteria with regard to HIV/AIDS.

Regarding altercations with seropositive persons, the transmission of HIV through open wounds has been documented in the medical literature (O'Farrell, Tovey, & Morgan-Capner, 1992). Although such cases are rare and have not involved criminal justice personnel, public safety workers are advised to follow CDC (1989) guidelines by keeping all open wounds bandaged and wearing gloves when anticipating contact with blood (or body fluids containing visible blood). Being wounded by HIV-contaminated needles also remains a concern of those working in criminal justice because such injuries do present a risk—albeit a relatively low one—of HIV transmission; experts recommend that safety procedures be followed to reduce the likelihood of these incidents (Richman & Richman, 1993).

Another popular myth suggests that HIV/AIDS is spreading rapidly within the correctional population. This myth is driven by the fear of homosexual rape and IV drug abuse among inmates, as well as by a general misunderstanding of how HIV is transmitted. The prevalence of homosexual rape in correctional facilities is greatly exaggerated. Even though transmission does occur during incarceration, it is a relatively infrequent event, and at this time, there is no evidence to support the claim that there is widespread transmission of HIV/AIDS among inmates (Hammett et al., 1994; Hammett & Moini, 1990; Vlahov et al., 1991; also see Blumberg, 1990a, 1990b; Blumberg & Langston, 1995).

Confronting myths about HIV/AIDS is important because misinformation can inflame fear and hysteria, resulting in discriminatory management practices. For instance, in 1992, Louise K. Nolley was awarded $155,000 for what a judge called humiliating and improper treatment at the Erie County jail where she was held on charges of forgery and passing a check without sufficient funds.

Staff placed Nolley in a forensic unit usually reserved for suicidal and mentally disturbed inmates, required that she wear plastic gloves when she used the typewriter in the jail library, and denied her regular attendance to Roman Catholic services. Jailers also attached red stickers on all her belongings, indicating that she had AIDS, a violation of a New York State law that prohibits the disclosure that a person has tested positive for HIV. Judge John T. Curtain concluded, "There is no question that the red sticker policy was developed, not in response to contagious diseases in general, but specifically in response to the hysteria over HIV and AIDS" (Sullivan, 1992, p. B4). Judge Curtain also cited the Erie County jail for violating regulations adopted by the New York State Department of Correction Services in 1987, under which inmates who test positive for HIV cannot be isolated from the general prison population. The basis of the ruling and award rested on compensatory and punitive damages for AIDS discrimination (*Nolley v. County of Erie*, 1991). Norman Siegel, executive director of the New York American Civil Liberties Union (ACLU) added, "We applaud Judge Curtain for his courageous and legally correct decision. It sends a strong message that such stigmatization will not be tolerated by the courts and that once and for all we must end this kind of hysteria" (Sullivan, 1992, p. B4).

The red sticker alert controversy in *Nolley v. County of Erie* (1991) is reminiscent of other correctional practices that blatantly stigmatize and humiliate unpopular prisoners. For more than 15 years, homosexual inmates held at the Polk County jail in Florida were segregated and required to wear pink bracelets symbolizing their sexual identity. In 1989, jail officials facing legal action discontinued the practice of tagging and segregating homosexuals. Six lesbians complained to the ACLU that being pink-tagged had limited their privileges and brought harsh treatment from jailers. According to ACLU attorney Jim West, "It reflects homophobia. . . . Labeling people's clothing based on a sexual preference seems an extreme response that doesn't warrant it" ("Pink Bracelets for Homosexuals," 1989, p. 35; "Red Tags for Gays," 1990). (Incidentally, in 1987, a federal court ruled against the segregation of homosexuals in Indiana correctional facilities.) Red tagging homosexual prisoners also should be understood in a larger social and historical context. During the Third Reich of the 1930s and 1940s, German Nazis held between 10,000 and 15,000 homosexuals in concentration camps, arrested for violating Paragraph 175 of the German criminal code, which called for the imprisonment of any "male who commits lewd and lascivious acts with another male." Under Nazi rule, homosexuality was referred to as being a sinful deviance and being sexually subversive. Homosexuals wore uniforms bearing pink triangles while in the camps where many were tortured and castrated: 60% of the incarcerated homosexuals died in the camps (Dunlop, 1995; Heger, 1972; Plant, 1986, 1989).

Mass Screening and Prisoner Stratification

Among the most controversial management issues in dealing with HIV/AIDS in corrections is mass screening: "the mandatory testing of all inmates, or all releases in the absence of clinical indicates" (Hammett & Moini, 1990, p. 4).

Proponents of mass screening often rely on exaggerated views or myths about HIV/AIDS to support their views. For instance, proponents assume that the rates of transmission are higher in correctional institutions than in the larger society and that screening is thereby necessary to identify infected inmates. Opponents of mass screening point out that there is no evidence of higher transmission rates in prisons and jails. More important, educational programs can be offered to all inmates without identifying infected prisoners. Hammett (1989) further emphasizes that mass screening can lead to the unnecessary and false stratification of the inmate population into a stigmatized class and a safe class. (This limitation of mass screening is particularly evident in light of the lengthy incubation period during which infected persons do not test positive.)

Mass screening also raises issues of confidentiality and reliability. Opponents assert that the confidentiality of test results is difficult to protect and that patient information (or rumors) can lead to victimization while incarcerated and to discrimination upon release (for example, in obtaining health insurance, housing, and employment). The reliability of testing has been questioned, and the cost of repeat tests to confirm cases is prohibitive, especially in large institutions (Carroll, 1992).

Legal issues related to mass screening also must be addressed. Opponents point out that mass screening (which involves involuntary testing) can be challenged on the basis of existing laws that require the person's informed consent. Considering these issues, voluntary (or on-request) testing for early detection (or if clinical symptoms are present) and therapeutic intervention has become the trend; arrangements for voluntary testing are made with local public health departments or other agencies. In addition, voluntary testing is also available to inmates and staff in response to possible transmission incidents. Mass screening creates additional funding difficulties for corrections and, in the end, often creates more problems than it solves (Hammett et al., 1994; Hammett & Moini, 1990).

Currently, each state, the District of Columbia, and the Federal Bureau of Prisons test their inmates for HIV based on certain criteria. Most jurisdictions (45 out of 52) test inmates if they have HIV-related symptoms or if the inmates request a test. Twenty-four states test inmates after they are involved in an incident, and 15 states test inmates who belong to specific high-risk groups. Sixteen states test all inmates who enter their facilities. Three of these states (Alabama, Missouri, and Nevada) and the Federal Bureau of Prisons test inmates upon their release. Rhode Island, Utah, and Wyoming test all inmates currently in custody. Massachusetts, New York, and the Federal Bureau of Prisons test inmates selected at random (Bureau of Justice Statistics, 1997).

Denial of Adequate Medical Care

Conforming to the punitive metaphor, the denial of adequate medical care to prisoners with HIV/AIDS constitutes a fringe punishment because it exacerbates both physical and emotional suffering among this population. Partially as a result of the penal harm movement, proposals to allocate health care dollars to corrections have become increasingly unpopular, especially when those requiring the expensive medications and services are infected with illnesses brought on by IV drug use and homosexual sex. Efforts to generate greater public concern for treating prisoners with HIV/AIDS often are hampered by a lack of awareness, apathy, and in some instances, hostility. According to Ronald Bogard, a former general counsel of the New York City Health Department, there has been little effort to determine the extent of the problem: "Not only do we not know, we don't really care, because of the people that are involved and the money that is involved" (Purdy, 1997, p. 28).

A particularly expensive feature of HIV/AIDS intervention is the distribution of azidothymidine (AZT), a medication which is believed to retard the progression of the disease in some patients. Due to its cost, however, correctional systems may not properly distribute AZT in ways required for effectiveness; for example, dosages may be improperly rationed. Hammett and Moini (1990) found that nearly one fourth of the prisons and jails do not dispense AZT to all prisoners who meet the eligibility requirements, even though physicians acknowledge that such behavior is unethical (see Purdy, 1997). A similar treatment gaining interest inside and outside of prison is the so-called HIV cocktail, a combination of medications designed to prevent the reproduction of the virus. However, financial barriers abound. In New Jersey, the annual expense for treating one prisoner with the HIV cocktail costs from $10,000 to $15,000, and the cost jumps to $70,000 for prisoners with full-blown AIDS. These and other medical costs have prompted New Jersey's Correctional Health Services—a private contractor—to renegotiate part of its contract. Currently, the medical plan covers annual expenses to the tune of $2,900 per inmate; in 1997, Correctional Health Services requested an additional $5 million to meet HIV-related expenses (Sforza, 1998b).

Overall, correctional health care is woefully inadequate or, even under the best circumstances, is marred by inconsistent care; indeed, the quality of medical services varies from state to state and from prison to prison. Whereas it is tempting to compromise medical care for inmates because of budgetary constraints, many administrators deal with these problems by lobbying state officials for additional funding. In some cases, litigation geared at increasing spending for medical services in corrections has yielded support from the courts. Attorneys representing prisoners with HIV/AIDS, often in class action suits, insist that the denial of adequate care constitutes cruel and unusual punishment, which is unconstitutional under the Eighth Amendment of the U.S. Constitution. "A sick person on the street can go to an emergency room. But these people can't because they're under lock and key, so that puts a big responsibility on the person holding the key," says Maddie LaMarre, clinical services coordinator for the Georgia prison system (Purdy, 1997, p. 28). Despite some important legal victories, financial obstacles combined with larger social forces (e.g., political apathy) and organizational forces (e.g., lack of equipment, supplies, and staff) continue to strain medical attention for inmates with HIV/AIDS (see Blumberg 1990a, 1990b; Blumberg & Mahaffey-Sapp, 1997; Bolonsky et al., 1994; Koehler, 1994; Thomas & Moerings, 1994). Michael Wiseman of the Prisoners Rights Project of the Legal Aid Society of New York reflects, "Prisons were never designed to deliver medical treatment, they were designed to keep people locked up. Before HIV prisons never gave good care. But with HIV, its turned a lot of them into death camps" (Gross, 1993, p. A12).

For several years, many prisoners with HIV/AIDS have formally complained to the courts that they have been denied adequate medical care. As a result of litigation, some medical services have improved. Nevertheless, disparities in treatment for HIV/AIDS persist because prisoners do not have a constitutional right to "every potential beneficial medical procedure" (Friedman, 1992, pp. 933-934; also see *Adams v. Poag,* 1995; Vaughn & Carroll, 1998). In *Harris v. Thigpen* (1991), the district court ruled that inmates are not entitled to state-of-the-art medical care and that reasonable care (determined by community standards) is constitutionally sufficient. Questions persist whether many prisoners with HIV/AIDS are receiving even basic medical attention: "Prisoners with AIDS live about half as long following diagnosis as persons in the community" (Committee on the Judiciary, 1991, p. 86; U.S. General Accounting Office, 1994; Vaughn & Carroll, 1998). Admittedly, the accelerated death rate among inmates also may be related to the poor health of inmates before entering prison (Marquart, Merianos, Cuvelier, & Carroll, 1996). Still, it is commonly argued that denial of medical care is the result of deliberate indifference to the prisoners' medical needs or in retaliation for exercising their right to contest the charges against them (*Proctor v. Alameda County*, 1992). Adhering to U.S. public health guidelines, the New Jersey Department of Corrections promised to provide HIV-positive prisoners with comprehensive medical care and education (*Roe et al. v. Fauver et al.*, 1992; also see *Fitzhugh v. Wyoming Board of Charities and Reform,* 1991). Remember, the quality of medical care for prisoners is uneven and varies from state to state and from facility to facility; relatedly, prisoners with HIV/AIDs at some institutions have been denied participation in programs and activities that present no risk of viral transmission, constituting clear examples of exclusion, rejection, and discrimination (Cauchon, 1995; for other legal issues pertaining to prisoners with HIV/AIDS, also see Jacobs, 1995; Middleton & Lee, 1997).

Related Forms of Discrimination

Many issues germane to prisoners with HIV/AIDS addressed thus far—stigma, victimization, segregation, and denial of adequate health care—share a common complaint, namely, discrimination. Indeed, discrimination toward prisoners with HIV/AIDS not only reinforces stigma and related manifestations of inequality but also is another fringe punishment. Whether intentional or unintentional, discrimination against prisoners with HIV/AIDS produces an added degree of suffering. Many discrimination lawsuits filed by prisoners with HIV/AIDS have reached the judiciary, resulting in complex and conflicting rulings. In addition to demanding adequate medical care, other chief areas of litigation are challenges to mandatory testing, confidentiality, segregation, and access to programs.

In resolving a complaint against Nevada's mandatory HIV-testing policy, the court reversed a district court's summary judgment holding that the state did not offer evidence that its policy was reasonably related to legitimate penological interests (*Walker v. Sumner*, 1990; also see *Turner v. Safley*, 1987). Conversely, the 10th circuit in 1989 rejected appellants' claims that they were unconstitutionally tested for HIV and segregated from the general prison population (*Dunn v. White*, 1989). Recognizing inmate confidentiality and privacy interests, a federal district court limited disclosure of medical records to those involved in litigation who had need for access to them (*Doe v. Meachum*, 1989; also see *Doe v. City of Cleveland*, 1991).

Segregation in correctional housing viewed as discrimination by prisoners with HIV/AIDS remains an ongoing issue in litigation. As noted previously in *Nolley v. County of Erie* (1991), the court ruled against the segregation of a female prisoner with AIDS; however, in *Harris v. Thigpen* (1991), the federal appeals court for the 11th circuit upheld the Alabama Corrections Department's (DOC) regulation requiring the HIV antibody testing and segregation of those determined to be HIV positive. The district court insisted that segregation was not a form of discrimination; rather, it was a necessary measure to protect all inmates from victimization. However, the HIV-positive inmates claimed that their blanket exclusion from prison education, employment, and community placement programs violated Section 504 of the Rehabilitation Act of 1973. Supporting DOC's policies, the district court determined that even after reasonable accommodations, a significant risk of HIV transmission would exist (see Dalrymple-Blackburn, 1995). Conversely, a consent decree in New Jersey (*Roe et al. v. Fauver et al.*, 1992) ceased segregation of inmates with AIDS from the general population and initiated the development of treatment and education programs.

In *Farmer v. Moritsugu* (1990), a federal court ruled that the Federal Bureau of Prisons did not violate equal protection rights because it prohibits HIV-positive inmates from working in prison hospitals and food services; the institution claims that such a policy is necessary to maintain order and security. However, a district court in Arizona determined that the state Department of Correction's prohibition against assignment of prisoners with HIV to food service jobs violated Section 504 of the Rehabilitation Act. The court permitted the Department of Corrections to institute individual determinations that would bar certain HIV-positive inmates from such employment (by demonstrating a significant risk) but could not enforce a blanket policy (*Casey v. Lewis*, 1991). In 1994, a federal appeals court overturned a federal judge's ruling allowing HIV-positive prisoners to serve food to the general prison population at the Vacaville penitentiary (California), citing the authorities' fears of a prison riot. "Other inmates will perceive a threat regardless of the scientific research or medical pronouncements"; this practice may result in "violent actions against the inmates who have the virus, inmates they perceive have the virus, or the staff that permits the perceived risk," said the U.S. court of appeals for the ninth circuit ("Limits Are Put On Prisoners," 1994, p. 40). ACLU attorney Matthew Coles said the ruling was "a serious setback for the rights of disabled prisoners" ("Limits Are Put On Prisoners," 1994, p. 40), thus reinforcing irrational fears and prejudice resulting in employment discrimination (see Lazzo & McElgunn, 1986).

Finally, the ongoing controversy over the distribution of condoms has become an ideological battleground in corrections. Many criminal justice officials oppose condom distribution, often citing reasons of morality. "It's ludicrous. If we issue condoms, then it would send a message that the Sheriff's Department would be responsible for illegal or immoral behavior," says Bergen County (New Jersey) Undersheriff Jack Quigley. Revealing his belief that homosexuality is wrong and that gays should be converted to straights, Quigley continues, "The most basic concept of rehabilitation is to accept responsibility for one's behavior" (Sforza, 1998a). Many public health experts, however, favor condom distribution, including New Jersey Governor's Advisory Council and the HIV Prevention Community Planning Group (PCPG), which offers recommendations to the state's health department. Gisele Pemberton of the HIV PCPG argues, "This is one of the populations already marginalized and discriminated against. They of all people should have access to condoms" (Sforza, 1998a, p. A12). Currently, only five correctional systems make condoms available to inmates; administrators defend this practice by arguing that they are not condoning the behavior but recognizing that sexual contact does occur in institutions (Hammett et al., 1994).

Conclusion

This article set out to explore the controversy over the correctional response to prisoners with HIV/AIDS. From a macrosociological perspective, attention was turned to the production of deviance in capitalist society and its mechanisms to socially control those who are marginalized. The correctional system serves a macrosociological function in the social control apparatus; still, its penal institutions are governed more by mesosociological and organizational forces that directly and indirectly shape the prison experience, a microsociological phenomenon. These levels of analysis contribute to a critical understanding of the correctional response to prisoners with HIV/AIDS, with particular relevance to the processing of deviance, stigmatization, and the production of suffering. In general, retribution against prisoners with HIV/AIDS is driven by a punitive metaphor of the illness, perpetuating the belief that those persons infected are being condemned by a higher power for having indulged in illegal drugs, promiscuity, or homosexuality. As Sontag (1989) notes, AIDS is "a theodicy as well as a demonology, it not only stipulates something emblematic of evil but makes this the bearer of a rough, terrible justice" (p. 57). Indeed, the stigma attached to prisoners with HIV/AIDS also is amplified by their status as lawbreakers. As a result, they are subjected to fringe punishments during their incarceration, including victimization and various forms of discrimination—

most notably, the denial of adequate medical care. Altogether, these fringe punishments intensify and heighten the suffering of prisoners with HIV/AIDS. As mentioned repeatedly, the war on drugs continues to transform significantly the size and scope of corrections. Not only are prison and jail populations growing at unprecedented rates but the influx of IV drug users infected with HIV/AIDS is also straining the traditional function of penal institutions because greater consideration is now being given to medical and health care. These transformations can be understood in terms of importation and deprivation in the prison world. According to the tenets of importation, the harsh character of prison society is shaped by the attributes of inmates imported from the street. Still, the suffering inherent to life behind bars is produced by the deprivations inherent to incarceration. Both perspectives apply to our analysis: The war on drugs imports offenders infected with HIV/AIDS into correctional facilities where they are deprived of, among other things, adequate medical attention.

Ironically, the problem of HIV/AIDS in corrections is escalated rather than resolved by larger social (macro) and criminal justice (meso) policies, namely, the criminalization of drugs and the reluctance (or inability) of institutions to administer adequate health care. This form of discrimination is fueled by the lack of general awareness on one hand and by apathy (or even hostility) against prisoners with HIV/AIDS on the other. According to John Miles, a special assistant for corrections and substance abuse at the CDC, "This is not just a hidden population. This is an invisible population. The public doesn't like to spend the money" (Purdy, 1997, p. 28). Due to the multiple and diverse problems generated by the war on drugs, correctional institutions are increasingly forced to function also as infirmaries for prisoners with HIV/AIDS; however, without sufficient funding for medical care, prisons have become mere monuments of misery where the production of suffering is prolific.

Note

1. In the United States, the HIV/AIDS epidemic was concentrated among urban gay men in the early 1980s; however, in the late 1990s, the course of the disease has shifted increasingly toward Blacks. "African-Americans make up 13 percent of the U.S. population. But they account for about 57 percent of all new infections with HIV, according to CDC" (Stolberg, 1998, p. A1). For people age 13 to 24, the estimate is even higher, at 63%. Currently, AIDS is the leading cause of death among Black people age 25 to 44 (Ireland, 1998; Stolberg, 1998).

References

Adams v. Poag, 61 F.3d 1537 (11th Cir. 1995).

Akerstrom, M. (1986). Outcasts in prison: The cases of informers and sex offenders. *Deviant Behavior, 7*, 1-12.

Bayer, R., & Kirp, D. (1992). The United States at the center of the storm. In D. Kirp & R. Bayer (Eds.), *AIDS in the industrialized democracies: Passions, politics, and policies* (pp. 7-47). New Brunswick, NJ: Rutgers University Press.

Becker, H. (1963). *Outsiders: Studies in the sociology of deviance*. New York: Free Press.

Blumberg, M. (1990a). *AIDS: The impact on the criminal justice system*. Columbus, OH: Merrill.

Blumberg, M. (1990b). The transmission of HIV: Exploring some misconceptions related to criminal justice. *Criminal Justice Policy Review, 4*, 288-305.

Blumberg, M., & Langston, D. (1995). The impact of HIV/AIDS and tuberculosis on corrections. In K. Haas & G. Alpert (Eds.), *The dilemmas of corrections: Contemporary readings* (pp. 572-584). Prospect Heights, IL: Waveland.

Blumberg, M., & Mahaffey-Sapp, C. (1997). Health care issues in correctional institutions. In M. Schwartz & L. Travis (Eds.), *Corrections: An issues approach* (4th ed., pp. 333-344). Cincinnati, OH: Anderson.

Bolonsky, S., Kerr, S., Harris, B., Gaiter, J., Fichtner, R., & Kennedy, M. (1994). HIV prevention in prisons and jails: Obstacles and opportunities. *Public Health Reports, 109*, 615-625.

Bureau of Justice Statistics. (1994). *Women in prison*. Washington, DC: Department of Justice.

Bureau of Justice Statistics. (1997). *HIV in prisons and jails, 1995*. Washington, DC: Department of Justice.

Bureau of Justice Statistics. (1999). *HIV in prisons, 1997*. Washington, DC: Department of Justice.

Carroll, L. (1992). AIDS and human rights in the prison: A comment on the ethics of screening and segregation. In C. A. Hartjen & E. E. Rhine (Eds.), *Correctional theory and practice* (pp. 132-145). Chicago: Nelson-Hall.

Casey v. Lewis, 773 F. Supp. 1365 (D. Ariz. 1991).

Cauchon, D. (1995, March 31). AIDS in prison: Locked up and locked out. *USA Today*, p. A6.

Centers for Disease Control and Prevention. (1988). Update: Universal precautions for prevention of transmission of human immunodeficiency virus, Hepatitis B virus, and other bloodborne pathogens in health-care settings. *Morbidity and Mortality Weekly Report, 37*, 2.

Centers for Disease Control and Prevention. (1989). Guidelines for prevention of transmission of HIV and Hepatitis B virus to health-care and public safety workers. *Morbidity and Mortality Weekly Report, 38*, S-6.

Clear, T. (1994). *Harm in American penology: Offenders, victims, and their communities*. Albany: State University of New York Press.

Cohen, S. (1973). *Folk devils and moral panics*. Herts, UK: Paladin.

Committee on the Judiciary, House of Representatives. (1991). *Medical care for the prison population*. Washington, DC: Government Printing Office.

Cullen, F. (1995). Assessing the penal harm movement. *Journal of Research in Crime and Delinquency, 32*, 338-358.

Dalrymple-Blackburn, D. (1995). AIDS, prisoners, and the Americans with Disabilities Act. *Utah Law Review, 717*, 839-885.

Doe v. City of Cleveland, 788 F. Supp. 979 (N.D. Ohio 1991).

Doe v. Meachum, 126 F.D.R. 444 (D. Conn. 1989).

Dunlop, D. (1995, June 26). Personalizing Nazis' homosexual victims. *The New York Times*, pp. A1, B4.

Dunn v. White, 800 F.2d 1188 (10th Cir. 1989).

Farmer v. Moritsugu, 742 F. Supp. 525 (W.D. Wisc. 1990).

Fitzhugh v. Wyoming Board of Charities and Reform, No. 91-CV-0106-B, DC Wyoming (1991).

Flanagan, T. (1996). Reform or punish: Americans' views of the correctional system. In T. Flanagan & D. Longmire (Eds.), *Americans view crime and justice* (pp. 75-92). Thousand Oaks, CA: Sage.

Flavin, J. (1998). Fear and policing in the age of HIV/AIDS. *The Critical Criminologist, 8*, 12-15.

Frankford, E., & Snitow, A. (1972). The trap of domesticity: Notes on the family. *Socialist Revolution, 9*, 83-94.

Friedman, M. (1992). Cruel and unusual punishment in the provision of prison medical care: Challenging the deliberate indifference standard. *Vanderbilt Law Review, 45*, 921-949.

Goffman, E. (1963). *Stigma: Notes on the management of spoiled identity*. Englewood Cliffs, NJ: Prentice Hall.

Gostin, L., & Lazzarini, Z. (1997). *Human rights and public health in the AIDS pandemic*. New York: Oxford University Press.

Gross, J. (1993, January 25). California inmates win better prison AIDS care. *The New York Times*, p. A12.

Hammett, T. M. (1989). *1989 update: AIDS in correctional facilities*. Washington, DC: National Institute of Justice.

Hammett, T. M., Harmon, P., & Maruschak, L. (1999). *1996-1997 update: HIV/AIDS, STDs, and TB in correctional facilities*. Washington, DC: National Institute of Justice.

Hammett, T. M., & Harrold, L. (1994). *Tuberculosis in correctional facilities*. Washington, DC: National Institute of Justice.

Hammett, T. M., Harrold, L., Gross, M., & Epstein, J. (1994). *1992 update: HIV/AIDS in correctional facilities*. Washington, DC: National Institute of Justice.

Hammett, T. M., & Moini, S. (1990). *Update on AIDS in prisons and jails*. Washington, DC: National Institute of Justice.

Harris v. Thigpen, 941 F.2d 1495 (11th Cir. 1991).

Heger, H. (1972). *The men with the pink triangle*. New York: Alyson.

Ho, D., Byington, R., Schooley, R., Flynn, T., Rota, T., & Hirsch, M. (1985). Infrequency and isolation of HTLV-111 virus from saliva in AIDS. *The New England Journal of Medicine, 313*, 1606-1616.

Huber, J., & Schneider, B. (1992). *The social contexts of AIDS*. Thousand Oaks, CA: Sage.

Ireland, D. (1998, April 20). Silence kills blacks. *The Nation, 269*, 6-7.

Irwin, J. (1985). *The jail: Managing the underclass in American society*. Berkeley: University of California Press.

Jacobs, S. (1995). AIDS in correctional facilities: Current status of legal issues critical to policy development. *Journal of Criminal Justice, 23*, 209-221.

Johnson, W., Bennett, K., & Flanagan, T. (1997). Getting tough on prisoners: Results from the National Corrections Executive Survey, 1995. *Crime & Delinquency, 43*, 24-41.

Juvelis, J. (1995). The stress factor for HIV+ prisoners. *AIDS & Society, 6*, 6,10.

Kappeler, V., Blumberg, M., & Potter, G. (1996). *The mythology of crime and criminal justice* (2nd ed.). Prospect Heights, IL: Waveland.

Koehler, R. (1994). HIV infection, TB, and the health crisis in corrections. *Public Administration Review, 54*, 31-35.

Lawrence, J., & Zwisohn, V. (1991). AIDS in jail. In J. A. Thompson & G. L. Mays (Eds.), *American jails: Public policy issues* (pp. 116-129). Chicago: Nelson-Hall.

Lazzo, M., & McElgunn, C. (1986). Recent developments: Public health and employment issues generated by the AIDS crisis. *Washburn Law Review, 25*, 505-535.

Limits are put on prisoners with H.I.V. (1994, November 6). *The New York Times*, p. A40.

Marquart, J., Merianos, E., Cuvelier, S., & Carroll, L. (1996). Thinking about the relationship between health dynamics in the free community and the prison. *Crime & Delinquency, 42*, 331-360.

Marx, K. (1967). *Capital: Vol. 1*. New York: International Publishers.

Masters, W., Johnson, V., & Kolodny, R. (1988). *Crisis: Heterosexual behavior in the age of AIDS*. New York: Grove.

McArthur, J. C. (1987). Neurological manifestations of AIDS. *Medicine, 66*, 407-437.

Middleton, J., & Lee, D. (1997). *1997 AIDS docket*. New York: American Civil Liberties Union AIDS Project.

New Jersey v. Smith, NJ Super. Ct., App. Div., No. A-636389-T4 (1993).

NJ inmate argues for reversal of 25-year AIDS bite jail sentence. (1992, December 22). *AIDS Litigation Reporter*, p. 1.

Nolley v. County of Erie, 776 F. Supp. 715 (W.D. N.Y. 1991).

O'Farrell, N., Tovey, S., & Morgan-Capner, P. (1992). Transmission of HIV-1 infection after a fight. *Lancet, 339*, 246-252.

Perez, H. (1996). Incarcerated populations: Have they been forgotten? *The Active Voice, 12*, 7-8.

Pink bracelets for homosexuals in Florida jail are challenged. (1989, December 3). *The New York Times*, p. A35.

Plant, R. (1986). *The pink triangle: The Nazi war on homosexuals*. New York: Henry Holt.

Plant, R. (1989, November 7). Nazis' forgotten victims: Gays. *The New York Times*, p. A23.

Potler, C. (1988). *AIDS in prison: A crisis in New York State corrections*. New York: The Correctional Association of New York.

Proctor v. Alameda County, Calif. Super. Ct., Alameda County, No. 693983-8 (1992).

Purdy, M. (1997, May 26). As AIDS increases behind bars, costs dim promise of new drugs. *The New York Times*, p. A1, A28.

Red tags for gays scrapped. (1990). *Civil Liberties, 369*, 7.

Richman, K., & Richman, L. (1993). The potential for transmission of human immunodeficiency virus through human bites. *Journal of Acquired Immune Deficiency Syndromes, 6*, 402-406.

Roe et al. v. Fauver et al., D. NJ No.88-1225-AET (1992).

Schneider, B. (1992). AIDS and class, gender, and race relations. In J. Huber & B. Schneider (Eds.), *The social contexts of AIDS* (pp. 19-43). Thousand Oaks, CA: Sage.

Schur, E. (1971). *Labeling deviant behavior: Its sociological implications*. New York: Harper & Row.

Secombe, W. (1973). The housewife and her labour under capitalism. *New Left Review, 82*, 3-24.

Sforza, D. (1998a, June 2). Jails prefer education, not condoms, to curtail HIV. *The Record*, p. A12.

Sforza, D. (1998b, June 2). Terms of treatment: Prisons tested by costs, burdens of HIV. *The Record*, pp. A1, A12.

Shilts, R. (1987). *And the band played on: Politics, people and the AIDS epidemic*. New York: St. Martin's.

Shover, N., & Einstadter, W. (1988). *Analyzing American corrections*. Belmont, CA: Wadsworth.

Sirica, J. (1988, May 19). Testimony on AIDS. *New York Newsday*, p. A14.

Sontag, S. (1980). *Illness as metaphor*. New York: Doubleday.

Sontag, S. (1989). *AIDS and its metaphors*. New York: Farrar, Straus & Giroux.

Spitzer, S. (1975). Toward a Marxian theory of deviance. *Social Problems, 22*, 638-651.

Stolberg, S. (1998, June 29). Eyes shut, Black America is being ravaged by AIDS. *The New York Times*, pp. A1, A12.

Sullivan, J. (1993, February 18). Inmate with HIV who bit guard loses appeal. *The New York Times*, p. B7.

Sullivan, R. (1992, August 26). Ex-inmate wins award in bias case. *The New York Times*, p. B4.

Thomas, E. (1985, September 23). The new untouchables: Anxiety over AIDS is verging on hysteria in some parts of the country. *Time*, 24-26.

Thomas, P., & Moerings, M. (1994). *AIDS in prison*. Aldershot, VT: Dartmouth.

Turner v. Safley, 428 U.S. 78, 107 S. Ct. 2254 (1987).

U.S. General Accounting Office. (1994). *Bureau of Prisons Health Care*. Washington, DC: Government Printing Office.

Vaughn, M., & Carroll, L. (1998). Separate and unequal: Prison versus free-world medical care. *Justice Quarterly, 15*, 3-40.

Vlahov, D., Brewer, T., Castro, K., Narkunus, J., Salive, M., Ullrich, J., & Munoz, A. (1991). Prevalence of antibody to HIV-1 among entrants to U.S. correctional facilities. *Journal of the American Medical Association, 265*, 1129-1132.

Walker v. Sumner, 917 F.2d 382 (9th Cir. 1990).

Weeks v. Texas, Texas Ct. Crim. App., No. 92-1154 (1992).

Welch, M. (1989). Social junk, social dynamite and the rabble: Persons with AIDS in jail. *American Journal of Criminal Justice, 14*, 135-147.

Welch, M. (1991a). Persons with AIDS in prison: A critical and phenomenological approach to suffering. *Dialectical Anthropology, 16*, 51-61.

Welch, M. (1991b). Social class, special populations and other unpopular issues: Setting the jail agenda for the 90s. In G. L. Mays (Ed.), *Setting the jail research agenda for the 1990s: Proceedings from a special meeting* (pp. 17-23). Washington, DC: Department of Justice, National Institute of Corrections.

Welch, M. (1994). Jail overcrowding: Social sanitation and the warehousing of the urban underclass. In A. R. Roberts (Ed.), *Critical issues in crime and justice* (pp. 251-276). Newbury Park, CA: Sage.

Welch, M. (1996). *Corrections: A critical approach*. New York: McGraw-Hill.

Welch, M. (1997). Tougher prisons? Newark Public Radio interviews Michael Welch. *The Critical Criminologist, 8*, 7-11.

Welch, M. (1999). *Punishment in America: Social control and the ironies of imprisonment*. Thousand Oaks, CA: Sage.

Welch, M., Fenwick, M., & Roberts, M. (1997). Primary definitions of crime and moral panic: A content analysis of experts' quotes in feature newspaper articles of crime. *Journal of Research in Crime and Delinquency, 34*, 474-494.

Welch, M., Fenwick, M., & Roberts, M. (1998). State managers, intellectuals, and the media: A content analysis of ideology in experts' quotes in featured newspaper articles on crime. *Justice Quarterly*, *15*, 101-123.

Zaretsky, E. (1973a). Capitalism, the family and personal life: Parts 1 & 2. *Socialist Revolution*, *10*, 69-126.

Zaretsky, E. (1973b). Capitalism, the family and personal life: Parts 1 & 2. *Socialist Revolution*, *11*, 19-70.

[15]

AN EMPIRICAL ASSESSMENT OF THE AIDS RISK REDUCTION MODEL (ARRM) EMPLOYING ORDERED PROBIT ANALYSES

MARK M. LANIER

Department of Criminal Justice and Legal Studies
University of Central Florida
Orlando, Florida 32816 USA

SCOTT GATES

Department of Political Science
Michigan State University
East Lansing, Michigan 48824 USA

ABSTRACT

The AIDS Risk Reduction Model (ARRM) is a conceptual model designed to explain the influence of knowledge and attitudes about AIDS/HIV on risk-related behaviors. This article measures the influence of the primary concepts associated with the ARRM (labeling, commitment, and enactment) on high-risk adolescent's knowledge, attitudes, and self-reported behaviors. Data were collected from 393 adolescents incarcerated in juvenile detention facilities. Ordered probit and ordinary least squares (OLS) analyses were conducted to determine which of several independent variables have the most impact on acceptance of the ARRM. Results indicated that the ARRM is effective for understanding the factors that influence AIDS risk avoidance. Findings also indicate that previous life experiences should be formally integrated into the model. Moreover, specific forms of enactment are associated with different factors. Suggestions as to how the ARRM may prove useful for promoting behavioral change among high-risk adolescents are provided.

INTRODUCTION

Acquired Immunodeficiency Syndrome (AIDS) is a severe manifestation of the Human Immunodeficiency Virus (HIV) (Hammett, Jaffe, and Johnson, 1987; Solomon and DeJong, 1986). There is no cure for AIDS and prevention is difficult, especially among certain populations where it is also spreading rapidly (e.g., adolescents and IV drug users) (Centers for Disease Control [CDC], 1995). Heightened awareness of the nature and transmission modalities of HIV among those who are not infected assumes ever-increasing importance. Currently, effective educational efforts motivating behavioral change are the best means of retarding the spread of HIV. Since high-risk behaviors are "partly under the control of conscious processes, (and) are potentially modifiable" (Gibson, Catania, and Peterson, 1991:62) effective interventions assume increasing importance. Hence social scientists, correctional administrators, and educators can play an increasingly vital role in helping slow down the spread of HIV (Bloom, 1988; Cleary et al., 1986).

When high-risk individuals are congregated in one location an ideal situation is created to provide AIDS education. Juvenile correctional facilities house large numbers of individuals who are at-risk due to their behaviors and lifestyle choices. Unfortunately, data are not available reporting the number of adolescents confined who are HIV positive. There were 2,354 AIDS cases among all youth aged 13–19 in December 1995 (CDC, 1995). Many more adolescents are HIV positive. There is more AIDS information available for adult inmates. Nationwide, 2.3 percent of all male inmates are HIV positive and 3.9 percent of female inmates are HIV positive (Office of Justice Programs, 1994). In 1994, AIDS accounted for over one-half (52.6 percent) of all inmate deaths in the Northeastern states[1] and AIDS was responsible for 35.1 percent of all inmate deaths nationwide (Office of Justice Programs, 1994). The rate of confirmed AIDS cases among inmates was seven times the rate found in the general United States population (Office of Justice Programs, 1994). Effective education targeting high-risk groups, such as those incarcerated, should be based on empirical assessments of theoretical models that show promise to modify behavior. The AIDS Risk Reduction Model (ARRM) is one such theoretical tool.

THEORETICAL MODEL

The constructs examined in this article are central to social psychological explanations concerning the impact that knowledge and attitudes have on behavior. The current examination builds on principles first associated with the now-classic Health Belief Model (HBM; Becker, 1974). The HBM was presented as a means to explain behaviors related to preventing illness (Rosenstock, 1974). Specifically, the HBM was developed to determine means to *prevent* illnesses common in the 1950s and early 1960s, such as tuberculosis. The HBM focuses on individual's susceptibility and psychological barriers. Consequently, inhibitions to taking health action are based on perceived benefits and barriers. In other words, the HBM analyzes, "an individual's motivation to act as a function of the expectancy of goal attainment in the area of health behavior" (Maiman and Becker, 1974:348). Thus, the HBM implies that individuals make decisions regarding their health following a *rationally* conducted, cost/benefit analysis. Consequently, health behaviors are a function of "people's perceived susceptibility and perceived severity of a health condition, and the perceived benefits and barriers to behavioral change" (Gibson, Catania, and Peterson, 1991:63).

Many theoretical extensions and empirical examinations of the traditional HBM have been presented (for a review of some of the variations see Maiman and Becker, 1974; Rosenstock, Strecher, and Becker, 1988; also see Feldman and Johnson, 1986, for other theoretical perspectives on AIDS). Conceptual schemes have been developed that may provide insight into factors most susceptible to manipulation in specific health areas. Variations of the HBM have been presented that deal with specific diseases (e.g., tuberculosis, cancer). Recent extensions involve AIDS/HIV prevention (see especially Cleary et al., 1986; Solomon and DeJong, 1986). A few studies of the HBM and HIV/AIDs have also been focused on adolescents (Petosa and Wessinger, 1989, 1990; Maticka-Tyndale, 1991). Hingson et al. (1990:298) postulated that, "some beliefs about HIV transmission and AIDS identified in the HBM predict whether adolescents will use condoms." Consequently, variations of the HBM should predict whether or not a person will adopt behavior to avoid HIV exposure (Hingson et al., 1990).

The AIDS Risk Reduction Model

The ARRM was first presented by Catania, Kegeles, and Coates (1990) to help explain motivations for altering sexual practices related to HIV transmission. The ARRM was developed to organize concepts related to the HBM, decision-making theory, and theories seeking to explain the role of interpersonal processes and emotions in behavior (Gibson, Catania, and Peterson, 1991:62–63). Consequently, the ARRM is a conceptual strategy created to help ascertain the role of these concepts as they relate to behavior change. While the ARRM was developed to examine sexual behaviors, "with minor modifications . . . it is also of relevance to other HIV risk behaviors" (Catania, Kegeles, and Coates, 1990:67).

There are three distinct stages in the ARRM: labeling, commitment, and enactment. During the labeling stage, the influences postulated to have the most effect are (1) transmission knowledge, (2) susceptibility, (3) aversive emotions, and (4) social influences. The primary outcome indicators associated with this stage seek to determine if the respondent's behavior places him or her at risk of HIV infection. During this first stage, knowledge is especially critical for providing sufficient motivation for behavioral change because awareness of high-risk behaviors must precede perceived threat. Susceptibility is related to knowledge because awareness that one is engaging in at-risk behaviors would logically succeed identification of these behaviors.

The second stage (commitment) focuses on measures of aversive emotions and social influences. The perceived benefits of making change (termed "response efficacy") and self-efficacy are included. Self-efficacy refers to a "person's perceived ability to implement recommended health practices" (Gibson, Catania, and Peterson, 1991:63). The outcome indicator here seeks to determine, "Do you expect to do *X* in the next 4 weeks?"

The final stage is enactment and adds communication skill to social influences and aversive emotions. The behavioral outcome asks, "What have you done?" Each of the three processes are "unidirectional and nonreversible" according to Catania, Kegeles, and Coates (1990). In other words, the ARRM is based on the premise that individuals will progress from stage one, to stage two, and, finally, stage three.

The ARRM has been empirically examined with a number of at-risk populations. Recent studies have utilized the ARRM to examine drug abusers (Bowen and Trotter, 1995; Longshore and Anglin, 1995; Malow et al., 1994; Kowalewski, Longshore, and Anglin, 1994), Asian and Pacific Island communities (Yep, 1993), unmarried heterosexual adults (Catania, Coates, and Kegeles, 1994), HIV positive people (Kline and VanLandingham, 1994) and African Americans (Malow et al., 1993). The studies most germane to this examination focused on juveniles (Breakwell, Millward, and Fife-Schaw, 1994). Boyer and Kegeles (1991) theoretically linked the ARRM with adolescent's risk and prevention.

Most assessments of the ARRM have supported the basic premises proposed by the model. Malow et al. (1993) found that higher levels of self-efficacy and communication skills affected safe sex choices as predicted by the ARRM. Kline and VanLandingham (1994) also presented data supporting the key constructs. Others have found only mixed support (Kowalewski, Longshore, and Anglin, 1994; Longshore and Anglin, 1995). With adolescent populations Breakwell, Millward, and Fife-Schaw (1994:206) also had mixed results concluding that "findings suggest that the parameters of the model deserve more formal specification."

PROBLEM STATEMENT

Adolescents who engage in intravenous drug use and sexual activity are at increased risk of HIV infection (Boyer and Kegeles, 1991; Lanier and McCarthy, 1989; Eiser, Eiser, and Lang, 1990). Concentrations of these high-risk adolescents are found in juvenile correctional facilities (DiClemente et al., 1991). Conventional educational efforts aimed at this population have often been relatively unsuccessful. Due to the sexual characteristics and drug use habits of this population effective AIDS education is especially vital. One multidisciplinary conceptual strategy that may prove useful with providing effective education is the ARRM. Basic concepts associated with this model have not been empirically verified, and the few studies examining the ARRM have found mixed results. It is necessary to examine the impact of the ARRM with various populations since, "models such as the ARRM may tell us quite different things, depending on which social group we are dealing with" (Gibson, Catania, and Peterson, 1991:73). The present study examines the primary constructs associated with the model on a group of high-risk adolescents. The study population may demonstrate differential knowledge levels, unique attitudes, and diverse behavioral intentions when compared to other populations. Basic assumptions underlying the ARRM may also be subject to revision.

For example, the ARRM is based on assumptions concerning the rationality of human behavior. According to Catania, Kegeles, and Coates (1990:60), "most people choose to engage in behaviors they believe will yield the greatest overall personal value relative to disvalue." Concerning possibly hedonistic adolescents who may harbor fatalistic attitudes, such a cost/benefit analysis may have little relevance. This may be especially true when they are faced with the prospect of immediate sexual and/or drug-induced gratification, opposed to the remote possibility of contracting a disease that may not manifest symptoms for several years. Others have also questioned the rationality of cognitive processes. For example, Cleary et al. (1986:324) noted, "Another problem with this type of model is the assumption that behavior is rational and that people usually act in ways that they think will result in the best possible outcome. . . . Much sexual behavior happens spontaneously and is prompted by emotional needs that may counteract cognitive decisions."

DATA COLLECTION

A six-page questionnaire, divided into four major sections, was administered to all juveniles in the custody of a southern state during the Spring of 1988. The survey included questions/statements that were designed to elicit information on the juveniles' objective/factual knowledge about HIV/AIDS, their attitudes toward HIV/AIDS, self-reported AIDS-related behaviors (e.g., drug use and sexual practices), and sociodemographic information. Most questions required a Likert-style response.

The instrument was administered to the juveniles by Department of Youth Services (DYS) personnel (a pre-test was administered to thirty-four incarcerated adolescents). Complete anonymity and confidentiality was afforded all respondents. Survey administration was completed at all DYS facilities during routine classroom situations. It was determined that this method would be practical and less disruptive for the DYS institutional routine than would be the case if outsiders were to administer the surveys. Optical scan sheets were provided to the respondents to fill in their answers, and each of the questions/statements were read aloud to the subjects.

In the present study, primary concepts associated with the ARRM were measured using several indicators of each variable (see Table 1). Consequently, an index was created for each concept. First, the labeling stage was measured by four transmission knowledge questions, two susceptibility questions, two measures of aversive emotions, and two indicators of social influences. Second, response efficacy and self-efficacy were measured using eight items from the questionnaire. Finally, while "enactment" cannot be measured in the current study, behavioral intentions were examined in six variables. One indicator of rationality was, "AIDS is a made up problem by the government to decrease drug use and sexual activity." In addition, several behavioral intentions can be regressed against high risk activities and perceived susceptibility to help measure rationality and/or irrationality.

Response Rate

A DYS census conducted two days after the administration of the survey showed that 455 juveniles were in the custody of DYS (415 in training schools and forty in regional group homes). A total of 363 surveys were returned from juveniles who were institutionalized (87.5 percent response rate) and forty surveys from the youth in the group homes were returned (100 percent response rate). The overall response rate for the survey was 86.4 percent. This resulted in a total of 393 individuals for analysis.

Demographic Characteristics

As shown in Table 2, over one-half of the respondents were from racial/ethnic minority groups.

Three-quarters of the respondents were male, and 80 percent were between the ages of fifteen and eighteen. Examination of HIV/AIDS at-risk behaviors revealed that the majority (85 percent) reported being sexually active, and over 10 percent reported having engaged in some form of homosexual activity. Twelve percent also reported having injected drugs.

A General Empirical AIDS Risk Reduction Model

One goal of this article is to specify a statistical model that is appropriate for evaluation of the AIDS Risk Reduction Model (ARRM) in general. In this section, the analysis of incarcerated juveniles enactment stage of the ARRM is outlined. In particular, the general behavior of these individuals toward reducing their risk as well as specific precautionary behaviors is examined by analyzing six models, including the propensity to ask sexual partners about their sexual history, to demand the use of a condom for self-protection, to demand the use of a condom for their partner's protection, to take precautions against acquiring AIDS, to have a blood test for HIV, and to have their friends tested for HIV.

The AIDS Risk Reduction Model and previous analysis were used to select a set of independent variables. From the ARRM, variables from the label stage, including knowledge about AIDS, attitudes toward the susceptibility to AIDS, respondents aversion to AIDS, and social influences, were analyzed. From the commitment stage, response efficacy and self-efficacy were examined. Drawing from other work on AIDS contraction, a set of variables from individual's life experiences were considered, including their gender, their race, the number of homosexual partners, the number of sexual partners, and whether they have "shot-up" drugs. To examine the general behavior of these incarcerated juveniles ordinary least squares (OLS) analysis was used. For the specific enactment behaviors ordered probit analysis was applied. These variables were measured along an ordinal dimension where respondents claim to partake in a particular activity frequently, sometimes, and never.[2] Ordered probit is a useful analytical technique for evaluating such limited-dependent qualitative variables. The statistical model is similar to

TABLE 1

MEASURES OF PRIMARY CONCEPTS

Variable	*Indicator*
Labeling	
Knowledge	"AIDS can be caught from kissing." "Mosquitoes can give you AIDS." "AIDS can be caught from sharing IV needles." "Using a condom will help prevent catching AIDS."
Susceptibility	"My chances of catching AIDS are great." "I worry a lot about catching AIDS."
Aversive emotions	"AIDS is a big problem in America." "AIDS is a made up problem...to decrease drug use and sexual activity."
Social influences	"Where did you learn the most about AIDS?" "Where have you heard the most talk about AIDS?"
Commitment	
Response efficacy	"If infected, I would/would not tell any sex partner, loved ones, close friends, anyone." "If infected I would not have sex."
Self-efficacy	"If you catch AIDS it's your own fault."
Enactment	
Behavioral intentions	"Demand the use of a condom for self-protection, partner's protection." "I take special precautions." "Ask sexual history of sex partners." "Would like a blood test for self, friends."

TABLE 2

DEMOGRAPHIC CHARACTERISTICS

	N	*Group %*	*Missing*
Gender			
Male	303	82.3	
Female	65	17.7	26
Age			
12 or under	8	2.1	
13–14	51	13.2	
15–16	169	43.9	
17–18	146	37.9	
19 or over	11	2.9	9
Ethnicity			
African American	217	55.9	
Caucasian	151	38.9	
Hispanic	9	2.3	
Other	11	2.9	26
Number of sexual partners			
None	50	13.0	
One	62	16.1	
2–5	73	19.0	
6–10	59	15.3	
Over 10	141	36.6	9
Homosexual activity			
Yes	42	10.9	
No	343	89.1	9
IV drug use			
Yes	43	11.7	
No	325	88.3	26
Total	393	100.0	0

logit or probit models used to evaluate binomial dependent variables, except that now there are dependent variables that possess choices that are inherently ordered into three categories. In fact, the ordered probit is a generalization of the binary threshold model. Ordered probit allows the inclusion of additional parameters that represent unobserved thresholds between categories in the dependent variables.

Ordered probit was used because of the ordered nature of the dependent variables. With regression analysis, the difference between never, sometimes, and always is assumed to be equal. For example, if "never" is coded as 0, "sometimes" as 1, and "always" as 2, regression analysis assumes that the distance between 0 and 1 is the same as 1 and 2. Yet, it cannot necessarily be assumed that the distance between "never" and "sometimes" is the same as between "sometimes" and "always." This underlying scale for each dependent variable makes ordered probit an appropriate analytical technique for determining the thresholds between "never," "sometimes," and "always." In other words, it allows one to express the probability of never asking, sometimes asking, and always asking about a partner's sexual history.[3] Ordered probit allows avoiding the bias that would result from regression analysis so that a more accurate estimation of the relative impacts of different variables is possible (McKelvey and Zavoina, 1975; Maddala, 1983; Greene, 1990).

RESULTS

In this section, the statistical results of the OLS and ordered probit analyses of each of the six dependent variables are presented. It begins with the OLS analysis and then turns to the ordered probit analyses of each of the specific dependent variables.

Results of OLS Analysis

Table 3 displays the OLS regression analysis of the general behavioral measure of AIDS risk reduction enactment and the independent variables described above. With this analysis, and for all the models to follow, both the statistical and substantive significance of the coefficients are important. Of the label variables, only knowledge was significant at $p \leq 0.05$. At the commitment stage, only response efficacy was significant, but at $p \leq 0.01$. As for life experiences, the race and gender of the respondent, as well as the number of homosexual partners, were also significant. More particularly, Caucasians were less likely to engage in AIDS risk reduction behavior, as is evident with the negative coefficient, which was significant at $p \leq 0.05$. Females are more likely to follow AIDS risk reduction behaviors than males; this coefficient was also significant at $p \leq 0.05$. Homosexual relations were marginally significant at $p \leq 0.1$, where the greater the number of homosexual partners was associated with a higher degree of AIDS risk behavior. From this analysis significant relationships between AIDS risk reduction behavior and knowledge, response efficacy, ethnicity, gender, and homosexual history were found. Significant variables are drawn from the labeling and

TABLE 3

OLS: GENERAL AIDS RISK REDUCTION BEHAVIOR

Independent Variable	*ARRM Estimated Coefficient*	
Constant	3.02281	(1.37900)
Knowledge	0.0876745	(0.04752)
Susceptibility	0.0537695	(0.04488)
Aversion	−0.0167876	(0.04163)
Social influence	−0.0362881	(0.05524)
Response efficacy	0.0925848	(0.03182)
Self-efficacy	0.0285276	(0.05867)
Caucasian	−0.36187	(0.21280)
Female	0.56060	(0.25780)
Sexual history	−0.0282405	(0.07037)
Homosexual relations	−0.23133	(0.17332)
IV drug use	−0.41066	(0.33575)
Number of observations	311	
R^2	0.10537	

commitment stages of the ARRM, and from the respondents' life experiences.

Results of Ordered Probit Analyses

Table 4 presents the results of the ordered probit analyses of the six dependent variables. The coefficients and levels of significance at $p \leq 0.10$, $p \leq 0.05$, and $p \leq 0.01$ are presented. The Likelihood Ratio Index (LRI) for each ordered probit model as an indicator of goodness of fit is also provided. This value is computed as:

$$LRI = 1 - \frac{\ln \hat{L}}{\ln L_0}$$

This measure takes the maximized value of the log-likelihood function and divides it by the log likelihood of only the constant term subtracted from 1. The LRI is thus bounded by 0 and 1. If all the slope coefficients equal zero, the LRI equals zero; as the LRI approaches one, a better fit is evident.[4] In addition to the LRI, the percent of the observations correctly predicted is given. Together these measures provide information about each ordered probit model as a whole. Table 4 presents the statistical results for each model.

Model 1: Asking About Partner's Sexual History

The propensity for the respondents to ask their partners about their past sexual history was examined first. Please refer to the column under "Ask" for the statistical results of this ordered probit model. For this model, response efficacy, Cauca-

TABLE 4

ORDERED PROBIT COEFFICIENTS FOR SPECIFIC AIDS RISK REDUCTION BEHAVIORS

	AIDS Risk Reduction Behavior					
Independent Variable	*Ask*	*Contraceptive for Self*	*Contraceptive for Others*	*Preventative Action*	*HIV Test for Self*	*HIV Test for Others*
Constant	−2.81371**	−0.54242	−0.23818	−0.94281	−1.36762*	−1.19124
Knowledge	0.05765**	0.03637	0.04698*	0.05549*	0.03508	0.06170**
Susceptibility	−0.00977	0.06335**	0.03437	−0.05625*	0.14579***	0.07850**
Aversion	−0.04639*	−0.02723	−0.03762*	−0.00633	−0.00154	0.00817
Social influence	−0.02561	−0.02542	−0.05317*	0.03906	0.01507	0.00903
Response efficacy	−0.07624***	0.03372*	0.03386*	0.04258**	0.04022**	0.04423**
Self-efficacy	−0.00500	0.05295*	0.00541	0.03547	0.01914	−0.00639
Caucasian	−0.40232***	−0.09252	−0.02992	0.14801	−0.12890	−0.16732
Female	0.49462***	0.23364	0.18949	0.02482	0.30102*	0.05511
Sexual history	0.13248***	−0.06735*	−0.08331**	0.08928**	−0.09099**	−0.09199**
Homesexual relations	0.04241	−0.20264**	−0.18323*	0.04578	0.09646	0.20249*
IV drug use	−0.18378	−0.23779	−0.20749	−0.39961*	−0.07370	−0.21569
Threshold 1	1.12159***	1.077558***	0.82107***	0.60530***	0.63091***	0.80204***
Number of cases	316	318	313	317	317	317
Likelihood ratio index	.2321	.2230	.2073	.2417	.2261	.1871
Percent correctly predicted	45.89	49.371	45.05	72.56	67.99	68.77

*Significant at $p \leq 0.10$; **significant at $p \leq 0.05$; ***significant at $p \leq 0.01$.

Note: Coefficient is reported in each box.

sian, female, and sexual history were all variable with coefficients highly significant at $p \leq 0.01$. Knowledge was significant at $p \leq 0.05$, and aversion was marginally significant at $p \leq 0.1$. Knowledge and aversion are statistically significant variables from the labeling stage of the ARRM. At the commitment stage of the ARRM, response efficacy was highly significant. Notice that the response efficacy was negatively associated with asking about a partner's sexual history; with all other dependent variables, response efficacy was positively related. Life experiences variables (Caucasian, female, and sexual history) were all highly significant. Caucasians were less likely to ask about a partner's sexual history; interestingly, asking was the only form of enactment where race played a statistically significant role. Females were more likely to ask than males. And a positive relationship exists between the number of sexual partners and the propensity to ask about a partner's sexual history. Note that these results differ from the OLS results from the analysis of the aggregate measure of AIDS risk avoidance behavior. It was found, specifically, that different independent variables were significant, including aversion and sexual history, as well as homosexual relations, which was not significant with respect to asking about a partner's sexual history. These results also differ from the other specific types of AIDS risk avoidance behavior.

Model 2: Use Contraceptive for Self-protection

The likelihood for the juvenile delinquents surveyed to say that they demand the use of a condom for their own protection are significantly related to their feelings of susceptibility to AIDS, their response efficacy, their self-efficacy, the number of sexual partners, and their homosexual history. These results are displayed on Table 4 under the column labeled "Contraceptive for Self." At the label stage of the ARRM, feelings of susceptibility were positively related to the propensity to demand the use of condoms for self-protection at a $p \leq 0.05$ level of significance. For the commitment stage, both response efficacy and self-efficacy were barely significant at $p \leq 0.1$. Life experience variables, sexual history, and homosexual relations were also significantly associated with demanding a condom for self-protection.

Model 3: Use Contraceptive for Partner's Protection

Interestingly, the likelihood for respondent youth to say that they demand a condom for their partner's protection was related to a different set of variables than those seeking self-protection as can be seen in Table 4 by comparing the columns under "Contraceptive for Self" and "Contraceptive for Others." For the label stage, knowledge, aversion to AIDS, and social influences were all statistically associated with demanding a condom for a sexual partner's protection. The only independent variable from this stage to not be significant is susceptibility, which was the only labeling variable to be significantly associated with demanding a condom for self-protection. Response efficacy from the commitment stage was marginally significant and positively associated with the dependent variable. The number of sexual partners and the number of homosexual relationships were also significantly related to demanding a condom for a partner's protection.

Model 4: Preventative Action

The results of the ordered probit model examining the propensity for the respondent to take preventative measures to avoid AIDS appear in Table 4 under the "Preventative Action" column. The general response to take precautions against contracting HIV was significantly associated with knowledge, susceptibility, response efficacy, the number of sexual partners, and IV drug use. At the label stage, knowledge and susceptibility were marginally significantly related. At the commitment stage, response efficacy was significantly associated with taking preventative measures to avoid contracting HIV. For life experiences, sexual history and IV drug use were statistically significant. As the number of sexual partners rises, the propensity to take precautionary measures rises. On the other hand, IV drug users are less likely to take precautions.

Model 5: HIV Test for Self

The statistical results of the ordered probit model of the desire to be blood-tested for HIV is presented on Table 4 under the "HIV Test for

Self" column. This desire for a blood test was significantly related to the number of sexual partners reported by these respondents and with females. Females were more likely to desire an HIV test for themselves. As the number of sexual partners rises, the propensity for asking for an HIV test declines. At the label stage of the ARRM, susceptibility was highly significantly related to the desire to have an HIV test. At the commitment stage, response efficacy was significant.

Model 6: HIV Test for Others

The propensity for these juveniles to want their friends to have a blood test for HIV was significantly related to a different set of variables as seen in the expressed desire for a blood test for themselves. Table 4 under the column, "HIV Test for Others," displays the results of this ordered probit model. The number of sexual partners and homosexual relations are both significantly related to the desire for others to have a blood test. At the label stage, knowledge and susceptibility were both statistically significant. At the commitment stage, response efficacy was significantly related.

ASSESSING THE AIDS RISK REDUCTION MODEL

The central conclusion is that while each component of the ARRM plays a role, certain parameters are more strongly associated with enactment than other factors. For example, in the labeling stage, knowledge and susceptibility play a more significant role than other variables at this stage (aversion and social influences). Aversion was associated with two specific AIDS risk reduction behaviors, asking about a partner's sexual history and demanding a condom for the protection of others. Social influence was significantly associated with demanding the use of a condom for a partner's protection. It is evident from these results that different aspects of labeling affect different forms of AIDS risk reduction behaviors differently.

A similar pattern was apparent at the commitment stage, where response efficacy was significantly related to every enactment variable. Self-efficacy, on the other hand, was only significantly associated with one dependent variable, to what extent the respondent used a condom for his/her own protection.

Life experience variables were also included in the analysis. Life experience variables were not, strictly speaking, part of the ARRM. Previous research of AIDS risk points to the importance of these variables. Indeed, the results indicate that several life experiences play a significant role in AIDS risk reduction behavior. Gender played an especially significant role in general risk reduction behavior and the propensity to ask a partner about his/her sexual history. Race and ethnicity were significantly associated with general risk avoidance behavior and asking about your partner's sexual history. The number of sexual partners a respondent had was significantly associated with every specific form of enactment. Having had homosexual partners was associated with general risk avoidance behavior, demanding a condom for self-protection and other's protection, as well as desiring that friends take an HIV test. Whether or not the respondent had used IV drugs was associated with only taking preventative measures against contracting HIV. Due to the degree to which these life experience variables played a significant role in shaping AIDS risk reduction behaviors, there is a strong argument for more formally incorporating life experiences into the ARRM. Further specification of the ARRM is thus needed.

Different independent variables are seen to be associated to specific AIDS risk reduction behaviors to varying degrees. Four independent variables, however, stand out as common factors across models. Sexual history and response efficacy were significantly associated with every aspect of AIDS reduction behavior; knowledge and susceptibility, although not significantly associated with every dependent variable, were highly associated with several specific AIDS reduction behaviors with high marginal influence.

DISCUSSION AND CONCLUSION

Given these results, what can be said about the ARRM? The ARRM serves as an effective construct for understanding the factors that influence AIDS risk avoidance. Nevertheless, there are some ways that the ARRM could be refined to add understanding of this salient public policy issue. First, previous life experiences should be formally integrated into the model. These factors play a consistently important role in shaping AIDS avoidance behavior. Sexual history plays a particularly relevant role. Second, the ARRM is associated with different types of AIDS avoidance behavior in an unconsistent manner. In other words, to understand the motivations for different forms of AIDS avoidance behavior, it must be recognized that all forms of enactment are not the same. Different aspects of labeling, commitment, and life experiences affect different forms of enactment. Refining the ARRM to account for these findings will contribute to developing public policies to deal with the AIDS crisis.

What implications do these results have for mitigating the spread of HIV? These findings point to the relevance and importance of education. Two of the most significant variables at the labeling stage include knowledge and susceptibility. Both of these factors that shape AIDS risk reduction behavior can be addressed through education specific to AIDS and the contraction of HIV. Education can serve a more general role in instilling values of response efficacy, which plays a big role at the commitment stage. These three factors constitute immediate points of intervention that could serve to slow the spread of this disease.

Finally, on a methodological note, several issues still need to be resolved. First, incarcerated adolescents are obviously a unique population. The study population may demonstrate differential knowledge levels, unique attitudes, and diverse behavioral intentions when compared to other populations. For one thing, their behaviors place them in a high-risk group. These findings need to be compared with samples of nonincarcerated youth to determine if the patterns identified persist. Second, a multistage progressive model, such as the ARRM, needs to be examined longitudinally. Ideally, a longitudinal comparative analysis needs to be conducted in diverse locations. Despite these obvious limitations, this study provides strong support for the ARRM, yet still suggests that some fundamental changes may be needed. Equally important, the importance of life experiences as a motivation for behavior change seems to be a vital aspect of the ARRM that requires further empirical inquiry.

ACKNOWLEDGMENT

The authors are grateful to Sherry Bennett Quiñones for her very helpful suggestions regarding our statistical analysis.

NOTES

1. Connecticut, Maine, Massachusetts, New Hampshire, New Jersey, New York, Pennsylvania, Rhode Island, and Vermont.

2. For the two variables regarding an HIV blood test for themselves and others, the three responses are no, don't know, and yes.

3. Because each dependent variable is measured along the same scale, with 0, 1, 2, the general model described here applies to each of the ordered probit models. The measures for each that form AIDS risk avoidance behavior are presented in Table 1.

4. The LRI, however, cannot equal one.

REFERENCES

Becker, M. (1974). The Health Belief Model and personal health behavior. *Health Education Monographs* 2:220–43.

Bloom, A. (1988). Acquired Immune Deficiency Syndrome in childhood. *Public Health* 102:97–106.

Boyer, C., and Kegeles, S. (1991). AIDS risk and prevention among adolescents. *Social Science and Medicine* 33:11–23.

Bowen, A., and Trotter, R. (1995). HIV risk in intravenous drug users and crack cocaine smokers: Predicting stage of change for condom use. *Journal of Consulting and Clinical Psychology* 63:238–48.

Breakwell, G., Millward, L., and Fife-Schaw, C. (1994). Commitment to "safer" sex as a predictor of condom use among 16–20 years olds. *Journal of Applied Social Psychology* 24:189–217.

Catania, J., Kegeles, S., and Coates, T. (1990). Toward an understanding of risk behavior: An AIDS Risk-Reduction Model. *Health Education Quarterly* 17:53–92.

Catania, J., Coates, T., and Kegeles, S. (1994). A test of the AIDS Risk Reduction Model: Psychosocial correlates of condom use in the AMEN cohort survey. *Health Psychology* 13:548–55.

Centers for Disease Control. (1995). *HIV/AIDS surveillance*. Atlanta, GA: U.S. Department of Health and Human Services.

Cleary, P., Rogers, T., Singer, E., Avorn, J., van Devanter, N., Perry, S., and Pindyck, J. (1986). Health education about AIDS among seropositive blood donors. *Health Education Quarterly* 13:317–29.

DiClemente, R., Lanier, M., Horan P., and Lodico, M. (1991). Comparison of AIDS knowledge, attitudes, and behaviors among incarcerated adolescents and a public school sample in San Francisco. *American Journal of Public Health* 81:628–30.

Eiser, C., Eiser, R., and Lang, J. (1990). How adolescents compare AIDS with other diseases: Implications for prevention. *Journal of Pediatric Psychology* 15:97–103.

Feldman, D., and Johnson, T. (1986). *The social dimensions of AIDS: Method and theory*. New York: Praeger Press.

Gibson, D., Catania, J., and Peterson, J. (1991). Theoretical background. In *Preventing AIDS*, eds. Sorensen et al. New York: Guilford.

Greene, W. (1990). *Econometric analysis*. New York: MacMillan.

Hammett, T., Jaffe, H., and Johnson, B. (1987). *The cause, transmission and incidence of AIDS* (AIDS Bulletin). Washington, DC: National Institutes of Justice.

Hingson, R., Strunin, L., Berlin, B., and Heeren, T. (1990). Beliefs about AIDS, use of alcohol and drugs, and unprotected sex among Massachusetts adolescents. *American Journal of Public Health* 80:295–99.

Kline, A., and VanLandingham, M. (1994). HIV-infected women and sexual risk reduction: The relevance of existing models of behavior change. *AIDS Education and Prevention* 6:390–402.

Kowalewski, M., Longshore, D., and Anglin, D. (1994). The AIDS Risk Reduction Model: Examining intentions to use condoms among injection drug users. *Journal of Applied Social Psychology* 24:2002–27.

Lanier, M., and McCarthy, B. (1989). AIDS awareness and the impact of AIDS education in juvenile corrections. *Criminal Justice and Behavior* 16:395–411.

Longshore, D., and Anglin, D. (1995). Intentions to share injection paraphernalia: An empirical test of the AIDS Risk Reduction Model among injection drug users. *The International Journal of the Addictions* 30:305–21.

Maddala, G. (1983). *Limited dependent and qualitative variables in econometrics*. New York: Cambridge University Press.

Maiman, L., and Becker, M. (1974). The Health Belief Model: Origins and correlates in psychological theory. *Health Education Monographs* 2:337–53.

Malow, R., Corrigan, S., Cunningham, S., West, J., and Pena, J. (1993). Psychosocial factors associated with condom use among African-American drug abusers in treatment. *AIDS Education and Prevention* 5:244–43.

Malow, R., West, J., Corrigan, S., Pena, J., and Cunningham, S. (1994). Outcome of psychoeducation for HIV risk reduction. *AIDS Education and Prevention* 6:113–25.

Maticka-Tyndale, E. (1991). Modification of sexual activities in the era of AIDS: A trend analysis of adolescent sexual activities. *Youth and Society* 23:31–49.

McKelvey, R., and Zavoina, W. (1975). A statistical model for the analysis of ordinal level dependent variables. *Journal of Mathematical Sociology* 4:103–20.

Office of Justice Programs. (1994). *HIV in prisons 1994*. Washington, DC: Department of Justice.

Petosa, R., and Wessinger, J. (1989). Using the Health Belief Model to assess the HIV education needs of junior and senior high school. *International Quarterly of Community Health Education* 10:135–43.

Petosa, R., and Wessinger, J. (1990). The AIDS education needs of adolescents: A theory-based approach. *AIDS E ducation and Prevention* 2:127–36.

Rosenstock, I. (1974). The Health Belief Model and preventive health behavior. *Health Education Monographs* 2:355–86.

Rosenstock, I., Strecher, V., and Becker, M. (1988). Social learning theory and the Health Belief Model. *Health Education Quarterly* 15:175–83.

Solomon, M., and DeJong, W. (1986). Recent sexually transmitted disease prevention efforts and their implications for AIDS health education. *Health Education Quarterly* 13:301–16.

Yep, G. (1993). HIV/AIDS in Asian and Pacific Islander communities in the U.S.: A review, analysis, and integration. *International Quarterly of Community Health Education* 13:293–315.

Part IV
Behavioural Interventions, Knowledge and Attitudes

[16]

Law enforcement responses to the HIV/AIDS epidemic

Selected findings and suggestions for future research

R. Alan Thompson and James W. Marquart

College of Criminal Justice, Sam Houston State University, Huntsville, Texas, USA

Since its discovery in 1981, acquired immune deficiency syndrome (AIDS) has become one of the USA's leading social and medical problems. To illustrate, the Centers for Disease Control (1997) recently reported that there were a total of 64,966 cases of AIDS contagion in the USA between July 1996 and June 1997. This figure, when combined with those gathered from previous years, results in a cumulative total of 612,078 reported AIDS cases in the USA since 1981 (CDC, 1997). Beyond these totals of annual and cumulative known AIDS cases, the CDC (1997) also reported that there are at least 239,000 individuals in the USA who are presently living with one or more AIDS-related opportunistic diseases. Each of these figures, however, dangerously misleading due to the fact that they under-represent at least two very important groups – not only those who have been diagnosed with HIV but have not yet developed an AIDS-related opportunistic illness thus escaping official reporting criteria, but also those infected with HIV who have yet to be either tested or identified. Combining the number of individuals in these two under-represented groups with those who are represented by the official statistics yields an incidence of HIV and AIDS contagion that undoubtedly extends far beyond the number of officially documented cases. This problem of under-reporting and under-representation is commonly referred to as the "dark figure" of HIV/AIDS contagion which, according to many experts, ranges somewhere on the order between one and one-and-a-half million unreported or unknown cases (Hombs, 1992)[1].

While these statistics regarding HIV/AIDS contagion are alarming and worthy of increased attention, what is perhaps even more disconcerting is the fact that the disease is no longer confined to members of the high-risk groups as was once the case. That is, whereas HIV/AIDS was once thought to only affect individuals who engaged in certain "risky" behaviours such as homosexual/bisexual conduct, prostitution, and intravenous drug use, it now poses a variety of concerns for many individuals who would remain otherwise unaffected by such issues. In fact, it is this very expansion of the disease from a relatively small number of socially isolated groups to the general population that has created a variety of both rational and irrational beliefs, perceptions and attitudes among individuals about the disease and its carriers. As a consequence, there presently exists a wide variation in the manner that both individuals and society respond to HIV/AIDS and its victims.

Considerable aggregate research has been conducted regarding the level and accuracy of knowledge, perceived threats, and stress caused by the HIV/AIDS epidemic within the American population. This early line of research has consistently revealed two notable findings, the first of which indicates that many Americans are relatively accurate in their knowledge regarding the major modes of transmission for HIV (Caron, *et al.*, 1992; Epstein, 1991; Fielstein, *et al.*, 1992; Kimmell and Keefer, 1991; LeBlanc, 1993; Singer, *et al.*, 1991). At the same time, however, the second notable finding from this line of research suggests that many Americans lack the comprehensive level of understanding about HIV/AIDS and its victims that is necessary in order to deal with both on a rational psychological basis (Caron, *et al.*, 1992; Epstein, 1991; Fielstein, *et al.*, 1992; Kimmell and Keefer, 1991; LeBlanc, 1993).

Additional research on these issues also indicates that older adults (LeBlanc, 1993; McCaig, *et al.*, 1991), males (Donnelly, *et al.*, 1996; LeBlanc, 1993; Lewis and Range, 1992; Wicks, 1991), members of racial and ethnic minority groups (Alcalay, *et al.*, 1989-90; Dicks, 1994; DiClemente, *et al.*, 1988; Friedman, *et al.*, 1987; Herek and Capitanio, 1994; Johnson, *et al.*, 1994; Kulwicki and Cass; 1994; Nicholas, *et al.*, 1994; Sobo, 1994) members of the lower socioeconomic classes (Flaskerud and Thompson, 1991; Sobo, 1994), those living outside of metropolitan areas (DiClemente, *et al.*, 1988; Donnelly, *et al.*, 1996; LeBlanc, 1993; McCaig, *et al.*, 1991; St Lawrence, *et al.*, 1989) who rely on the mass media as their primary source of information about the disease (Cline and Engel, 1991; Reardon and Richardson, 1991), generally exhibit lower levels of HIV/AIDS-related knowledge, higher levels of stress, and increased perceptions of threat than are average among the general population.

Given these facts, it comes as no surprise to find that similar perceptions are not uncommon among individuals vested with the professional responsibility to treat and handle persons affected by the disease on a daily basis. One obvious group of individuals with such obligations are those employed in the medical and related health care professions (Connors and Heaven, 1995; Gallop, *et al.*, 1992; Henry and Thurn, 1991; Kelly, *et al.*, 1987; Link, 1988; Shapiro *et al.*, 1992). It should be noted, however, that physicians, nurses and other personnel within the medical profession are not alone in experiencing the variety of adverse psychological and physical effects that accompany HIV/AIDS. That is, there exists a number of other occupations whose practitioners face the negative physical threats, personal prejudices and psychological stresses posed by HIV/AIDS as a result of routine contact with its victims. One such occupation is that of law enforcement.

Although not a single law enforcement officer within the USA has yet to test positive for HIV/AIDS as the result of a work-related exposure, a review of the published literature nonetheless indicates that there currently exists a paucity of empirical research on the attitudes and perceptions of these professionals regarding the topic as compared to that which has occurred in other occupations. Compounding this general lack of research regarding HIV/AIDS within the law enforcement profession is the fact that the amount of attention which the topic has received may be best characterized as either conjectural or topical at best (see

Aaron, 1991; Bigbee, 1987, 1993; Blumberg, 1990, 1993; Edwards and Tewksbury, 1996; Frost *et al.*, 1989; Gates and Lady, 1991; Hammett, 1987; Kennedy *et al.*, 1990; Laszlo and Smith, 1991; Lester and Pitts, 1991; Marsh, 1987a, 1987b, 1987c, 1987d, 1987e, 1988; Yearwood, 1992). In response to this apparent need for increased empirical attention to the issue, the authors analyzed survey data from a sample of Texas peace officers assigned to patrol duties regarding their beliefs, perceptions and attitudes about HIV/AIDS in relation to the performance of their everyday law enforcement duties. The results of this analysis, presented below, are interpreted and discussed within the context of future implications for the law enforcement profession. Finally, suggestions regarding the continued need and direction of further empirical research in this important area are given.

Method

Instrument

A review of the published literature revealed that there existed little empirical information aimed at assessing or responding to the HIV/AIDS-related concerns of this particular segment of the population. Drawing on the nature of issues addressed by existing studies of both the general population and medical profession, combined with discussions generated through a series of focus groups involving several law enforcement practitioners and experts, the instrument used in this study was the Law Enforcement and AIDS Survey (LEAS).

The LEAS consisted of 54 questions divided into six specific areas of inquiry:

(1) an evaluation of subjects' primary sources of HIV/AIDS information as well as accuracy of their knowledge regarding major modes of exposure;

(2) prevalence of HIV/AIDS-related, profession-specific training and protective devices with which subjects were provided;

(3) perceived adequacy of departmental policies guiding subjects' behaviour in potentially infectious situations;

(4) frequency with which subjects face a risk of exposure to the virus, practical measures taken during these contacts to diminish risk of contagion, and the perceived levels of psychological concern which arise from these encounters;

(5) inquiry into subjects' personal health histories with regard to HIV testing; and

(6) an assessment of changes made in subjects' practical behaviours and perceived ethical responsibilities precipitated by the fear of HIV/AIDS contagion.

Procedure

Respondents were administered the LEAS during the course of officer attendance at in-service training or shift briefings. Instructions were given regarding the necessity for providing as complete and accurate responses as possible, as well as the assurance of anonymity for individual respondents.

However, because some items contained within the instrument addressed admittedly sensitive and personal issues, a limited number of responses were omitted by subjects. Analysis of these missing responses revealed no systematic pattern or error. As a result, all completed instruments were included in the final analysis whether or not they contained missing data.

Subjects

Subjects (N = 142) for this study represent a convenience sample of law enforcement officers drawn from six central Texas agencies. The sizes and missions of these agencies differed somewhat and represented members from various state, municipal, and institutional branches of the law enforcement profession. Not surprisingly, 90 per cent of the subjects were males. Roughly 77 per cent were white, 5 per cent black, and 17.3 per cent represented other racial/ethnic groups with a mean of 34 years of age. Subjects, all of which were assigned to general patrol duties at the time of instrument administration, reported a mean tenure of 8.5 years in the law enforcement profession. Slightly less than three-fourths of the subjects (74 per cent) occupied the rank of patrol officer, while slightly greater than one-fourth of those remaining (26 per cent) occupied supervisory positions within the patrol division at the rank of corporal or above. Although based on non-probabilistic sampling methods, the demographic characteristics of the officers who participated in this study are roughly representative of those employed by many state, local and institutional law enforcement agencies (Bureau of Justice Statistics, 1996).

Results

Sources of information and knowledge of HIV/AIDS exposure

The first area of interest addressed by the LEAS not only sought to identify subjects' primary sources of information about HIV/AIDS, but to also assess the accuracy of their knowledge regarding its major modes of transmission. With respect to the former of these two objectives, the greatest percentage of subjects (78.4 per cent) reported that the mass media was their primary source of information about HIV/AIDS. Given this overwhelming reliance on the mass media, only a small number of the remaining subjects reported having received their information about HIV/AIDS through other primary sources such as: medical/scientific journals (6.3 per cent); departmental training (5.6 per cent); friends and everyday conversation (3.5 per cent); consultations with medical experts (2.8 per cent); professional/law enforcement related journals (2.1 per cent), and; special interest groups (0.7 per cent). Comparison of these results with the findings from existing research regarding the relative dangers involved in using the mass media as a primary source of information about the disease suggests that those officers who reported primary reliance on this medium are at least equally susceptible to experiencing the same elevated levels of psychological stress and increased perceptions of threat from the virus as the general population.

PIJPSM
21,4

652

Subjects were also asked to indicate with whom they had previously discussed the issue of HIV/AIDS as it related to the performance of their duties. Analysis of this data revealed that 85.9 per cent had discussed the issue with fellow officers, and 70.4 per cent reported having done so with a family member. A noticeably smaller percentage of subjects reported having discussed the issue with a doctor (26.1 per cent), while even less had done so with a religious leader (7.7 per cent).

Analysis of the data also revealed that subjects were not as well-informed as they could be. Specifically, 37.1 per cent of the officers represented believed that unprotected heterosexual contact is the primary source of HIV/AIDS exposure, followed second by IV drug use (35 per cent), and third by contact involving male homosexual/bisexual behaviour (19.3 per cent). Of those remaining, 7 per cent reported "other" unidentified means as the primary source of HIV/AIDS exposure, while only 1.4 per cent reported the belief that the disease was primarily transmitted through accidental body fluid exposures. Interestingly, zero subjects expressed the belief that HIV/AIDS exposures occur through contaminated blood transfusions and tissue transplants.

Comparison of these results with official data reveals differences between subjects' rank ordering of the primary modes of HIV/AIDS exposure and the frequency with which they actually occur in the general population. Specifically, CDC (1997, Tables III and XI) figures for July 1996 through June 1997 indicated that the most frequently reported HIV/AIDS exposure category was contact involving male homosexual/bisexual behaviour (24,146 cases), followed by IV drug use (16,150 cases), "other" unidentified means (11,807 cases), unprotected heterosexual contact (8,816 cases), blood transfusions and tissue transplants (489 cases), and accidental body fluid exposures among health care workers (52 cases) respectively.

Given these results concerning subjects' sources of information about HIV/AIDS and their relatively inaccurate knowledge regarding the major modes of exposure, the results of an additional item also included in the LEAS bear mention. Specifically, subjects were asked to indicate how accurate they believed physical appearance alone was for predicting HIV/AIDS infection in an individual. Slightly less than one-half (49.3 per cent) of the officers surveyed were largely sceptical about the use of such subjective criteria and reported the belief that visual perception of physical appearance alone could not be used with any degree of accuracy in predicting an individual's health status. More interesting, however, was the finding that slightly less than one-third of the subjects (30.2 per cent) were more confident in the accurate use of such subjective criteria. Specifically, 6.4 per cent reported the perception that physical appearance could be used to accurately predict a person's health status either "most" or "all" of the time, while an additional 23.9 per cent indicated that this measure could at least be used with a relative degree of accuracy for such purposes "some of the time." Of those remaining, 20.4 per cent reported that they were largely undecided on the use of a person's physical appearance as an accurate predictor of HIV/AIDS infection.

Prevalence of HIV/AIDS-related training and availability of protective devices
In terms of training, analysis of the data indicated that 42.3 per cent of the subjects reported having received any formalized in-service training on the issue of HIV/AIDS as related to the performance of their law enforcement duties. With regard to the availability of protective devices, 95.1 per cent of the subjects reported that they were regularly provided with latex gloves. An even smaller percentage reported that they were regularly provided with CPR delivery devices (50.7 per cent), facial shields/masks (43 per cent), decontamination/ cleansing liquids (33.8 per cent), tactical search gloves (12 per cent), or contamination suits (7 per cent). From this, it is apparent that few officers are being provided with access to the full range of devices that are necessary in order to ensure effective protection from the risk of accidental HIV/AIDS contagion on the job.

Perceived adequacy of departmental policies governing officers' responses
The third area of interest addressed by the LEAS focused on subjects' perceptions regarding the perceived adequacy of departmental policies governing their response to potentially infectious individuals and situations. Although several subjects reported the perception that their agency's guidelines were either "somewhat" (18.4 per cent) or "adequately" (5 per cent) comprehensive, a larger percentage evaluated them as being either "totally inadequate" (47.5 per cent) or "somewhat inadequate" (29.1 per cent). Interestingly, no subjects reported the perception that their agency's policies in this area were "totally comprehensive."

Frequency of risk exposure, protective measures taken and resulting psychological concerns
The fourth area of interest addressed by the LEAS assessed the perceived seriousness and potential for HIV/AIDS infection as a function of an officer's daily law enforcement responsibilities and duties. This general objective was met by assessing subjects' responses to a series of three specific items. The first of these three items asked subjects to report the frequency with which they encounter certain situations that place them at high risk for exposure to the virus. The second item asked them to indicate the various individual or combined measures they typically employ to protect themselves from exposure during such high-risk situations. The third item requested that they indicate the perceived levels of psychological concern experienced as a result of such encounters. Results for these three items are reported in Tables I-III.

Close inspection of the results contained within these three tables reveals several notable findings. With specific regard to Table I, it is apparent that the officers reported a rather high frequency of contact with what are traditionally referred to as members of the "high-risk groups" – known IV drug users, prostitutes, and homosexuals/bisexuals[2]. Less frequent were contacts in which the officer is required to arrest a known seropositive (HIV+) person, or is bitten, spat on, or threatened with infection by an arrestee/suspect. Even less

	Never No. (%)	1 to 5 times per year No. (%)	1 to 5 times per month No. (%)	Over five times per month No. (%)
IV drug users (n = 142)	1 (0.7)	32 (22.6)	44 (31)	65 (45.8)
Known prostitutes (n = 142)	8 (5.6)	59 (41.5)	35 (24.7)	40 (28.2)
Known homosexuals/ bisexuals (n = 136)	1 (0.7)	34 (25)	54 (39.7)	47 (34.6)
Arresting known seropositive (HIV+) person (n = 140)	22 (15.7)	91 (65)	22 (15.7)	5 (3.6)
Threatened by seropositive (HIV+) person (n = 139)	63 (45.3)	66 (47.5)	7 (5)	3 (2.2)
Arrestee/suspect spitting on officer (n = 140)	23 (16.4)	101 (72.1)	13 (9.2)	3 (2.1)
Arrestee/suspect biting officer (n = 137)	64 (46.7)	70 (51.1)	1 (0.7)	2 (1.5)
Administer first-aid where risk of HIV/AIDS is present (n = 141)	64 (45.4)	61 (43.3)	13 (9.2)	3 (2.1)

Table I.
Frequency of reported contact by subjects with certain high-risk individuals and activities

frequent still are situations in which an officer is required to administer critical first-aid where the risk of HIV/AIDS contagion is present.

Examination of Table II reveals that in four of the seven potentially hazardous situations – dealing with known drug users, prostitutes, homosexuals/bisexuals, and the administration of critical first-aid – the primary measure most frequently taken by officers to minimize the risk of exposure during contact with the arrestee/suspect/victim involves the use of one or more protective devices previously described. The second most frequent measure which officers employ in these situations is to treat the individual as they would any other. It should not be surprising to find that the three exceptions to this general trend are situations in which the officer is either bitten, spat on, or threatened with HIV/AIDS exposure by an arrestee/suspect. When this occurs, officers more frequently employ what may be best referred to as alternative control tactics, which generally involves the application of one or more forms of non-lethal force intended to gain compliance from the aggressor. An additional measure that is also relatively frequently utilized by officers either in combination or the presumed failure/absence of protective devices, indifferent treatment, and alternative control tactics involves the use of verbal commands – a tactic employing the issuance of specific oral directives for behavioural compliance to the arrestee/suspect by the officer, who ideally remains at a safe distance from the individual. Interestingly, only in a rare number of instances did any of the subjects report letting the arrestee/suspect freely leave the scene without the officer attempting to effect an arrest where, it can be presumed, one was necessary.

	Use protective devices No. (%)	Verbal commands only No. (%)	Alternative control tactics No. (%)	Let subject go without arrest No. (%)	Treated subject as any other No. (%)
IV drug users	78 (54.9)	28 (20.4)	33 (23.2)	4 (2.8)	41 (28.9)
Known prostitutes	69 (48.6)	34 (23.9)	28 (19.7)	4 (2.8)	45 (31.7)
Known homosexuals/ bisexuals	62 (43.7)	29 (20.4)	27 (19)	6 (4.2)	45 (31.7)
Threatened by seropositive (HIV+) person	60 (42.3)	21 (14.8)	67 (47.2)	2 (1.4)	18 (12.7)
Arrestee/suspect spitting on officer	41 (28.9)	12 (8.5)	72 (50.7)	1 (0.7)	27 (19)
Arrestee/suspect biting officer	40 (28.2)	10 (7)	69 (48.6)	1 (0.7)	25 (17.6)
Administer first-aid where risk of HIV/ AIDS is present	105 (73.9)	14 (9.9)	10 (7)	9 (6.3)	14 (9.9)

Table II. Frequency of reported measures taken by subjects to reduce the risk of infection during contact with certain high-risk individuals and activities

Table III also presents several findings which may help to further illuminate an important dimension suspected of influencing officers' behavioural responses to HIV/AIDS following initial exposure to one or more of the high-risk situations described above. This important dimension is the level of perceived psychological concern experienced by the officer following their involvement in a potentially infectious encounter. Specifically, the results reported in Table III indicate that anywhere from 39.6 per cent to 79.1 per cent of the officers represented reported being "very" to "extremely" concerned following involvement in any of the seven situations. Conversely, only a maximum of 5.8 per cent of the respondents reported experiencing no psychological concern following such encounters.

A second finding to be taken from Table III indicates that while officers have a high frequency of contact with known IV drug users, prostitutes and homosexuals/bisexuals (see Table I), their levels of psychological concern following such encounters do not seem to subside. Given this observation, it is not surprising to find that officers also exhibit elevated levels of psychological concern over involvement in less frequent but more potentially infectious situations such as being threatened, spat on, or bitten by an arrestee/suspect, or having to administer critical first-aid where the risk of HIV/AIDS exposure is present.

As a result of these response patterns, two common beliefs regarding the nature of officers' psychological responses to potentially infectious situations are in need of closer empirical scrutiny. The first common belief in need of such examination is that which presumes officers eventually become psychologically desensitized over time to the risk of HIV/AIDS infection from what may be

Table III.
Frequency of reported levels of concern among subjects following contact with certain high-risk individuals and activities

	No concern No. (%)	Very little to some concern No. (%)	Very to extremely concerned No. (%)
IV drug users (n = 140)	3 (2.1)	63 (45.5)	74 (52.8)
Known prostitutes (n = 139)	6 (4.3)	78 (56.1)	55 (39.6)
Known homosexuals/bisexuals (n = 137)	8 (5.8)	59 (43.1)	70 (51)
Threatened by seropositive (HIV+) person (n = 133)	6 (4.5)	41 (30.8)	86 (64.6)
Arrestee/suspect spitting on officer (n = 132)	3 (2.3)	41 (31.1)	88 (66.7)
Arrestee/suspect biting officer (n = 129)	3 (2.3)	24 (18.6)	102 (79.1)
Administer first-aid where risk of HIV/AIDS is present (n = 134)	2 (1.5)	26 (19.4)	106 (79.1)

regarded as fairly routine and repeated contacts with members of the traditional at-risk groups (e.g. known IV drug users, prostitutes, and homosexuals/ bisexuals). The second common belief in need of examination is that which assumes there exists some qualitative difference between the various types of high-risk situations that officers encounter in terms of the resulting levels of psychological concern which each produces. That is, it is very likely that officers do not make a clear distinction between levels of exposure risk based on the situation. Instead, each encounter in which the risk of HIV/AIDS contagion is present is considered as equally dangerous as any other.

Finally, chi-square analysis revealed that there exists no significant difference between officers based on demographic variables with regard to the likelihood of experiencing various levels of psychological concern following exposure to the situations described above. This suggests that all officers – despite differences in tenure, rank, age, gender, education, or race – are equally likely to experience the same levels of psychological concern as their peers to any form of potential HIV/AIDS exposure.

Taken together, there are several conclusions to be drawn from the results presented in Tables I-III. First, while the law enforcement officers in this sample come into relatively frequent contact with members of the high risk groups, they less frequently experience situations in which they are required to administer critical first-aid where the risk of HIV/AIDS is present or where they are bitten, spat on, or threatened with HIV/AIDS exposure by an arrestee/ suspect. Second, depending on the nature of the particular situation, officers are likely to employ those measures which they perceive as being most effective for protecting them from exposure to HIV/AIDS. In most situations where outward aggression by the arrestee/suspect is absent, officers are more likely to simply use measures such as protective devices and/or indifferent treatment. Conversely, in situations where outward aggression against the officer by the arrestee/suspect is present, officers are more likely to use independent or combined measures such as alternative control tactics, protective devices, and verbal commands to protect themselves from potential exposure. A final conclusion to be drawn from these results is that in all but one situation – contact with known prostitutes – greater than one-half of the subjects reported being "very" to "extremely" concerned following such encounters. This particular finding raises questions regarding the assumption that officers eventually become desensitized to concerns over the threat of contagion as their frequency of exposure to such situations increases.

Incidence and reasons underlying HIV testing among officers
The fifth area of interest addressed by the survey examined subjects' personal health histories with regard to HIV testing. Specifically, this section assessed the frequency with which subjects reported having submitted to an HIV antibody test in the past and the various reasons that formed the basis for this decision. Analysis of this data indicated that 70.4 per cent of the subjects reported having submitted to an HIV antibody test in the past. The most commonly cited reason among subjects for having the test was to alleviate concern over a suspected work-related exposure (16.2 per cent), followed second by having the test as part of a routine physical examination (15.5 per cent), and third as a prerequisite for donating blood (14.8 per cent). The fourth most frequent reason cited by subjects for undergoing an HIV test was that it was required as part of a work-related physical examination (14.1 per cent). Concern over an unprotected sexual encounter was the sixth most common reason (6.3 per cent). Finally, submitting to the test as a prerequisite for receiving medical treatment was the least cited reason (3.5 per cent).

Additional analysis indicated that some officers were more likely to report having undergone an HIV test than others. Specifically, subjects 30 years of age or younger were more likely than those over 31 to report having an HIV test (Pearson's chi-square = 32.67, df = 1, $p < 0.001$) (Table IV). Similarly, subjects who reported having ten years and less experience in the profession were more likely to report having had an HIV test than those with 11 or more years on the job (Pearson's chi-square = 10.62, df = 1, $p = 0.001$) (Table V).

	Reported having submitted to HIV testing	Reported *not* having submitted to HIV testing
Officers 30 years of age and younger	$f_o = 50$ $f_e = 35.3$	$f = 0$ $f_e = 14.7$
Officers 31 years of age and older	$f_o = 48$ $f_e = 62.7$	$f = 41$ $f_e = 26.3$

Table IV. Expected and obtained frequencies of occurrence for reported HIV testing among officers by age

PIJPSM
21,4

658

Fear of exposure and the transformation of officers' behaviours and beliefs

The sixth area of interest assessed a range of officers' attitudes regarding the fear of HIV/AIDS contagion and the changes that such concerns have precipitated in both their practical behaviours and perceived ethical responsibilities. Specifically, this area of interest contained four items which queried subjects about their:

(1) concern for receiving a needle puncture or cut from a sharp object while conducting a search;

(2) degree of change in conducting various types of searches based on concern for accidental HIV/AIDS transmission;

(3) stated support for having HIV/AIDS information disclosed by law following suspected work-related exposures; and

(4) belief regarding the ethical responsibility to act in situations that pose a high risk of HIV/AIDS contagion.

With regard to the first of these items, it was expected that a majority of the subjects would report elevated levels of concern over the risk of receiving a needle puncture or cut from a sharp object while conducting searches. Analysis of the data supports this expectation by finding that 80.3 per cent of the subjects reported being "very" to "highly" concerned with this particular risk for HIV/AIDS exposure. A notably smaller percentage (18.3 per cent) indicated that the risk of receiving a puncture or cut caused them "some" to "very little" concern, while only 1.4 per cent reported experiencing no concern whatsoever over this source of potential exposure.

Given both the expected and confirmed elevation of concern among officers for the risk of receiving a needle puncture or cut while conducting a search, it was anticipated that subjects would also report adopting mild to dramatic changes in conducting various physical searches of persons, places, and property. Again, the results obtained for this item were largely supportive of the expected response pattern. Specifically, 20.6 per cent of the subjects indicated that they had adopted a completely new method for conducting searches, with an additional 71.6 per cent reporting having adopted a range of moderate to dramatic changes in the manner which they conduct searches. By comparison, a relatively small percentage of subjects reported having made only limited (6.4 per cent) or no changes whatsoever (1.4 per cent) in their search techniques.

Table V.
Expected and obtained frequencies of occurrence for reported HIV testing among officers by years of experience in the law enforcement profession

	Reported having submitted to HIV testing	Reported *not* having submitted to HIV testing
Officers with ten years and less professional experience	$f_o = 75$ $f_e = 66.7$	$f = 20$ $f_e = 28.3$
Officers with 11 years and more professional experience	$f_o = 24$ $f_e = 32.3$	$f = 22$ $f_e = 13.7$

A third item asked subjects to indicate whether or not they were likely to support legislation referred to as "police protection" statutes which would allow officers to be informed of an arrestee's or suspect's health status following a potential work-related exposure to HIV/AIDS. As might be expected, an overwhelming majority of the subjects (98.6 per cent) responded favourably to such a proposition. Additional analysis revealed that subjects at the rank of patrol officer were statistically more likely ($p = 0.003$) to support this type of legislation than were subjects of higher rank. This distinction between the ranks is perhaps explained by the qualitative differences that exist in the nature of the duties each performs.

The final item in this area of interest sought to assess subjects' perceived ethical responsibility to act in situations (such as the delivery of critical first-aid) that pose a high risk of HIV/AIDS contagion. The largest percentage of subjects (39.3 per cent) indicated that they had the same perceived degree of responsibility to act in such a situation as in any other. An additional 19.3 per cent reported feeling that they have at least a moderate degree of responsibility to act in situations which pose a high risk of contagion. However, it was disturbing to find that 41.4 per cent of the subjects reported feeling that they have only a limited degree or no responsibility whatsoever to act in situations that pose a threat to their personal health as far as the risk of HIV/AIDS exposure is concerned. Further data analysis revealed that officers over 31 years of age were more likely to report feeling a stronger sense of ethical responsibility to act in situations which pose a risk of HIV/AIDS exposure than were their younger counterparts (Pearson's chi-square = 18.84, df = 3, $p < 0.001$) (Table VI).

Discussion

With little disagreement, the results presented above strongly suggest that HIV/AIDS poses a number of emerging implications for the law enforcement profession and its practitioners. While the methodology employed in the present study precludes drawing any specific conclusions regarding the causal factors underlying officers' response patterns, it is possible to identify several areas of concern in need of increased attention if the risks posed by HIV/AIDS are to be minimized to a level that is psychologically tolerable. Through devoting greater

	No responsibility to act	Some responsibility to act	Moderate responsibility to act	Same responsibility to act
Officers 30 years and younger	$f_o = 4$ $f_e = 5.8$	$f_o = 26$ $f_e = 15$	$f_o = 8$ $f_e = 9.5$	$f_o = 12$ $f_e = 19.7$
Officers 31 years and older	$f_o = 12$ $f_e = 10.2$	$f_o = 15$ $f_e = 26$	$f_o = 18$ $f_e = 16.5$	$f_o = 42$ $f_e = 34.3$

Table VI. Expected and obtained frequencies of occurrence for officers' reported degree of ethical responsibility to act in situations which pose a threat of HIV/AIDS exposure by age

attention to the beliefs, perceptions and attitudes of law enforcement officers who are required to deal with the issue of HIV/AIDS on almost a daily basis can we hope to develop positive responses to the delicate and potentially life-threatening issues involved. In this regard, future attention should be directed toward at least two areas. These include:

(1) enhancing the current state of profession-specific training on HIV/AIDS and availability of protective devices; and

(2) developing policies and procedures that ensure the safe and unbiased delivery of law enforcement services to the public.

Enhancing profession-specific training and increasing the availability of protective devices

Similar to challenges previously encountered by the profession, perhaps the most logical measure first to be taken in counteracting the negative implications posed by the HIV/AIDS epidemic is that of increasing the amount and quality of profession-specific training that officers currently receive on the issue. Given the finding that primary reliance on the mass media for information about HIV/AIDS is associated with misinformation and increased levels of fear and stress about the disease, combined with the finding that only a relatively small number of officers from the present sample reported having received any agency-provided training on the topic, it is apparent that improvement in this general area is needed. Specifically, future training for officers should focus on:

(1) the known means of HIV/AIDS transmission and the relative risk involved with each;

(2) the appropriate use of alternative methods for minimizing risk of exposure in differing law enforcement situations;

(3) proper handling of contaminated evidence; and

(4) procedures for decontamination following suspected exposure.

In addition, officers need to be given adequate access to equipment with which they can perform their duties in a safe and efficient manner. Failure to adequately provide protective devices may contribute to situations where officers refuse to perform the duties required of them, thus triggering otherwise avoidable public scrutiny of the agency and disciplinary actions against the parties involved.

While instituting training and issuing protective devices may constitute a sizable expense for many agencies, particularly those serving larger jurisdictions, the dividends to be realized clearly outweigh the potential costs that may arise if they are neglected. While avoidance of litigation is a foreseeable benefit, one of the greatest dividends is improving the psychological health of those officers who deliver law enforcement services to HIV/AIDS affected populations on a regular basis. To this important end, future research should seek to assess the qualitative effects of enhancing profession-specific training efforts as well as the availability of protective devices for purposes of reducing negative psychological conditions associated with exposure to HIV/AIDS populations.

Developing policies and procedures to ensure safe and unbiased delivery of services

Given the potentially lethal health consequences posed by HIV/AIDS for officers who are vested with the responsibility of providing law enforcement services to members of the high-risk populations on an almost daily basis, it is imperative that agency administrators confront the variety of practical and ethical challenges that such encounters pose. One of the most effective methods of confronting and resolving potentially troublesome issues such as HIV/AIDS before they become manifest, as well as exacting compliance by those most directly affected by the issues raised, is through the formulation and implementation of policies and procedures. To be considered at least adequate, agencies should develop what may be best described as "infection control" policies and procedures that encompass a variety of critical issues, three of which may be readily surmised from the findings of the present study.

Perhaps the most obvious issue to be addressed is the specification of measures that ensure officer safety during the performance of practical law enforcement duties such as criminal investigations, arrest of suspects, and the delivery of critical first-aid. Such policies should directly address the issue of use of force against a suspect who presents a threat of HIV/AIDS exposure to the officer. Failure to do so may result in an officer's over-reaction to a real or perceived threat that may not pass legal muster, thus exposing both the agency and officer to liability litigation. Equally important are policies which outline the procedures for reporting potential exposures as well as providing confidential employee testing and counselling. Such policy initiatives seem to logically fit hand in glove with training efforts such as those noted above which are designed to alleviate officer concern over perceived infectious encounters. Finally, and perhaps most problematic, is the formulation of policies that ensure officer performance of duties. As the findings of the present study indicate, law enforcement officers are highly cautious around individuals and circumstances which they perceive as posing a threat of exposure to HIV/AIDS. In fact, officers are cautious to the point where many feel that their ethical responsibility to act in such situations is justifiably diminished. In order to avoid charges of unequal treatment and discrimination by citizens against officers, agencies would be wise to develop policies which seek to provide the most professional level of services possible to all individuals regardless of their health status. Future research in this general area should seek to assess the extent to which agency guidance not only influences officers' beliefs, perceptions and attitudes, but also their attending individual behaviours both before and after policy implementation.

PIJPSM
21,4

662

Conclusion

Although generally considered remote, the risk of HIV/AIDS contagion has emerged as a new source of psychological stress and physical risk for members of the law enforcement profession. As such, the virus has directly influenced the manner in which officers not only perceive but also perform the various tasks associated with their duties including, but not limited to: interactions with suspects, conducting searches of the person, effecting arrests, and delivering critical first-aid to victims. Perhaps the most concerning illustration of the extent to which HIV/AIDS has negatively affected officers' perceptions regarding their role in protecting society is the finding of the present study that some 40 per cent of the subjects felt they only had limited or no responsibility whatsoever to act in situations that posed a threat of HIV/AIDS exposure.

Today, officers can no longer rely on mere visual cues emanating from a suspect's physical gestures for purposes of assessing the relative presence or absence of danger. Instead, officers now have to be equally if not more concerned with the threat posed by what is physically imperceptible within the suspect's body as compared to that which is visually perceptible outside of it. In fact, it is not unreasonable to suggest that law enforcement officers may be more concerned about the long-term health risks that are posed by their interactions with members of certain groups than they are with the short-term risks of assault and minor physical injury. All of this is to say that while the formulation and implementation of "infection control" policies such as those described above can certainly assist officers and agencies in confronting the range of adverse implications posed by the disease for the profession, they may be less helpful in narrowing the gap that HIV/AIDS has created between the police and the public which they are intended to serve.

On a more encouraging note, it is important to point out that law enforcement officers across the nation have had virtually millions of interactions with the public since the discovery of this deadly disease in 1981 and thus far not a single officer has become infected with HIV/AIDS as the result of a work-related exposure. This observation is by no means intended to minimize the importance of HIV/AIDS as a critical issue for the profession. Rather, the intent of this article has been to illuminate the range of beliefs, perceptions and attitudes of law enforcement officers whose responsibility it is to deal with this public health issue on a daily basis. Through gaining a better understanding of the various psychological dimensions can we respond to them with effective measures that minimize the potential risks for officers in the future.

Notes

1. To further illustrate the extent of AIDS contagion on the national level, CDC (1997) statistics rank Texas as reporting the fourth largest number of AIDS diagnoses during the one year period between July 1996 through June 1997. Specifically, Texas – which reported 4,928 known AIDS cases – was led by New York (12,525), California (8,177) and the District of Columbia (6,725) respectively. While there admittedly exists both a quantitative as well as qualitative difference in each of these jurisdictions' AIDS contagion figures, it is

generally agreed that Texas – along with those few jurisdictions that exceed its record – bears the undesirable task of dealing with the disease as a serious public health and safety concern.

2. Although the disease is not exclusively limited to the members of these three groups, official CDC figures indicate that such individuals consistently experience the highest proportion of HIV/AIDS contagion; hence the rationale underlying the attention given in the present analysis to police contacts with such individuals.

References

Aaron, T. (1991), "AIDS education in law enforcement", *Law and Order,* Vol. 39 No. 3, pp. 35-6.

Alcalay, R., Sniderman, P.M., Mitchell, J. and Griffin, R. (1989-90), "Ethnic differences in knowledge of AIDS transmission and attitudes towards gays and people with AIDS", *International Quarterly of Community Health Education,* Vol. 10 No. 3, pp. 213-22.

Bigbee, D. (1987), *The Law Enforcement Officer and AIDS,* US Government Printing Office, Washington, DC.

Blumberg, M. (1990), "The transmission of HIV: exploring some misconceptions related to criminal justice", *Criminal Justice Policy Review,* Vol. 4 No. 4, pp. 288-305.

Blumberg, M. (1993), "The AIDS epidemic and the police: an examination of the issues", in Dunham, R.G. and Alpert, G.P. (Eds), *Critical Issues in Policing,* 2nd ed., Waveland Press, Prospect Heights, IL, pp. 208-19.

Bureau of Justice Statistics (1996), *Local Police Departments 1993,* US Department of Justice, Washington, DC.

Caron, S.L., Davis, C.M., Wynn, R.L. and Roberts, L.W. (1992), "America responds to AIDS, but did college students? Differences between March, 1987 and September, 1988", *AIDS Education and Prevention,* Vol. 4 No. 1, pp. 18-28.

Centers for Disease Control and Prevention (1997), *HIV/AIDS Surveillance Report,* Vol. 9 No. 1, pp. 1-37.

Cline, R.J.W. and Engel, J.L. (1991), "College students' perceptions of sources of information about AIDS", *Journal of American College Health,* Vol. 40 No. 2, pp. 55-63.

Connors, J. and Heaven, P. (1995), "Health beliefs and attitudes toward people living with HIV/AIDS", *Journal of Applied Social Psychology,* Vol. 25 No. 10, pp. 922-31.

Dicks, B.A. (1994), "African American women and AIDS: a public health/social work challenge", *Social Work in Health Care,* Vol. 19 No. 3-4, pp. 123-43.

DiClemente, R.J., Boyer, C.B. and Morales, E.S. (1988), "Minorities and AIDS: knowledge, attitudes and misconceptions among black and Latino adolescents", *American Journal of Public Health,* Vol. 78 No. 1, pp. 55-7.

Donnelly, J., Donnelly, M., Kittleson, M.J. and Procaccino, A.T. (1996), "Assessing variability of HIV transmission attitudes and behaviours at an urban northeastern university", *Psychological Reports,* Vol. 78 No. 2, pp. 375-83.

Edwards, T.D. and Tewksbury, R. (1996), "HIV/AIDS: State police training practices and personnel policies", *American Journal of Police,* Vol. 15 No. 1, pp. 45-62.

Epstein, R. (1991), "Patient attitudes and knowledge about HIV infection and AIDS", *Journal of Family Practice,* Vol. 32 No. 4, pp. 373-7.

Fielstein, E.M., Fielstein, L.L. and Hazlewood, M.G. (1992), "AIDS knowledge among college freshmen students: need for education?", *Journal of Sex Education and Therapy,* Vol. 18 No. 1, pp. 44-5.

Flaskerud, J.H. and Thompson, J. (1991), "Beliefs about AIDS, health and illness in low-income white women", *Nursing Research,* Vol. 40 No. 5, pp. 266-71.

Friedman, S.R., Southeran, J.L., Abdul-Quader, A., Prim, B.J., Des Jarlais, D.C., Kleinman, P., Mauge, C., Goldsmith, D.S., Elsadr, W. and Maslansky, R. (1987), "The AIDS epidemic among blacks and Hispanics", *The Milbank Quarterly,* Vol. 65 Sup. 2, pp. 455-99.

Frost, M., Moore, M. and Crowe, G. (1989), "AIDS education for California law enforcement", *The Police Chief,* Vol. 56 No. 12, pp. 25-8.

Gallop, R.M., Lancee, W.J., Taerk, G., Coates, R.A. *et al.* (1992), "Fear of contagion and AIDS: nurses' perceptions of risk", *AIDS Care,* Vol. 4 No. 1, pp. 103-9.

Gates, D.F. and Lady, K.E. (1991), "Enhancing AIDS awareness in Los Angeles", *The Police Chief,* Vol. 58 No. 3, pp. 44-7.

Hammett, T.M. (1987), *AIDS and the Law Enforcement Officer: Concerns and Policy Responses,* National Institute of Justice, Washington, DC.

Henry, K. and Thurn, J. (1991), "HIV infection in health care workers: how great is the risk? What can be done before and after exposure?", *Postgraduate Medicine,* Vol. 89 No. 3, pp. 30-8.

Herek, G.M. and Capitanio, J.P. (1994), "Conspiracies, contagion and compassion: trust and public reactions to AIDS", *AIDS Education and Prevention,* Vol. 6 No. 4, pp. 365-75.

Hombs, M.J., (1992), *AIDS crisis in America,* ABC-CLIO, Santa Barbara, CA.

Johnson, E.H., Gilbert, D. and Lollis, C. (1994), "Characteristics of African-American college students with HIV/AIDS", *Journal of the National Medical Association,* Vol. 86 No. 12, pp. 931-40.

Kelly, J.A., St Lawrence, J.S., Smith, S., Hood, H.V. and Cook, D.J. (1987), "Medical students' attitudes towards AIDS and homosexual patients", *Journal of Medical Education,* Vol. 62 No. 7, pp. 549-56.

Kennedy, D.B., Homant, R.J. and Emery, G.L. (1990), "AIDS concerns among crime scene investigators", *Journal of Police Science and Administration,* Vol. 17 No. 1, pp. 12-9.

Kimmell, A.J. and Keefer, R. (1991), "Psychological correlates of the transmission and acceptance of rumors about AIDS", *Journal of Applied Social Psychology,* Vol. 21 No. 19, pp. 1608-28.

Kulwicki, A.D. and Cass, P.S. (1994), "An assessment of Arab-American knowledge, attitudes and beliefs about AIDS", *IMAGE: Journal of Nursing Scholarship,* Vol. 26 No. 1, pp. 13-17.

Laszlo, A.T. and Smith, B.E. (1991), "Evaluating criminal justice training addressing AIDS policy", *Crime and Delinquency,* Vol. 37 No. 1, pp. 19-35.

LeBlanc, A.J. (1993), "Examining HIV-related knowledge among adults in the US", *Journal of Health and Social Behaviour,* Vol. 34 No. 3, pp. 23-36.

Lester, D. and Pitts, J. (1991), "Who would have a test for HIV: a study of police officers", *Psychological Reports,* Vol. 69 No. 1, p. 198.

Lewis, L.S. and Range, L.M. (1992), "Do means of transmission, risk knowledge and gender affect AIDS stigma and social interactions?", *Journal of Social Behaviour and Personality,* Vol. 7 No. 1, pp. 211-16.

Link, R.N. (1988), "Concerns of medical and pediatric house officers about acquiring AIDS from their patients", *American Journal of Public Health,* Vol. 78 No. 4, pp. 455-67.

Marsh, T.O. (1987a), "AIDS: a police nightmare?", *Law and Order,* Vol. 35 No. 8, pp. 78-80.

Marsh, T.O. (1987b), "AIDS: a police nightmare? Part two", *Law and Order,* Vol. 35 No. 9, pp. 76-80.

Marsh, T.O. (1987c), "AIDS: a police nightmare? Part three", *Law and Order,* Vol. 35 No. 10, pp. 48-50.

Marsh, T.O. (1987d), "AIDS: a police nightmare? Part four", *Law and Order,* Vol. 35 No. 11, pp. 66-71.

Marsh, T.O. (1987e), "AIDS: a police nightmare? Part five", *Law and Order,* Vol. 35 No. 12, pp. 49-52.

Marsh, T.O. (1988), "AIDS: a police nightmare? Part six", *Law and Order,* Vol. 36 No. 1, pp. 185-7.

McCaig, L.F., Hardy, A.M. and Winn, D.M. (1991), "Knowledge about AIDS and HIV in the US adult population: influence of the local incidence of AIDS", *American Journal of Public Health*, Vol. 81 No. 12, pp. 1591-5.

Nicholas, L.J., Tredoux, C. and Daniels, P. (1994), "AIDS knowledge and attitudes toward homosexuals of black first-year university students: 1990-1992", *Psychological Reports*, Vol. 75 No. 2, pp. 819-23.

Reardon, K.K. and Richardson, J.L. (1991), "The important role of mass media in the diffusion of accurate information about AIDS", *Journal of Homosexuality*, Vol. 21 No. 1-2, pp. 63-75.

Shapiro, M.F., Hayward, R.A., Guillemont, D. and Jayle, D. (1992), "Residents' experiences in and attitudes toward, the care of persons with AIDS in Canada, France and the United States", *Journal of the American Medical Association*, Vol. 268 No. 4, pp. 510-5.

Singer, E., Rogers, T.F. and Glassman, M.B. (1991), "Public opinion about AIDS before and after the 1988 US Government public information campaign", *Public Opinion Quarterly*, Vol. 55 No. 2, pp. 161-79.

Sobo, E.J. (1994), "Attitudes toward HIV testing among impoverished inner-city African-American women", *Medical Anthropology*, Vol. 16 No. 1, pp. 17-38.

St Lawrence, J.S., Hood, H.V., Brasfield, T. and Kelly, J.A. (1989), "Differences in gay mens' AIDS risk knowledge behaviour patterns in high and low AIDS prevalence cities", *Public Health Reports*, Vol. 104 No. 4, pp. 391-5.

Wicks, T.G. (1991), "Comparing behaviour patterns/social styles and gender in students' perceptions of AIDS", *College Student Journal*, Vol. 25 No. 3, pp. 351-3.

Yearwood, D.L. (1992), "Law enforcement and AIDS: knowledge, attitudes and fears in the workplace", *American Journal of Police*, Vol. 11 No. 2, pp. 65-83.

Further reading

Becker, M.H. and Joseph, J.G. (1988), "AIDS and behavioural change to reduce risk: a review", *American Journal of Public Health*, Vol. 78 No. 4, pp. 394-410.

Bigbee, D. (1993), "Pathogenic microorganisms: law enforcement's silent enemies", *FBI Law Enforcement Bulletin*, Vol. 62 No. 5, pp. 1-5.

Carroll, L. (1991), "Gender, knowledge about AIDS, reported behavioural change and the sexual behaviour of college students", *Journal of American College Health*, Vol. 40 No. 1, pp. 5-12.

[17]

POLICE AND HIV/AIDS: The Risk, the Reality, the Response

JEANNE FLAVIN†
Fordham University

ABSTRACT: *Risk and fear have been examined empirically and theoretically in the policing literature. To date, however, there has been minimal effort to examine these concepts in the context of HIV/AIDS. Since the HIV/AIDS epidemic was first detected nearly 20 years ago, relatively little attention has been given to the complex issues it presents for police officers. The following discussion draws from both the policing and epidemiological literatures to examine police officers' fear and risk of occupational HIV transmission and individual and departmental responses to this fear. Important elements of educational programs and policies are also addressed.*

INTRODUCTION

The relationship between risk and fear of danger has been examined empirically and theoretically in the policing literature (Cullen, Link, Travis & Lemming, 1983; Gross, 1991; Jermier, Gaines, & McIntosh, 1989; Manning, 1977) but has rarely been addressed in the context of HIV/AIDS. Existing sources of information on police officers and HIV/AIDS fall short in three respects. First, general sources of information on preventing occupational HIV transmission do not take into account the unpredictable and uncertain nature of much police work, or the wide range of situations an officer may encounter. Second, many law enforcement-specific sources are outdated. Because new information about HIV/AIDS is continually emerging, up-to-date materials are needed that reflect the most current information available, and address new concerns. For example, in the 1980s, the National Institute of Justice published a series of reports addressing workers' concerns about HIV/AIDS, including *AIDS and the Law Enforcement Officer* (Hammett, 1987) and *AIDS in Probation and Parole* (Hunt, 1989). Even though much of the information contained in these reports has not changed over time, it needs to be reinforced by reference to recent medical and legal findings. Given the rate at which new HIV-related information becomes available, sources that are several years old lack

† Direct all correspondence to: Jeanne Flavin, Fordham University, Department of Sociology and Anthropology, 440 East Fordham Road, Bronx, NY 10458.

credibility and generate distrust. As one police officer observed, "With a disease like this, 100% fatal and no cure imminent, there is no room for error and misinformation" (Barr & Warshaw, 1994, p. 59).

Finally, many police-specific sources of information are too narrow in scope, focusing on officers' HIV/AIDS-related knowledge, fear, or behaviors rather than exploring the links among the three. The existing literature also tends to focus uncritically on how officers *should* respond to people with HIV (in order to avoid HIV infection or a lawsuit), without addressing the legal and social implications of responding to HIV with prejudice and fear rather than professionalism.

The aforementioned shortcomings in the literature may contribute to officers' overestimating their risk of occupational HIV infection and experiencing heightened levels of fear. This fear in turn contributes to some officers' mistreatment of persons thought or known to be infected with HIV (cf. Flavin, 1998). This article explores the source of police officers' fear of HIV as well as their actual risk of HIV infection. It also examines individual and departmental responses to the fear and considers the important role played by policy and education programs. The policing literature on fear and risk and the epidemiological literature on HIV transmission suggest that officers' fears are not based so much on their objective risk of becoming infected. Instead, they may stem from the uncertain and unpredictable nature of police work and possibly from officers' discomfort with HIV's association with homosexuality and drug use.

FEAR, DANGER, AND UNCERTAINTY

Cullen et al. (1983) describe the "paradox in policing": Even though most officers in their study did not believe that physical injury occurred frequently in police work, nearly four-fifths believed they worked at a dangerous job and two-thirds thought policing was more dangerous than other kinds of employment. Similarly, many officers' perceptions of the danger of being exposed to HIV in the workplace do not match their actual risk. The following section compares HIV/AIDS to other occupational dangers officers face and attempts to explain the discrepancy between officers' fears of occupational transmission of HIV and the reality.

Danger and risk are important in shaping the policing occupational role. The emphasis on risk and danger of the occupation is used to reinforce safety messages, transforming everyday routines into a "craft of identifying threats to public and officer safety" (Crank, 1998, p. 110). Danger may serve to make work more enriching, meaningful, and interesting (Jermier et al., 1989; Roberts, 1993). Also, the threat of danger serves to solidify relationships among members of the police subculture because an assault or accident that hurts one officer affects other members of the squad (Crank, 1998).

Three elements characterize a dangerous setting: the inherent degree of physical and emotional danger, the potential for accidental and delayed harm, and the objective and subjective nature of the danger (Jermier et al., 1989). Using these criteria, policing would definitely be categorized as a dangerous occupation although incidents of bodily harm to police officers are infrequent; most injuries to police are the result of accidents, not assaults; and most injuries are relatively minor (Brandl, 1996; Crank, 1998; Cullen et al., 1983). Assessing exposure to harmful agents must take into account not only the likelihood of the occurrence of harm, but also the potential severity of the harm. For example, the risk of a police officer being shot is similar to the occupational risk faced by nuclear power plant workers and airline pilots. Although the probability of being killed in the line of duty is low, the harm is potentially catastrophic, producing a level of physical danger comparable to someone (such as a professional boxer or a sanitation worker) who has a higher chance of being harmed, but faces a less catastrophic harmful event (Jermier et al., 1989).

In some respects, HIV/AIDS poses a unique occupational threat to police officers. First, the source of the risk is an invisible microbe, not a visible (if unexpected) assailant. Second, the officer does not know what harm he or she has suffered until 3-6 months later, when sufficient time has elapsed for antibodies to be detected in testing. Also, given the nature of HIV infection, an officer who becomes infected could remain healthy for a decade or more (if not indefinitely) before showing symptoms of HIV infection. Furthermore, unlike a black eye or a broken bone, HIV infection is incurable and potentially makes the police officer subject to prejudice and discrimination. And while a vaccine is available to protect against death by hepatitis, there is no vaccine that can provide preemptive protection against HIV infection.

In other respects, HIV transmission can be viewed as just one of the myriad of occupational dangers an officer faces. As with other injuries, it may stem from an assault or from an accident (Brandl, 1996). Moreover, the perceived danger posed by HIV is defined not only by the risk presented by various modes of transmission, but also by personal and social constructions of risk. That is, perceptions of danger are shaped by an officer's knowledge of HIV transmission and his or her control over the situation (Jermier et al., 1989).

As will be discussed later, officers' exposure to HIV while on the job is a relatively rare event and the actual incidence of occupational transmission of HIV is extremely low. Still, the fear of HIV among police officers is substantial. A study by Burgess et al. (1992) compared differences in the fear of occupational exposure to HIV among six groups of workers: law enforcement personnel, correction officers, emergency nurses, emergency physicians, social workers, and rape-crisis workers. Fear of becoming HIV positive in the workplace was rated on a widely used scale ranging from 1 ("not at all fearful") to 10 ("extremely fearful"). Even after controlling for sex, years of experience, and experience with HIV/AIDS, emergency nurses were found to have the highest mean level of fear (5.6), followed by law enforcement personnel (5.2), emergency physicians (4.9), and corrections officers (2.9). Similarly, a Swedish study reported that police officers expressed greater fear of becoming infected than either nurses or the general public (Herlitz & Brorsson, 1990).

For most officers, the fear of HIV does not match their realistic risk of occupational exposure. Studies of law enforcement officers in California and North Carolina found that low knowledge of HIV/AIDS was linked to a higher self-assessment of risk (Gellert, Maxwell, Higgins, Barnard, & Page, 1994; Yearwood, 1992). In a New York City study, only around 10% of the officers thought it likely that HIV would be transmitted by working near someone with HIV. Yet, over one-third of the officers reported being afraid of contracting HIV by working with someone who has AIDS, which suggests that "some fears may override factual information" (Barr & Warshaw, 1994, p. 60). There also is evidence that even though an officer may intellectually "know" that HIV is not transmitted by a particular behavior, he or she may still suspect that infection might be transmitted in this way. For example, Herlitz and Brorsson (1990) reported that one-third of all respondents said they would demand a separate toilet for an HIV+ colleague even though only one-fifth thought public toilets might pose a risk of infection.

As with other sources of danger, however, apparently it is not the actual incidence of occupational HIV transmission so much as the *potential* for risk that contributes to fear among officers (Crank, 1998; Cullen et al., 1983; Jermier et al., 1989). Police work is marked by unpredictability and uncertainty (Manning, 1977; McNulty, 1994). No procedures or policies can anticipate the wide range of circumstances or situations in which police may find themselves (Kennedy, Homant, & Emery, 1990). The knowledge that should infection occur, it could have fatal consequences no doubt contributes to heightened levels of fear and anxiety, as does the knowledge that universal precautions cannot provide protection in every situation where there is a risk of HIV transmission.

THE RISK AND THE REALITY

According to the concept of universal precautions, all human blood and certain body fluids (including semen, vaginal secretions, cerebrospinal fluid, pleural fluid, and any unidentifiable body fluid) should be treated as if they contain HIV, HBV, or other bloodborne pathogens. That is, personal protective equipment such as gloves or a mask should be used in the presence of blood or other potentially infectious materials. Universal precautions do not apply to sweat, sputum, tears, urine, feces, or vomitus unless these body fluids contain visible blood. The unpredictable and uncertain nature of police work limits the application of universal precautions and thus contributes to the fear that officers experience regarding HIV/AIDS. Police officers often find themselves in emergent situations involving fights and assaults during which there may be insufficient time to take adequate precautions (Hoffman, Henderson, O'Keefe, & Wood, 1994; Pagane, Chanmugam, Kirsch, & Kelen, 1996). For example, when responding to a domestic dispute, the officer may encounter a range of situations that may or may not involve blood or that may become bloody if one or both parties become combative.

A study of Denver police officers conducted from December 1989 through March 1991 documented 42 exposures to blood. Two-thirds of the 42 blood exposures occurred in circumstances in which the officer was either restraining or being assaulted by a suspect and did not have time to put on protective gloves and clothing or in which gloves would not have been protective because of penetration by needles (Hoffman et al., 1994). In other words, while precautionary routines are helpful, they cannot address the full range of situations an officer may encounter (Whitmire & McCall, 1994). It is important, then, to examine the risk associated with officers in instances where no precautions are exercised.

In general, workplace-related risk of HIV exposure can be divided into three categories (Crutcher, Lamm, & Hall, 1991; Department of Health and Human Services, 1987). Category I applies to those workers at greatest risk of occupationally acquired HIV infection, such as health care workers, including emergency medical workers. Police officers and correctional personnel fall into Category II, where there is intermittent exposure potential. Although police officers can be exposed to HIV by coming into contact with blood or other body fluids at a crime scene or by being injured by a needlestick or other sharp object during a search, their exposure is not routine. Workers such as office personnel who have rare or no exposure potential fall into Category III.

Even though health care workers (HCWs) are considered to be at substantially higher risk for occupational exposure to HIV relative to police officers, HCWs' incidence of occupational HIV transmission is still low. Over a 19-year period (from January 1978 to December 1996), there were only 52 documented cases of occupational transmission of HIV infection and 111 cases of possible occupational transmission (CDC, 1996a). Of the 15 types of HCW reported, emergency medical technicians (EMTs) and paramedics arguably are the most similar to police officers in the *nature* (but not the *frequency*) of their exposure. Both, for example, are present at bloody crime scenes and may have contact with "sharps" such as syringes, knives, razor blades, and broken glass. Interestingly, the Centers for Disease Control and Prevention (CDC) has documented no occupational transmission cases among EMTs and paramedics and only 10 cases of possible occupational transmission.

No studies have systematically and comprehensively evaluated the risk of police officers who come in direct contact with persons infected with HIV. However, studies of health care workers provide some idea of the probability of transmission through various exposure routes. The two main routes of occupational transmission are those involving exposure that is either percutaneous (i.e., via a needlestick injury or a cut with a sharp object such as a scalpel or lancet) or mucocutaneous (i.e., via nonintact skin or mucous membranes including those that line the mouth, eyes, and nostrils). While the estimated transmission risk for both routes of exposure is extremely low (with infection occurring in fewer than one-third of 1% of all cases), several factors influence the transmission risk of a specific exposure event (CDC, 1995; Gerberding, 1998).

First, the risk of transmission increases with the quantity of blood involved in the exposure (e.g., a device visibly contaminated with the infected person's blood; a deep injury; or a procedure involving a needle placed directly in a vein or artery). Second, the risk of HIV infection increases if the source of the blood was someone who died of AIDS within 60 days after the exposure. This is thought to be due to the higher "viral load" (i.e., a higher concentration of HIV) present in the source-person's blood. Also, the risk of infection was *reduced* by nearly 80% if the health care worker used zidovudine (AZT or ZDV) following exposure. Current research is also investigating whether prolonged duration of contact with blood or the immunological response of the exposed person influences the probability of infection (CDC, 1995; Gerberding, 1998). Additional factors influencing the risk of infection in individual cases may emerge with additional research, prompting one researcher to conclude that "risk assessment remains, at best, an art"

(Gerberding, 1998, n.p.). The following section describes the incidence of officers' exposure to HIV, as well as the risk of infection associated with possible modes of officers' occupational exposure.

Incidence of Officers' Exposure to HIV

While police officers do face the risk of becoming infected with HIV via occupational exposure (albeit a comparatively small one), as of July 1997 the Centers for Disease Control and Prevention (CDC) Business and Labor Resource Service had no confirmed cases of a police or correctional officer whose workplace exposure resulted in HIV infection (CDC BLRS, 1997a). Federal Bureau of Investigation personnel conducted a survey of all law enforcement agencies in the United States and its territories with the aim of identifying the extent to which officers contracted HIV or hepatitis B while performing their official duties between 1981 and 1991 (Bigbee, 1993). The law enforcement agencies reported seven cases of HIV infection that they deemed to have occurred via occupational transmission. Three of the cases were reported to have occurred when the officer absorbed infected blood through a break in the skin, two from needlestick injuries, and one from a blood transfusion. In one case, no details were provided regarding the circumstances of the reported occupational transmission. The CDC, however, did not find sufficient evidence that any of these officers contracted the infection while on the job.

Although this evidence indicates that the likelihood of a police officer becoming *infected* with HIV while on the job is low, a police officer's risk of being *exposed* to HIV is higher. Some studies have tried to estimate officers' frequency of exposure to HIV. In Orange County, California, law enforcement officers reported 292 occupational exposures to blood and body fluids from May 1989 to November 1992 (Gellert, Higgins, Maxwell, & Barnard, 1993). Upon investigation of these suspected exposures, no actual risk of HIV transmission was found for 29% of the cases, and exposure was doubtful in 34% of the cases. Law enforcement officers and first responders most commonly were exposed to HIV during the handling of sharps and the management of open soft-tissue injuries. Five percent of reported exposures involved an HIV+ source, suggesting the risk to personnel is real. However, during the study no officers were identified as HIV positive, and no transmission of HIV to public safety officers (including first responders) was documented.

Similarly, a retrospective analysis of exposure to bloodborne infectious organisms (including HIV, hepatitis B, and hepatitis C) among New York City police officers examined self-reported incidents of injuries (Pagane et al., 1996). During 1992, officers reported 121 transcutaneous exposures, of which 106 resulted from human bites and 15 from needlestick injuries. Officers assigned to patrol or narcotics were exposed to blood at a rate of approximately 43.6 exposures for every 10,000 police officers. No significant differences were found in the exposure rate between men and women officers. The study did find that officers between the ages of 20 and 29 had a significantly higher rate of exposure than did officers of other ages.

A Denver study sought to measure police officers' risk of exposure to blood and HIV and to document how exposures occurred. As in the New York City study, the authors found that in every type of assignment, police officers were exposed to blood. The rate of exposure, however, was quite small, ranging from .09 to 1.52 per 10,000 person-days, or one exposure every 40 years (Hoffman et al., 1994, p. 915). Although the rate of officers' exposure in the study was small, the percent of source persons with HIV was high (15.6%). This finding prompted the study's authors to conclude that "Denver police officers rarely have percutaneous or mucosal exposures to blood, but when they do, their risk of exposure to HIV-infected blood is relatively high" (Hoffman et al., 1994, p. 916).

Possible Routes of Occupational Exposure to HIV

Studies of needlestick injuries suggest that they present a small but significant risk of HIV infection. The average risk of HIV transmission associated with needle punctures or other percutaneous injuries is 0.32% (21 infections following 6,498 exposures) (CDC, 1995; Gerberding, 1995). Some studies have investigated the impact of needle and syringe legislation on officers' risk of needlestick injuries. For example, Connecticut enacted laws that permit the purchase in pharmacies of up to 10 needles and syringes at one time and the possession of up to 10 clean needles and syringes. Prior to legislation, purchase and possession of needles and syringes without a prescription had been illegal. Concern was raised that the increased likelihood of IDUs carrying needles and syringes on the streets might place Hartford police officers at greater risk for needlestick injuries. However, a comparison of needlestick injury rates among officers in the months preceding and following the new legislation revealed similar injury rates (CDC, 1993; Groseclose et al., 1995). In fact, Groseclose et al. (1995) reported that the injury rates actually dropped from six injuries in 1,007 drug-related arrests in the six months prior to the introduction of the new laws, to two in 1,032 arrests in the six months after the new laws were enacted.

Police officers also have expressed fear that in the course of breaking up a fight they may receive a cut that could expose them to HIV (Blumberg & Langston, 1991). Gerberding (1998) reports findings from a study of health care workers that estimate that the measured mucocutaneous transmission risk is 0.03% (one infection following 2,885 exposures through mucous membranes or nonintact skin).

Richman and Rickman (1993) report two cases involving contact with flesh wounds that may have resulted in HIV transmission. The first involved a fight in which a man sustained several facial injuries with profuse bleeding. In a second incident, a soccer player was discovered to have HIV one month after colliding with an HIV-infected soccer player and suffering skin wounds involving copious bleeding. In the latter case, however, public health officials could not rule out the presence of other risk factors that may have accounted for the infection. In sum, "transmission of HIV has occurred through contaminated blood on broken skin, albeit rarely" (Richman & Rickman, 1993, p. 405). HIV infection has never been linked to cutaneous exposure involving intact skin or casual contact with people with HIV (Gerberding, 1998).

According to the CDC, HIV has not been recovered from the sweat of HIV-infected persons, so sweat does not present a risk of HIV transmission. HIV has been found in tears in only minute quantities from some people with HIV/AIDS. Contact with tears or airborne droplets (as in a sneeze) has never been shown to result in transmission of HIV.

Exposure to saliva uncontaminated by blood is considered to be a very rare mode of HIV transmission for several reasons: (1) HIV-inhibiting factors are found in the saliva of both people infected and uninfected with HIV; (2) HIV rarely exists in the saliva of HIV+ persons; (3) none of the cases of AIDS reported to CDC has been attributed to saliva alone; (4) levels of HIV are low in the saliva of HIV+ persons; and (5) there have been no documented cases of HIV transmission in association with kissing in studies of nonsexual household contacts of HIV-infected persons (CDC, 1997; Richman & Rickman, 1993). The risk of HIV transmission via spitting is considered extremely low.

Biting presents more of a risk of HIV transmission than does spitting. One study found that officers were more afraid of being bitten by someone with HIV than being spat upon or having to restrain someone with HIV (Yearwood, 1992). Typically, the biter is at greater risk of becoming infected than the person who is bitten because the former comes into contact with the victim's blood while the reverse may not be the case. Because HIV and HIV-infected immune cells can exist in saliva, there is a theoretical possibility that exposing saliva to the bloodstream could cause HIV infection. Richman and Rickman reviewed 13 cases in which people had been bitten by HIV-infected individuals and found no one became infected. The authors concluded that "the transmission of HIV through human bites is biologically possible but remains unlikely, epidemiologically insignificant, and, as yet, not well documented" (Richman & Rickman, 1993, p. 402).

There have been at least two published cases in which HIV transmission through bites may have occurred. One case involved a person with AIDS experiencing a grand mal seizure who unintentionally bit someone offering first aid to prevent airway obstruction. Experts concluded that the blood present in the source patient's saliva was probably crucial for HIV transmission in this case (Vidmar et al., 1996). In another incident in 1994, an HIV+ woman bit a 91-year-old man three times. The bite victim initially tested negative, but tested HIV+ within 40 days after the assault. The woman had bleeding gums and tore the man's skin, causing bleeding and extensive tissue damage. There is no evidence the victim was infected by other routes, and DNA studies show the two people's strain of HIV are closely related (Liberti et al., 1996). In both biting incidents, the nature of the incident suggests HIV was passed via blood-to-blood transmission, a common and well-documented method of HIV infection rather than from a newly documented method of transmission (Liberti et al., 1996; Vidmar et al., 1996). As mentioned earlier, the likelihood of HIV transmission by needlestick is extremely low. Yet, needlesticks are estimated to transmit, on average, 20 times more HIV-infected cells than a human bite (Richman & Rickman, 1993). It should be noted, however, that the presence of blood in the saliva heightens the theoretical risk of HIV transmission through human bites.

In sum, there are a number of occasions in which officers may be afraid of being exposed to HIV. For example, there may be large amounts of blood, body fluids, and tissue present at scenes where physical force was used to inflict injury. These conditions may present HIV exposure but can be managed by employing precautions such as wearing latex gloves and a waterproof gown or overalls and wearing protective eyewear and disposable masks if there is a chance of blood splashes (Laszlo & Ayres, 1990). Similarly, exposure to HIV while administering CPR can be significantly reduced through use of a pocket mask with a one-way valve (Laszlo & Ayres, 1990). These and other protective guidelines for searching and transporting arrestees, conducting crime scene investigations, or performing CPR and other first aid measures have been documented extensively elsewhere (see CDC, 1989; Gerberding & Rankin, 1994; Laszlo & Ayres, 1990).

Still, it is important to acknowledge that many situations are volatile and unpredictable and, thus, do not permit police officers to take appropriate precautions. For example, an officer may come into unexpected contact with a needle (either as the result of a deliberate assault with a syringe or accidental contact during a search), may experience blood-to-blood contact during a fight or scuffle, or may be spat upon or bitten. Because of the fragility of the virus when outside the human body, however, the risk associated with each of these ranges from virtually nonexistent to very small, especially in comparison with the risk associated with sharing injection equipment or engaging in unprotected sex. According to the CDC, 99.7% of needlestick/cut exposures and 99.9% of eye, nose, or mouth exposures do *not* lead to infection. The risk after exposure of the skin to HIV infected blood is estimated to be less than 0.1% (CDC 1997). Even though the risk of infection is low, the physical and social stakes associated with being infected are very high, so the importance of taking precautions must be stressed.

THE RESPONSE

Some level of fear and danger may be useful because it inspires workers to take the necessary precautions and to remain vigilant to potential risks (Burgess et al., 1992; Crank, 1998; Cullen et al., 1983). High and unwarranted levels of fear, however, have been associated with stress and emotional exhaustion, which can compromise a person's ability to do his or her job (Cullen et al., 1983; Jermier et al., 1989). Further, and of central interest in this paper, fear may result in discriminatory treatment of suspects, offenders, and even fellow officers known or suspected to have HIV.

Police Response to Civilians and Offenders with HIV/AIDS

Among the most adverse reactions to HIV/AIDS have been the reluctance to administer first aid and the violation of suspects' rights to privacy. Thirty percent of the police officers in one study reported they would avoid helping people in need out of fear of contact with infected blood (Herlitz & Brorsson, 1990). Leinen (1993) found that the majority of the 41 officers he interviewed to approach injury cases with caution, minimizing their exposure to wounds by taking precautionary measures such as wearing rubber gloves. Nonetheless, he found evidence that fear of HIV/AIDS does on occasion interfere with an officer's duty to assist accident and injury victims. One officer described a situation in which a person came into the station with a head injury and covered with blood. His initial response was to help the man but then:

> I physically, for the first time in my life, stopped. I thought that the guy may be a junkie and I don't want to go over and touch him. I got an ambulance. I'm not putting my mouth on anybody, and I'm not touching anybody's blood or saliva. (Leinen, 1993, p. 61)

Much of the reluctance to administer first aid — even while wearing gloves — reflects ignorance and reliance on false information. An officer reports, "My partner, he's got the idea that even if a person looks at you, you can get AIDS from him. I've tried to talk to him time and time again, but there's no telling him. He knows what he knows" (Leinen, 1993, pp. 58-59). Another officer reports that "straight cops have all the *mis*information that all the straight people have. They have the information that you're going to get [AIDS] by touching somebody" (Leinen, 1993, p. 59).

Anecdotal reports from individual departments in several states also suggest the existence of an unofficial practice of including HIV status on police records. When the police dispatcher gets a call, the dispatcher will notify the patrol car that the person is HIV+, frequently by use of a code. Presumably, this policy exists to protect the officer from unknowingly becoming exposed to HIV. In reality, such practices actually *reduce* the safety of police officers by providing them with a false sense of security. Police dispatchers will not know the HIV status of most of the individuals with whom the officers will come into contact. Therefore, it cannot be assumed that because no warning is given that the suspect is not infected with HIV. Instead of providing better protection for the officers, such protocols undermine the basic principle of universal precautions: to assume that everyone is potentially infectious.

This raises another concern: that fear, ignorance, and prejudice may lead some officers to violate individuals' rights to privacy and confidentiality. HIV continues to be associated with lifestyles that have been deemed "unacceptable" by mainstream society. As a result, HIV+ individuals often experience discrimination. Even infected heterosexual nondrug users, who comprise less than 20% of those infected with HIV, may be stereotyped as being either injection drug users or gay. Because of the high potential for discrimination, maintaining the confidentiality of one's HIV status is of primary concern to those infected (Souza, 1995).

Doe v. Borough of Barrington (1990) and *Doe v. Town of Plymouth* (1993) held that an officer and his or her police department can be held liable for a police officer's disclosure of an individual's HIV status without compelling reason to do so. In both cases, the town was held responsible for its alleged failure to train and supervise police officers in the protection of privacy rights of individuals with HIV/AIDS. In general, the plaintiff's rights to confidentiality are balanced against the state's interest in disclosure. Typically, the personal right to privacy is found to outweigh the governmental interest (Souza, 1995). For example, in *Doe v. Borough of Barrington*, the officer asserted that his concern for preventing the transmission of the disease prompted his disclosure of a citizen's HIV status to a neighbor. The court acknowledged that preventing transmission is an appropriate objective, but it concluded that this objective was not served by the disclosure since HIV is not spread by casual contact. Consequently, the court ruled that the release of the personal information violated the plaintiff's privacy rights.

The case of A.L.A. illustrates some of the harmful social consequences of unauthorized disclosure. A.L.A. was arrested for passing a bad check at a retail store. During a search incident to the arrest, Officer Johnson discovered a piece of paper in A.L.A.'s wallet indicating he was HIV positive. Later, Johnson told A.L.A.'s sister and his two housemates, at least one witness at the store, and the jailer that A.L.A. was HIV+, even though A.L.A. had not engaged in any conduct that would have placed any of these people at risk. As a result of Johnson's disclosures, A.L.A.'s friends and family shunned him, and fellow prisoners and the guards harassed him. While in jail, A.L.A. underwent testing that revealed that he was not and had never been infected with HIV. The district court's ruling was eventually reversed, and the plaintiff was permitted to sue for unauthorized disclosure of the false information that he was infected with HIV (*A.L.A. v. West Valley City*, 1994).

In Indiana, a waiter lost his job as a result of a police officer's disclosure. "John Doe" filed suit against a city police officer who repeatedly visited the restaurant but would not allow Doe to wait on him because Doe has AIDS. The officer's comments and threats prompted Doe to leave the restaurant and Doe was fired. Doe sued the police officer for disclosing his HIV status to workers and customers and intentionally inflicting emotional distress. The City of Kokomo was also named for failing to properly train officers about HIV confidentiality. As part of the out-of-court settlement, police were ordered to pay $60,000 and the City was ordered to educate police officers on confidentiality (*Doe*, 1997; "Police Must Pay," 1997).

Another privacy issue involves the testing for HIV antibodies of suspects who may have exposed a police officer to HIV/AIDS. These cases require that the privacy rights of the suspect be balanced between curbing the spread of HIV and the emotional and physical health of the officer. Many courts have assigned greater weight to public health interests and permitted minimally invasive, minimally risky blood and saliva tests of persons charged with needle-use and sex crimes. Several courts, however, have required statutory authorization to test defendants. Where no statute exists, some courts have permitted testing only if it is reasonably related to establishing the allegations. In these cases, the Ninth Circuit has held that HIV testing requires a proper search warrant (Gostin, 1996, pp. ix-x).

A number of cases suggest that police who may have been exposed to HIV are not entitled to test a person's blood without first obtaining a warrant. For example, both *Walker v. Upper Merion Police Department* (1996) and *Barlow v. Ground* (1992) involved instances where the suspect scuffled with or bit police officers. Subsequently, the suspect's blood was drawn to be tested for HIV, but no warrant was obtained. In both cases, the court found the drawing of blood violated the plaintiff's Fourth Amendment rights against illegal searches and seizures. The courts reasoned that evidence of a person's HIV infection (i.e., HIV antibodies) would not disappear and, therefore, there was no pressing element of time.

Even if a warrant is issued, there is no guarantee that its justification will survive close scrutiny by the courts. For example, police obtained a warrant to test a defendant for HIV who bled on several officers during an arrest for car theft. The jury was convinced that the police lacked probable cause to suspect that the defendant was HIV+, and awarded $5,000 to the defendant ("Jury Faults Police," 1995).

Police Response to Fellow Officers with HIV/AIDS

The consequences of fear and prejudice are not confined to officers' treatment of citizens, but may also affect their treatment of fellow officers who have or are perceived to have HIV/AIDS. HIV/AIDS is a particularly sensitive subject among police not only because of the possibility of occupational HIV transmission, but also because of the law enforcement taboos against homosexuality and drug use (Boxall, 1996; Buhrke, 1996; Flavin, 1998; Leinen, 1993). This creates a particularly difficult situation for HIV+ police officers, most of whom have contracted HIV off-duty through unprotected sexual activities (Suraci, 1997). To date, very little research has been conducted on HIV+ officers, precluding an extensive discussion.

Local, state, and federal law enforcement personnel with AIDS are protected from discrimination by Section 504 of the Rehabilitation Act of 1973 and the Americans with Disabilities Act of 1990 (Goldfein & Hanssens, 1996). The purpose of these acts is to assure civil rights protections to qualified people with disabilities. The ADA is modeled after the Rehabilitation Act, so the two acts are very similar in scope. The main difference between them is found in the sectors to which they apply. In very general terms, the ADA prohibits disability-based discrimination in the private sector and in state and local government, whereas the Rehabilitation Act applies to employers and organizations receiving federal assistance.

In spite of the protections provided by federal legislation, harassment and discriminatory treatment occurs. Experiences reported by gay police officers suggest that fear of HIV/AIDS may be aligned with homophobia. For example, a gay Miami Beach police officer, Pete Zecchini, described how in 1995 he was reassigned to patrol duty after being transferred to the front desk ostensibly out of concern for his safety. He subsequently was tear gassed in an area restricted to authorized personnel and specially admitted personnel. He observed:

> Realizing that I would be even less safe on the streets, I reluctantly resigned from the police department. I believe I was discriminated against because my lover of thirteen years is totally disabled with AIDS, and some officers perceived I was HIV-positive. I have begun litigation against the City of Miami Beach in hopes of making some difference (Buhrke, 1996, p. 272).

Law enforcement officials also justified placing "John Doe," a straight New York Police Department detective with AIDS, on restricted duty by citing a concern for his well-being. Doe reported he was relegated to mopping precinct floors, cleaning toilets, and changing tires on squad cars following an anonymous tip to the Internal Affairs Bureau reporting his condition in 1995. Doe also claimed that six police officers wearing body armor and gloves beat him up because he has AIDS. A 14-year veteran, Doe filed a suit against the City seeking $20 million in damages, his reinstatement to active duty, back pay, and compensation for his legal fees (Guart, 1997).

Not all experiences of HIV+ officers have been negative. Preliminary evidence suggests a wide range of experiences coping with the demands of being a police officer, being HIV+, and, for some, being gay. For example, a 16-J. year veteran of the San Francisco Police Department (SFPD) who decided to disclose his HIV status only to a few close friends observed, "If anyone asked, I was prepared to tell the truth. However, only one person ever did. . . . Whatever people knew, they respected my privacy in the matter" (J. Land, personal communication, July 23, 1997).

Before his death in 1995 of AIDS-related complications, Lee Jensen also was a police officer in San Francisco. Jensen reported that when his AIDS diagnosis prompted him to take an extended medical leave, city and county employees (including other police officers) donated over 200 hours of leave to him (Buhrke, 1996). Elsewhere, an HIV+ officer in an unnamed metropolitan police department described his department's response to his 18-month disability leave as "incredibly supportive" (Buhrke, 1996, p. 265). In San Francisco, the response to HIV+ officers may be shaped in part by the prevalence of HIV in the area and general attitudes to gays and lesbians. A patrolman with the SFPD for over 15 years explained:

> Here, it is widely assumed that half the gay male population has HIV. . . In San Francisco, everyone knows gay people, so the fears were frequently addressed with compassion and concern. Then, gay cops started to die. Some of them were well loved and respected, some were not. But everyone seemed truly shaken by the loss of these young men (J. Land, personal communication, July 23, 1997).

Some officers have organized in an effort to address the multitude of issues surrounding HIV infection. For example, in 1994, the Gay Officer's Action League-New York (GOAL-NY) held its first annual International Conference of Gay and Lesbian Criminal Justice Professionals. Among the workshops offered was one focusing on the impact of HIV/AIDS on gay police personnel. In the New York City area, Jack Lambe, a retired New York City police officer with AIDS, spearheaded the effort to form an off-hours support group for police officers with HIV/AIDS called "Positive Police" (Boxall, 1996). The group helps officers deal with such issues as feelings of isolation, fear of losing one's job, and concerns about failing strength or possibly infecting others if one is hurt and bleeding. While laudable, these individual efforts are limited in the impact they can have on police officers' fear and attitudes. As discussed in the following section, departmental educational programs and policy development are essential components in promoting widespread, lasting, and humane treatment of people with HIV/AIDS.

THE IMPORTANCE OF HIV/AIDS-RELATED TRAINING AND POLICY

The single most important factor influencing uniformed police officer's workplace attitudes toward HIV/AIDS is their level of knowledge about HIV transmission (Barr & Warshaw, 1994). Officers gain information about HIV from a variety of sources, including the media. A 1989 study found that nearly all of the 445 New York City police officers used the media as a source of HIV/AIDS-related information

(Barr & Warshaw, 1994). Results from a 1987 survey of 728 police officers who attended AIDS education training indicate that around 60% of officers report newspapers or magazines as their primary information source on AIDS (Sheridan, Lyons, Fitzgibbon, Sheridan, & McCarthy, 1989). While the mass media may be a good source of general information about how HIV is and is not transmitted, it rarely addresses police-specific concerns about, for instance, whether HIV can be transmitted through a bite. For example, news reports of assaults by needlestick often emphasize the sensationalized "newsworthy" aspects of the incident rather than the low probability of transmission. Thus, the media should not be assumed to serve consistently as a reliable, disinterested source of HIV/AIDS-related information.

Officers' frequent contacts with hospital personnel suggest that the medical community may also have a significant impact on officers' fear and perceived risk (Whitmire & McCall, 1994). Around one-quarter of officers in a "large urban department" report their primary source of information is health professionals (Sheridan et al., 1989). The reliance on health professionals may be related to the prevalence of HIV in the surrounding area. For example, nearly three-quarters of New York City police officers working in an area of higher prevalence of AIDS cited a physician or health specialist as an extremely or somewhat informative source as compared to only around one-third of the officers in an area with a much lower AIDS prevalence (Barr & Warshaw, 1994). It should not be assumed, however, that the information hospital personnel convey is always accurate. For example, one rural police officer reported that "a doctor had told her that AIDS can be transmitted through the air, and if a doctor said that, [then] it must be true" (Whitmire & McCall, 1994, p. 150).

Misinformation about the way HIV is transmitted may contribute to officers' fears and prejudices. Studies of police officers in Orange County, California, and New York City (Gellert et al., 1994; Barr & Warshaw, 1994) suggest that notions that HIV can be transmitted through casual contact persist in spite of public health messages to the contrary. While able to identify the major modes of HIV transmission, significant percentages of officers respond incorrectly to items regarding means that do *not* transmit HIV, such as being bitten by a mosquito or other insect, being coughed or sneezed on by someone with HIV, eating at a restaurant where the cook has HIV, or sharing eating utensils with someone who has HIV. For example, around one-third of the New York City sample and almost 80% of the Orange County sample incorrectly thought it was very or somewhat likely that HIV/AIDS could be transmitted through a cough or a sneeze (Gellert et al., 1994; Barr & Warshaw, 1994).

Court rulings also may promulgate inaccurate information about the transmission of HIV. Such decisions undermine attempts at educating police officers and other law enforcement officials to the actual risk. Assisted by his colleagues on the AIDS Litigation Project, Lawrence Gostin of Georgetown University Law Center examined cases litigated in federal and state courts from 1991 through 1996 that involved the intentional exposure of another person to HIV (Gostin, 1996). He found that prosecutors typically invoke two types of criminal charges against persons who risk transmitting HIV: assault and attempted murder. People with HIV have been criminally convicted for various behaviors, not all of which have been scientifically found to pose a significant risk of transmission.

These convictions reflect in part that the issue of intent is more salient to the courts than is the issue of transmission likelihood. For example, *State v. Smith* (1993) upheld the conviction of attempted murder for biting a correctional officer. The court reasoned that the conviction is based upon the defendant's criminal intent at the time of the act, *not* the actual chance of transmission. Similarly, in *People v. Caine* (1995), the court held that saying "I'll give you AIDS" while sticking someone with a syringe was sufficient to convict for attempted second-degree murder, regardless of whether or not the syringe actually contained HIV. The issue is further complicated by the fact that "notably absent in many judicial opinions is a careful differentiation between significant and remote risks of transmission. Although courts enunciate a 'deference' to scientific opinion, they also may grant 'expert' status to testimony that is loosely grounded in solid science" (Gostin, 1996, pp. 24-25). For example, in *Burk v. State* (1996), the court upheld the felony reckless endangerment conviction of an HIV+ individual who attempted to bite a police officer. The court relied, in part, on the misleading testimony of Burk's treating physician who asserted that it was

> *very strongly probable* that someone could get the HIV virus if bitten by an infected person. [The physician] further testified that *although he was not aware of any known reports of anyone contracting AIDS through the transmission of saliva*, the HIV virus had been found in saliva and he did not see why it could not be transmitted that way (p. 531, emphases added).

Although not addressed in the literature, officers probably also serve as a source of misinformation about HIV. Research suggests that officers attach particular importance to the informal learning that occurs "on the street" versus the formal book learning that takes place in the police academy (Hunt, 1985; McNulty, 1994). For example, one officer noted that "quite a few guys have told me that they wouldn't [administer first aid to] *anyone* who looks like a junkie or a fag, no matter who they were" (Leinen, 1993, p. 60).

Whether the result of the police personality (Skolnick, 1994) or the police culture (Crank, 1998), suspicion accounts for many officers' distrust of factual information being disseminated (Barr & Warshaw, 1994; Whitmire & McCall, 1994). Thus, probably the best means of lessening unnecessary fear about HIV transmission and the negative consequences that stem from this fear is to provide officers with accurate information via training. Appropriate educational programs not only teach officers about the epidemiology, transmission, and prevention of HIV, but may appropriately alter their perceptions of risk (Sheridan et al., 1989). Evidence suggests, however, that not all police departments are providing adequate educational programs. In 1992, 70 law enforcement supervisors attending the FBI National Academy were informally surveyed about their policies regarding bloodborne diseases, including HIV/AIDS and hepatitis B. More than half of those surveyed indicated they did not have a comprehensive departmental policy in place regarding bloodborne diseases, were unaware of recent OSHA regulations requiring employers to provide vulnerable employees with protective equipment (e.g., gloves), and had not provided at least four hours of training on bloodborne diseases to each employee within the past four years (Stewart, 1993). Similarly, a 1992-1994 national study found that half of the 337 police chiefs surveyed thought that at least "moderate" improvement was needed in their police officers' training on infectious diseases (McEwen, 1996).

Edwards and Tewksbury (1996) surveyed the directors of 49 state police training academies and 49 state police personnel directors. They found that most state police agencies offer basic HIV/AIDS instruction to recruits, and through in-service training. The two primary reasons for initiating HIV/AIDS instruction are to meet legal requirements and to address safety concerns of officers and other agency personnel. The quality and quantity of instruction, however, vary widely. For example, course materials ranged from a brief, handwritten outline, to elaborate training materials and professionally produced videotapes.

Edwards and Tewksbury observe that standardizing training by either the national medical or law enforcement community is "essential," given the lack of uniformity in instructional content (1996, p. 58). Among other things, experts recommend that HIV/AIDS education programs accomplish the following:

(1) provide accurate information about how HIV is and is not transmitted;

(2) defuse unwarranted fears and anxieties about contact with HIV-infected persons, including coworkers;
(3) educate officers on universal precautions, as well as the potential for infection during arrest, first aid, search, and crime scene processing activities;
(4) tie the content explicitly to departmental policies and procedures regarding the rights of employees with HIV/AIDS, HIV-antibody testing, confidentiality, and other HIV/AIDS-related issues;
(5) involve staff in the development of training programs and materials to lend credibility to the program and ensure the program addresses the issues raised by the staff;
(6) adopt a proactive stance, that is, education should take place prior to a job-related exposure incident;
(7) be offered on an ongoing basis;
(8) contain an evaluation component to assess the content, quality, and effectiveness of the training program; and
(9) be provided to all officers, regardless of their assignment, given that assignment does not appear to be correlated with risk of exposure (Barr & Warshaw, 1994; Hammett, 1987; Stewart, 1993).

Furthermore, education programs should acknowledge that — compared to other work settings — the police work environment has a higher degree of uncertainty. Thus, not only should officers be trained in the use of universal precautions, but police training programs also must acknowledge the limitations of universal precautions if they are to have credibility with the officers.

Programs should reflect the particular concerns and needs of the police officers and should relate to situations they encounter in their daily activities. Officers are not expected to engage in kissing or other sexual activity on the job, so educational messages about the relative risk associated with sexual activity are of limited utility in quelling fears and minimizing the risk of occupational HIV transmission. The risk associated with administering CPR, being bitten by someone with HIV, or having blood splash into one's eyes, however, is another story (Flavin, 1998). Further, updated information should be used to clarify the risk of infection associated with certain situations.

Because police officers are trained to be suspicious and distrustful, another prerequisite for an effective educational campaign is ensuring that police officers are confident in the source that distributes the information (Herlitz & Brorsson, 1990). The educators should be considered by the police officers to have a high level of integrity.

In addition to educational programs, departmental policies can ensure both the safety of officers and the fair and humane treatment of people with HIV/AIDS. Montgomery and Lewis's (1995) study of 558 hospitals found that fear levels are lower in organizations with policies that directly address the type of knowledge uncertainty held by employees. The authors emphasize that the education of workers about modes of transmission may help reduce uncertainty about how HIV is transmitted, but is inadequate in dealing with uncertainty about how HIV+ persons in the workplace should be treated.

While information on law enforcement HIV/AIDS-related policies is scant, evidence exists to suggest that this too is an area in which there is much room for improvement. For example, in 1992 the Police Executive Research Forum prepared a model police statement on the Americans with Disabilities Act as a guide to law enforcement agencies (PERF, 1992). Although reference is made to impairments commonly associated with advanced stages of HIV infection, such as visual and mobility impairments, nowhere in the 19-page document is HIV or AIDS specifically mentioned. This oversight is particularly noticeable in the sections addressing officer response to emergency calls for service.

Most agencies with educational programs and policies initiated these efforts because of legal requirements (e.g., mandates from OSHA) and a desire to protect personnel (Edwards & Tewksbury, 1996). Only 10% of agencies, for example, cited a desire to treat citizens with HIV/AIDS fairly as a reason for developing an HIV/AIDS-related policy. Similarly, while 29 agencies have policies addressing how to handle a person with HIV, only nine of these policies address the employment of people with HIV.

As with educational programs, a department seeking to develop a humane and comprehensive workplace HIV/AIDS policy does not need to start from scratch. A number of resources are available. Among the major issues that an HIV/AIDS-related policy should address are the following:

(1) antidiscrimination in employment practices and reasonable accommodations;
(2) antidiscrimination in services to public;
(3) HIV-antibody testing and counseling;
(4) confidentiality of HIV-related information for both employees and the public;
(5) infectious disease control procedures; and
(6) availability and content of HIV/AIDS-related training (Hammett, 1987; Laszlo & Ayres, 1990; Laszlo & Smith, 1991).

Such policies should be adaptable to changes in current knowledge on medical transmission and the law. Further, they should specify the schedule by which the policy will be reviewed periodically and amended as necessary. Anecdotal evidence suggests that the police officers with HIV/AIDS are themselves instrumental in the development of humane responses to HIV/AIDS. John Land describes his experience with the San Francisco Police Department:

> Those who died early forged departmental and city policies regarding HIV disabilities. [For me, it] was a simple matter to request a disability retirement, even though my health remained relativity good. I could have stayed on, and would have been accommodated in countless ways, such as low stress assignments, donated sick time, flexible scheduling, as well as more personal acts of compassion (J. Land, personal communication, July 23, 1997).

CONCLUSION

HIV/AIDS presents a serious and often complex set of challenges for both public health officials and law enforcement officers. Yet, these issues are not adequately addressed in either the existing policing literature regarding risk and fear or the epidemiological literature. This article has attempted to provide an overview of these issues and to summarize significant recent findings related to the fear, knowledge, and risk of HIV transmission and the treatment of both suspects and police officers who have or are perceived to have HIV/AIDS. This discussion stresses the important roles that policy and education play in reducing fear and risk and ensuring the compassionate and fair treatment of people with HIV/AIDS.

ACKNOWLEDGMENTS: The author wishes to thank Mary Bosworth (Fordham University), Lillian Dote (Temple University), and Greg Fallis for their substantive criticism of earlier drafts of this paper. Also, this paper would not have been possible without the insight and encouragement provided by John Land, formerly of the San Francisco Police Department.

REFERENCES

Barr, J. K., & Warshaw, L. J. (1994). Worksite AIDS education: A case study of the New York City police. *AIDS Education and Prevention, 61*(1), 53-64.

Bigbee, D. (1993). Pathogenic microorganisms. *FBI Law Enforcement Bulletin,* May, 1-5.

Blumberg, M., & Langston, D. (1991). Mandatory HIV testing in criminal justice settings. *Crime and Delinquency, 37*, 5-18.

Boxall, B. (1996, March 11). Officer infected with HIV is torn between serving and protecting LAPD. *The Los Angeles Times,* B6.

Brandl, S. G. (1996). In the line of duty: A descriptive analysis of police assaults and accidents. *Journal of Criminal Justice, 24*(3), 255-264.

Burgess, A. W., Jacobsen, B. S., Baker, T., Thompson, J., & Grant, C. (1992). Workplace fear of acquired immunodeficiency syndrome. *Journal of Emergency Nursing, 18*(3), 233-238.

Buhrke, R. A. (1996). *A matter of justice: Lesbians and gay men in law enforcement.* New York: Routledge.

CDC Business and Labor Resource Service (1997, July 17). Personal communication with Sherryl Zemo via electronic mail.

Centers for Disease Control (1989). Guidelines for prevention of transmission of human immunodeficiency virus and hepatitis B virus to health-care and public-safety workers. *MMWR, 38*(S-6), 1-37.

Centers for Disease Control (1993). Impact of new legislation on needle and syringe purchase and possession — Connecticut, 1992. *MMWR, 42*(8), 145-148.

Centers for Disease Control (1995). Case-control study of HIV seroconversion in health-care workers after percutaneous exposure to HIV-infected blood — France, United Kingdom, and United States, January 1988-August 1994. *MMWR, 44*(50).

Centers for Disease Control (1996). *HIV/AIDS surveillance report, 8*(2).

Centers for Disease Control (1997). Transmission of HIV possibly associated with exposure of mucous membrane to contaminated blood. *MMWR, 46*(27).

Crank, J. P. (1998). *Understanding police culture.* Cincinnati, OH: Anderson Publishing.

Crutcher, J. M., Lamm, S. H., & Hall, T. A. (1991). Prevention of HIV transmission in the workplace: Categorization of jobs and tasks by risk of HIV infection. *American Industrial Hygiene Association Journal, 52*(1), 14-16.

Cullen, F., Link, B., Travis, L. T., & Lemming, T. (1983). Paradox in policing: A note on perceptions of danger. *Journal of Police Science and Administration, 11*, 457-462.

Department of Labor/Department of Health and Human Services (1987, October 19). *Joint advisory notice. Protection against occupational exposure to hepatitis B virus (HBV) and human immunodeficiency virus (HIV).* Washington, DC: Office of Information and Consumer Affairs.

Edwards, T. D., & Tewksbury, R. (1996). HIV/AIDS: State police training practices and personnel policies, *American Journal of Police, 15*(1), 45-62.

Flavin, J. (1998). Fear and policing in the age of HIV/AIDS. *Critical Criminologist, 8*(3).

Gellert, G. A., Higgins, K. V., Maxwell, R. M., & Barnard, R. (1993). Assessment of the impact of an HIV occupational exposure program among law-enforcement officers and first responders. *AIDS and Public Policy Journal* 8(2), 62-72.

Gellert, G. A., Maxwell, R. M., Higgins, K., Barnard, R., & Page, B. (1994). AIDS knowledge, occupational precautions, and public education activities among law enforcement officers and first responders. *Journal of Public Health Policy, 4*, 460-469.

Gerberding, J. L. (1998). Transmission of HIV to health care workers. In *The AIDS knowledge base: A textbook on HIV disease* (3rd ed.). San Francisco: University of California and San Francisco General Hospital. On-line document: http://hivinsite.ucsf.edu/akb/1997/.

Gerberding, J. L. (1995). Management of occupational exposures to blood-borne viruses. *New England Journal of Medicine, 332*, 444-451.

Gerberding, J. L., & Rankin, R. (1994). HIV and public safety workers. Section 10.5 in *The AIDS knowledge base: A textbook on HIV disease* (2nd ed.). San Francisco: University of California and San Francisco General Hospital. On-line document: http://hivinsite.ucsf.edu/akb/1994/10-5/index.html.

Goldfein, R. B., & Hanssens, C. (1996). Protecting HIV-positive workers: Whose Act is it anyway? *Trial,* February, 26-31.

Gostin, L. G. (1996). *The AIDS Litigation Project II: A look at HIV/AIDS in the courts of the 1990s.* Washington, DC: Georgetown University Law Center.

Grosclose, S. L., Weinstein, B., Jones, T. S., Valleroy, L. A., Fehrs, L. J., & Kassler, W. J. (1995). Impact of increased legal access to needles and syringes on practices of injecting-drug users and police officers —Connecticut, 1992-1993. *Journal of Acquired Immune Deficiency Syndromes and Human Retrovirology, 10,* 82-89.

Gross, P. R. (1991). The structure of occupational fears in police recruits. *Police Studies, 14*(4), 176-179.

Gruzen, T. (1996, August 1). Crime scenes often as deadly as the act itself, *The Chicago Tribune,* p. 4.

Guart, A. (1997, October 18). AIDS cop hits city with $20m bias suit. *The New York Post,* p. 3.

Hammett, T. M. (1987). *AIDS and the law enforcement officer: Concerns and policy responses.* Washington, DC: National Institute of Justice.

Herlitz, C., & Brorsson, B. (1990). Facing AIDS: Reactions among police officers, nurses and the general public in Sweden. *Social Science Medicine, 30*(8), 913-918.

Hoffman, R. E., Henderson, N., O'Keefe, K., & Wood, R. C. (1994). Occupational exposure to human immunodeficiency virus (HIV)-infected blood in Denver, Colorado, police officers. *American Journal of Epidemiology, 139*(9), 910-917.

Hunt, D. E. (1989). *AIDS in probation and parole.* Washington, DC: National Institute of Justice.

Hunt, J. (1985). Police accounts of normal force. *Urban Life, 13*(4), 315-341.

Jermier, J. M., Gaines, J., & McIntosh, N. J. (1989). Reactions to physically dangerous work: A conceptual and empirical analysis. *Journal of Organizational Behavior, 10,* 15-33.

Jury faults police for forcing defendant to undergo testing. (1995). *AIDS Policy and Law, 10*(16), 4.

Kennedy, D. B., Homant, R. J., & Emery, G. L. (1990). AIDS concerns among crime scene investigators. *Journal of Police Science and Administration, 17*(1), 12-19.

Laszlo, A., & Ayres, M. (1990). *AIDS: Improving the response of the correctional system* (2nd ed.). Alexandria, VA: National Sheriff's Association.

Laszlo, A. T., & Smith, B. E. (1991). Evaluating criminal justice training addressing AIDS policy. *Crime and Delinquency, 37*(1), 19-35.

Leinen, S. (1993). *Gay Cops.* New Brunswick, NJ: Rutgers University Press.

Liberti, T., Lieb, S., Scott, R., Nolan, J., Malecki, J., Kalish, M., & Jaffe, H. (1996). Blood-to-blood transmission of HIV via bite. *International Conference on AIDS* (abstract no. Mo.D. 1728), *11*(1), 179.

Manning, P. (1977). *Police work: The social organization of policing.* Cambridge, MA: MIT Press.

McEwen, T. (1996). *National Assessment Program survey of criminal justice agencies in the United States, 1992-1994* [computer file]. ICPSR version. Alexandria, VA: Institute for Law and Justice [producer], 1994. Ann Arbor, MI: Inter-university Consortium for Political and Social Research [distributor].

McNulty, E. W. (1994). Generating common-sense knowledge among police officers. *Symbolic Interaction, 17*(3), 281-294.

Montgomery, K., & Lewis, C. E. (1995). Fear of HIV contagion as workplace stress: Behavioral consequences and buffers. *American College of Healthcare Executives, 40*(4), 439-456.

Pagane, J., Chanmugam, A., Kirsch, T., & Kelen, G. D. (1996). New York City police officers' incidence of transcutaneous exposures. *Occupational Medicine, 46*(4), 285-288.

Police Executive Research Forum. (1992). *Model policy: Americans with Disabilities Act.* PERF. September. Washington, DC: Bureau of Justice Assistance.

Police must pay $60,000 for revealing waiter's HIV status. (1997). *AIDS Policy Law, 12*(7), 6-7.

Richman, K. M., & Rickman, L. S. (1993). The potential for transmission of human immunodeficiency virus through human bites. *Journal of AIDS, 6*(4), 402-406.

Roberts, J. T. (1993). Psychosocial effects of workplace hazardous exposures: Theoretical synthesis and preliminary findings. *Social Problems, 40*(1), 74-89.

Sheridan, K., Lyons, J. S., Fitzgibbon, M., Sheridan, E. P., & McCarthy, M. J. (1989). Effects of AIDS education on police officers' perceptions of risk. *Public Health Reports, 104*(5), 521-522.

Skolnick, J. (1994). A sketch of the policeman's working personality. In *Justice without trial: Law enforcement in democratic society* (3rd ed., pp. 41-68). New York: Wiley.

Souza, J. M. (1995). Doe v. Town of Plymouth and Officer Paul Tibbetts: When is the disclosure of HIV status beyond the call of duty? *New England Law Review, 29*, 391-424.

Stewart, J. D. (1993). Bloodborne diseases: Developing a training curriculum. *FBI Law Enforcement Bulletin, May*, 11-15.

US Department of Justice (1997). Law enforcement officers killed and assaulted, 1995. *FBI Uniform Crime Reports.* Washington, DC: Government Printing Office.

Vidmar, L., Tomazic, J. D., Poljak, M., Seme, K., Kristancic, L., Klavs, I., & Maticic, M. (1996). A human bite: Possible mode of HIV-1 transmission. *International Conference on AIDS* (abstract no. Tu.C.2563), *11*(1), 362.

Whitmire, J. T., & McCall, P. L. (1994). Determinants of perceived risk for HIV infection among police officers. *Applied Behavioral Science Review, 2*(2), 139-156.

Yearwood, D. L. (1992). Law enforcement and AIDS: Knowledge, attitudes, and fears in the workplace. *American Journal of Police, 11*(2), 65-83.

CASES CITED

ALA v. West Valley City, 26 F. 3d 989; 10th Cir. (1994)

Barlow v. Ground, 943 F.2d 1132 (9th Cir. 1991), *cert. denied*, 505 U.S. 1206 (1992)

Burk v. State, 223 Ga. App. 530; 478 S.E.2d 416; Ga App. (1996)

Doe v. Borough of Barrington, 729 F. Supp. 376 D.N.J. (1990)

Doe v. Town of Plymouth, 25 F. Supp. 1102. D.Mass. (1993)

Doe v. Kokomo, 729 F. Supp 376. (1997)

People v. Caine, 652 So. 2d 611. (La. Ct. App.), *cert. denied* 661 So.2d 1358 (1995)

58 POLICE AND HIV/AIDS

State v. Smith, 621 A. 2d 493. (N.J. Super. Ct. App. Div.), *cert. denied*, 634 A.2d 523 (1993)

Walker v. Upper Merion Police Department, Civil Action No. 94-4888, 1996 U.S. Dist. LEXIS 940 (E.D.Pa. Jan. 26, 1996)

[18]

INJECTION DRUG USERS AND HIV RISK BEHAVIORS: CRIMINAL JUSTICE PROFESSIONALS' ROLE IN IDENTIFYING AND RESPONDING TO RISK BEHAVIORS†‡

Richard Tewksbury
Gennaro F. Vito
Scott Cummings
University of Louisville

ABSTRACT

This research uses data from a community wide assessment of knowledge, attitudes and behaviors to determine risks for HIV infection among traditional high risk populations. This analysis is based upon a sample of self-identified injection drug users. It examines the multiple avenues to infection that threaten this population. The role of criminal justice practitioners in the control and reduction of the likelihood of HIV transmission by this population is also considered. Policy makers should reevaluate traditional methods of compelling interactions between offenders and revise their means and systems for communicating information about HIV to injection drug using offenders.

---

†Presented at the annual meetings of the Southern Criminal Justice Association, October 1995, Gatlinburg, Tennessee.

‡Funding for this project was provided by a grant from the United States Conference of Mayors Collaborative HIV Prevention Grants Program.

INTRODUCTION

The continued presence of HIV/AIDS underscores the need for diversified prevention/education programs to slow its spread. Human service professionals must recognize the need for more sophisticated knowledge of the manner in which HIV/AIDS impacts their agencies, clients and personnel. In particular, criminal justice practitioners interact with one specific population at high risk for HIV infection - injection drug users (IDUs). Prevention and intervention methods should be developed to reduce the spread of HIV in this population.

As of June, 1996, more than 548,000 Americans had been diagnosed with AIDS (Centers for Disease Control and Prevention (CDC), 1996). The number of persons infected with HIV, but not yet diagnosed with AIDS is unknown, but according to the CDC (1995) it is estimated that approximately one million Americans are HIV infected. AIDS does not attack individuals in a completely indiscriminate manner. While it strikes the entire fabric of American society, this disease is more likely to be present among urban residents, young adults, persons of color and men.

While primary attention has been devoted to the major epicenters of the HIV epidemic (e.g., New York, San Francisco, Los Angeles, Miami), there is a growing concern about how HIV and efforts to prevent its transmission in smaller cities can be understood (Bell, 1991; Hobfoll, Jackson, Lavin, Britton and Shepherd, 1993; Kelly, St. Lawrence, Brasfield, Stevenson, Diaz and Hauth, 1990; Ruefli, Yu and Barton, 1992; Silvestre, 1992; Tewksbury, 1994, 1995). The present research is based upon a community-wide assessment of HIV knowledge, attitudes, risk behaviors and utilization of education/prevention providers in Louisville, Kentucky. Metropolitan Louisville provides a unique opportunity for HIV prevention and education professionals to understand the outcomes of their efforts; Louisville has a generally low rate of AIDS cases (a total of 766 reported AIDS cases as of 6/30/96; 1,024 cases of HIV infection as of 6/30/96). It has an active gay community and medium levels of drug abuse and addiction.

Nationwide, since the start of the epidemic the majority (58%) of known cases of AIDS have been attributed to male-male sexual transmission. However, in the 1990s heterosexual contacts (8%) and injection drug use (32%) are increasingly common methods of HIV transmission in the United States (CDC, 1996)[1]. In Kentucky, figures are lower than the national average. Eighteen percent of diagnosed cases of AIDS were attributed to injection drug use (Department for Health Services,

1996). In Jefferson County, 16 percent of AIDS cases and 12 percent of all asymptomatic HIV infection cases were attributed to injection drug use (Jefferson County Health Department, 1995).

In the industrialized world, the United States has one of the highest rates of illicit drug use (Hammett, Hunt, Gross, Rhodes, and Moini, 1991). Injection drug users are frequent clients of the criminal justice system. In some cities three-quarters of arrestees test positive for one or more illicit substances (United States Department of Justice, 1992). Correspondingly, arrestees who use drugs have been shown to be more likely than non-drug using arrestees to engage in more HIV risk behaviors (Magura, Rosenblum and Joseph, 1991), including having more sex partners than non-drug using arrestees (Decker and Rosenfeld, 1992; Huebert and James, 1992). Therefore, it may be assumed that addicts in the criminal justice system are more likely than other addicts to at risk for, or already HIV infected (see Decker and Rosenfeld, 1995).

Offenders and inmates with HIV infection and AIDS are not uncommon in our criminal justice system. At a minimum, 4.6 percent of all AIDS cases in the United States have occurred among inmates (Hammett, et. al., 1994). In 1993, 2.2 percent of state and federal prison inmates were reported to be HIV infected. More recently, DeGroot, Hammett and Scheib (1996) have reported that at least eleven state prison systems have HIV infection rates approaching or exceeding 8 percent. Fully one-third (33.2%) of all deaths in state prisons during 1993 were AIDS-related (U.S. Department of Justice, 1995a). Finally, the individual rate for AIDS among state and federal inmates is twenty times greater than in the general population (U.S. Department of Justice, 1995b). However, the vast majority of these are individuals whom come to the criminal justice system already infected, these are not individuals who become infected due to, or during their detention, adjudication, or incarceration.

Within the criminal justice system, IDUs represent the population most likely to present exposure and transmission risks to staff. Although the actual risk presented may be very slight, fears and apprehensions on the part of personnel can have very real repercussions. Interestingly though, despite this perceived threat to criminal justice agencies, the importance of policies for and training about HIV is unrecognized (Edwards and Tewksbury, 1996).

Since a cure is not on the horizon, the key to stemming the consequences of HIV must be focused on the prevention of infection (see Stevens, 1993). The policy emphasis upon prevention is one aspect that HIV and injection drug use have in common. Behavioral and attitudinal changes are necessary to stem the effects of both problems.

4 Journal of Crime and Justice

Policies directed at IDUs other than prevention and education have legal implications. Most notable here are the calls for distribution of disinfectant supplies (e.g., bleach) and needle exchange programs (see Haverkos and Jones, 1994 and Vlahov, 1995). While research shows such programs can be very effective in controlling the spread of HIV (Des Jarlais, Marmor, Paone, Titus, Shi, Perlis, Jose, Friedman, 1996; Des Jarlais, Friedman, Sotheran, Wenston, Marmor, Yancovitz, Frank, Beatrice, and Mildvan, 1994a), nonetheless, political and legal opposition to such programs makes these especially difficult to implement and maintain. While some locations have effectively implemented needle exchange programs and made sterile needles more widely available, such programs remain very limited in number. In some locations, such as Kentucky, such programs are considered by public health officials as "unworkable." As argued in the National Institute of Justice's *1994 Update: HIV/AIDS and STDs in Correctional Facilities*,

"...The challenge of providing effective HIV education and prevention for correctional inmates is thus heightened by a central tension: the best programs seem to be those that are most explicit about particular precautionary and preventive measures yet correctional regulations often prohibit such explicit messages and, in any case, almost universally prohibit the distribution of condoms, bleach and other materials needed to implement them" (Hammett, Widom, Epstein, Gross, Sifre and Enos, 1995).

While we do not dismiss the efficacy potential for programs including needle exchanges and bleach/condom/spermicidal distribution, in the correctional setting there are numerous conflicts of interest presented by such for criminal justice professionals. Consequently, in the criminal justice community, it appears that the only widely available option for controlling or minimizing HIV infection risks from injection drug users may be preventive education. At present, the only criminal justice agencies consistently providing HIV prevention programming is corrections; these "programs" most often rely on distribution of written or audio-visual materials to inmates (Hammett, Widom, Epstein, Gross, Sifre, and Enos, 1995). The CDC transmission statistics show that many persons do not have simply one possible or likely means of becoming infected with HIV. To assume that injection drug users are at risk *only* from their needle use would be dangerous. Instead, such individuals must be viewed as having many of the same risk factors as anyone else, *besides* risks due to injection drug use.

Two studies from the National AIDS Demonstration Project (NADR) funded by the National Institute of Drug Abuse (NIDA) have revealed dramatic information about the linkages between IDUs and HIV. The purpose of this project was to reach street drug users who were not in treatment and develop and test AIDS prevention activities aimed at reducing high risk behaviors for HIV infection. For example, a study of 413 street IV drug users in Miami, Florida found that half of the group who injected drugs at least four times per day were seropositive for HIV antibodies. The majority (87.4%) of this group had been incarcerated in jail in the last five years. Although some (13.5%) reported that they had obtained AIDS information in jail, few were exposed to AIDS prevention programs or received treatment services during their incarceration (McBride and Inciardi, 1990:270-272).

Similarly, a study based upon a sample of 879 Midwestern IDUs, not in treatment, revealed a number of variables were significantly related to the amount of time spent in jail. Specifically, these variables were: (1) initiation to drug injection at an early age; (2) having multiple sex partners; (3) having a history of an STD; (4) being a daily drug user; (5) daily injection of cocaine, heroin, or speedball; (6) inconsistent use of condoms; and (7) using rented needles (Siegal, Wang, Forney, Falck, and Carlson, 1994). In addition, the most active IDUs with the highest HIV risk behaviors were those most likely to spend time in jail.

Most recently, Decker and Rosenfeld (1992) have profiled injection drug users arrested in twenty cities, and report significant rates of risk behaviors. Especially notable of their findings is the fact that fully one-half of injecting drug users report sharing needles. Programs focusing on reducing rates of needle-sharing behaviors appear to face formidable obstacles, although the dynamics of addiction may not be central. However, needle-sharing behavior may, in fact, be a "pragmatic response to needle scarcity" (Koester, 1994:287) rather than a cultural norm, as often widely believed.

Based on these findings, and the official estimate that only 15-20 percent of IDUs may pursue drug treatment (U.S. Department of Health and Human Services, 1991) the criminal justice system emerges as the most logical place to initiate HIV prevention services for IDUs. This, coupled with the fact that a growing body of research shows that interventions can lead to behavior changes among IDUs (Des Jarlais, Choopanya, Vanichsein, Plangsringarm, Sonchai, Carballo, Friedman, and Friedman, 1994b; Desjarlais, Hagan, Friedman, Friedman, Goldberg, Frischer, Green, Runving, Ljungberg, Wodak, Ross, Purchase, Millson, and Myers, 1995; Mandell,

Vlahov, Latkin, Carron, Oziemkowska, and Reedt, 1994), points out the clear need for interventions to be pursued. This point, and the captive nature of a correctional audience, has lead one researcher to conclude that:

"...HIV prevention programs within jail settings provide excellent opportunities to interact with hard-to-reach IDU populations. Although the actual jail setting may pose problems, such as logistical and ethical barriers, space, access to inmates, and necessary adjustments to curriculum it also provides the opportunity to involve individuals who are at risk for HIV... in ... intervention" (Stevens, 1993:388).

RESEARCH METHODS

To examine these issues, our research explored the variety and degree of risks for HIV infection encountered by injection drug users in a low-incidence, mid-sized city (Louisville, KY). The purpose was to identify the HIV risk behaviors of injectable drug users. Special attention was given to the proportionality of infection risk attributable to drug use and sexual activities. The goal was to determine the means by which criminal justice professionals can identify HIV infection risks in this specialized population. This knowledge could then lead to informed decisions about the allocation of resources to and prevention efforts within this population.

The data for this research come from a larger community-wide, multi-population assessment of HIV education/prevention needs in Jefferson County (Louisville), Kentucky. This endeavor, funded by the United States Conference of Mayors, sought to identify the risk behaviors and knowledge and utilization of HIV information sources in the community. A total of 674 individuals was included in the larger, targeted sample[2]. The present analysis centers only on the portion of the sample who self-identify as users of injection drugs.

All data come from face-to-face, structured interviews conducted between August 1994 and February 1995. Interviews were administered by a team of interviewers specially trained in HIV/AIDS issues, techniques for interviewing on sensitive topics and cultural sensitivities. In the vast majority of instances, interviews were conducted in public settings (public parks, soup kitchens, social service agency lobbies, etc.). Interviews lasted between 15 and 45 minutes in length. All interviews were voluntary and anonymous, with no remuneration offered in exchange for participation.

Table 1

Demographic Characteristics, Injection Drug Users

Demographic Characteristics	Percent of Sample
Sex	
Male	59.7%
Female	40.3%
Race[4]	
Caucasian	44.1%
African-American	50.0%
Other Races	5.9%
Mean Age	36.8%
Parents	71.6% 55% with 2+ children
Education	
High School or Less	66.2%
Post High-School	33.8%
Employment Status	
Employed Full-time	19.1%
Employed Part-time	23.5%
Unemployed	57.4%
Sexual Orientation	
Heterosexual	70.6%
Bisexual	13.2%
Lesbian/Gay	16.2%

Sample

A total of 68 injection drug users is included in the sample, representing both those in treatment programs (inpatient and outpatient) and those who are not in treatment. The research team included consultants from two community groups whose role included ensuring the cultural sensitivities of all questions and facilitating access to the African-American and gay/lesbian/bisexual communities. All individuals in this sample self-identify as individuals who have used needles to inject drugs in the previous three years.[3] Table 1 reports the demographic characteristics of this sample. Nearly two-thirds (61.8%) of the respondents reported that they knew someone (either living or dead) with HIV/AIDS. In fact, these individuals knew an average of 5.2 persons who were HIV positive. Furthermore, 4.5 percent of injection drug users admitted that they were HIV infected. Based on the small number of cases included in this analysis, readers are cautioned regarding the generalizability of these findings.

FINDINGS

Identification of Risk Behaviors

There are three risk factors that put injection drug users at significantly increased risk of contracting HIV and transmitting it to others. In addition to the obvious risks associated with the highly efficient transmission of HIV via sharing of needles, syringes and works, there are identifiable contextual conditions that place IDUs at heightened risk of infection. These three risk factors are:

1. High rates of high risk sexual activities. For example, Siegal and his colleagues (1994:93) reported that the majority (92.7%) of their Midwestern city sample of IDUs had engaged in sexual activities with one or more partners in the six months prior to the interview. Over half of these subjects had sex with another IDU. Less than seven percent reported regular use of condoms during sexual contact.

2. Negative attitudes regarding HIV risk reduction activities.

3. Low levels of knowledge concerning HIV, and a perception of credibility and accessibility for information sources of questionable value.

The effects of these three risk factors are significant in themselves. In the IDU population, they combine to yield a potentially deadly outcome (HIV infection).

Table 2

Rates of Sexual Behaviors and Condom Use

Sexual Behavior	% of Sample	Never	Rarely	Some times	Usually	Always
Mastur-bation	86.7%	94.0%	2.0%	2.0%	2.0%	2.0%
Mutual Mastur-bation	38.2%	87.0%	4.3%	8.7%	0.0%	0.0%
Touched, No Penetration	54.4%	83.3%	10.0%	3.3%	3.3%	0.0%
Vaginal Intercourse	83.6%	39.2%	19.6%	33.3%	5.9%	2.0%
Performed oral sex	71.6%	75.0%	9.1%	11.4%	4.5%	0.0%
Received oral sex	80.9%	79.6%	8.2%	10.2%	2.0%	0.0%
Performed anal sex	35.8%	52.2%	4.3%	8.7%	17.4%	17.4%
Received anal sex	22.4%	28.6%	7.1%	14.3%	35.7%	14.3%
Sex with 2+ others	17.9%	not asked	not asked	not asked	not asked	not asked
Been paid for sex	19.4%	30.8%	7.7%	53.8%	0.0%	7.7%
Paid for sex	6.0%	50.0%	50.0%	0.0%	0.0%	0.0%
Sex with a stranger	31.3%	31.6%	5.3%	31.6%	15.8%	15.8%

High Rates of High-Risk Sexual Activities

Table 2 presents a summary of the participation rates of injection drug users in 14 forms of sexual behavior, for the preceding six months. Additionally, Table 2 also presents the condom utilization rates for injection drug users for each sexual behavior in which participation is reported.

Injection drug users engaged in a wide range of sexual activities at rates high enough to arouse concern among public health and criminal justice professionals. Again, consistent with previous research (Decker and Rosenfeld, 1995; Stevens, 1993), IDUs report very low levels of condom use. In addition to their wide range of sexual activities, injection drug users reported a very high mean number of annual sex partners: 9.9, and a median of 3.0.[5] Previous researchers (Stevens, 1993) have reported large numbers of lifetime sexual partners (52.2), but report no data on annual averages. In addition, an important interaction between injection drug use, race and sexual orientation was revealed. Injection drug users of color reported a significantly and substantially larger mean number of annual sex partners than white injection drug users (14.9 vs. 4.0, p=.035). Also, self-identified gay/lesbian/bisexual injection drug users reported an annual mean number of sexual partners that is nearly nine times larger than that reported by heterosexual injection drug users (27.1 vs. 3.3, p=.014). In the previously cited Midwestern study, the IDUs reported an annual mean number of sex partners of 6.9 (Siegal, et. al, 1994:94).

Another indicator of HIV risk behavior is the frequency of sexual activities. Table 3 demonstrates that the IDUs in general were sexually active and that the IDUs of color had particularly pronounced rates of sexual conduct. However, once again, the small sample size warrants caution in generalizing these findings.

These data reveal a great potential for sexual transmission of HIV (and other sexually transmitted diseases) by this population. This group of individuals shows a high level of possibility for disease transmission and infection, at least in part due to its unique demographic characteristics. This is especially true for injection drug users of color.

Consistent with these findings, IDUs reported high levels of sexually transmitted diseases. Fully 30.9 percent of the sample reported at least one STD diagnosis - most commonly, gonorrhea (36.8 percent of diagnoses) syphilis (31.6%) or chlamydia (15.8%). Also, IDUs of color (36.8%) were more likely their white counterparts (23.3%) to report an STD diagnosis. However, there is some consolation in the finding that this population showed some concern about their sexual health. Almost three of every four (73.5%) injection drug users reported having been tested for HIV antibodies[6]. This concern also carried over to sexual and needle-sharing behaviors. Only 7.6 percent of the sample reported sharing needles with *anyone* in the past six months. Only 7.3 percent of the IDUs reported *ever* sharing a needle with someone they knew to be HIV positive. Additionally, less than one in five (17.1%) injection drug users reported sexual contact with a person who was known to be HIV positive. These relatively low rates of highest risk behaviors suggest that it may well be possible to conduct effective intervention strategies with injection drug users. Some racial differences did emerge, however. IDUs of color were more likely to share needles and white injection drug users were more likely to report sex with a HIV-positive partner.

Table 3

Reported Frequency of Sexual Activity

Frequency of Sexual Activity	% of All Injection Drug Users	% of White Injection Drug Users	% of Injection Drug Users of Color
No sex in past one year	1.5% (N=1)	3.3% (N=1)	0.0%
One to three times monthly	63.3% (N=43)	73.3% (N=22)	55.2% (N=21)
Once per week or more often	35.2% (N=24)	23.4% (N=7)	44.8% (N=17)

In Table 4, we see that the vast majority of injection drug users reported that they were using either alcohol or other drugs when they engaged in sexual activities. Injection drug users (particularly those of color) consistently reported being intoxicated when having sex.

Attitudes Regarding Risk Reduction Activities

Here, individuals were asked to respond to twelve Likert scale attitudinal items on risk reduction activities. Their response to these items were summed to yield a safer sex attitude score for each respondent[7]. Injection drug users reported a mean attitude score of 37.6 (of a total possible of 60). There were no statistically significant differences in mean safer sex scaled scores between white and of color injection drug users or divisions based on education, income or sexual orientation. However, females reported a average score 3.4 points higher than male injection drug users (39.5 vs. 36.1, p=.006).

Table 4

Frequency of Using Alcohol/Drugs when Sexually Active

Frequency of Using Alcohol/Drugs When Sexually Active	All Injection Drug Users	White Injection Drug Users	Of Color Injection Drug Users
Always	16.2% (N=11)	10.0% (N=3)	21.1% (N=8)
Usually	48.5% (N=33)	43.3% (N=13)	52% (N=20)
Sometimes	20.6% (N=14)	23.3% (N=7)	18.4% (N=7)
Rarely	5.9% (N=4)	10.0% (N=3)	2.6% (N=1)
Never	8.8% (N=6)	13.3% (N=4)	5.3% (N=2)

Knowledge of HIV/AIDS

All respondents were asked to respond to ten items designed to assess their personal knowledge of HIV and AIDS issues and facts[8]. Each respondent's total number of correct responses was summed, yielding a scaled knowledge score ranging from 0 to 10. Generally speaking, injection drug users displayed generally low levels of knowledge of HIV/AIDS. The mean scaled knowledge score for the sample of injection drug users was 5.04 (of a possible 10)[9]. Three demographic variables produce statistically significant differences in scale knowledge scores. Racial distinctions did not yield statistically significant differences in scaled knowledge scores. Gay/lesbian/bisexual injection drug users had a 1.1 point higher mean score than heterosexual injection drug users (p=.002). Respondents with more than a high school education had scaled mean knowledge scores 0.9 points higher than injection drug users with a high school or less education (p=.004).

The most important finding regarding knowledge of HIV/AIDS is that injection drug users hold some common misperceptions about possible modes of HIV transmission that may place them at increased risk of contracting HIV disease. This misperception is especially significant in light of their high rates of high-risk sexual activity. Yet, injection drug users believed themselves to be well-informed regarding HIV/AIDS issues. As shown in Table 5, more than 70 percent of injection drug users believe they are either very well or fairly well informed. However, the previous data on their risk behaviors reveals that their confidence is obviously misplaced.

Table 5

Self-Perceived Knowledge of HIV/AIDS

Self-Perceived Level of Knowledge	Percent of All Injection Drug Users
Very Well Informed	23.5% (N=16)
Fairly Well Informed	48.5% (N=33)
Know Only a Few Things	25.0% (N=17)
Know Very Little/Nothing	2.9% (N=2)

With what appears as a relatively high degree of confidence in their knowledge of HIV/AIDS, it is not surprising that injection drug users saw themselves at generally low levels of risk for HIV infection. However, by their own admission, this population is at very high risk of contracting HIV. Table 6 shows that nearly 60 percent of injection drug users believe they have little or no chance of becoming HIV infected. This perception appears strongest among IDUs of color. Despite their apparently higher rate of sexual activity and resultant increased risk for HIV infection, and their higher rate of STD diagnosis, injection drug users of color were more likely than white IDUS to perceive themselves at low risk of contracting HIV.

Table 6

Self-Perceived Risk of Contracting HIV Infection

Self-Defined Risk	Percent of All Injection Drug Users	Percent of White Injection Drug Users	Percent of Injection Drug Users of Color
No Chance	13.4% (N=9)	6.9% (N=2)	18.4% (N=7)
Low	46.3% (N=31)	44.8% (N=13)	47.4% (N=18)
Medium	29.9% (N=21)	31.0% (N=10)	28.9% (N=11)
High	6.0% (N=4)	10.3% (N=3)	2.6% (N=1)
Already HIV+	4.5% (N=3)	6.9% (N=2)	2.6% (N=1)

Examination of crosstabulations of individuals' tested knowledge levels and self-perceived chances of contracting HIV infection show no discernible differences in any category of perceived vulnerability correlated with tested knowledge level. Actual knowledge regarding HIV transmission methods and trends do not influence how vulnerable an individual injection drug user sees himself.

ACCESS AND UTILIZATION OF INFORMATION SOURCES

There are a wide range of sources of HIV-related information in our society. Some are more active in disseminating information than others. Some sources also have more controls on what they publicize and others may be more likely to be disseminating accurate information. Table 7 reports on the responses of the sample of injection drug users concerning where individuals have learned about HIV/AIDS. As seen, the most common places for people to learn about HIV//AIDS is from mass media outlets and health professionals and educators, as well as discussions with friends. Not surprisingly, injection drug users have commonly received at least some HIV/AIDS information from substance abuse counselors. This source was accessed by only a small portion of all other populations of concern in this study.

Table 7

Sources of Information about HIV/AIDS

Source of Information	Percent of Injection Drug Users Accessing Information from Source
Doctors/nurses/clinics	80.0% (N=52)
Drug/alcohol counselors	76.9% (N=50)
Friends	76.9% (N=50)
Television	76.9% (N=50)
Brochures or pamphlets	72.3% (N=47)
Health educators/outreach workers	66.2% (N=43)
Magazines or newspapers	64.6% (N=42)
Sexual partners	50.8% (N=33)
Family members	49.2% (N=32)
Radio	40.0% (N=26)
HIV/AIDS organizations	36.9% (N=24)
Spouse/lover/boyfriend/ girlfriend	35.4% (N=23)
School	24.6% (N=16)
Gay magazines or newspapers	18.5% (N=12)
Church	10.8% (N=7)

Injection drug using respondents were also asked to indicate how likely they would be to believe information about HIV/AIDS that they might receive from each of these sources. What we see is that IDUs reported very high levels of trust in the information they might receive from all sources. The only source approaching general distrust is gay community media outlets (30.5 percent unlikely to believe at least *some* of what they access from such sources). The sources granted the highest credibility are family members, schools, doctors/nurses/clinics, brochures/pamphlets, (and encouragingly) substance abuse counselors and health educators/outreach workers.

Factor analysis identified three primary types of information sources that injection drug users look to, and are willing to believe, when receiving information regarding HIV/AIDS issues. One factor is composed of those sources representing mass media or the medical community (doctors, HIV organizations, schools, friends, radio and television). A second factor shows that some persons look to personal contacts (whether or not medically educated) for credible information (family, significant others, sexual partners, church contacts, health educators and substance abuse counselors). Finally, a third group of similarly viewed sources of information is composed solely of written materials concerning HIV/AIDS (brochures/pamphlets, magazines/newspapers and gay community magazines/newspapers).

In addition, the IDU respondents were asked to identify the one source that had taught them the most about HIV/AIDS. A total of 17 different varieties of sources were offered, ranging from significant others, friends, AIDS service organizations, medical personnel and correctional facilities. These various open-ended responses were collapsed into seven categories of specific locations. The most commonly offered source that had provided the most information to respondents was easily medical sources, followed by personal/family contacts. There are no substantial differences in attributed value for sources by race of injection drug using respondents.

Implications for Criminal Justice Agencies/Practitioners

Although this research is based on a small sample size, they nonetheless suggest that injection drug users engage in high rates of high-risk behavior, have low levels of knowledge regarding HIV/AIDS (although such is not recognized by IDUs), and often receive their information from sources of unknown credibility (family/partners and mass media). There are also some indications here for possibilities of prevention/intervention program efficacy. Most notably, this sample of IDUs report very low rates of needle-sharing and sexual contact with known HIV+ persons. There are three important implications in this data. First, we must realize that injection drug users may be the most likely population to be at risk for (and to already have) an HIV infection. Injection drug users' continued practice of high risk sexual activities have been shown before (Vlahov, 1994), although generally not in smaller, lower-incidence cities such as here. Second, reiterating the findings of Decker and Rosenfeld (1995), there is a significant need to address injection drug users' minimal perception of vulnerability for HIV infection. Third, criminal justice practitioners may be uniquely equipped to fill the identified gap in HIV education/prevention programming; while some may believe drug treatment programs would be the most appropriate venue for such, however, only 15-20 percent of IDUs may pursue treatment (U.S. Department of Health and Human Services, 1991).

In order to provide effective prevention/intervention programming, however, it is first necessary to alter the perceptions of injection drug users in the criminal justice system regarding the realistic possibilities of their infection. To accomplish such attitudinal/perceptual changes, through it is necessary not just to provide "factual" information, but rather to present the threat of HIV as a reality. Such attitudinal adjustments can be accomplished by directly showing individuals others like them who have been infected. When combined with easily understood (i.e. non-clinical) information about how sexual and injection activities can and do lead to virus transmission, it is possible to reach those who may initially seem unreachable.

The key to HIV prevention programming in any setting is this: HIV is a threat to all of us. While some populations may actively place themselves at greater risk of infection (and subsequent passing of infection to others) through their behaviors, attitudes and knowledge levels, prevention cannot be limited to only certain specified populations. As human service providers we have an important responsibility -- to maintain the quality of life in our communities, including contributing to the public health of our communities.

ENDNOTES

1. Totals do not sum to 100 percent as some individuals report more than one possible means of infection. However, in addition, 9 percent of cases are of either unknown transmission mode, due to hemophilia/blood coagulation disorders or blood transfusions.

2. In an attempt to ensure the inclusion of injection drug users in the larger research sample a total of fifteen different points of contact, including drug treatment facilities, soup kitchens, correctional facilities and street outreach efforts were accessed. Locations were selected on the advice of local health department and drug treatment officials.

3. Three-fourths (75.4%) of this group reports having been in a substance abuse treatment at least once in their lives. These individuals are fairly evenly split between those who would be considered active injection users (40%) and those who report being free of injection drugs in the last 6 months (60%).

4. Because of the small percentage of respondents that identify as neither Caucasian or African-American, and the fact that the community in which the research was conducted is generally considered racially dichotomous, all references to racial differences refer to white and "of color" respondents.

5. Contrary to the expectations of some, "only" 19.4 percent of self-identified IDUs report having traded sex for money, drugs or goods.

6. Most (88%) of these individuals who were tested report knowing the results of the HIV antibody test.

7. Higher mean scaled scores indicate more positive attitudes regarding safer sex practices.

8. The ten items used to assess individuals' knowledge of HIV/AIDS included nine true/false items and one open-ended question. These items are as follows:

You can get HIV from kissing someone who already has HIV/AIDS.
You can get HIV from a mosquito bite.
You can get HIV from having sex with someone who has it already.
You can get HIV from a blood transfusion.
There is a vaccine (shot) that can prevent you from getting AIDS.
You can *not* get AIDS from oral sex.
If I use any form of birth control whenever I have sex I know I will not get AIDS.
Needles can be cleaned of HIV by rinsing them with soap and water.

White people are more likely to get HIV/AIDS than African-Americans. What do the letters H-I-V stand for?

9. Compared with mean scores for other high risk populations in Louisville, IDUs have a statistically significant lower score (5.04) than men who have sex with men (5.9), high risk women (5.5) and high risk youth (5.5).

REFERENCES

Baxter, S. (1991). "AIDS Education in the Jail Setting." *Crime and Delinquency* 37:48-63.

Bell, N.K. (1991). "Social/Sexual Norms and AIDS in the South: Ethics and the Politics of AIDS: Lessons for Small Cities and Rural Areas throughout the U.S." *AIDS Education and Prevention* 3:164-180.

Burris, S., H.L. Dalton, J.L. Miller and the Yale AIDS Law Project (1993). *AIDS law today: A new guide for the public.* New Haven: Yale University Press.

Centers for Disease Control and Prevention (1996). *HIV/AIDS Surveillance Report* 6:5.

Centers for Disease Control and Prevention (1995). *HIV and AIDS: Trends in the Epidemic.* Atlanta: U.S. Public Health Service.

Decker, S. and R. Rosenfeld. (1992). "Intravenous Drug Use and the AIDS Epidemic: Findings from a 20-City Sample of Arrestees." *Crime and Delinquency* 38:492-509.

Decker, S. and R. Rosenfeld (1995). "'My Wife is Married and So Is My Girlfriend': Adaptations to the Threat of AIDS in an Arrestee Population. *Crime and Delinquency* 41:37-53.

DeGroot, A.S., T. Hammett and T.G. Scheib (1996). "Access to HIV Services in Prisons and Jails: A Public Health Concern." Unpublished paper presented at Centers for Disease Control and Prevention's HIV Community Planning Groups Co-Chairs Prevention Summit. Atlanta, GA. (March)

Department for Health Services (1995). *AIDS in Kentucky*. Frankfort, KY: Surveillance and Investigations Branch, Division of Epidemiology.

Department for Health Services (1996). *1997 Kentucky HIV Prevention Plan*. Frankfort: Division of Epidemiology: HIV/AIDS Branch.

Deren, S., M. Beardsley, W.R. Davis and S. Tortu (1993). "HIV Risk Factors Among Pregnant and Non-Pregnant High Risk Women in New York City." *Journal of Drug Education* 23:57-60.

Des Jarlais, D.C., S.R. Friedman, J.L. Sotheran, J. Wenston, M. Marmor, S.R. Yancovitz, B. Frank, S. Beatrice and D. Mildvan (1994a). "Continuity and Change within an HIV Epidemic: Injecting Drug Users in New York City, 1984 through 1992." *The Journal of the American Medical Association* 271:121-127.

Des Jarlais, D.C., K. Choopanya, S. Vanichseni, K. Plangsringarm, W. Sonchai, M. Carballo, P. Friedman and S.R. Friedman (1994b). "AIDS Risk Reduction and Reduced HIV Seroconversion among Injection Drugs Users in Bangkok." *The American Journal of Public Health* 84:452-455.

Des Jarlais, D.C., H. Hagan, S.R. Friedman, P. Friedman, D. Goldberg, M. Frischer, S. Green, K. Tunving, B. Ljungberg, A. Wodak, M. Ross, D. Purchase, M.E. Millson and T. Myers (1995). "Maintaining Low HIV Seroprevalence in Populations of Injecting Drug Users." *Journal of the American Medical Association* 274:1226-1231.

Des Jarlais, D.C., M. Marmor, D. Paone, S. Titus, Q. Shi, T. Perlis, B. Jose and S.R. Friedman (1996). "HIV Incidence among Injecting Drug Users in New York City Syringe Exchange Programs." *The Lancet* 347:987-991.

Edwards, T. and R. Tewksbury (1996). "HIV/AIDS: State Police Training Practices and Personnel Policies." *American Journal of Police* 15:45-62.

Hammett, T., D. Hunt, M. Gross, W. Rhodes and S. Moini (1991). "Stemming the Spread of HIV among IV Drug Users, Their Sexual Partners and Children: Issues and Opportunities for Criminal Justice Agencies." *Crime and Delinquency* 37:101-124.

Hammett, T., L. Harrold, M. Gross and J. Epstein (1994). *1992 Update: HIV/AIDS in correctional facilities.* Washington, DC: National Institute of Justice.

Hammett, T., R. Widom, J. Epstein, M. Gross, S. Sifre and T. Enos (1995). *1994 Update: HIV/AIDS and STDs in correctional facilities.* Washington, DC: National Institute of Justice.

Haverkos, H.W. and T.S. Jones (1994). "HIV, Drug-Use Paraphernalia, and Bleach." *Journal of Acquired Immune Deficiency Syndromes* 7:741-742.

Hobfoll, S. E., A.P. Jackson, J. Lovin, P.J. Britton and J.P. Shepherd (1993)."Safer Sex Knowledge, Behavior, and Attitudes of Inner-City Women." *Health Psychology* 12:481-488.

Huebert, K. and D. James (1992). "High-Risk Behaviors for Transmission of HIV among Clients in Treatment for Substance Abuse." *Journal of Drug Issues* 22:885-901.

Jarvis, R.M., M.L. Closen, D. H.J. Hermann and A.S. Leonard (1991). *AIDS Law in a Nutshell.* St. Paul: West Publishing.

Jefferson County Health Department (1995). *Quarterly AIDS/HIV Surveillance Report.* Louisville, KY: AIDS/HIV Surveillance Program.

Kelly, J.A., J.S. St. Lawrence, T.L. Brasfield, L.Y., Stevenson, Y.E. Diaz and A.C. Hauth (1990). "AIDS Risk Behavior Patterns among Gay Men in Small Southern Cities." *American Journal of Public Health* 80:416-418.

Koester, S.K. (1994). "Copping, Running and Paraphernalia Laws: Contextual Variables and Needle Risk Behavior among Injection Drug Users in Denver." *Human Organization* 53:287-295.

Magura, S., A. Rosenblum and H. Joseph (1991). "AIDS Risk among Intravenous Drug-Using Offenders." *Crime and Delinquency* 37:86-100.

Mandell, W., D. Vlahov, C.A. Latkin, D. Carran, M.J. Oziemkowska, and L. Reedt (1994). "Changes in HIV Risk Behaviors among Counseled Injecting Drug Users." *Journal of Drug Issues* 24:555-567.

McBride, D.C. and J.A. Inciardi (1990). "AIDS and the IV Drug User in the Criminal Justice System." *Journal of Drug Issues* 20:267-280.

Sibthorpe, B. (1992). "The Social Construction of Sexual Relationships as a Determinant of HIV Risk Perception and Condom Use among Injection Drug Users." *Medical Anthropology Quarterly* 6:255-270.

Siegal, H.A., J. Wang, M.A. Forney, R.S. Falck, and R.G. Carlson (1994). "Incarceration and HIV Risk Behaviors among Injection Drug Users: A Midwestern Case Study." *Journal of Crime and Justice* 17:85-101.

Silvestre, A. (1992). *HIV Rates and Differences in Behavior Over Time among Men Entering an HIV Disease Cohort Study.* Pittsburgh: University of Pittsburgh.

Stevens, S. (1993). "HIV Prevention Programs in a Jail Setting: Educational Strategies." *The Prison Journal* 73:379-390.

Tewksbury, R. (1995). "Sexual Adaptations among Gay Men with HIV." In *Men's Health and Illness: Gender, Power and the Body,* D. Gordon and D. Sabo (eds.). Thousand Oaks, CA: Sage.

Tewksbury, R. (1994). "'Speaking of Someone with AIDS...' Identity Constructions of Persons with HIV Disease." *Deviant Behavior* 15:337-355.

United States Department of Health and Human Services (1991). *Drug Abuse and Drug Abuse Research.* Washington, DC: Department of Health and Human Services.

United States Department of Justice (1995a). *HIV in Prisons and Jails, 1993.* Washington, DC: Bureau of Justice Statistics.

United States Department of Justice (1995b). *Managing Prison Health Care and Costs.* Washington, DC: National Institute of Justice.

Vlahov, D. (1994). "HIV Seroconversion Studies Among Intravenous Drug Users." *AIDS* 8:263-265.

[19]

HIV/AIDS: STATE POLICE TRAINING PRACTICES AND PERSONNEL POLICIES

Terry D. Edwards

Richard Tewksbury
University of Louisville

INTRODUCTION

In 1981, the US Center for Disease Control[1] (CDC) noted outbreaks of Kaposi's Sarcoma and Pneumocystis Carinii Pneumonia (Bigbee, 1993; Jarvis et al., 1991). Although the number infected was less than 400, CDC identified the patterns as "unusual". By 1984, the outbreaks continued to alarm the CDC and the number of cases was reported as over 5,000. The condition was collectively referred to as Acquired Immune Deficiency Syndrome (AIDS) and the suspected infecting agent subsequently given the term Human Immunodeficiency Virus (HIV).[2] By the end of 1993, CDC reported over 361,000 cases of AIDS and over 220,000 deaths (US Department of Health, 1994). New diagnoses increased 125 percent from 1992 to 1993 (US Department of Health and Human Services, 1994). Repeatedly, leading medical scholars referred to HIV/AIDS as the most serious public health problem in the United States today. In the face of this meteoric rise in HIV/AIDS cases and related fatalities, and given the alarm raised by the medical community, the question becomes "How has the criminal justice system as a whole, and the law enforcement community in particular, responded to HIV/AIDS?"

The 1980s witnessed a relative dearth of research on HIV/AIDS as they relate to the criminal justice community, although a few research studies were generated (Bigbee, 1987; Hammett, 1987a; 1988; Laszlo and Ayers, 1986). Furthermore, the early criminal justice research agenda almost always focussed on corrections settings (Hammett, 1987a; 1988). The watershed work addressing HIV/AIDS and the law enforcement community was the 1987 study by the National Institute of Justice (Hammett, 1987b). The NIJ report quickly generated a keen interest in, and concern for, the risks encountered by public safety workers in general, and the law enforcement community in particular (e.g. California Department of Health Services, 1988; US Department of Health and Human Services, 1989). The 1987 NIJ report was followed in 1988 by an outline from the CDC for meeting the training needs of public safety workers (US Department of Health and Human Services, 1989). By December 1989, law enforcement's concerns about HIV/AIDS were addressed when the International Association of Chiefs of Police (IACP) promulgated a model policy entitled "Communicable disease". With awareness, training and officer safety as the cornerstones, law enforcement entered the 1990s with a keen sense of the issues related to HIV/AIDS.

The 1990s saw the issuance of a plethora of policies and standards regarding the transmission of infectious diseases. Some policies dealt with the HIV/AIDS issue as part of a broad agenda involving infectious diseases and the general population; others addressed specifically the law enforcement's concerns regarding HIV/AIDS. In June 1990, the IACP model policy from the previous year was followed by a "Concepts and Issues Paper", which laid to rest any doubt about whether HIV/AIDS posed a threat to the law enforcement community when it declared: "The [IACP Model] policy deals particularly with acquired immunodeficiency syndrome (AIDS)" (IACP, 1990:1).

In December 1991, the Federal government joined those expressing concern for job-related HIV/AIDS issues when the Department of Labor's Occupational Safety and Health Administration (OSHA) promulgated its final regulations in the Code of Federal Register. OSHA's "Occupational Exposure to Bloodborne Pathogens" (29 CFR Part 1910.1030) became effective in March 1992, and quite clearly applied to the vast majority of police departments in the United States. This Federal mandate was followed by the adoption of the IACP's model policy "Prevention of Bloodborne Diseases" in October 1992, and the accompanying "Concepts and Issues" paper, released in May 1993.

This activity relating to the development and implementation of standards and policies on communicable diseases paralleled the opening of a virtual "floodgate" of research addressing specifically the effects, past and future, of HIV/AIDS on the law enforcement community (Barr and Warshaw, 1994; Benny, 1993; Bigbee, 1991; 1993; Blumberg, 1990; Gates and Lady, 1991; Kennedy et al., 1990; Kime, 1993; Sheridan et al., 1989; Sinkfield and Houser, 1989; Stewart, 1993; Yearwood, 1992). Evidence emerged indicating law enforcement agencies could benefit from HIV/AIDS education programming (Barr and Warshaw, 1994; Yearwood, 1992). It quickly became apparent from these efforts that the law enforcement community needed to become involved in HIV/AIDS issues, given the real likelihood of one or more of the following legal issues arising:

- departmental liability for job-related infection of officers;
- the department's responsibility for preventing the spread of HIV infection by, and among, prisoners; and
- finally, the potential for criminal charges stemming from intentional or negligent HIV infection (Hammett, 1987b).

Yet, despite the research, preventive efforts, policies and national standards, it was simply a matter of time before the law enforcement community experienced HIV/AIDS work-related exposure, transmission and infection. However, general disagreement existed among researchers as to whether law enforcement had incurred any job-related HIV/AIDS deaths. Although Hammett (1994) reports no deaths, at least one author reported that between 1981 and 1991 seven cases had been documented where police officers had become exposed to, or actually tested positive for, HIV and at least three officers had died from AIDS (Bigbee, 1993). Details and specifics regarding numbers and outcomes aside, given the focus on HIV/AIDS and law enforcement over the past three years, the numerous legal and administrative issues that had arisen and the actual and potential threat being faced by the law enforcement community, the stage was set for research such as this; research exploring the response of the law enforcement community to the HIV/AIDS issues.

By design or default, virtually all previous research involving police organizations focussed on larger, metropolitan or urban police departments. Why, then, assess or evaluate the efforts of state police organizations when policing the traditional "high risk" populations (intravenous drug users, gay men, immigrants, minorities, lower income) is usually associated with larger, metropolitan and urban, police agencies? State police organizations are usually identified with the delivery of police services to rural locations, populated primarily by the white middle class (Wrobleski and Hess, 1990). Additionally, most police scholars would agree that state police organizations are "conservative" when it comes to adopting new instructional techniques and, historically, have been remiss in addressing cultural or controversial issues such as HIV/AIDS (Edwards, 1993). What, then, is to be gained from this study of state police agencies?

It is precisely because of their inherent "conservatism" and lack of identification with the populations with high rates of infections that the state police organizations lend themselves to this study. By late 1993, the time of this survey, over 13 years had elapsed since the initial recognition of the issues involved with HIV/AIDS and policing. Additionally, over five years had elapsed since the IACP first addressed the issue of communicable disease. Furthermore, several months had transpired since the adoptions of OSHA's standards and the IACP model policy. Surely by late 1993 responsible law enforcement agencies would have responded to and implemented a variety of training policies to address these concerns. Furthermore, agencies surely would have implemented personnel policies regarding hiring and retention of personnel who were HIV positive or diagnosed as having AIDS. A true test of the efforts by national health and law enforcement agencies to increase awareness of HIV/AIDS issues among law enforcement agencies would be to determine whether state police organizations, often perceived as the "last to change", had adopted changes in training and/or policies in response to the available information.

Probably the most important reason for assessing state police organizations is that state police organizations, as opposed to most metropolitan agencies, have more control over their recruitment and in-service training processes. The vast majority of state police organizations conduct training in academies they, rather than some state training board, control. Instructors are usually all sworn officers from the state police agency, not "civilians" from "centralized" state training programs. Because of the control and "ownership" of the training facilities, the state police organizations determine both the course content and methodology of the instruction (Edwards, 1993), as opposed to the majority of urban agencies whose training needs are met by state-operated, centrally controlled training councils. Therefore, the presence or absence of instruction relating to HIV/AIDS in a particular state police training program truly reflects the agency's perceived need, or lack thereof, for instruction on that topic, while the presence or absence of HIV/AIDS instruction in a training program not controlled by the agency may or may not be reflective of the agency's needs.

The depth and breadth of these changes by state police organizations would be evidence, and a fairly accurate measure, of how serious the law enforcement community perceived the threat. This research represents an assessment of the depth and breadth of that response.

METHODS

Two different survey instruments were employed in this study. The first, sent to the directors of the 49[3] state police training academies, was a two-page document. The academy directors were asked whether or not their agencies were offering training (either for new recruits or as part of in-service programs) related to HIV/AIDS. If they indicated either type of training was being offered, they were then asked to explain why it was initiated, what problems had been encountered, the methods used, sources, and to provide copies of materials. If either was not offered, they were asked to give reasons. Finally, they were asked whether or not instruction was offered regarding infectious diseases or conditions other than HIV/AIDS.

A second two-page survey was sent to the 49 state police personnel directors. They were asked whether or not their agency had implemented policies addressing:

- officers dealing with, or encountering, persons known to be, or suspected of being, HIV positive or diagnosed with AIDS; and
- the hiring and/or employment of persons testing positive for HIV or diagnosed with AIDS.

If policies existed, agencies were ask to provide a copy; if no policy existed they were asked to explain why such policy had not been implemented.

The surveys, and subsequent clarifying telephone interviews in some cases, resulted in the completion of usable instruments as follows: 42 of the 49 academy directors and 44 of the 49 personnel directors responded to one or more questions (however, not every question was answered by all respondents). For 37 state police organizations, the surveys were completed, to some degree, by *both* the academy and personnel director. At least one survey from each of the 49 states with a state police organization was usable. The resulting data set was evaluated and used to generate both quantitative assessments and a more general descriptive account of "the state of the art" relating to HIV/AIDS training and personnel practices.

As an aside, numerous training and personnel policies were provided by the agencies. In fact, the agencies generously provided us with copies of various training manuals, brochures, flyers, course outlines and even video tapes.

FINDINGS

Training

Forty-two academy directors responded to the question about HIV/AIDS instruction to recruits. A substantial majority (*N* = 36, 86%) reported they were offering basic training to their recruits. Of the six directors reporting no instruction was being offered, four indicated they were considering such training and two indicated they had no plans to offer such training. Forty-one academy directors responded to the question about HIV/AIDS instruction being offered as part of in-service training. Although the number was smaller (*N* = 32, 78%), again a substantial majority of the academy directors reported offering in-service training (Table 1).

Thirty-one academy directors indicated instruction was being offered to both recruits and through in-service training. Four directors indicated training was being offered only to recruits and one reported offering training only in-service. Five directors reported they offered no training, either to recruits or as part of in-service, while one academy

Table 1
PREVALENCE OF RECRUIT/IN-SERVICE TRAINING REGARDING HIV ISSUES

Variable (# Responding)	Yes	No
Instruction Offered: Recruit (42)	36 (86%)	6 (14%)
Instruction Offered: In-Service (41)	32 (78%)	9 (22%)

reported offering training to recruits but failed to indicate whether in-service training was being offered.

It is of interest to note 36 agencies reported offering instruction to recruits, while only 32 agencies reported offering in-service instruction to current officers. Furthermore, four agencies offer instruction *only* to recruits. This training focus on recruits suggests these agencies perceive the risks of HIV infection as less serious than do agencies offering training for all officers. This perspective is further reinforced by the fact that, of the nine agencies not currently offering HIV issues as part of in-service training, only four indicate having given any serious consideration to developing such training. The most common rationale provided for not developing and delivering in-service training is that the anticipated costs (both financial and in terms of manpower) are seen as too great, given the small risk involved.

The academy directors who offered training, either recruit or in-service, were asked to explain why such training was initiated. About the same number of directors responded for both recruit ($N = 23$) and in-service training ($N = 29$). Two primary reasons for initiating HIV/AIDS instruction emerged:

(1) to meet legal requirements (recruit, $N = 12$; in-service, $N = 20$); and

(2) to address concerns of safety for officers and other agency personnel (recruit, $N = 11$; in-service, $N = 9$).

When queried about problems regarding the delivery of instruction to recruits, academy directors overwhelmingly ($N = 29$, 80%) reported they had not encountered any significant problems. However, the results are somewhat different with regards to potential problems with the delivery of in-service training. Of the 32 agencies offering in-service training, slightly over one half ($N = 19$, 59%) report no problems. When problems are encountered, for both recruit and in-service training, they are generally reported to be related to issues of students' attitudes and resistance to such information. As might be anticipated, veteran officers are expressing their objections more frequently than are the new recruits. This reflects the consequences of both occupational socialization and the fact that the (presumably) younger and better educated recruits have more exposure to HIV/AIDS issues.

A review of the course materials (both recruit and in-service) provided by the agencies suggests that topics, course materials and instructional methods vary greatly from agency to agency. Generally, the topics offered as part of HIV/AIDS training, whether to recruits or as part of in-service, are the origin and history of HIV/AIDS, decontamination procedures, transmission processes and risks, protocols for prevention of transmission, statistics, medical terms and definitions, officer safety, confidentiality of information and records, supplies/equipment requirements, notification procedures, administrative (paperwork) requirements and evidence handling. Course materials also vary dramatically. One agency utilizes a brief, handwritten outline; others use elaborate training manuals (some over 100 pages), color handouts, and even videos. Frequently, the instruction regarding HIV/AIDS is part of general training on infectious diseases, including Hepatitis-B. Most instruction was based on course outlines or manuals prepared by the agency and supplemented with information, flyers, or handouts from state or federal agencies. Some agencies did have very detailed and professionally produced brochures specifically addressing HIV/AIDS and their agency. A few agencies reported instruction was conducted by medical personnel, most often registered nurses. The effective date on most policies and materials was 1992, with a few dating to 1990. One agency, however, had course materials dating from 1986.

Finally, the academy directors were asked whether or not they were offering instruction on how to deal with infectious diseases other than HIV/AIDS. Thirty-nine academy directors responded, with 35 indicating they were offering other instruction and four indicating no other instruction was being offered.

Analysis also focussed on identifying differences in instruction by type of agency ("state police" or "highway patrol") and by regions of the country. For the purpose of this analysis the classification of agencies recognized by the International Association of Chiefs of Police (IACP) was employed (IACP, 1975). Of the 49 state law enforcement agencies, 23 are classified as "state police" and 26 are classified as "highway patrol".[4] Regional breakdowns follow the model used by the United States Census Bureau. Four regions are identified: East, Midwest, West, and South.[5]

As Table 2 indicates, there is little difference in whether or not instruction, either recruit or in-service, is being offered based on the type of agency. Furthermore, when the reasons for conducting recruit training are examined by type of agency, there are virtually no differences between state police and highway patrol agencies (Table 3). However, when the reasons for conducting in-service training are reviewed, just over half of the state police agencies report legal requirements as the reason, while more than three-fourths of the highway patrol agencies reported legal requirements as the reason.

Although virtually no differences in the distribution of reasons for initiating recruit training by type of agency were identified, some differences were discerned in the distribution of reasons for initiating such training when reasons are examined by region of responding agency (Table 4). Furthermore, the reasons for initiating in-service training vary

Table 2
NUMBER OF STATE POLICE/HIGHWAY PATROL AGENCIES OFFERING HIV/AIDS TRAINING

Type of Training	State Police	Highway Patrol
Recruit	Yes = 17 No = 5	Yes = 19 No = 1
In-Service	Yes = 16 No = 4	Yes = 16 No = 5

Table 3
REASONS FOR INITIATING RECRUIT AND IN-SERVICE HIV/AIDS TRAINING

Reason for Initiating Training (*N*)	State Police	Highway Patrol
Recruit Training		
Meeting Legal Requirements (12)	6 (50%)	6 (50%)
Concerns of/for Officers (11)	6 (55%)	5 (45%)
In-Service Training		
Meeting Legal Requirements (20)	8 (40%)	12 (60%)
Concerns of/for Officers (9)	5 (56%)	4 (44%)

Table 4
NUMBER OF AGENCIES, BY REGION: REASONS FOR INITIATING RECRUIT AND IN-SERVICE HIV/AIDS TRAINING

Reason for Implementation	East	Midwest	West	South
Recruit Training (N = 23)				
Meeting Legal Requirements (*N* = 12)	1	3	3	5
Concerns of/for Officers (*N* = 11)	3	3	1	4
In-Service Training (N = *29)*				
Meeting Legal Requirements (*N* = 15)	1	4	4	6
Concerns of/for Officers (*N* = 14)	3	5	2	4

somewhat by region. Agencies in the East and Midwest regions reported offering in-service training more due to concerns of/for officers; in the West and South regions, the most frequently offered reason for conducting HIV/AIDS related in-service training is to meet legal requirements.

Personnel Policies

In addition to evaluating the instructional activities of state law enforcement agencies, it was also important to examine the development and implementation of policies and standardized procedures regarding interactions with HIV positive individuals across agencies. Forty-one personnel directors responded to the question regarding whether or not their agency had implemented a policy addressing how to deal with persons suspected of being HIV positive or having AIDS. Twenty-nine personnel directors (71%) reported their agency had adopted such a policy. An interesting note is that while 36 agencies reported offering HIV/AIDS instruction either to new recruits or as part of in-service training, only 29 agencies opted to adopt a policy on the topic (Table 5).

Evidently these agencies not adopting policies are assuming the training and instructional recommendations for such encounters are sufficient to ensure adequately the health and safety of officers and the legal protection of HIV positive citizens, rather than through proscriptive or restrictive policies. There are virtually no differences in whether such a policy was adopted by type of agency (Table 6), and only minimal differences were noted when examining the regions (Tablc 7).

Among those agencies that have developed and implemented policies, more than one-half (55%) report doing so in order to meet legal requirements (usually citing mandates from the Occupational Safety and Health Administration). Other agencies report adopting such policies in

Table 5
Prevalence of Policies Regarding HIV Issues

Variable (# Responding)	Yes	No
Implement Policy: How to Handle HIV Positive Persons (41)	29 (71%)	12 (29%)
Implement Policy: Employment of HIV Positive Persons (36)	9 (25%)	27 (75%)

patrol agencies report having no policies regarding the employment of HIV positive individuals. When implementation of employment policy is addressed by region, it is disturbing that no region has more than 30 percent (18% of East, 30% of Midwest, 28% of West and 25% of South) of its state police organizations reporting the implementation of such a policy.

A look at the reasons cited by types of agencies and region further support the idea that rationales for policy development or non-development are consistent across agencies. In both state police and highway patrol agencies the most frequent reason provided for not having implemented policies regarding the employment of HIV positive persons was a lack of perceived need (50% and 43% respectively). Regional analysis shows in the East, Midwest and South the primary cited reason for not having a policy on the employment of HIV positive individuals is a lack of need (50%, 50% and 66% respectively). However, in the West region the only cited reason is a belief the Americans with Disabilities Act and/or Equal Employment Opportunity Commission prohibit such policies. Interestingly, the only other references to these reasons are provided by 38 percent of the East region agencies without such a policy.

CONCLUSIONS

Over a decade has passed since the medical and law enforcement communities first became aware of, and concerned about, the implications of HIV/AIDS for police officers. As a result of these concerns, a number of policies and standards have been implemented specifically addressing the training and employment issues relating to what the medical community has labeled the most serious public health threat today. Although a majority of state police organizations have implemented training, fewer agencies have adopted policies informing sworn officers how to deal with persons suspected of, or known to have, HIV/AIDS, even though national standards and model policies have existed for over a year. Even fewer agencies report having policies addressing the employment of HIV/AIDS employees, although no single reason for not having such policies surfaces.

While the clear majority of state police agencies are offering some training to their officers, either in basic or in-service training, the instruction varies widely in terms of both quality and quantity, and a wide variety of source materials currently exist. Course materials range from simple handwritten outlines to elaborate training manuals over 100 pages in length. Some incorporate superb, professionally produced, video tapes. A handful even offer instruction by personnel from the medical community. Further evaluation of the content of the instruction is not only needed but warranted by the noticeable lack of uniformity. Standardization, by either the national medical or law enforcement community, is essential. While training, and to some degree course content, has been mandated by OSHA and developed by the IACP, little has been done to ensure agencies, state or otherwise, are adhering to the federal mandates or instructing recommended topics.

Many state police organizations have been woefully remiss in implementing policies addressing the employment of HIV/AIDS employees. Furthermore, the dearth of policies cannot be traced to a universal underlying reason founded in either law or practice. Rather, a variety of reasons are offered. Ironically, federal statutes such as the ADA are cited both as a reason *for* adopting employment policies and as a reason *not* to adopt such a policy. Agencies without policies appear to be offering excuses, rather than justifications, for their lack of implementation, or it could be argued that these agencies are engaged in collective denial of the simple reality that HIV positive persons will be in their employ. Given the breadth and depth of the HIV/AIDS issue, common sense dictates agencies should be considering the implications of having employees who have HIV disease. Although the risk of a job-related infection for an employee appears to be nearly infinitesimal (certainly significantly less than the risk of contracting Hepatitis-B, for instance), the law enforcement community must acknowledge and address the real likelihood that:

- HIV/AIDS applicants will seek employment; and
- current employees may contract HIV through non-job related transmission processes.

Furthermore, given the current costs of, and efforts to reorganize, health insurance, state (as well as municipal and urban) agencies must seriously consider the HIV/AIDS implications for health insurance.

In conclusion, law enforcement leaders must ask, as virtually every other employer has – how will HIV/AIDS affect my employees and my business? What can I do now to minimize liability and increase employee safety? Are my training practices sufficient to meet the needs of my employees? Are we meeting national standards and adhering to federal and state training requirements? Are my policies and practices in compliance with current legal mandates? To date, this evaluation of state police efforts seems to suggest that the law enforcement community in general, and many state police organizations in particular, are unable, or unwilling, to address some of these questions.

NOTES

1. Now known as the US Centers for Disease Control and Prevention.

2. It is beyond the scope of this research paper to address the medical background of either HIV or AIDS. Numerous articles and books exist addressing, in great detail, such medical issues as theories regarding origins, methods of transmission, how the human body is affected, which groups are "at risk", symptoms, testing and research, and incidence. For a superb discussion of the medical issues related to HIV/AIDS, see Blumberg (1990).

3. Hawaii has no police organization equivalent to a true state police agency.

4. States classified as "state police" are: Alaska, Arkansas, Connecticut, Delaware, Idaho, Illinois, Indiana, Kentucky, Louisiana, Maine, Maryland, Massachusetts, Michigan, New Hampshire, New Jersey, New Mexico, New York, Oregon, Pennsylvania, Rhode Island, Vermont, Virginia and West Virginia. States classified as "highway patrol" are: Alabama, Arizona, California, Colorado, Florida, Georgia, Iowa, Kansas, Minnesota, Mississippi, Missouri, Montana, Nebraska, Nevada, North Carolina, North Dakota, Ohio, Oklahoma, South Carolina, South Dakota, Tennessee, Texas, Utah, Washington, Wisconsin and Wyoming.

5. West region states are: Alaska, Arizona, California, Colorado, Idaho, Montana, Nevada, New Mexico, Utah, Oregon and Washington; Midwest region states are: Indiana, Illinois, Iowa, Kansas, Michigan, Nebraska, North Dakota; Minnesota,

Missouri, Ohio and South Dakota; East region states are: Connecticut, Delaware, Maine, Maryland, Massachusetts, New Hampshire, New York, New Jersey, Pennsylvania, Rhode Island and Vermont; South region states are: Alabama, Arkansas, Florida, Georgia, Kentucky, Louisiana, Mississippi, North Carolina, Oklahoma, South Carolina, Tennessee, Texas, Virginia and West Virginia.

REFERENCES

Barr, J.K. and Warshaw, L.J. (1994), "Worksite AIDS Education: A Case Study of the New York City Police", *AIDS Education and Prevention*, 6(1):53-64.

Benny, D.J. (1993), "The Bloodborne Pathogens Act", *FBI Law Enforcement Bulletin*, May 62(5):16-18.

Bigbee, D. (1993), "Pathogenic Microorganisms: Law Enforcement's Silent Enemies", *FBI Law Enforcement Bulletin*, May 62(5):1-5.

Bigbee, D. (1991), *The Law Enforcement Officer and AIDS*, Washington, DC: Federal Bureau of Investigation.

Bigbee, D. (1987), "Collecting and Handling Evidence Infected with Human Disease Causing Organisms", *FBI Law Enforcement Bulletin*, July 56(7): 1-5.

Blumberg, M. (1990), *AIDS: The Impact on the Criminal Justice System*, Columbus, OH: Merrill Publishing Company.

California Department of Health Services (1988), *Public Safety Workers and AIDS*, (3rd ed.) May: California Firefighters Foundation.

Department of Labor, Occupational Safety and Health Administration (1991), *Occupational Exposure to Bloodborne Pathogens*, 29 CFR 1910.1030. Washington, DC: Department of Labor, Occupational Safety and Health Administration.

Edwards, T.D. (1993), "State Police Basic Training Programs: An Assessment of Course Content and Instructional Methodology", *American Journal of Police*, 12(4):23-45.

Gates, D.F. and Lady, K.E. (1991), "Enhancing AIDS Awareness in Los Angeles", *The Police Chief*, 18 (3):44-47.

Hammett, T.M. (1987a), *AIDS in Correctional Facilities: Issues and Options*, Washington, DC: National Institute of Justice.

Hammett, T.M. (1987b), *AIDS and the Law Enforcement Officer: Concerns and Policy Responses*, Washington, DC: National Institute of Justice.

Hammett, T.M. (1988), *1988 Update: AIDS in Correctional Facilities*, Washington, DC: National Institute of Justice.

Hammett, T.M. (1994), *1992 Update: HIV/AIDS in Correctional Facilities*, Washington, DC: National Institute of Justice.

International Association of Chiefs of Police (1975), *Comparative Data Report – 1974*. Alexandria, VA: IACP, Division of State and Provincial Police.

International Association of Chiefs of Police (1989), *Model Policy – Communicable Disease*, Alexandria, VA: IACP, National Law Enforcement Policy Center.

International Association of Chiefs of Police (1990), "Communicable Disease", *Concepts and Issues Paper*, Alexandria, VA: IACP, National Law Enforcement Policy Center.

International Association of Chiefs of Police (1992), *Model Policy – Prevention of Bloodborne Diseases*, Alexandria, VA: IACP, National Law Enforcement Policy Center.

International Association of Chiefs of Police (1993), "Prevention of Bloodborne Diseases", *Concepts and Issues Paper*, Alexandria: IACP, National Law Enforcement Policy Center.

Jarvis, R.M., Closen, M.L., Hermann, D.H.J. and Leonard, A.S. (1991), *AIDS Law*, St. Paul, MN: West Publishing Company.

Kennedy, D., Homant, R. and Emery, G. (1990), "AIDS Concerns among Crime Scene Investigators", *Journal of Police Science and Administration*, 17(1):12-19.

Kime, R.C. (1993), "New Regulations Covering Emergency Response Employees", *The Police Chief*, 2 (12):12.

Laszlo, A. and Ayers, M. (1986), *AIDS: Improving the Response of the Criminal Justice System*, Alexandria, VA: National Sheriffs Association.

Sheridan, K., Lyons, J.S., Fitzgibbon, M., Sheridan, E. and McCarthy, M. (1989), "Effects of AIDS Education on Police Officers' Perceptions of Risk", *Public Health Reports*, 104:521-522.

Sinkfield, R.H. and Houser, T.L. (1989), "AIDS and the Criminal Justice System", *The Journal of Legal Medicine*, 10(1):103-125.

Stewart, J.D. (1993), "Bloodborne Diseases: Developing a Training Curriculum", *FBI Law Enforcement Bulletin*, May 62(5):11-15.

US Department of Health and Human Services (1989), *A Curriculum Guide for Public-Safety and Emergency Response Workers*, Atlanta, GA: US Department of Health and Human Services, Center for Disease Control.

US Department of Health and Human Services (1994), *HIV/AIDS Surveillance Report*, 5(4). Atlanta, GA: US Department of Health and Human Services, Center for Disease Control.

Wrobleski, H. and Hess, K. (1990), *Introduction to Law Enforcement and Criminal Justice* (3rd ed.), St. Paul, MN: West Publishing.

Yearwood, D.L. (1992), "Law Enforcement and AIDS: Knowledge, Attitudes, and Fears in the Workplace", *American Journal of Police*, 11(2): 65-83.

[20]

HIV/AIDS EDUCATION NEEDS ASSESSMENT: A COMPARATIVE STUDY OF JAIL AND PRISON INMATES IN NORTHWEST FLORIDA

KATO B. KEETON
CHERYL SWANSON

To ascertain HIV/AIDS knowledge levels and the education needs of inmates in four jails and two state prisons in northwest Florida, a needs assessment instrument was administered on-site. Because prison inmates receive HIV/AIDS education at intake, it was hypothesized that this group would have greater knowledge levels than jail inmates. On the whole, knowledge levels were good in both groups, with prison inmates scoring somewhat better than jail inmates. Of the 24 items on the questionnaire, only six questions resulted in statistically significant differences. Of these, three were questions representing high-risk situations, two were low-risk situations, and one represented a no-risk or minimal-risk situation. Item analysis of the questions on which there were lower percentages of correct answers or a somewhat large percentage of not sure responses resulted in the conclusion that HIV/AIDS education needs to focus more on discriminating between differing levels of risk and identifying appropriate behaviors for varying risk levels. Specific recommendations for HIV/AIDS education in jails and prisons are offered.

Although HIV/AIDS is considered a serious health problem for the nation at large, the problem is amplified within America's jail and prison facilities, where the rate of HIV infection has been estimated to be as great as six times that of the general population (Vlahov, 1990). The reason for this is that incarcerated populations exhibit high-risk behavior, primarily because of intravenous drug use. In 1994, 22.3% of inmates in state correctional facilities were incarcerated for drug-related offenses (Bureau of Justice Statistics, 1996). Clientele with high-risk profiles for HIV infection also frequent local jails (i.e., those arrested on drug-related charges and for prostitution), usually as short-term residents. Among jail inmates who have been tested for HIV/AIDS, those held for drug offenses are the most likely to be HIV positive (Maruschak, 1997). In 1993, the incidence of AIDS among a sample of correctional facilities was estimated at 11,656 inmates, an increase of 66% over the numbers reported in 1990 (Hammett & Daugherty, 1991; Hammett, Harold, Gross, & Epstein, 1994). Recent estimates from the Bureau of Justice Statistics (Maruschak, 1997) place the percentage of all state and federal prison inmates with AIDS at 2.3% at year-end 1995. A survey of jail inmates in 1996 showed that almost 6 of 10 had been tested for AIDS, and among that population, 2.2% were HIV positive (Maruschak, 1997).

Inmates in correctional facilities are considered good candidates for meaningful AIDS prevention through education. Because the vast majority of inmates will eventually reenter society, it makes sense to use the time they are incarcerated productively to educate inmates about the dangers of HIV/AIDS and precautions that can be taken to reduce the risk of infection (Martin, 1995). Although many jail detainees are technically not guilty and are classified as pretrial, in 1996, 49% of inmates under jail supervision had been convicted and were serving sentences of a year or less in the facility, serving a sentence in an alternative program outside a jail facility, or awaiting sentencing (Gilliard & Beck, 1997). Of 1,630,940 persons incarcerated in 1996, one third were held in local jails (Gilliard & Beck, 1997). Thus, the jail as well as the prison population should be considered candidates for AIDS education.

The levels of knowledge of HIV and AIDS among incarcerated populations are not well documented, particularly among jail inmates. This study reports the results of a needs assessment survey designed to ascertain levels of knowledge about HIV and AIDS among jail and prison inmates in northwest Florida. Because jails are locally operated correctional facilities that confine persons before and after adjudication, it was predicted that inmates in the state prison system—with its more stable population, long-term residents, central administration, and more established education policies—would have better knowledge of HIV and AIDS. Attention was given to the content of the inmates' knowledge base in both types of institutions, with particular concern for facts and skills necessary to assess levels of risky behaviors and then determine appropriate behavior modification. Recommendations are made for more effective HIV/AIDS education in correctional facilities.

PREVIOUS RESEARCH ON HIV/AIDS EDUCATION IN CONFINEMENT FACILITIES

A number of comparative descriptive studies have attempted to survey AIDS education in U.S. prisons. A study by Martin, Zimmerman, and Long

(1993) found that most states provided some form of AIDS education for inmates, but few prison systems actually knew what kind of impact their programs were having. In a 1994 review of HIV/AIDS education programs in prisons and jails, Hammett (1996) used a twofold classification of these programs—interactive (e.g., peer-led programs and instructor-led sessions such as lectures, discussions, or question-and-answer periods) and passive programs (e.g., use of videotapes, other audiovisual materials, or written materials). Hammett found that many facilities have not provided interactive programs, noting in particular that peer-led programs may be more credible and effective than those provided by staff employed by the corrections facilities. Additional problem areas have been identified with AIDS education in prisons. These include the fact that attendance in programs is not always mandatory (Hammett & Daugherty, 1991), many inmates may receive as little as 1 hour of AIDS education during a year (Hammett & Daugherty, 1991), and many educational efforts do not provide specific information about reducing the risks of HIV transmission (Hammett & Daugherty, 1991; Martin & Zimmerman, 1990; Vaid, 1987).

As mentioned, very few corrections systems have conducted evaluations of their programs. Some studies have attempted to measure the knowledge level of inmates about AIDS transmission. Inferences are then made about strengths and deficits in corrections education programs. Zimmerman, Martin, and Vlahov (1991) reported that among Pennsylvania prisoners, inmates were very knowledgeable about high-risk behaviors related to contracting the HIV virus. However, they were much less knowledgeable about behaviors that pose a low risk or no risk of HIV transmission. Zimmerman et al. note that these kinds of knowledge deficits can pose a problem in prison settings where unsubstantiated fears can contribute to management problems in the institutions. The authors point to the importance of scoring AIDS knowledge questions separately by content areas, including general AIDS knowledge, normal HIV transmission routes, unlikely AIDS transmission routes, and HIV prevention methods (Zimmerman et al., 1991, p. 239). Using anecdotal information from a counseling session with inmates in a county jail, Hogan (1994) observed that although inmates had a high knowledge of HIV/AIDS subject matter in general, most misinterpreted how to apply the basics to their own lives.

In a comparative study of HIV knowledge among incarcerated youth in San Francisco and Alabama (considered high- and low-risk locales, respectively), Lanier, Diclemente, and Horan (1991) reported similar findings. Youth in both sites had fairly good knowledge levels about high-risk behaviors and basic knowledge about AIDS. However, accuracy rates were considerably lower for unlikely transmission routes. After reviewing several studies

(Celentano, Brewer, Sonnega, & Vlahov, 1990; Lanier et al., 1991; Valdiserri, Hartl, & Chambliss, 1988; Zimmerman et al., 1991) on HIV knowledge among prisoners, Martin et al. (1993) concluded that

> although it is true that, in some areas, knowledge levels are consistently high (e.g. general knowledge about HIV and AIDS), there are other knowledge domains in which inmates (and others) still exhibit deficits and misconceptions (e.g. unlikely routes of transmission). (p. 107)

The authors note that there continues to be a substantial amount of fear and anxiety about contracting the disease. As mentioned earlier, these emotions can be particularly problematic in a corrections setting.

Finally, there are very little data on the behavioral impact of prison-based AIDS education programs. Lanier et al. (1991) found that although knowledge about reducing the risk of contracting HIV was higher among incarcerated youth in San Francisco than among the Alabama sample, Alabama youth were more likely to report the use of condoms during sexual intercourse. This suggests that knowledge is not a sufficient motivator of behavior change. Similar implications were reported for a study of Scottish prisoners (Power, Markova, McKee, & Kilfedder, 1996) where high levels of knowledge were positively correlated with high-risk behaviors. Mahon (1996) reports similar findings among New York state prisoners. This suggests the need to target prison-based education programs to "realistic risk reduction strategies" (Lanier et al., 1991).

THE STUDY

To learn more about HIV/AIDS knowledge levels and education needs among jail and prison populations, inmates of four county jails and two state prisons located in northwest Florida were studied in an HIV/AIDS education needs assessment. A 25-item paper-and-pencil questionnaire was administered; 23 items measured HIV/AIDS knowledge, 1 item measured attitudes toward persons with HIV/AIDS, and 1 item gauged the number of formal classes each inmate had experienced. Additional information on gender and institution was recorded separately by the researchers. A goal of a random sample from each of the six facilities could not be fully met. With each facility, participation of inmates had to be on a voluntary basis.

The largest jail, with an inmate population of 1,400, randomly generated the names of 100 individuals to participate in the study. However, only 30 showed up when small groups were escorted to a classroom. Jail personnel were not interested in identifying a second sample. The other three jails are much smaller (populations ranging from 75 to 440), and procedures for surveying inmates targeted the entire population. In two of the three locations, the researchers, accompanied by one or two correctional officers, administered the survey in the dormitories/cells. In the smallest facility, inmates were allowed to leave the dormitory areas to convene in the cafeteria. Approximately two thirds of the inmates in each of the smaller jails participated in the study.

The two state prisons (average population 1,000) were handled somewhat like the largest jail in that a random sample of 100 inmates was generated, and prisoners were escorted in small groups to a classroom. Participation rates were significantly higher, with 98 of the 100 inmates at each facility attending a session in which the survey was administered. Work details precluded full participation.

Because of concerns about participation in the study, information that might be construed as personal was not asked of inmates. Thus, data on age and race are estimated. Record keeping by the researchers on gender and the facility of incarceration was done during data collection, resulting in precise data (see Table 1). The majority of inmate participants (both males and females) at the largest jail are African American, and the majority of participant inmates (both males and females) at the smaller jails are White. The typical age of all jail inmates is early to mid-20s. The majority of participants in the two state prisons are African American and male. About 5% are Hispanic. The typical age of state prisoners participating in the study is mid-20s to early 30s. The race and age characteristics of participants are consistent with the characteristics of the jail and prison populations.

The jails have no AIDS education policy, whereas all inmates entering a Florida state prison are exposed to AIDS education at intake. In viewing data on AIDS education classes taken, inmates in the jails averaged almost one class less than those in the prisons. However, the number of prisoners saying they had no AIDS education class was just more than 30%, even though they were told that the AIDS education exposure they experienced at intake counted as one. Several inmates made a statement to the effect that they did not consider what was provided at intake as an AIDS class.

The survey instrument measured knowledge about HIV/AIDS and the transmission of HIV in clusters of questions that are categorized as high- or low-risk situations. Another cluster of questions measured knowledge of HIV/AIDS that gauged situations of minimal or no risk. One no-risk question measured attitudes toward persons with HIV/AIDS. Response choices were true, false, and not sure. For many questions, not sure was circled by a very small proportion of participants (5% or less). Thus, for purposes of statistical analysis, this answer choice is not included. However, in a general discussion

TABLE 1: Characteristics of Jails and Prisons Inmates

	Jails	*Prisons*
Male (%)	85.5	100
Female (%)	14.5	0
Mean number of HIV/AIDS classes	.8	1.7
% of those having zero classes	64.2	30.3
n	310	195

of the responses and in providing recommendations for HIV/AIDS education in jail and prison settings, not sure responses representing at least 10% of participants in either group are discussed.

Prior to administering the survey, time was spent talking with each group of inmates to gain greater participation and attempt to build some rapport with each group. The survey was administered in small groups to same-gender inmates. The instrument's questions were written in short statements using language that was simple and familiar to inmates. A font size of 16 was used to make reading the instrument easier. In addition, the questionnaire was read aloud to all groups. Inmate translators were available in the state prisons to work with the Hispanic participants who did not speak English. In the process of administering the survey, if a term was not fully understood, that term was explained. At the conclusion of the survey, all instruments were collected, and then a discussion session was held. Inmates could ask questions about the survey or other HIV/AIDS-related questions they thought of during the completion of the survey.

DATA ANALYSIS

General information on percentages of the correct or preferred response to questions is provided in Table 2. To test for hypothesized differences in HIV/AIDS educational levels between jail and prison populations, a t test was used. Because of the paucity of literature from jail settings and concerns about the quality of HIV/AIDS education in the two prisons studied, a two-tailed test of significance was adopted. Results on statistically significant differences ($p \leq .05$) of individual questions representing each cluster (high-, low-, and minimal- or no-risk situations) are reported in Tables 3 through 5. To provide a basis for specific HIV/AIDS education recommendations, an item analysis of the questions on which less than 80% gave the correct or preferred responses is presented later in Table 6.

TABLE 2: Jails and Prisons Inmates' Responses to HIV/AIDS Education Needs Assessment Questions

	% True		*% False*		*% Not Sure*	
Questions	*Jails*	*Prisons*	*Jails*	*Prisons*	*Jails*	*Prisons*
From sitting next to someone with AIDS	1.9	0.5	95.5[a]	99.0	2.6	0.5
From intimate sex between heterosexuals	94.2[a]	92.3	4.2	4.6	1.6	3.1
From intimate sex between homosexuals	97.1[a]	99.0	2.3	0.5	0.6	0.5
From food prepared by someone with AIDS	14.3	5.6	73.6[a]	82.1	12.1	12.3
From mosquito and other insect bites	26.4	18.7	55.4[a]	67.4	18.2	14.0
From kissing	25.1	18.0	60.3[a]	73.2	14.7	8.8
From sharing plates, knives, and forks	10.7	8.8	76.1[a]	86.1	13.3	5.2
From saliva (spitting, drinking after someone with AIDS)	36.7	27.7	45.9[a]	58.5	17.4	13.8
From selling or donating blood	68.2	62.4	28.2[a]	34.5	3.6	3.1
From money handled by someone with AIDS	2.6	3.1	95.5[a]	95.9	1.9	1.0
From sneezes and coughs	10.4	4.7	78.0[a]	88.1	11.7	7.3
From having sex with someone you know	86.1[a]	85.1	10.6	14.4	3.2	0.5
From having sex while under the influence of drugs/alcohol	80.7[a]	87.7	14.1	10.3	5.2	2.1
From sharing needles	99.4[a]	99.5	0.6	0.0	0.0	0.5
From tattooing or body piercing	81.4[a]	95.4	10.1	0.5	8.5	4.1
From a monogamous/ faithful partner	49.3	37.2	41.7[a]	51.8	8.9	11.0
From having unprotected anal sex	94.5[a]	98.5	3.2	0.5	2.3	1.0
From a blow job	66.8[a]	66.0	18.6	18.6	14.7	15.5
From the first time having sex with an infected person	94.8[a]	92.3	2.6	2.1	2.6	5.7
Sex with a condom reduces the risk of AIDS infection	90.3[a]	94.3	6.2	5.2	3.6	0.5
Early testing may prolong the life of a person with AIDS	76.5[a]	81.5	12.1	8.7	11.4	9.7
Males are more likely to get AIDS than females	13.4	21.8	63.1[a]	54.9	23.5	23.3
The AIDS virus is easy to kill	16.8[a]	18.5	78.6	77.9	4.5	3.6
Persons with AIDS should be quarantined from those who don't have AIDS	31.0	35.1	56.5[a]	53.6	12.4	11.3

NOTE: Jails: $n = 310$. Prisons: $n = 195$. Total: $N = 505$.
a. Represents correct or preferred response.

A review of Table 2 shows that, in general, HIV/AIDS education levels among jail and prison inmates are high. This is consistent with the literature, most of which reports data gathered from prisons on site-specific programs (e.g., Lanier et al., 1991; Martin et al., 1993; Zimmerman et al., 1991). For most questions, a majority gave the correct or preferred answer, with prison inmates doing somewhat better than those in the county jails. Despite the reluctance to count the AIDS education provided at intake, apparently exposure to information about HIV/AIDS at intake has some effect on prisoners' knowledge levels.

The most glaring exceptions to the generalization about reasonably high knowledge levels are questions gauging the risk of donating or selling blood (clearly differentiated from a blood transfusion in administering the survey) and ease of killing the virus that causes AIDS. The statement, "The AIDS virus is easy to kill," was considered a trick question by some inmates. During the debriefing in which questions were answered, it was explained that this is a highly discriminating question, albeit a difficult one. The only situation in which one can talk about killing the virus is outside the body; we have no known evidence that HIV can be killed while in the body.

NOT SURE RESPONSES

Ten percent or more of participants (in at least one group) answered not sure (see Table 2) to 11 questions. These are the following:

1. food prepared by someone with HIV/AIDS;
2. mosquito and other insect bites;
3. kissing;
4. sharing plates, knives, and forks;
5. saliva;
6. sneezes and coughs;
7. monogamous/faithful partner;
8. blow job;
9. early testing may prolong the life of an infected person;
10. males are more likely to get AIDS than females; and
11. persons with AIDS should be quarantined.

One of these questions, blow job, involves a high-risk behavior situation; three involve low-risk behaviors (numbers 3, 5, and 6); and eight involve minimal- or no-risk situations (numbers 1, 2, 4, and 7-11).

It is clear from the number of minimal- or no-risk questions in which not sure was answered (7 of the 11 questions identified above) that HIV/AIDS

TABLE 3: *t* Test of Jail and Prison Inmates' Responses to HIV/AIDS Education Needs Assessment Questions Measuring High-Risk Situations

Questions	t *Value*	df	*Two-Tailed Significance*
Under influence of drugs/alcohol	2.40	485	.017
Tattoo	4.06	499	.0009
Anal sex	2.11	501	.036

NOTE: Only statistically significant differences at $p \leq .05$ reported.

education needs to emphasize minimal- and no-risk situations. Similarly, low-risk situations need attention, too. Indeed, 10 of the 11 questions comprising this not sure analysis fall into these two risk categories. These findings are consistent with those of Zimmerman et al. (1991) and Hogan (1994).

Apparently, participants are fairly confident of their knowledge of high-risk situations, judging from the relatively few not sure responses to questions representing this category. Analysis of the correct or preferred responses on these questions confirms that 90% or more replied correctly to most high-risk questions. These results are consistent with findings of earlier studies (e.g., Celentano et al., 1990; Hogan, 1994; Lanier et al., 1991; Martin et al., 1993; Valdiserri et al., 1988; Zimmerman et al., 1991).

CLUSTERS MEASURING RISK LEVELS

Nine behaviorally related questions measured high-risk situations for the transmission of HIV. Table 3 reports statistically significant responses between jail and prison inmates. Of the nine questions, answers to three were significantly different to meet the test of statistical difference. These are AIDS can be gotten from (a) sex while under the influence of drugs/alcohol, (b) tattooing, and (c) anal sex. On each question, significantly more prison inmates answered correctly when compared with jail inmates.

A cluster of six low-risk questions was analyzed to ascertain differences between responses of jail and prison inmates. Responses to two questions were statistically different. These questions asked about HIV transmission from a faithful partner and the use of condoms in preventing HIV infection. Again, prison inmates were more knowledgeable (see Table 4).

The final cluster of nine questions measured no- or minimal-risk situations. Of these, only one resulted in statistically significant responses between jail and prison inmates. The question asked whether HIV/AIDS can be gotten from food prepared by an infected person. As with the previous questions measuring high- and low-risk situations, more prison inmates answered this question correctly (see Table 5).

TABLE 4: *t* Test of Jail and Prison Inmates' Responses to HIV/AIDS Education Needs Assessment Measuring Low-Risk Situations

Questions	t *Value*	df	*Two-Tailed Significance*
Faithful partner	−2.38	491	.018
Using condoms	2.30	499	.022

NOTE: Only statistically significant differences at $p \leq .05$ reported.

TABLE 5: *t* Test of Jail and Prison Inmates' Responses to HIV/AIDS Education Needs Assessment Measuring No-Risk Situations

Questions	t *Value*	df	*Two-Tailed Significance*
Food prepared by infected person	−2.40	500	.042

NOTE: Only statistically significant differences at $p \leq .05$ reported.

ITEM ANALYSIS

Table 6 contains those questions that were answered correctly by less than 80% of the jail and/or prison inmates. The 80% target was selected to reflect differences in educational levels and expected retention levels among participants.

Of the 13 questions on which less than 80% of correct or preferred responses were made by at least one group (jail inmates, prison inmates), 8 (61.5%) fall into the minimal- or no-risk category, and 4 (30.8%) are representative of low-risk situations. Only one high-risk behavior question (HIV infection from oral sex/blow job) was answered incorrectly by a large number of inmates. Approximately one third of the participants in each group did not know that HIV infection can occur through oral sex.

Interesting patterns evolve from the analysis of items in Table 6. First is the number of minimal- or no-risk questions with which participants had problems. The myth of HIV infection from a mosquito or other insect bite is alive and well, as is confusion between blood transfusions and donating blood. Concern about food prepared by persons with AIDS (PWAs) and sharing plates and utensils with PWAs was higher among jail inmates.

A second interesting pattern is the lack of ability to discriminate between similar situations that fall within the same risk classification. Participants had problems with questions relating HIV transmission via saliva, sneezes and coughs, and kissing—all activities involving saliva dispersion. In addition, a number of participants responded not sure to these three items. More correct

TABLE 6: Item Analysis of Less Than 80% Correct or Preferred Responses

Question	*% Correct Jail Inmates*	*% Correct Prison Inmates*
Food prepared by person with AIDS (PWA)[a]	73.6	82.1
Sharing plates and utensils[a]	76.1	86.1
Saliva[b]	45.9	58.5
Sneezes and coughs[b]	78.0	88.1
Kissing[b]	60.3	73.2
Faithful partner[b]	41.7	51.8
Blow job[c]	66.8	66.0
Mosquito/insect bites[a]	55.4	67.4
Selling/donating blood[a]	28.2	34.5
Benefits of early testing[a]	76.5	81.5
Males more likely to get AIDS[a]	63.1	54.9
AIDS virus easy to kill[a]	16.8	18.5
Quarantine PWAs[a]	56.5	53.6

a. Indicates questions that measure no- or minimal-risk situations for contracting HIV or measure objective knowledge about HIV.
b. Indicates questions that measure low-risk situations for contracting HIV.
c. Indicates questions that measure high-risk situations for contracting HIV.

responses were given to the sneezes and coughs question followed by kissing. Markedly fewer respondents answered the saliva question correctly, and more indicated they were unsure about saliva and HIV transmission.

CONCLUSIONS

A clear outcome of this research is the relatively high levels of knowledge about HIV/AIDS in incarcerated populations, regardless of exposure to formal AIDS education programs. As discussed earlier, this conclusion is consistent with studies of AIDS education programs in prison settings. To our knowledge, similar studies of jail populations are virtually nonexistent.

However, a major problem identified in this research is the inability of jail and prison inmates to differentiate between risk situations, thereby possibly creating various levels of uncertainty as to appropriate behaviors. This inability is evident in divergent responses to various questions alluding to similar situations (e.g., saliva) and was underscored in discussions with inmates that followed the administration of the survey.

Given the substantial dollar amounts devoted to AIDS education in Florida and elsewhere, the question that looms is, Why do HIV infection rates continue to increase when HIV/AIDS knowledge levels are relatively high? And, particularly, why are certain populations (incarcerated individuals) considered at higher risk and, indeed, higher rates of HIV are showing up in these populations?

The plethora of reasons underlying this phenomenon of increasing rates of HIV infection will not be explored here. The focus of this study is AIDS education needs. It is apparent that current HIV/AIDS education is not effective among this high-risk population. That is, behavior changes are not consistent with knowledge levels. A review of the state of Florida's AIDS education curriculum (State of Florida, 1996) and observation of dozens of training sessions reveal that AIDS information and specific scenarios are presented, but no tools and experiences are provided to participants whereby they learn to discriminate between different risk situations. Thus, through rote memorization, typical participants know that "you can't get AIDS from money handled by someone with AIDS," yet many do not know the high risk of infection via oral sex. Indeed, oral sex is not a behavior addressed in the Florida curriculum (Florida Department of Health, 1995). Without question, analysis of the questions about the transmission of HIV via saliva, sneezes and coughs, and kissing underscores the lack of ability to discriminate.

The number of high-risk persons "passing through" our jails strongly suggests the need for an HIV/AIDS education policy in each local jail. And, as with those in the general population (Keeton & Brewton, 1995), it is clear that AIDS education should be radically revised for jail and prison inmates and recognize differing needs of men and women. In fact, Florida law (Sec. 381.0038, Fla. Stat., 1995) requires training sessions to be modified to address the needs of diverse groups. However, there is no evidence (from telephone interviews with corporate executive officers of AIDS education and service organizations throughout the state) that this law is widely adhered to by those providing education.

Given that general knowledge of HIV and AIDS is quite good, AIDS education delivered in a corrections setting should review the basic facts and devote the majority of sessions to teaching inmates about the characteristics of HIV (e.g., the environment required for it to survive and multiply) and how to differentiate between risk situations. Thus, knowing that HIV requires a warm, moist, white blood cell rich environment to flourish and cannot survive for longer than 60 seconds outside that environment, it becomes easy to assess the risks of infection from food prepared by PWAs compared to engaging in oral sex, for example. Similarly, providing information on why HIV is not transmitted through mosquito or other insect bites should help convince individuals of that fact. Also, more detailed information about collection procedures used by blood banks should dispel the widespread notion that one is at high risk for HIV if selling or donating blood. Furthermore, information should clarify differences between fresh blood on an open cut, the one-way process of giving blood in a sterile environment, and the now limited risks of blood transmissions. Finally, AIDS education should focus on the various types of sexual behavior and why all are high-risk situations. Clearly, the general statement that HIV infection occurs through the exchange of body fluids is not sufficient information for the typical inmate to assess the various types of sexual behavior accurately and without hesitation.

In addition, the literature (e.g., Hogan, 1994; Saltz, Perry, & Cabral, 1994; Shaw, 1988) notes the importance of repetition and varying methodologies of teaching for individuals of diverse backgrounds and intellectual capabilities to learn. Consistent with Hammett's (1996) conclusions in a study of prison inmates, this suggests that HIV/AIDS education in jails and prisons needs to be delivered in multiple sessions and via teaching methods appropriate for this group. A conversation with one of the jail nurses underscored the need for diverse teaching methods. For jail inmates, her experiences led to the recommendation of the almost exclusive use of audiovisuals. In particular, she suggested the use of videotaping to maximize involvement of inmates from the beginning of the education sessions.

RECOMMENDATIONS

Analyses of surveys and conversations with inmates and jail/prison staff suggest the following actions:

- Adopt a policy of HIV/AIDS education programs delivered in jail settings.
- Ascertain specific information requirements (e.g., using needs assessment techniques such as surveys and focus groups) in addition to the basic information that would be delivered in HIV/AIDS education sessions.
- Deliver HIV/AIDS education in multiple sessions over time.
- Incorporate active learning techniques in the delivery of education.
- Teach skills to discriminate between risk levels of a wide range of situations.
- Teach the hows and whys of HIV/AIDS risk situations/behaviors.
- Focus HIV/AIDS education on topics consistent with the needs of the target population (e.g., IV drug use, oral and anal sex, infection risks from fighting).

REFERENCES

Bureau of Justice Statistics. (1996). *Correctional populations in the United States, 1994.* Washington, DC: U.S. Department of Justice.

Celentano, D., Brewer, T., Sonnega, J., & Vlahov, D. (1990). Maryland inmates knowledge of HIV transmission and prevention: A comparison with the U.S. general population. *Journal of Prison and Jail Health, 9,* 45-54.

Florida Department of Health. (1995). *AIDS-104 instructor's guide*. Tallahassee, FL: Department of State.

Florida Statute. Sec. 381.0038 (1995).

Hammett, T. (1996). HIV/AIDS education and prevention programs for adults in prisons and jails and juveniles in confinement facilities—United States, 1994. *Morbidity and Mortality Weekly Report, 45*, 268-271.

Hammett, T., & Daugherty, C. (1991). *1990 update: AIDS in correctional facilities*. Washington, DC: U.S. Department of Justice.

Hammett, T., Harold, L., Gross, M., & Epstein, J. (1994). *1992 update: HIV/AIDS in correctional facilities*. Washington, DC: National Institute of Justice.

Hogan, N. (1994). HIV education for inmates: Uncovering strategies for program selection. *The Prison Journal, 74*, 220-243.

Keeton, K., & Brewton, D. (1995). A comparative analysis of AIDS related attitudes between public and private sector employees. *Review of Public Personnel Administration, 15*, 44-59.

Lanier, M., Diclemente, R., & Horan, P. (1991). HIV knowledge and behaviors of incarcerated youth: A comparison of high and low risk locales. *Journal of Criminal Justice, 19*, 257-262.

Mahon, N. (1996). New York inmates: HIV risk behaviors: The implications for prevention policy and programs. *American Journal of Public Health, 86*, 1211-1215.

Martin, R. (1995). A content assessment and comparative analysis of prison-based AIDS education programs for inmates. *The Prison Journal, 75*, 5-45.

Martin, R., & Zimmerman, S. (1990). Adopting precautions against HIV infection among male prisoners: A behavioral and policy analysis. *Criminal Justice Policy Review, 4*, 330-348.

Martin, R., Zimmerman, S., & Long, B. (1993). AIDS education in U.S. prisons: A survey of inmate programs. *The Prison Journal, 73*, 103-129.

Maruschak, L. (1997). *HIV in prisons and jails, 1995*. Washington, DC: U.S. Department of Justice.

Power, K., Markova, I., McKee, K., & Kilfedder, C. (1996). Correlates of HIV/AIDS knowledge in a Scottish prison sample. *Health Education Research, 11*, 287-297.

Saltz, E., Perry, A., & Cabral, R. (1994). Attacking the personal fable: Role-play and its effect on teen attitudes toward sexual abstinence. *Youth and Society, 26*, 223-242.

Shaw, N. (1988). Preventing AIDS among women: The role of community organizing. *Socialist Review, 100*, 77-92.

State of Florida. (1996). *AIDS 104*. Tallahassee, FL: Department of State.

Vaid, U. (1987). Prisons. In B. S. Dalton & Yale AIDS Law Project (Eds.), *AIDS and the law* (pp. 235-250). New Haven, CT: Yale University Press.

Valdiserri, E., Hartl, A., & Chambliss, C. (1988). Practices reported by incarcerated drug abusers to reduce risk of AIDS. *Hospital and Community Psychiatry, 39*, 966-972.

Vlahov, D. (1990). HIV infection in the correctional setting. *Criminal Justice Policy Review, 4*, 306-318.

Zimmerman, S., Martin, R., & Vlahov, D. (1991). AIDS knowledge and risk perceptions among Pennsylvania prisoners. *Journal of Criminal Justice, 19*, 239-256.

Part V
Future Trends, Global Impact and Ethical Issues

[21]

Linking the Structure of African American Criminalization to the Spread of HIV/AIDS

ANTHONY J. LEMELLE JR.
University of Wisconsin–Milwaukee

This article is organized in two parts. In the first, the author presents the racialized social system conceptual framework for understanding links between the criminalization of Blacks and the spread of HIV/AIDS. In the second, the author presents data from a focus group and in-depth interviews that collaborate that conceptual framework. The major findings are (a) the racialized social system manufactures a Black criminalized profile and contributes to the spread of AIDS; (b) the distrust of authority and lack of faith in institutional order is nothing short of a legitimation crisis for the society coming from the men in this sample; (c) the men expressed a profound lack of trust in public health; (d) they sincerely believe that Whiteness is out to annihilate them; (e) and they have made a commitment to fight back. The author argues these orientations will make HIV/AIDS intervention and prevention programs largely unsuccessful.

Keywords: *Racism, HIV/AIDS, African American health, African American criminal justice, White supremacy and crime, infectious disease and race, crime and infectious disease*

PART 1: INTRODUCTION

This article is organized in two sections and is designed to link empirical findings demonstrating African American processes of criminalization with the spread of HIV/AIDS among African Americans. A conceptual framework is presented in the first section of the article. The second section presents focus group and in-depth interview data collected between 2000 and 2001 with a group of HIV-positive African American males.

This research was supported by a grant from the Indiana Minority Health Coalition. I am also grateful to the Department of Africology, College of Letters and Science, University of Wisconsin–Milwaukee for providing moral and facility support to complete the final product.

The latest AIDS statistics show the staggering toll of HIV/AIDS on people of African descent in the United States. Although Blacks represent around 12% of the total population, we account for 37.7% of the accumulated AIDS cases, and more than 50% of new AIDS cases. In 2000, Black men made up 40% of the new AIDS cases among males; Black women represented 62% of the reported AIDS cases among females; and 6.2 of every 10 children reported with AIDS in the United States were Black (Wilson, 2002, p. 153). Wilson goes on to point out among Black gay or bisexual males, at least 30% are already infected with HIV. He indicated most of the Black gay or bisexual males were recently infected (Wilson, 2002, p. 153).

The HIV/AIDS pattern in Blacks mocks public health because the rates of infection in White gay males decreased significantly as a result of gay community mobilization during the same time the rates were increasing in African Americans. Gay White males received considerable policy and social support that racial minorities were denied (Wohlfeiler, 2000). In fact, their political class emerged as controllers of the HIV/AIDS service organizations (Lemelle, 2002). For African Americans to be disproportionately affected by HIV means they would have to be made so (Bourdieu, 1989). Groups that are ill and incarcerated are to be made. They are not a given in "social reality" (Bourdieu, 1989). The White political class has more cultural capital and it consequently dominates the social space in which they wage a symbolic struggle to maintain the subordination of African Americans. This results in another layer of external control of public health for African Americans. In the racialized social system that relies on oppression, subordination and stigmatization of people of color is found a lack of social control over social institutions among the oppressed (Blauner, 2001; Lemelle, 2002).

The central way to accomplish the subordination of African Americans is through the use of state resources. "Whiteness" uses the criminal justice arm of the state to represent Blackness as a criminal class. This allows a White political class to amass symbolic capital by naming Blacks as a social problem of criminology, and thereby Whiteness performs a diagnostic function in the criminal class discourse. The White political class can then increase surveillance of African Americans as part of the administrative function of the criminology discourse that will ultimately lead to authorize accounts that we find in the so-called official records of African American disreputability. Here, then, two groups are created: one powerful and the other less so. But each group develops its perception of the making of their group, and Whiteness prevails as the powerful and reasonable perception. By Whiteness I mean a framework of perception, appreciation of practices, cognitive, and evaluative structures that are acquired from cultural heritage and sustained over the years based on its social position. That is, Whiteness is a social position with inordinate social capital. And when it comes to the making of

Blacks as a group plagued by pathologies of criminality and disease, Whiteness, through its cultural capital, plays the pivotal role.

In the foregoing sense, African Americans are criminalized in ways that Whites are not (Ruffins, 2002). During the escalating Black HIV/AIDS prevalence period, the criminal justice system was exponentially increasing Black incarceration. Much of this is related to the war on drugs that instrumentally served the White political state in its making of a Black political group disproportionately affected by HIV/AIDS (Kelley, 2000; Russell, 1998; Staples, 2002). Black males are particularly affected by a turnstile incarceration system that instrumentally serves as an occupation-like organization keeping the entire Black community in its place. The social structures organized for the mass arrests of Blacks affects dating, marriage, and family among them, and it also affects the organization of recreational and sexual activities. For example, sociologist Orlando Patterson (1998) in his study of Black marriage patterns found that a night ever spent in jail for Black males reduces their odds of ever marrying by 76% (p. 82). Similarly, there is a dialectical relationship between employment, arrest, and incarceration. In communities in which we find high arrest and incarceration rates, lower levels of middle-class dating, marriage, and family, and high rates of unemployment we also find higher rates of HIV/AIDS, less community control over HIV/AIDS intervention and prevention, and less access to and utilization of health care services (Amaro, Raj, Vega, Mangione, & Perez, 2001; Aral & Blanchard, 2002; Williams & Collins, 2001). For these reasons, the HIV/AIDS trajectory for African Americans must be conceptualized differently than it has been conceptualized for Whites. Fundamentally, this trajectory must be linked to the racialized nature of criminal justice and solutions for HIV/AIDS intervention and prevention must also be conceptualized differently.

The micro-level and behavioral models for conceptually framing the spread and prevention work against HIV/AIDS are widespread (Bowser, 2002; Heffernan, 2002). But these models have done little to thwart the spread of AIDS among African Americans (HealthWatch, 1999). Increasingly, it is suspected that a relationship is present between jails and prisons and HIV. At the same time, transmission of HIV in prisons has been empirically demonstrated to be minimal (Braithwaite, Hammett, & Arriola, 2002). More empirical research is needed on HIV transmission in jails and prisons. Much of the work omits an analysis of how high rates of incarceration affect communities outside the prison walls. In communities in which incarceration rates are high, we find HIV rates are high. To present this conceptual framework, in this article, I use published research, facts, and figures to construct a reasonable explanation of the relationship between African American criminalization and HIV/AIDS. Figure 1 is a graphic presentation of this con-

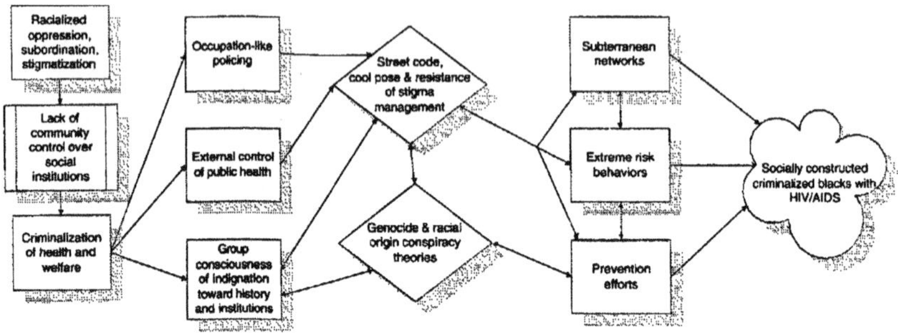

Figure 1 The Racialized Social Structure Production Linking Black Criminalization to HIV/AIDS

ceptual framework. The theoretical foundation guiding the model is a racialized social system approach. By racialized social system, I mean a society in which part of the stratification system is designed to rank people based on their racial classification (Bonilla-Silva, 2001; Feagin & Hernán, 1995). In such societies, there are other ways that people are hierarchically ranked. These include ranking by gender, class, and sexual orientation (Bonilla-Silva, 2001). Yet, the primary ranking is racialized, and even when these other rankings are taken into consideration, they do not explain away the racialized hierarchy.

The most important function of the racialized ranking system is the domination of the groups that are subordinated. Racial domination means that based on race, individual and group movements are controlled (Blauner, 2001). For the controlled, full participation in society is restricted. Roles and activities are determined by stereotypes and norms that sort people of color into less powerful positions. In addition, dominated groups organize to oppose their domination. To interpret the social system as racialized, the focus must be on the social structure. By social structure I mean the networks of interactional relationships that people are organized into to perform certain roles. These roles then determine how they will relate to each other and conduct daily affairs. These are related to socially meaningful characteristics of actors and aggregates of actors (Bourdieu, 1984; Whitmeyer, 1994). Therefore, to view the social system as racialized adds knowledge to the structural ways criminality and HIV are linked and is a closer explanation of how the system really operates. This knowledge provides opportunities to reframe ineffective and outworn intervention methodologies and public health policies.

OCCUPATION-LIKE POLICING

The race to punish that began in the mid-1970s overwhelmed African Americans, particularly males. The rate of imprisonment rocketed to new historical highs. Between 1975 and 1995, the prison population increased from approximately 204,593 to 1,085,363, a 430% increase. The incarceration rate increased from 11 to 411 inmates per 100,000 during that time. There were also nearly one half million inmates in local jails in 1995, and that was close to twice as many as in 1985 (U.S. Department of Justice, 1996). Blacks consist of 13% of the national population but 30% of citizens arrested, 41% of those in jail, and 49% of those in prison (Beck & Mumola, 1999). Of all Black adults, 9% are under some form of correctional supervision including jail, parole, prison, or probation compared with 2% of White adults (U.S. Department of Justice, 1998, Table 6.2). Of Black males between the ages of 20 and 29, 33% were either in jail or prison or on parole or probation in 1995 (Mauer, 1995). Of all Black males in their 20s and early 30s, 10% are in prison or jail (Mauer, 1999).

The rate at which Black males are incarcerated is a national scandal. The work of Hawkins and Hardy (1989) argued that the percentage of a state's Black population that is urban may be the best predictor of incarceration rates rather than crime rates. That is, Northern states have larger urban concentrations than Southern states and have higher racial disparities in their incarcerated population. In short, nationwide, there are 4,630 Black men in prison per 100,000 Black men in the population, whereas the rate for White men is 482, and between 1985 and 1995, the Black male rate increased at 10 times the White male rate (Tonry, 1998, p. 15). These skyrocketing rates of incarceration are primarily because of the skyrocketing war on drugs and not because of an increase in violent crime.

HIV surveillance among incarcerated populations is rudimentary. Currently there are few estimates. However, Table 1 presents some of the best data and methods counting characteristics of incarcerated persons 13 years and older with HIV. It shows most HIV (80%) and AIDS (94%) among the incarcerated are in males. And it shows that incarcerated African Americans lead HIV/AIDS infections. The rate of HIV in prisons is 5 times greater than the rate among the general population (Ross, 2001). African American inmates are twice as likely as Whites to test HIV positive (Ross, 2001).

In addition to the high rate of Black incarceration that is largely related to the war on drugs is the pattern now to criminalize HIV. The data for this emerging pattern are concealed under the cover of police arrests. It would require a search of each jurisdictional district to uncover the arrests and convictions related to HIV. However, several cases have made the front pages of newspapers. One example is the case of college freshman Nikko Briteramos,

TABLE 1
Race and Gender Characteristics of Incarcerated Persons Aged 13 Years or Older, by Disease Status at Initial Diagnosis—25 States With HIV Reporting Since 1994 Disease Status at Initial HIV Diagnosis

	HIV		*AIDS*			
Characteristic	N	%	N	%	*Total*	%
Gender						
Male	5,912	80	922	94	6,834	87
Female	928	14	62	6	990	13
Race						
Black	4,868	71	682	69	5,550	71
White	1,346	20	170	17	1,516	19
Hispanic and other	626	9	132	14	758	10

SOURCE: Abridged from Dean, Lansky, and Fleming (2002).

a 6-foot-5, 18-year-old Black male from Chicago, Illinois. Briteramos was a freshman at Si Tanka-Huron University in South Dakota. He was recruited to play basketball there. In March 2002, he decided to donate blood and was told by the health department that he had tested HIV positive. Health workers came to his dorm room where he was in boxer shorts with a girlfriend, and they called the police on him, claiming he had been discovered in flagrante delicto. South Dakota is 1 of 31 states to have criminalized HIV transmission. The law penalizes those who know they are positive and intentionally expose another person to infection. Briteramos faces 45 years of prison for not disclosing his HIV status before sex (Stukin, 2002).

The case of Briteramos is a striking one. There are other remarkable cases, including the notorious case of Nushawn Williams, who was arrested in 1997 for knowingly infecting nine women and girls with HIV in upstate New York. Many states have instituted such laws as the face of AIDS changed. The Illinois HIV statute is one example of the draconian laws many states passed that is poised to unequally affect racialized groups. The statute could impose criminal penalties on any behavior that might be found to transmit HIV. The law was approved in 1989 and it allows state prosecutors to bring felony criminal charges against anyone who, knowing he or she is infected with HIV, engages in activities—including intimate contact, donating blood, or sharing dirty needles—that could transmit HIV (Grady, 1993). The penalty for conviction in Illinois is 3 to 7 years in prison. It is not necessary to actually transmit HIV to be prosecuted under the law. Such laws are available to profile and arrest African Americans, in much the same way that powder and crack cocaine federal statutes were used to unevenly prosecute African Americans.

EXTERNAL CONTROL OF PUBLIC HEALTH

The changing of HIV/AIDS into a disease that mostly affects people of color and treatments that have transformed it from a deadly disease into a chronic condition have resulted in less attention being paid to the disease. This racialized situation has historical precedence. From the very beginning of HIV/AIDS, race relations between public health and medical workers and racial minorities were strained. Western medicine had taken a paternalistic position toward African Americans as a part of its practitioners' civilizing mission. These racialized images have been an inextricable part of Western medical consciousness that conceived of African Americans as trapped in contagion, degradation, and disease (McBride, 1991). In the process, African Americans were often described as dirty, disease-filled, hypersexual animals, immature, indolent, and sexually perverted (Comaroff, 1993).

The view that African Americans were somehow different from other humans had resulted in one emblematic episode of racism in public health. The Tuskegee Syphilis Study followed some 600 low-income African American males—about 400 of whom were infected with the disease—from 1932 to 1972. Although during this time penicillin was identified as a treatment for the deadly disease, the scientists conducting the study decided not to administer antibiotics on the grounds that it would interfere with their research on untreated syphilis. Many of the men—between 28 and 100—died of syphilis. It is therefore no coincidence that some in the African American community think of AIDS as a government invention that was part of a larger genocidal strategy (Epstein, 1997; Jones, 1993; Krouse, 1999). This suspicion comes from years of racial bias in public health. It contributes to significantly less medicine, less therapeutic intervention, and shorter survival time for African American HIV/AIDS patients. In addition, there is a lack of trust of the medical establishment. As a result, African Americans have lower receptivity to prevention efforts and there is less involvement of African Americans in clinical trials.

An example of the organization of race-based practices is the manner that funds are allocated for HIV/AIDS prevention and treatment. In 1988 in New York City, for example, the community-based service organization Gay Men's Health Crisis (GMHC) had a $10 million budget and a staff of about 75. At the same time, the Minority Task Force on AIDS had a budget of $1 million and a staff of 8, even though half the cases of AIDS in New York City involved people of color. GMHC was criticized for failing to reach bisexual and gay men of color, although many of the workers there and many of their clients were people of color (Kayal, 1993). Now GMHC has changed to place more people of color in prestigious positions in their organization and, because of the change in the face of the disease, to have as their clients mostly people of color (Wilson, 1995). Yet, it remains a White–male arranged and founded organization (Cameron & Lee, 1999; Chambré, 1991; Gambe & Getzel, 1989).

A color-blind attitude would dismiss this observation as being of little importance (Lemelle, 2001). However, the policies that became part of the structure of the organizational culture of GMHC and organizations like it are grounded in a particular set of values and viewpoints that are significantly different from those of African Americans. In short, African American public health is controlled by outside groups, organizational structures, and institutions.

In 1993, the National Institutes of Health (NIH) implemented the NIH Revitalization Act. The law requires that women, members of minority groups, and their subpopulations must be included in all NIH-supported biomedical and behavioral research projects involving human subjects, unless there is clear and compelling justifications and rationales why their inclusion would be inappropriate. Although this standard increased attention to African Americans, there remained a problem in the proposals for behavioral studies and clinical trials as to what merits funding. Both explicit and implicit institutional biases in the normal screening process of awarding grants continue to exclude African American researchers.

A number of other programs have been instituted with soft support, including a minority supplement program in which a funded program could apply for another line of money to support a minority researcher. This form of institutional tokenism limits the amount of funds that flow to African Americans because it is designed for all minorities. To participate in the minority supplement programs, African American researchers must network with more established White researchers. Under these constraints, it is virtually impossible to introduce atypical conceptual knowledge. And it is likely that a struggle against HIV among African Americans will call for different than normal concepts. These concepts and groups are usually considered peripheral by mainstream HIV intervention researchers.

GROUP CONSCIOUSNESS OF INDIGNATION AND CONSPIRACY THEORIES

One reaction to the social relations between racialized representatives of the state and African Americans is the widespread attitude among African Americans that HIV/AIDS is a secret genocidal plot to annihilate them. One of the major proponents of the conspiracy theory is Boyd Ed Graves. For Graves, HIV was produced in a laboratory as part of biological warfare that was globally directed against Africans. According to Graves, the U.S. government used tax dollars to secretly develop HIV in a lab and then spread it as a biological weapon to kill Blacks (Whitfield, 2000, p. 46). Graves's claims caused many to believe public health services might still engage in spreading disease. Some decided not to accept condoms or clean needles because they suspected they might be tainted with HIV. Graves was named as one of the 25 most influential citizens by the major African American newspaper in Cleveland, Ohio (Whitfield, 2000).

In 1998, the Reverend Al Sharpton called a meeting in Harlem to discuss AIDS. Surprisingly, others shared the view that HIV was a genocidal plot directed against African Americans. In a 1999 study funded by the National Institutes of Health, it was reported that 25% of African Americans surveyed believed the U.S. government created HIV to eliminate Blacks (Whitfield, 2000, p. 48). The Southern Christian Leadership Conference found in a survey that 54% of Blacks view HIV testing as a way to infect them with the virus (p. 48). A survey of Black church members in 1990 found that 35% believed AIDS was a form of genocide ("The AIDS 'plot' against Blacks," 1992). A *New York Times*/WCBS-TV News poll in 1990 found that 1 Black in 10 believes the AIDS virus was "deliberately created in a laboratory to infect Black people," and an additional 2 in 10 thought that might be so ("The AIDS 'Plot' Against Blacks," 1992; Cooper, 1990).

Health educators Sandra Crouse Quinn and Stephen B. Thomas reported to the American Public Health Association that conspiracy belief theories among Blacks in Washington housing projects and clinics, and among Black college students were high. "In all these samples, somewhere around 30 to 35 percent are agreeing that AIDS is a form of genocide and 30 percent are unsure" (Key, 1995). Because of such beliefs, Blacks are less likely to get tested, less likely to use condoms, and less likely to participate in clinical trials (Key, 1995). In addition, now that medications have been found to be effective in the management of HIV, Blacks are less likely to comply with treatment protocols.

STREET CODE AND STIGMA MANAGEMENT

Incarceration, economic, and dating patterns result in specific lines of behaviors among African Americans that have been associated with recent Black culture. For example, Majors and Billson (1992), in their profound study of dilemmas of Black masculinity in America, developed the concept of masking. With regard to many Black men, they wrote, "He learned to play that role with a finesse and artistry that became part of his culture . . . the art of concealment, his mask constructed, as Kochman observes, of innocence and ignorance, childishness and humility, and obedience and deference" (p. 59).

If it is indeed accurate to characterize concealment as a feature of African American masculine culture, the institutional processes of disproportionately imprisoning Black males might potentially serve as an incubator for the spread of HIV in Black communities. Such masking is likely to occur when males strive to avoid the stigma of the gigolo, homosexual, intravenous drug user (IDU), or prostitute label but are engaged in such activities nevertheless (HealthWatch, 1999; also, for some of the best data on gay Blacks on the street and meaningful constructions, see Pettiway, 1996). The latest Bureau of Justice statistics showed that 7 million are incarcerated, and the HIV rate in jails and prisons is 10 times greater than in the outside population. AIDS accounts for one third of all prison deaths (Maddow & Greenspan, 2000, p. 29). About one fifth (19%) of people with AIDS (PWAs) in the United States have spent time in prison. Although some studies found transmission in prison to be minimal, there is little doubt that considerable HIV transmission is occurring in prisons. For one thing, sexual activities and rapes in prison are widespread (Human Rights Watch, 2001). Some of the inmates are pimped by other inmates in the prison for a profit. There is injection use in prisons. There is also considerable tattooing behavior that results in the exchange of bodily fluids in jails and prisons. With such a large proportion of African American males passing from prison to the community and back to prison again, many males mask the experiences they had while in prison; they do not identify with stigmatizing labels and attempt to establish regular heterosexual relations soon after they leave prison. These institutional conditions contribute to an increase in African American HIV/AIDS cases. The mass media assists in promoting the norms, roles, and values that are clustered in institutional organizations. African Americans are left with little space, in the context of these structures, to direct their own destinies.

If Black males are not incarcerated, the community internalizes the norms and values associated with the possibility of incarceration. These practices become diffused in the isolated and segregated communities in which Blacks reside. Although network analyses assist us in tracking the core pattern of transmissions, they do little to help us understand the ideological complex associated with different structures. The latter can help us to understand structures in which individuals become caught up in risky situations. These situations are patterned, and individuals' behaviors often become subordinated to the patterned activities of the risky situations. This is not to say that structures completely control line of behaviors, but individuals have a "sense of one's place" and a "sense of the place of others" in risky social situations (Bourdieu, 1989). This is why Bourdieu wrote, "agents classify themselves, expose themselves to classification, by choosing, in conformity with their taste, different attributes (clothes, types of food, drinks, sports, friends) that go well together and that go well with them or, more exactly, suit their position" (p. 19).

MAKING CRIMINALIZED BLACK HIV/AIDS IDENTITIES

Taken all together, the social structure of Black marginalization that relies so heavily on the social manufacturing of a Black criminal class is intricately tied to the spread of HIV/AIDS among Blacks. The unanticipated consequences of using criminal law to control leisure behaviors among marginalized groups require considerable study. Theoretically, individuals who violate the law are prevented from future transgressions by imprisonment (incapacitation); individuals obey the law primarily because they want to avoid being caught and punished (instrumental/deterrence); and individuals obey the law primarily because the law establishes what is "right" or fair, regardless of the likelihood or severity of punishment (norm-setting) (Lazzarini, Bray, & Burris, 2002). Whatever the merits of these theoretical frameworks, when large numbers of Blacks are repeatedly having criminal justice contact, normative social structure is affected. Reactionary journalist Hanna Rosin (1995) summed it up in this way:

> Race itself does not affect one's chances of contracting HIV. . . . But inner-city ills do. For example, one-quarter of all Black men in their 20s, and 15 percent adult males, rotate through prison. Among inmates, unprotected anal sex is common. Prison is thus a place where the virus can spread to men who may have sex with men while in jail and with women when they get out. In 1990, doctors at Rikers Island conducted what is called a blind seroprevalence test. They took the nametags off blood samples used in mandatory syphilis tests and checked them for HIV. A quarter of both male and female samples tested positive, a result since replicated in other big city prisons. (pp. 21-23)

Law plays a broad role in public health, but it is likely not the ills of the inner city as much as it is the structure of White supremacy that affects public health outcomes. At bottom, it has to do with power, for it is unlikely that any community would take it on itself to criminalize so many of its citizens as we find in the United States, where Whites control and benefit from the prison industrial complex and Blacks inhabit the positions of subordination in the prison industrial structure. The criminalization bureaucracy defines power and jurisdiction of health agencies, and it influences norms that shape individual behavior (Gostin, Burris, & Lazzarini, 1999). In the case of African Americans, a broader conceptual framework must be considered linking the criminalization process to the spread of AIDS. A revealing comment appeared recently at the end of a research article on correctional facilities and infectious disease published in the *American Journal of Public Health* (Hammett, Harmon, & Rhodes, 2002):

> Prevalence statistics for inmates by race and ethnicity are generally lacking, so it was not possible to develop estimates of disease burden by racial and ethnic group. However, the disproportionate incarceration rates experienced by African Americans and Latinos and the already disproportionate burden of the diseases under study among the same groups combine to produce a situation in which the vast majority of inmates and releasees are African American and Latino. In New York State correctional facilities, 48% of inmates diagnosed with AIDS in 1997 were Black and 45% were Hispanic, compared with the proportions of these groups in the total population of the state of 18% and 14%, respectively. (pp. 1792-1793)

PART 2: PROCEDURES AND SAMPLE

The conceptual framework presented in Part 1 partially emerged from observations and ethnographic studies of Black males. What follows are parts of two qualitative interview techniques: focus groups and individual interviews during the years 2000 and 2001. A group of Black, HIV-positive males was approached and told about the study's interest in attitudes, knowledge, and behaviors that might place someone at risk for contracting HIV. The men were given a 42-item questionnaire that queries background demographics, sexual behaviors, AIDS knowledge, schooling, drug use, and gang-related behaviors. From the larger group, a focus group ($N = 7$) was formed. They were asked a set of open-ended questions about arrests and incarcerations, sexual behaviors, fear of AIDS and knowledge about it, gang and drug use activities, schooling, and neighborhoods. Questions were also asked about life feelings and personal satisfaction. The questionnaire items were entered in a SPSS spreadsheet, and focus group and individual interviews were transcribed and entered into ATLAS.ti software. From the focus group, 4 males were selected that our research team identified as representative of the focus group, and we held individual, in-depth 1-hour interviews with them. Each participant was paid $25 for their participation, and participants in the in-depth interviews were paid an additional $50. The interviews were conducted at a community social services center that referred and temporarily housed HIV positive males on the southwest side of Chicago.

The interview strategy followed models proposed by Fullilove, Lown, and Fullilove (1992) and Post, Roy-Byrne, and Uhde (1988) for the simultaneous depiction of prior HIV/AIDS knowledge, drug use, HIV/AIDS risk behaviors, and treatment noncompliance. The data are qualitative and collected from a small number of males. It is incomplete in that no full histories detailing HIV knowledge, traumatic events, drug use, and treatment compliance are collected for all the interviewed males. In this regard, there are obvious limitations in ability to generalize from these data. Nonetheless, these data are worth reporting because they provide immediate implications for future data-gathering activities. They will provide urgently needed guideposts for HIV/AIDS intervention and prevention concepts in the context of Black inner-city ethos.

The 7 men who participated in the focus group were between 41 and 50 years old and all are HIV positive. The median age was 43. All of the men worked irregularly at dead-end jobs. Two of the men recently had been released from prison and were under state parole supervision. One of the men worked part-time as an HIV counselor. He had been offered the position after learning of his blood status. Four of the men were unemployed. Two of them lived in public housing near downtown Chicago. They both receive food subsidies. All of the men expressed a desire to find regular work. Three of the men reported their parents were married and together when they were growing up. One said his parents were separated, 1 said he only knew one parent, 1 said his parents were never married, and 1 had no answer for the question about parents' marriage status. All of the men have brothers and sisters. The median number of brothers is 2 and the median number of sisters is 3.

The men ranged in formal education between the 9th grade to having completed college. Two had not graduated from high school. Four had educations between completing high school and 3 years of college.

Five of the men in this sample reported having sex in the last 12 months. Three said they were 100% heterosexual; 1 mostly heterosexual; 1 bisexual/ equally attracted to men and women; 1 mostly homosexual; and 1 reported being 100% homosexual. Three reported having sex with an HIV-positive male. One said he had done so between 1 and 10 times, 2 said the question did not apply to them, and 4 had no answer. When the men were asked how often they used a condom while having sex with an HIV-positive male, 1 said all the time, 2 about one half the time, 2 said the question did not apply, and 2 had no answer. None of the men reported having sex with an HIV-positive woman. When they were asked how often they use a condom with a woman, 2 said always, 1 said never, 2 said sometimes, 1 said he did not have sex with women; and 1 did not answer the question.

Four of the men said they had been taught in school about safe sex. They said they had been taught about it before graduating from high school. Three said they had at least 10 hours of AIDS instruction, 2 said they had more than 40 hours. One said you could get AIDS from sharing an apartment, none said you could get AIDS from shaking hands, all said you could get AIDS from sex, and all said you could get AIDS from having a penis in the mouth.

RESULTS

Knowledge, sexual relations, sex in prison, and stigma are the four themes that emerged from this study. First, there were knowledge issues the men stressed as important. A large part of their knowledge base was grounded in conspiracy theories. None of the men were educated about sex by their parents or parental surrogates. Sex was a hidden topic, and they would sneak to learn about it. When asked how he learned about sex, 1 of the men represented what the others expressed when he said, "I used to peep through the door." These men expressed shame and secretive identification with sexual knowledge. For them, it was as though sex itself is a necessary transgression, "Yeah, I can recall my mother telling me not to put my hands between no women's legs." One of the men made it clear that sharing sexual knowledge was not part of his familial experience:

> Well, now I learned exactly from my peers. I had a daddy too. And we was tight until the day I buried him, which was a couple of years ago. He was always in the household, but there was certain thangs that he would not go into. I watched him and I admire him. But I learned about sex behaviors out in the streets. Mom never talked about it.

The knowledge of HIV was intricately related to theories of conspiracy in these men. One of the participants said,

> Myself, I believe that it was planned that way. Because our people are most of the major ones that's infected with this. You know, even over seas, you don't see this high percent in Caucasian community. It's only in the African American communities that you see these diseases. Our people are dying off, it seems that they are producing pills or something for themselves, where they're having 4 or 5 babies, and we're steadily dying off.

The men also expressed the conspiracy theme. The majority of the men felt the government, as a genocidal plot against African Americans, designed the disease, others felt money was the driving force behind the spread of disease among Blacks:

> I'd find out about the Reagan administration and everything. I thought it was fascinating how one guy went all the way over to France and everything and admitted that he stole information about when they called it HLTV I and II. How he stole the information from Atlanta Centers for Disease Control, and took it over there and got it patent and got money, and Ronald Reagan and the media covered it up. I found that fascinating, so then I started getting into it. So I'm somewhat like person no. 3, except for I think it was

more about getting money and everything, instead of telling people, letting it get wide-spread, so they could then they start using this group of people and everything as the poster child for this year, to get more money and everything.

SEXUAL RELATIONS

The men agreed on the importance of maintaining a distance between their emotions and sexual relations. They framed sexual relations as a getting-over competition. In this competition, drugs played a central role. On one hand, the men admitted enjoying sex and drugs. On the other hand, they pointed out the importance of drugs for making sexual contacts. On the latter point, one of the men said,

> The females out there, I mean, they'll do anything for it [drugs]. And I believe that's what broke me. Most of us, including myself, might have contracted that from . . . because they would have sex with anybody, and almost anything for that. . . . [I've] heard some stories that I don't even care to repeat.

The men realize their drug-using sexual behaviors place them at great risk but were entrapped in relaxation and leisurely activities that are widespread in urban communities. However, sex combined with intoxication was most prevalent for this group of men,

> because I pretty much stay isolated all my life. And when I was having sex, let's just admit it, I was mostly drunk all the time . . . so it was nothing but sex . . . [and] then it wasn't really fulfilling because it was a drunk sex. I had sex three times while I wasn't high.

These men associated sex and drugs with power positions. On one hand, power played a role between men and women and sex and drugs. Using this logic, the men said they used drugs to attract women who would do "anything." On the other hand, the men revealed they would also do "anything." In this sense, the men referred to their activity as "the hustle." One example was explained by one of the men who engaged in homosexual prostitution for drugs and money:

> It was all a part of it. Just like to me, I'll just be they'll big trophy. They had to show me off, and they had to keep me shining. So it never was a dull moment. No matter what. It never was a dull moment. I didn't have to want for anything. Basically, they took me in just like a little slave. It was a sense of power, that's what it completely was. A complete sense of power, where

> you had control, and that was sort of amusing. These people sitting up here making all this money and everything, and in no more than 5 years, they'll spend it all or give it all to me. Just to keep me over every other weekend.

The power over someone who is weak appears to add excitement to the game of sexual conquest. The men spoke of this excitement in context of the streets and prison. Money and drugs are tied to these risky sexual behaviors that would presumably be impossible to accomplish, in terms of opportunity and socialization, were it not for their marginal position to educational institutions and the labor market. The question becomes, "so most of the guys who are participating in homosexual activity are usually using drugs?" Hence, the answers are usually using drugs. It is all about money to get the drugs.

> It's an easy way to get the money to get the drugs, and if you get one that really got money, you gone have it made every week, because they gone make sure you got $200-$300 a we . . . each night. That's the tuff part, each night so you can really stay high. I'm taking care of you, just keep on coming back. The money is always be there.

The men associated the sexual and drug play with masculinity. Being able to have what they wanted when they wanted was a form of masculine power. One of the men represented this when he said,

> I was a crack-head, and I smoked a lot of crack, and I had crack to get females. I had to have both. It wasn't . . . if I couldn't have one, I didn't want the other, they were simultaneous. I will make this observation that when the rise of crack in our neighborhood came, so did the rise of HIV among heterosexuals. It's something that my spiritual, by the grace of God, I'm no longer there. But I know, I know, I know, I know, that that's where I contracted, from which woman, I don't know. But it was some woman that was with the disease. Yeah, baby I could blow up $500 worth on some crack rock and your girlfriend, you understand? But I ain't buying no rubber and I want what I want, when I want it. No questions asked.

This masculine power was channeled as power over women in their minds.

> When I got about 13 or 14, I was hanging with a crowd, about 6 or 7 of us males and 7 or 8 girls, and we did rituals. Go to the show and did the dance and things, we fought over the chicks in our neighborhood, we pulled trains on chicks, when one was ready to go, we took her and had sex with her, you know. As a matter of fact, I saw the first woman I ever boned in my life about a week and a half [ago] at McDonald's.

The men have been socialized into a subterranean culture in which a "down low," meaning secretive, attitude is stressed in terms of sexual relations. Sexual relations are associated with the criminality of drug use and the criminality of HIV transmission. Prevention models would necessarily have to penetrate these subterranean norms.

SEX IN PRISON

The men who had been in prison reported considerable sexual activity among inmates. The sexual activity was related to power, as was the street sexual activity the men talked about. One of them remarked,

> I guess when a person has a long-term sentence; it's just to the fact where this is home. I might as well make the best of it. So whatever's gone happen, I ain't getting out no way, so I'm gone try to talk him out of it or give him something where he got to pay me back in return. Or, I'm a take it.

Institutionalization results in same-sex encounters. Similar to the encounters in the neighborhoods, the power relationships guide prison encounters. The central idea is that a sexual manipulation is likely to occur when someone has taken something from another inmate and now owes a favor. They reported favors such as older men protecting younger men, allowing a man to watch a television show he desired to see, or sharing commissary goods.

> I fittin' [about] to get me some fresh booty hole. Or, get my edge—you know what I mean? Give me some face, or something, you know. But I guess if a person mind his business, they can kind of go through there real easy, you just can't be taking nothing from nobody. Mind your own business, respect the people in there, the gangs in there, go your way. And if you see something and don't see something, you got a lot of people who go in there and come out with no problems.

The men explained the prison environment as one marked by fear and intimidation. Intimidation is the instrumental used to spread HIV/AIDS. One of the men described his observations about the way AIDS is spread in context of the sexual stratification that happens in prison:

> I've been in the penitentiary, and by it being like that, I was in Statesville and men get sexually active in there, because they're basically dealing with each other, you know. And they find somebody that's weak, you know, and 9 times out of 10, a person is not revealing their [HIV] status because they scared. And you got a population of 8-9-1000 people or something you know, each cell house holds 500 people, and once somebody attack 'em and

if he don't belong to nobody, he belongs to everybody. And so if you tell somebody you got it, they would probably kill 'em and you know, so they just keep it hush, hush. They end up liking it and keep on going with 'em. Some people go in there just to be with a man. So it is spreading more—so in the penitentiary out there.

The men tied the prison sexual scene and the fact that condoms are not distributed in prison back to the racialized social system and a possible genocidal conspiracy.

When they talk about they having sex in prison, or you shouldn't give condoms to kids, that's the biggest bunch of crock I ever heard. Because you know they're sexually active, so why don't you give it to 'em, so they don't get this. And in no way in the world they gone sit up there and say they not having sex in prison. There's no way they can even look nobody dead in the eye and say, it ain't going on. That's stuff right there . . . that's like asking me, myself, not to go through this back door because you said, don't go through that back door. Just because you told me not to go through that back door, I'm a go through that back door, just to let you know I can go through that back door.

Another one of the men followed up on masculine expression of resistance, genocide, and the subterranean values associated with prison sexual stratification:

I want to say something about that. It's a funny thing, that's just common knowledge, but it's a funny thing how they can come up . . . you say this was on TV [a discussion of distributing condoms in prison], it was brought up. That was just admitting to their [White power structure] participation and genocide against our culture, our people. Why they couldn't talk about some programs or something a little positive. They want to come up like they're really doing something to really help somebody out in prison, giving them rubbers. And talking about the young people, that's almost admitting exposing their hand what they really all about. And then they want to try and put it out there on you like you're making the decisions on what you think about it. You know this goes on, you know this was going on before they got that. What were you [Whites in power] doing about that, that's not brought out? Programs and other things that will be helpful or indications that's not brought out. Then when you hear something like that, that should be a warning, a wake-up call to you, that's what they're doing to you.

One other dimension to the prison sexual stratification that spreads HIV that the men talked about is the selling of men to one another:

> Well, look, you give me some sex, I'll make sure don't nobody else continue to bother you—you know, stuff like that. Well, okay, if you ain't gone tell nobody. And you break 'em in, and by you being a fresh person on the block, they may sell him for $3-400, because everybody be wanting to have sex with him. And they sell people in the joint. You know, for $3-400, for the first time, or if you don't have no man, he belong to everybody, and then everybody come at him.

The men stated it would be useless to attempt to use authority to control prison sexual stratification:

> Well, they find out old boy done got him, then my turn. It's like a dog eat dog world. And running to the police trying to protect him in custody. Ain't no protective custody. It's not safe because the majority of the guards are hooked-up too. And you might have some on the side and some under the take. So, one might say, well man, let me out my cell and let me go down there with that fresh young White boy down there. And they'll open the cell and be down there with him about an hour, come on back down there in his cell—you know?

STIGMA

The men clearly knew the importance of hiding their HIV status. They expressed the stigma that exists. The fear begins in their family life. One of the men expressed this when he said,

> if I told my mother, then I would have to spend the rest of my life explaining to her what happened to me. Too much energy. Just let it roll as it is, let the chips fall where they may, rather than to say, okay, I'm diagnosed. And once I say I'm diagnosed with HIV, they'd go why-y-y-y, then I got all this energy I have to use to explain to them.

Yet, another man said,

> I never did tell them about my status, but I think my mother knew and got a phone call from them last Christmas, saying Merry Christmas and heard about all the things that I was doing. I was mad, but I haven't let my momma know that I was mad about it because I still think on one thing, I should have been the one to tell 'em, but I just let it go. I won't tell her nothing about it.

He felt stigmatized by revealing his status to her:

> But she would always think that she got to start to pamper me and everything. If I take a bath, she want to grease my back down and everything. She's doing all these little things. I mean it was nice but she made it seem like I was sick. It was uncomfortable for me, because she was worried, she didn't have to be worried.

In addition to the stigma of HIV identification was the expressed fear of being identified as gay. The men were annoyed by the forms that asked them if they were gay. One of the men said,

> Naw, I ain't gay. Yeah, I turn tricks with men because that's what we did when we was getting high. A gay approached us and everything, you got money, a whore says you can have it as long as you got money.

These fearful feelings fuelled the men's need to remain secretive about their blood status and their sexual orientations. Likewise, it fuelled their ways of acquiring sex that could be read as largely criminal that clearly contributes to the spread of HIV/AIDS.

CONCLUSION

The accounts from the data support the conceptual framework of a racialized social system that manufactures both the Black criminalized profile and the spread of AIDS. The distrust of authority and lack of faith in institutional order is nothing short of a legitimation crisis for the society coming from the men in this sample. The men express a profound lack of trust in public health. They sincerely believe that Whiteness is out to annihilate them. They have made a commitment to fight back. Much of the fighting back is in the context of masking their behaviors as identities. Expressing a commitment to insubordination, particularly when it came to matters of control over their bodies. Accomplishing their resistance, the men promote a system of norms and values that place them in extremely risky situations. These situations are then masked and become secretive spaces of behavioral and symbolic expression.

The only way to make a difference among these populations is to empower them. However, the rules of the racialized social system are designed to prevent just the kind of empowerment that would be necessary to effectively reduce the spread of AIDS. This, then, will be the greatest accomplishment of the AIDS service industry—the ability to share power. Unfortunately, Whiteness is committed to another set of values.

REFERENCES

The AIDS "plot" against Blacks. (1992, May 12). *New York Times*, p. A22.

Amaro, H., Raj, A., Vega, R. R., Mangione, T. W., & Perez, L. N. (2001). Racial/ethnic disparities in the HIV and substance abuse epidemics: Communities responding to the need. *Public Health Reports, 116*, 434-448.

Aral, S. O., & Blanchard, J. F. (2002). Phase specific approaches to the epidemiology and prevention of sexually transmitted diseases. *Sexually Transmitted Infections, 78*, i3-i13.

Beck, A. J., & Mumola, C. J. (1999). *Prisoners in 1998*. Washington, DC: Bureau of Justice Statistics, Department of Justice.

Blauner, R. (2001). *Still the big news: Racial oppression in America*. Philadelphia: Temple University Press.

Bonilla-Silva, E. (2001). *White supremacy & racism in the post-civil rights era*. Boulder, CO: Lynne Rienner.

Bourdieu, P. (1984). *Distinction*. Cambridge, MA: Harvard University Press.

Bourdieu, P. (1989). Social space and symbolic power. *Sociological Theory, 7*(1), 14-25.

Bowser, B. P. (2002). The social dimensions of the AIDS epidemic: A sociology of the AIDS epidemic. *International Journal of Sociology and Social Policy, 22*(4,5,6), 1-20.

Braithwaite, R. L., Hammett, T., & Arriola, K. R. J. (2002). Introduction to the special issue: HIV/AIDS in correctional settings. *AIDS Education and Prevention, 14*, 1-6.

Cameron, T., & Lee, Y. (1999). Women with AIDS: Will it change AIDS service organizations? *Policy Studies Journal, 27*(4), 872-889.

Chambré, S. M. (1991). Volunteers as witnesses: The mobilization of AIDS volunteers in New York City, 1981-1988. *Social Science Review, 65*(4), 531-547.

Comaroff, J. (1993). The diseased heart of Africa: Medicine, colonialism, and the Black body. In S. Lindenbaum & M. Lock (Eds.), *Knowledge, power & practice* (pp. 305-329). Berkeley: University of California Press.

Cooper, M. (1990). The return to the paranoid style in American politics: Why some Blacks and gays fear "genocide." *U.S. News & World Report, 108*, 30-31.

Dean, H. D., Lansky, A., & Fleming, P. L. (2002). HIV surveillance methods for the incarcerated population. *AIDS Education and Prevention, 14*, 65-74.

Epstein, S. (1997). AIDS activism and the retreat from the "genocide" frame. *Social Identities, 3*(3), 415-438.

Feagin, J. R., & Hernán, V. (1995). *White racism: The basics*. New York: Routledge.

Fullilove, M. T., Lown, E. A., & Fullilove, R. E. (1992). Crack 'Hos and skeezers: Traumatic experiences of women crack users. *Journal of Sex Research, 29*, 275-287.

Gambe, R., & Getzel, G. (1989). Group work with gay men with AIDS. *Social Casework, 70*(3), 172-179.

Gostin, L. O., Burris, S., & Lazzarini, Z. (1999). The law and the public's health: A study of infectious disease law in the United States. *Columbia Law Review, 99*(1), 59-128.

Grady, W. (1993, November 9). ACLU says AIDS law too vague. *Chicago Tribune*, p. 2C1.

Hammett, T. M., Harmon, M. P., & Rhodes, W. (2002). The burden of infectious disease among inmates of and releasees from U.S. correctional facilities, 1997. *American Journal of Public Health, 92*(11), 1789-1794.

Hawkins, D. F., & Hardy, K. A. (1989, winter). Black-White imprisonment rates: A state-by-state analysis. *Social Justice, 164*(38), 75-94.

Heffernan, C. (2002). HIV, sexually transmitted infections and social inequalities: When transmission is more social than sexual. *International Journal of Sociology and Social Policy, 22*(4,5,6), 159-176.

HealthWatch. (1999). *AIDS & African-Americans: It's time for action! A strategy development project for HIV prevention and risk reduction for African-Americans*. New York: State Department of Health AIDS Institute.

Human Rights Watch. (2001). *No escape: Male rape in U.S. prisons*. New York: Author.

Jones, J. H. (1993). *Bad blood: The Tuskegee syphilis experiment*. New York: Free Press.

Kayal, P. M. (1993). *Bearing witness: Gay men's health crisis and the politics of AIDS*. Boulder, CO: Westview.

Kelley, R. D. G. (2000). Slagin' rocks . . . Palestinian style: Dispatches from the occupied zones of North America. In J. Nelson (Ed.), *Police brutality: An anthology* (pp. 21-59). New York: Norton.

Key, K. K. (1995). Conspiracy theories about HIV puts individuals at risk. *Infectious Disease Weekly, 11/13*, 14.

Krouse, M. B. (1999). Feminist discursive pivoting: Charting the politics of AIDS. *Humanity and Society, 23*(1), 32-48.

Lazzarini, Z., Bray, S., & Burris, S. (2002). Evaluating the impact of criminal laws on HIV risk behavior. *Journal of Law, Medicine & Ethics, 30*(2), 239-253.

Lemelle, A. J. (2001). Black masculinity and colorblind ideology. In L. L. Bethel (Ed.), *Africana: An introduction and study* (pp. 304-321). Dubuque, IA: Kendall/Hunt.

Lemelle, A. J. (2002). Racialized social system and HIV infection: The case of African Americans. *International Journal of Sociology and Social Policy, 22*(4,5,6), 133-158.

Maddow, R., & Greenspan, J. (2000). In the BIG house. *HIV Plus, 6*, p. 29.

Majors, R., & Billson, J. M. (1992). *Cool pose*. New York: Touchstone.

Mauer, M. (1995). *Young Black Americans and the criminal justice system: Five years later.* Washington, DC: The Sentencing Project.

Mauer, M. (1999). *Race to incarcerate*. New York: New Press.

McBride, D. (1991). *From TB to AIDS: Epidemics among urban Blacks since 1900*. New York: State University of New York Press.

Patterson, O. (1998). *Rituals of blood*. Washington, DC: Civitas.

Pettiway, L. E. (1996). *Honey, honey, Ms. Thang: Being Black, gay, and on the streets*. Philadelphia: Temple University Press.

Post, R. M., Roy-Byrne, P. P., & Uhde, T. W. (1988). Graphic representation of the life course of illness in patients with affective disorder. *American Journal of Psychiatry, 145*, 844-848.

Ross, H. (2001, December). HIV in prisons is 5 times the rate of general population: Public health efforts coordinate with corrections. *HIV Impact*, pp. 1-2, 4.

Rosin, H. (1995). The homecoming. *The New Republic, 212*, 21-23.

Ruffins, P. (2002). Fighting to be heard: Black criminologists seek proper context to explain racism's influence on Black crime. *Black Issues in Higher Education, 18*(24), 20-31.

Russell, K. K. (1998). *The color of crime: Racial hoaxes, White fear, Black protectionism, police harassment, and other macroaggressions*. New York: New York University Press.

Staples, R. (2002). White racism, Black crime, and American justice: An application of the colonial model to explain crime and race. In S. L. Gabbidon, H. T. Greene, & V. D. Young (Eds.), *African American classics in criminology & criminal justice* (pp. 161-168). Thousand Oaks, CA: Sage.

Stukin, S. (2002). Sex crimes. *POZ, 7/8*, 13-14.

Tonry, M. (1998). Crime and punishment in America. In M. Tonry (Ed.), *The handbook of crime and punishment* (pp. 1-30). London: Oxford University Press.

U.S. Department of Justice. (1996). *Sourcebook of criminal justice statistics*. Washington, DC: Bureau of Justice Statistics.

U.S. Department of Justice. (1998). *Sourcebook of criminal justice statistics*. Washington, DC: Bureau of Justice Statistics.

Whitfield, L. (2000). The secret plot to destroy African Americans. *POZ, 12*, 45-51.

Whitmeyer, J. (1994). Why actors are integral to structural analysis. *Sociological Theory, 12*, 153-165.

Williams, D. R., & Collins, C. (2001). Racial residential segregation: A fundamental cause of racial disparities in health. *Public Health Reports, 116*, 404-416.

Wilson, P. A. (1995). AIDS service organizations: Current issues and future challenges. *Journal of Gay and Lesbian Social Services, 2*, 3-4.

Wilson, P. (2002). In the fight of our lives: Notes on the AIDS crisis in the Black community. In H. Boyd (Ed.), *Race and resistance: African Americans in the 21st century*. Boston: South End Press.

Wohlfeiler, D. (2000). Structural and environmental HIV prevention for gay and bisexual men. *AIDS, 14*, s52-s56.

Anthony J. Lemelle Jr. is professor and chair of the Department of Africology at the University of Wisconsin–Milwaukee. He is author of Black Male Deviance *and coeditor of* Readings in the Sociology of AIDS.

[22]

"Come back when you're dying:" the commodification of AIDS among California's urban poor

Johanna Crane[a,*], Kathleen Quirk[b], Ariane van der Straten[c]

[a] *Department of Medical Anthropology, University of California San Francisco, Box 0850, San Francisco, CA 94143, USA*
[b] *Cornerstone Consulting, San Francisco, CA, USA*
[c] *Center for AIDS Prevention Studies and Department of Obstetrics, Gynecology, and Reproductive Sciences, University of California, San Francisco, CA, USA*

Abstract

As with any other long-term illness, the decline in health that accompanies symptomatic HIV infection often has a profound negative impact on employment and personal finances. However, research to date on the financial consequences of AIDS has focused largely on middle-class working individuals, and cannot account for the experiences of those who are already poor and unemployed at the time of their infection. We conducted in-depth qualitative interviews with 33 Californian heterosexual couples in which one partner was infected with HIV and the other was HIV-negative. Most couples interviewed were low-income, marginally housed, and either former or active substance users. Unlike their middle-class counterparts, it became clear through the course of our study that many participating couples were living in a world in which a positive HIV antibody test or an AIDS diagnosis could result in an *improved* quality of life by allowing for increased access to Supplemental Security Income, subsidized housing, food and services. This situation is in part a consequence of recent policy decisions related to the "War on Drugs" and welfare reform. These policies have contributed to the creation of an economy of poverty in which the sick, needy, and addicted must compete against each other for scarce resources. Within such an economy, an HIV or AIDS diagnosis may actually operate as a commodity.

Keywords: HIV seropositivity; Heterosexuals; Poverty; Qualitative interviews; Supplemental security income; California; USA

As with any other long-term illness, the decline in health that accompanies symptomatic HIV infection often has a profound impact on employment and personal finances. A number of studies have shown that both work hours and income decrease significantly as HIV progresses (Yelin, Greenblatt, Hollander, & McMaster, 1991; Massagli, Weissman, Seage, & Epstein, 1994; Kass, Munoz, Chen, Zucconi, & Bing, 1994; Leigh, Lubeck, Farnham & Fries, 1995). This phenomenon is also reflected by AIDS magazines such as *POZ* and *A&U*, the pages of which are filled with advertisements for viatical companies[1] offering to help alleviate the "financial disease" of HIV. However, this depiction of AIDS as financially devastating is based largely on the experiences of individuals who were consistently employed prior to their infection and cannot account for the experiences of those who were already poor and unemployed when diagnosed with HIV. As the AIDS epidemic in the US becomes increasingly concentrated among economically disenfranchised groups—particularly low-income drug addicts and their sexual partners—it is crucial that we incorporate an understanding of poverty, addiction, and marginality into AIDS research. How might the consequences of HIV infection be

*Corresponding author.
E-mail address: jcrane@epi.ucsf.edu (J. Crane).

[1] Viatical companies buy the life insurance policies of the terminally ill in exchange for a percentage of the policy's benefit.

different among the poor and unemployed than among the working middle class, and what are the implications of these differences for AIDS prevention?

Using data from a qualitative study of 33 HIV serodiscordant[2] heterosexual couples, we will examine the often contradictory relationship between HIV status, disease progression, and financial stability as it is experienced by predominantly low-income drug addicts and their partners. In part due to recent changes in welfare eligibility criteria, many active and former substance users (both HIV-positive and HIV-negative) are finding it increasingly difficult to access federal disability benefits. In addition, those who are HIV-infected (but not AIDS diagnosed) sometimes find themselves restricted from AIDS-related services because they have not suffered the health problems (low T-cell count, opportunistic infections) that define an AIDS diagnosis. Unlike their middle-class counterparts, it became clear through the course of our study that many participating couples were living in a world in which a positive HIV antibody test or an AIDS diagnosis could result in an *improved* quality of life by allowing for increased access to disability benefits, subsidized housing, food and services. This suggests that the most economically disenfranchised segments of society may be being placed in the difficult position of experiencing AIDS both as a threat and as a means of financial survival.

Methodology: the Partners Qualitative Study

The Partners Qualitative Study was initially developed in order to supplement quantitative data being collected by the California Partners Study II (CPSII), a larger behavioral intervention trial for heterosexual HIV-serodiscordant couples.[3] A subset of 33 couples who had participated in CPSII were recruited into the Partners Qualitative Study. In all cases except one, both partners in each couple were interviewed for a total of 65 individual qualitative interviews. (In one case, the male partner in a couple could not be seen because he was arrested on a parole violation en route to the interview.) Two-thirds of this sample (23 couples) had received a risk-reduction counseling intervention while participating in CPSII. The remaining one-third (10 couples) consisted of couples who were screened for CPSII but, because they did not report any unprotected vaginal or anal sex in the six months prior, received only a baseline interview and no risk-reduction intervention.

The interview guide used in the Qualitative Study consisted of open-ended questions designed collaboratively by the three study staff. Couples could elect to be interviewed either at their homes, provided they had sufficient space to allow for privacy, or at a local clinic or AIDS service organization. Partners in a couple were interviewed separately, by two different female interviewers. Interviews lasted approximately an hour and a half and covered four main topic areas: an evaluation of CPSII (for those who had participated in the intervention); the centrality of HIV in daily life, including questions on financial and social support, stigma, and disclosure of serodiscordant relationship to others; knowledge of and experiences with HIV treatments and medications, particularly protease inhibitor cocktails; and the impact of HIV on sexual and emotional intimacy. Participants were paid US$30 each after completing the interview. All interviews were conducted in English and were tape-recorded and transcribed, with the exception of three cases in which the participant refused to be taped. In these cases, notes were taken during the interview and expanded afterwards. Analysis was conducted through a systematic reading of all interviews by the three study staff and the development of a series of codes corresponding to dominant themes. The interviews were then coded according to their content and inputted into FolioViews, a data management program.

In addition to the qualitative interview, each participant was given a short sociodemographic survey. More extensive demographic information as well as information on drug use, sexual practices, and medical history was also available from baseline interviews conducted by CPSII. Most of the 65 Partners Qualitative Study participants were African American (45%) or white (43%), and lived in San Francisco (38%) or Alameda County (23%), although couples living in seven other San Francisco Bay Area counties were interviewed as well. Participants were predominantly low-income, with 46% reporting an annual household income of under $10,000, and another 25% reporting household incomes of less than $19,000 annually. Sixty-six percent received income from Social Security (see Table 1). During their interviews, most participants described some form of financial hardship, reliance on welfare programs such as General Assistance (GA) and Supplemental Security

[2] In other words, heterosexual couples in which one partner was HIV-positive and the other was HIV-negative.

[3] The CPS II was the second of two large studies of HIV-serodiscordant heterosexual couples headed by epidemiologist Dr. Nancy Padian of the University of California, San Francisco. The purpose of the study was to measure the effectiveness of a brief counseling intervention in reducing behaviors that could result in the transmission of HIV from an HIV-positive to an HIV-negative partner in a heterosexual relationship. Couples who reported unprotected vaginal or anal sex within the last six months at baseline were enrolled in the intervention study. Enrolled couples were followed for 1 yr, with the risk-reduction intervention taking place within the first 3–6 months of this time. All participants were given HIV and STD tests (and standard test counseling) as well as an extensive quantitative interview detailing their sexual and drug practices at baseline, 6 and 12 months.

Table 1
Sociodemographics, $N = 65$ participants

	N	%
Annual gross household income		
$0–9000		
$10,000–19,000	30	46
$20,000–29,000	16	25
$30,000 and over	12	18
	7	11
Income from social security	43	66
Ethnicity		
White	25	39
African American	25	39
Latino/a	5	8
Native American	1	2
Asian/Pacific Islander	1	2
Multiracial	8	12
Female	33	50
HIV-positive	33	50
Other serious health problem	31	48
Ever injected drugs	41	63

Income (SSI), and/or housing instability and reliance on low-income housing programs.

Poverty and vulnerability

Although quantitative sociodemographic data are helpful in describing our study sample, poverty and social marginality cannot be adequately understood by quantitative data alone. Indeed, the richest source of information about the daily realities experienced by our study participants came from the qualitative interviews themselves. In general, the couples we interviewed for the Partners Qualitative Study described considerable economic, social, and physical vulnerability. Whether HIV-positive or HIV-negative, many participants faced much more immediate threats to their well-being than AIDS. Indeed, as we began to interview couples, it was at times striking how little people talked about AIDS. Although many participants were clearly distressed about the possibility of contracting or transmitting HIV within their relationship, there were often many other equally compelling dangers in their lives as well.

Lack of housing, inadequate housing, lack of money, struggles to obtain or maintain benefits, negotiations with the child welfare system, staying out of prison, avoidance of neighborhood gunfire, the management of heroin/crack/speed addiction and/or alcoholism, mental illness, suicidality, violence, abuse, chronic pain, and a variety of disabling and life-threatening illnesses (i.e., hepatitis, cancer, sickle-cell anemia, gout, cirrhosis, diabetes, hemophilia, multiple sclerosis, emphysema) are all among the issues that study participants raised during their interviews. One homeless participant described his and his partner's situation as follows:

> It comes to a point where you have so little money that it is cheaper to go down to the Goodwill and get a pair of jeans for a buck—everything is a buck—and a hooded sweatshirt and a T-shirt and to spend $4 on yourself and $4 on her than it would be for use to go out and pay $4 for a box of Tide and then all the quarters to wash them. I mean it costs like $3.50 for one of those big loads, and then the money to dry them. It costs less to have disposable clothing, especially the way we live going from one place to another. You can't be carrying these big bags around. So it becomes less that we just go down, we pay for new clothes every other day or whatever. And then we go to a public shower or a shelter, shower, throw the new clothes on, and leave the other clothes for somebody else if they need them or throw them away. And that is how you end up living. You live like an animal.
>
> Patrick, HIV-negative, white, 41-yr old, San Francisco

Although most couples we interviewed were not in quite such dire financial straits as this, many did rely on some form of public assistance and/or low-income housing subsidies in order to remain housed and some were, like Patrick (all person and place names have been changed) and his partner, living alternately on the street and in low-income Single Room Occupancy hotels (SROs).

In addition to financial instability and vulnerability to homelessness, the lives of many couples interviewed were shaped by drug addiction and/or alcoholism. At entry into CPSII, 63% of participants reported having a history of injection drug use—a number which may be artificially low, as researchers disagree as to the accuracy of self-reported information (Bourgois, Lettiere, & Quesada, 1997; Darke, 1998). The impact of drugs on participants' lives extended beyond individual use and abuse, as many couples inhabited neighborhoods steeped in the drug economy and the crime and violence that frequently accompany it. Melissa, a crack user who had been living with HIV for 10 yr at the time of her interview described her home as follows:

> Hey I live at [street name] and [street name], ok? I have more of a chance of getting shot by drive-by than from me dying of this [HIV]. For real. I mean I've looked out my window and seen two drive-bys. And people got shot, out my window, ok? And my little daughter, she is 14. She is sitting at our window ledge, looking out on the corner. She goes, "Momma, that boy is cute". I said, "Honey, that boy is a crack dealer. Leave him alone, ok?"

Melissa, HIV-positive, white, 43-yr old, San Francisco

Both this proximity to and involvement in the drug trade made many Qualitative Study participants subject to frequent incarceration and/or street violence—both of which are arguably more immediately disruptive and dangerous than HIV infection, which for many years poses only a remote threat of pain and illness.

In addition to the physical vulnerability that comes from living in a violent environment, many study participants were physically quite fragile due to medical problems other than HIV. Nearly half of the Qualitative Study participants, both HIV-positive and HIN-negative, described serious non-AIDS-related illnesses. In fact, in some couples, the HIV-negative partner was actually in much poorer health than the HIV-positive partner. (Interestingly, over 25% of HIV-negative participants described that they had felt "very unwell" or "fairly unwell" in the month prior to their qualitative interview, versus only 9% of HIV-positive participants). For example, Lisa, a 35-yr-old Filipina woman living in San Francisco, was heavily reliant on her partner Steve, a 39-yr-old white man with HIV, for care following a suicide attempt that made it difficult for her to walk on her own. At the time of her interview she was still using a wheelchair due to serious injuries to her back and feet sustained a year earlier when she had jumped from a window after being arrested for selling drugs. In addition, she suffered from Hepatitis C. Simply based on appearance only, the state of her health seemed much more fragile than that of her partner, whose healthy-looking muscular body sharply contrasted with her wasted and frail appearance.

Similarly, an HIV-negative participant named Diane was in much poorer health than her HIV-positive partner Jerome, who drove her to and from kidney dialysis three times a week as well as to the methadone clinic on a daily basis. Another woman in San Francisco explained that her HIV was rarely a topic of conversation anymore since her partner had been diagnosed with multiple sclerosis:

> Interviewer: Well how's the HIV in terms of your priorities now? Is it like your top concern?
>
> Larissa: It's like no, he ain't even worried about it. It's like I don't even have no disease, with him. Because now it's all about his MS.
>
> Larissa, HIV-positive, African American, 33-yr old, San Francisco

Her partner, heavily depressed since his diagnosis, echoed her statements:

> 'Cause I don't even think about HIV anymore, really, with Larissa...' Cause I have my own medical problems that I have to worry about, unrelated to HIV or anything. I think in a lot of ways my medical problems way outweigh [her] HIV.
>
> Stan, HIV-negative, white, 39-yr old, San Francisco

There were also several HIV-positive study participants for whom HIV was a secondary medical worry in comparison to, for example, the daily monitoring and treatment of insulin-dependent diabetes or the threat of heart failure due to endocarditis (a deterioration of the heart valves that can result from long-term injection drug use). This was most dramatically demonstrated by the case of Joyce, a 50-yr-old African American woman who had recently become infected with HIV. A crack user for the past 10 years and a heroin addict for the past 3 years, Joyce felt that HIV had little impact on her life, as she was "dying anyway" from breast cancer. In the context of the myriad of other health problems she was dealing with (which included Hepatitis C as well as those she mentions below), she portrayed HIV as making little difference in terms of her daily life and survival:

> Interviewer: What are your concerns in your everyday life, like day-to-day, what are the main things that you're dealing with?
>
> Joyce: Nothing really. Not HIV. I have so many other things I'm involved in, HIV is the least thing on my mind. Okay? I don't even trip on HIV. If I do, I would probably be mentally ill at the moment. Okay? I'd be in somebody's mental institution if I did, but I don't, so it doesn't bother me.
>
> Interviewer: So since HIV isn't the main thing, what are the other things?
>
> Joyce: Oh see I have cancer, I have high blood pressure, I have an enlarged heart. I have every other thing except, y'know I'm not worried about HIV... People don't understand HIV is just another disease, that's all. There's nothing you can do about it, there's no need to sit up and discuss it, what for? I mean I don't understand why people go all out their heads and minds to simply discuss HIV. There's no reason to. Discuss cancer—what can you do about cancer? Nothing. What you're gonna do about your heart? Nothing.
>
> Joyce, HIV-positive, African American, 50-yr old, San Francisco

At first glance, Joyce's assertion that "there's no reason to sit up and discuss [HIV]" might appear irrational—and certainly at odds with the goals of medicine and public health. If anything, discussing HIV seems to be especially important in Joyce's case given the already fragile state of her health. However, an alternative interpretation is to see her categorization of

HIV as "just another disease" as a challenge to behavioral approaches to AIDS education and prevention, which tend to focus narrowly on "risk behaviors" that might lead to infection, but rarely consider the larger context of risk (risk of other illness, risk of violence, risk of overdose, risk of homelessness, risk of arrest, etc.) in which many of those most vulnerable to HIV live.

The experiences described by our study participants reflect the shifting impact of the AIDS epidemic in the United States. Since AIDS in the United States was first recognized among fairly privileged communities of white gay men, initial prevention and service responses reflected the needs of this socially marginalized yet relatively financially affluent group. Indeed, the threat posed by the epidemic helped spur a powerful mobilization and politicization of gay and lesbian communities that has resulted in political and cultural changes reaching far beyond the issue of disease prevention. However, as HIV becomes increasingly focused among the most *economically* marginalized members of society, it is crucial that we re-examine our assumptions about service needs and prevention strategies in relation to what one activist has called the "second epidemic" (Anderson in Harris, 1999).

Substance abuse, social security, and the commodification of illness

Study participants repeatedly named income and housing as two major sources of stress in their lives. Two-thirds of those interviewed were dependent upon income from the Social Security Administration, and many had been greatly affected by recent welfare reform legislation changing the eligibility requirements for Supplemental Security Income SSI, the federal government's benefits program for the low-income disabled. The SSI program provides financial support to the ill and disabled who, due to their lack of significant work history, do not qualify for Social Security Disability Insurance (SSDI). In California, where the federal grant may be augmented by state money, SSI pays between approximately US$500 and US$800 a month depending on the amount of the state supplement. It also allows recipients to receive medical coverage through Medi-Cal (California's version of Medicaid, the federal health insurance program for the poor).

Until January 1, 1997, it was possible to receive SSI (or SSDI) for disabilities related to drug addiction and alcoholism (DA&A). Since these addictions were often easier to document than physical or mental illnesses (which require a medical paper trail often difficult to trace among uninsured people with sporadic health care), low-income addicts who may have had numerous qualifying disabilities often sought SSI on the basis of their addiction (or a dual diagnosis which included addiction) rather than other illnesses. During the late 1980s and early 1990s, states with large numbers of substance users—such as California—began to encourage low-income drug addicts and alcoholics to apply for SSI as a way of shifting the cost burdens of supporting them from state to federal programs. As a result, "between 1989 and 1995, the number of SSI beneficiaries classified as drug addicts and/or alcoholics increased from 16,100 to 130,924" (Bluthenthal, Lorvick, Kral, Erringer, & Kahn, 1999).

Unlike other recipients of SSI, DA&A recipients were required to have a representative payee responsible for managing their benefits and preventing their checks from being spent on drugs or alcohol. In addition, DA&A recipients were required to participate in drug treatment while receiving benefits. However, the rapid increase in addicts and alcoholics on SSI in the early 1990s (an increase of over 500% in the first half of the decade) combined with studies showing low participation in drug treatment and the questionable effectiveness of payees led to a backlash against the program.[4] With the "War on Drugs" in full swing and lawmakers taking an increasingly punitive stance towards both substance abusers and welfare recipients, legislation was passed in 1996 eliminating SSI and SSDI benefits on the basis of drug addiction or alcoholism as of January 1, 1997. This legislation was a part of the Republican Congress's "Contract with America" and sought to alleviate concerns that benefits were being spent on drugs and that taxpayer money was being used to subsidize addiction.[5] Of those who lost their benefits, approximately, one-third were successful in re-qualifying under another diagnosis while another one-third appealed and were denied. The remaining one-third did not respond to letters notifying them of the termination of benefits. California—as the state with the largest number of DA&A recipients (25% of the national total)—was particularly impacted by this legislation (Gresenz, Watkins, & Podus, 1998).

Too many T-cells

The situations of a number of those interviewed for the Partners Qualitative Study demonstrate these

[4]Even those who supported giving benefits to substance abusers were troubled by the "perverse incentive" of terminating benefits upon successful completion of drug treatment (Gresenz et al. (1998)).

[5]Ironically, this law may actually increase rates of drug addiction as those who lose their benefits also lose their Medicaid or Medi-Cal, leaving them with no health insurance and thus no means by which to pay for drug treatment. In San Francisco, most methadone maintenance programs cost over $200 a month.

consequences of the 1996 legislation, as well as some additional concerns particular to those living with HIV. Some participants who had been DA&A recipients lost their SSI eligibility, while others who tried to qualify under non-drug related medical or psychiatric diagnoses found that their drug use made the Social Security Administration reluctant to grant them benefits. Jerome, an HIV-positive man who had been receiving SSI for an addiction-related disability, found his check discontinued with the enactment of the law in 1997. Although he had been HIV-positive when he initially applied for SSI, he had been granted benefits on the basis of his heroin addiction. "When I first found out that I was HIV-positive, my T-cells was 1700, so I knew I couldn't get on [SSI] for that", he recounted during his interview. "So I used the drugs and alcohol, and I got it. Then I was on about 2 years when the law came up, and they put me off. " Unable to qualify medically—based on his HIV—Jerome attempted unsuccessfully to qualify under mental illness by arguing that he was suffering from depression as a result of being HIV-positive. However, the simple fact of his drug use seemed to jeopardize his re-qualification under another disability. He blamed the rejection of his claim on his lawyer, who told the judge at his hearing that Jerome was using drugs, even after Jerome had warned him not to:

> That [lawyer]... went right in there and said something about me using drugs, and that's the reason they refused me. 'Cause I was trying to get it on being, how you say, you know things that bother you all the time. You know, you be depressed. Being depressed and stuff like that all the time. The judge wrote a letter back and said he believed... if I would quit using drugs, I wouldn't be depressed, and I could work. And that's why he turned me down.[6]
>
> Jerome, HIV-positive, African American, 53-yr old, Alameda County

At the time of his interview Jerome was on methadone maintenance and rarely used heroin anymore. His time was taken up by providing care for his partner Diane, who was in very poor health and required dialysis three times weekly, and raising Diane's young nephew. The three of them were sharing a one-bedroom apartment with Diane's son and brother. Their chief source of income was Diane's SSI, which she received due to her kidney disease. As a result of Jerome's disqualification from SSI, the car that the couple needed for transportation to and from the methadone and dialysis clinics they visited regularly was in jeopardy of being repossessed, forcing him to hide it:

> Jerome: Lately a lot of my time has been going trying to get good transportatation. Diane has to go to dialysis three times a week, and I need transportation to take her back and forth. And also, we go to the methadone clinic every morning. And I got, my SSI got cut off.
>
> Interviewer: When the law changed?
>
> Jerome: Yeah. And it's been, the financial thing has been kind of rough for us. The car I had, they want to repossess it. I hid it out.

When asked what he saw as the biggest problem in his and Diane's relationship, Jerome responded, "Money". When asked to elaborate, he explained, "She got a steady income, and I don't have one". He implied that being cut off of SSI made him dependent on his partner's income for support, and as a result it was hard for him to fulfill his desired role of family provider. Although he had received General Assistance (the government benefit program for those who are unemployed but do not meet disability eligibility requirements) in the past, he had been disqualified after 6 months when the program learned that he had earned outside money by taking a job delivering telephone books for two weeks. Instead, Jerome did what he could to contribute to the household income in other ways—mainly through his food stamps and money he "hustled up on" to pay their electricity bills. Although both on methadone, Jerome and Diane still injected heroin occasionally, and it was to the drug economy that Jerome turned when he needed to earn money:

> Jerome: [My] food stamps buys groceries enough for the whole house for a month. I give her that and usually I pay the electricity bills. I hustle up on that.
>
> Interviewer: What kinds of things, what ways do you make money?
>
> Jerome: Doing a little something for someone, taking somebody somewhere, somebody need to buy some drugs and I go cop [buy] it for them, you know. And I'm not gonna go cop it if I'm not gonna make

[6] Although it was sometimes difficult to tell whether participants actually felt they suffered from depression or mental illness or whether they simply saw such a diagnosis as a strategy to access a stable income, certainly mental illness among the poor, addicted, and HIV-infected is not uncommon. In a study of 2500 SSI recipients with DA&A-related diagnoses, one study found that 50% reported serious depression, serious anxiety, and memory and concentration problems in the prior 30 days, 40% had been prescribed psychiatric medication, and 30% had attempted suicide (McKay, McLellan, Durell, Ruetsch, & Alterman, 1998). These high rates of mental illness among substance abusers are not surprising given that many psychologists argue that a significant portion of the mentally ill may "self-medicate" through the use of alcohol and illicit drugs (Kasten, 1999; Castaneda, Galenter, & Franco, 1989; Khantzian, 1985).

nothing.... Usually if I go do something for somebody, I'm gonna make $50 or more, or else I'm not doing it.... I been in that life for twenty, thirty years, something like that, so I know all the ups and downs, ins and outs about it. And if there's some way to make some money on messing with it in any kind of way, I know it.

In Jerome's case, his continued reliance on the drug economy for income also fed his and Diane's heroin habit, as even though he rarely spent much money on drugs any more, he would occasionally accept heroin as part of his payment for buying drugs for someone else:

Jerome: Very seldom [do I] spend some money on drugs now. Very seldom.

Interviewer: If you're going to cop for someone else, will they give you some as like a part of your payment?

Jerome: Yeah. Mm-hmm. A lot of times I won't take the drugs, or if I get the drugs, I sell them. I always make some cash money. Always some cash money, but sometimes I make drugs and money. Like I need about $300 to get this car all situated so I can get it registered right.

Though Jerome felt that he had been "doing the right things" since being diagnosed with HIV in 1991 and was happy that he had successfully stayed out of prison for the last 8 years, his disqualification from SSI made it necessary for him to turn to the drug economy he knew so well in order to make ends meet in his household. In this way—contrary to the intension of the 1996 legislation—losing his check actually served to drive him back into the drug economy rather than keep him out of it.

Steve, an HIV-positive San Francisco resident, had also been unsuccessful in qualifying for SSI under either HIV or mental illness. Like Jerome, Steve had received SSI in the past but lost it when the law changed:

Steve: I was discontinued from Social Security because there was a history of drugs and alcohol, and the new law in 1997.

Interviewer: They cut you off SSI?

Steve: Mm-hmm. And my HIV status is not disabling enough to qualify so now I'm on GA. And I used an attorney from AIDS Benefit Counselors to do a hearing and an appeal and I'm still with them but I just lost an appeal. My psychiatrist, my therapist feels I'm unemployable because of psychological reasons as well as physical but that doesn't fit into the category that the government sees, so therefore I'm in this gray area.

Steve, HIV-positive, white, 39-yr old, San Francisco

Steve felt that his application for SSI had been denied partly on the basis of his physical health, which was generally good despite his HIV infection:

Interviewer: Your Social Security, you had it before based on addiction?

Steve: My HIV and addiction. It was a dual diagnosis.

Interviewer: But then even once they said ok we're not giving people SSI for addiction, your HIV wasn't enough?

Steve: Exactly. I wasn't ill enough. My T-cells were too high.

Ironically, because qualification for SSI also automatically qualifies recipients for Medi-Cal coverage, when Steve "wasn't ill enough" to retain his SSI, his health care coverage was also threatened. Although still receiving Medi-Cal at the time of our interview, Steve feared that it would be discontinued shortly as he had just lost his appeal for SSI.

The situations of Jerome, Steve, and other study participants who were unable to qualify for SSI are in part the result of the current punitive attitude towards drug addiction in US politics. This attitude has resulted in a public welfare system that punishes substance users for their addiction but essentially rewards them for other illnesses. Rejected on the claims of one disability, they turn to others—real or exaggerated—in an attempt to access a stable, legal monthly income and (by extension) adequate housing.[7] As their situations demonstrate, simply being HIV-positive does not automatically entail eligibility for SSI. Being able to claim other chronic illnesses or disabilities in addition to HIV or having a diagnosis of AIDS increase the likelihood that an individual will qualify for benefits, provided that one of these disabilities is not drug addiction or alcoholism. Thus, within the context of scarcity and addiction in which many study participants lived, declining health status became a commodity.[8]

[7]The loss of SSI had a serious impact on participants' ability to pay for housing, particularly in San Francisco's inflated housing market, where even rooms in low-income residence hotels—often the last resort before the street—frequently cost US$500 a month or more. One 1995 survey of injection drug users in the Bay Area found the rate of homelessness among those who did not receive SSI to be double that of those who did (Bluthenthal et al., 1999).

[8]This commodification of illness among the poor is not limited to HIV/AIDS nor is it solely an issue among substance abusers. See Estroff (1981) for a discussion of a similar "professionalization of patienthood" among the low-income mentally ill.

The commodification of AIDS

Jerome and Steve both felt that their T-cell counts had been too high to allow them to qualify for SSI based on their positive HIV-status. Although the epidemiological definition of AIDS used by the Centers for Disease Control (CDC) includes having a T-cell count of less than 200, the Social Security Administration has its own criteria for an AIDS disability diagnosis that is not linked to the CDC's and is based primarily on opportunistic infections rather than T-cell count. Nonetheless, it is true that sicker individuals (who often have low T-cell counts, in addition to various opportunistic infections) are more likely to qualify as AIDS diagnosed by Social Security Administration. As a result, some study participants who had successfully qualified for SSI based on an AIDS diagnosis worried that health improvements would jeopardize their disabled status and thus their eligibility for benefits. Dorothy was a recovering heroin and crack addict who was living on and off in residence hotels with her partner at the time of her interview. Dually diagnosed with both disabling HIV and a psychiatric disability, Dorothy's eligibility came in to question when her HIV did not progress:

> As far as like the HIV, my attorney got like a letter two years ago from the Social Security office, and they wanted to know how come I was still receiving SSI, because they had supposedly lost my file. When my lawyers wrote them back that I was getting SSI for being HIV-positive and for psychiatric, they wanted to know what my T-cell count and stuff was and how long I had been positive. So when they told them, Social Security was like, well, how come she's still getting SSI, there's nothing wrong with her as far as her being HIV-positive. They were trying to cut me off.
>
> Dorothy, HIV-positive, African American, 38-yr old, Alameda County

In this case, with the help of her lawyers, Dorothy was able to maintain her benefits on the basis of her psychiatric diagnosis. However, her story suggests that even when SSI is awarded based on HIV-related illness, continued eligibility may be somewhat tenuous. The Social Security Administration does periodically review disability cases to verify that recipients are still eligible for benefits. Recently, the Administration has increased the number of "continuing disability reviews" it conducts, from 157,000 reviews in 1996 to 792,000 in 1999. Of the reviews conducted in 1999, nearly 97,000 individuals had their benefits terminated (Social Security Administraton, 2000).

This possibility of losing or being denied benefits on the basis of improving health has created a situation in which chronic illnesses are essentially commodities that the poor must use to barter with the public welfare system in order to obtain a stable income (SSI) and access to health care (Medi-Cal or Medicaid). In the case of HIV, the diagnosis appears to become more "valuable" as the disease progresses. Among those interviewed for the study, this was most graphically demonstrated by Christopher, who purposefully refused to take antiretroviral medication until his T-cells dropped below 200 in order to secure his SSI benefits. An HIV-positive heroin addict living in an SRO in California's agricultural Central Valley, Christopher had originally been awarded SSI on the basis of his addiction but risked losing it with the passage of the 1996 legislation. In an effort to requalify for medical reasons, Christopher attempted to maximize his HIV disease:

> In fact I wouldn't take any medication for the first 18 months I was positive. I absolutely refused to take anything for it.... My check was going through being changed over. They're taking up from everybody for drugs and alcohol and I was trying to get on [for] medical reasons, so I made sure my CD4 count was low. I mean I would not do anything to help myself. Like I used to tell everybody, I would rather expire before the check expires. That was my whole attitude, period. I don't want to be around without that check, I'd rather die first.
>
> Christopher, HIV-positive, white, 40-yr old, San Joaquin County

This strategy proved successful and Christopher's SSI was continued for medical reasons. As soon as his check was no longer in jeopardy, Christopher acquiesced to his doctor's recommendation that he begin treatment:

> I finally went in and said, okay, I got SSI straightened out, and they're gonna do the change-over, now we'll start medicating me. Y'know 'cause maybe I was driving [my doctor] nuts. Here he got a guy coming in that don't want no medicine, y'know and he couldn't understand that. I guess if you're making 40,000 or 50,000 a year, you got money, it doesn't seem that important. But when you don't have it, you want it. And he couldn't understand that this check was more important than months of my life were.

Christopher's case is an extreme example of the way in which poor health may become a bargaining chip used by the very poor in order to negotiate for income and services. Although Christopher's logic is unsettling, it is not irrational. Though he risked dying from AIDS by refusing medication, in the end, Christopher's gamble paid off. As a self-declared "dope fiend" who spent a significant portion of his SSI check on heroin, Christopher's case is the type that originally generated the 1996 legislation eliminating benefits to addicts. However, it is important to recognize the possibility that even though he was using a portion of his SSI benefits to buy drugs, Christopher's health and well-being were perhaps better off than they would have been had he lost his check, which easily could have left him homeless, sick from heroin withdrawal, and more likely to take desperate and dangerous measures—such as needle-sharing—to ensure his next fix (Bourgois et al., 1997). These consequences, in turn, would have made it extremely difficult to adhere to his complex antiviral regimen, thus further endangering his health and survival. Christopher's willingness to risk developing AIDS in order to secure his SSI check was atypical but nonetheless indicative of the way that the benefits system may actually reward illness.

In addition, for those participants who were feeling well and expressed interest in returning to work, the system seemed to punish their improved health. Several Qualitative Study participants expressed a desire to work at least part-time, but feared that the Social Security Administration would learn of their earnings and either discontinue their benefits or decrease their checks. As a result, a number of participants on SSI and SSDI worked under the table as a way of making ends meet. For example, one low-income HIV-positive participant who received a combination of SSI and SSDI benefits was also working under the table as an independent painting contractor in order to pay the rent and support his partner, who was unemployed at the time.

Because SSI and SSDI eligibility are linked to Medicaid eligibility, participants interested in working feared losing their health care coverage in addition to their benefits checks. Susan, an HIV-positive recovering heroin addict, had returned to school to become trained and certified as a drug and alcohol counselor. However, she feared that if she joined the work force, she would no longer have health insurance:

> Susan: I'm just leaving it up to God and the faith as to whether I'll ever be able to work. I don't know. I don't know what health I'll be in. I don't know if I'll have the stamina for working. It has affected me so that I have to live on $640 a month [her SSI and SSDI payments] and somehow make that work... That's how I feel limited, and I feel like it's going to be tough, even with the certificate, getting a job once that [HIV] is disclosed.
>
> Interviewer: And your [HIV] drugs are paid for?
>
> Susan: That's a blessing. Thank God. And if I did get a job, I better have damn good coverage. 'Cause I can't almost afford to go to work unless they're going to totally cover these pills.
>
> Interviewer: Right. That's the catch-22.
>
> Susan: And you know, that little bit where you go on probation with most jobs—they want to make sure you work out before medical kicks in. Well, I couldn't afford to drop my Medi-Cal and wait for that 6 months.
>
> Susan, HIV-positive, white, 43-yr old, San Joaquin County

Ironically, it was around this issue of entering the work force that the experience of lower income but upwardly mobile participants seemed to dovetail with those of more middle class (but, due to HIV, downwardly mobile) participants. Robert, an HIV-positive participant who lived in a wealthy Bay Area suburb, was supplementing his disability benefits by doing part-time computer work under the table. His concerns echoed Susan's:

> The [HIV] drugs that I take cost over $1000 a month, and that's come down, you know. I get that from ADAP [AIDS Drug Assistance Program],[9] and the reason I qualify for ADAP is because I'm on disability. So, if I were to go back to work, I would lose my ADAP drug assistance. I would lose my health insurance, which is Medicare HMO right now. At some point I may be able to enroll in some sort of company health plan if I were to do that, but then they all have pre-existing condition stuff. Even if they signed me on, there's a waiting period of 6 months to a year.
>
> Robert, HIV-positive, white, 40-yr old, Santa Clara County

Although the very poor may find that their disability status opens the door to a degree of upward mobility through access to SSI, those such as Susan who try to further their mobility by increasing their legal income beyond their benefits grant may find that they are trapped. Some, like Robert, may choose to risk working under the table in order to maintain their standard of living. Those with fewer resources may find it easier to return to illegal sources of income, as Jerome did when he lost his General Assistance eligibility because of a legal job delivering telephone books. The result is that both poor and middle-class individuals in need of disability benefits may be forced to pretend that they are sicker than they really are or poorer than they really are in order to maintain a livable income and health care coverage.[10]

[9] ADAP, the AIDS Drug Assistance Program, is a federally funded program that helps people with HIV and AIDS cover the cost of their antiretroviral medications.

[10] In 1999, the US Congress passed legislation allowing states to continue providing Medicaid to employed individuals with a "medically improved disability" who no longer qualify for SSI. However, states are not required to do so.

"Come back when you're dying"

SSI is not the only potential financial benefit that can come with HIV or AIDS. Access to housing, food, and social services are also more easily obtained by those with HIV. Frequently, as with SSI, an AIDS diagnosis is more "valuable" that an HIV-positive serostatus, and can open the door to even more resources and support. Nathan, who had been diagnosed with HIV only a year earlier, was working as a welder and living in a shelter in Sonoma County at the time of his interview. He and his wife, both recovering drug addicts, had lost their apartment due to a drug relapse in the previous year. In addition, he had suffered two recent heart attacks. Once back in recovery and working again, Nathan's main concern was securing a place for himself and his wife to live. However, his attempts to seek housing assistance from AIDS service organizations were unsuccessful:

> Our main concern is finding a place to stay because it's just like they said, they have some services, but it's like if you're not, what they call it, if you're not, if your T-cell count is above 200 or you're not symptomatic, you can't get help. It's like, ok, you had a virus but you're not dying so there's nothing we can do for you. Come back when you're dying, you know.
>
> Nathan, HIV-positive, African American, 47-yr old, Sonoma County

Other rent subsidy programs did not consider disease stage as part of their eligibility, but were difficult to access for other reasons. Some AIDS housing programs have restrictions, such as requiring the subsidy recipient to live alone. Christopher experienced this with his government rent subsidy:

> In June I got the letter, June the sixth, retro dated to June the first. You're cut off. We're no longer funding you because you violated Rule Four. So I called and I go, "What's Rule Four?" and they tell me, having somebody live with you.

Christopher's violation was having Emily, his partner, share his subsidized SRO room. Although he was generally happy to obtain any HIV-related benefits he could, Christopher spoke bitterly about what he experienced as hostility on the part of housing services saying, "they want you to die alone". Jerome also experienced difficulty accessing an AIDS housing program in Alameda County, which would have paid 70% of his rent for 18 months. His partner was allowed to live with him, but the program refused his application because he and Diane did not have legal custody of their 2-yr-old nephew for whom they had been caring for the past year.

As both Christopher's and Jerome's experiences indicate, accessing HIV-related services such as housing affected not only their own life circumstances but also those of their HIV-negative partners and other family members. In this way, HIV-negative partners are also affected by the commodification of illness that can result from rules regarding service provision to the poor and HIV-infected. Some HIV-negative study participants spoke very favorably about the vicarious benefits that they had been able to access through their partner's HIV status:

> Interviewer: I know that you're HIV-negative, but has having a partner who is HIV-positive affected—has there been a financial effect from HIV?
>
> Kevin: Financial effect? Yeah. We get money! [laughs] We get paid. God damn like we get paid!
>
> Kevin, HIV-negative, African American, 45-yr old, San Francisco

At the time of our interview, Kevin—an HIV-negative crack user—was living in a cheap SRO room in what he described as a "nice area" of downtown San Francisco, an upgrade from his previous residence in the Aurora Hotel, which burned down in late 1996 and has yet to be rebuilt. His 2 year relationship with his white, HIV-positive girlfriend, Melissa—also a crack user—was on the wane. Even though he no longer considered her to be his girlfriend, he maintained his official status as her caregiver, for which he was paid by a program providing in-home health care for the disabled:

> Interviewer: So what kinds of benefits did you guys get?
>
> Kevin: Well. I'm her caregiver. So we get, I get paid.
>
> Interviewer: So, how does that work? I didn't know about that.
>
> Kevin: You apply for it. IHSS.[11] It is like, the state or something like that. They call you, you're their caregiver... I'll always be her caregiver.

Patrick, Lois's partner, also extolled the benefits that he had been able to access through his partner's HIV-positive status:

> Interviewer: Has it affected you financially at all? Her being HIV-positive?
>
> Patrick: No, not at all. Actually, the only thing it has ever done is good for me. You know it has gotten me

[11] In-Home Support Services (IHSS) is a non-profit organization that provides home health care for the chronically ill and disabled. Those who are prescribed home health care by their doctor can choose their own caregiver, who will be paid by IHSS.

food at times, it has gotten me shelter at times, you know, when we were down.

Interviewer: We're just trying to figure out if financially it is a burden on you, or you know?

Patrick: It has not been any burden on me. It has been nothing but an asset because, like I say, they've helped her out and in turn it has helped me out because we're together.

These perspectives are in sharp contrast to the experiences of the few middle-class Qualitative Study participants, several of whom had to stop or at least disrupt their employment in order to cope with their declining health and had thus experienced a marked financial loss due to HIV.

On the other hand, many HIV-negative partners deeply resented their lovers' improved access to resources and services of which they themselves were equally in need. Vanessa, a 27-yr-old mother of two, was living with her children in a run-down apartment in Stanislaus County at the time she was interviewed. She was struggling to pay the rent and support her sons on money she earned by working nights. Her HIV-positive husband, Anthony, was living and working 2 h away in San Mateo County, where he was required to finish serving his parole. Vanessa expressed resentment for her partner's increased access to resources due to his HIV:

I mean if we were [living] together, we would probably get into a lot more things together but what really pisses me off [is that] a lot of the services that are offered are only available to him. Even though I'm his wife, they are only for him.... That's messed up. And actually, one time I got really mad at him, because he's HIV positive and they give him all this free stuff, and here I am a single mother struggling with two kids, trying my hardest to get out of being homeless, and working, and they fuckin' give it to him for free.

Vanessa, HIV-negative, African American, 27-yr old, Stanislaus County

Later in the interview, she spoke specifically about their unequal access to housing—a major concern of hers as she and her two young sons had been homeless and living in a shelter when she first met her husband 2 years before, and had since suffered displacement from the house they had moved into with Anthony when it caught fire and burned down:

Vanessa: The only reason I got help that time when Community Shelter helped me pay my rent in December was because of Anthony. Anthony wasn't really living in the home; she wasn't supposed to give me that check 'cause he wasn't living in the house.

Interviewer: So it's because he's positive?

Vanessa: Yep, and guess what? And that's why I wish he was living here. If he was living here, they would pay our rent 8 months of the year. They would pay our rent. Like right now, I'm going to be behind... my rent is $530 and I'm already $123 behind from since I moved here... I'm going to be another $130 behind, so I'm going to be $260 behind [this month].

Other HIV-negative participants also expressed anger over their partners' access to services. This was the case with Ruth, an HIV-negative participant who shared a low-rent San Francisco apartment with her HIV-positive partner Luis and her brother, who was dying of AIDS. A heroin addict on methadone maintenance like her partner, her own health problems included breast cancer, neuropathy, and depression:

Ruth: I only have my counselor at the methadone clinic, that's it.

Interviewer: Yeah, but you could use some other people to talk to about the HIV and about your breast cancer and things like that.

Ruth: Well I know all I can; I keep up on the latest thing of AIDS and HIV preventions. And how to deal and take care of people who are HIV or full-blown AIDS affected. I just never think of myself anymore. I've been so depressed to the point where if I don't start seeing somebody—I don't know. Maybe I'll become suicidal. That's a joke [slight laugh]. I would never take the coward's way out. But I could suffer in silence. I'm tired of doing that.

Interviewer: Yeah. Well, you don't have to. There are people out there to help you.

Ruth: Yeah. But it seems like there's never anybody out there for us that are not infected. You don't need us. That's not fair.

Ruth, HIV-negative, white, 48-yr old, San Francisco

Ruth's accusation that "You don't need us" speaks to the commodification of AIDS. She recognizes what has come to be known in the literature as "AIDS exceptionalism"—the differential response to AIDS in comparison to other diseases. Initially, the term "AIDS exceptionalism" arose in reference to HIV testing which—unlike testing for other sexually transmitted diseases in the US—was voluntary, anonymous, not reported to public health agencies and did not require partner notification. These exceptional policies were upheld as necessary to protect privacy and avoid "driving AIDS underground" given the stigma and discrimination associated with an HIV-positive serostatus (Bayer, 1999; Scheper-Hughes, 1993). More recently, the term has been used to describe the exceptional medical services (such as ADAP) offered to AIDS patients versus people suffering from cancer or other diseases—a situation that is particularly salient in the US, which lacks universal health care coverage (Casarett & Lantos, 1998). In addition, the preferential provision of food and housing to people with AIDS, as described by our study participants, provides yet another example of AIDS exceptionalism. Although we by no means advocate the reduction of HIV and AIDS-related benefits, the denial of services to those who are HIV-negative but otherwise in equally dire straits (financially and medically) is extremely problematic, particularly in the context of an economy of poverty. In other words, the ethical problem of AIDS exceptionalism is not "special treatment" of those with AIDS, but rather the failure to provide adequate assistance to all of the chronically ill (Bayer, 1999).

Implications for prevention

At its most extreme, the commodification of AIDS may actually encourage those with minimal resources and little to lose to become HIV-infected as a means by which to meet basic needs. In her interview, Dorothy expressed concern that her partner was purposely trying to become infected in order to access the benefits that she was able to receive for being HIV-positive. In recovery herself, she left the homeless shelter where she and her partner had been living when her partner was kicked out for drug use. Since then, the couple had been living on and off in residence hotels. Frustrated with her partner's continued crack use and worried about her upcoming heart surgery for endocarditis, Dorothy was planning to move into a subsidized housing situation for which she—but not her partner—was eligible due to her HIV. For her, the incentive for her partner to become infected created by preferential access to services was one of the most difficult aspects of her relationship:

> Interviewer: What's hardest about being in a mixed-status couple, where your partner's negative?
>
> Dorothy: That he always wants to, he always talks about he wants to get it.
>
> Interviewer: He does?
>
> Dorothy: Yeah. I think he's crazy.
>
> Interviewer: Why does he say that, do you think?
>
> Dorothy: Because he looks at all the benefits and stuff that I get. He looks at it, well, you get housing. You get this, you know? I told him, I said but that's no reason to want to get the virus just to want to get anything. It's like all the time he tells me, "I wish I had the virus too". ... I just think it's the drugs talking sometimes. He goes through this phase where, you know, he wants to catch the virus.

Even for those who would not take such drastic measures, the increased access to income and housing afforded by a positive HIV test may make condom-and-bleach public health prevention messages appear weak by comparison.

Furthermore, this commodification of AIDS may have other less linear but nonetheless equally significant implications for HIV prevention. This is particularly true in relation to SSI eligibility. As argued by Gresenz et al. (1998), one possible consequence of the 1996 law eliminating SSI and SSDI benefits for drug and alcohol-related disabilities is that fewer substance abusers will access drug treatment, either because they are no longer required to as a condition of receiving benefits or because they cannot afford to as a result of being discontinued from Medi-Cal or Medicaid. Indeed, one San Francisco study examining the impact of the withdrawal of benefits from injection drug users showed that only 11% of those not on SSI were participating in drug treatment, versus 33% who did receive SSI (Kral, Lorvick, & Bluthenthal, 1997). This decreased access to treatment combined with the stress of losing benefits and—as a potential consequence—housing, may actually serve to increase rather than decrease rates of substance abuse (and thus transmission of HIV via shared drug paraphenalia). Again, this is supported by the San Francisco study in which those receiving SSI reported fewer injections than those who did not receive benefits (Kral et al., 1997).

What are the implications of these connections for AIDS prevention? Firstly, this analysis demonstrates that prevention efforts must understand and respect the life circumstances of target populations. This includes the recognition that, for some, HIV or AIDS may represent one of the few available means by which to access the income and housing that middle-class populations may take for granted. As such, traditional behavioral approaches to prevention may be inappropriate and alienating to low-income drug addicts. By focusing on individual decision-making processes, behavioral prevention models advocating condom literacy and risk reduction counseling often ignore the larger social and economic forces that may affect risk-taking. An alternative approach would allow us to see those "at risk" for HIV not as isolated individuals practicing risky behaviors, but rather as individuals who are one part of a larger social structure which shapes their choices and behavior in complex and often contradictory ways. According to this approach, policy decisions such as the 1996 law eliminating SSI eligibility for substance abusers are seen as linked to HIV prevention through the impact that they may have on the daily lives of infected and at-risk individuals. Similarly, policy decisions affecting the availability of drug treatment or the construction of affordable housing are also seen as critical to HIV prevention as those whose lives are chaotic due to drug addiction and/or homelessness may be less concerned with or less able to reduce behavioral risks such as needle sharing or condomless sex. It is through the documentation of the effects of adverse policy decisions on the HIV risk of individuals that AIDS prevention research might better address the root causes of the epidemic among the urban poor.

Acknowledgements

We would like to thank Nancy Padian and Cynthia Gómez for their support through the development and implemention of this study, as well as Andy Williams and Kelly Knight for their thoughtful review of an earlier version of this manuscript. Thanks also to our 65 study participants, whose openness and insight made this research possible.

This research was supported by the Center for Disease Control and Prevention, Grant # U64/CCU912270

References

Bayer, R. (1999). Clinical progress and the future of HIV exceptionalism. *Archives of Internal Medicine, 159*, 1042–1048.

Bluthenthal, R. N., Lorvick, J., Kral, A., Erringer, E. A., & Kahn, J. G. (1999). Collateral damage in the war on drugs: HIV risk behaviors among injection drug users. *The International Journal of Drug Policy, 10*(1), 22–38.

Bourgois, P., Lettiere, M , & Quesada, J. (1997). Social misery and the sanctions of substance abuse: Confronting HIV risk among homeless heroin addicts in San Francisco. *Social Problems, 44*(2), 155–173.

Casarett, D. J., & Lantos, J. O. (1998). Have we treated AIDS to well? Rationing and the future of AIDS exceptionalism. *Annals of Internal Medicine, 128*, 756–759.

Castaneda, R., Galenter, M., & Franco, H. (1989). Self-medication among addicts with primary psychiatric disorders. *Comprehensive Psychiatry, 30*(1), 80–83.

Darke, S. (1998). Self-report among injecting drug users: A review. *Drug and Alcohol Dependence, 51*, 253–263.

Estroff, S. (1981). *Making it crazy: An ethnography of psychiatric clients in an American community*. Berkeley: University of California Press.

Gresenz, C. R., Watkins, K., & Podus, D. (1998). Supplemental Security Income (SSI), Disability Insurance (DI), and substance abusers. *Community Mental Health Journal, 34*(4), 337–350.

Harris, P. (1999). The degaying of AIDS? *A&U, 8*(4), 46–49.

Kass, N. E., Munoz, A., Chen, B., Zucconi, S L., & Bing, E. G. (1994). Changes in employment, insurance, and income in relation to HIV status and disease progression. *Journal of Acquired Immune Deficiency Syndrome, 7*(1), 86–91.

Kasten, B. (1999). Self-medication with alcohol and drugs by persons with severe mental illness. *Journal of the American Psychiatric Nurses Association, 5*(3), 80–87.

Khantzian, E. J. (1985). The self-medication hypothesis of addictive disorders: Focus on heroin and cocaine dependence. *American Journal of Psychiatry, 142*(11), 1259–1264.

Kral, A., Lorvick, J., & Bluthenthal, R. (1997). *Impact of withdrawal of SSI disability benefits for injection drug users in the San Francisco Bay Area*. Paper presented at the Eighth International Conference for the Reduction of Drug Related Harm, Paris, France.

Leigh, J. P., Lubeck, D. P., Farnham, P. G., & Fries, J. F. (1995). Hours at work and employment status among HIV-infected patients. *AIDS, 9*(1), 81–88.

Massagli, M. P., Weissman, J. S., Seage, G. R., & Epstein, A. M. (1994). Correlates of employment after AIDS diagnosis in the Boston health study. *American Journal of Public Health, 84*(12), 1976–1981.

McKay, J. R., McLellan, A. T., Durell, J., Ruetsch, C., & Alterman, A. (1998). Characteristics of recipients of Supplemental Security Income (SSI) benefits for drug addicts and alcoholics. *Jounal of Nervous and Mental Disease, 186*(1), 290–298.

Scheper-Hughes, N. (1993). AIDS, public health, and human rights in Cuba. *Lancet, 342*, 965–968

Social Security Administraton. (2000). The supplemental security income program at the millenium. Available: www. ssa.gov/policy/programs/SSI/millenium/index. html.

Yelin, E. H., Greenblatt, R. M., Hollander, H., & McMaster, J. R. (1991). The impact of HIV-related illness on Eemployment. *American Journal of Public Health, 81*(1), 79–84.

[23]

Context, Culture, and Collaboration in AIDS Interventions: Ecological Ideas for Enhancing Community Impact

Edison J. Trickett[1,2]

The paper describes developments in preventive interventions in AIDS/HIV that signal the emergence of a new perspective focusing on community-level intervention and community-level impact. These developments are reviewed, and a ecological framework from community psychology is offered as an integrating and guiding mind-set for future community impact interventions. Key ingredients are community assessment, the ecology of lives lived in different sociocultural communities, the development of collaborative relationships, and enhancing community empowerment through the development of local community resources. The perspective is outlined using existing examples of AIDS/HIV preventive interventions, which focus on such community-level issues as norms regarding sexual risk behavior. The paper concludes with a call to explore more fully the wisdom found in existing community-level work in the AIDS/HIV area and to develop an ecological mind-set when engaging in preventive community interventions.

KEY WORDS: culture; context; collaboration; ecology; AIDS.

INTRODUCTION

In a somewhat paradoxical fashion reminiscent of the scientific benefits emerging from the necessities of World War II (Sarason, 1981), the continuing public health crisis of the AIDS pandemic may well be a watershed for furthering preventive interventions responsive to the real world in which people live. The behavioral science response to this crisis has, in many ways, been shaped by the "normal science" (Kuhn, 1970) paradigm, reflected in a conceptual focus on what Sarason (1981) has called the "acultural, asocial, ahistorical individual." As such,

[1]University of Illinois at Chicago, Chicago, IL.
[2]Address correspondence to Edison J. Trickett, University of Illinois at Chicago, Chicago, IL.

it has emphasized the importance of individual-level outcomes and theory-driven investigator control of both questions and methods.

As experience within this perspective has accumulated, however, questions have been raised about the degree to which individual behavior change can be sustained no matter what the context (Rhodes, Stimson, & Quirk, 1996). Further, the adequacy of such interventions to counteract the multifaceted sets of environmental risk factors that contribute to both the incidence of risk behavior and "relapse" after intervention has been questioned (Latkin, 1998; Tawil, Verster, & O'Reilly, 1995; Singer and Weeks, 1996; Choi and Coates, 1994; Kegeles, Hays, and Coates, 1996; Altman, 1995).

In response, a new perspective is emerging that localizes interventions in specific sociocultural community contexts, focuses on how preventionists can collaborate with local citizens and organizations, and locates specific interventions in the context of a long-range strategy for community development. Here the emphasis is increasingly on the sociocultural community context, drawing attention to those extra-individual forces and resources which affect the lived experience in communities. They may include racism, the availability of adequate health care, the quality of schools, neighborhood violence, and the norms enforced by social support systems. Culture is in community norms around sex-role prerogatives, strategies of coping with social inequality, beliefs about the role of professional versus indigenous helpers when one is in trouble, and how preventionists who are outsiders to the community are viewed.

The core of this perspective is provided by Singer and Marauch-Rodriquez (1996): "The starting point for AIDS prevention is recognition that AIDS is only a cover term for a complex set of intertwined local epidemics that differentially impact diverse subgroups in varied local settings based on their sociopolitical location, social and sexual networks, specific configuration of risk behaviors (e.g. sexual practices and patterns), attitudes and beliefs, and prior health status (e.g. stressors, nutrition, exposure to other sexually transmitted diseases)" (p. 141). Adds Aggleton (1993): "HIV/AIDS health promotion is always context-bound, taking place within discrete communities and in specific settings. The impact of health promotion is always contingent, being mediated by social expectations, popular prejudices, and group norms . . . An understanding of the social context is therefore essential when it comes to making sense of the varying ways in which people respond to health promotion intervention" (p. 186).

The goal of the perspective involves impact at the community as well as individual level. The task is to design interventions which both aid populations at risk and contribute to the development of community resources for longer-range local development. Such longer-range resources can include preventive interventions self-consciously designed to leave a community infrastructure in place when the specific intervention has run its course. They may involve creating new community settings designed to serve hard-to-reach populations. Resources are also created when the skill level of local citizens recruited to carry out preventive interventions is enhanced, or when interventions are aimed at changing local norms around the importance of safe sex behavior. Each in its own way contributes to the local resource pool and to what Iscoe (1974) called the "competent community."

Achieving this level of impact suggests a collaborative and empowering relationship between preventionists and community members. Beeker, Guenther-Grey, and Raj (1998) use the term "paradigm drift" to signal this aspect of the new perspective. "A community empowerment intervention seeks to effect community-wide change in health-related behaviors by organizing communities to define their health problems, to identify the determinants of those problems, and to engage in effective individual and collective action to change those determinants." This definition is predicated on three assumptions: first, that health problems have multiple determinants, often including those which lie beyond individual volition and skill; second, that communities must participate in both the definition and solution of health problems; and third, that the success of an intervention depends on the capacity of the community to engage in effective action. (Beeker et al., 1998).

There is an increasingly visible body of preventive work within the AIDS arena that illustrates this concern with community impact. This work documents the imprint of culture and context on the expression of risk and the design of interventions, the value of empowerment as process and goal, and the necessity of collaboration in the spirit of creating community impact. Included here are preventive interventions which focus on multiple-component interventions with gay men (Kegeles, Hays, & Coates, 1986) designed to orchestrate, integrate, and enhance local resources. Other studies have successfully changed peer group and community norms around safe-sex behavior (Treadway & Yoakam, 1992, Kelly, St. Lawrence, Diaz, Stevenson, Hauth, Brasfield, Kalichman, Smith, & Andrew, 1991; Kelly, St. Lawrence, Stevenson, Hauth, Kalichman, Diaz, Brasfield, Koob, & Morgan, 1992), as well as norms in the social networks and support systems of at-risk individuals (Power, Jones, Kearns, Ward, & Pierce, 1995; Latkin, 1998; Latkin, Mandell, Oziemkowska, Celentano, Vlahov, Ensminger, & Knowlton, 1995).

Taken together, these studies show the power of context and the social relations of at-risk individuals to influence individual behavior and the promise of intervening in those contexts. They encompass a variety of populations in both urban areas and smaller cities, use both qualitative and quantitative methods (Carey, 1993), and, in general, provide both an empirical and conceptual base for further community-level work.

The purpose of this paper is to further this "paradigm drift" toward community-level interventions by describing a perspective from community psychology which directly addresses the community impact issue. It is an ecological perspective, which provides an overarching framework within which to locate such community-level interventions as described above. It further directs attention to certain kinds of questions of relevance to the design and evaluation of preventive interventions, which include community-level impact as a goal. In so doing, this perspective complements thc comparable efforts of scholars representing different fields to move the level of analysis and intervention in AIDS/HIV to one focusing on community change and community impact (Altman, 1995; Singer & Weeks, 1996; Tawil, Verster, & O'Reilly, 1995; Kegeles, Hays, & Coates, 1996; Walker & Small, 1991).

An Ecological Perspective and Community Impact

Ecology has historically focused on the nature of the environment and person-environment transactions. Emphasis has rested on methods of describing environments and studies of how contrasting environments affect the development and well-being of those in them (e.g. Bronfenbrenner, 1979; Moos, 1974, 1975, 1979; Barker, 1968). Within community psychology, however, Kelly and colleagues (Kelly, 1968, 1970, 1986) and elaborated by the author (Trickett, Kelly, & Todd, 1972; Trickett, 1984; Trickett, Kelly, & Vincent, 1985; Trickett & Birman, 1989; Trickett, 1996) have linked this emphasis on environmental assessment to designing preventive interventions intended to have community impact. The spirit of community development is key.

Kelly's work draws on ecological processes developed in field biology, where the biological community, not the individual plant, is the level of analysis. The ecological processes of adaptation, cycling of resources, interdependence, and succession are more fully outlined elsewhere (Kelly, 1968; Trickett, Kelly, & Todd, 1972; Trickett, Kelly, & Vincent, 1985; Kelly, 1986; Trickett & Birman, 1989; Trickett, 1996). Each focuses on differing aspects of the community context. Together, they represent a framework for assessing community norms and structures, latent and manifest personal and social resources in the community, how differing aspects of the community fit together in reciprocal interaction, and the sociocultural history and future hopes of the community and its varying groups.

From this perspective, community-level intervention includes three additive and complementary sets of activities: (1) environmental assessment of the community context and the ecology of individual lives in that context; (2) developing collaborative relationships between the preventionist and the setting or community where the intervention occurs, and (3) designing interventions through processes which serve the goal of community development by enhancing local resources. (Trickett & Schmid, 1992; Trickett & Birman, 1989).

The spirit of these activities is commensurate with Altman's (1995) description of the goals of a public health perspective on community intervention: "(1) integrate interventions into a community infrastructure, (2) use comprehensive, multilevel intervention approaches, (3) facilitate community participation and promote community capacity-building, and (4) conduct thorough needs assessment/environmental reconnaissance in order to tailor interventions to the community context" (p. 229).

The perspective has been applied to diverse research and intervention domains such as social networks and social support (Mitchell & Trickett, 1979; Trickett & Mitchell, 1993), traumatic stress (Trickett, 1995), community consultation (O'Neill & Trickett, 1983; Trickett, Barone & Watts, 2000), adolescent coping in high school (Kelly and Associates, 1979), the provision of community mental health services (Kelly, 1966), and school-community relationships (Trickett, 1997). In each case the intent has been to provide a sociocultural surround or context within which more discrete psychological phenomena occur. Each case represents an effort to shift the level of analysis from the more personological to the more contextual and cultural.

The remainder of the paper elaborates on how these topics form a foundation for designing preventive AIDS interventions which show community impact.

ENVIRONMENTAL ASSESSMENT: THE COMMUNITY CONTEXT AND THE ECOLOGY OF LIVES

Community Context

From an ecological perspective, the sine qua non for approaching the concept of community impact involves an understanding of what the community of interest is like. The community may be defined as a single setting like a school or neighborhood organization; it may encompass a geographical area served by local organizations, or it may be defined as a neighborhood bound together by shared cultural experiences and traditions. Whatever the local definition, developing concepts for assessing the community and processes for gaining such understanding are primary. Such community assessment becomes the knowledge base for the development of preventive interventions aiming for community impact. It provides data for such questions as:

(1) What range of possible community-level interventions can the community tolerate and support?
(2) What different groups or social settings in the community can be engaged in the intervention to coordinate various additive and incremental change efforts?
(3) What other existing community organizations have comparable goals and resources to collaborate with over time?
(4) What processes are necessary to ensure that the intervention project meshes with the hopes and aspirations of the community?
(5) What community-level outcomes are locally relevant which can be targeted and assessed in terms of intervention impact?

The four different ecological processes of Kelly's perspective sharpen the community assessment process. The adaptation principle directs attention to the community's broad demand characteristics and opportunity structures—the environment which surrounds the individual. The distribution and availability of behavior settings (Barker, 1968) relevant to risk behavior, the degree of neighborhood collective efficacy (Sampson, Raudenbush, & Earls, 1997), and the cultural norms supportive homophobia are examples of the nature of the community context within which individuals must function.

The cycling of resources principle emphasizes the importance of identifying, conserving, managing, and creating resources at the community level of analysis. Community resources may include effective interorganizational connections, well-respected citizens who care about what is good for the community, traditions for coping with adversity, or social settings that facilitate the resolution of community conflict. They may include religious institutions that serve both the spiritual and tangible needs of those unwilling to deal with the formal service system. Thus, not only people, but settings and events (Trickett, Kelly, & Vincent, 1985) are potential resources for the development of AIDS interventions designed to have community impact.

The interdependence principle focuses on the interconnectedness of aspects of the community; of formal helping agencies and informal supportive networks of individuals at risk for HIV; of the cooperative or competitive connections among agencies which may influence how services are delivered; of the compatibility of commitments of the intervention team and the expectations of community agencies. The ecological assumption is that even individually-based interventions have ripple effects and unintended consequences in the community since they represent an intrusion into the ongoing processes of community life. Thus, how different relevant facets of the community of interest fit together to form a coherent and ongoing context for individuals helps inform how to construct an integrative, community-level intervention strategy. It further advocates for unearthing the unintended consequences of interventions by ongoing assessment of the ripples they create in the community context.

The final principle is succession, a reminder that institutions and communities have histories and hopes for the future just as individuals do. This principle recognizes the powerful role of culture and tradition as forces at both the individual and group level which frame the kinds of interventions which are acceptable and comprehensible from a community's perspective. The potency of such forces is well articulated by Stevenson and White (1994) in their discussion of the historical antecedents of African-American suspicion of government-sponsored AIDS interventions fueled by the infamous Tuskegee experiment of years ago. Preventive interventions are grafted onto an ongoing cultural and community history and offer the potential opportunity of tapping into the hopes for a better tomorrow. Thus, getting to know this history and hopes for the future represents time well spent when developing interventions intended to have community impact.

The importance of community assessment is highlighted in the AIDS literature. One strand of this work focuses on the intervention implications of differences among communities and the behavior settings in them. Aggleton (1993) comments: "The communities within which interventions take place are not homogeneous, but socially and culturally fragmented—by age, by class, by culture, and in some cases by gender. This renders any simple notion of community development problematic. It is, for example, absurd to talk about carrying out HIV/AIDS health promotion within the 'injecting drug using community,' within the 'gay community,' or even worse, within the 'heterosexual community' " (p. 195).

Further, the assessment of critical behavior settings in the community provide a contoured perspective on risk-related phenomena and potential sites for intervention. Matricka-Tyndale, Elkins, Haswell-Elkins, Rujkarakorn, Kuyyakanond and Stam (1997) present data on the contexts and patterns of men's commercial sexual partnerships in over 30 villages in northeastern Thailand based on observations, structured face-to-face interviews, focus groups, informal interviews with key informants, and surveys. Four different contexts for purchase of sexual services were identified, all of which were related to peer group activity and alcohol consumption: brothels, festivals, sugarcane camps, and cattlemarkets. Within each of these settings "the key factor was that 'sexual servicing' was considered part of entertainment, much like eating and drinking were" (p. 211). Their intervention suggestions flowed from their understanding of the contexts in which sexual activity occurred.

Latkin, Mandell, Vlahov, Oziemkowska, Knowlton, and Celentano (1994) studied the differential impact on HIV-related risk behavior. Through interviews with intravenous drug users these authors identified five different settings affecting injection practices: one's own, friends, and mother' residences, shooting galleries, and semipublic areas. These settings differed from one another both in terms of frequency of use (e.g. injecting at home or in a friend's home occurred with greatest frequency) and injection practices (e.g. friends' residence and shooting galleries were most positively related with the frequency of sharing unhygienic needles). They conclude that HIV related behaviors may differ by environmental setting and suggest that systematic study of drug behavior settings will, by clarifying the social dynamics of risk behaviors, inform the design of interventions.

Not only do different types of settings differ in the kinds of risk-related behavior they promote; the same type of setting may differ depending on community factors. Friedman and colleagues (Friedman, Neagius, des Jarlais, Sotheran, Woods, Sufian, Stepherson, & Sterk, 1992) studied such differences in shooting galleries. Differences included whether or not they were residential or non-residential, quasi-residential, where clientele are highly restricted, or "crack spots," apartments in which there is a permanent crack party. "These different kinds of high-risk drug use locations, then, may well be associated with different patterns of viral spread among and across friendship circles, and do seem to be associated with different levels of risk behavior and risk reduction" (pp. 195–6).

These kinds of studies provide roadmaps for assessing select aspects of community structures and norms. Additional community assessment strategies are also found in the AIDS literature as well. Higgins, O'Reilly, Tashima, Crain, Becker, Goldbaum, Elifson, Galavotti, and Guenther-Grey (1996) describe formative community assessment research as a prelude to intervention design and implementation. They outline a series of steps through which information about the community was gained from a variety of sources. In addition to conducting literature reviews and focus groups, they held meetings with "interacters" (those in touch with the target community who were not themselves part of the community), "gatekeepers" whose sanction was important for community access, and "key participants" or members of the community. On the basis of this environmental assessment, semistructured interviews were then constructed to assess the ecology of the everyday lives of community members, including questions about the activities of daily life, media usage, and where and with whom they spent their time. The authors suggest that such a lengthy and inclusive procedure produced necessary insider information relevant to instrument development and increased access to community members (see also Aral & Fransen, 1995; Feldman, O'Hara, Baboo, Chitalu, & Lu, 1997; Asthana & Oostvogels, 1996 for other community assessment strategies).

The commitment to community assessment thus includes not only the task of gaining substantive knowledge about where interventions may occur but also developing relationships with insiders who can serve as key informants about community life. Through such activities the interventionist can develop a sense of who to count on, what settings need to be created to enhance local problem-solving, and how discrete interventions can be placed into a larger community-relevant plan for reducing relevant risk factors and promoting proactive community action.

The Ecology of Lives: Contextual and Cultural Influences on Individual Experience

An ecological perspective on community impact not only directs attention to the nature of communities themselves; it focuses on the lived experience of individuals in their community contexts. From an ecology of lives perspective, the meaning of risk behavior cannot be separated from the context in which it occurs. Further, behavior occurring in any one area of an individual's life is understandable only in the context of other situations the individual must negotiate. As Kelly and Kalichman (1995) argue with respect to the interpersonal context of HIV risk behaviors, "research on situational antecedents of high-risk sex underscores the fact that sexual behavior does not occur in isolation from other events in people's lives, and that these other events can serve as important risk cofactors" (p. 911).

One important aspect of individuals in varying community contexts involves their cultural identification. While the degree of this group identification varies greatly within any culture or subculture, the cultural context has been resourcefully employed in many AIDS interventions to increase cultural validity. For example, in discussing AIDS interventions among the African communities in Canada, Nakyonyi (1993) focuses on how culturally-linked norms such as keeping problems to oneself, discussing sex only with those of similar age, and homophobia affected the development of HIV/AIDS education workshops. Guydish and Sanstad (1992) discuss the concept of familismo in Hispanic communities as a cultural resource to draw on in the design of interventions. Here, concern for family members may provide both a motivation and a strategy for intervening with IV drug users about AIDS and transmission issues (see also Singer & Marxauch-Rodriquez, 1996; Weeks, Schensul, Williams, Singer, & Grier, 1995; Herdt & Boxer, 1991; Singer, Willms, Adrien, Baxter, Brabazon, Leaune, Godin, Maticka-Tyndale, & Cappon, 1996 for additional examples).

While the ecology of lives perspective is relevant to the design of interventions across levels of analysis, its particular relevance with respect to community impact lies in its focus on extraindividual forces which create a context for individual risk behavior. With respect to broad cultural forces, for example, considerable attention has been focused on the disempowered position of women, particularly women who are also ethnic minorities.

Drawing on the findings of 17 studies in developing countries worldwide, Gupta and Weiss (1993) conclude that "in many settings, the cultural norms that demand sexual fidelity and docile and acquiescent sexual behavior among women permit—and sometimes even encourage—early sexual experimentation, multiple partnerships, and aggressive and dominating sexual behavior among men" (p. 399). They specify a number of cultural norms, such as condoms signifying a lack of trust and intimacy and being associated with illicit relationships. "Together with women's social and economic dependency, (these norms) can limit a women's ability to negotiate safer sex with her partner, restrict her access to information and knowledge about her body, force her to sometimes barter sex for survival, increase her vulnerability to physical violence in sexual interaction, and compromise her self-esteem" (p. 399) (see also Amaro, 1995).

A similar concern with disenfranchisement is voiced with respect to African-American communities. Friedman, Neaigus, Des Jarlais, Sotheran, Woods, Sufian, Stepherson, and Sterk (1992) present a stark assessment of the relationships among patterns of risk behavior, risk reduction, and race. "On a structural level, race shapes the entire life-situations of everyone in a multi-racial society, and thus shapes hopes, fears, and options that can affect the probability of high-risk behaviors" (p. 396). These same authors speculate that the differing patterns in white and black risk behaviors reported in the literature may, in part, be understood "in terms of the simultaneous processes of social inequality and survival cultures" (p. 397).

Such macro forces are reflected in the everyday lives of individuals and the roles they play. De Zalduondo (1991) suggests their implications for prostitution, defined as "an institution or pattern of impersonal and/or time-limited transactions between socially unrelated individuals involving purchase and sale of sexual services at an acknowledged and agreed upon unit price" (p. 229). She suggests that "since the concept hinges on the presence of sex disconnected from a social relationship, it is doubtful that a useful understanding of prostitution can be constructed without reference to social stratification, family structures, gender roles, and other sociocultural variables that define normative sociosexual roles and relations" (p. 230).

Herdt and Boxer (1991), in a study of African-American and Latina women, add to these macro forces additional concerns for immigrant women who are not fluent in English. They emphasize that in order to cope with recurrent dangers facing them "sexuality... may become, at times, a source of employment, a method for establishing proprietary rights in a relationship, or a means of establishing tangible or emotional support" (p. 179). They describe the crucial role of ethnographic knowledge in developing culturally sensitive programs in terms of finding credible community sources to deliver interventions, locating them in familiar and trusted community institutions such as churches, and developing community outreach programs to reach populations not typically identified or seen by service providers. Such a stance provides an early detection perspective on how proposed interventions mesh with community norms and hopes. (see also Singer & Marxauch-Rodriquez, 1996). Out of these cultural contexts came "culturally targeted interventions (which) were designed to bring about behavior change through a conscious incorporation of each group's key concepts, beliefs, and values into the content and presentation format of the program" (p. 256).

In addition, Herdt and Boxer (1991) suggest that this knowledge affected the recruitment strategies used for African-American and Latina women and the decision to conduct interventions in different sites to accommodate the lives of different groups of women (e.g. using women's houses for the Latino intervention, particularly for sex partners of IDU men). Initial findings comparing their culturally-grounded intervention with a standard intervention showed that both initiation and retention rates for Latina women were improved by the option in the Latino culturally targeted program to provide intervention in the women's homes. This was particularly true for women with small children and those not engaging in drug use.

While considerable work has been conducted in varying ethnic minority sociocultural contexts, less has focused specifically on how the acculturative stresses facing immigrant groups affects their risk-behavior. "Most ethnocultural communities differ considerably from the dominant culture in their approach to sex education, dating relationships, and expectations of sexual behavior in young people.

Both parents and young people expressed frustration over the conflicting directions for behavior. Traditional ways are threatened by youths' adoption of dominant cultural perspectives and behavior" (Singer, Willms, Adrien, Baxter, Brabazon, Leaune, Godin, Maticka-Tyndale, & Cappon, 1996, p. S29).

The concept of acculturation has been extended to include the gay culture as well. Using such acculturation criteria as the regular reading of gay newspapers and belonging to organizations for gay men, Seibt, Ross, Freeman, Krepcho, Hedrich, McAllister, and Fernandez-Esquer (1995) found a relationship between level of acculturation into the gay culture and both talking to sexual partners about HIV risk reduction and frequency of condom use for anal sex. In like manner Dowsett (1995) describes "community attachment strategies" to complement the community intervention strategies developed by gay organizations in Australia. The overall community interventions strategies focus on the use of community leaders, entertainers, and gay media to "link gay men to a safe sex culture invoking the notion of a community acting to protect itself" (p. 247). As Dowsett (1995) describes it: "Safe sex culture cannot be reduced to sexual practice: it is context for practice and, as such, has been remarkably successful in sustaining a high degree of compliance for safe sex by most men with most partners most of the time in Australia" (p. 247). Both studies suggest the power of social integration into the gay culture as a protective factor and reinforce the importance of understanding the norms of that culture and how to foster their protective aspects.

The ecology of lives, then, draws attention to the varied ways in which individuals in differing social and cultural contexts experience pressures, opportunities, and constraints which influence the range of behaviors they exhibit, the meanings of those behaviors, and the kinds of choices they see as possible and unthinkable. Such knowledge is relevant for interventions at any level of analysis. The particular relevance of the ecology of lives for community-level intervention, however, lies in its ability to illuminate how local culture, supports, resources, pressures, and the local meaning of high risk behaviors may be incorporated into interventions. These interventions can draw community resources and settings into the community change process while simultaneously targeting extraindividual forces relevant to individual risk.

The Intervention Relationship: Creating Collaborative Relationships and Empowering Processes

The preceding provides a variety of examples of the importance of understanding community, contextual, and cultural influences in designing interventions which mesh with community culture and create conditions for community impact. This represents the first aspect of the ecological perspective mentioned earlier in the paper; namely, the importance of community assessment and the ecology of lives. The second emphasis of the ecological perspective focuses on how to enact the intervention relationship with the community in ways that facilitate the durability, effectiveness, sustainability, and community impact of the intervention.

From an ecological perspective, the social values and epistemological premises of the preventionist are nowhere better illuminated than in the kind of research relationship formed with participating groups or communities. The spirit of this relationship is concretized by the amount of energy devoted to collaborative relationship building, the degree to which the community is allowed influence in selecting problems and research strategies, and the vigilance adopted by the researcher in seeking out both positive and negative ripple effects in the local ecology.

The epistemological assumptions behind the value of collaboration involve the belief that effective collaborations can: (a) increase the preventionist's knowledge of the community context and community concerns and hopes, (b) increase the chances that the intervention taps into hopes for the future, (c) improve the quality and validity of the data gathered, and (d) provide an opportunity for ongoing feedback about the effects of the intervention on the setting. Pragmatically, these outcomes increase the likelihood that, because the intervention is responsive to local influence, it will be more sustainable when the project ends or the grant runs out (see Trickett, 2000 for an overview) and thus become an enduring community resource.

By creating dialogue between the "theory class" and citizens, collaboration serves the additional purpose of reducing the disconnect between research and practice. As Freudenberg, Eng, Flay, Parcel, Rogers, and Wallerstein (1995) state in their assessment of AIDS interventions in the United States: "The discrepancy between published evaluations and community practice was striking. With a few notable exceptions, the evaluated programs were generally too simplistic or superficial to make a significant impact on the continued transmission of infection or too unique to be valuable . . . Almost none looked at the impact of multiple interventions that bombarded vulnerable populations in many communities or compared the impact on different subpopulations. Yet the most creative, intensive, and innovative community-based interventions were rarely evaluated, leaving these programs to repeat the same mistakes, unable to share their successes or failures with others" (p. 300).

Various models of collaboration have been proposed. For example, Reed and Collins (1994) developed a "three communities model" resting on the assertion that "research on the effectiveness of interventions . . . cannot be conducted without the participation of those who design the research, those who deliver the interventions, and those who receive the interventions" (p. 69). These authors outline in detail how the differing professional life style demands and goals of the research community, the CBO community, and the Persons with HIV/Persons with AIDS communities cause inevitable and predictable tensions in the collaborative process (see also Grace, Fernandez, Battjes, Sloboda, & Genser, 1994).

From an ecological perspective, however, the critical task is to understand how varying models of collaboration play out in differing ecological contexts. Research reports of this issue suggest that while it is perhaps easy to tout collaboration as an unalloyed good, in practice it is a complex, context-bound phenomenon. For example, surveys of survey researchers (e.g. Weiss, 1976) suggest a common wisdom about the importance of hiring indigenous interviewers. However, Huygens, Kajura, Seeley, and Barton (1996), in portraying the role of local interviewers in a series of studies in Uganda, state that while "local interviewers played a crucial role in the translation of the questionnaire into Luganda and helped to a large extent in understanding cultural meanings for the data collected . . . there is evidence to suggest that respondents were sometimes reluctant to talk to local interviewers about sensitive issues" (p. 225).

At the same time, these authors also provide many examples of the useful role of collaboration. They show how anthropological understanding can complement and enrich quantitative survey data. Referring to the multiple meanings of such terms as "abstinence," they conclude: "Our results show that 'abstinence' was actually a concept that included various sexual practices (such as coitus interruptus and using a condom for over 20% of their sample). The number of people equating it with total avoidance from physical contact in sex was relatively small. This should stimulate AIDS workers to re-think carefully what we are proposing when we promote 'abstinence' as a strategy for behavior change" (p. 228).

Within the broad band of collaborative models, the concept of empowerment is emerging as a goal of AIDS interventions (Beeker, Guenther-Grey, & Raj, 1998; Freudenberg & Zimmerman, 1995). A strong case has been made for the empowerment paradigm as a perspective which can affect community health and well–being more generally (e.g. Altman, 1995; Rappaport, 1987) and AIDS intervention more specifically (Airhihenbuwa, DiClemente, Wingood, & Lowe, 1992; Asthana & Oostvogels, 1996). However, the issue of whether or not one group can ever truly empower another has been raised (Gruber & Trickett, 1986) as is the question of whether or not an empowerment ideology is always one shared by certain groups of stakeholders in the intervention.

With respect to the latter, for example, Lackey, Moberg, and Balistrieri (1997) found in their evaluation of community organizations that the issue of the credibility of the evaluation led some community groups, particularly those concerned with group advocacy (e.g., receiving recognition, attracting funding), "to surrender evaluation ownership to the institutionally-based, professional evaluators, particularly when they anticipated favorable evaluation findings" (p. 137). In these ecological conditions it was more useful in terms of the organization's goals to renounce empowerment as commonly conceived in favor of a strategy which the organization felt preserved evaluator credibility.

Thus, collaboration may unlock the door to conceptual and pragmatic advances in AIDS interventions which aspire to community impact. However, the collaborative process involves a complex undertaking whose intricacies are just beginning to be explored. From an ecological perspective, however, they represent critical endeavors and ones which need to be explored more fully in differing sociocultural contexts.

CONCLUSION: COUPLING ECOLOGY WITH COMMUNITY IMPACT

The thrust of the preceding is that increasing the community impact of AIDS interventions rests on an appreciation of the community context, the ecology of lives of targeted groups, and the development of reciprocal, collaborative relationships in the design, conduct, and evaluation of interventions. In reviewing AIDS interventions, at least two different literatures have emerged. One, quite rigorous, and representing "normal science," deals primarily with individual-level interventions. The other, more descriptive, non-comparative, and qualitatively rich, portrays the adventuresome effort of community-based organizations, activist groups, action researchers, and service sector settings more generally to create locally meaningful and responsive interventions whose effectiveness and community impact is often unknown.

The ecological perspective focusing on community impact does not argue against the "normal science" concern with scientific rigor, hard data, and causal explanation. However, it does imply numerous paradigm-stretching activities. These include the active involvement of stakeholders in a collaborative process and conceptual attention to the nature of the sociocultural context of the community. It demands an appreciation of the insider perspective on the lives of those whose behavior is the object of change and a willingness, indeed eagerness, to make sure that preventive interventions are appropriate for local conditions. It further rests on the ability of those controlling external resources to consider how to promote both scientific accountability and programmatic flexibility so that preventionists can be responsive to local concerns and adapt accordingly. Finally, it requires a time frame and longitudinal commitment which embeds any efforts at the quick fix into a larger plan for the long haul of community development.

The ecological perspective and the selective review of literature is offered not as a blueprint but as a stimulus for thought about how to embed current work on AIDS interventions within the critical task of community development. Doing so will push further the boundaries of normal science and add to the already palpable impact that AIDS interventions have had on behavioral science more generally. Emerging work within the AIDS prevention community, which addresses community-level impact, suggests that investigators are implicitly if not explicitly using ecological premises as they develop preventive interventions dealing with HIV/AIDS. This work is creating new ideas, methods, and knowledge about the complexities of attempting to change community structures, norms, and dynamics.

As such, it represents a resource for all of us concerned with the development of prevention as a community-building activity.

REFERENCES

Aggleton, P. (1993). Promoting whose health? Models of health promotion and education about HIV disease. *Advances in Medical Sociology*, 3, 185–200.

Airhihenbuwa, C.O., DiClemente, R.J., Wingwood, G.M., & Lowe, A. (1992). HIV/AIDS education and prevention among African-Americans: A focus on culture. *AIDS Education and Prevention 4(3)*, 267–276.

Altman, D. G. (1995). Strategies for community health intervention: Promises, paradoxes, pitfalls. *Psychosomatic Medicine*, 57, 226–233.

Amaro, H. (1995). Love, Sex, and Power: Considering women's realities in HIV prevention. *American Psychologist*, 50(6), 437–447.

Aral, S.O., & Fransen, L. (1995). STD/HIV prevention in Turkey: Planning a sequence of interventions. *AIDS Education and Prevention, 7(6)*, 544–553.

Asthana, S., & Oostvogels, R. (1996). Community participation in HIV prevention: Problems and prospects for community-based strategies among female sex workers in Madras. *Social Science and Medicine, 43(2)*, 133–148.

Barker, R. G. (1968). *Ecological psychology: Concepts and methods for studying the environment of human behavior*. Stanford, CA: Stanford University Press.

Beeker, C., Guenther-Grey, C., & Raj, A. (1998). Community empowerment paradigm drift and the primary prevention of HIV/AIDS. *Social Science Medicine, 46* (7), 831–842.

Bronfenbrenner, U.(1979). *The ecology of human development: Experiments by nature and design*. Cambridge: Harvard University Press.

Carey, J. W. (1993). Linking qualitative and quantitative methods: Integrating culture factors into public health. *Qualitative Health Research*, 3(2), 298–318.

de Zalduondo, B.O. (1991). Prostitution viewed cross-culturally: Towards reconceptualizing sex work in AIDS intervention research. *Journal of Sex Research*, 28(2), 223–248.

Dowsett, G. (1995). Sexual contexts, HIV prevention and gay men. *Venereology, 8(4)*, 243–250.

Feldman, D. A., O'Hara, P., Baboo, K. S., Chitalu, N. W., & Lu, Y. (1997). HIV prevention among Zambian adolescents: Developing a value utilization/norm change model. *Social Science and Medicine*, 44(4), 455–468.

Friedman, S. R., Neaigus, A., de Jarlais, D. C., Sotheran, J. L., Woods, J., Sufian, M., Stepherson, B., & Sterk, C. (1992). Social intervention against AIDS among injecting drug users. *British Journal of Addiction*, 87, 393–404.

Freudenberg, N., Eng, E., Flay, B., Parcel, G., Rogers, T., & Wallerstein, N. (1995). Strengthening individual and community capacity to prevent disease and promote health: In search of relevant theories and principles. *Health Education Quarterly*, 22(3), 290–306.

Freudenberg. N. & Zimmerman, M.A. (Eds.) (1995). *AIDS prevention in the community: Lessons from the first decade*. American Public Health Association: Washington, D.C.

Grace, W.C., Fernandez, I., Battjes, R.J., Sloboda, Z., & Genser, S.G. (1994). Organizational psychology perspectives on Enhancing National HIV prevention research among drug abusers. *Psychology of Addictive Behaviors, 8(3)*, 191–197.

Gruber, J. & Trickett, E.J. (1987). Can we empower others? The paradox of empowerment in the governing of an alternative public school. *American Journal of Community Psychology, 15*, 353–372.

Gupta, G.R., & Weiss E. (1993). Women's lives and sex: Implications for AIDS prevention. *Culture, Medicine, and Psychiatry, 17*, 399–412.

Guydish, J., & Sanstad, K. H., (1992). Behavior change among intravenous drug users: The role of community-based interventions. *Psychology of Addictive Behaviors*, 6(2), 91–99.

Herdt, G. & Boxer, A. M. (1991). Ethnographic issues in the study of AIDS. *Journal of Sex Research*, 28(2), 171–187.

Higgins, D. L., O'Reilly, K., Tashima, N., Crain, C., Beeker, C., Goldbaum, G., Elifson, C. S., Galavotti, C., & Gunther-Grey, C. (1996). Using formative research to lay the foundation for community level HIV prevention efforts: An example from the AIDS community demonstration projects. *Public Health Reports*, 3(Supplement 1), 28–35.

Huygens, P., Kajura, E., Seeley, J., & Barton, T. (1996). Rethinking methods for the study of sexual behavior. *Social Science and Medicine, 42(2)*, 221–231.

Iscoe, I. (1974). Community psychology and the competent community. *American Psychologist*, 29, 607–613.

Kegeles, S.M., Hays, R.B., & Coates, T.J. (1996). The Mpowerment project: A community-level HIV prevention intervention for young gay men. *American Journal of Public Health, 86(8)*, 1129–1136.

Kelly, J. A. & Kalichman, S. C. (1995). Increased attention to human sexuality can improve HIV-AIDS prevention efforts: Key research issues and directions. *Journal of Consulting and Clinical Psychology*, 63(6), 907–918.

Kelly, J.A., St. Lawrence, J.S., Diaz, Y., Stevenson, L.Y., Hauth, A.C., Brasfield, T.L., Kalichman, S.C., Smith, J.E., & Andrew, M.E. (1991). HIV risk behavior reduction following intervention with key option leaders of population: An experimental analysis. *American Journal of Public Health, 81(2)*, 168–171.

Kelly, J.A., St. Lawrence, J.S., Stevenson, Y., Hauth, A.C., Kalichman, S.C., Diaz, Y.E., Brasfield, T.L., Koob, J.J., & Morgan, M.G. (1992). Community AIDS/HIV risk reduction: The effects of endorsements by popular people in three cities. *American Journal of Public Health, 82(11)*, 1483–1489.

Kelly, J. G. (1986). Content and process: An ecological view of the interdependence of practice and research. *American Journal of Community Psychology*, 14, 581–589.

Kelly, J. G. (1979). *Adolescent boys in high school: A psychological study of coping and adaptation.* Hillsdale, NJ.: Erlbaum.

Kelly, J. G. (1970). Antidotes for arrogance: Training for a community psychology. *American Psychologist*, 25, 524–531.

Kelly, J.G. (1968). Toward an ecological conception of preventive interventions. In J.W. Carter, Jr. (Ed.). *Research contributions from psychology to community mental health.* New York, NY: Behavioral Publications.

Kelly, J. G. (1966). Ecological constraints on mental health services. *American Psychologist*, 21, 535–539.

Kuhn, T. H. (1970). *The structure of scientific revolutions.* Chicago: University of Chicago Press.

Lackey, J. F., Moberg, D. P., & Balistrieri, M. (1997). By whose standards? Reflections on empowerment evaluation and grassroots groups. *Evaluation Practice, 18* (2), 137–146.

Latkin, C. (1998). Outreach iin natural settings: The use of peer leaders for HIV prevention among injecting drug users' networks. *Public Health Reports* (Supplement 1), 151–159.

Latkin, C., Mandell, W., Oziemkowska, M., Celentano, D., Vlahov, D., Ensminger, M., & Knowlton, A. (1995). Using social network analysis to study patterns of drug use among urban drug users at high risk for HIV/AIDS. *Drug and Alcohol Dependence, 38*, 1–9.

Latkin, C., Mandell, W., Vlahov, D., Oziemkowska, M., Knowlton, A., & Celentano, D. (1994). My place, your place, or no place: Behavior settings as a risk factor for HIV-related injection practices of drug users in Baltimore, Maryland. *American Journal of Community Psychology*, 22, 415–430.

Maticka-Tyndale, E., Elkins, D., Haswell-Elkins, M., Ruikakoirn, D., Kuyyakanond, T., & Stam, K. (1997). Contexts and patterns of men's commercial sexual partnerships in Northeastern Thailand: Implications for AIDS prevention. *Social Science and Medicine*, 44(2), 199–213.

Mitchell, R.M., & Trickett, E.J. (1980). Social networks as mediators of social support: An analysis of the determinants and effects of social networks. *Community Mental Health Journal, 16*, 27–44.

Moos, R. H. (1974). *Evaluating treatment environments: A social ecological approach.* New York: Wiley.

Moos, R. H. (1975). *Evaluating correctional and community settings.* New York: Wiley.

Moos, R. H. (1979). *Evaluating educational environments.* San Francisco: Jossey-Bass.

Nakyonyi, M. M. (1993). HIV/AIDS education participation by the African community. *Canadian Journal of Public Health*, Supplement 1, S19–S23.

O'Neill, P. & Trickett, E. J. (1982). *Community consultation.* San Francisco: Jossey-Bass.

Power, R., Jones, S., Kearns, G., Ward., J, Perera, J. (1995). Drug users networks, coping strategies, a HIV prevention in the community. *The Journal of Drug Issues, 25(3)*, 565–581.

Rappaport, J. (1987). Terms of empowerment/exemplars of prevention: Toward a theory for community psychology. *American Journal of Community Psychology, 15*(2), 121–148.
Reed, G.M., & Collins, B.E. (1994). Mental health research and service delivery: A three communities model. *Psychosocial Rehabilitation Journal, 17(4)*, 69–81.
Rhodes, T., Stimson, G. V., & Quirk, A. (1996). Sex, drugs, intervention, and research: From the individual to the social. *Substance Use and Misuse*, 31(3), 375–407.
Sampson, R., Raudenbush, S., & Earls, F. (1997). Neighborhoods and violent crime: A multilevel study of collective efficacy. *Science*, 277, 918–924.
Sarason, S. B. (1981). *Psychology misdirected.* New York: Free Press.
Seibt, A.C., Ross, M.W., Krepcho, M., Hedrich, A., McAlister, A., & Ferna'ndez-Esquer, M.E. (1995). Relationship between safe sex and acculturation into the gay subculture. *AIDS Care, 7*(Suppl. 1), s85–s88.
Singer, M. & Marxuach-Rodriquez, L. (1996). Applying anthropology to the prevention of AIDS: The Latino Gay Men's Mental Health Project. *Human Organization*, 55(2), 141–148.
Singer, M. & Weeks, M. (1996). Preventing AIDS in communities of color: Anthropology and social pervention. *Human Organization*, 55(4), 488–492.
Singer, S.M., Willms, D.G., Adrien, A, Baxter, J., Brabazon, C., Leaune, V., Godin, G., Maticka-Tyndale, & Cappon, P. (1996). Many voices: Sociocultural results of the ethnocultural communities facing AIDS study in Canada. *Canadian Journal of Public Health, 87*(Supp. 1), s26–s32.
Stevenson, H.C., & White, J.J. (1994). AIDS prevention struggles in ethnocultural neighborhoods: Why research partnerships with community based organizations can't wait. *AIDS Education and Prevention, 6(2)*, 126–139.
Tawil, O., Verster, A., & O'Reilly, K. R. (1995). Enabling approaches for HIV/AIDS prevention: Can we modify the environment and minimize the risk? *AIDS*, 9, 291–306.
Treadway, L. & Yoakam. J. (1992). Creating a safer school environment for lesbian and gay students. *Journal of School Health*, 62(7), 352–357.
Trickett, E. J. (2000). Collaboration and Social Inquiry: The Multiple Roles of Relationships in Creating Useful and Valid Knowledge. Unpublished paper, University of Maryland.
Trickett, E.J. (1997). The Interdependence of Schools and Communities: Developing an Ecological Mind-Set on School-Community Collaboration. In W. Martin and J. Swartz (Eds.), *Applied Ecological Psychology for Schools within Communities: Assessment and Intervention.* (Pp. 139–166), Mahwah, NJ: Lawrence Erlbaum.
Trickett, E.J. (1996). A future for community psychology: The contexts of diversity and the diversity of contexts. *American Journal of Community Psychology*, 24(2), 209–229.
Trickett, E.J. (1995). The community context of disaster and traumatic stress: An ecological perspective from community psychology. In S.E. Hobfoll and M. deVries (Eds.). *Extreme Community Stress: Impact and Intervention.* The Hague, The Netherlands, Martinus Nijhof.
Trickett, E.J. (1984). Towards a Distinctive Community Psychology: An Ecological metaphor for Training and the Conduct of Research. *American Journal of Community Psychology, 12*, 261–279.
Trickett, E. J., Barone, C., & Watts, R. (2000). Contextual influences in mental health consultation: Toward an ecological perspective on radiating change. In J. Rappaport & E. Seidman (Eds), *Handbook of Community Psychology* (pp. 303–330). New York: Kluwer Academic/Plenum Publishers.
Trickett, E. J. & Birman, D. (1989). Taking ecology seriously: A community development approach to individually-based interventions. In L. Bond and B. Compas, (Eds.), *Primary prevention in the schools*. Hanover, NH: University of New England Press.
Trickett, E. J., Kelly, J. G., & Todd, D. M. (1972). The social environment of the high school: Guidelines for individual change and organizational development. In S. Golann & C. Eisdorfer (Eds.), *Handbook of commuity mental health* (pp. 331–406). New York: Appleton-Century-Crofts.
Trickett, E.J., Kelly, J. G. & Vincent, T. A. (1985). The spirit of ecological inquiry in community research. In E. Susskind & D. Klein (Eds.), *Community research: Methods, paradigms, and applications*. New York: Praeger.
Trickett, E.J. & Mitchell, R.E. (1993). An ecological metaphor for research and intervention in community psychology. In Gibbs, M.S., Lachenmeyer, J.R. and Sigal, J. *Community Psychology: Theoretical and Empirical Approaches*, 2nd edition, New York, Wiley.

Trickett, E.J. & Schmid, K. (1993). The social context of the school: An ecological perspective on school, adolescents in schools, and intervention in schools. In P. Tolan and B. Cohler (Eds.) *Handbook of Clinical Research and Practice with Adolescents*. New York: Wiley & Sons.

Walker, G. & Small, S. (1991). AIDS, crack, poverty, and race in the African-American community: The need for an ecosystem approach. *Journal of Independent Social Work*, 5(3–4), 69–91.

Weeks, M. R., Schensul, J. J., Williams, S.S., Singer, M., & Grier, M. (1995). AIDS prevention for African-American and Latina women: Building culturally and gender-appropriate intervention. *AIDS Education and Prevention, 7(3),* 251–263.

Weiss, C. H. (1977). Survey researchers and minority communities. *Journal of Social Issues, 33* (4). 20–35.

[24]

Everyday life with AIDS/HIV: surveys in the social sciences

Janine Pierret*

Centre de Recherche Médecine, Sciences, Santé et Société, CNRS/INSERM/ÉHÉSS, 182 bd de la Villette, 75019, Paris, France

Abstract

Research on persons infected with HIV is critically assessed by using the notions developed in the sociology of illness. Has this research stimulated new questions or led to reformulations in research paradigms? Methodological problems related to data collection are pointed out, namely: the recruitment of HIV-positive participants for such studies and the stance they adopt during interviews. The contributions made by studies that have focused on adjustment strategies or resorted to the notions of stigmatization, identity and illness trajectory are also discussed. In conclusion, questions are raised about what implications the new HIV/AIDS treatments will have on this field of social science research.

Keywords: HIV; Stigmatization; Time; Illness trajectory; Identity

Introduction

Whereas the consequences of chronic illness on patients' daily lives has, over the past few decades, been a subject of inquiry in the social sciences, the consequences of HIV infection and AIDS on the everyday lives of those concerned has drawn less attention. Of course, numerous research about the psychological and social impact of HIV infection have been published in the AIDS specialized literature. Because the analysis of HIV infection and AIDS however raises questions of interest for the whole community of social scientists, the focus, in this review paper, is rather put on publications in the academic field of social sciences.

Research in the social sciences on persons living with HIV/AIDS has produced a limited number of studies that often lack a firm footing in existing analytical frameworks. This research will be critically reviewed by using notions developed in the sociology of illness. What concepts have been used to analyze AIDS as an illness? And what impact has this illness had on current sociological inquiry? Will paradigms shift as a result of studies about the consequences of AIDS on the everyday lives of HIV-infected persons? These questions will be examined with respect to both the methodological limits encountered in collecting and analyzing data and to the theoretical limits of the notions used in this research.

Since Strauss and Glaser (1975), the sociology of illness has turned toward the problems the ill have had to cope with as they manage everyday activities. It has thus drawn attention to "chronic illnesses", which have become a major health problem in Western societies since the 1960s. Unlike acute illness, a chronic condition is not an episode in a life; instead, it tends to become the person's very

* Tel.: +33-1-5372-8034; fax: +33-1-5372-8049.
E-mail address: pierret@ext.jussieu.fr (J. Pierret).

life. These often crippling conditions last, acute phases alternating with relatively calm spells. In the place of the symptom–diagnosis–treatment–healing model, a new paradigm has emerged with open, uncertain prospects related to the state of relevant medical knowledge, which, in many cases, is still making advances. The idea of "illness management" has thus replaced the notion of "healing" (Baszanger, 1986). This management entails changes in doctors' and nurses' work. It reaches beyond the world of medicine and into all aspects of the patient's life for an indefinite period of time. Owing to their characteristics, these illnesses lead to a situation poorly defined not only for health professionals but also for the ill themselves (Herzlich and Pierret, 1984).

For more than a decade, sociologists — in studies of illnesses as different as epilepsy, chronic renal failure, diabetes, multiple sclerosis, cancer and polyarthritis — have concentrated on the patient's viewpoint (Anderson and Bury, 1988). They have worked out approaches that Conrad (1987) formulated as the "experience of illness". This formulation has been helpful in two ways. First of all, it has — through the concepts of stigma, uncertainty, shared knowledge and information, biographical work and self-reconstruction — helped explain the problems persons suffering from long-term illness encounter in various fields of life. Secondly, it has — thanks to the concepts of illness career or illness trajectory — helped us understand the strategies worked out by these persons.

This sort of research is based on what we might call the illness-event model. Accordingly, illness is an individual hardship with a social meaning; and it implies a high degree of social mobilization (Augé, 1984). When it occurs in a person's life, it creates a watershed separating "before" and "after". Previously taken for granted activities now become problems. Such an illness takes on meaning in the person's life story through the answers given to the questions: "Why me?" "Why now?" Though unique for the individual, the illness is always interpreted with reference to social values and norms. In order to live with an illness of this sort, sometimes for many years, persons will tap various resources so as to rearrange living conditions and adjust to the new situation. They give thought to their relations with others and work out new self-images. Such an illness experience can alter the individual's biography and serve as the basis for a sense of identity (Charmaz, 1987). Public authorities and non-governmental organizations (henceforth NGOs) have also become actively involved in the search for more or less institutionalized solutions (such as specific benefits under health insurance or social security, appropriate health-care centers or self-help groups) to the problems caused by such illnesses (Bury, 1982, 1991).

Frameworks used for analyzing the HIV/AIDS experience

Sociological research has focused on the consequences that known chronic illnesses have on the lives and identities of the persons who have to manage, day in day out, the illness situation. However, the outbreak in the early 1980s of a transmissible infection for which there was no known medical treatment, a disease causing death in the relatively short term and related to the behaviors, practices and ways of life of young men, forced social scientists to question whether existing concepts were pertinent for studying this new illness's impact on the everyday lives of those infected (Pierret, 1992, 1997). AIDS as an illness has characteristics that distinguish it from the illnesses normally studied in sociology.

First of all, AIDS (and even more so HIV-infection) covers a wide range of situations and medical conditions. As medical science soon discovered, the period of time before an infected person develops diseases associated with the immunodeficiency syndrome varies widely. This would, as of 1984 when the first tests for detecting the virus were invented, set HIV-infection apart from most illnesses, which are diagnosed whenever symptoms break out. This situation may be compared with that of the healthy carriers of genetic conditions for which there are now tests. Furthermore, it is known that those who are HIV-positive may have no clinically symptoms many years after infection. Following what has long been characterised as an "asymptomatic" period, the illness period starts, itself marked by several phases running up to the terminal period. In this respect, the AIDS experience can shed light on general problems in the field of predictive medicine.

Secondly, the mass media presented this deadly illness as an epidemic in a context where chronic ailments represented the prevalent form of illness (Herzlich and Pierret, 1993). But could the characteristics of the AIDS experience be detected with the same means used to study chronic illness?

Thirdly, owing to its transmissibility and the cognitive representations surrounding it, AIDS turned out to be an illness that threatens the person's relationships. And unlike previously studied chronic illnesses, AIDS is not an illness which occurs randomly among isolated individuals: it has smitten groups or networks of persons owing to their medical history (blood transfusion, haemophilia) or way of life.

The first studies of the everyday lives of persons

with AIDS focused on the secret of their being infected and the sharing of this secret. In the 1990s, studies in terms of adjustment processes concentrated on the strategies people who were HIV-positive worked out to lead a life in conditions of uncertainty. As the population being infected with HIV diversified, along with the living conditions and socioeconomic statuses of the infected, more recent studies have turned toward the social inequality related to AIDS and health care.

Thanks to highly active antiretroviral therapies (HAART) including protease inhibitors introduced as of March 1996, a growing proportion of HIV-infected persons remain without any clinical symptoms and HIV-related morbidity, and persons with AIDS are living longer and staying in better physical conditions. By becoming a long-term illness, the AIDS experience, once again, forces questions upon us. For example, studies of compliance with prescriptions have been made for several years now in North America (Baekeland and Lundwall, 1975; Haynes, 1979; Rees, 1985). By referring to the theory of "social representations", a study of compliance in clinical trials has shown the limits of the North American approach in terms of behavior and emphasized the importance of the "prescription context" (Morin and Moatti, 1996). The continuation of research on how treatments are followed and how they affect patients' everyday lives might help us better understand what it means to live with a long-term, onerous treatment in the case of a transmissible disease (Chesney et al., 2000). In particular, studies of illness trajectories could help us focus on the work performed by HIV-positive people and by the persons close to them during various phases of their illness and on the process of negotiating with various health professionals.

Methodological questions and issues

The development of quantitative surveys on the general population's behaviors toward AIDS has, in most countries, aroused debate about how such studies are implemented and how the data thus collected are analyzed. On the other hand, qualitative inquiries into the everyday lives of persons who live with HIV or AIDS have seldom raised new methodological questions of this sort.

In the book edited by Boulton (1994), twelve British research groups have debated methodological questions raised by studies of the social aspects of HIV/AIDS, in particular, in relation to prevention work. According to Blaxter (1994, p. 243), social science inquiries in this field have been conducted

> "in an atmosphere of urgency, with the greatest possible openness to different disciplines and new approaches, and an unusual lifting of the dead hand of the conventional in academic research".

They have made significant contributions to the analysis of health behavior and behavioral change. Although studies specifically focused on those who are HIV infected and people with AIDS (PWAs) have been more limited, they did draw attention to new problems such as "personal choice in treatment and the self-management of serious disease" or "responsibility for the health of others, not just self-responsibility" (Blaxter, 1994, p. 250).

Qualitative studies of HIV-positive people and PWAs have not drawn as much attention to methodological problems as the quantitative surveys devoted to health behaviors or large-scale longitudinal studies like the UK SIGMA Project. Nonetheless, they raise questions of a different sort. They are based on in-depth interviews or autobiographical accounts obtained from a small number of individuals or from "focus-group" members (e.g., Weitz, 1989, 1990, 1993; Green, 1994, 1995, 1996; Carricaburu and Pierret, 1992, 1995; Delor, 1997; Crawford et al., 1997). In this interpretative research into experiences and their meanings, the theoretical approach used, data collection and data analysis are all closely related to each other. Few of these studies, however, raise questions about either the conditions for collecting data or the nature of the data collected. For instance, how to establish contacts with a range of persons who, owing to their origins, preferences or behaviors, want to keep their infection or its cause secret? Access to research subjects raises problems in many countries because of special legal and ethical constraints relating to confidentiality.

Depending on whether the social scientist can establish contacts through doctors, AIDS organizations or personal networks, the recruitment of interviewees will be skewed toward or away from certain categories, e.g. those who have a regular doctor or those who avoid doctors; those who are actively involved in NGOs or those who are not. As a channel of recruitment, Weitz (1993, p. 103) used "both physicians who treat HIV disease and the four community AIDS organizations in Arizona". However she did not obtain access to the doctors' mailing lists. Nor could she compare the characteristics of the 14 women interviewed with the others who had been initially contacted. By passing through doctors in HIV-related hospital services in Paris, Carricaburu and Pierret (1992) sought out asymptomatic HIV-positive interviewees infected through sexual relations or blood-derived products for treating hemophilia. But they had little control over the way doctors made their selections. Despite his diversified sources, Delor (1997) reported difficulties in forming a group of HIV-positive persons in Brussels.

Crawford et al. (1997, p. 3) pointed out how reluctant Australian women were to talk about their sexual lives. In broader terms, these difficulties reflect the heterogeneity of target populations and differences with respect to illness phases and the origins of infection. The analyses of these data often do not sufficiently take this heterogeneity into account. They fail to discern differences or compare situations between individuals — as if the fact of being a man or woman infected with HIV or suffering from AIDS did not have any incidence on the strategy the interviewee worked out. Might the results of qualitative studies not carry more weight if they took into account characteristics of the illness and differences between those infected with HIV?

Questions should also be raised about the conditions for carrying out interviews, since they also affect the type of data collected, as Holland et al. (1994) have shown in their study of the sexual lives of women, 16–21 years old, living in Manchester and London. Although this study did not focus on women with HIV and AIDS, it raised relevant questions for any qualitative survey of "private" matters such as sexual behavior or illness. An interview may well provide an opportunity for talking. But each interviewee may understand this opportunity differently. It may be a time for bearing witness or telling life stories with reference to general or activist values (Pollak, 1988, 1990). It may also be a time for breaking silence and breaking out of solitude by sharing one's secret through the sociologist (Pierret, 1994). When the interview is part of a medical research project, it may take on special meaning as a way to obtain additional tests in the quest to explain an exceptional situation, namely a long period of life with the virus (Pierret, 1998a,c). Finally, it may also be a time for seeking help and counseling. These different stances adopted by interviewees must not be overlooked insofar as they determine what the person has to say and thus affect the data actually collected.

Collecting and analyzing this type of qualitative data must lead beyond the description of individual experiences so as to both reveal the "logic" that organizes what an interviewee has to say and shed light on similarities and dissimilarities between interviewees' accounts. The aim should be to reconstitute major categories of analysis and to bring to light the beliefs that, running through interviewees' accounts, enable us to compare them. But we must bear in mind that the results do not correspond to persons but to structures in what individuals have to say in an interview setting as part of a research project (Demazière and Dubar, 1997).

Everyday life with HIV and adjustment strategies

AIDS/HIV-related studies in the social sciences have concentrated on prevention work and behavioral change, but few of them have focused on how persons cope with infection. Moreover, PWA-centered studies have mainly been conducted in clinical and social psychology (Nilsson-Schönnesson, 1995) in an effort to bring to light the individual characteristics, personality traits and behaviors related to the effort to cope with infection. But why have so very few in the social sciences shown interest in the consequences of AIDS on the lives of the infected? Can this scarcity be set down to characteristics of the illness itself (the ways it is transmitted, the morbidity rate, the lack of medical treatment) or to the sociological methods needed to develop such studies? Several studies have however been made by persons involved in the fight against AIDS and by persons closed to people with HIV (Bennett et al., 1998).To answer the question "How do people live with HIV/AIDS?", existing approaches have to be broadened so as to study the relations between the ill person's individual history, forms of collective action (especially in associations) and arrangements for social and political interventions. This means analyzing the processes whereby HIV-positive people and PWAs mobilize resources so as to build up the hope necessary for living. It entails bringing to light individuals' trajectories and their strategies for bargaining with health-care professionals and dealing with existing arrangements. Research conducted early in the epidemic focused on reactions to the AIDS/HIV stigma; but more recent studies have turned toward analyzing illness trajectories and strategies for managing the stigma, as we now shall see.

Keeping the secret and reacting to the stigma

For nearly ten years now, research in various countries has studied how individuals have kept their HIV-infection secret. Such studies initially focused on homosexuals, who were the first and most numerous among HIV-infected people and PWAs. The keeping of the secret was analyzed in relation to stigmatization (Pollak, 1988; Weitz, 1990; Siegel and Krauss, 1991). As of 1988 (Kowalewski, 1988), the notion of a "double stigma" was formulated to explain how a stigmatized group (homosexuals) was reacting to the new stigma (AIDS). What was actually studied, however, was not the stigma itself but the keeping of the secret in reaction to stigmatization. Although the notion of stigma should be understood in terms of relations and not of attributes (Goffman, 1963), AIDS turned out to be an illness that was stigmatized owing to certain characteristics.

For one thing, talk was rife about AIDS as a "divine punishment", "the new leprosy" and "the curse of modern times". The press was busy shaping this social discourse before anything was actually known about this new illness's symptoms and social repercussions, in fact before its first victims were visible. A moralizing discourse about deviant behavior and life-styles put the blame on the infected (Herzlich and Pierret, 1988). As Frankenberg (1986) pointed out, the illness experience always forces patients to cope with the metaphors produced and imposed by society. But the association made between AIDS and death — all the more in that it involved the death of young people in societies where the life expectancy had been rising continually — entailed stigmatization.

For another thing, the "felt stigma" (Scambler and Hopkins, 1986) is especially important in the case of AIDS inasmuch as the body is infected by a virus that it can also transmit. The concerned may have internalized the stigma and anticipate negative reactions by keeping their infection secret. This is the case, in particular, of the asymptomatic who, with no visible sign of illness, are "discreditable" (Carricaburu and Pierret, 1995).The social discourse constructed around death, fear and deviant behavior and the potential danger related to the HIV-positive are so many characteristics that help us explain the stigma.

These characteristics of the stigma attached to AIDS account for the extent of the rejection of and discrimination against HIV-infected persons (loss of jobs, travel controls, insurance problems). They have been studied at the workplace. The fear of being dismissed from work or rejected by fellow-workers may have a tenacious hold, even when labor laws provide quite strong protection (Fabre, 1994, Bertau et al., 1997). This research has shown how the informal arrangements made with colleagues, especially with those who share the secret, are important, even when labor laws exist. Since such arrangements are precarious, we can raise questions about the effectiveness of existing protection and, in particular, about "confidentiality" at the workplace, which varies depending on the country and occupation (Pollak, 1992). Barbour (1994), for example, has brought to light inter- and intraoccupational variations in four towns in Scotland. In some firms, employee educational campaigns have been launched; and organizational arrangements, made for protecting those who are HIV-positive (Barr, 1993). From a macrosocial perspective, Goss and Adam-Smith (1994) have proposed distinguishing between two broad policy approaches, defensive and humanistic, in the United Kingdom.

Studies of reaction to the stigma were broadened to cover different populations so as to take into account various social factors: the poverty associated with immigrants from different ethnic groups, the conditions of women (Weitz, 1993; Sherr et al., 1996) and conditions in families with HIV-positive children (Melvin and Sherr, 1993; Melvin, 1996). Green (1996) and Boulton (1998) have found that HIV-positive women in these circumstances feel shame about assuming the role of mother and taking care of their children. Crawford et al. (1997) have shown how ashamed and guilty HIV-positive women in Australia feel: they feel they are "dirty" and a "polluted source of infection". And the close association which is still perceived between AIDS and homosexuality, in various countries like Australia, makes it even harder to reveal one's serostatus to sexual partners. Green (1994) has defined three types of "sexual careers" among HIV-positive people: "the path to celibacy"; the denial that one can infect others along with the failure to modify behavior; and the "path of behavior modification". These sexual career choices vary over time depending on the illness and on changing circumstances in the person's life. Green (1995) has related these sexual careers to an emotional context, and pointed out the tensions around issues such as reproduction and the desire to have children; but the primacy of personal relationships was emphasized. This research, like Hankins' (1996) proposals, should lead to the development of empirical studies of HIV-positive women's sexual lives and of their choices regarding reproduction. HIV-transmission from mother to fetus has considerably decreased in Western lands (Lisann Bedimo et al., 1998) despite the isolation of these women, their lack of access to health care, their difficulty following treatment or even their refusal to take AZT (Weitz, 1993; Crystal and Sambamoorthi, 1996; Siegel and Gorey, 1997). As the HIV-positive population is diversifying, the ability of health-care services to treat persons in precarious circumstances and the conditions where under the latter obtain care are becoming major issues (Rosman, 1994, 1996; Crystal and Glick Schiller, 1993; Huby, 1997).

A particularly interesting orientation in research has been to study stigmatization as a dynamic process. Alonzo and Reynolds (1995) have used the phrase "stigma trajectory" to conceptualize how HIV-infected people and PWAs experience the stigma and to show how biophysical changes affect this experience. Such individuals are stigmatized because their illness is "associated with deviant behavior", "viewed as the responsibility of the individual", "tainted by a religious belief as to its immorality", "perceived as contagious", "associated with an undesirable and an unaesthetic form of death", "not well understood by the lay community", and "viewed negatively by health-care providers" (Alonzo and Reynolds, 1995). As a function of these characteristics of the stigma and of the four stages of HIV-infection, the HIV-stigma trajectory is said to have four distinct biopsychosocial phases: "at risk: pre-stigma and the worried well"; "diagnosis: confronting an altered identity"; "latent: living between health and illness"; and "manifest: passage to social and physical death" (Alonzo and Reynolds, 1995). Here, the stigma is not static; it results from the person's struggle to renegotiate and redefine life during each illness phase.

The stigmatization process also lies at the center of a recent study of 139 gay/bisexual American men that discerned ten "stigma management strategies" ranging from reactive to proactive, depending on the degree to which the strategy challenges or acquiesces to social values and norms that tend to discredit the infected (Siegel et al., 1998). The ten strategies are: concealment, selective disclosure, personal attribution, gradual disclosure, selective affiliation, discrediting the discreditors, challenging moral attributions, preemptive disclosure, public education, and social activism. These authors have wondered whether their results are relevant to other HIV-positive groups. In conclusion, they call for turning attention to "the role of proactive coping strategies among resource-poor communities of persons coping with AIDS-related or other stigmas" (Siegel et al., 1998, p. 22).

The two aforementioned studies open interesting perspectives for analyzing the processes at work in the strategies that HIV-positive people and PWAs use to fight against the stigma. AIDS research into the effects of the new therapies should take into account changing social values and this illness's biological characteristics. This approach could even be extended to other chronic illnesses, such as cancer, or transmissible ones, such as hepatitis.

The organization of everyday life, time and identities

Research on the processes whereby HIV-positive people struggle against the infection and reorganize their lives has been based on the idea of resources. The notion of "capital" has served to study the adjustments between the individual and social spheres; and the concept of "resources", to account for extreme situations characterized by unpredictability and uncertainty (Pollak, 1990). Before analyzing how resources are tapped and managed, it is necessary to name and classify them. They are relatively diverse: physical, psychological, emotional and relational. They are related to the person's being part of various networks and groups. Nor should we forget cognitive and informational resources. For some HIV-positive persons and PWAs, occupational or religious commitments and involvement in NGOs serve as resources (Pollak, 1988). Carricaburu and Pierret (1995) have distinguished two ways that resources are put to work (using existing resources or tapping new ones) and two objectives (making arrangements in everyday life or reinforcing the ability to face an uncertain future). Might this formulation of the notion of resources not be relevant to the idea of empowerment?

By conducting their study in terms of coping and adjustment, Pantzou et al. (1998) have focused on the ways those who are HIV-positive and PWAs handle the uncertainty of everyday life. They have shed light on three tendencies related to the conceptions of, perception of, and attitudes toward the management of everyday life. The first is negative: AIDS comes to interrupt and destroy a life-course. The second is more positive: AIDS comes to interrupt, change and sometimes improve a way of life. And the third is neither negative nor positive: life is perceived as continuing, and no major changes are made. It would have been interesting had these authors taken into account the diversity of interviewees' situations.

In a more obvious way than for other illnesses, HIV forces the infected to face up to uncertainty (Weitz, 1989), a notion that can serve as the basis for studies of time and its meaning to HIV-positive people and PWAs. This uncertainty is of two sorts: the uncertainty related to the development of full-blown AIDS and the uncertainty related to the life expectancy of those who are PWAs. One study has shown that some HIV-positive homosexual men use the asymptomatic period as a temporal resource to put off the start of illness. This has been analyzed as the passage from a biological to a social category, from having an HIV-positive blood test to being an HIV-positive person (Pierret, 1996). From a different perspective but one close to an analysis in terms of adjustment, Davies (1997) has brought to light, among members of the National Long-Term Survivors' Group in Great Britain, "compensatory" ways for handling time under the threat of death. She pointed out three temporal orientations: living with a philosophy of the present, living in the future, and living in the empty present.

Attention should be drawn to the opportunity for social scientists to use the cohorts established by physicians for following up HIV-positive persons over a long period of time. Studies of such cohorts in Great Britain and France have developed original approaches to these persons' experience of time. Crossley (1997) has distinguished two main types of "theories" that long-term HIV-positive people work out to reply to the question of why they have lived for so long: interpersonally oriented (normalizing, activity-based and enjoyment-based) and intrapersonally/intrapsychically oriented. Pierret (1998b) has brought to light three ways that thirty long-term nonprogressors in France have talked about the passing of time since learning they were infected. Some of them organized their stories around the idea of continuing as life moves on; and in this case, keeping one infection secret was a precondition. Other stories came out of a questioning of the AIDS/HIV experience; and such accounts tended to be organized around the idea of giving meaning to certain events that had occurred over the years. In the third type, accounts of misfortune, or worse, were organized around the breaches that HIV-infection had wrought in the person's life. These three ways interviewees organized their accounts were neither directly nor obviously correlated with the characteristics of the person's initial situation or with the objective conditions at the time when they learned they were HIV-positive. In other words, whether the persons had learned they were HIV-positive before the age of 25 (and thus started out adult life with the virus), or had learned it later (once they had settled down) did not affect the interview's form. Let us insist however that interviewees, regardless of their type of accounts, wanted to show they were leading "normal lives". Elsewhere, Pierret (1998c, 2000) has shown how being accepted as part of a medical cohort, because it legitimates the situation resulting from the exceptionally long life span, enables people both to give meaning to their lives since infection and to talk about how they have constructed their lives in conditions of uncertainty.

HIV/AIDS raises the painful question of imminent death from a transmissible disease. PWAs belong to networks or groups whose ranks have been decimated. For this reason, studies have been made of the "AIDS survivor syndrome", in particular among homosexuals (Wright, 1998). This notion, borrowed from studies of survivors from Nazi concentration camps, refers to individual symptoms, signs and behaviors (death anguish, psychological fragility, guilt feelings, isolation, etc.). As Pollak (1990) pointed out, the impossibility of communicating and sharing what was experienced in concentration camps (experiences placed outside of space and time) lies at the center of this syndrome. This is a far cry from the HIV/AIDS experience, which is happening now. This "live" experience is highly visible in society even though HIV-positive people themselves may be shut up inside silence. Moreover, as Pollak insisted, survivors' experiences and the social possibilities for managing memories vary widely from person to person. For this reason, we can hardly imagine uniformly applying the survivor's syndrome to all victims of either AIDS or concentration camps. Crossley (1997) has emphasized how discordant the idea of a survivor is with the philosophy of empowering long-term HIV-positive people, since it refers back to debates about survivors and victims and, in general terms, to conceptions of self and others.

Besides the issues of empowerment or resource mobilization and management, the question has also been studied of how persons rearrange their biographies and rework their identities when confronted with HIV-infection and AIDS. In Carricaburu and Pierret's (1995) inquiry into the emergence of a "HIV patient identity", men infected following homosexual relations or through blood-derived products against hemophilia did not reconstruct their life stories around their infection. On the contrary, by questioning their pasts before the time of infection, they rearranged their lives so as to continue living as normally as possible. These sociologists have proposed the concept of biographical reinforcement to understand the complex process of reconstructing the individual and, too, collective pasts by accenting certain elements, related to hemophilia or homosexuality, of their previous identity.

Studying the relationships between trajectories and identities, Delor (1997) tried to see how the identities of homosexual HIV-positive men in Belgium are structured. He considered forms of identity to be a social arrangement of different but more or less similar elements that vary over time and space. Four major poles of identity were thus identified: repression of one's homosexual preference; acceptance of this preference but while managing one's social identity in secret; acceptance of this preference while managing one's social identity as a compromise; acceptance of this preference while managing one's social identity as an assertion. It would be worthwhile to extend this type of analysis so as to take into account various phases in the illness trajectory.

Whereas this research has mainly concentrated on the consequences on the everyday lives of those who are HIV-positive and PWAs, other studies, taking the family to be a system, have focused on the consequences on organizing family life as a function of the evolution of the illness. The rearrangements in families where a parent or child is HIV-positive are not easy to make. They are related to the family's expectations about how the illness will evolve and to the plans it makes for children (Dumaret et al., 1995a,b; Melvin, 1996). In these families, tensions arise between different family members' needs (Melvin and Sherr, 1993). Poor families from sub-Saharan Africa encounter, in addition, ethnic discrimination (Boulton, 1998). Studies have also been conducted of how members of the wider family (grandparents, uncles, aunts, etc.) take part in caring for children (depending on whether or not they are orphans) whose mothers are HIV-positive. A sense of duty and blood ties tend to hide the difficulties in extended families (Dumaret and Donati, 1998).

Conclusion

Most of the aforementioned studies were conducted before the new treatments for AIDS. Changes in therapy since the spring of 1996 bring up new questions about how to analyze the consequences of the

HIV/AIDS experience on everyday life. What arrangements (biographical, material and organizational) will have to be made by persons who are going to live longer and longer with HIV, and some of whom will be living in precarious social situations?

To answer these questions and understand how people adjust over time to the illness, large-scale longitudinal studies, as in the UK and the USA, will have to be carried out to follow up patients. The repetition and accumulation of qualitative studies that analyze in-depth what a relatively small number of interviewees have to say no longer suffice. To further our knowledge significantly, the social sciences must draw the lessons from previous studies of those who are HIV-positive and PWAs so as to analyze the problems now cropping up as HIV/AIDS is becoming "ordinary". The "sick role" or "empowerment" alternative that Crossley (1998) described for long-term survivors now carries more weight. As an analysis of the press has shown (Lupton, 1999), the persistence of stigmatization and of negative reactions toward HIV-positive people, who are now living longer with an illness that can be transmitted between sexual partners and from mother to child, forces us to address the issues of mass and group reactions and of social policy responses to HIV/AIDS.

Research on the sexual activities of HIV-positive people should be pursued not only for prevention purposes (Schiltz and Sandfort, 2000) but also with the aim of furthering the analysis of sexuality as a social activity — an activity that is a full-fledged part of the efforts made by those who are HIV-positive to rework their biographies and reorganize everyday life. These efforts challenge the separation between the intimate and public spheres of life, and raise questions about social processes such as visibility and dissimulation. In broader terms, studies of the consequences of AIDS in the world of work and on the organization of family life should continue so as to analyze the forms of solidarity and rearrangements in family and work life. Such analyses can develop only by taking into account the mobilization by NGOs as well as public policies and interventions. The work of constructing hope performed by the individual as he/she taps available resources in order to avoid the onset or aggravation of the illness and to fight against uncertainty cannot be analyzed without bringing these political, social, collective interventions under consideration. To end this review of studies in the social sciences about everyday life with HIV/AIDS, I would like to ask a question. How can the knowledge produced by "experts" be linked to the knowledge coming from the direct experiences of patients themselves? This question, though often asked in research on illness and disability in English-speaking lands, does not arouse much debate in France or southern European countries, even though, owing to AIDS, the situation is changing somewhat.

Acknowledgements

Translated from French by Noal Mellott, CNRS, Paris.

References

Alonzo, A.A., Reynolds, N.R., 1995. Stigma, HIV and AIDS: An exploration and elaboration of a stigma trajectory. Social Science and Medicine 41 (3), 303–315.

Anderson, R., Bury, M., 1988. Living with Chronic Illness. Unwin Hyman, London.

Augé, M., 1984. Ordre biologique, ordre social: La maladie, forme élémentaire de l'événement. In: Augé, M., Herzlich, C. (Eds.), Le sens du mal. Anthropologie, histoire, sociologie de la maladie. Editions des Archives Contemporaines, Paris, pp. 35–91 (Translation, 1995: The Meaning of Illness. Harwood Academic).

Baekeland, F., Lundwall, L., 1975. Dropping out of treatment: A critical review. Psychology Bulletin 82 (5), 738–783.

Barbour, R.S , 1994. A telling tale: AIDS workers and confidentiality. In: Aggleton, P., Davies, P., Hart, G. (Eds.), AIDS: Foundation for the Future. Taylor and Francis, London, pp. 147–158.

Barr, J.K., 1993 Organizational response to AIDS in the workplace. In: Albrecht, G , Zimmerman, R. (Eds.), Advances in Medical Sociology. The Social and Behavioral Aspects of AIDS, vol. 3. Jai Press, Greenwich, Conn, pp. 143–164.

Baszanger, I., 1986 Les maladies chroniques et leur ordre négocié. Revue Française de Sociologie 27, 3–27.

Bennett, L , Rose, D., Jackson, A., Thomas, S., 1998. Psychological and socio-medical aspects of HIV/AIDS: a reflection on publications in: AIDS Care (1989–1995). AIDS Care 10 (1), 115–121.

Bertau, P., Favrot-Laurens, G., Sanchez, F., 1997. Les situations de handicap liées au sida en milieu de travail. Facteurs sociaux de maintien et d'exclusion de la vie professionnelle, a report. Toulouse, ANRS, 368 pp.

Blaxter, M., 1994. Towards the mainstreaming of HIV/AIDS research. In: Boulton, M. (Ed.), Challenge and Innovation: Methodological Advances in Social Research on HIV/AIDS. Taylor and Francis, London, pp. 243–251.

Boulton, M. (Ed.), 1994. Challenge and Innovation: Methodological Advances in Social Research on HIV/AIDS. Taylor and Francis, London.

Boulton, M., 1998. Coping with a Chronic Illness: The Experience of Families of HIV-Infected Children. Working paper for synthesis session 12, Second European Conference on Methods and Results of Social and Behavioural Research on AIDS, Paris.

Bury, M , 1982. Chronic illness as a biographical disruption. Sociology of Health and Illness 4, 167–182.

Bury, M., 1991. The sociology of chronic illness: A review of research and prospects. Sociology of Health and Illness 13, 451–468.

Carricaburu, D., Pierret, J., 1992. Vie quotidienne et recompositions identitaires autour de la séropositivité, a report. Paris, CERMES-ANRS, 277 pp.

Carricaburu, D, Pierret, J., 1995. From biographical disruption to biographical reinforcement: The case of HIV-positive men. Sociology of Health and Illness 17, 65–88.

Charmaz, K., 1987. Struggling for a self· Identity levels of the chronically ill. Research in the Sociology of Health Care 6, 283–321.

Chesney, M., Morin, M., Sherr, L, 2000. Adherence to HIV combination therapy, Social Science and Medicine 50(11), 1599–1605.

Conrad, P., 1987 The experience of illness: Recent and new directions. Research in the Sociology of Health Care 6, 1–31.

Crawford, J., Lawless, S., Kippax, S., 1997. Positive women and heterosexuality: Problems of disclosure of serostatus to sexual partners. In: Aggleton, P., Davies, P., Hart, G. (Eds.), AIDS, Activism and Alliances. Taylor and Francis, London, pp 1–14.

Crossley, M., 1997. "Survivors" and "victims": Long-term HIV-positive individuals and the ethos of self-empowerment. Social Science and Medicine 45 (12), 163–173 (born Davies).

Crossley, M., 1998. "Sick role" or "empowerment"? The ambiguities of life with an HIV-positive diagnosis. Sociology of Health and Illness 20 (4), 507–531.

Crystal, S., Glick Schiller, N., 1993. Stigma and homecoming: Family care-giving and the "disaffiliated" intravenous drug user In: Albrecht, G., Zimmerman, R. (Eds.), Advances in Medical Sociology The Social and Behavioral Aspects of AIDS, vol. 3. Jai Press, Greenwich, Conn, pp. 165–184.

Crystal, S., Sambamoorthi, U., 1996. Care needs and access to care among women living with HIV. In: Sherr, L., Hankins, C, Bennett, L. (Eds.), AIDS as a Gender Issue. Psychosocial Perspectives. Taylor and Francis, London, pp. 191–196.

Davies, M., 1997. Shattered assumptions: Time and the experience of long-term HIV-positivity. Social Science and Medicine 44 (5), 561–571.

Delor, F., 1997. Séropositifs. Trajectoires identitaires et rencontres du risque. L'Harmattan, Paris.

Demazière, D., Dubar, C., 1997. Analyser les entretiens biographiques. L'exemple des récits d'insertion. Nathan, Paris.

Dumaret, A., Donati, P., 1998. Enfants concernés par le sida: Implications des familles élargies et retentissements sur les modes de vie et les dynamiques familiales. Les Cahiers du CTNERHI. Handicaps et Inadaptations 77, 3–24.

Dumaret, A., Boucher, N., Torossian, V., Donati, P., Rosset, D., 1995a. Children born to HIV-positive mothers: Family environment, social support and care. Early Child Development and Care 112, 65–76.

Dumaret, A., Boucher, N., Rosset, D., Donati, P., Torossian, V., 1995b. Enfants nés de mère séropositive au VIH. Éditions INSERM, Paris.

Fabre, G., 1994. L'infection á VIH dans les parcours professionnels, a report. Aix-en-Provence, CNRS-ANRS, 295 pp.

Frankenberg, R, 1986. Sickness as cultural performance: Drama, trajectory and pilgrimage, root metaphors and the making social of disease. International Journal of Health Services 16, 603–626.

Goffman, I., 1963. Stigma. Prentice-Hall, Englewood Cliffs, NJ.

Goss, D., Adam-Smith, D., 1994 Empowerment or disempowerment The limits and possibilities of workplace AIDS policy. In: Aggleton, P., Davies, P, Hart, G. (Eds), AIDS: Foundation for the Future. Taylor and Francis, London, pp. 33–47.

Green, G., 1994. Positive sex: Sexual relationships following an HIV-positive diagnosis. In: Aggleton, P., Davies, P., Hart, G. (Eds.), AIDS: Foundation for the Future Taylor and Francis, London, pp. 136–146.

Green, G., 1995. Sex, love and seropositivity: Balancing the risks. In: Aggleton, P., Davies, P., Hart, G. (Eds.), AIDS: Safety, Sexuality and Risk. Taylor and Francis, London, pp. 144–148.

Green, G., 1996. Stigma and social relationships of people with HIV: Does gender make a difference? In: Sherr, L, Hankins, C., Bennett, L. (Eds.), AIDS as a Gender Issue. Psychosocial Perspectives. Taylor and Francis, London, pp. 46–63.

Hankins, C., 1996. Sexuality issues, reproductive choices and gynaecological concerns affecting women living with HIV. In: Sherr, L., Hankins, C., Bennett, L. (Eds.), AIDS as a Gender Issue. Psychosocial Perspectives. Taylor and Francis, London, pp. 1–15

Haynes, R.B., 1979. Determinants of compliance. The disease and the mechanisms of treatment. In. Haynes, R B, Taylor, D.W., Sackett, D L (Eds.), Compliance in Health Care. Johns Hopkins University Press, Baltimore, pp. 46–62.

Herzlich, C., Pierret, J., 1984. Malades d'hier, malades d'aujourd'hui. De la mort collective au devoir de guérison Payot, Paris (Translation, 1987 Illness and Self in Society Johns Hopkins University, Baltimore).

Herzlich, C., Pierret, J., 1988. Une maladie dans l'espace public. Le sida dans six quotidiens français Annales ESC 5, 1109–1134.

Herzlich, C., Pierret, J., 1993. From epidemic to modern illness: The social construction of AIDS in France In: Albrecht, G., Zimmerman, R. (Eds.), Advances in Medical Sociology. The Social and Behavioral Aspects of AIDS, vol. 3. Jai Press, Greenwich, Conn, pp. 59–76.

Holland, J., Ramazanoglu, C., Scott, S., Sharpe, S, Thomson, R., 1994. Methodological issues in researching young women's sexuality. In: Boulton, M. (Ed.), Challenge and Innovation: Methodological Advances in Social Research on HIV/AIDS. Taylor and Francis, London, pp. 219–239.

Huby, G., 1997. Interpreting silence, documenting experience: An anthropological approach to the study of health service users' experiences with HIV/AIDS care in Lothian, Scotland. Social Science and Medicine 44 (8), 1149–1160.

Kowalewski, M.R., 1988. Double stigma and boundary maintenance: How gay men deal with AIDS. Journal of Contemporary Ethnography 17 (2), 211–228.

Lisann Bedimo, A., Bessinger, R., Kissinger, P., 1998. Reproductive choices among HIV-positive women. Social Science and Medicine 46 (2), 171–179.

Lupton, D, 1999. Archetypes of infection: People with HIV/AIDS in the Australian press in the mid-1990s. Sociology of Health and Illness 21 (1), 37–53

Melvin, D., Sherr, L., 1993. The child in the family-responding to AIDS and HIV. AIDS Care 5 (1), 35–42

Melvin, D., 1996. Don't forget the children: Families living with HIV-Infection. In: Sherr, L., Hankins, C., Bennett, L. (Eds.), AIDS as a Gender Issue. Psychosocial Perspectives. Taylor and Francis, London, pp. 215–234.

Morin, M, Moatti, J.P., 1996. Observance et essais thérapeutiques: Obstacles psychosociaux dans la recherche sur le traitement de l'infection par le VIH. Natures, Sciences, Sociétés 4 (3), 228–240.

Nilsson-Schönnesson, L., 1995. Living with HIV: Dead end and/or turning point. In: Friedrich, D., Heckman, W. (Eds.), AIDS in Europe: The Behavioural Aspect, vol. 1. Edition Sigma, Berlin, pp. 89–101.

Pantzou, P., Tselepi, C., Metallinou, O., Agrafiotis, D., 1998. Constraints and modes of adaptation of HIV-carriers in everyday life. Working paper for synthesis session 12, Second European Conference on Methods and Results of Social and Behavioural Research on AIDS, Paris.

Pierret, J., 1992. Coping with AIDS in everyday life. In: Pollak, M., Paicheler, G., Pierret, J (Eds.), AIDS: A Problem for Sociological Research. Sage, London, pp. 66–84.

Pierret, J., 1994. Dites-leur ce qu'il ne m'est pas possible de dire. Je suis homosexuel et séropositif. Discours Social/Social Discourse 6 (34), 33–45.

Pierret, J., 1996. Maladie, sciences et société: L'expérience des personnes atteintes par le VIH Natures, Sciences, Sociétés 4 (3), 218–227.

Pierret, J., 1997. Un objet pour la sociologie de la maladie chronique: La situation de séropositivité au VIH? Sciences sociales et santé 15 (4), 97–120.

Pierret, J., 1998a. Uncertainty and secrecy among long-term AIDS non-progressors. Oral communication, Second European Conference on Methods and Results of Social and Behavioural Research on AIDS, Paris.

Pierret, J., 1998b. Constructing Discourses out of long-term AIDS non-progressors' accounts of their past. Poster 24158, Twelfth World AIDS Conference, Geneva.

Pierret, J., 1998c. Vivre longtemps avec le VIH. Récits sur la longue durée de vie et reconstruction du temps. Paris, CERMES-ANRS, 126 pp

Pierret, J., 2000 Interviews and biographical time: The case of persons who have lived with the HIV for a long time. Submitted for publication.

Pollak, M., 1988. Les homosexuels et le sida. Sociologie d'une épidémie. Métailié, Paris.

Pollak, M., 1990. L'expérience concentrationnaire. Métailié, Paris.

Pollak, M., 1992. Organizing the fight against AIDS. In: Pollak, M., Paicheler, G., Pierret, J. (Eds.), AIDS: A Problem for Sociological Research. Sage, London, pp. 36–65.

Rees, D.W., 1985 Health beliefs and compliance with alcoholism treatment. Journal of Studies on Alcohol 46 (6), 517–524.

Rosman, S., 1994 Profil social et trajectoires des résidents de l'association APARTS. In: ANRS (Ed.), Les personnes atteintes: Des recherches sur leur vie quotidienne et sociale, pp. 53–60. Paris.

Rosman, S., 1996. Maladie et précarité: Une association d'aide aux malades du sida au carrefour du médical et du social. PhD dissertation in sociology, ÉHÉSS, Paris.

Scambler, G., Hopkins, A., 1986. Being epileptic: Coming to terms with stigma. Sociology of Health and Illness 8, 26–43.

Schiltz, M.A., Sandfort, T., 2000. HIV-positive people, risk and sexual behaviour, Social Science and Medicine 50(11), 1571–1588.

Sherr, L., Hankins, C., Bennett, L. (Eds.), 1996. AIDS as a Gender Issue. Psychosocial Perspectives. Taylor & Francis, London.

Siegel, K., Krauss, B., 1991. Living with HIV-infection: Adaptive tasks of seropositive gay men. Journal of Health and Social Behavior 32 (3), 17–32.

Siegel, K., Gorey, E., 1997. HIV-infected women: Barriers to AZT use. Social Science and Medicine 45 (1), 15–22.

Siegel, K., Lune, H., Meyer, I.H., 1998. Stigma management among gay/bisexual men with HIV/AIDS. Qualitative Sociology 21 (1), 3–24.

Strauss, A., Glaser, B., 1975. Chronic Illness and Quality of Life. Mosby, St. Louis.

Weitz, R., 1989. Uncertainty and the lives of persons with AIDS. Journal of Health and Social Behavior 30 (11), 270–281.

Weitz, R., 1990. Living with the stigma of AIDS. Qualitative Sociology 13 (1), 23–38.

Weitz, R., 1993. Powerlessness, invisibility and the lives of women with HIV disease. In: Albrecht, G., Zimmerman, R. (Eds.), Advances in Medical Sociology. The Social and Behavioral Aspects of AIDS, vol. 3. Jai Press, Greenwich, Conn, pp. 101–121.

Wright, M.T., 1998. AIDS Survivor Syndrome and Being HIV-Positive. Working paper for synthesis session 12, Second European Conference on Methods and Results of Social and Behavioural Research on AIDS, Paris.

Name Index

For Product Safety Concerns and Information please contact our EU representative GPSR@taylorandfrancis.com Taylor & Francis Verlag GmbH, Kaufingerstraße 24, 80331 München, Germany

Batch number: 10726404

Printed by Printforce, the Netherlands